QuickBooks® 2006 Bible

QuickBooks® 2006 Bible

Jill Gilbert Welytok
C.P.A., Attorney, Llm in Taxation

WILEY
Wiley Publishing, Inc.

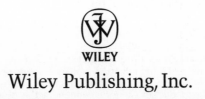

QuickBooks® 2006 Bible

Published by
Wiley Publishing, Inc.
10475 Crosspoint Boulevard
Indianapolis, IN 46256
www.wiley.com

Published simultaneously in Canada

ISBN-13: 978-0-471-78380-0
ISBN-10: 0-471-78380-3

Manufactured in the United States of America

10 9 8 7 6 5 4 3 2 1

1B/RZ/QR/QW/IN

For general information on our other products and services or to obtain technical support, please contact our Customer Care Department within the U.S. at (800) 762-2974, outside the U.S. at (317) 572-3993 or fax (317) 572-4002.

Library of Congress Cataloging-in-Publication Data

Welytok, Jill Gilbert.
Quickbooks 2006 bible / Jill Gilbert Welytok.
p. cm.
Includes index.
ISBN-13: 978-0-471-78380-0 (pbk.)
ISBN-10: 0-471-78380-3 (pbk.)
1. QuickBooks. 2. Small business—Accounting—Computer programs—Handbooks, manuals, etc. 3. Small business—Finance—Computer programs—Handbooks, manuals, etc. I. Title.
HF5679.W45 2006
657'.9042028553—dc22

2005032776

Wiley also publishes its books in a variety of electronic formats. Some content that appears in print may not be available in electronic books.

To my husband, Dan, and my little writing buddies, Tara, Julia, and Daniel

About the Author

Jill Gilbert Welytok is both a certified public accountant and an experienced tax attorney. She also has a Masters Degree in Computer Science. Jill's articles have appeared in numerous professional and technical publications, as well as a popular community news column, "Tax Talks." In addition, she teaches continuing education classes for attorneys, accountants, and financial professionals, and provides consulting and accounting services to small businesses.

Credits

Executive Editor
Chris Webb

Acquisitions Editor
Katie Mohr

Senior Development Editor
Kevin Kent

Technical Editor
Thomas J. Lieven, C.P.A.

Production Editor
Kenyon Brown

Copy Editor
Kathryn Duggan

Editorial Manager
Mary Beth Wakefield

Production Manager
Tim Tate

Vice President and Executive Group Publisher
Richard Swadley

Vice President and Executive Publisher
Joseph B. Wikert

Project Coordinator
Ryan Steffen

Graphics and Production Specialists
Carrie Foster
Lauren Goddard
Stephanie D. Jumper
Lynsey Osborn
Heather Ryan
Ron Terry
Julie Trippetti
Erin Zeltner

Quality Control Technicians
John Greenough
Leeann Harney
Jessica Kramer
Joe Niesen
Brian H. Walls

Proofreading and Indexing
TECHBOOKS Production Services

Contents at a Glance

Contents

Part IV: Managing Your Business with QuickBooks 243

Part VI: Banking and Credit Card Transactions 451

Preface

Welcome to *QuickBooks 2006 Bible* — a comprehensive source that discloses pretty much everything you need to know about QuickBooks. Most QuickBooks users concur it's helpful to be told how to perform an accounting function—but it's invaluable when someone also reminds you when and why to perform it, particularly if you're not a seasoned accountant. And if you are an accounting maven, this book is also written with you in mind. It provides legal analysis and coverage of advanced features.

Why This Book Is Essential to Your Business

Most entrepreneurs don't give it much thought, but as your business (or any business) grows, it faces three issues unrelated to producing the goods and services it sells. This inevitable trilogy of headaches includes legal, accounting, and marketing decisions. If your small business is like most, you probably cannot afford to call on expensive professionals whenever you'd like. You need to be able to handle as many of these issues as possible on your own. And besides, many business issues are so interrelated that they defy attempts at delegation. This book recognizes that QuickBooks is not used in a vacuum; everyone in a small business environment needs to know a little bit about what everyone else does. And if you are the owner, you need an aerial view of all the issues.

QuickBooks 2006 Bible is designed to give you valuable background in the accounting and legal concepts that help you optimize the value of the software. For example, you may not be inclined to go to the library to research the different types of business entities, or have the funds to hire a professional advisor at the start. But QuickBooks asks you to enter your choice of business entity at the outset, and you need enough background to take a decent stab at the question. *QuickBooks 2006 Bible* comes to your rescue in this and similar scenarios.

Who Should Read This Book

Every book makes some assumptions about its readers. You might be interested in knowing what I've assumed about you:

- You are familiar with Windows and Windows-based software programs, and you understand how to perform such basic operations as opening files and maneuvering through them.
- Although you may not be the owner of the business, you have some sort of personal stake in its ongoing health and financial vitality, even if that stake extends only as far as your own job. Hence, the repeated references to "your" company or "your" business.
- The purchasers of this book, as a group, have widely varying levels of familiarity with accounting concepts. Some have never heard the term *balance sheet*, whereas others have spent a good part of their lives producing and analyzing them. This book is intended to give background information to the novice and added insight to the expert.
- Everyone reading this book has a competent tax advisor, even if that advisor is you. Federal and state taxation are areas that require years of study to attain a level of competence. This book can't make you a tax expert if you aren't one already, but it will identify issues to raise with your tax advisor (or for you to think about if you are one).
- You are buying this book because you want to learn about accounting concepts relevant to your business, not about accounting in general. For example, if you are a restaurant doing a cash trade, you don't want to have to wade through a chapter on accounts receivable — it has no relevance to your business or your life. In fact, I don't think a single person out there actually intends to read this book cover to cover. Taking that into account, each chapter is written as a standalone reference source. I try to give information to you on a need-to-know basis. In instances where you do need some background from another chapter, cross-references direct you to the information.

Helpful Icons

This book uses four types of icons as visual cues to annotate the contents of the text:

You'll see this icon any time an accounting term is introduced that might not be familiar to a layperson.

This icon warns you when to watch out or when to take particular care when performing a procedure.

Most people won't read this book cover to cover, instead zeroing in on the chapter or information they need. This icon tells you that information relevant to the topic you're reading about is located elsewhere in the book.

Note

This icon offers an aside or extra information about a topic.

Tip

This is perhaps the most important icon. It signals the kind of information that saves you time, money, and aggravation.

How This Book Is Arranged

If I have done my job right, this book will be your ultimate reference source. The initial chapters are intended to give you an overview of the system and get you up and running as quickly and painlessly as possible; they're written with the assumption that you'd rather be working on the system than reading about it. Subsequent chapters are divided according to accounting function so you can tailor your reading to the character and needs of your business. Advanced legal and accounting topics are also given thorough treatment in their own chapters, so as to not bog down the reader who's trying to catch the basics or bore the more sophisticated professional with introductory information.

The book is divided into the following seven main parts, with related chapters in each part:

- Part I, "The QuickBooks System and Generally Accepted Accounting Practices," is calculated to give insight into the logic and structure of the program.
- Part II, "Establishing Your QuickBooks Business," attempts to address all of the obstacles you need to overcome in both the start of a new business and the introduction of a new accounting system.
- Part III, "Preferences and Data Management," covers those features available for customizing and optimizing your QuickBooks accounting system and maintaining the integrity and security of stored data.
- Part IV, "Managing Your Business with QuickBooks," introduces you to the program features that keep you in control of the day-to-day operations of the business.
- Part V, "Payroll and Taxes," covers the range of knowledge necessary to pay your employees and track taxes attributable to them. It also covers sales taxes.
- Part VI, "Banking and Credit Card Transactions," contains everything you need to know about online banking, bill payment, and credit card transactions.
- Part VII, "Analyzing Business Performance," provides an aerial view of business performance to high-flying entrepreneurs.

In addition, the appendixes guide you through the installation process, discuss how to download tax forms from the Internal Revenue Service Web site, and provide you with contact information for the various Internal Revenue Service Centers.

How to Reach the Author

If you have comments about the book, I encourage you to e-mail me at `taxtalks@wi.rr.com`. Your input will be gratefully received and will provide a great service to readers of future editions.

PART

I

The QuickBooks System and Generally Accepted Accounting Practices

✦ ✦ ✦ ✦

In This Part

✦ ✦ ✦ ✦

CHAPTER 1

Quick Insights and Program Overview

✦ ✦ ✦ ✦

In This Chapter

The QuickBooks program philosophy and design

The QuickBooks Chart of Accounts

Registers — the basic documentation file created by QuickBooks

Lists — the QuickBooks answer to database management

Items — the QuickBooks indexing system

Reports for analysis and budgeting

✦ ✦ ✦ ✦

QuickBooks is a complete business accounting system designed to accommodate nearly two dozen types of industries, ranging from small service-based firms to large retail and manufacturing companies. For each type of company, QuickBooks offers a preselected Chart of Accounts that automatically sets up most of the accounts necessary to run a particular enterprise. When you record a business transaction, QuickBooks instantly adjusts the balances of all affected accounts and can generate reports summarizing the updated financial information for your company at any time with a click of your mouse. QuickBooks offers several tools to help you organize and manage complex accounting data, including lists, items, registers, forms, and reports. This chapter provides an overview of these powerful program features.

QuickBooks Program Philosophy and Design

QuickBooks is marketed as a program for businesses. But this shouldn't lead you to believe that it is in any sense a program of limited scope or capability. QuickBooks is a powerful electronic accounting program that is adequate for the needs of many high-volume and sophisticated businesses. Nonaccountants who need to manage and record the day-to-day financial transactions of a business have helped create the program design. The Windows-based graphical user interface (GUI) makes the processing of transactions intuitive. With QuickBooks, you can generate sophisticated reports even if you don't have any prior accounting experience. It's assumed, however, that these reports will be submitted to your CPA for review and income tax preparation. QuickBooks facilitates the preparation of income tax returns by maintaining accurate, readily available information that can be transferred directly to your tax return form, but it is not a tax preparation program. It is unlikely that QuickBooks will replace your accountant. It will, however, minimize the cost of professional services by enabling you to directly access financial information about your business without using your accountant as an intermediary.

The QuickBooks Chart of Accounts: The Starting Point

The framework for recording information about your business is the Chart of Accounts, shown in Figure 1-1.

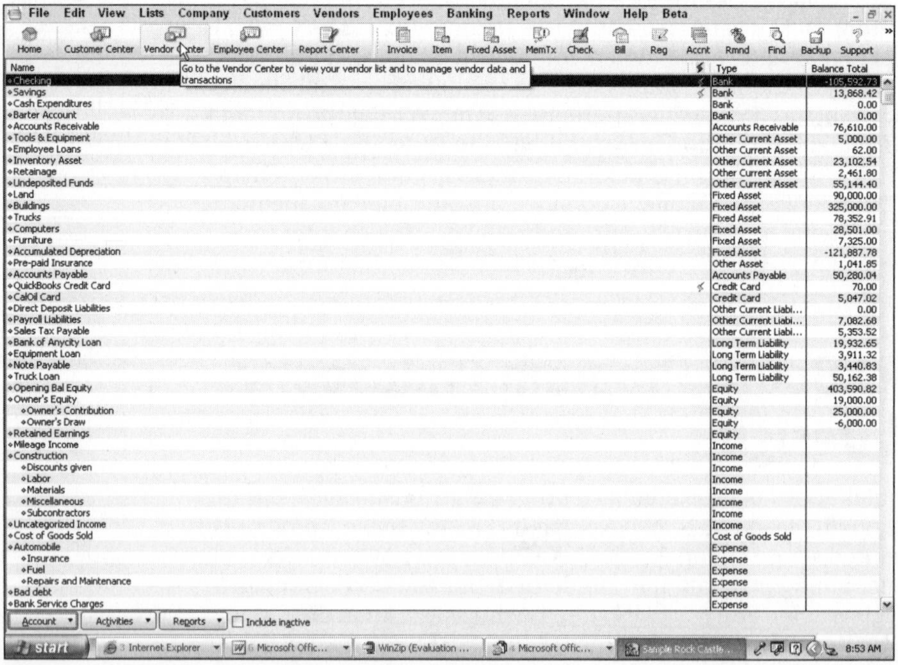

Figure 1-1: This Chart of Accounts window shows accounts to record inventory, sales discounts, cost of goods sold, and sales tax liability.

Chart of Accounts refers to a complete list of all the accounts in which you record information about the activities of your business. Every business has its own customized Chart of Accounts. The types of accounts and their names vary, as does the type of information in each account. Some businesses maintain very detailed Charts of Accounts where many different accounts are used to track highly specific types of information (for example, sales or expenses associated with each type of product or service). Other businesses find it more convenient to maintain a chart with fewer, more general accounts that track less detail but that may also be easier to maintain.

Accounts are named and identified according to their type – for example, Office Expense or Payroll Tax Account Equipment. Many businesses have a hundred or more accounts, which compose their Chart of Accounts. The topics of setting up and customizing your Chart of Accounts are discussed in Chapters 5 and 6.

As business transactions are recorded, QuickBooks automatically adjusts the balances of all affected accounts. A *register* (discussed in detail later in this chapter) contains a chronological list of all transactions affecting an account balance for a particular account. Registers reflect what your business owns and what it owes. It is important to establish appropriate accounts for your business at the outset to ensure accurate and logical recording of information. Companies differ greatly as to their individual Chart of Accounts. There are three main types of enterprises — service companies, retail companies, and manufacturing companies — and understanding the differences between them provides insight as to the makeup of their individual Chart of Accounts.

Service-based companies

As the name indicates, service companies derive their revenue from fees charged for services such as consulting. Service companies often do not maintain any inventory accounts tracking goods on hand for use or sale to customers. Similarly, service companies may not be required to pay sales tax. For example, a Chart of Accounts for an accounting firm generally has few or no inventory accounts and has no sales tax account.

Product-based companies

Product-based companies include both retail and manufacturing companies.

Retail companies

Retail companies must maintain both sales tax accounts and inventory accounts reflecting goods for resale.

Manufacturing companies

Manufacturing companies derive revenue from manufacturing or producing goods for wholesale. Generally, these companies do not sell goods directly to the public, and thus they are not required to pay sales tax. QuickBooks Premier and QuickBooks Pro do not offer the extensive inventory costing and tracking capabilities needed by a large manufacturing plant. However, the QuickBooks Premier edition contains more extensive inventory-tracking features that allow larger manufacturing operations to track inventory components used in various phases of the manufacturing process and to "build assemblies." This Premier version also allows you to assign minimum inventory reorder points to alert you when it's time to reorder. It also offers a special Manufacturing & Wholesale Chart of Accounts that is especially helpful in setting up manufacturing businesses.

Creating Your Chart of Accounts

Fortunately, with QuickBooks, you don't need to know very much about accounting to set up your Chart of Accounts. Most of the accounts are automatically created when you create a new company using the dialog box shown in Figure 1-2. This dialog box appears on-screen the first time you open the QuickBooks program.

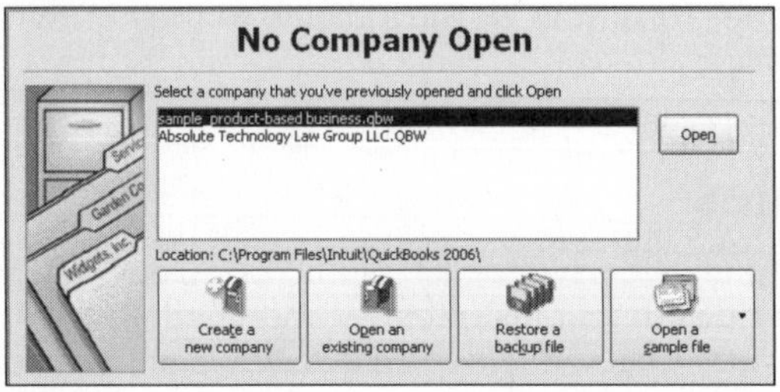

Figure 1-2: This screen appears, with a button for you to create a new company, the first time you open QuickBooks.

Click the Create a New Company button to begin the QuickBooks EasyStep Interview. This unique feature asks you questions about your business relevant to setting up your Chart of Accounts. The dialog box that appears to take you through the EasyStep Interview appears in Figure 1-3.

Some standard accounts, such as Accounts Receivable, are automatically created for all new companies. Other accounts, such as sales tax or inventory accounts, are created as needed by your particular business based on your answers to the questions on the EasyStep Interview. In addition to saving time, the preselected standard charts offer the benefit of added professional expertise. Sophisticated accountants with specialized industry knowledge have developed each chart — the same people who would normally charge you exorbitant hourly rates to come to your office and help you set up an accounting system.

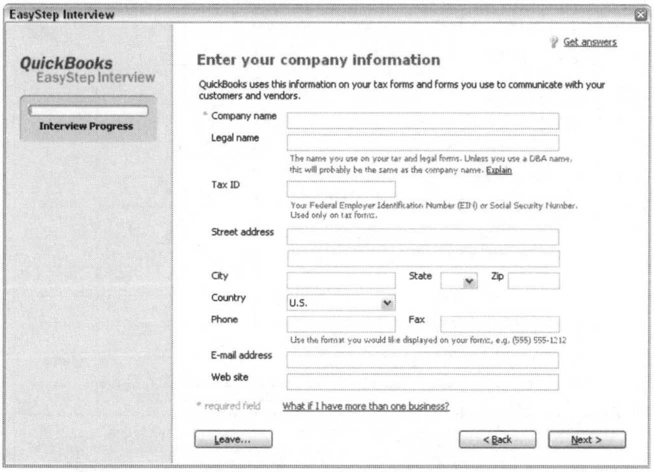

Figure 1-3: The EasyStep interview prompts you for all information needed to set up your basic Chart of Accounts.

Registers: Tracking Your Asset and Liability Accounts

As defined earlier, a register is a chronological list of transactions for each asset and liability account maintained by a company. Each asset and liability account has its own register. The register shows you all the transactions that affect the balance in the account. A QuickBooks register is conceptually identical to your checkbook register, which records the activity in your checking account.

Asset and liability accounts, as their name implies, track the assets and liabilities of your company. In other words, they tell you what the company owns (including cash balances) and what it owes. Asset and liability accounts are reported on your company's balance sheet, as discussed in more detail in Chapters 28 and 29.

By viewing the account register, you can review all the transactions that have affected the balance in the account since the beginning of the accounting period (the start date). For example, the window for your Accounts Receivable register displays information about invoices, customer payments, returns, finance charges, and credit memos (see Figure 1-4). QuickBooks automatically updates the account balance shown in the register after each accounts receivable transaction.

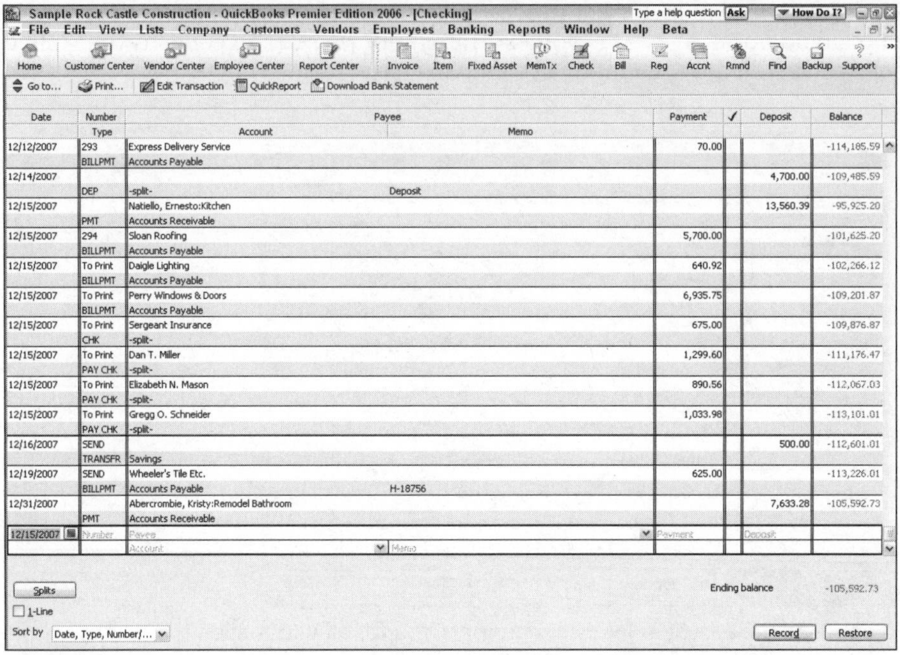

Figure 1-4: This check window reveals the transactions that affect the account and its current balance.

Cross-Reference

Chapter 19 includes a detailed discussion of registers.

Organizing with Lists

Lists are the QuickBooks answer to database management. Using lists, you can easily maintain databases of important information that allows you to organize customers, vendors, employees, and jobs into categories and types. Figure 1-5 shows a list of vendor types maintained by a QuickBooks company. All list windows follow the same general format and have two important menu buttons, located at the bottom, for accessing drop-down menus. The first menu button is labeled with the same name as the list itself and allows you to edit the list; in the case of Figure 1-5, the button is labeled Vendor Type. Use this button to update and change the list (such as add or delete a vendor) by clicking the button in the bottom left corner of the window. Use the second button, labeled Activities, to perform transactions related to the information on the list — such as recording receipts and payments. On some screens, a button labeled Reports appears, which allows you to access information about the entry (such as the contact information for vendors) and historical transactions that pertain to each list entry.

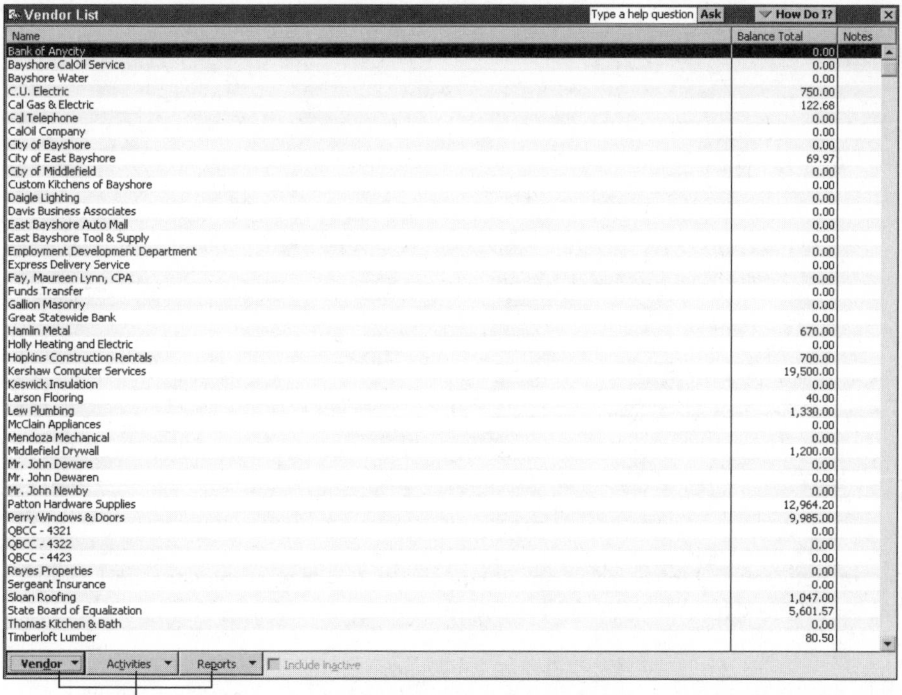

Click these buttons to access menus for list-related activities

Figure 1-5: QuickBooks allows you to create lists, such as this list of different types of vendors, as a database management tool. Each list has buttons that allow you to access pop-up menus for information and transactions related to each item on the list.

Taking Control with Centers

QuickBooks organizes information about vendors, customers, employees, and reports into databases called *centers*, which can be accessed from the icons below the menu bar, as shown in Figure 1-6. The Customer Center screen, shown in Figure 1-7, allows a user to view a list of customers (on the left of the screen) and detailed information about each customer in the list simply by clicking on it. The customer center contains historical and billing information about each customer, similar to a Rolodex or cabinet containing paper files on customers. Your Customer List might include, for example, names, addresses, and billing information. Similarly, an Employee List contains the names of personnel and all of the information necessary for preparing payroll checks and withholding payroll taxes

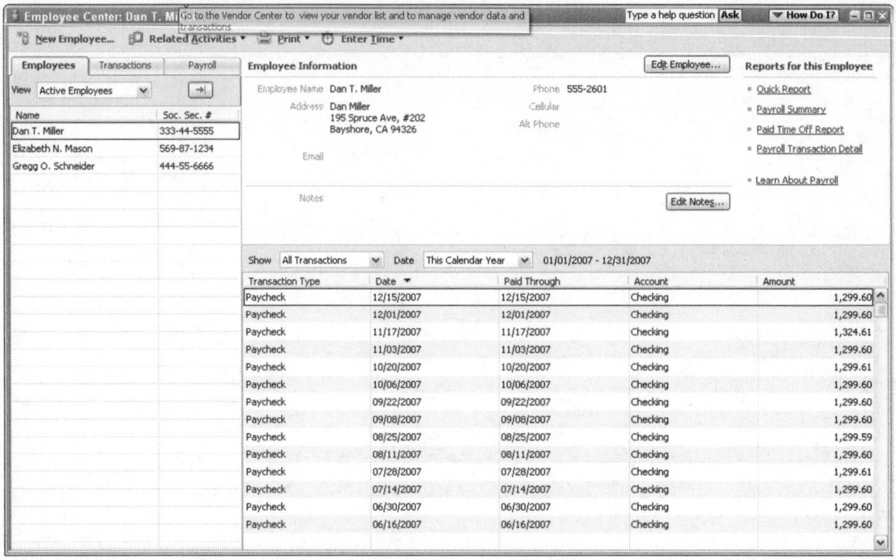

Figure 1-6: Detailed information about customers, vendors, employees, and reports can be accessed from the QuickBooks centers.

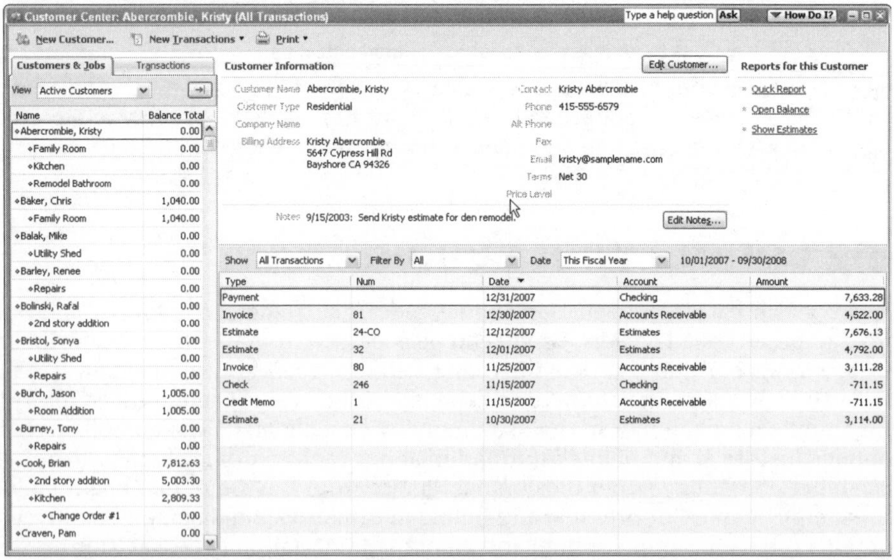

Figure 1-7: View detailed information about customers on a single screen.

Custom fields identify the specific information that will be maintained on each customer, employee, vendor, or job in your centers. For example, in your Employee Center, you might decide to include these custom fields for each employee included on your list:

✦ Name

✦ Address

✦ Social Security number

✦ Date of birth

✦ Date of hire

✦ Job title

✦ Date of termination

You can easily add a new listing of information maintained in each center (such as a new employee or customer) by clicking an icon on the screen, as shown previously in Figure 1-7, to access the dialog box shown in Figure 1-8.

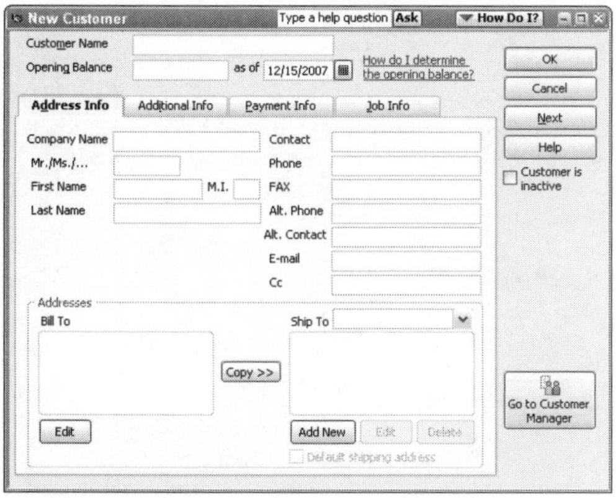

Figure 1-8: You can customize the columns of information maintained in your lists.

Cross-Reference

Chapter 8 explains how to create, edit, organize, and maintain lists. Additionally, Chapter 22 contains specific information about Employee Lists.

Indexing with Items

Items comprise the indexing system used for tracking the services and products that you regularly sell, resell, or purchase for use in your business. You can also use Items to standardize recurring calculations such as discounts or sales taxes imposed by various locales.

When you are completing an invoice for a customer, you can quickly enter each service or product by accessing a drop-down menu. Each Item selected from the list contains additional information about the product. You can also access any applicable discounts or taxes from the Items menu. QuickBooks automatically calculates an amount due based on the cost of the Item and the quantity entered. Figure 1-9 shows a list of Items maintained by a construction company. Chapter 10 explains the types and uses of QuickBooks Items.

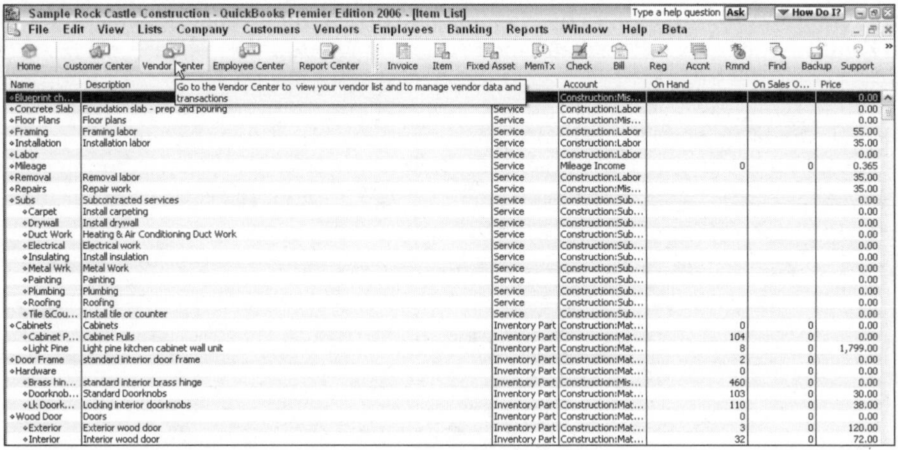

Figure 1-9: A sample list of items.

Figure 1-10 shows the window that appears when a sample Item (a cabinet pull) is right-clicked from the list shown in Figure 1-9. When you choose an Item from a drop-down list accessed directly from the sales form, QuickBooks automatically enters all relevant descriptive information on the form.

QuickBooks also uses previously entered information about the Item to automatically adjust the balances in the appropriate income, expense, and inventory accounts, which can be adjusted as previously shown in Figure 1-9.

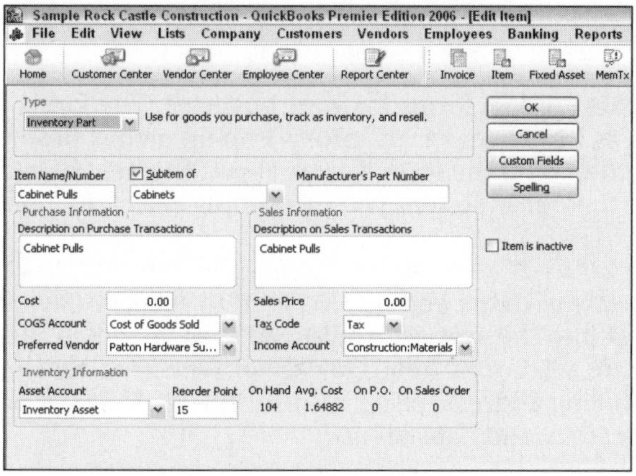

Figure 1-10: This Edit window for cabinet pulls allows you to edit information for transactions in which this Item is used.

Reports and graphs, discussed in Chapter 30, can provide additional insight as to which service and product Items are most profitable for your business. Figure 1-11 shows a QuickReport for the Inventory Item, cabinet pulls, which is you access by clicking the Reports button on the bottom of the Item screen and selecting QuickReport:Cabinet Pulls or by pressing Ctrl+Q.

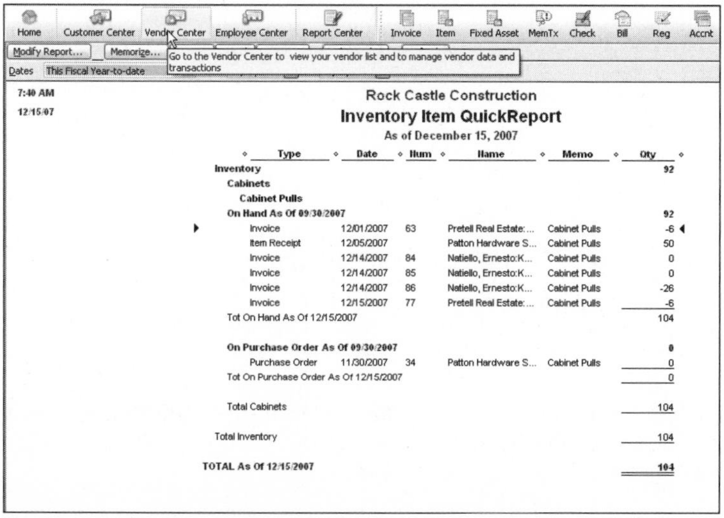

Figure 1-11: A sample QuickReport for an Item.

Using Forms

You can use QuickBooks to create custom forms for your business. The forms contain blanks to be filled in, such as for names or inventory. Pop-up menus prompt you for the information to be entered on the form. For example, the Item blank on an invoice causes the Item List to appear so that you can simply select an Item from the list rather than typing it.

Appropriate accounts are instantly updated and recalculated to reflect relevant transactions as they are entered into the system. Additionally, as you fill in the standard form fields with a name from a list or an Item, QuickBooks automatically enters other information such as the billing address, price, or description. This not only saves time but also ensures accuracy and consistency.

The custom forms that you create and save are called *templates*. QuickBooks also comes with standard form templates, which you can modify and save as your business needs dictate. Figure 1-12 shows the available standard templates.

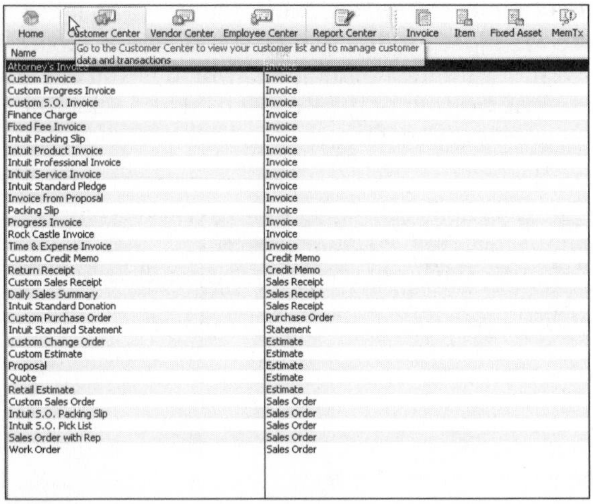

Figure 1-12: To access the standard templates, choose Templates from the Lists menu.

Cross-Reference

Chapter 5 tells you, in depth, how to create, edit, and use QuickBooks forms to document your business transactions.

Time-Saving Features

QuickBooks has a number of features designed to record and document the daily transactions of a business and to make it fast and easy to do so. For example, convenient drop-down menus for lists and Items make it easy to find information. QuickBooks has a number of features that you can use to minimize data entry on your forms and provide instant access to routinely needed information. These features are discussed in the following sections.

Quick Add

Quick Add is a handy feature that enables you to add customer, employee, vendor, and job information on-the-fly. For example, if you are completing a form for a new customer whose name does not appear on your Customer List, QuickBooks prompts you to add that customer information now.

The appearance of the prompt screen showing the Quick Add and Set Up options is a reminder to ensure that Customer, Vendor, and Employee Lists are kept current. If you want to enter only a name on the list, choose Quick Add. To enter additional relevant information, such as an address and billing information, choose the Set Up option.

Quick Fill

You may be familiar with this feature from other Windows-based programs. In QuickBooks, if you type the first few letters of a name or Item, QuickBooks automatically fills in the rest of the word and other stored information, such as the customer name or address or the price of an Item.

Quick Recall

When activated by a Preference menu command, Quick Recall fills in data from the last transaction, such as the recording of a sale or a check. This is useful, for example, if you are processing a number of customer rebate checks or identical employee bonus checks. You can still change individual fields when this function is activated, but you don't need to enter recurring data.

Quick Math

To make basic calculations, you can perform a simple Quick Math calculation in any numeric field. This very simple, but extremely useful, function is often overlooked.

Take note of it now. You will use it often. To use Quick Math to calculate a transaction, follow these steps:

1. Click in the field where you want to make the calculation.
2. Type a number followed by one of these operators: =, ∞, +, *, or /.
3. Continue typing numbers and mathematical operators to complete the desired calculation. An image of a paper adding machine tape appears showing the numbers you entered.
4. Press Tab or Enter to display the result of the calculation in your numeric field.
5. Press C to clear the calculation when you are finished.

The Find function

QuickBooks has a sophisticated Find feature that you can access from the Edit menu. You can locate transactions and other information in the program using a name, amount, date, memo, or other transaction information. Figure 1-13 shows the QuickBooks Find window, which is accessed through the Edit menu.

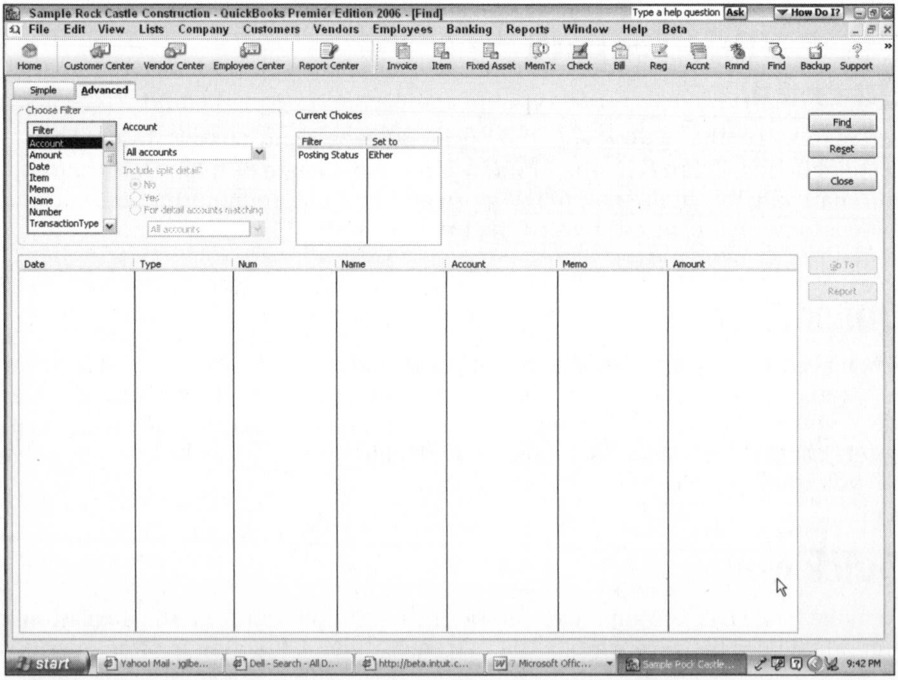

Figure 1-13: You can search for specific transactions using the QuickBooks Find window.

To use the Find option, follow these steps:

1. Choose Find from the Edit menu.
2. Click the Advanced tab, select one of the filter criteria displayed in the Find window using the Filter scroll box, and indicate the criterion for your search.
3. Click Find.
4. Select the transactions that you want to see from among those meeting your search criterion. To see the original form where the transaction was entered, you can double-click any transaction that appears on the list.
5. Click Reset if you want to enter additional criteria or Close if you are finished and want to close the screen.

Memorized transactions

You can "memorize" recurring transactions, such as the monthly rent for your office or a recurring monthly billing for a regular customer. Memorized transactions are discussed in Chapter 14.

Reports and Graphs

QuickBooks generates over 50 types of standard reports and graphs to help you analyze the performance of your company. Reports organize and summarize the data from the transactions you enter. These reports give you a snapshot of your business's profitability and value.

You can generate reports directly without the benefit of an accountant or professional financial advisor. You can access this data at any time, but typically you would review and compare your company's performance over a set period of time such as a weekly, monthly, or quarterly cycle. This section provides a brief sampling of the many available types of reports and graphs.

The Profit and Loss Statement

The Profit and Loss Statement shows the profitability of your business for the relevant period by summarizing all of the data entered in the income and expense accounts. The information on the statement is updated instantly each time a transaction is entered, and you can view year-to-date information at any time. Figure 1-14 shows a sample QuickBooks Profit and Loss Statement.

Rock Castle Construction

Profit & Loss

December 1 - 15, 2007

	Dec 1 - 15, 07	
Ordinary Income/Expense		
Income		
Construction		
Labor	15,066.00	
Materials	31,898.01	
Miscellaneous	2,232.03	
Subcontractors	22,122.01	
Total Construction		71,318.05
Total Income		71,318.05
Cost of Goods Sold		
Cost of Goods Sold		4,669.78
Total COGS		4,669.78
Gross Profit		66,648.27
Expense		
Automobile		
Fuel	71.02	
Total Automobile		71.02
Bank Service Charges		10.00
Freight & Delivery		104.60

Figure 1-14: The Profit and Loss Statement is also referred to as the Income Statement.

The Balance Sheet

The Balance Sheet shows the value of your business as of a certain date. It is sometimes called a *statement of financial position* because it depicts a snapshot of a company's financial position as of the report date. It displays and summarizes the balances of all of the asset and liability accounts. Figure 1-15 shows a sample QuickBooks Balance Sheet.

The sales report by Item

The sales report is a breakdown of your company's sales. It reveals the percentage of total sales and gross profit attributable to each Item that your business sells. Sales reports can be generated in several different formats, such as by Item or by customer. An analysis of a sales report by Item enables you to identify your most profitable products. Figure 1-16 shows a Sales by Item Summary Report presented by Item.

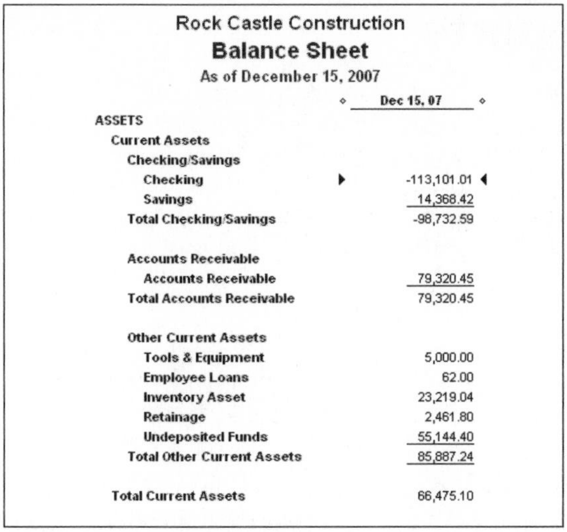

Rock Castle Construction

Balance Sheet

As of December 15, 2007

	Dec 15, 07
ASSETS	
Current Assets	
Checking/Savings	
Checking	-113,101.01
Savings	14,368.42
Total Checking/Savings	-98,732.59
Accounts Receivable	
Accounts Receivable	79,320.45
Total Accounts Receivable	79,320.45
Other Current Assets	
Tools & Equipment	5,000.00
Employee Loans	62.00
Inventory Asset	23,219.04
Retainage	2,461.80
Undeposited Funds	55,144.40
Total Other Current Assets	85,887.24
Total Current Assets	66,475.10

Figure 1-15: The Balance Sheet summarizes the assets and liabilities of your business.

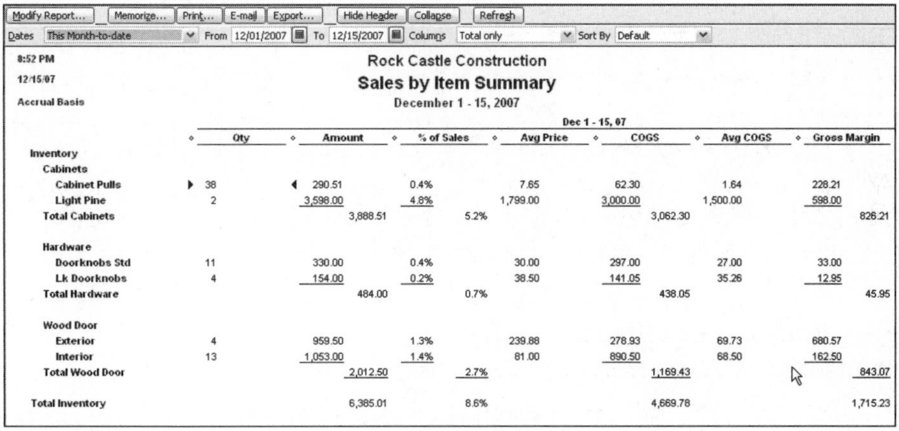

Modify Report... Memorize... Print... E-mail Export... Hide Header Collapse Refresh

Dates This Month-to-date From 12/01/2007 To 12/15/2007 Columns Total only Sort By Default

8:52 PM

12/15/07

Accrual Basis

Rock Castle Construction

Sales by Item Summary

December 1 - 15, 2007

	Dec 1 - 15, 07						
	Qty	Amount	% of Sales	Avg Price	COGS	Avg COGS	Gross Margin
Inventory							
Cabinets							
Cabinet Pulls	38	290.51	0.4%	7.65	62.30	1.64	228.21
Light Pine	2	3,598.00	4.8%	1,799.00	3,000.00	1,500.00	598.00
Total Cabinets		3,888.51	5.2%		3,062.30		826.21
Hardware							
Doorknobs Std	11	330.00	0.4%	30.00	297.00	27.00	33.00
Lk Doorknobs	4	154.00	0.2%	38.50	141.05	35.26	12.95
Total Hardware		484.00	0.7%		438.05		45.95
Wood Door							
Exterior	4	959.50	1.3%	239.88	278.93	69.73	680.57
Interior	13	1,053.00	1.4%	81.00	890.50	68.50	162.50
Total Wood Door		2,012.50	2.7%		1,169.43		843.07
Total Inventory		6,385.01	8.6%		4,669.78		1,715.23

Figure 1-16: This sales report presented by Item shows which products have the highest percentage of sales.

Generating QuickReports

QuickReports are useful summaries of information contained in the account registers. You can access the QuickReports function from the Employee and Vendor Centers, shown in Figures 1-17 and 1-18, whenever you display a list, an account register, or a form with a name field. Simply click the QuickReports button on the list, register, or form to create summaries of account activity (such as receivables or payables) or customer and vendor histories. Figure 1-18 shows a QuickReport of a customer history.

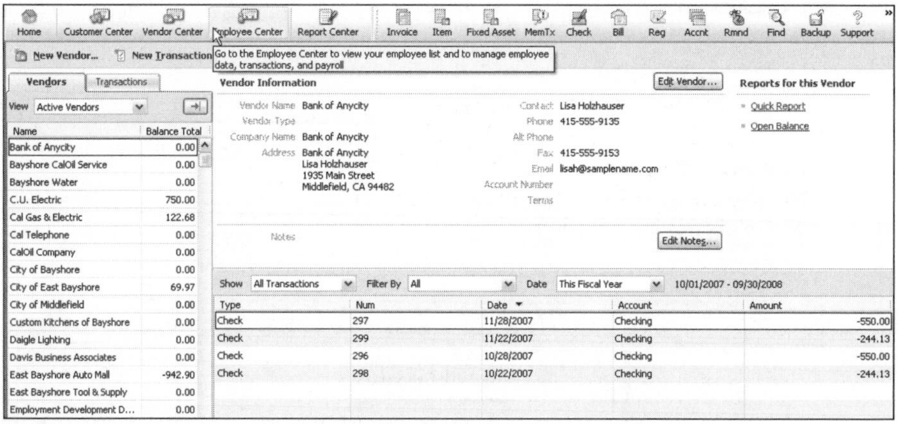

Figure 1-17: You can access Quick Reports from the Vendors and Customers Center by clicking on a link.

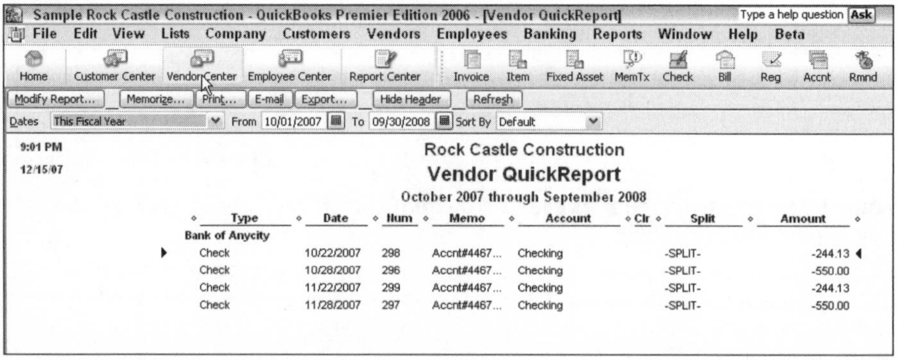

Figure 1-18: Quick Reports summarize information about a specific vendor or customer for the period you specify.

Analyzing Information with Graphs

QuickBooks generates several kinds of graphs. *Graphs* give you an immediate picture of the relationships among various pieces of information. QuickBooks provides graphs showing Income and Expenses, Sales, Accounts Receivable, Net Worth, Budget vs. Actual, and Accounts Payable. Figure 1-19 shows a graph of sales for a sample company.

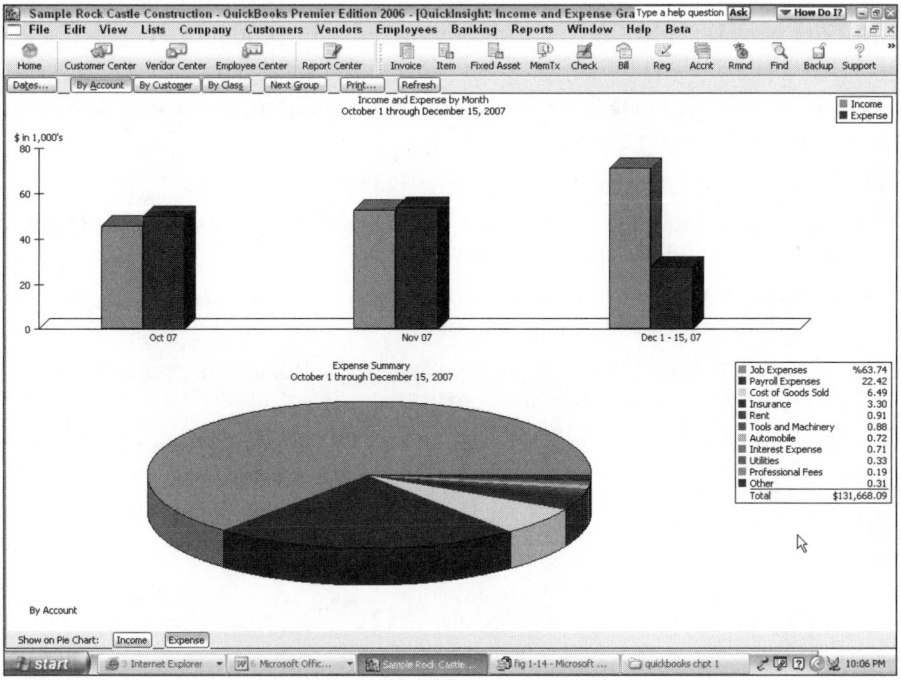

Figure 1-19: Create graphical representations of reports.

Budgeting with QuickBooks

QuickBooks enables you to set up a budget showing your projected income and account balances. You can then compare your company's actual performance with the anticipated amounts shown in your budget. Chapter 31 explores the process of setting up a budget.

Summary

QuickBooks is a complete accounting system that enables nonaccountants and accountants to record, process, and analyze accounting data. Nonaccountants can use QuickBooks without the ongoing assistance of an accountant or financial professional. A few of the QuickBooks features that you learned about in this chapter included the following:

- The Chart of Accounts meets the needs of any business entity.
- Lists perform convenient database functions for products, customers, and other information essential to your business.
- The Items menu makes it easy to index and standardize information about products, inventory, and services.
- Standardized forms streamline business documentation.
- QuickBooks has several easy-to-use, time-saving features, such as Quick Add, Quick Fill, Quick Recall, and Quick Math.
- Registers maintain up-to-date account balances and historical information for individual asset and liability accounts
- With a click of your mouse, you can create graphical representations of financial information contained in reports.
- The QuickBooks budgeting feature allows you to compare the actual performance of your business to the projected performance.

✦ ✦ ✦

CHAPTER 2

Twenty Minutes to Navigating QuickBooks

In This Chapter

Welcome screen options

QuickBooks Navigator

Navigating sales and customers

Getting plenty of help

Entering a practice transaction

It is a peculiarity of the QuickBooks program that to access and browse its features you must first open a data file for a company — any company. Sample company ata files are included for both QuickBooks and QuickBooks Pro. This sample company is called the Rock Castle Construction Company. Using sample data gives you the luxury of experimenting and exploring without the risk of doing any lasting damage to a real company's records.

Opening the Sample Company File

The sample company data provides a great opportunity for you to experiment with different types of transactions. You can open the files for these fictitious companies either from the Welcome screen or from the File menu. To access the sample company data from the Welcome screen, follow these steps:

1. After launching QuickBooks, Go to File ⇨ Open a New Company and select Sample Product Based Business from the dialog box that appears on your screen, as shown in Figure 2-1.
2. The warning screen shown in Figure 2-2 appears. Click OK.

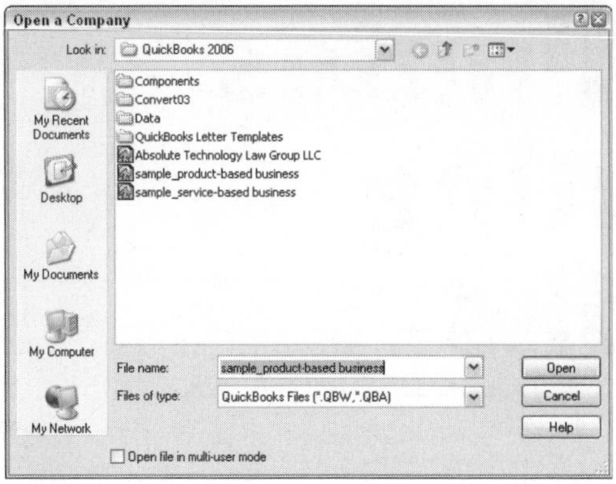

Figure 2-1: Opening a sample data company.

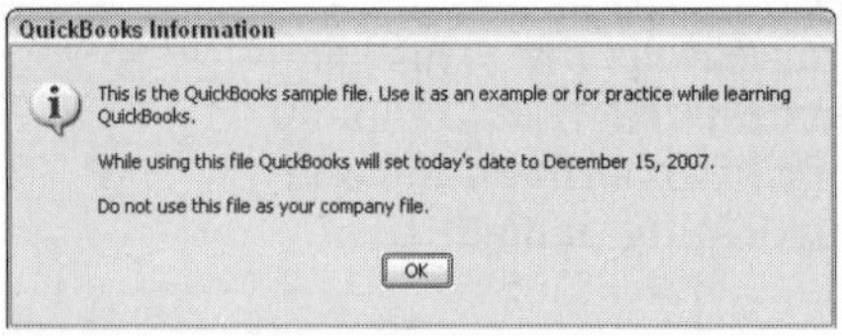

Figure 2-2: This warning appears to let you know you are opening a sample data company.

The Company Navigator screen for the sample data company appears as shown in Figure 2-3.

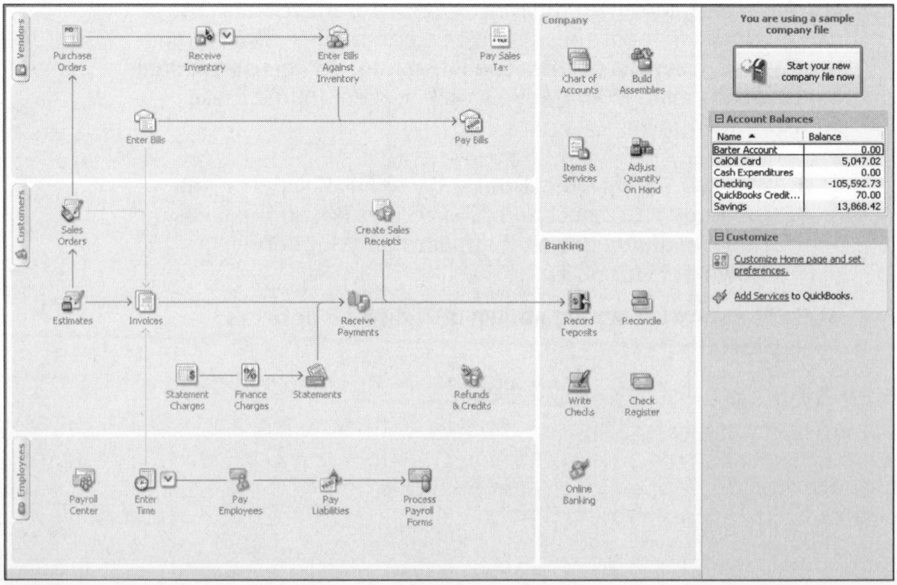

Figure 2-3: The Company Navigator screen.

QuickBooks Navigator

Most QuickBooks users view the Navigator as a faster and more efficient alternative to the standard menus, and many also find that it gives them a better understanding of the flow of transactions, the accounting cycle, and the underlying data that appears on their reports.

Navigating basics

The QuickBooks Navigator is a visual alternative to the standard Windows-based menus. But it is more than a pretty face. The Navigator affords fast and powerful access to every feature of QuickBooks by logically grouping Activity icons in the five major sections of the screen.

The tasks and workflow shown on the Home page reflect how you use QuickBooks to run your business. The version of the Home page you see when you start QuickBooks is based on your company file preferences or how you answered the questions about your business in the EasyStep Interview.

Accessing preferences to change the Navigator screen

You can change these icons to serve the needs of your particular business by following these steps:

1. Click Home to go to the Home page.
2. In the Customize box, click Customize Home Page.
3. On the Company Preferences tab, select or clear the check boxes for the task icons you want to show or hide. At the bottom of the Company Preferences tab is a list of the QuickBooks features that you can enable or disable. Next to each feature name is an indicator of its current status (on or off). To turn a feature on or off, click the blue link and then make the appropriate changes.
4. Click OK.

The following is a discussion of the five different Navigator sections, all of which you will want to become familiar with.

The Company Navigator Section

The Company section of the Navigator screen, shown in Figure 2-4, includes icons and access to the program sections based on your answers to the EasyStep Interview. You can also edit what appears on this screen by using the Preferences option, as shown in Figure 2-5.

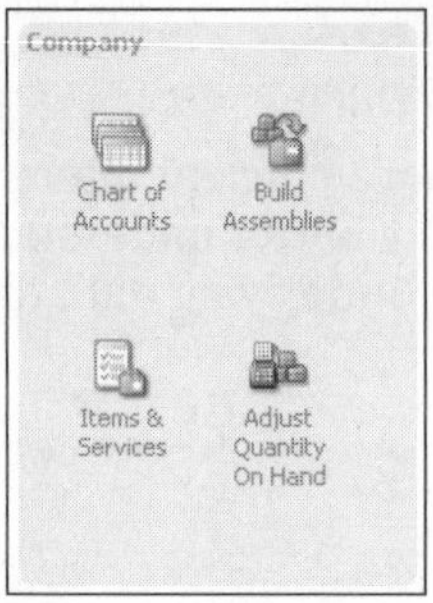

Figure 2-4: The Company Navigator screen allows you to quickly access the company's Chart of Accounts and initiate its most significant inventory and service transactions.

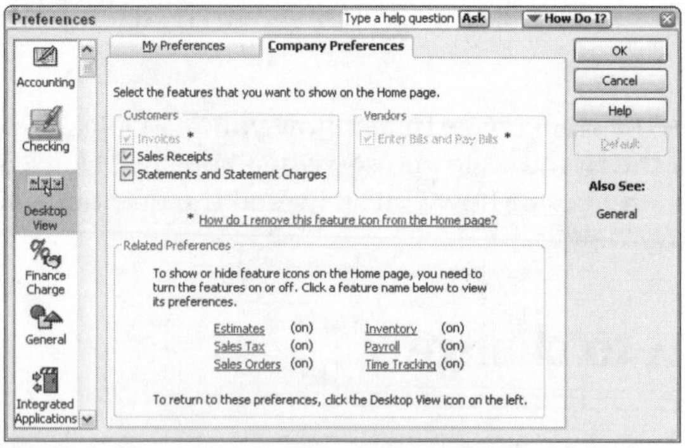

Figure 2-5: Edit the Company section of the main navigator screen using this Preferences window.

Almost always, the icons shown in this section include:

- ✦ **Chart of Accounts:** The Chart of Accounts is a listing of all of the income statement and balance sheet accounts maintained by your company. You can make changes to your Chart of Accounts directly from this section of the Navigator screen.
- ✦ **Items & Services:** You can access lists and make adjustments to inventory and service items.

The Customers Section of the Navigator

The icons shown in Customers section of the Navigator screen shown in Figure 2-6 allow you to access program sections relevant to your company's cycle of providing a product or service. It allows you to access all of the program features and information you need to service and track your customers. Functional icons are organized in a convenient flowchart format that reflects the chronological order of a customer sale cycle. Working clockwise, to the right of those icons, you can access links for customer-related activities such as invoicing, sending forms, and processing payments. Just below the activity links, you find a menu for accessing various types of customer reports. And to the left, in the lower left-hand corner, QuickBooks promotes its other convenient services (available to you for an extra fee) by providing you with links to them, including a credit-checking service and a link to buy more software from Intuit, the makers of QuickBooks.

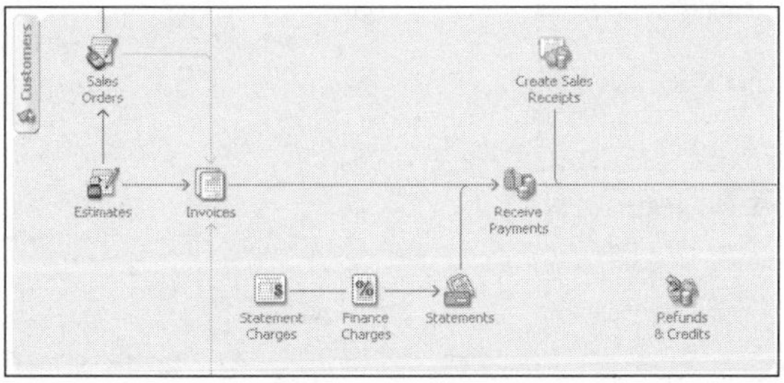

Figure 2-6: Preferences for information that appears in the Customers section of the Navigator screen.

The Vendors Navigator

The Vendors section of the Navigator screen, shown in Figure 2-7, is similar to the Customers section screen discussed in the previous section.

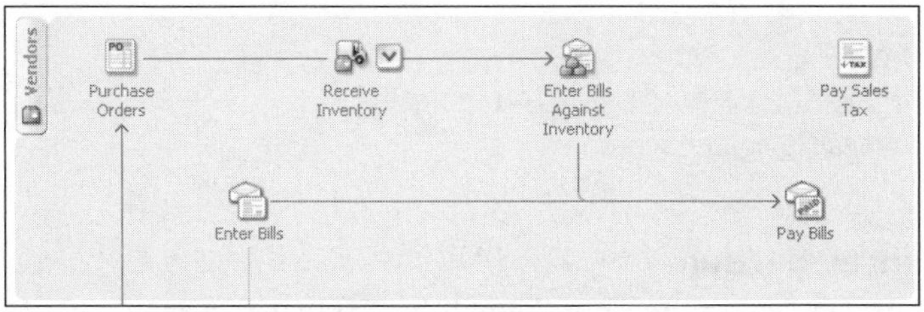

Figure 2-7: The Vendors section of the Navigator screen.

The Vendors section of the Navigator screen allows you to access all program features and information you need to service and track transactions with your vendors. Functional icons are organized in a convenient flowchart format that reflects the chronological order of transactions with your vendor: generating a purchase order, receiving your bill, paying your bill, and so on. You can change the icons that appear in the Vendors section of the Navigator screen using the Purchases & Vendors Preferences screen shown in Figure 2-8.

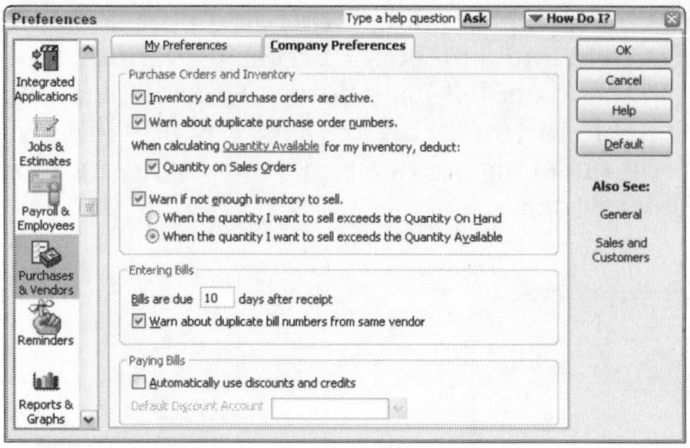

Figure 2-8: The Purchases & Vendors Preferences screen.

The Employees Navigator

The Employees section of the Navigator screen, shown in Figure 2-9, is the "human resources" department of QuickBooks. It contains an icon section to access program features for tracking time, payroll liabilities, and payments to employees. The Related Activities section contains links that allow you to launch specific tasks relative to managing your employees.

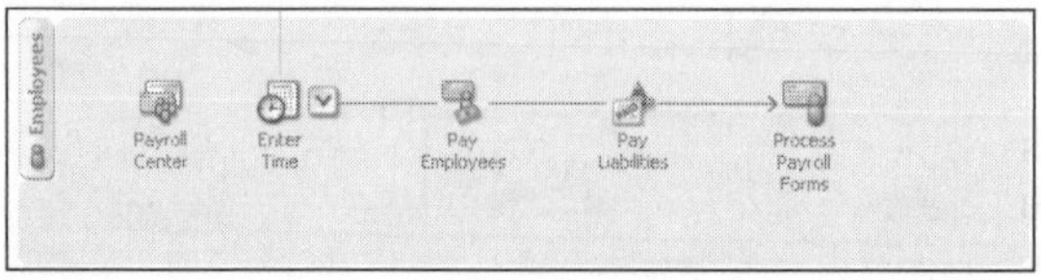

Figure 2-9: The Employees Navigator screen.

The Account Balances Section

The Account Balances section on the right side of the Navigator screen, shown in Figure 2-10, displays the current balance all of your checking and other cash accounts. You can click any account to display a register of transactions for the account (which looks like a checkbook register) as shown in Figure 2-11.

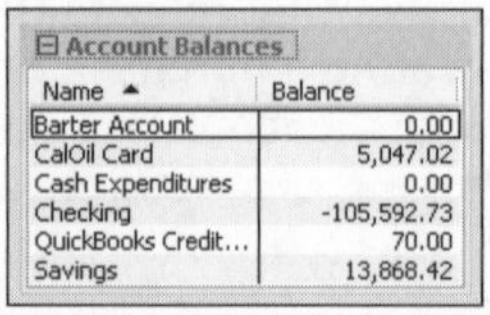

Account Balances
Name
Balance
Barter Account 0.00
CalOil Card 5,047.02
Cash Expenditures 0.00
Checking -105,592.73
QuickBooks Credit... 70.00
Savings 13,868.42

Figure 2-10: The Account Balances Section of Navigator screen.

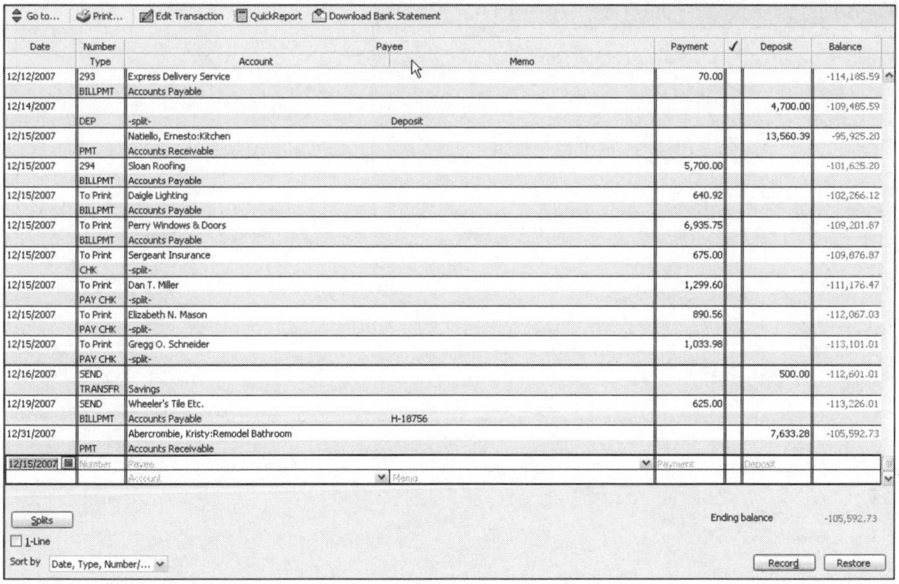

Go to...
Print...
Edit Transaction
QuickReport
Download Bank Statement
Date
Number
Type
Payee
Account
Memo
Payment
Deposit
Balance
12/12/2007 293 BILLPMT Express Delivery Service Accounts Payable 70.00 -114,185.59
12/14/2007 DEP -split- Deposit 4,700.00 -109,485.59
12/15/2007 PMT Natiello, Ernesto:Kitchen Accounts Receivable 13,560.39 -95,925.20
12/15/2007 294 BILLPMT Sloan Roofing Accounts Payable 5,700.00 -101,625.20
12/15/2007 To Print BILLPMT Daigle Lighting Accounts Payable 640.92 -102,266.12
12/15/2007 To Print BILLPMT Perry Windows & Doors Accounts Payable 6,935.75 -109,201.87
12/15/2007 To Print CHK Sergeant Insurance -split- 675.00 -109,876.87
12/15/2007 To Print PAY CHK Dan T. Miller -split- 1,299.60 -111,176.47
12/15/2007 To Print PAY CHK Elizabeth N. Mason -split- 890.56 -112,067.03
12/15/2007 To Print PAY CHK Gregg O. Schneider -split- 1,033.98 -113,101.01
12/16/2007 SEND TRANSFR Savings 500.00 -112,601.01
12/19/2007 SEND BILLPMT Wheeler's Tile Etc. Accounts Payable H-18756 625.00 -113,226.01
12/31/2007 PMT Abercrombie, Kristy:Remodel Bathroom Accounts Receivable 7,633.28 -105,592.73
12/15/2007
Splits
1-Line
Sort by Date, Type, Number/...
Ending balance -105,592.73
Record
Restore

Figure 2-11: A register of transactions is displayed when you click an account in the Account Balances section of the Navigator screen.

Getting Plenty of Help

Even if you are not a Help enthusiast because the Help features in other Windows programs have disappointed you, continue to read this section. You'll find some of the QuickBooks Help features to be truly useful.

Standard Help

Similar to other Windows programs, QuickBooks contains a standard Help menu that can be accessed from the taskbar at the top of the QuickBooks window, as shown in Figure 2-12.

You can resize and move the Help window. Use the tile option in the upper-right corner of the screen to reduce the size of the Help window. Simply click the border until a double arrow appears and then drag the Help window to where you want it.

The QuickBooks Learning Center

The Business Learning Center contains instructive articles, such as the Customers & Sales tutorial shown in Figure 2-13, on QuickBooks features and related accounting topics. It can be accessed through the Help menu. Select a general topic area by clicking the program area tabs on the left side of the screen, and then choose a link to a specific tutorial topic. The estimated time to complete each tutorial appears next to its link.

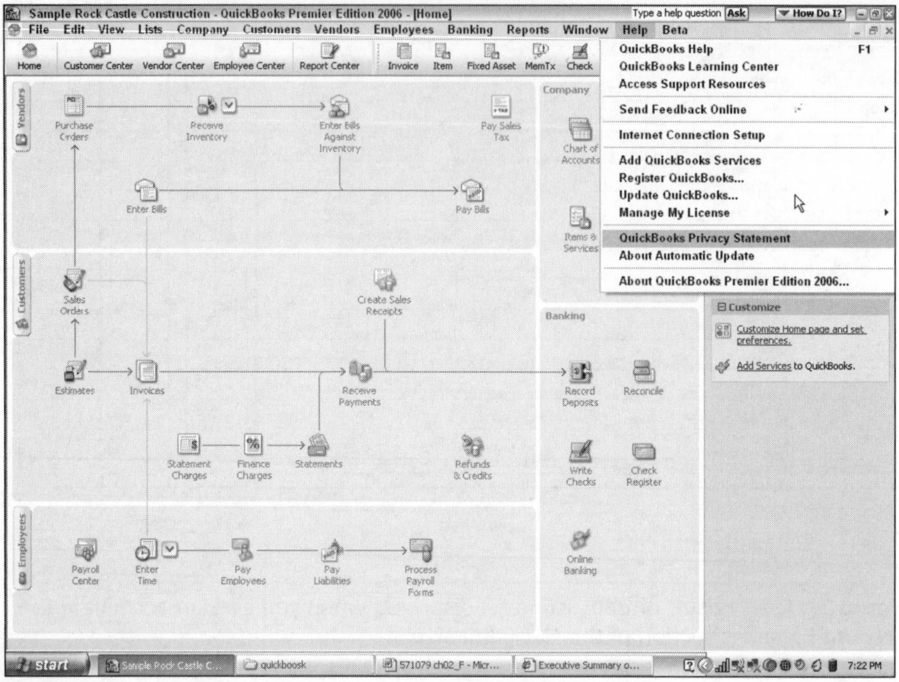

Figure 2-12: The QuickBooks Help features.

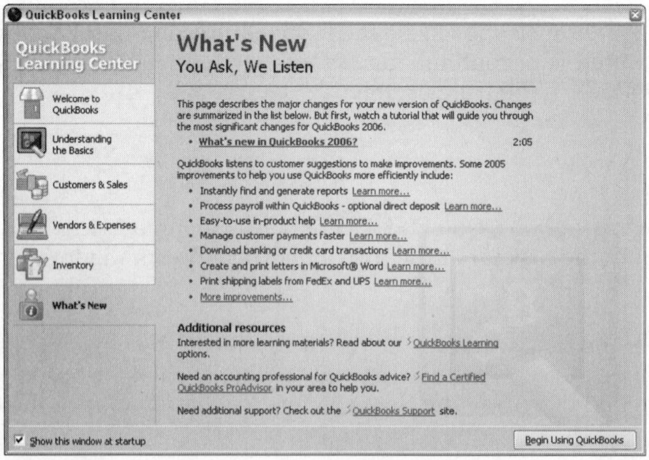

Figure 2-13: Access tutorials from the QuickBooks Learning Center.

Entering a Transaction

Your short tour of some of the main Navigator screens, centers, and menus and the sample company data has given you an overview of the sophisticated accounting and business management tools available in QuickBooks. One of the system's key features is that it instantly updates all affected accounts and records each time a transaction is entered. To get a feel for this, enter a simple practice transaction—a cash payment on an account—and then check the sample company's records to see that it was properly reflected.

A good transaction to start with is a simple cash payment on an open invoice. This is an easy transaction both to enter and to verify. Here's how:

1. Take a look at the outstanding account balance and aging information for a specific customer. In the Customer section of the Navigator screen, click the Receive payments icon. A Customer Payment window, such the one shown in Figure 2-14, appears.

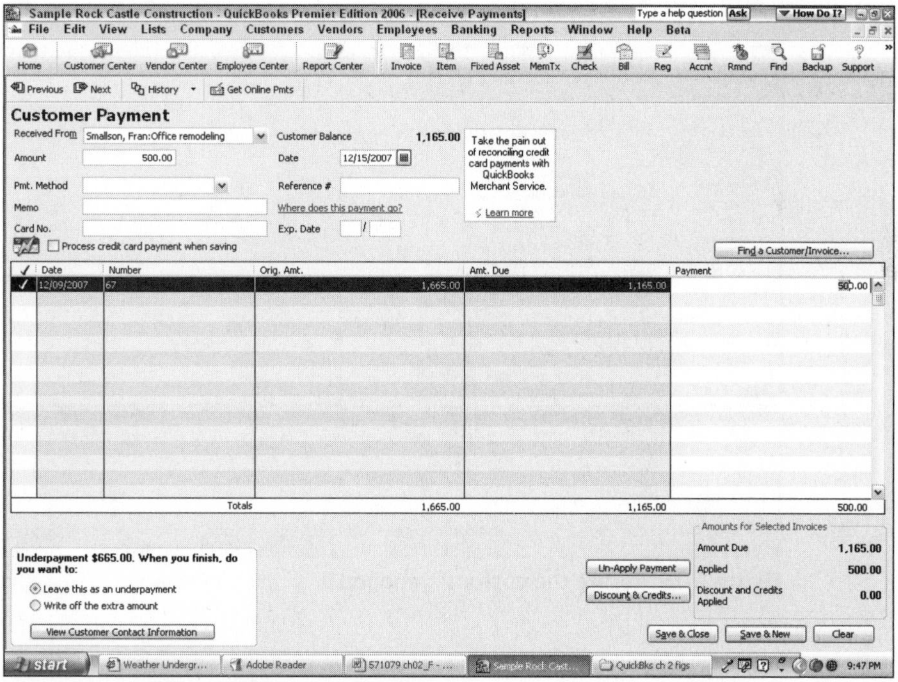

Figure 2-14: The Customer Payment window.

2. Locate the customer, the Smallson Fran: office remodeling, and the other information for the date, amount, and amount due.
3. Click Save & Close to apply the payment and adjust the account balances.
4. From the Navigator Screen, click the Customers icon on the left side of the screen to access the Customer Center screen.
5. Locate Smallson Fran: office remodeling and right click, as shown in Figure 2-15.
6. Select Use register. A customer register window appears.
7. Scroll to the bottom of the register, as shown in Figure 2-16, to locate the payment you entered and to view how this entry affects the account register for Fran Smallson.

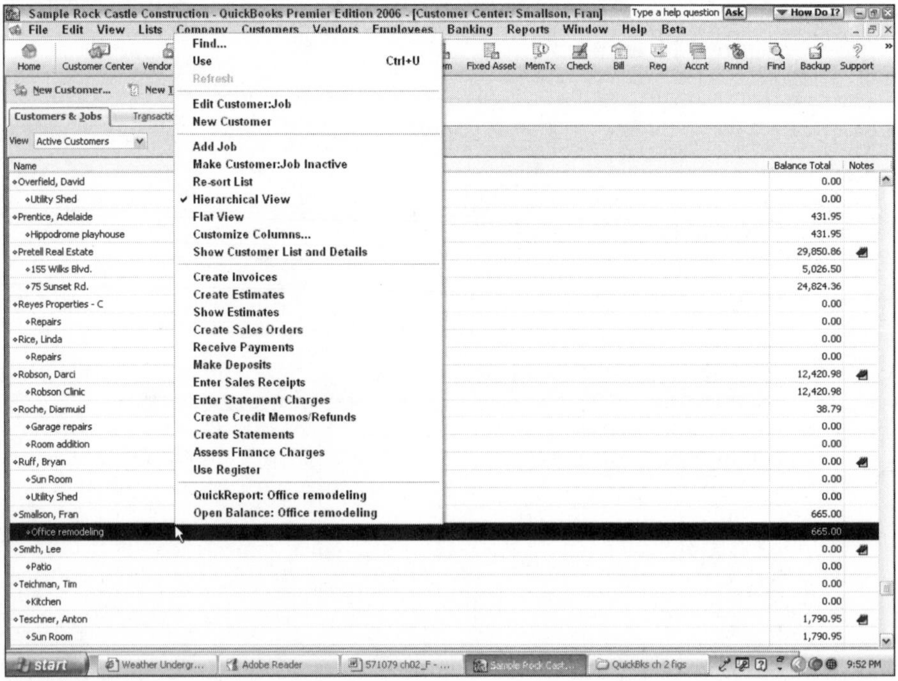

Figure 2-15: Locate the customer and job.

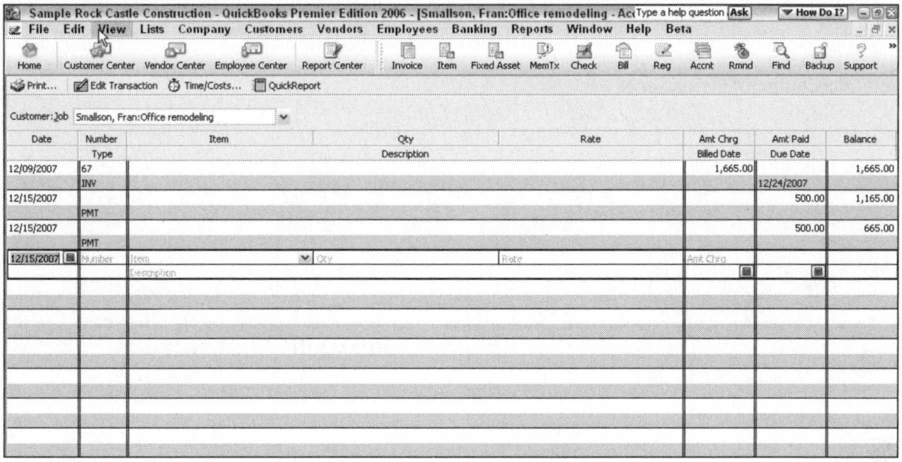

Figure 2-16: Locate the payment you have just entered.

Accessing Detailed Information via Centers

QuickBooks allows you to access detailed information about customers, vendors, employees and reports by using multifunctional screens, called *Centers*, within the program. Centers can be accessed from the menu bar, or by clicking icons on the Navigator screen as shown in Figure 2-17.

The Customer Center

You can use the Customer Center to access, from one screen, information about all of your customers and their transactions. From the default view of the Customer Center, shown in Figure 2-17, you can find customer contact information, past purchases and what invoices have been paid, outstanding balances, and more. In the default view of your Customer Center, the Customers & Jobs list is displayed on the left side of the Center, and the detailed information and transactions list for the selected customer or job is displayed on the right.

From the Customers & Jobs tab you can:

- ✦ Add or edit a job
- ✦ Add or edit notes about a customer or job
- ✦ Run an Open Balance report and other useful reports for your customers and jobs
- ✦ View some or all transactions for the selected customer

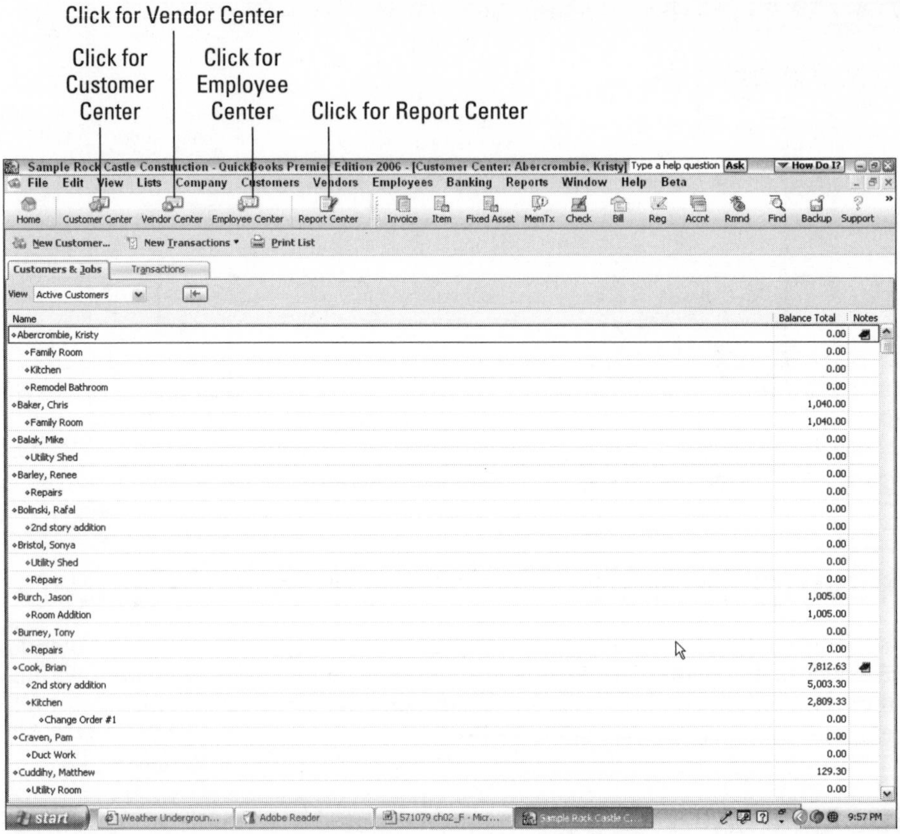

Figure 2-17: Access QuickBooks Centers from the Navigator screen or menu bar.

You can click the Transactions tab, shown in Figure 2-18, to access information about specific transactions.

Note

In QuickBooks, a *customer* is anyone who pays you for goods or services. A job is a specific project or scope of work that you want to track. Add or edit a customer.

The Vendor Center

The Vendor Center, shown in Figure 2-19, displays, in a single place, information about all of your vendors and their transactions. From the default view of the vendor center, you can add a new vendor, add a transaction to an existing vendor, or print the Vendor list or transaction list. You can also edit vendor information and notes.

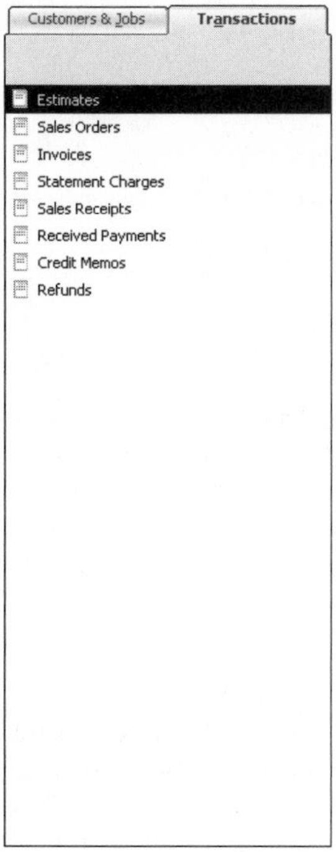

Figure 2-18: The Transactions tab.

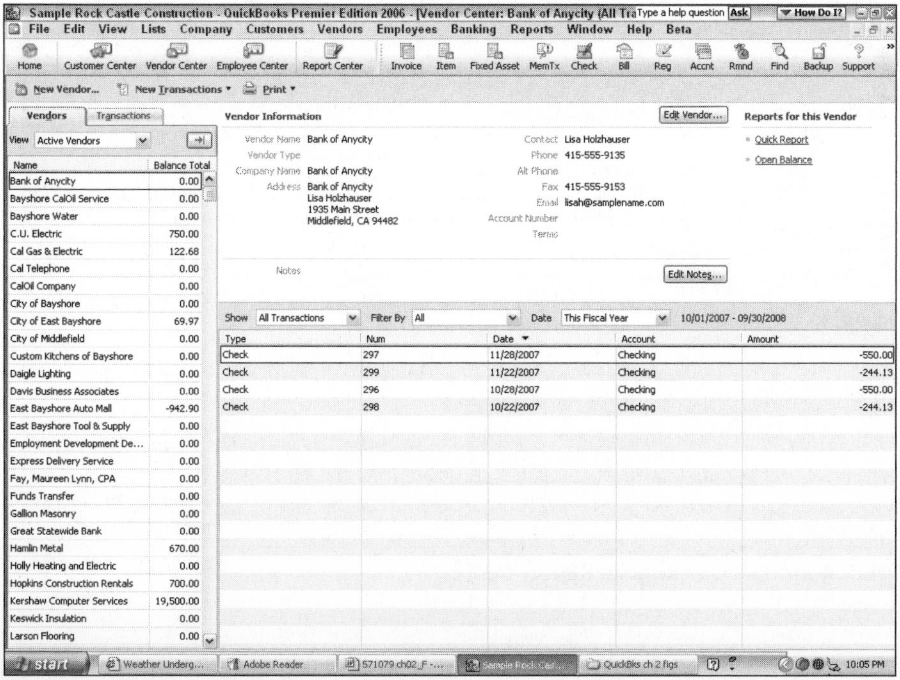

Figure 2-19: The QuickBooks Vendor Center.

On the Vendors tab of the Vendor center, you can:

✦ Edit a vendor's information

✦ Modify the contents of the Vendor list

✦ Run a Quick Report or Open Balance report for a vendor

✦ View and filter the list of transactions for a vendor

The Report Center

QuickBooks provides many preset reports that focus on all aspects of your business finances. You can find the Reports you need in order to provide instant information about your business from the Report Center shown in Figure 2-20.

The Employee Center

The Employee Center, shown in Figure 2-21, displays, in a single place, information about all of your employees and their transactions. You can add a new employee, add a transaction to an existing employee, or print employee and transaction information. You can also edit an employee's information or edit a note for the employee.

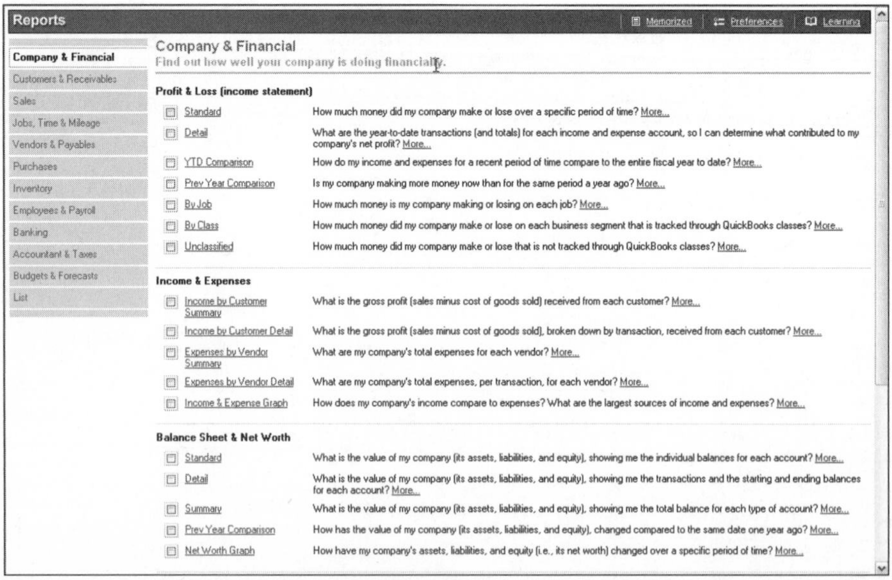

Figure 2-20: The QuickBooks Report Center.

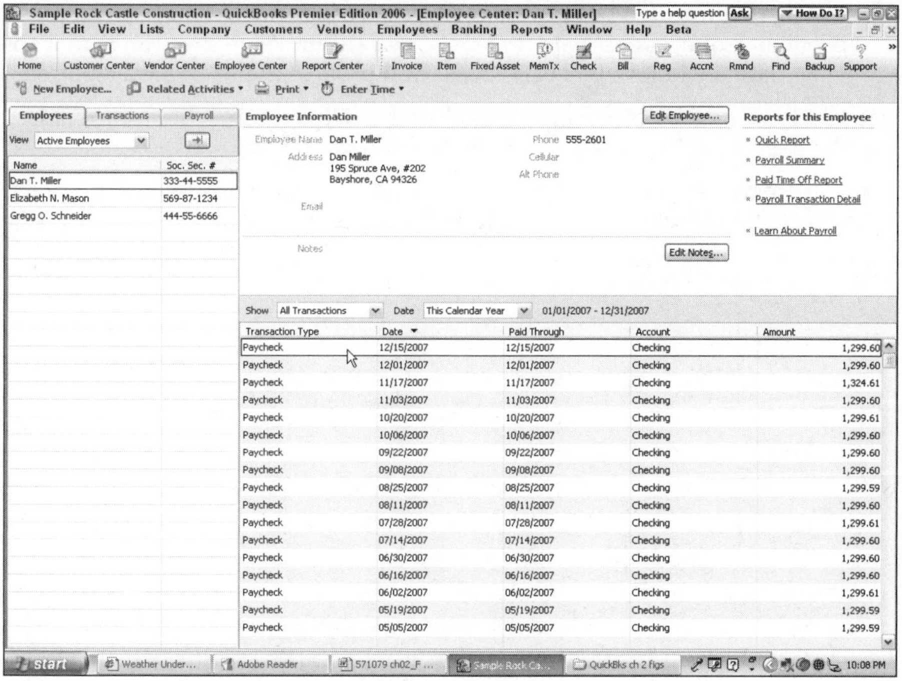

Figure 2-21: The QuickBooks Employee Center.

From the Employees tab, you can:

✦ Edit an employee's information

✦ Modify the contents of the Employee list

✦ View a list of active and released employees

✦ View and filter the list of transactions for an employee

Summary

This chapter introduced you to the QuickBooks Navigator and started you thinking about the advantages that it may offer over the standard menu format. It also showed you that QuickBooks is more than accounting software; it is a complete business management program with sophisticated tools for financial analysis and decision-making.

- You were introduced to the Welcome screen's options and the program's peculiar requirement that you must open either a sample or an actual company data file before you can access and browse the program's features.
- You toured some of the unique and useful Help features, informational databases, and tutorials that QuickBooks has to offer.
- You entered a sample transaction and saw that QuickBooks does, indeed, automatically update all relevant accounts and reports.

✦ ✦ ✦

CHAPTER 3

Choosing the Correct Legal Entity and Avoiding Tax Penalties

✦ ✦ ✦ ✦

In This Chapter

Choosing basic types of business entities

Federal tax identification numbers

Avoiding tax penalties for late filers and nonfilers

QuickBooks Reminders

Choosing a QuickBooks start date

Checklist of issues

✦ ✦ ✦ ✦

QuickBooks is a complete accounting system that will correctly record information about your day-to-day business transactions. But you must first define your business entity and secure its recognition under the laws of your state and the regulations established by the Internal Revenue Service. QuickBooks asks you to provide information as to your form of business and taxpayer reporting identification number when you first set up your company. This chapter ensures that you are prepared to answer such questions. It also provides insight as to the impact of these initial decisions on your future tax-reporting practices

Basic Types of Business Entities

Before the late 1980s, accounting and law professors taught their students about three types of business entities: sole proprietorships, partnerships, and corporations. Each was taxed in a distinct manner, and only corporations were afforded limited liability. Limited liability status means that creditors do not have any claim on the personal assets of the business owners; liability is limited to the extent of the assets of the business entity. But in the last 10 years, the law has blurred some of the advantages, disadvantages, and tax-reporting procedures traditionally associated with each type of entity.

In particular, there is a new kid on the block, the limited liability company (LLC). This entity, which is recognized in all 50 states, can be taxed as a partnership but, legally, is entitled to limited liability status. So these days, to make an informed decision about your choice of business entity, you not only need to know about sole proprietorships, partnerships, and corporations, but you also must consider a hybrid type of entity, the limited liability company.

Currently there are five standard types of business entities:

✦ **Sole proprietorships:** Owners do not maintain a distinct legal entity from themselves and report income and loss on their personal tax returns.

✦ **Corporations:** A legal entity that has limited liability but that must file a corporate return and pay tax at the corporate level. Shareholders generally are subject to tax on their individual returns for amounts from dividends and distributions.

✦ **S corporations:** These are special types of corporations that offer the advantages of limited liability, but there is no tax on the corporate level. This type of entity is limited to 100 or fewer shareholders. A husband and wife are considered one shareholder, and corporations are not allowed to be shareholders.

✦ **Partnerships and limited partnerships:** A partnership reports no income or loss at the entity level; income is reported on the returns of its partners. Standard partnerships do not offer limited liability, unless they are established as limited liability partnerships.

✦ **Limited liability companies:** These entities are taxed as partnerships (that is, there is no tax at the entity level) but offer limited liability. They are recognized in all 50 states and have become a more popular alternative to limited partnerships because of favorable and relatively uniform state laws.

Each type of business entity has distinct requirements for formation, maintenance, and reporting. For example, limited liability companies generally must file an annual report in the state in which they are established, and they must pay a fee at that time.

Consider a hypothetical entrepreneur named Norm. Norm decides to open his own business, a vegetarian catering service called Quit Meating Like This. (He has always loved to cook.)

Norm buys a copy of QuickBooks to help him keep track of his accounts receivable, accounts payable, inventory, and the payroll for his assistants. After installing the program, Norm is uncertain how to answer some of the questions in the EasyStep Interview prior to setting up his Chart of Accounts. Most notably, he cannot decide how to answer the question as to which type of income tax reporting form his new business uses. Is he a sole proprietorship, partnership, or corporation? Norm decides to exit the program and do some research as to which entity type is most suitable for his business before proceeding further.

In deciding what type of entity to choose for his business, entrepreneurs such as Norm will generally consider issues such the following:

- **Liability issues:** Some type of entities (such as corporations) allow the owners to insulate their personal assets from liability in the event that the business is sued. The owners and the business generally must comply with specific types of legal requirements in order to keep their assets separate from those of the business.
- **Cost of complying with the legal formalities necessary to maintain the entity:** For example, corporations must keep certain types of books and records, depending on the state in which they are incorporated.
- **Tax issues:** Corporations classified as C corporations pay tax at the corporate level, and their shareholders must pay again on their individual returns. S corporations, limited liability companies, and partnerships are types of businesses that do not pay taxes, but instead pass their profits and losses to their owners who report the income (or loss) on their individual tax returns.

This list of considerations is by no means complete. The choice of entity is a decision that depends on a myriad of factors specific to a business. Also, any business is potentially subject to the laws and regulations of each of the states in which they are established, are located, or do business. States have different legal and regulatory requirements, which may vary significantly.

It is important that Norm makes this decision at the time he first sets up his new company data file so that QuickBooks can automatically associate the account balances to the correct lines of the tax form. This means that the program keeps track of the balances in the accounts and where they go on the tax forms. For example, the "office expense" account may be associated with the line on the Schedule C tax form for "office expense." Or multiple types of office expenses can be tracked in different accounts, and all these different accounts can be associated with the same line on the tax return to arrive at the total office expense to be reported for income tax purposes.

What if Norm starts out as a sole proprietorship and decides to change to a different entity later in the year (for example, change from a sole proprietorship to a corporation)? If he does this, all of the associations between the accounts and the tax lines are reset to Unassigned.

Cross-Reference

If Norm wants to associate accounts with specific lines on tax forms, it is best for him to turn on this preference when first setting up his company's Chart of Accounts. Otherwise, he will need to manually reassociate each account with the appropriate line on the correct tax form, as discussed in Chapter 6.

The sole proprietorship

Norm, like many new businesses, decides to start out as a sole proprietorship. Norm opens a separate checking account for his business and handles all business expenses and deposits through that account. A sole proprietor reports business on Schedule C of Form 1040, the individual's income tax return.

Accounting Jargon

A *sole proprietorship* is an entity owned by one person; it is the simplest form of business record keeping and reporting. At the end of the year, Norm will total his revenues and review his expenses to categorize them for reporting expenses on his Schedule C. The difference between the revenue and expense amounts will determine Norm's taxable income.

Sole proprietors must pay both income and self-employment tax. The rate on self-employment income is currently 15.3 percent. This is a combined rate that consists of 12.4 percent for old-age, survivors, and disability insurance (OASDI) and a 2.9 percent component for Medicare. This rate is subject to change and is computed on Schedule SE of Form 1040. The OASDI tax is currently imposed on the first $90,000 of income for 2006. This amount is referred to as the *OASDI wage base* and it changes annually.

Tip

You can learn more about self-employment taxes by obtaining a free copy of IRS publication 533 from any IRS office or by accessing it online at `http://www.irs.gov/formspubs`.

Self-employed persons may subtract self-employment tax liability as a business expense from their adjusted gross income. For 2004, the amount that may be subtracted is 50 percent of the self-employment (SE) tax. This amount is scheduled to increase a little at a time each year until it reaches 100 percent in 2007. This deduction of SE tax is not treated as a business expense but is taken as an adjustment in arriving at the adjusted gross income on the sole proprietor's Form 1040 individual income tax return.

QuickBooks can help Norm track all of his day-to-day business transactions, including the correct amount of payroll tax withholding for his employees. To prepare his tax return, Norm is likely to submit several reports he has generated using QuickBooks to his accountant, including a Profit and Loss Statement. The accountant will determine Norman's self-employment tax and federal income tax liability based on these reports.

Cross-Reference

The Profit and Loss Statement is discussed in detail in Chapter 4.

As a sole proprietorship, Norm and his business do not have a separate legal identity. If Norm inadvertently dishes up some salmonella with the broccoli cheese puffs, he may find himself served with a lawsuit. He is personally liable—all of his assets are at risk—to creditors and claimants of his business.

The partnership

Imagine that Norm decides not to embark on the new business venture alone, but that he will make his assistant an equity partner. A partnership, unlike a sole proprietorship, is an entity with a distinct legal identity from that of its owners. A partnership, as a separate entity, files its own tax return.

Like a sole proprietorship, a partnership determines its profit or loss by subtracting its expenses from its revenue. The gain or loss from the partnership is divided, for reporting purposes, among the partners in proportion to their ownership interest or some other basis agreed on in a partnership agreement. The partners report their share of the gain or loss from the partnership on their individual income tax returns. The partners are taxed at their individual income tax rates. The partnership income may also be subject to the self-employment tax discussed previously.

Partners, generally, are liable for the debts and claims against the partnership entity. There is no limited liability except in the case where a partnership agreement provides for a special class of partners called *limited partners*. Limited partners share in the profits and losses of the partnership, as provided in the partnership agreement, but their personal assets are not at risk to creditors.

Much law governing partnerships can be found in the Uniform Partnership Act (UPA), which is a model act adopted by most states. In the absence of a formal partnership agreement, the UPA, as adopted by a particular state in which the partnership is located, governs. The laws of most states assume that each partner has equal control over the management of the business unless the partnership agreement provides otherwise.

Caution

Individual partners may be liable for unpaid tax bills and obligations of a partnership, which can place their individual assets at risk.

Partnerships are usually less expensive to maintain than corporations. The law imposes fewer reporting requirements on them. Additionally, there is not a separate return to prepare for the entity, as there is with a corporation.

Limited partnerships are a special kind of partnership, recognized in all 50 states. There are usually very strict formalities for establishing a limited partnership. If a business is set up as a limited liability partnership, a special class of partners receives limited liability. This means that they do not place their assets at risk. Limited partnerships are required to have at least one general partner.

The corporation

The corporation, unlike the sole proprietorship or the partnership, affords limited liability status to the owners. There are two types of corporations, C corporations (referring to a Subchapter C of the Internal Revenue Code) and S corporations. S corporations are small corporations that must have 100 or fewer shareholders and must meet other specifically established criteria in order to receive favorable tax treatment.

Generally, creditors and claimants of the corporation can proceed only against the assets of the corporation. They cannot collect a judgment from the assets of the owners.

For the C corporation, this protection comes at a price—higher taxes. Unlike sole proprietorships and partnerships where the owners simply divvy the income or loss on their individual returns, a corporation is subject to an entity level tax. This means that a tax is imposed on the corporate entity as well as on the individual owners who are generally taxed on any dividends. This is sometimes referred to as double taxation, and its impact is significant. The maximum individual tax rate is 35 percent. The maximum combined individual and corporate tax rate is approximately 70 percent. (And this does not even consider the double-taxation issue with respect to state taxes!)

S corporations

Because of the double-taxation issue, it is desirable for corporations having 75 or fewer shareholders and meeting the other tests set forth in the Internal Revenue Code to elect S corporation status. An S corporation pays no corporate income tax. Rather, this type of corporation receives limited liability status just like a C corporation, but it is taxed like a partnership or sole proprietorship. Income from the S corporation "flows through" to the individual tax returns of the shareholders and is taxed at their individual rates, thus avoiding that onerous double-taxation issue.

The limited liability company

In recent years, many state legislatures have come to the conclusion that businesses should not have to make the painful choice between limited liability status and favorable individual (as opposed to corporate) rates. Accordingly, most states have passed legislation creating a sort of hybrid type of entity: the limited liability company (LLC). This is especially good news for entities that for one reason or another cannot meet the rather stringent requirements for S corporations. The LLC receives limited liability status. It is also taxed as a partnership, which means that there is no double-taxation issue as with corporations.

Federal Tax Identification Numbers

Every taxpayer or tax-reporting entity must record an identifying number on the required return. If your business is a sole proprietorship, the only number that you need is your Social Security number. Because they are considered separate legal entities, partnerships and corporations must apply for separate Employer Identification Numbers (EINs). To obtain a taxpayer identification number for your corporation, partnership, or LLC, you need to file IRS Form SS-4.

Tip

If you need to obtain a taxpayer identification number quickly, you can call 1-816-926-5999 to obtain one by phone. Fill out the SS-4 form and have it with you when you call so that you can provide the required information verbally. The IRS agent will provide you with an EIN over the phone. The procedure requires that you submit the SS-4 form by facsimile within 24 hours.

Remember that if you are a sole proprietorship, you do not need a separate taxpayer identification number for your business. It creates a lot of confusion if you file for an identification number that you do not need; the IRS will be looking for a return for an entity that does not exist.

In addition to determining whether you need a separate tax identification number for your business, you are legally responsible for providing the IRS with correct Social Security numbers for persons who work for you. This requirement is the underpinning of the most widespread audit program of the IRS — the matching program. Here is how it works. Your business must report to the IRS the total amount of wages and withholding taxes paid for each employee on a W-2 form such as the one shown in Figure 3-1. The employee also receives a copy.

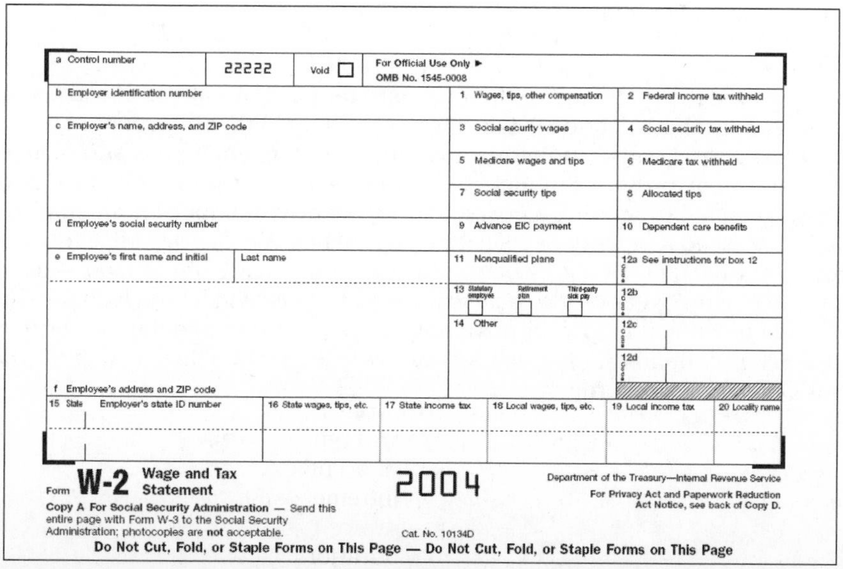
a Control number 22222 Void ☐ For Official Use Only ► OMB No. 1545-0008
b Employer identification number
1 Wages, tips, other compensation
2 Federal income tax withheld
c Employer's name, address, and ZIP code
3 Social security wages
4 Social security tax withheld
5 Medicare wages and tips
6 Medicare tax withheld
7 Social security tips
8 Allocated tips
d Employee's social security number
9 Advance EIC payment
10 Dependent care benefits
e Employee's first name and initial | Last name
11 Nonqualified plans
12a See instructions for box 12
13 Statutory employee ☐ Retirement plan ☐ Third-party sick pay ☐
12b
14 Other
12c
12d
f Employee's address and ZIP code
15 State | Employer's state ID number | 16 State wages, tips, etc. | 17 State income tax | 18 Local wages, tips, etc. | 19 Local income tax | 20 Locality name

Form **W-2** Wage and Tax Statement **2004**
Department of the Treasury—Internal Revenue Service
For Privacy Act and Paperwork Reduction Act Notice, see back of Copy D.
Copy A For Social Security Administration — Send this entire page with Form W-3 to the Social Security Administration; photocopies are not acceptable.
Cat. No. 10134D
Do Not Cut, Fold, or Staple Forms on This Page — Do Not Cut, Fold, or Staple Forms on This Page

Figure 3-1: Employers must file a W-2 form for each employee.

In addition to reporting wages paid to employees, your business must report payments made to nonemployees, such as vendors and independent contractors, who received more than $600 during the calendar year. Generally, you are not required to withhold taxes from amounts paid to someone who is categorized as an independent contractor rather than an employee. The 1099-Misc form, shown in Figure 3-2, is used for reporting amounts paid to nonemployees. QuickBooks prepares both W-2 and 1099-Misc forms for your business.

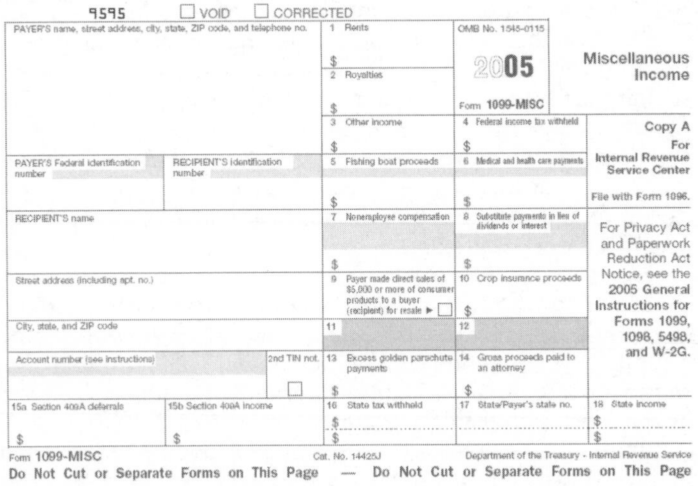

9595 ☐ VOID ☐ CORRECTED

PAYER'S name, street address, city, state, ZIP code, and telephone no.

1 Rents $

2 Royalties $

3 Other income $

OMB No. 1545-0115

2005

Form 1099-MISC

Miscellaneous Income

4 Federal income tax withheld $

Copy A For Internal Revenue Service Center

File with Form 1096.

PAYER'S Federal identification number

RECIPIENT'S identification number

5 Fishing boat proceeds $

6 Medical and health care payments $

RECIPIENT'S name

7 Nonemployee compensation $

8 Substitute payments in lieu of dividends or interest $

For Privacy Act and Paperwork Reduction Act Notice, see the 2005 General Instructions for Forms 1099, 1098, 5498, and W-2G.

Street address (including apt. no.)

9 Payer made direct sales of $5,000 or more of consumer products to a buyer (recipient) for resale ▶ ☐

10 Crop insurance proceeds $

City, state, and ZIP code

11

12

Account number (see instructions)

2nd TIN not. ☐

13 Excess golden parachute payments $

14 Gross proceeds paid to an attorney $

15a Section 409A deferrals $

15b Section 409A income $

16 State tax withheld $ $

17 State/Payer's state no.

18 State income $ $

Form 1099-MISC   Cat. No. 14425J   Department of the Treasury - Internal Revenue Service

Do Not Cut or Separate Forms on This Page — Do Not Cut or Separate Forms on This Page

Figure 3-2: Payments to vendors and independent contractors must be reported on a 1099-Misc form.

Now here's where the matching part comes in. The IRS looks at the Social Security number shown on the W-2 and 1099 forms and compares that information to the information reported on the individual tax returns of the employees and recipients of the W-2 and 1099 forms. If the reported amounts do not match, the IRS assesses a deficiency. If you fail to provide a correct Social Security number for an employee, you will be assessed a penalty of $50.00 per erroneous W-2 or 1099-Misc form, to a maximum of $100,000. This may be the case even if you are not at fault — as in a situation where employees (such as illegal aliens) have provided you with false information or documents. It is to your advantage to request documentation verifying the Social Security numbers that employees provide to you before you enter them into your QuickBooks records.

Caution

If you do not have the taxpayer identification number of the person for whom you have issued the 1099-Misc, you are required to pay backup withholding at a rate of 31 percent.

As an employer, you are required to withhold the employee's portion of tax on wages whether or not the money is actually collected from the employee. If you do not collect or pay withholding tax for an employee, you can be assessed a penalty equal to 100 percent of the amount of the tax that should have been paid. This is important to remember when you are trying to decide whether an individual who performs services for you is an employee or an independent contractor. If you make a mistake and treat someone who is legally an employee as an independent contractor and fail to withhold the proper amounts, you may find yourself liable for 100 percent of the tax that should have been paid by the employee.

Tip

Are you unsure whether to treat someone as an employee or an independent contractor? The IRS offers several publications relating to this topic. Visit `http://www.irs.gov/publications/p15a/ar02.html#d0e298` for information, or go to `www.irs.gov` and type **Independent Contractor** in the Search IRS Site for text box.

Tax Penalties for Late Filers and Nonfilers

The following, somewhat depressing, information is certainly not essential to implementing the program, but it may help you avoid traps that new businesses (especially service businesses) often fall into. Or maybe you always wondered what actually happens to people who don't file their taxes (or who file them late). This is a partial list of the penalties and assessments that late filers and nonfilers can look forward to:

- **Failure to file:** 5 percent per month up to a maximum of 25 percent per month; if more than 60 days have passed, the penalty may not be less than the lesser of $100.00 or 100 percent of the tax due on the return. In cases of fraudulent failure to file, the penalty is 15 percent per month to a maximum of 75 percent.
- **Substantial understatement:** 20 percent of the total tax for understatement. An understatement of your tax liability is "substantial" if it exceeds 10 percent of the total tax due or $5,000. This penalty will not be imposed if you can convince the IRS that the position you took in preparing your return and in reporting your liability was based on reasonable authority.
- **Failure to pay tax when due:** One-half of 1 percent for each month the tax remains unpaid to a maximum of 25 percent.

- **Frivolous return:** $500.00. (I always think of a guy I know that used to write a lengthy antigovernment statement on the face of his return and then file it—without any numbers. That's the only time that I've actually seen this penalty imposed.)
- **Failure to file information returns:** 15 percent for returns filed within 30 days of the due date, 30 percent for returns filed after the due date but by August 1, or 50 percent for returns either filed after August 1 or never filed.
- **Failure to supply an accurate Social Security or taxpayer identification number:** $50.00 per return to a maximum of $100,000. (This penalty also applies to returns that are otherwise incomplete or incorrect.)
- **Underpayment of estimated taxes:** Estimated taxes are legally required for taxpayers that have substantial income during the year that is not subject to withholding. An individual return can be avoided by (1) paying 105 percent of the tax that was due on the prior year's return or (2) paying 105 percent of the prior year's return. Special rules apply to taxpayers with income over $150,000, and different due dates apply to corporations. The underpayment penalty is equal to interest but can be waived if due to reasonable cause and not willful neglect. (No penalty is imposed if an individual taxpayer's tax due is $1,000 or less, or if a corporate taxpayer's tax due is $500 or less.)
- **Penalties for failure to withhold or pay payroll taxes:** Employers who fail to withhold may be liable for 100 percent of the tax due plus a 100 percent penalty. Any responsible person (for example, corporate officer or employee) may be individually liable for the penalty, and this debt is not dischargeable in bankruptcy. Also, late deposit penalties apply as follows:
  - 5 days or less — 2 percent of the tax due
  - 6 to 15 days — 5 percent of the tax due
  - More than 15 days — 10 percent of the tax due
  - 10 days after first delinquency notice — 15 percent of the tax due

The foregoing penalties are easily avoided using the QuickBooks Reminders feature, described in the next section.

Choosing a QuickBooks Start Date for Your Business Entity

The first decision that a QuickBooks user makes is a choice as to when to switch the company over from its current method of accounting. The choice of start date is critical for two reasons. It determines what records and data will be available in the system for generating reports and comparing financial information. Also, it determines how much work you will have to do entering historical transactions. For example, if you purchase the program in December, and your company does its tax and financial reporting on a calendar-year basis, you may want to wait until January 1 of the following year to start using the program. That way, you won't have to enter any historical data. What if you purchase the program midyear? If you want to be able to generate reports for the full year, you will have to enter historical transactions—such as sales, receipts, and payments—from the beginning of the year.

Because the start date that you select determines the data available for generating all future QuickBooks reports, select a start date that corresponds to the beginning of a logical accounting period such as the beginning of a tax year or quarter. Most existing businesses choose January 1 of the current year as their start date. If you choose this start date, enter data for all transactions that occurred on or after January 1 into the system, and this information is then available to generate QuickBooks reports for the current 12-month accounting period and quarterly reporting periods within that year.

Ask yourself the following questions when selecting a start date for an existing QuickBooks company:

- **Is today's date closer to the beginning or the end of the company's reporting period?** If it is close to the end, you may want to wait until the beginning of the next year to implement a QuickBooks accounting system because of the daunting task of entering all transactions since the start of the accounting year.
- **How much time do you have to devote to entering historical data?** If time is not an issue, you may even want to enter data from previous years so that it is available to compare with the current year's performance.
- **Has the company been keeping its books on a cash or accrual basis?** It is generally easier to enter historical data for cash-basis taxpayers because they record only payments and receipts. Cash-basis taxpayers recognize revenue on their books when it is received and expenses when they are paid. In contrast, accrual-basis taxpayers recognize income on their books that they have a legal right to collect, even if it has not been paid, and expenses that they have an obligation to pay. They record the event giving rise to the obligation as well as payment and receipt, which means that there is a lot more historical data to enter.

Tip

The concepts of cash and accruals are discussed in full detail in Chapter 4.

- **Is data available for prior periods?** Many businesses don't keep exemplary records. You need to realistically decide whether it is even practical to access the necessary data concerning historical transactions.

A Checklist of Issues

This section is intended to provide a practical list of the issues and considerations for deciding on the type of your business entity and determining the tax requirements for that entity. Here are some questions that will help you get it all together before setting up your QuickBooks account:

- What type of entity is the business for tax-reporting purposes (for example, sole proprietorship, partnership, S corporation, or C corporation)?

Caution After you have selected a business entity in QuickBooks, you cannot change entities. To change business entities, you must establish a new Company file, repeating the EasyStep Interview process in Chapter 2 and entering data from your start date.

- Which income tax–reporting tax form is used for the business (for example, Schedule C, partnership return, corporate return, and so on)?
- Does the business need a federal or state tax identification number?
- What policies and procedures do you currently have in place for billing your customers and assessing finance charges? Have you included provisions in your customer contracts and agreements that would impact your billing procedures?
- What recurring expenses do you have each month (for example, rent, telephone, and utilities)?
- What would be an appropriate start date for the business to convert to using QuickBooks software?
- Does the business need to keep track of inventory (that is, goods and supplies consumed or sold to customers)?
- Do you have documents showing the current balances for all accounts maintained by the business?
- Do you have the necessary information to compute amounts currently owed by the business?
- Do you need to maintain payroll records for the business, and if so, do you have accurate Social Security numbers, addresses, telephone numbers, and withholding information for each of your employees?

If you are able to answer all these questions, you are prepared to establish a QuickBooks accounting system for your business. If you do not know the answer to any of these questions, take steps to resolve them now. Don't try to wing it and then blame the software.

Summary

This chapter helped you identify some of the main criteria for electing one form of business entity over another. It also provided background information as to the importance of obtaining and using correct federal taxpayer reporting numbers. Finally, it alerted you to some of the penalties that often entrap the relatively naïve owners of new businesses and showed you a practical QuickBooks feature that can be used to avoid them.

- You are now familiar with the basic types of tax-reporting forms and entities — the sole proprietorship, partnership, corporation, and LLC.
- You understand the significance of federal taxpayer identification numbers and how to obtain one for your business if it is needed.
- You are aware of some tax-reporting penalties that might ensnare a less-informed entrepreneur or office manager (who has not read this book).
- You have been introduced to QuickBooks Reminders, a help feature that may assist you in avoiding penalties.
- You have been given a list of business issues that must be resolved before implementing any accounting system.

✦ ✦ ✦

CHAPTER 4

Accounting Basics for QuickBooks Companies

In This Chapter

Generally accepted accounting principles (GAAP)

Types of accounts and their functions

Format of basic financial statements

Journal entries

Cash versus accrual

This chapter offers an overview of basic accounting principles and methods that affect how a company keeps its books and prepares its financial reports. Although Congress determines tax laws, the accounting principles that determine how your company keeps its books are developed in a far less public and more stable manner. Unlike tax laws, which are the product of Congress's whims, basic accounting principles are relatively unchanging. So if, for example, the idea of closing out retained earnings seems hard to grasp initially, take heart. Once you master any generally accepted accounting principle (GAAP), it is yours indefinitely — unlike this year's election-year tax-cut legislation that may fall to the wayside in preparing next year's return.

A Matter of Principle: GAAP and Your Business

Businesses are like children — they are all different. Each type of business has its own peculiar types of transactions. For example, construction companies record reimbursable expenses, retail companies record sales taxes and a variety of discounts, farmers have a lot of different profit-making activities within their business entity, and so forth. Each of these industries must adopt certain accounting conventions so that their records can be understood and interpreted by outsiders. That is the purpose of generally accepted accounting principles, or GAAP.

QuickBooks and Your Industry is a database on the Help menu. This invaluable resource is an industry-specific analysis of accounting rules and conventions for particular types of businesses, such as farming, law firms, construction, and so on. QuickBooks has been designed to record day-to-day business transactions in accordance with GAAP. The QuickBooks and Your Industry articles provide additional guidance as to the principles that apply to your business.

All about Accounts

Business transactions are the lifeblood of the accounting cycle, and accounts in which the data are recorded are its skeletal framework. A well-planned Chart of Accounts is the backbone of a good accounting system. As you record each business transaction, QuickBooks automatically updates the affected account balances. For example, if you bill a client for a service, QuickBooks automatically increases the balances in your revenue and accounts receivable accounts. These updated account balances are then reflected on your company's financial statements to provide a measure of the business's overall performance for that period.

Start with the Chart

You may have gotten the impression from earlier chapters that the Chart of Accounts is a concept unique to QuickBooks. It is not. All accounting systems utilize a Chart of Accounts as a starting point. It is simply a listing of all of the accounts used by the business entity to categorize different types of transactions. Any accounting system begins with the selection of the accounts to be used for subsequent recording of transactions.

Minding Your Business

Do you wonder just who is responsible for GAAP? GAAP embodies all of the written and unwritten pronouncements and policies of the following:

- The American Institute of Certified Public Accountants (AICPA)
- Financial Accounting Standards Board (FASB)
- Securities and Exchange Commission (SEC)
- American Accounting Association (AAA)
- The Public Company Accounting Oversight Board, recently created under the Sarbanes-Oxley Act of 2002
- Other bodies such as Financial Executives Institute (FEI), American Institute of Certified Public Accountants (AICPA), National Association of Accountants (NAA), and state boards that regulate the accounting profession

The processes of setting up and customizing a QuickBooks Chart of Accounts are discussed in detail in Chapters 5 and 6.

When you set up your business using the EasyStep Interview, QuickBooks automatically provides a standard Chart of Accounts for your industry. This saves a lot of time, and you can further customize the Chart of Accounts for your individual business. Figure 4-1 illustrates the Chart of Accounts window for Larry's Landscaping & Garden Supply.

Name		Type	Balance Total
◆Checking	↯	Bank	-78,925.64
◆Cash Expenditures		Bank	225.23
◆Savings	↯	Bank	5,987.50
◆Barter Account		Bank	0.00
◆Accounts Receivable		Accounts Receivable	35,730.02
◆Prepaid Insurance		Other Current Asset	500.00
◆Employee advances		Other Current Asset	100.00
◆Inventory Asset		Other Current Asset	6,937.08
◆Undeposited Funds		Other Current Asset	0.00
◆Truck		Fixed Asset	12,025.00
◆Accumulated Depreciation		Fixed Asset	-1,725.00
◆Original Purchase		Fixed Asset	13,750.00
◆Accounts Payable		Accounts Payable	2,578.69
◆CalOil Card		Credit Card	1,403.99
◆QuickBooks Credit Card		Credit Card	70.00
◆QBCC Field Office	↯	Credit Card	45.00
◆QBCC Home Office	↯	Credit Card	25.00
◆QBCC Sales Dept	↯	Credit Card	0.00
◆Payroll Liabilities		Other Current Liabi...	4,265.09
◆Direct Deposit Liabiliti		Other Current Liabi...	0.00
◆Payments on Account		Other Current Liabi...	-1,520.00
◆Sales Tax Payable		Other Current Liabi...	2,086.50
◆Bank of Anycity Loan		Long Term Liability	19,932.65
◆Equipment Loan		Long Term Liability	3,911.32
◆Bank Loan		Long Term Liability	5,369.06
◆Opening Bal Equity		Equity	-29,248.48
◆Owner's Equity		Equity	-5,000.00
◆Owner's Contributions		Equity	0.00
◆Owner's Draw		Equity	-5,000.00
◆Retained Earnings		Equity	

Figure 4-1: The Chart of Accounts window for Larry's Landscaping displays a special icon to denote online banking or online payment.

Types of accounts

The Chart of Accounts is composed of five general types of accounts: assets, liabilities, owner's equity, revenue, and expenses. Any account that you establish for your business will fall into one of these broad categories. It is therefore worthwhile to learn the essential characteristics of each type of account and forever commit their names to memory.

Income

Income accounts are used to track the earnings of your business as measured by both money that comes into the company and the increase in its accounts receivable balance, which reflects money owed to the company by others. *Income* is a term that is often confused with *profit*. A business's profit (or loss) is determined after subtracting expenses from income. You may also have heard the terms *gross income* and *gross profit*. These terms refer to all of the income that comes into the business prior to deducting expenses such as the cost of goods sold.

Cost of goods sold is a term that refers to the cost of all goods held in inventory to produce the products that were sold. You will note that the income statements for the QuickBooks sample companies subtract cost of goods sold from the business's total income to arrive at a number called gross profit.

The portion of the Profit & Loss Statement reflecting income, cost of goods sold, and gross profit for Larry's Landscaping is shown in Figure 4-2.

Larry's Landscaping & Garden Supply
Profit & Loss
December 1 - 15, 2007

	Dec 1 - 15, 07
Cost of Goods Sold	
Cost of Goods Sold	1,777.46
Total COGS	1,777.46
Gross Profit	16,923.31

Figure 4-2: Gross profit refers to the difference between cost of goods sold and total income.

Accounting Jargon

QuickBooks refers to the process of including a transaction in an account, for the purpose of recalculating the account balance to reflect the transaction, as *posting* the transaction to the account.

To view a chronological list of all of the transactions that have been posted to an account, follow these steps:

1. Go to the Company Navigator screen (Home screen).
2. Click the Chart of Accounts icon located at the top of the Company section of the Navigator window.
3. Select any account in the Chart of Accounts and click the Report button at the bottom of the Chart of Accounts window. A drop-down menu appears.
4. Select QuickReport. A summary appears, such as the one shown in Figure 4-3 for the interest expense account of Larry's Landscaping.

8:58 PM
12/15/07
Accrual Basis

Larry's Landscaping & Garden Supply
Account QuickReport
October 1 through December 15, 2007

Type	Date	Num	Name	Memo	Split	Amount
Interest Expense						
Bill	10/16/2007	14	Great Statewide B...		Accounts Pa...	66.77
Check	10/22/2007	1461	Bank of Anycity	Accnt#4467...	Checking	28.95
Check	10/28/2007	1459	Bank of Anycity	Accnt#4467...	Checking	117.01
Bill	11/17/2007	15	Great Statewide B...		Accounts Pa...	60.97
Check	11/22/2007	1462	Bank of Anycity	Accnt#4467...	Checking	27.52
Check	11/28/2007	1460	Bank of Anycity	Accnt#4467...	Checking	114.57
Total Interest Expense						415.79
TOTAL						415.79

Figure 4-3: All of the transactions that have been posted to the interest expense account are summarized in this QuickReport.

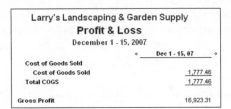

Expense

Expense accounts track the resources that a company is spending to carry on its business operations. As with income accounts, you can view a list of transactions posted in the expense account. To do so, perform the same steps as described in the previous section used to view the summary of asset account transactions—but pick an expense account to look at this time.

Asset

Assets are things of value that your company owns. QuickBooks distinguishes between two types of assets: current assets and fixed assets. *Current assets* include cash accounts and assets that you could convert to cash within one year. Inventory items that you hold for sale to customers are an example of current assets. Your *accounts receivable*, which is the money that customers owe to you, is another example of a current asset.

Fixed assets are assets that you won't convert to cash within the year. Examples of fixed assets are equipment, machinery, trucks, desks, and cash registers. Fixed assets are often depreciated, which means that the business will spread the cost of the asset over a number of years or accounting periods. *Depreciation* is the accounting method used to offset a portion of the original cost of the asset against a business's income each year. For example, if you purchase a $10,000 photocopy machine that makes collated, stapled, and scented copies of all of your legal documents, you might depreciate that asset, or "write it off" over a five-year period. This method would assume that at the end of five years, the machine will have no value because it is worn out or obsolete.

To determine the value of an asset at any time during its useful life, you would subtract the amount in the accumulated depreciation account from the original cost. In other words, depreciation is an expense that does not reduce the balance in any cash account. Instead, it reduces the value of the fixed asset being depreciated. Take a look at how this works. Figure 4-4 shows how a partially depreciated truck is represented on Larry's Landscaping's Balance Sheet.

Liability

Liability accounts reflect your company's debts—what is owed to others. Similar to assets, liabilities are categorized as "current" or "long-term." *Current liabilities* are those that must be paid within one year. *Long-term liabilities* are debts your company will take more than one year to pay off. Examples of current liabilities include accounts payable to vendors and income, payroll, and sales taxes. Long-term liabilities include obligations such as a property mortgage, a long-term loan, or a major equipment lease.

Larry's Landscaping & Garden Supply
Balance Sheet
As of December 15, 2007

		Dec 15, 07
Total Accounts Receivable		35,730.02
Other Current Assets		
Prepaid Insurance		500.00
Employee advances		100.00
Inventory Asset		6,937.08
Total Other Current Assets		7,537.08
Total Current Assets		-28,770.81
Fixed Assets		
Truck		
Accumulated Depreciation	-1,725.00	
Original Purchase	13,750.00	
Total Truck		12,025.00
Total Fixed Assets		12,025.00
TOTAL ASSETS		-16,745.81

Figure 4-4: Larry's Landscaping's Balance Sheet shows the original cost of a fixed asset, a truck, offset by the amount of accumulated depreciation.

Liabilities can also include an obligation to provide goods or services. For example, receipt of payment in advance may give rise to a corresponding liability on the part of your company. Figure 4-5 shows the liability section of Larry's Landscaping's Balance Sheet.

Larry's Landscaping & Garden Supply
Balance Sheet
As of December 15, 2007

		Dec 15, 07
LIABILITIES & EQUITY		
Liabilities		
Current Liabilities		
Accounts Payable		
Accounts Payable		2,554.57
Total Accounts Payable		2,554.57
Credit Cards		
CalOil Card		1,403.99
QuickBooks Credit Card		
QBCC Field Office	45.00	
QBCC Home Office	25.00	
Total QuickBooks Credit Card		70.00
Total Credit Cards		1,473.99
Other Current Liabilities		
Payroll Liabilities		4,265.09
Payments on Account		-1,520.00
Sales Tax Payable		2,086.50
Total Other Current Liabilities		4,831.59
Total Current Liabilities		8,860.15
Long Term Liabilities		
Bank of Anycity Loan		19,932.65
Equipment Loan		3,911.32
Bank Loan		6,013.06
Total Long Term Liabilities		29,857.03

Figure 4-5: The liabilities section of the Balance Sheet is divided into current and long-term liabilities, to distinguish between obligations that must be met within one year of the reporting date and those that will be met in more than one year.

Retained earnings and equity

Equity accounts are definitely the most interesting — and complicated — of the five account types.

An *equity account* represents the value of the business to its owners. Equity accounts include both contributions to capital, or money contributed to the business by its owners, and earnings that are retained in the business rather than withdrawn (thus the term *retained earnings*). Equity is synonymous with ownership when used in connection with financial statements.

The *retained earnings account* tracks all of the net profits earned by the business from the date it was formed. It is the total of all earnings that have been retained by the business as opposed to distributed to the owners. The retained earnings account appears on the Balance Sheet. Figure 4-6 shows this account on the sample Balance Sheet for Larry's Landscaping in Figure 4-6.

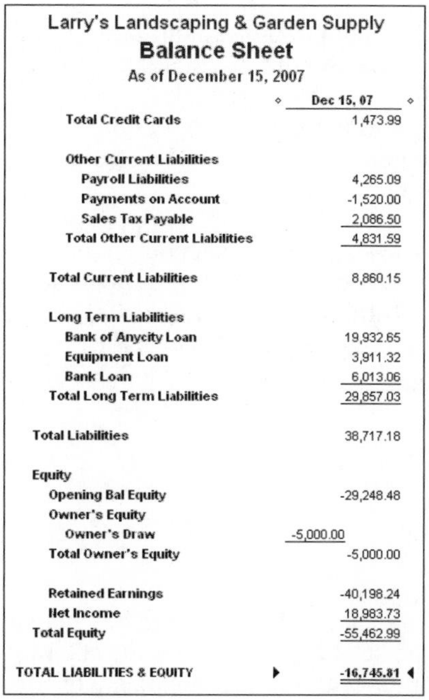

Larry's Landscaping & Garden Supply
Balance Sheet
As of December 15, 2007

		Dec 15, 07
Total Credit Cards		1,473.99
Other Current Liabilities		
Payroll Liabilities		4,265.09
Payments on Account		-1,520.00
Sales Tax Payable		2,086.50
Total Other Current Liabilities		4,831.59
Total Current Liabilities		8,860.15
Long Term Liabilities		
Bank of Anycity Loan		19,932.65
Equipment Loan		3,911.32
Bank Loan		6,013.06
Total Long Term Liabilities		29,857.03
Total Liabilities		38,717.18
Equity		
Opening Bal Equity		-29,248.48
Owner's Equity		
Owner's Draw	-5,000.00	
Total Owner's Equity		-5,000.00
Retained Earnings		-40,198.24
Net Income		18,983.73
Total Equity		-55,462.99
TOTAL LIABILITIES & EQUITY		-16,745.81

Figure 4-6: The retained earnings and owner's equity accounts appear on Larry's Landscaping's Balance Sheet.

QuickBooks automatically adds the retained earnings and owner's equity accounts to the Chart of Accounts whenever a new Chart of Accounts is established. At the end of each fiscal year, QuickBooks automatically transfers the amount of net income (or loss) for the year to the retained earnings account so that it increases the balance of the retained earnings account for the following year.

Temporary versus permanent accounts

At this point, I'll give you the benefit of an insight that seems to help my clients understand the interrelationships among different types of accounts. Accounts can be viewed as either permanent or temporary. Temporary accounts are "closed" at the end of the year (or accounting period) and start the next period with a zero balance. Permanent accounts stay open indefinitely and have cumulative balances year after year.

Asset, liability, and equity accounts are considered *permanent* accounts. They are permanent because the balances in them carry over from one accounting period to the next. In contrast, revenue and expense accounts are *temporary* accounts because they are "closed out" at the end of an accounting period.

An *accounting period* is usually the company's fiscal year, but it can be a shorter period such as monthly or quarterly. A *fiscal year* is a one-year period that the company uses for reporting purposes. The fiscal year may or may not correspond to the calendar year.

It may be helpful to consider some specific examples of permanent and temporary accounts. An equipment account is a good illustration of a permanent account. The balance in your equipment account will be there on December 31, 2005, and still be there on January 1, 2006. In contrast, revenue and expense accounts are temporary accounts because they are "closed out" at the end of one accounting period and start with a zero balance in the next accounting period.

But what happens to the balance in the revenue and expense accounts — that is, the temporary accounts — when they are zeroed out at midnight on December 31? The answer is that the difference between the total income and the total expenses for the year will be used to determine the company's income or loss for the fiscal year. The income or loss for the current fiscal year will then be added to (or subtracted from) the permanent retained earnings account, which is shown on the Balance Sheet.

Financial Statements

Most businesses prepare two major types of financial statements: the Balance Sheet and the Profit and Loss (Income) Statement. These statements are generally prepared at the end of each fiscal year. Permanent accounts with cumulative balances are shown on the Balance Sheet. These are the assets, liabilities of the business, and the retained earnings and owner's equity accounts discussed earlier. The Profit and Loss Statement lives up to its name by showing the balances in the temporary accounts, which are the income and expense accounts, for the applicable reporting period.

Profit and Loss Statements

The *Profit and Loss Statement* (also called the *Income Statement*) reports the revenues and expenses of the business over the fiscal year. A new Profit and Loss Statement is prepared at the end of each fiscal year. In other words, businesses start with a fresh Profit and Loss Statement each accounting period, and each account has a zero balance at the beginning of the new accounting period.

Every Profit and Loss Statement is made up of three sections: Income, Expenses, and Net Profit or Loss. The information on any income statement for any company can be summarized by the following standard accounting equation:

Income – Expenses = Profit / Loss

The income section may include information about returns, allowances, discounts, and cost of goods sold. This can be confusing, because you would think that these items should appear in the expense section. Don't let this throw you; GAAP allows them to be shown as part of the income section of the Profit and Loss Statement when the company feels that it makes the information easier to understand. The difference between sales and cost of goods sold is called *gross profit*, and this figure is usually clearly shown on a Profit and Loss Statement.

The expense section of the Profit and Loss Statement shows the costs of goods and services used by the company to produce income or revenue. This section includes selling, general, and administrative expenses.

The number that you get when you subtract selling, general, and administrative expenses from net income is sometimes referred to as *income from operations*. This is income earned in the normal course of doing business.

Sometimes a company has income from events that are not a normal or ongoing part of its business, such as the sale of an asset. These items may be shown as "other revenue and expenses" to give readers a clearer picture of the company's performance. When a firm is organized as a corporation, income tax liability is also shown on the Profit and Loss Statement. The following is the standard format for a basic Income Statement:

Ordinary Income/Expense Income

```
Less: Cost of Goods Sold
= Gross Profit

Less Expenses
= Net Ordinary Income

Add Other Income/Expense
= Net Income
```

Closing the books

The profit or loss at the end of each year is summarized in the retained earnings account.

The process of reducing the income and expense accounts to a zero balance and determining the net income or loss is sometimes called "closing the books."

This can be a complicated process. QuickBooks, unlike many other accounting programs, does not require a series of confusing procedures to close your books at the end of an accounting period. QuickBooks automatically updates data as you enter it and allows you to obtain a report at any time within an accounting period. QuickBooks automatically transfers the net income or loss into retained earnings at the end of a fiscal year.

You may, however, want to protect the records of a prior accounting period from tampering or accidental change. QuickBooks enables you to do this by using a password to restrict access to records maintained for prior accounting periods. By requiring a password, you restrict casual or unauthorized access to valuable prior records for your company, but you can still make necessary corrections to these records. Using passwords to close an accounting period is discussed further in Chapter 13.

With a click of your mouse, QuickBooks enables you to compare your company's profit and loss for this year to the profit and loss for the same period last year. To view this valuable comparative information, follow these steps:

1. Click the QuickBooks navigator icon (always located in the upper-right corner of the screen) and then go to the Reports section of the Taxes and Accountant Navigator window.
2. Click the Profit and Loss Report icon that appears in the Reports section located at the bottom of the Navigator window. A drop-down menu appears.
3. Choose Prev Year Comparison from the drop-down menu.

Viewing the Profit and Loss Statement

In addition to preparing financial statements for each fiscal year, QuickBooks allows you to view a year-to-date Profit and Loss Statement at any time. To do so, follow these steps:

1. Click the QuickBooks Navigator icon (always in the upper-right corner of the screen) and go to the Reports Center and then the Company & Financial section of the Taxes and Accountant Navigator window.
2. Click the Profit and Loss Report icon that appears in the Reports section, at the bottom of the Navigator window. Then go to the Profit & Loss (income statement) section, the first section on the list.
3. Choose Prev Year Comparison from the menu that appears.

You can also view the income and expense information that is shown on the Profit and Loss Statement in the form of a graph, so you can literally see how your year is going. You can also use the buttons at the bottom of the graph window, which is shown in Figure 4-7, to view breakdowns of expenses to get a better sense of where the company's resources are going.

To see your Profit and Loss Statement information presented in the form of a graph, follow these steps:

1. From the Reports menu, choose Company & Financial and then choose Income and Expense Graph. A graph appears, as shown in Figure 4-7.
2. Click the Income button at the bottom of the screen to display a breakdown of the income items on the Profit & Loss screen. Click the Expense button to view a breakdown of expenses.

```
Balance Sheet Format
Dec. 15, '05
```

ASSETS

```
Current Assets
Checking/Savings
Accounts Receivable
Other Current Assets
Total Current Assets
Fixed Assets

TOTAL ASSETS
```

LIABILITIES AND EQUITY

```
Liabilities
Current Liabilities
Accounts Payable
Credit Cards
Other Current Liabilities
Total Liabilities
Equity

TOTAL LIABILITIES AND EQUITY
```

It is hard to imagine anything more entertaining than the ability to turn financial statements into colorful graphs. But QuickBooks takes this art form even further. The window for the income and expenses graph has a "zoom" function that allows you to select a specific income or expense account that is shown on the Income Statement and create a graph just for that account.

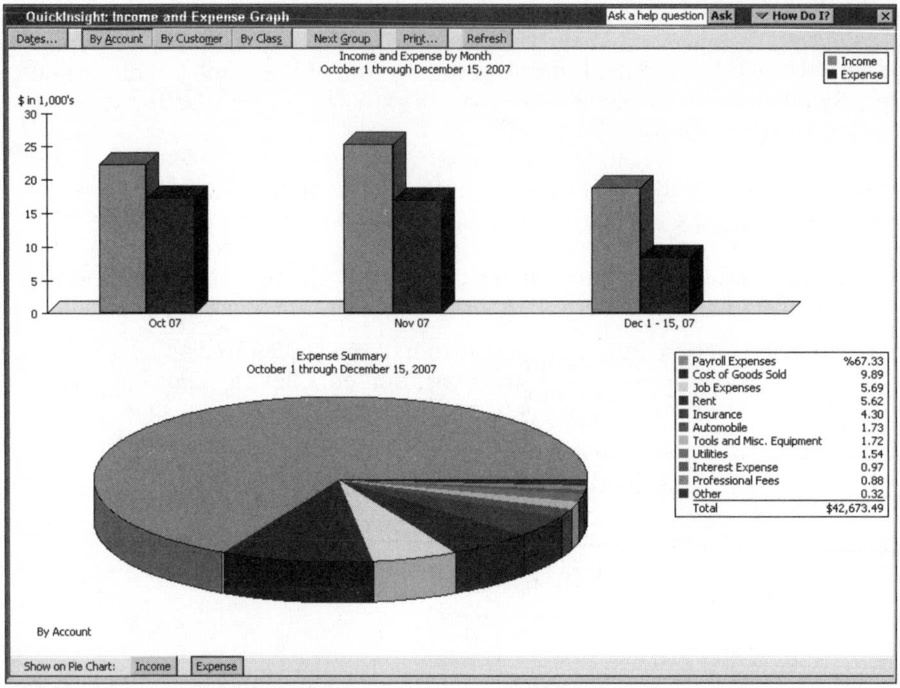

Figure 4-7: The QuickBooks graph window shows breakdowns of expenses.

The Balance Sheet

The Balance Sheet provides a snapshot of the company's financial position as of a certain date.

The *Balance Sheet* is also sometimes referred to as the *Statement of Financial Condition*. It presents information as to the balances in the business's asset, liability, and owner's equity accounts.

The balance sheet accounts — assets, liabilities, and equity — are all permanent accounts. This means that the year-end balances carry forward, rather than being "zeroed out" like Income Statement accounts. The year-end balance in the net income account shown on the Profit and Loss Statement is added to the retained earnings account in the equity section of the Balance Sheet.

The information shown on a Balance Sheet is always presented in a specific order. First, assets are presented, followed by liabilities, and finally the owner's equity accounts. The information shown on the Balance Sheet reflects this equation:

Assets + Liabilities = Owner's Equity

Within the asset, liability, and equity classifications, the accounts are further subdivided. Assets are shown as current or fixed assets, depending on whether they will be converted to cash within the year. Similarly, liabilities are broken down into short-term and long-term obligations, depending on whether they will be repaid within one year.

The equity section generally includes accounts reflecting the owner's contributions to capital, owner's withdrawals of money from the company (or *draws*), and retained earnings. The presentation of the equity section of the Balance Sheet varies from company to company depending on whether it is for a sole proprietorship, partnership, LLC, or corporation. For example, a corporation may use the term *stockholder's equity* to reflect the value of the shareholder's ownership interest in the company.

You can view a graphic representation of a company's assets, liabilities, and net worth. You can compare each month of the current year, compare this information to prior years, or track the increase in your company's value over a number of other time periods that you select. To view a graph depicting your company's net worth over a period of time, follow these steps:

1. Go to the Reports menu and select Company & Financial.
2. Select Net Worth Graph from the Reports submenu. The window shown in Figure 4-8 appears.

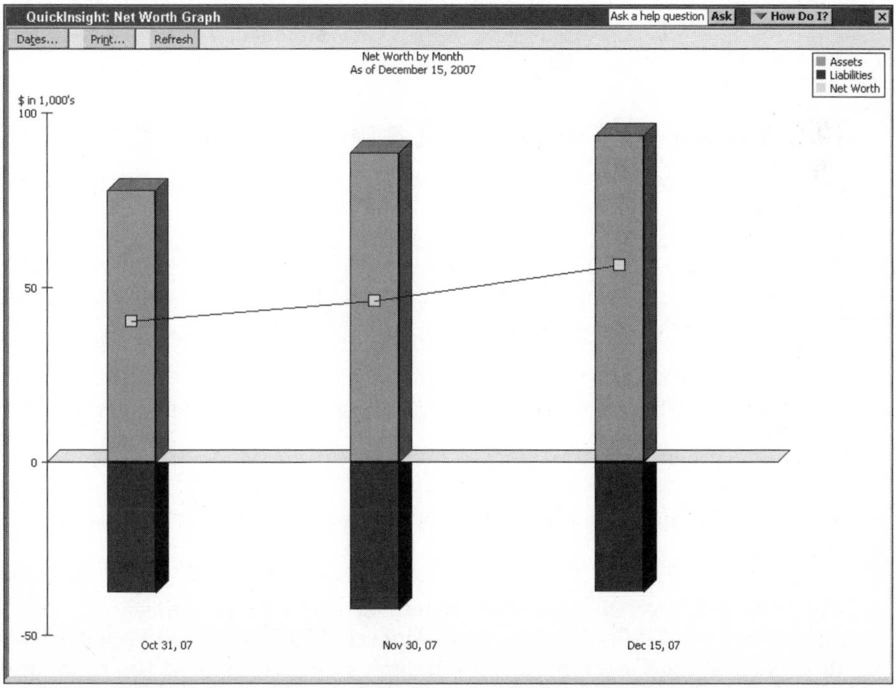

Figure 4-8: Comparative net worth data for three months for Larry's Landscaping. To select the period that you want to use for comparison, click the Dates button and use the Graph Dates drop-down menu to make your selection.

Journal Entries and T Accounts

A journal is a chronological record of each transaction that occurs in a business; it is the original point of entry into the accounting system because it is the first point at which the transaction is recorded. In traditional accounting systems, the journal had two columns—one for debits and one for credits. Entries are made to indicate which accounts were debited and which were credited.

In a traditional journal, a sample entry record rent expense for the month of February might appear as follows:

Date	*Account Title*	*Debit*	*Credit*
2/1/05	Office Expense	$1,000	
	Rent Payable		$1,000

In QuickBooks, the original point of entry for a transaction is not the traditional two-column journal. Rather, entries are recorded as checks and invoices. QuickBooks has a special General Journal Form for transactions that are not conveniently entered on the standard forms, such as the sale of a depreciated asset (see Figure 4-9). If you make adjustments directly to asset or liability account registers, QuickBooks labels them as GENJRNL.

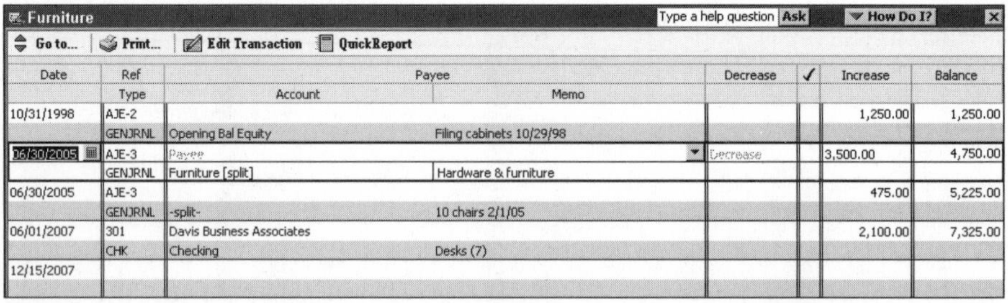

Figure 4-9: How an entry to reflect the purchase of a fixed asset might appear in the register.

Cross-Reference

General Journal entries are discussed more specifically in Chapter 28.

The traditional terms—debits, credits, and T accounts—have only marginal relevance to the QuickBooks user. *T account* refers to a two-column journal format. The debit side of the T account is the left side. The credit side is the right side. Every transaction must be recorded in two parts, a debit and a credit, so there is a corresponding and offsetting increase or decrease in two different accounts for every transaction entered. For example, a cash payment results in an increase in the cash account and a decrease in accounts receivable.

Debit refers to the process of increasing an expense or asset or decreasing a liability, equity, or revenue account by making an entry in the left column of the T account format. A *credit*, which is an entry in the right column of the T account, increases liabilities, revenues, and equity. Credits also decrease assets and expenses. These rules are summarized in Table 4-1. This system of recording transactions by using offsetting entries and a two-column format showing debits and credits is traditionally known as *double-entry bookkeeping*. QuickBooks automatically debits and credits the appropriate accounts when you enter a transaction, freeing you from the need to understand debits and credits.

Table 4-1
Rules of Debits and Credits

Debits	*Credits*
Increase:	Increase:
Expense Accounts	Liability Accounts
Asset Accounts	Equity Account
	Revenue Accounts
Decrease:	Decrease:
Liability Accounts	Expense Accounts
Equity Accounts	Asset Accounts
Revenue Accounts	

Minding Your Business

Some terminology has been made obsolete by QuickBooks. The ledger is used in traditional accounting systems, but it does not have a lot of relevance to the QuickBooks system. You won't find this term in its Glossary or Help Index, but it is a commonly used term, so it bears a mention and an explanation of its absence. A *ledger* is used to summarize the transactions recorded in a journal and to update the balance in each individual account affected by the transactions for a period of time, for example, weekly or monthly. Because QuickBooks instantly updates each affected account balance at the time that a transaction is entered, no ledger is necessary.

Cash versus Accrual Accounting

There are two methods for calculating the account balances shown on financial statements and reports. The two methods are the cash basis and the accrual basis.

In the *cash basis* of accounting, revenue is recorded only when cash is received; expenses are recorded only when cash is paid.

Cash-basis reports reflect income only if the company has received a cash equivalent as payment for the goods or services. So, for example, accounts receivable would not be included in a cash-basis report.

Reports prepared on the *accrual basis* reflect income and expenses at the time that a legal right or obligation for payment arises.

Revenue from a sale made to a customer who will be billed at a later date would be recognized using the accrual method. In the accrual method, receipt of income and payment are recorded as two separate events. In the cash basis, they would be reported as a single event. You will determine whether you want your company's Profit and Loss Statement to be shown on a cash or accrual basis during the initial company setup, as discussed in Chapter 5.

QuickBooks' default settings show all summary reports on an accrual basis unless you specify that you want them to be shown on the cash basis. Summary reports summarize groups of transactions and contain the term "Summary."

To show Summary reports on the cash basis, follow these steps:

1. Click the Customize Home Page and Set Preferences link on the right side of the Navigator screen as shown in Figure 4-10.
2. Open the reports and graphs preferences.
3. Click the Company Preferences tab.
4. Under Summary Report Basis, click the accounting basis (cash or accrual) you want for summary reports and graphs, as shown in Figure 4-10.
5. Click the Reports & Graphs subarea.
6. Click OK.

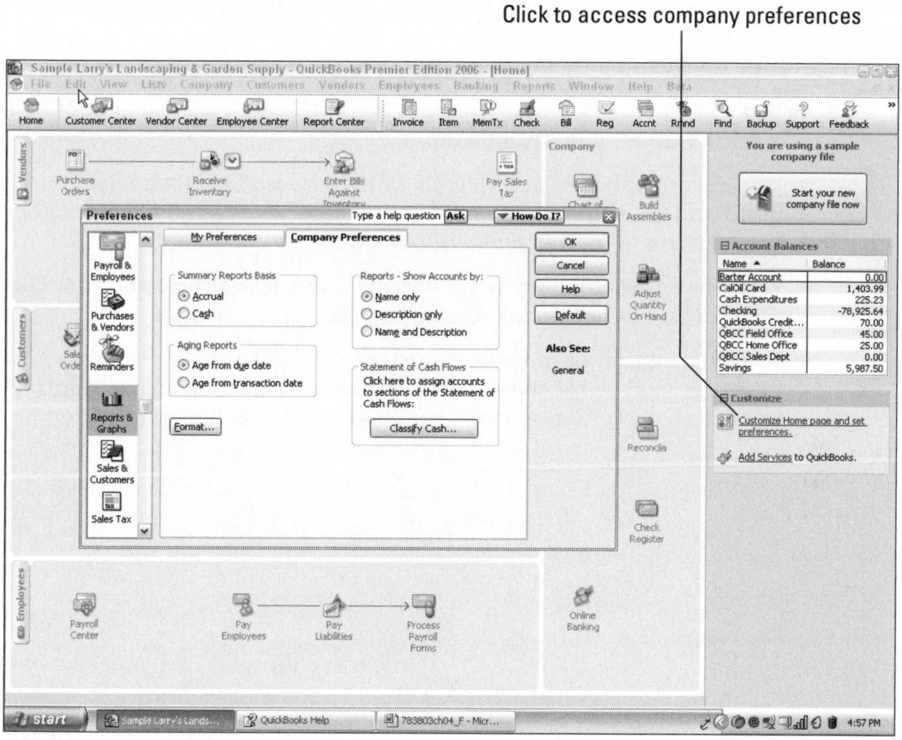

Figure 4-10: Changing reports from cash to accrual.

Traditionally, the cash-basis method of accounting has been viewed as an easier method of record keeping because you recognize transactions only at the time of payment — that is, when you pay the bill. If you are keeping books on the accrual basis, you must make two entries to reflect the same transaction; you record both the receipt and the payment of the bill. By streamlining the procedures and minimizing the time required to record accounting transactions and events, QuickBooks makes it easy to use either method. Accrual-based reports give you a better idea of how well your company is doing, which is why QuickBooks displays reports on the accrual basis by default.

Summary

This chapter introduced you to those accounting concepts that are relevant to maintaining records for a QuickBooks company. You now understand why a transaction is reported in a particular manner instead of just mechanically entering it into the system.

- ✦ You learned about generally accepted accounting principles, or GAAP, and now know that all companies keep their books using these conventions (if they are keeping them correctly).
- ✦ You learned the characteristics of the five basic types of accounts: income, expense, asset, liability, and equity.
- ✦ You learned the format and logic of the two major financial statements — the Profit and Loss Statement and the Balance Sheet — and can comfortably read or create them for any QuickBooks company.
- ✦ You now know what a general journal and a ledger are, and how QuickBooks renders these traditional accounting concepts obsolete.
- ✦ You learned that cash-basis reporting recognizes a transaction only when money is paid or received, and accrual-basis accounting recognizes income or expenses anytime a right or obligation for payment is created.

✦ ✦ ✦

PART II

Establishing Your QuickBooks Business

✦ ✦ ✦ ✦

In This Part

✦ ✦ ✦ ✦

CHAPTER 5

Setting Up Your QuickBooks Company

✦ ✦ ✦ ✦

In This Chapter

Simplify life with the EasyStep Interview

Completing the Welcome and General sections

Deciding about income and expense

Entering opening balances

Payroll

Bypassing the EasyStep Interview

✦ ✦ ✦ ✦

Setting up a QuickBooks company is a bit like unpacking your belongings in a new house. The more advance thought you have put into the project, the less rearranging you will need to do in the future. But if you do have to rearrange a bit to make your surroundings (or accounting system) more comfortable, it isn't the end of world. This chapter gives you the basics on setting up a QuickBooks company and tells you which initial decisions are easily reversed and which ones can be undone only by starting from scratch and reentering your company data. Fortunately, very few decisions fall into the latter category.

Tasks for Setting Up a New Company

Different versions of QuickBooks offer different ways to set up your company file. Depending on the version you use and the nature of your company, you need to perform most or all of the following tasks to set up your QuickBooks company.

- **Decide on a start date for your company:** This is the date you begin operations and start tracking account balances for your company. It is distinct from your tax year and is the date you may select later for closing your books.
- **Set up accounts for your company:** You need to set up accounts to track all income, expenses, assets, and liabilities for your company.

- **Enter historical transactions:** To ensure that your accounts, as of today's date, have correct balances, you need to enter all of the historical transactions for each account as of the start date.
- **Create customer, vendor, and Item lists:** QuickBooks enables you to track customer, vendor, and Item information. (Items include things like inventory, services and charges to customers.)
- **Enter banking and credit card information:** QuickBooks needs information about your bank and credit card balances in order to be able to give you up-to-date information at any time.
- **Set up your payroll:** QuickBooks enables you to track and compile the 1099 and W-2 information you need in order to properly pay and withhold taxes for employees.

Other optional steps that you may want to incorporate in the initial set-up of your business include:

- **Optional adjustments to accounts:**
- **Set up forms and templates:** QuickBooks allows you to create a custom business form and templates for routine business transactions, invoices, credit memos, sales receipts, sales orders, purchase orders, and estimates, depending on your business needs.

If you haven't previously set up any company data files in QuickBooks, when you start the program, the Welcome screen gives you the option of creating a new company, as shown in Figure 5-1.

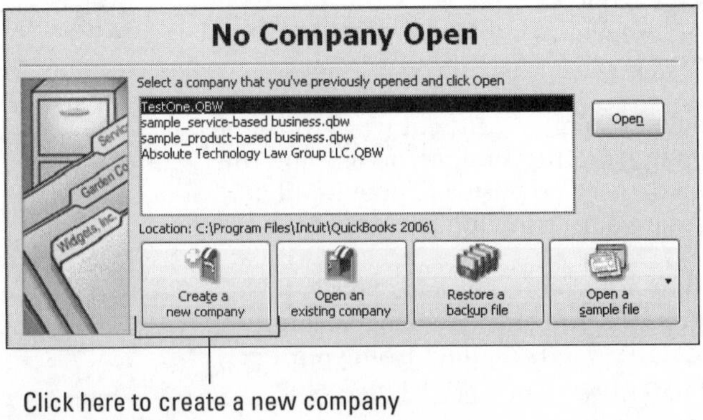

Figure 5-1: When you open QuickBooks, this screen gives you the option of creating a new company.

After you click the Create a New Company button, the interview window shown in Figure 5-2 appears, inviting you to get started. Click the Start Interview button.

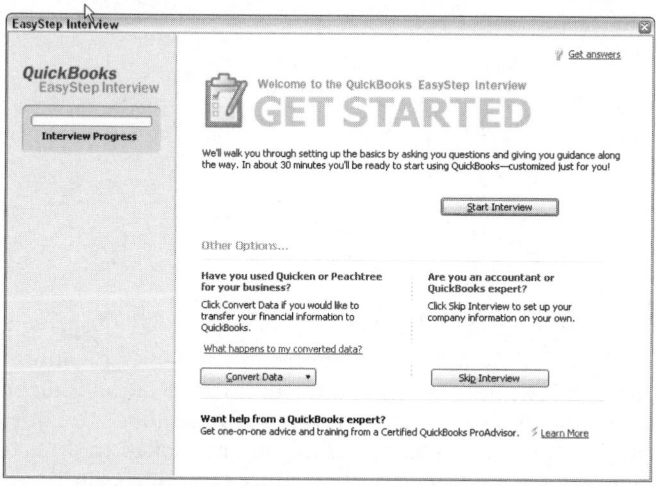

Figure 5-2: Initial interview screen to create a new company.

Why use the interview?

The interview is a carefully developed logical series of queries that prompt you to provide all of the information required to begin recording transactions and to successfully maintain records for a business entity. Why reinvent the wheel and painstakingly create your own checklist of information to enter, when the EasyStep Interview has already been provided to ensure that you omit nothing of consequence? After you complete the interview, you'll know that everything is in place for you to begin entering day-to-day transactions. If you don't find this rationale for using the interview sufficiently compelling, the last section in this chapter tells you how to skip it altogether when setting up a company.

This chapter presumes that you have given careful consideration to the list of issues for establishing a new business that appears at the end of Chapter 3 and that you are familiar with the essential accounting terminology introduced in Chapter 4. If you have not addressed an issue that is essential to setting up an accounting system for your company, the interview will force you to confront it. While the interview is designed to keep you from consternating and stalling, numerous Help features can be accessed directly from the interview that help resolve those troublesome issues. For example, if you are unsure whether you need a tax identification number or how to select a fiscal year, you can access Help directly from the interview screen. And, better yet, this feature is context-sensitive, which means that it gives you options directly related to the questions on that particular interview screen.

Progressing through the interview

The interview asks important questions relevant to setting up the following features of an accounting system that meets the specific needs of your company:

- ✦ Company Information
- ✦ Income & Expenses
- ✦ Income Details
- ✦ Opening Balances
- ✦ What's Next

The Company Information page

The Company Information page of the Interview, shown in Figure 5-3, prompts you to enter critical tax-reporting information and to set up your initial Chart of Accounts. As with any pop quiz, it is helpful to know something about the questions before they appear on the screen. The first thing you are asked to do is to enter your company name and legal name. If there is more than one company, you need to open a separate QuickBooks data file for each company. You are also required to file an appropriate tax form for each entity. What if you have only one company that has a number of different profit-making activities, and you want to track the income and expenses of each separately? In that case, it is appropriate to open a single QuickBooks data file for the company and to use a tool called Classes to track the different profit-making ventures of the business.

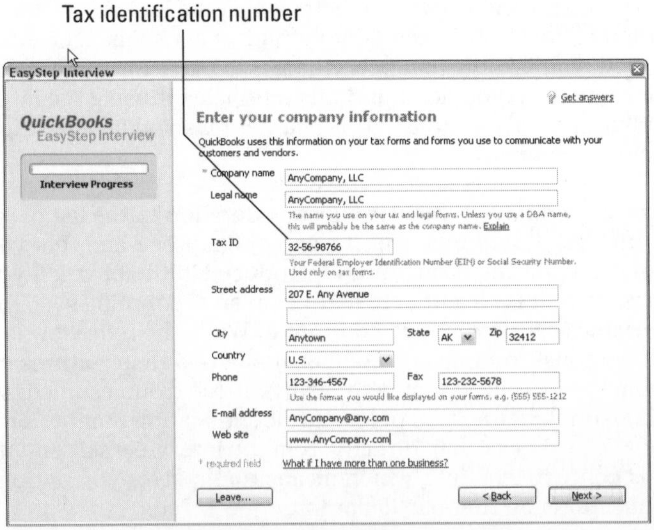

Figure 5-3: Identifying your company.

Cross-Reference Classes are discussed in Chapter 28.

Identifying your business by name

What if your company uses different names or acronyms to identify itself? These are commonly called *DBAs* (which stands for "doing business as"). You can register your DBA, as well as your company name, in most states so that no one else can use it. The interview screen asks you to enter the legal name of your company. This is the name that appears on the legal documents establishing your company.

Tax identification number

You must enter a tax identification number for your business in this portion of the interview as previously shown in Figure 5-3.

When you are done, click Next, and a page appears inviting you to create an administrator password, as shown in Figure 5-4.

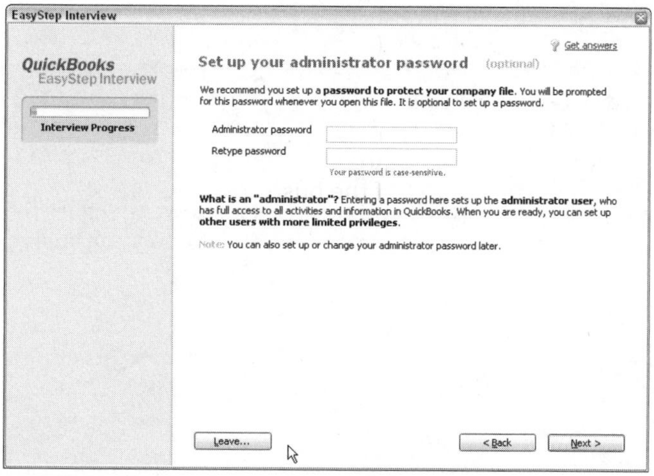

Figure 5-4: Create an administrator password.

Administrator password

The *administrator password* is the password that must be entered by anyone who wants to add or change certain aspects of your QuickBooks system. As you set up certain elements later in the program, you are asked whether you want to require persons who access them in the future to use an administrator password. Click Next when you've entered your chosen password.

Entering information about your company file

QuickBooks next prompts you to indicate where you want to store QuickBooks accounting records for your company. You can browse and select a location on your computer as shown in Figure 5-5.

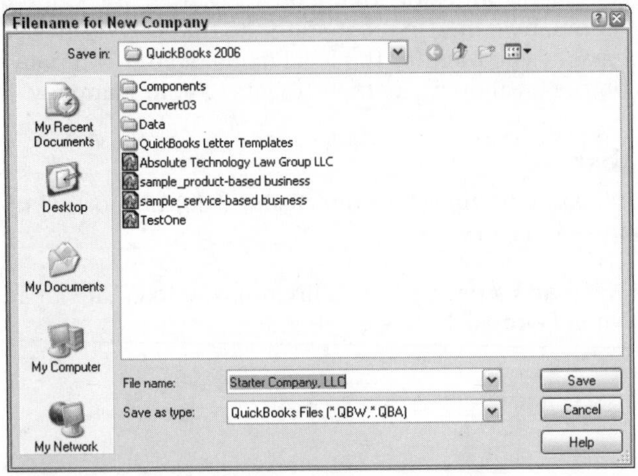

Figure 5-5: Browse to select a location on your computer to store QuickBooks data.

Once you've selected a location, click Next, and the screen shown in Figure 5-6 appears. This page asks you to select an industry type relevant to your business.

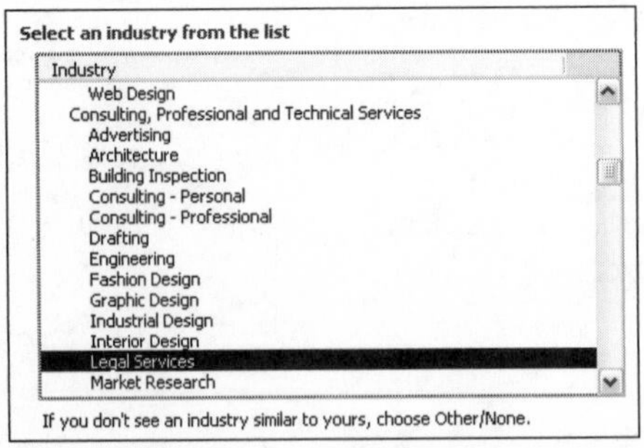

Figure 5-6: Selecting an industry.

The Industry option is used to determine, for the balance of the interview, questions that enable features that work best for your business. QuickBooks will recommend features that can best meet your business needs, such as:

- ✦ Enabling sales tax for retail businesses
- ✦ Using estimates in QuickBooks for some service-based businesses
- ✦ Managing inventory in QuickBooks for wholesalers and manufacturers
- ✦ Creating income and expense categories
- ✦ Enabling sales orders for businesses that take pre-sales product orders

Figure 5-6 reflects an industry selection of legal services (such as for a law office). On the next screen, shown in Figure 5-7, you have options for businesses that sell services only, products only, or both (indicating that this particular business will be providing both products and services, such as legal publications or materials). This option means that you can set up accounts relevant to services and inventory in the remainder of the interview.

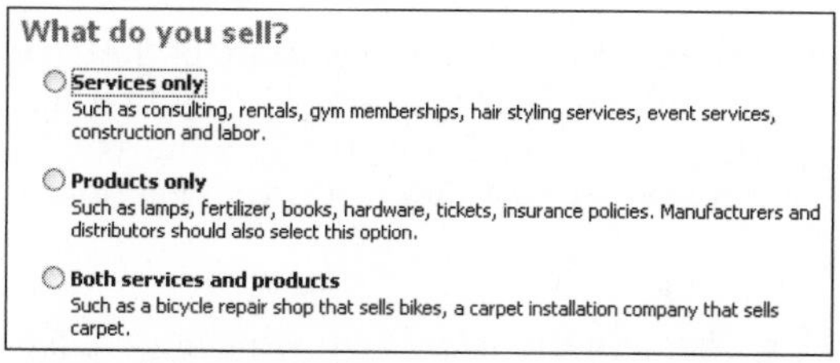

Figure 5-7: This interview screen determines whether service accounts, inventory accounts, or both, will be set up in the remainder of the interview.

On the screen that follows, shown in Figure 5-8, the option is selected that indicates it is not necessary to set up accounts for online sales at this time (you can always set up these accounts for this later).

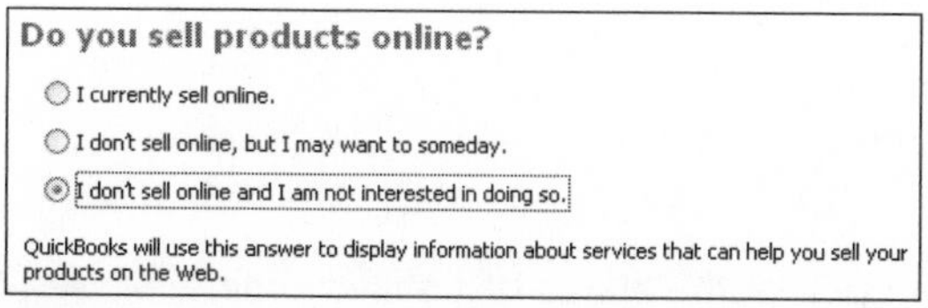

Do you sell products online?
I currently sell online.
I don't sell online, but I may want to someday.
I don't sell online and I am not interested in doing so.
QuickBooks will use this answer to display information about services that can help you sell your products on the Web.

Figure 5-8: This option tells QuickBooks not to set up accounts for online sales at this time.

Setting up accounts to handle sales tax

On the next several screens, you're prompted to indicate whether QuickBooks should set up accounts for handling sales taxes, estimates, and tracking orders, invoices, progress statements, and customer reminders and bill management (by tracking balances and issuing reminders). Simply selecting Yes initiates the set-up process to take care of establishing all of the accounts your business needs to do these things. Figure 5-9 shows the first of these screens, for setting up sales tax accounts.

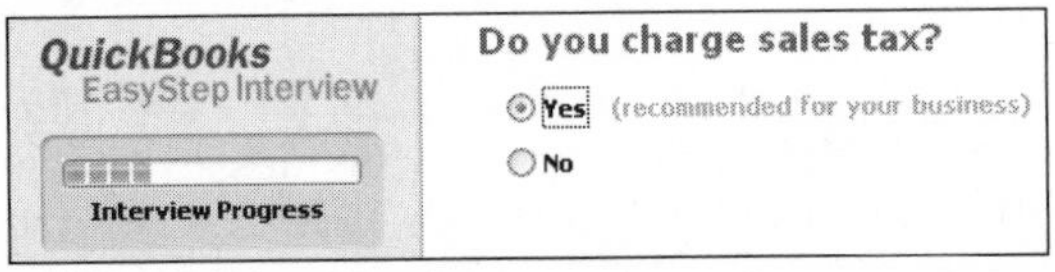

Figure 5-9: The option to set up sales tax accounts.

Tracking inventory

If you click Yes on the sales tax screen, the next screen that appears is the inventory tracking screen, as shown in Figure 5-10. This screen asks you if you want to track inventory in QuickBooks. If you click Yes, QuickBooks tracks what you receive from vendors and the quantities on hand and provides you with various options for valuing the amount of the inventory.

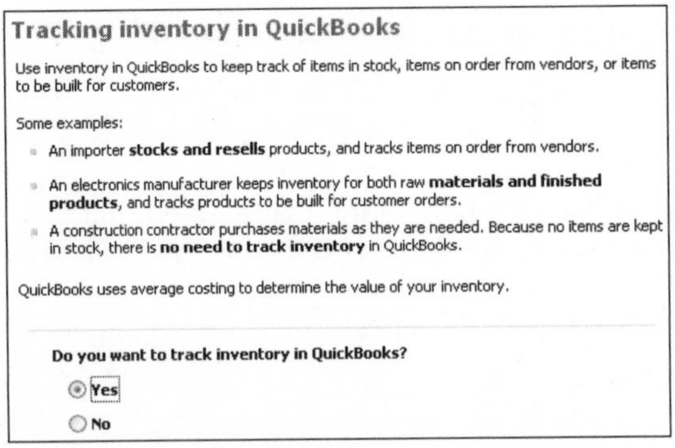

Figure 5-10: Options for tracking inventory.

Note

Order tracking means keeping track of the status of unfilled orders, converting invoices to show when they have been filled, and adjusting inventory accordingly.

Tracking time and wages

QuickBooks has convenient time tracking features that are activated from the Interview screen shown in Figure 5-11.

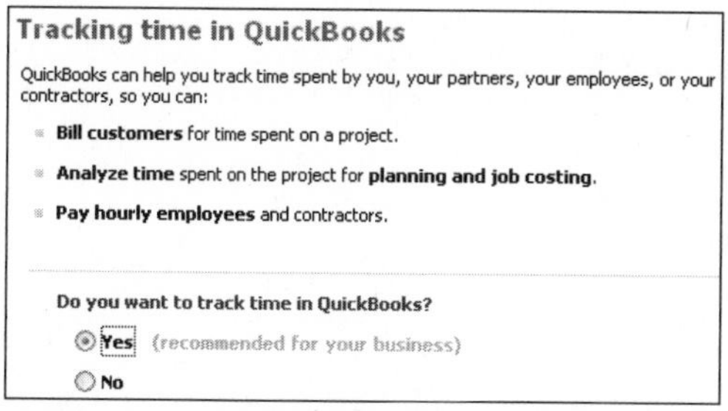

Tracking time in QuickBooks
QuickBooks can help you track time spent by you, your partners, your employees, or your contractors, so you can:
Bill customers for time spent on a project.
Analyze time spent on the project for planning and job costing.
Pay hourly employees and contractors.
Do you want to track time in QuickBooks?
Yes (recommended for your business)
No

Figure 5-11: Activating time tracking in QuickBooks.

On the screen that follows, shown in Figure 5-12, you are asked to indicate whether you have employees (subject to withholding) or want to track wages for independent contractors (which may not be subject to withholding).

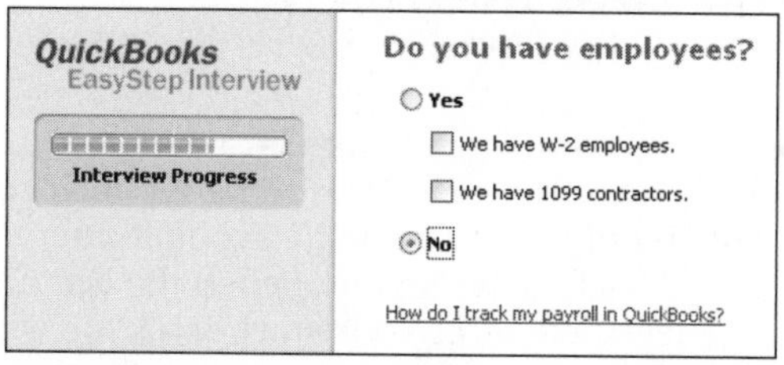

Interview Progress

We have W-2 employees.

How do I track my payroll in QuickBooks?

Figure 5-12: Activating withholding options for employees and independent contractors.

Entering your company's start date

A critical Interview question is the one that asks you to enter a start date, on the screen shown in Figure 5-13. What should you choose as a start date? You should have bank and credit card statements showing accurate balances as of the start date, as well as information regarding any outstanding transactions, as of the statement date, that did not appear on the statements. For example, if your most recent checking account statement as of the start date does not include several outstanding checks, you need to obtain and enter information about those outstanding checks. You also need to know the amount of any unpaid balances or obligations and the amounts that customers owed you as of the start date. When you can confidently nod yes to having all of this information, proceed to entering your start date. If you don't have the required records, consider starting at a later date.

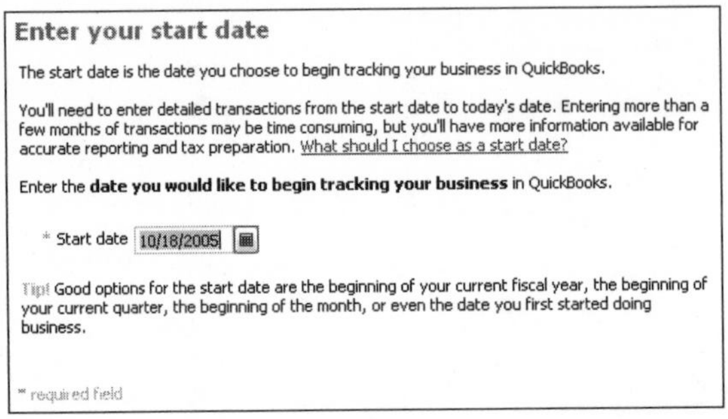

Figure 5-13: The start date is a critical accounting decision.

Cross-Reference

Chapter 4 provides guidance on choosing a start date.

Setting up bank and credit card accounts for your company

In the series of screens beginning with the one shown in Figure 5-14, you are prompted to enter information about bank and credit card accounts for your company. It helps to have account statements handy for referencing account numbers and beginning balances. You are also asked to indicate if you opened the accounts before or after your start date. If you opened them after your start date, you will not need to enter beginning balance information as of the QuickBooks start date.

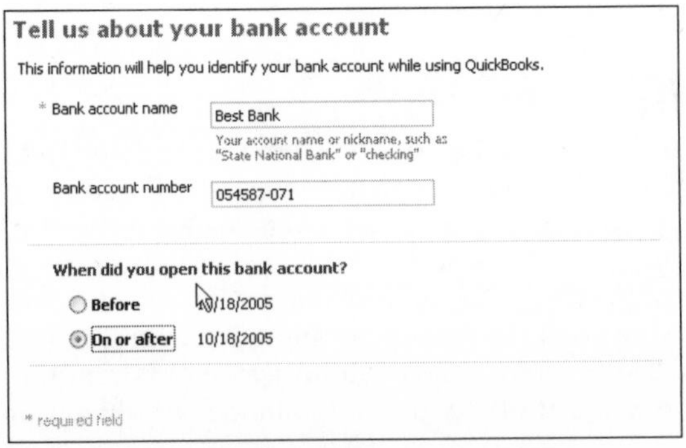

Figure 5-14: Setting up bank and credit card accounts for your company.

The screen shown in Figure 5-15 allows you to review information about each account you create.

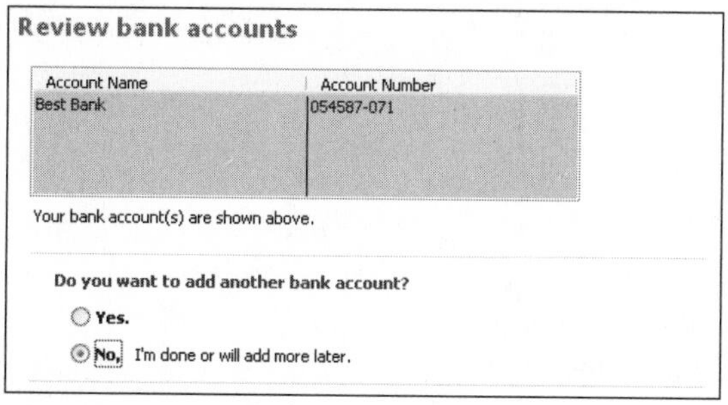
Review bank accounts
Account Name
Account Number
Best Bank
054587-071
Your bank account(s) are shown above.
Do you want to add another bank account?
Yes.
No, I'm done or will add more later.

Figure 5-15: The balance in each account is shown as of the start date.

Creating and previewing your Chart of Accounts

The screen shown in Figure 5-16 is the first in a series that allows you to preview the Chart of Accounts QuickBooks has created for you based on your previous interview questions.

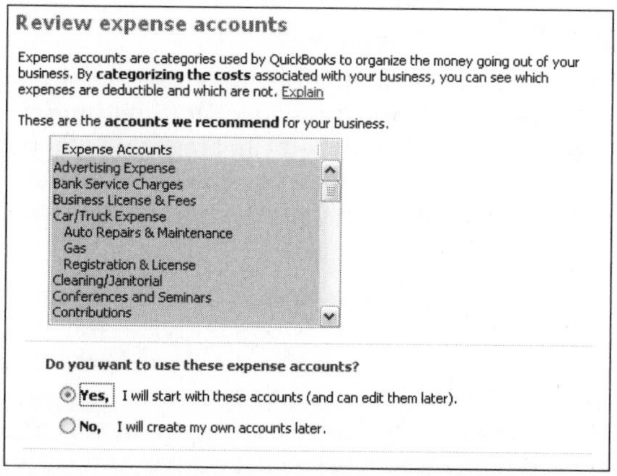
Review expense accounts
Expense accounts are categories used by QuickBooks to organize the money going out of your business. By categorizing the costs associated with your business, you can see which expenses are deductible and which are not. Explain
These are the accounts we recommend for your business.
Expense Accounts
Advertising Expense
Bank Service Charges
Business License & Fees
Car/Truck Expense
Auto Repairs & Maintenance
Gas
Registration & License
Cleaning/Janitorial
Conferences and Seminars
Contributions
Do you want to use these expense accounts?
Yes, I will start with these accounts (and can edit them later).
No, I will create my own accounts later.

Figure 5-16: Reviewing expense and income accounts QuickBooks has created for you.

Congratulations!

After reviewing the expense and income accounts QuickBooks has created for you, your company set up is complete. The screen shown in Figure 5-17 congratulates you.

Figure 5-17: This screen signals the end of the setup process.

Optional Adjustments

After you've created your company file, you might need to make a few adjustments as of your start date. Depending on how your particular company operates, you might need to:

- **Enter any sales tax liability:** If you collect sales tax, record in the Sales Tax Payable account register the sales tax owed as of your start date. Make sure that each sales tax agency is a vendor on your Vendor list.
- **Adjust the Uncategorized Income and Uncategorized Expense accounts (for accrual basis only):** When you enter unpaid balances for customers, QuickBooks assigns the income to an account called Uncategorized Income. Similarly, when you enter unpaid balances for vendors, QuickBooks assigns the expenses to the Uncategorized Expenses account based on how you keep your books.
- **Adjust for current income and expenses if your start date is not at the beginning of the fiscal year:** If you are setting up with a midyear start date and you know what your income and expenses are for the period from the beginning of the fiscal year through the start date, you can enter an adjustment for them. Then, your QuickBooks Profit and Loss Statement will be accurate for the period starting with the beginning of the fiscal year and ending on any date after your start date. To get this information, have your accountant create a year-to-date profit and loss statement for the current fiscal year through your start date.

✦ **Distribute earnings and equity before your start date:** After you have entered all opening balances and made other adjustments, you may want to move the amount in your Opening Balance Equity account to your other equity accounts if you want to identify retained earnings or the equity of several owners.

Bypassing the Interview

I strongly recommend using the EasyStep Interview the first time that you set up a QuickBooks company. But if you are an experienced QuickBooks user and feel you can save time by setting up a company on your own, be my guest. Here's how:

1. Choose File ⇨ New Company. The Interview window appears.
2. Click Next to bypass the next two interview screens. The Setting Up a New QuickBooks Company screen appears.
3. Click the Skip Interview button.
4. Enter your company name, fiscal year, and other information in response to the prompts that appear, and specify your Chart of Accounts and filename choices.

Summary

Your company is now up and running on the QuickBooks system. The Interview has not only prompted you with the right questions but also provided you with on-screen help and prominent Warning dialog boxes to make sure you stay on track. This chapter offered additional information to make sure that you fully understand the system you have created through the setup process.

✦ You now have a sense of when it is helpful to use the interview, how to maneuver through it, and how to exit and reenter it. You also know how to bypass it when you find it expedient to do so.

✦ You know that it is generally more time-efficient to start with a standard Chart of Accounts and improve on it than to start from scratch and painstakingly enter all of your own accounts, one by one.

✦ You have set up any necessary additional accounts for tracking all of your company's income and expenses, either by adding these accounts directly to the Chart of Accounts or by setting up Items.

✦ ✦ ✦

CHAPTER 6

Customizing Your Chart of Accounts

✦ ✦ ✦ ✦

In This Chapter

Automatically created accounts

Adding and deleting accounts

Making accounts inactive

Numbering accounts

Editing account information and opening balances

Combining accounts

Optional adjustments

✦ ✦ ✦ ✦

The Chart of Accounts is the skeletal framework of any accounting system. All transactions must be recorded in appropriate accounts. But what if you do not have the clairvoyance and vision at the outset to anticipate every type of transaction that the company will enter and, hence, every type of account that will be needed? QuickBooks acknowledges this human frailty in two ways. First, the program allows you to confidently create needed accounts as you enter new types of transactions. Second, it makes the process of adding, deleting, and changing the Chart of Accounts extraordinarily simple.

Creating and Maintaining Accounts

Chapter 4 introduced the concept of an account and dissected it like a biology class frog. If you read that chapter, you learned that there are five basic types of accounts: income, expense, asset, liability, and owner's equity. You learned that permanent accounts, for which balances are cumulative and carry over from one fiscal year to the next, appear on the Balance Sheet. Temporary accounts, which start with a zero balance at the beginning of each fiscal year and reflect only the activities of the business for the current fiscal year, appear on the Profit and Loss Statement.

Generally, you can add an account to your Chart of Accounts in one of three ways:

- **Accounts established during the initial Interview or initial company setup:** When setting up your company initially, you either select a preset Chart of Accounts or create your own. Some accounts, such as retained earnings, are established for every QuickBooks company. Other types of accounts, which appear on the standard chart, are dictated by the characteristics of your industry type.
- **Accounts you create:** The process of doing this is discussed later in this chapter. These are accounts you create specifically to meet the needs of your business. For example, you may create a special Coupon Promotion account for discounts.
- **Accounts that QuickBooks automatically creates for you:** Be aware of this third category of accounts — the ones that QuickBooks automatically creates for your business after completion of the initial setup such as those for cash, retained earnings, undeposited funds, and so on. These automatically created accounts vary with the type of business you are setting up. They are accounts that are most frequently used for your type of business, based on the questions you answered in the Interview, and include accounts such as Service Revenues, Work-in-Process, and so on.

Automatically Created Accounts

QuickBooks takes the liberty of adding several types of asset accounts to your chart. It creates the Accounts Receivable account the first time you create an invoice, if it was not created during the Interview in response to questions about whether your customers pay your company at the time they receive goods and services. QuickBooks creates an Inventory Asset account the first time you add an inventory Item, and you can rename it to be more specific and descriptive. QuickBooks automatically creates an Undeposited Funds account, shown in Figure 6-1, the first time you receive payment from a sale and do not deposit it into a bank account. Funds remain in this account until you deposit them in a bank account.

QuickBooks automatically shows the Uncategorized Income and Uncategorized Expense accounts on the Profit and Loss Statement as of your start date if you keep your books on the accrual basis. These accounts reflect opening and outstanding balances for customers and vendors, respectively. If you maintain your books on a cash basis, QuickBooks does not create these accounts. These amounts simply show up on your Profit and Loss Statement when payment occurs, as mentioned in the Chapter 4 discussion of cash versus accrual. Because these income and expense amounts are really attributable to the year prior to the start date, you may want to make the optional adjusting entries discussed at the end of this chapter.

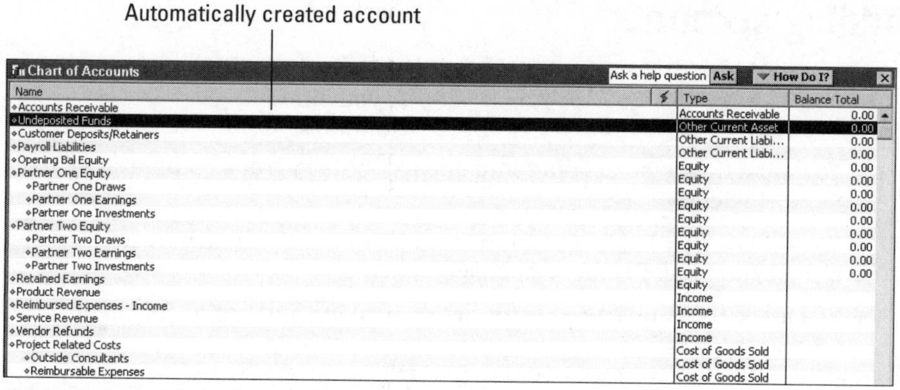

Automatically created account
Chart of Accounts
Ask a help question Ask
How Do I?
Name
Type
Balance Total
Accounts Receivable
Accounts Receivable
0.00
Undeposited Funds
Other Current Asset
0.00
Customer Deposits/Retainers
Other Current Liabi...
0.00
Payroll Liabilities
Other Current Liabi...
0.00
Opening Bal Equity
Equity
0.00
Partner One Equity
Equity
0.00
Partner One Draws
Equity
0.00
Partner One Earnings
Equity
0.00
Partner One Investments
Equity
0.00
Partner Two Equity
Equity
0.00
Partner Two Draws
Equity
0.00
Partner Two Earnings
Equity
0.00
Partner Two Investments
Equity
0.00
Retained Earnings
Equity
Product Revenue
Income
Reimbursed Expenses - Income
Income
Service Revenue
Income
Vendor Refunds
Income
Project Related Costs
Cost of Goods Sold
Outside Consultants
Cost of Goods Sold
Reimbursable Expenses
Cost of Goods Sold

Figure 6-1: QuickBooks automatically creates this account the first time you receive a payment and do not record a deposit.

Cross-Reference

Chapter 4 contains an explanation of the differences and similarities of these two accounting methods.

QuickBooks automatically creates the Cost of Goods Sold account the first time that you enter an inventory Item for the company. Cost of goods sold is an amount shown on the Income Statement as a reduction of sales revenue. It actually reflects an aggregate of expense accounts. It is the cost of goods and materials held in inventory and then sold.

Finally, QuickBooks creates a Purchase Orders account the first time you create a purchase order. A purchase order documents a customer's request for a good or service. It does not represent a legal right to payment. Accordingly, it is reflected as a special "nonposting" account. This means that you can track the total of purchase orders written by checking the balance of this account in its register, but the amounts shown in this register don't appear on either the Income Statement or the Balance Sheet.

Adding and Deleting Accounts

In Chapter 5, you were encouraged to use the Interview to set up your Chart of Accounts. You were also given the option of setting up your own Chart of Accounts from scratch. Choosing a preset Chart of Accounts frees you from the mental effort of adding each account, one by one. And even if the standard chart for your industry does not precisely reflect your business needs, it is more time-efficient to customize it with appropriate additions and deletions.

Adding accounts

You may want to create a new account for the following reasons:

- ✦ You require an additional account to track another income or expense item.
- ✦ You must divide an account into subaccounts to track income and expenses more efficiently.
- ✦ You open a new bank account or acquire a new credit source and must create a corresponding Balance Sheet account.
- ✦ You are setting up accounts for online banking and online payment.

To add a new income or expense account, follow these steps:

1. Go to the Company Navigator screen (which is the Home screen) and click the Chart of Accounts icon, as shown in Figure 6-2. Your Chart of Accounts appears.

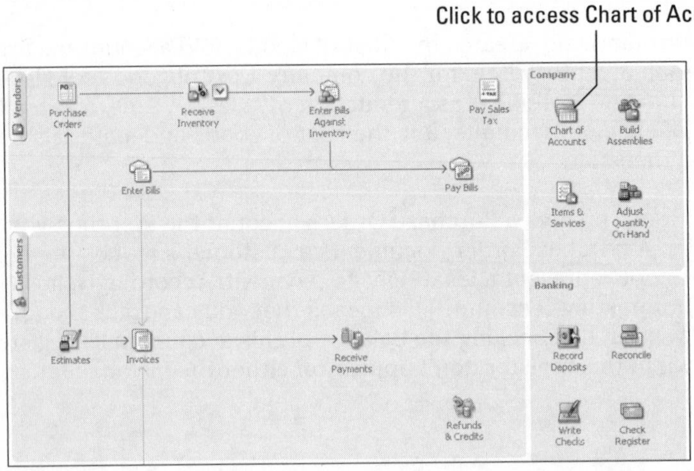

Figure 6-2: Click the Chart of Accounts icon on the Company screen.

2. Click the Account button located on the lower left corner of the Chart of Accounts, as shown in Figure 6-3.
3. Select New from the pop-up menu to open the New Account window.
4. Enter the account type (for example, bank, income, or expense).

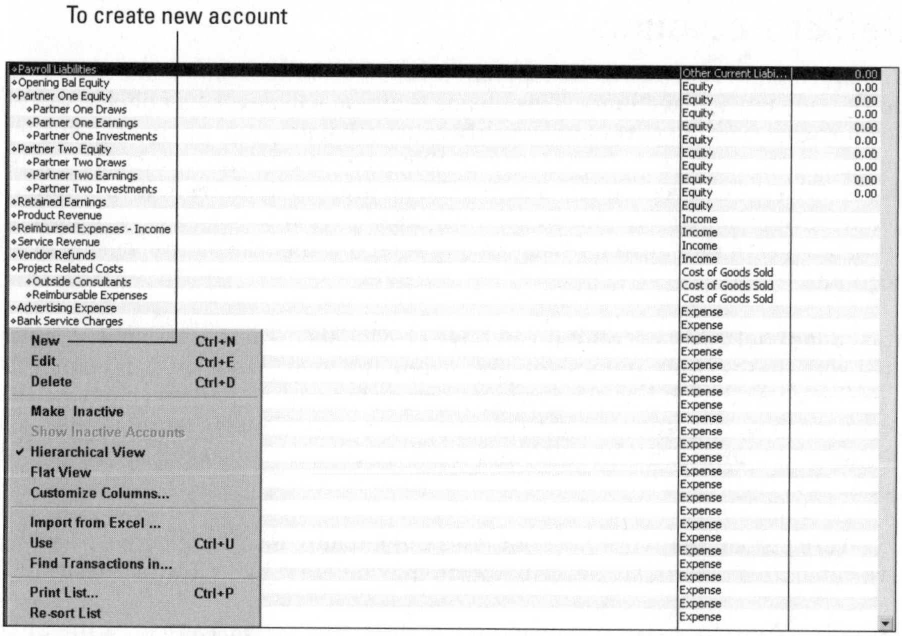

Figure 6-3: Click the Account button for options to change your Chart of Accounts.

5. Assign an appropriate name to the account.
6. If this account is to be a subaccount of another account, check the subaccount box and enter the name of the parent account.
7. For income and expense items, elect either the appropriate income tax line with which to associate the account or the Not Tax-Related option. Note that although the program refers to a line, you are actually indicating the correct form or schedule in the type of tax return you specified during the initial setup of the company. If you are, for example, a sole proprietor using a Form 1040, you enter Schedule C in this field.
8. Enter the opening balance of the account as of your start date.
9. If you have previously activated Track Reimbursed Expenses as a preference Item, additional fields appear on the New Account screen. Indicate in these fields whether you want to track reimbursable expenses and in which account you wish to track them.
10. Click Next to create another account or OK to close the New Account window.

Deleting accounts

The most important rule to remember about deleting accounts is that you can delete only unused accounts. This means that you will never be able to delete an account that has any sort of balance, because a balance means that the account is being used to reflect those transactions that gave rise to the balance. You must make sure that an account has a zero balance prior to deleting it. If you want to delete an account with a balance, you will need to first reenter every transaction associated with that account balance and rerecord the transactions using different accounts.

You cannot delete an account if you have previously created an Item that is associated with that account unless you first delete the Item. Similarly, you cannot delete a parent account that has subaccounts associated with it, and you cannot delete accounts that are associated with memorized transactions. (Chapter 7 discusses memorized transactions.) You cannot delete accounts that have associated online messages.

If you are certain that your account does not fall into any of the active or associative categories previously described, you may delete it by following these steps:

1. Go to the Navigator screen (which is the Home screen) and click the Chart of Accounts icon, as previously shown in Figure 6-2. Your Chart of Accounts appears.
2. Click the Account button located on the lower left corner of the Chart of Accounts.
3. Select Delete from the pop-up menu.

If you attempt to delete an account that cannot be deleted because it has a balance or because it is associated with subaccounts, online messages, or payroll Items, a warning icon and specific explanation about why the account cannot be deleted appears. Figure 6-4 illustrates the warning that appears when you attempt to improperly delete an account that is associated with an inventory Item.

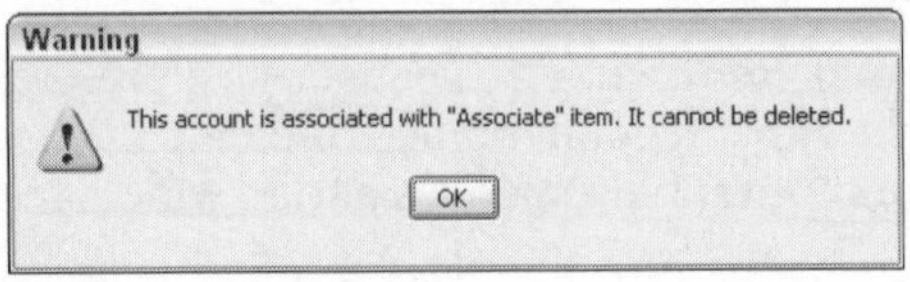

Figure 6-4: The warning icon and specific information displayed when you improperly attempt to delete an account.

If you still want to delete an account after you have received a message that it cannot be deleted because it is active, you need to first locate the transactions that are reflected in the account balance. If the account you are trying to delete is a Balance Sheet account, look in the register for that account.

Making Accounts Inactive

You can inactivate or hide an account so that it does not show up on your Chart of Accounts without actually deleting it. You can do this even if there is currently a balance in the account. When you make an account inactive, QuickBooks retains all of the information associated with the account but removes it from all lists and drop-down menus. You can make the account active again at any time.

To make an account inactive, do the following:

1. Go to the Company Navigator screen and click the Chart of Accounts icon (previously shown in Figure 6-2). Your Chart of Accounts appears.
2. Select the account that you want to make inactive.
3. Click the Account button located on the lower left corner of the Chart of Accounts.
4. Select Make Inactive from the pop-up menu.

You can view a complete Chart of Accounts, including inactive accounts, at any time. To view inactive accounts, follow these steps:

1. Go to the Company Navigator screen and click the Chart of Accounts icon (previously shown in Figure 6-2). Your Chart of Accounts appears.
2. Click the Account button located in the lower left corner of the Chart of Accounts.
3. Select Show Inactive Accounts from the pop-up menu. A special X icon appears next to each inactive account, as shown in Figure 6-5.

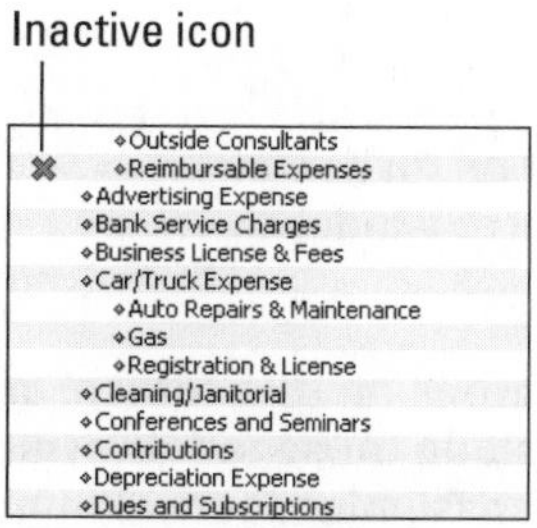

Figure 6-5: The special X icon appears next to inactive accounts when the Show Inactive Accounts option is active.

Numbering Accounts

You may find it convenient to assign numbers to each account in your Chart of Accounts. One reason you might want to number your accounts is because as your Chart of Accounts becomes lengthy, it is easier to locate individual accounts if they are numbered. If you activate the Numbering Accounts preference, QuickBooks displays the appropriate field in the New Account window each time you create a new account. The numbers assigned to the accounts are shown on your Chart of Accounts and on all reports.

Activating Account Numbering

To take advantage of the Account Numbering features and turn numbers on or off, follow these steps:

1. Go to Edit ➪ Preferences. In the Preferences window, select Accounting from the list on the left.
2. Select the Company Preferences tab. Select the Use Account Numbers check box as shown in Figure 6-6.

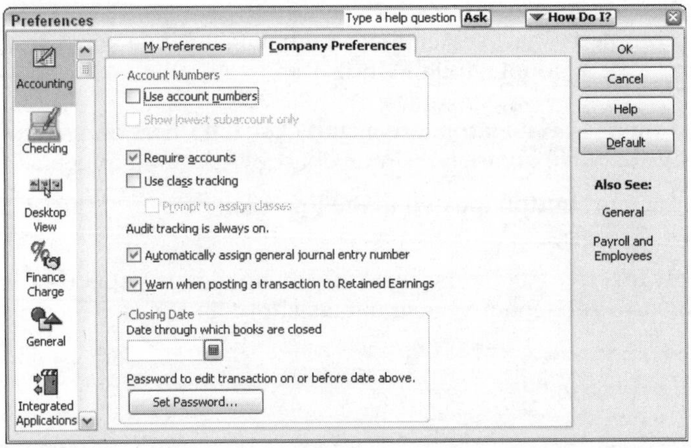

Figure 6-6: You can turn the Account Numbering function on or off at any time through the Accounting Company Preferences window.

3. You may also want to choose some of the other options on this screen, as discussed in the following sections. These options include those for showing only the lowest subaccount, creating an audit trail, assigning journal numbers, and so on.
4. Click OK.

Special Features to Help You Track Account Information

QuickBooks has a number of special features that allow you to analyze account information, as well as simply record it. These features include creating an audit trail, viewing subaccount detail, and tracking classes.

Creating an audit trail

You can have QuickBooks keep a record of all the changes made to transactions. Such a record is called an *audit report.* To view the audit report, choose Accountant & Taxes from the Reports menu, and then select Audit Trail. An audit trail is shown in Figure 6-7.

6:08 PM
12/15/07

Larry's Landscaping & Garden Supply
Audit Trail
Entered/Last Modified December 15, 2007

Num	Entered/Last Modified	Last modified by	State	Date	Name	Memo	Account	Split	Amount
					Accumulated Depr...		Depreciation	Accumulated...	575.00
Modified General Journal, ID #771									
A99	12/15/2007 17:01:17	Admin	Latest	09/30/2006			Accumulated Depr...	Depreciation	-575.00
							Depreciation	Accumulated...	575.00
New General Journal, ID #773									
	12/15/2007 12:21:13	Admin	Latest	09/22/2007		Account Op...	Equipment Loan	Opening Bal E...	-4,343.11
						Account Op...	Opening Bal Equity	Equipment Lo...	4,343.11

Figure 6-7: This screen shows a QuickBooks audit trail.

QuickBooks maintains a record of all the additions, deletions, and modifications made to transactions in your accounts, called an Audit Trail Report. The Audit Trail Report provides an accurate record of changes to all of your QuickBooks data. QuickBooks maintains the following information in the Audit Trail Report:

- ✦ The action taken (modified, new, or deleted)
- ✦ The type of transaction (deposit, check, bill payment, and so on)
- ✦ The internal QuickBooks number of the transaction (ID#)

Note

QuickBooks sorts the Audit Trail Report by the date a transaction was created, not by the date it was modified or deleted. This date appears in the Entered/Last modified column.

The Audit Trail Report consists of two sections. The first section shows all transactions that are currently active and whether they are new or modified. The second section lists all deleted transactions.

Viewing subaccount detail

QuickBooks Account Numbering preferences, edited from the window previously shown in Figure 6-6, allow you to view your Chart of Accounts in various levels of detail, such as subaccounts. *Subaccounts* track specific information within main accounts, which can be very useful when viewed in conjunction with audit trails or Class Tracking features. To activate this feature and track information in subaccounts, follow these steps:

1. Go to Lists menu ⇨ Chart of Accounts. Click the Account button, and choose New.
2. Enter the type and name of the account. The account type must be the same as the parent account. For example, if the parent account is an expense account, the subaccount must also be an expense account.
3. If applicable, enter the starting balance and starting balance date of the account.
4. Select the Subaccount Of check box. From the drop-down list, choose the account that you want to be the parent account. The subaccount inherits the active or inactive status of the parent account.
5. For income and expense accounts, from the Tax Line drop-down list, choose the appropriate tax line or Not Tax-Related.

Caution To avoid duplication in your income tax reports, do not associate both the parent account and subaccounts to tax lines.

6. Click OK.

Tip If you have numbered all your accounts, you can view a more concise version of your Chart of Accounts (while still keeping track of detail in subaccounts) by clicking the Show Lowest Subaccount Only option on the screen previously shown in Figure 6-6.

Using the Class Tracking feature

You can manage and analyze information about your company's accounts by using the Class Tracking feature. This feature allows you to track income and expenses by department, business office or location, or any other meaningful breakdown or segment of your business.

Note QuickBooks frequently reminds you of the option to assign classes when performing transactions.

After you activate this feature, you can view your profits and losses in either of the following two ways:

- ✦ **Profit and Loss by Class Report:** Shows the profit and loss of each aspect of your business that you are tracking by class in QuickBooks.
- ✦ **Profit and Loss Unclassified Report:** Shows the profit and loss from all transactions that are not classified. You can use this report to identify unclassified transactions in your company file.

You can access both of these reports from the Reports menu by selecting Company & Financial and then the type of report you want to view.

Figure 6-8 is a sample Profit and Loss by Class Report.

6:10 PM
12/15/07
Accrual Basis

Larry's Landscaping & Garden Supply
Profit & Loss by Class
October 1 through December 15, 2007

	Design	Landscaping	Maintenance	Overhead	Unclassifi
Ordinary Income/Expense					
Income					
Landscaping Services					
Design Services	13,510.00	0.00	0.00	0.00	0.00
Job Materials					
Misc Materials	0.00	141.30	0.00	0.00	0.00
Decks & Patios	45.00	0.00	0.00	0.00	0.00
Fountains & Garden Lighting	0.00	6,657.90	0.00	0.00	145.50
Plants and Sod	0.00	4,655.70	186.00	0.00	500.25
Sprinklers & Drip systems	0.00	3,887.21	0.00	0.00	0.00
Total Job Materials	45.00	15,342.11	186.00	0.00	645.75
Labor					
Installation	0.00	19,654.00	3,159.00	0.00	1,594.00
Maintenance & Repairs	0.00	609.00	1,317.00	0.00	1,638.50
Total Labor	0.00	20,263.00	4,476.00	0.00	3,232.50

Figure 6-8: A sample Profit and Loss by Class Report.

Editing Account Information and Opening Balances

Generally, you can edit information from the Chart of Accounts window previously depicted in Figure 6-5 by clicking the Account button and selecting New from the pop-up menu. There are, however, limits with respect to three types of accounts. You cannot change the account type if an account is an accounts payable, an accounts receivable, or an automatically created account. (Examples of automatically created accounts include retained earnings, sales tax, undeposited funds, and purchase orders.) The reason you cannot change the type designation of these accounts is that they are essential to accurately record certain transactions for your business. If you change their account type, you will not have the necessary accounts on your chart to reflect these essential transactions. On the other hand, if you attempt to change a current asset to a fixed asset, or an income Item to an asset, you are not omitting any account classifications necessary to record essential transactions such as the creation of accounts payable and receivable, inventory Items, and sales tax.

If you would like to edit basic account information, follow these steps:

1. Go to Lists ➪ Chart of Accounts, and then select the account that you want to edit.
2. From the Account menu button, choose Edit. Make your changes in the Edit Account window.
3. Click OK.

You may find that you made an error in entering the opening balance of an account. To change an opening balance for any account, follow these steps:

1. Go to Lists ➪ Chart of Accounts, and select the account for the opening balance to be changed.
2. Click any account to open its Register window.
3. Locate the account opening balance and change the amount shown to reflect the correct opening balance.
4. Click the Record button in the lower right corner of the Register window to save the changes.

Merging Accounts

If you find you are using two accounts to record similar types of transactions, you can simplify your Chart of Accounts by merging them. It is helpful to merge accounts if you've been using two similar accounts and want to see those accounts represented by a single line in your reports. Keep in mind, however, that merging accounts is irreversible.

To merge two accounts of the same type, follow these steps:

1. Go to Lists ➪ Chart of Accounts, and select the account with the name you no longer want to use.
2. Choose Edit from the Account menu.
3. Change the account name so that it is the same as the account you're merging it with.
4. Click OK and then click Yes to confirm that you want to merge the two accounts.

Special Start-Up Issues for Accrual-Based Taxpayers

The concepts of uncategorized income and uncategorized expenses are no doubt the most difficult for some QuickBooks users to understand without already having a lot of familiarity with accounting practices. You don't have to worry about these concepts if you have maintained an accrual-based accounting system in the past and have accurate accrual-based financial statements as of your start date. But what if you are like many QuickBooks users who first implement an accounting system after their business is up and running? What about income earned and expenses incurred prior to your start date? If your start date corresponds to the beginning of a fiscal year, these amounts are not really part of the current year's income and expenses, as reported on an accrual basis. The optional adjustments discussed in this section address this issue.

When you set up a company initially, you are asked to enter unpaid balances for customers. QuickBooks assigns this income to an account called Uncategorized Income. Similarly, unpaid balances owed to vendors as of the start date are assigned to the Uncategorized Expenses account. If you keep your books on a cash basis, these amounts will not appear on your financial statements until they are paid.

If you are an accrual-basis taxpayer, however, you may want to make an adjustment so that certain cash received or paid is not included in the current (start) year's income and expenses. As you may recall from Chapter 4, these amounts really belong on the Profit and Loss Statement for the prior year. According to the accrual method, these amounts should have been recognized on the financial statement and included in income in the year that the legal rights and obligations to payment were created, not in the year the cash is received. As Chapter 4 explained, the owner's equity account includes the cumulative earnings of the company for all prior years.

Accordingly, you may want to make an optional adjustment to your books for the first year that you use QuickBooks to ensure that these amounts are reflected correctly under the accrual method. This involves making an appropriate adjustment to the opening balance shown on the owner's equity account — that is, increasing it or decreasing it to show what the effect should have been on retained earnings had these amounts been properly included in the prior year's income.

Adjusting the Uncategorized Income account

If you are adjusting for uncategorized income, you want to increase the opening balance in the owner's equity account to show that this income is attributable to a prior year. To adjust for uncategorized income, follow these steps:

1. Go to Lists ➪ Chart of Accounts and then select the Uncategorized Income Account.

2. Go to Reports ⇨ QuickReport. If the report doesn't list any amounts, change the Dates field to ALL.
3. Scroll to the bottom of the report and locate the total amount for all the customer opening-balances.
4. Return to the Chart of Accounts window and select the equity account called Opening Bal Equity.
5. From the Activities menu, choose Use Register.
6. In the empty transaction at the bottom of the register, enter a transaction and then enter your start date.
7. From the Account drop-down menu in the Account field, choose Uncategorized Income, as shown in Figure 6-9.

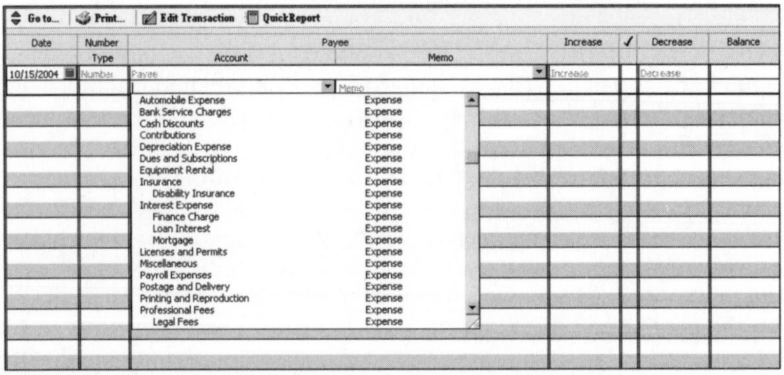

Figure 6-9: The Account field has a drop-down menu from which you can select a type of account.

8. In the Increase field, enter the total amount from the Uncategorized Income QuickReport.
9. Click Record to record the transaction.

Adjusting for uncategorized expenses

When you are switching from a cash-based system to an accrual-based system or are setting up QuickBooks for an ongoing business, you may also have accrued (uncategorized) expenses. To record these expenses, follow these steps:

1. Go to Lists ⇨ Chart of Accounts and select Uncategorized Expenses.
2. Go to Reports ⇨ QuickReport. If the report doesn't list any amounts, change the Dates field to ALL.

3. Scroll to the bottom of the report, and write down the total amount for all the vendor opening-balance transactions.
4. Return to the Chart of Accounts window and select the equity account called Opening Bal Equity.
5. Go to Activities ➪ Use Register. In the empty transaction at the bottom of the register, enter a transaction.
6. Enter your start date.
7. From the drop-down menu in the account field list, choose Uncategorized Expenses.
8. In the Decrease field, enter the total amount from the Uncategorized Expenses QuickReport.
9. Click Record to record the transaction.

Summary

This chapter focused on program features and accounting practices that enable you to customize your accounting system to meet your unique business needs. The information provided in this chapter enables you to manage your Chart of Accounts more efficiently and ensures that balances shown on the Profit and Loss Statement and Balance Sheet accurately reflect your company's performance and financial position.

- QuickBooks automatically adds certain accounts to your Chart of Accounts as you enter transactions, such as Undeposited Funds, Uncategorized Income and Expenses, and Cost of Goods Sold.
- You can always add accounts, but you can delete accounts only if they do not have positive balances and are not associated with any Items, subaccounts, or online messages.
- Implement a numbering system if you need to quickly locate specific accounts or rearrange accounts into logical groups as your Chart of Accounts grows larger.
- You can simplify your Chart of Accounts by merging or combining accounts.
- Making accounts inactive enables you to remove them from all lists and drop-down menus until you want to view them by using the Show All Accounts option.
- To correctly match revenue and expenses to the year in which they are appropriately recognized, you may make optional adjustments directly to the opening balance shown in the owner's equity register.

✦ ✦ ✦

CHAPTER 7

Entering Historical Transactions and Data

✦ ✦ ✦ ✦

In This Chapter

Entering past sales and accounts receivable

Entering past accounts payable information

Entering historical bank transactions

Entering opening balances for asset and liability accounts tracked on your company's Balance Sheet

✦ ✦ ✦ ✦

The task of entering historical data as of your start date is time-consuming, but there is no way around it. In Chapter 2, I acknowledged that in choosing a start date, a major consideration for many businesses is the amount of work involved in entering historical data. The more recent your QuickBooks start date, the less historical data you are required to enter. On the other hand, the more historical data you have at your disposal, the more information you can use for creating graphs, charts, and budgets.

Record-Keeping Goals

The integrity and reliability of your QuickBooks accounting system depend on the accuracy of the historical data that you enter in the system. Its scope and flexibility as a tool for budgeting and analysis also depend on the start date you choose and how much historical data you have entered. When entering historical data in the system, you are always entering all transactions from the start date to the current date.

Assume that you choose January 1 of the current year as your start date, and today is March 15. You would enter all transactions as of January 1 through March 15. You then have records identical to those that you would have had if you had actually started using QuickBooks on January 1. If you want to compare your company's performance in the current year to its performance in the prior year, you would have to enter all transactions for the prior year to generate comparative reports, charts, and graphs.

Compiling and entering historical information is labor intensive and requires thought and familiarity with the business. How far back in time should you go? How much historical information is enough?

If you enter the data indicated at the end of this chapter, you can rely on your accounting system to help you with four questions that every small business must be able to answer:

- **Do I have sufficient working capital to meet my liabilities? What is my current bank account balance?** QuickBooks calculates accurate balances for your bank accounts, which you can use to reconcile your bank statement to the account balance shown on the QuickBooks system.
- **Am I making a profit?** QuickBooks gives you an accurate year-to-date Profit and Loss Statement at any time — updated as of the very last transaction entered into the system.
- **Are my payroll and sales tax liabilities current?** No small business can afford to fall behind in paying its payroll and sales tax liabilities. Chapter 3 gave you a feel for the different types of penalties imposed on late filers — and how quickly they mount. With QuickBooks, sales tax and payroll records are a mouse click away if you have properly entered the relevant historical data.
- **Do I have sufficient cash flow to meet my current obligations?** With QuickBooks, you can generate reports about your accounts receivable and accounts payable at any time to see what your customers owe you and what you owe to vendors.

The Essential Order for Entering Data

Does it make a difference which types of transactions you decide to enter first? Generally, you will want to enter transactions in the order in which they generally occur — such as bills before payments. For example, you want to do the following:

- **Enter bills from vendors before you enter payments.** If you don't do this, QuickBooks cannot tell which bills you are paying and where to apply the payments.
- **Enter customer invoices before you enter customer payments.** Again, QuickBooks must have information about the outstanding bills so that it can apply the customer payments properly.
- **Enter accounts payable before accounts receivable.** Do this if you track reimbursable expenses.

- **Enter bank account transactions last.** The reason is that as you enter accounts payable, accounts receivable, and payroll transactions, your bank balance is automatically adjusted to reflect them. All you need to do, at the very end, is enter any transactions affecting the bank account balance that are not attributable to accounts payable, accounts receivable, or payroll.

Tip

If it will take several days or weeks to enter historical data for a company, begin entering current transactions as you go, so that you don't fall further behind. QuickBooks recognizes that entering historical data is a time-consuming task and that in the meantime you still have a business to run. Just remember that the account balances will not be accurate until you finish entering all of the historical data since the start date.

A Checklist for Establishing Your Opening Balances

You can save time and streamline the task of entering opening-balance information if you have the correct information on hand. The following is a partial checklist of information to compile from the start date to the current date:

- Invoices, sales receipts with sales tax, and other information relevant to customer
- Customer return documentation
- Records of payments received from customers
- Deposits made since the start date
- Payments of sales tax
- Bills received from vendors
- Credits for payments from vendors
- Outstanding bills
- Bill payments you have made since your start date

Entering Opening Balances

If you have a company that existed prior to your QuickBooks start date, you must enter information to accurately reflect assets and liabilities.

To enter opening balance information for an asset or liability account you have created during the initial interview:

1. Go to the Lists menu and click Chart of Accounts.
2. Double-click the account.
3. Click in the blank entry at the end of the register as shown in Figure 7-1.

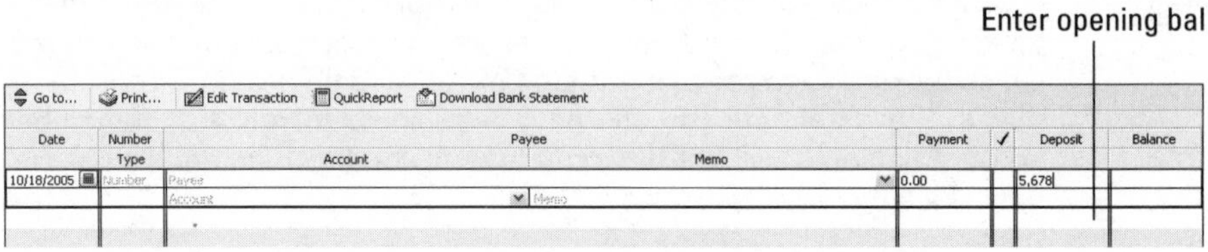

Figure 7-1: Entering the opening balance for a bank account.

4. Change today's date to your QuickBooks start date.
5. Leave the Number and Payee fields blank.
6. Enter the opening balance amount as follows:
   - For bank accounts, enter the amount in the Deposit column.
   - For asset, liability or equity accounts, enter the amount in the Increase column.
   - For credit card accounts, enter the amount in the Charge column.
7. Click the Account field, and choose Opening Bal Equity from the drop-down list.
8. Click Record.

Tip

If you do not know the opening balances of your accounts receivable and payable, either select a different start date for which you do know the opening balance.

The procedure for entering opening balances for income and expense accounts is slightly different than for the asset and liability accounts. To enter opening balance information for these accounts:

1. Go to the Lists menu and click Chart of Accounts.
2. Double-click the Opening Bal Equity account.
3. Go to the blank line at the bottom of the register, as shown in Figure 7-2.
4. In the Decrease column, enter the total year-to-date amount of your income.
5. Click Splits.

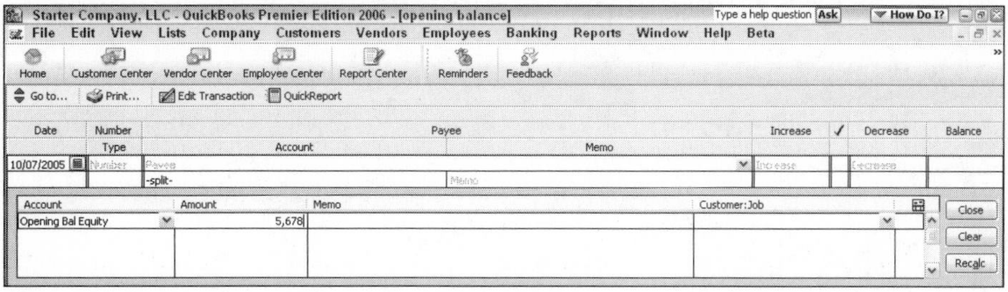

Figure 7-2: Entering the opening balance for a year-to-date income amount.

6. In the Account column, enter an income account.
7. In the Amount column, enter the amount received to date for this account.
8. Repeat steps 6 and 7 for all income accounts with a balance.
9. Click Record when done.

Summary

This chapter integrated a discussion of data entry with more fundamental accounting concepts. The process of entering historical data allowed you to consider the chronology and interrelationship of various accounting transactions.

✦ Accurate historical data is necessary for a business to have an accurate picture of its ability to meet cash-flow requirements and to gauge its profitability.

✦ All assets and liabilities are valued and tracked on your company's Balance Sheet, and the balance in your owner's equity account is established based on the asset and liability information you enter.

✦ ✦ ✦

CHAPTER 8

Using Lists

QuickBooks manages customer, vendor, employee, and product information in lists. These lists maintain information about all the people and companies you do business with so you can easily create new transactions and reports. Even though each of these lists contains different information, the procedures for using them are similar. After you've mastered the Customer List, for example, the Vendor List should present no problem.

In This Chapter

How lists manage your data

Adding list records

Creating custom fields

Merging lists

Making list entries inactive

Printing lists and generating list reports

What Lists Are Available?

Lists perform a database function in QuickBooks, helping you update, track, organize, and access accumulated information that is essential to the operation of your business. QuickBooks offers the following types of lists, which you can access directly from the Lists menu shown in Figure 8-1:

- **Chart of Accounts:** This list, discussed in Chapter 6, shows all your accounting categories.
- **Item List:** Use this list to define and keep track of the products and services that you bill for on invoices and to track the flow of inventory, if your business requires it.
- **Fixed Asset Item List:** Displays information about fixed assets (furniture, equipment, buildings, and vehicles) such as the date of purchase and cost.
- **Price Level List:** The Price Level list stores all the price levels you've created. It includes the name and type (either fixed percentage or per item).
- **Sales Tax Code List:** This list contains information about your sales taxes.

✦ **Other Names List:** If you need to keep a list of names that do not fall neatly into one of the other "people" categories (Employees, Vendors, or Customers), you can keep it here. For example, perhaps you maintain a list of technical experts you call for quotes to include in articles you write.

✦ **Customer & Vendor Profile Lists:** These lists allow you to maintain databases of sales representatives, customer types, vendor types, job types, messages to send to customers, sales terms you offer customers, shipping information, payment methods, and information about any vehicles used or owned by your company. The lists available under this option are as follows:

- **Sales Rep List:** This list allows you to track your sales representatives' initials, names, and types.
- **Customer Type List:** This list includes all of the different types of customers your business services (for example, "corporate" or "institutional") for easy designation on business forms.
- **Vendor Type List:** This list includes all of the different types of customers your business services (for example, "office supplies" or "metal work") for easy designation on business forms.
- **Terms List:** If you use special terminology in your business, you can track and define those terms using this list.
- **Customer Message List:** You can create a list of standardized messages for communicating with customers via this list (for example, "this account is 39 days overdue").
- **Payment Method List:** This list allows you to track information about the different payment types your business accepts.
- **Ship Via List:** Use this list to track all the different shipping methods and vendors your business uses.
- **Vehicle List:** This list tracks the vehicles you use in your business.

✦ **Payroll Item List:** This is a database of payroll-related items such as vacation pay, sick pay, overtime pay, and so on.

✦ **Templates:** This list contains the various templates you can use to generate invoices and statements. Chapter 15 shows you how to work with these templates.

✦ **Memorized Transaction List:** You can save time when entering transactions by telling QuickBooks to "memorize" those transactions you enter often. For example, if you pay rent on your office space every month, you might have QuickBooks memorize that transaction. (See Chapter 17 for more on this list.)

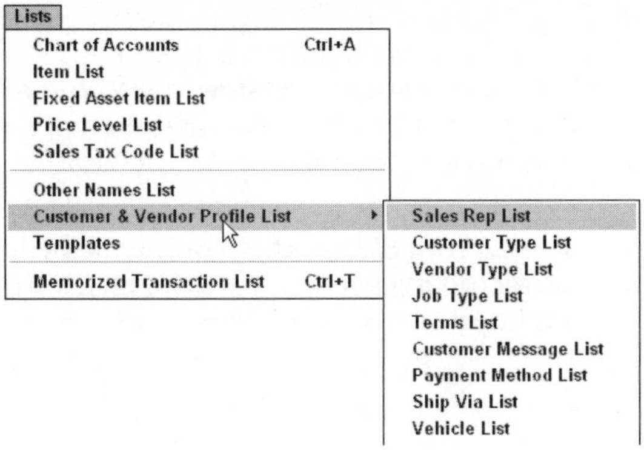

Figure 8-1: The QuickBooks Lists menu.

Where Do List Entries Come From?

You can enter an entry on a QuickBooks list either ahead of time or on-the-fly— that is, as you work on a transaction. For example, suppose you want to invoice a customer. You could either set up the customer before you create the invoice, or you could start creating the invoice first and then enter the customer information when prompted.

Which is better? It all depends on your preferences. If you have an existing list of customers (perhaps from your old accounting system), you may want to spend an afternoon entering them into QuickBooks and be done with it. This works well for companies that have the same customers over and over.

On the other hand, if you seldom work with the same customer more than once, you may not find it worth your time to set up customers beforehand. You may want to enter a customer only when it becomes necessary (that is, when you are entering a transaction for him or her). The disadvantage to this method is it takes time to enter a new customer, so this process can slow down your invoice entry somewhat. If you are dealing with a repeat customer, and he or she is standing there waiting, it can make you look bad.

Viewing Lists

To view any list, open the Lists menu and pick the list you want. A window containing the entries on the list appears, similar to the screen shown in Figure 8-2, which is a sample Employees list. Each list has the following three buttons:

✦ **List button:** The List button changes its name depending on the list you are looking at. For example, in the Sales Rep List this button is Sales Rep. The button opens a menu of list-management commands that allow you to add Items to your list; delete, edit, and modify Items; and otherwise perform functions that allow you to maintain the list as a complete, reliable, and accurate database.

✦ **Activities button:** This button opens a menu of QuickBooks activities you can perform on the list entries, such as record a payment or write a check. For example, on the Activities menu for Chart of Accounts, you'll find commands for creating new transactions that include an account you select from the list.

✦ **Reports button:** Click this button to display a menu of reports that can be generated from each list.

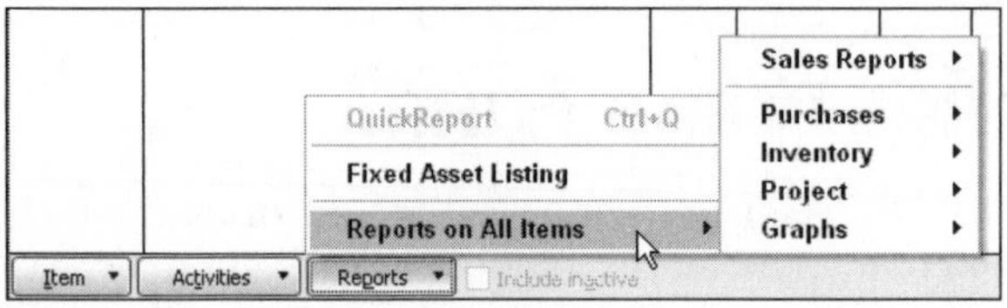

Figure 8-2: A sample list (Fixed Asset Item List).

Tip Just as in other Windows programs, you can resize the window by dragging one of its borders. By making it longer, you can see more list entries at once without scrolling. You can also maximize the window for a full-screen view of the list.

Adding Entries to a List

Adding new items to a list is a simple process for which QuickBooks provides meaningful prompts so that you do not forget to include key information.

When any list is displayed, you can click the list button to open its menu and add new entries. Simply follow these steps:

1. Display the list to which you want to add an entry by selecting it from the Lists menu or by accessing it from the appropriate Navigator screen.
2. In the lower left corner of the list, click the List button. One or more dialog boxes appear asking you for information relative to the list with which you are working, such as customer contact information for Customer lists. Fill in the fields.
3. Click Next when you finish entering the information for your entry to add it to your list and enter another entry. Click OK if you are finished making entries.

This general procedure for adding items is a little different for every list with which you are working. It's helpful to look at a few examples. The concepts illustrated in the following sections work well for all types of lists.

Example: Adding a vendor type

If you frequently do business with the same vendors, you may want to set them up formally in QuickBooks, rather than simply entering them on-the-fly. By entering a vendor's information beforehand, you can enter much more complete and thoughtful information because you won't be in a hurry to complete a transaction.

To enter a new vendor type, do the following:

1. Choose Lists ➪ Customers & Vendor Profile List ➪ Vendor Type List to open the Vendor List. Or, if you want to access this list from the Vendor Navigator screen, click the Vendors icon.
2. Click the New Vendor link (see Figure 8-3) and fill in the vendor contact information.

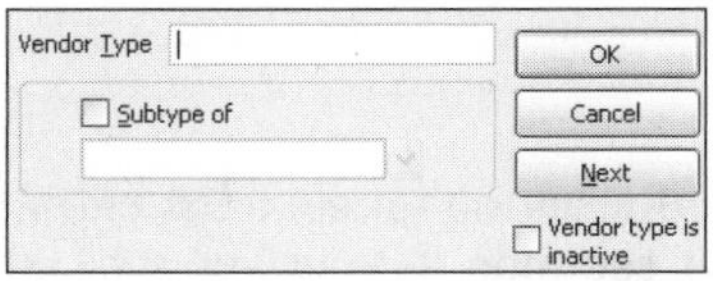

Figure 8-3: Fill in the contact information for the new vendor.

3. Click OK to close the dialog box, or click Next to start a new vendor entry.

Adding list entries as you go

You can also add entries to lists while in the middle of activities, such as creating invoices or writing checks. Suppose you want to create a new vendor while you're writing a check, as shown in Figure 8-4.

Simply open the Customer:Job drop-down list. Notice that Add New appears on that list. This Add New option also appears on the drop-down lists for bank accounts and the Pay to the Order of field. If you want to create a new customer, job, or bank account while you're working on a transaction, choose this option.

Tip

Keep this in mind: No matter what activity you are performing—be it writing checks, creating invoices, entering inventory, and so on—certain fields will always pull information from lists. Whenever you're dealing with such fields, the Add New option is always available, so you can make new entries as you go.

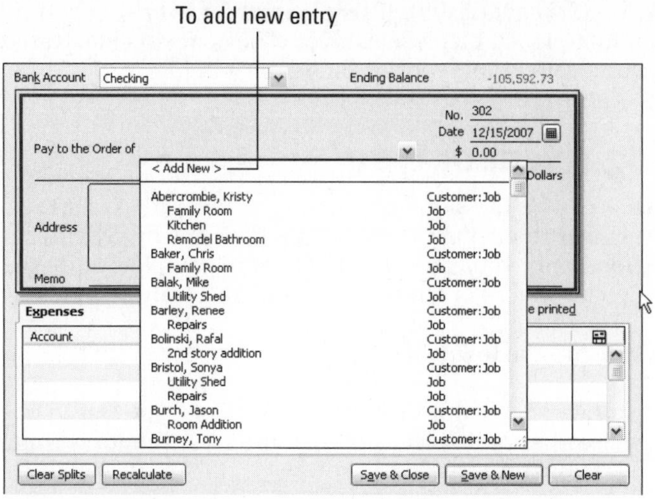

Figure 8-4: Many drop-down lists provide an Add New option for creating new list entries on-the-fly

Creating Custom Fields

You can use custom fields to keep track of information for each list entry that does not fit neatly into one of the other fields. For example, in your Vendor List, you may want to enter which county each vendor is located in for tax purposes.

Note

Custom fields are available for vendors, employees, customers, and Items. For employees, vendors, and customers, the procedure is similar. For Items, it's a little different.

Although you create custom fields for Employee, Vendor, and Customer Lists in the New dialog box, the custom fields you create apply to all entries on the list, not just the new entry being created. For example, if you define a custom field called County, it automatically appears on the Additional Info tab for all vendors. That's because QuickBooks assumes that if you want to indicate some special information for one list entry (one particular vendor, for example), you must also want to track that same bit of information for all others, too, for comparison. It isn't important, for example, that Acme Corporation is in Marion County unless other vendors are in different counties.

When you create a custom field for one list (Employee, Vendor, or Customer), you can also make it available to either or both of the other two lists by clicking the appropriate check box. This, too, happens because QuickBooks is anticipating your needs. If you are interested in tracking certain information about customers, it's likely that you are also interested in tracking that same information about your vendors and/or employees.

To create a custom field, follow these steps:

1. Open the list for which you want a custom field.
2. Double-click the entry to display a screen like the one shown in Figure 8-5. (This one is for editing the Fixed Asset List.) Double-click an existing one to edit it.

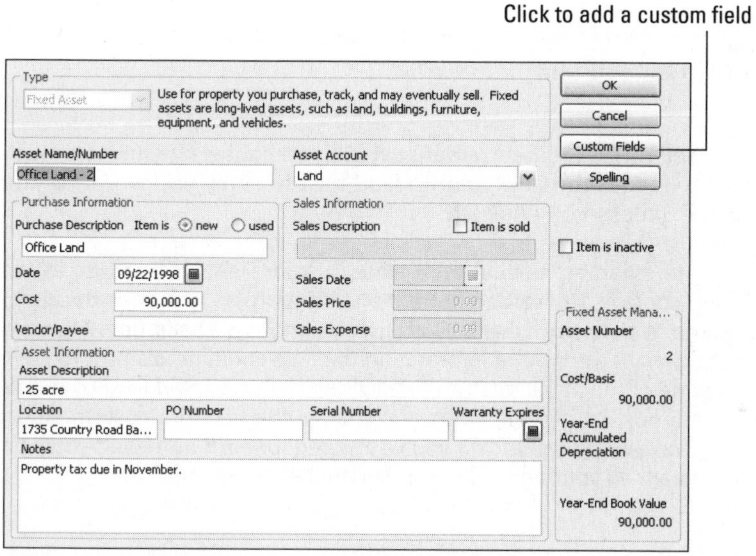

Figure 8-5: Click any list entry to display this screen.

3. Type the new field name in the first blank or empty row.
4. Select or deselect the check boxes as needed to indicate in which lists you want the new field included (Customers:Jobs, Vendors, and Employees).
5. Enter any additional fields needed.
6. Click OK. The new fields appear in the Custom Fields area of the dialog box shown in Figure 8-6.
7. Complete the list entry and click OK, or click Cancel if you do not want to create or edit the entry.

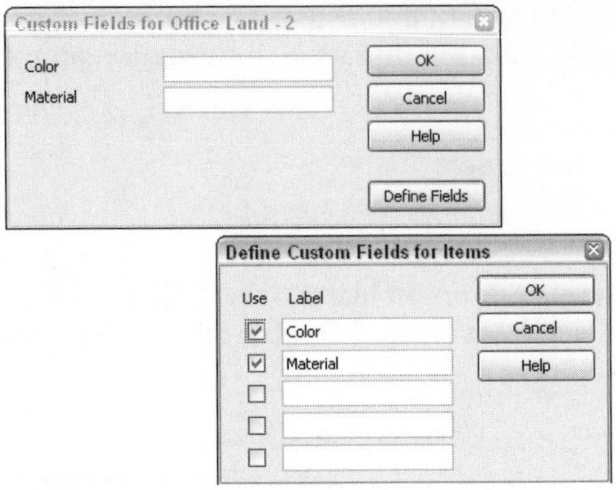

Figure 8-6: Enter information in this dialog box to create a custom field for a list.

The custom fields you created remain even if you cancel the new entry. However, if you entered data into the new custom field for the entry you were working with, it will not "stick" unless you click OK.

Caution

It's okay to rename a field in the Define Custom Fields dialog box, as long as the field still contains the same information. For example, you may decide to change the name Warehouse Location to just Warehouse. That's fine. However, if you need to change the type of information the field contains, it's best to create a new field in one of the blank rows and deactivate the unwanted field by deselecting its Use check box. Otherwise, when you change the title of a custom field, the field will still contain the same data you've entered for each Item, and you'll have to go back through all your Items and modify the field's content.

Organizing Lists

When you start out with QuickBooks, you may have only a few entries on each list, but as things heat up, you're going to end up with hundreds of entries on some lists. In my own business, I have noticed the Vendor List multiplies especially quickly, as every time I write a check the recipient is added to this list. In the following sections, you'll learn how to organize and sort your lists to keep them under control.

Rearranging individual list entries

Because you'll do most of your work in QuickBooks by selecting entries from various lists, it's important that you keep the list entries you use most frequently handy. By default, all list entries appear in alphabetical order, from A to Z. However, many people choose to move their most frequently used entries to the top of their lists so those entries are more immediately available. You may also want to make a subentry a main entry or turn a main entry into a subentry.

Caution

You can't rearrange all lists. The ones that you can are Chart of Accounts, Class, Customer:Job, Customer Type, Item, Job Type, Memorized Transactions, and Vendor Type.

To rearrange your lists by moving items, follow these steps:

1. Open the list in which you want to rearrange entries (from the List menu). Notice the little diamonds next to each list entry. The diamonds indicate that these entries can be rearranged.
2. Point the mouse pointer at the diamond next to the entry you want to move. The mouse becomes a four-pointed arrow.
3. While holding down the mouse button, drag the entry to the desired spot and drop it there. To move an entry with all of its subentries, drag the main (parent) entry. To make a subentry a main entry, drag it to the left; to make a main entry a subentry, drag it to the right.
4. Repeat the previous step for any other entries that you want to move.

There are important limits on how and what you can rearrange in some lists. For example, when you're working with the Item List, you must keep Items within the same type. You can't mix up Inventory Parts, Non-Inventory Parts, and Services. However, within those groupings, you can rearrange entries.

To put a list back the way you found it (that is, in alphabetical order), click the list button (for example, the Customer:Job button on the Customers:Job List) and choose Re-sort List from the menu that appears.

Sorting entire lists

QuickBooks puts lists in alphabetical order, but you don't have to stick to this format. You may want the option to sort lists by amount, put active accounts first, and so on depending upon the List. Table 8-1 describes the list sorting options and how to carry them out. The same sort of table is also included in QuickBooks Help Menu for convenient use while you're working in QuickBooks.

Table 8-1
Sorting Options for QuickBooks Lists

To . . .	*Do This*
Return to the order you started with	Click the large diamond in the column title.
Sort a column in ascending order	Click the column heading so that the arrow points up.
Sort a column in descending order	Click the column heading so that the arrow points down.
Sort or rearrange a long list	Choose Flat View from the list's menu button, and then click the column you want to sort.
Sort a list while viewing subentries (not available in all lists)	Choose Hierarchical View from the list's menu button, and then click the column you want to sort.

Making list entries inactive

A good trick for simplifying a cumbersome list is to make some items inactive, so you don't have to view them every time you access the list. You may not want to delete list entries entirely, because they may have transactions associated with them. In fact, QuickBooks won't let you delete an entry with associated transactions. This is for your own protection. For example, if you deleted a customer who is now out of business, there might be a problem displaying invoices for that customer if you ever needed to look back at your old records. Instead, you should make inactive any list entries you don't plan on using anymore.

When an entry is inactive, it does not appear on any drop-down lists in activities, but it is still in the system. To inactivate an entry, display the appropriate list and then right-click the list entry you want to inactivate. Choose Make Inactive from the shortcut menu that appears.

If you want to hide the inactive entries, go to Edit ➪ Show Inactive Customers. The inactive entry immediately disappears from the list. If you want to see the complete list, including the inactive entries, click the Show All check box. Inactive entries reappear, with a symbol next to them (see Figure 8-7). To make an inactive entry active again, right-click it and choose Make Active, or just click the ghost symbol to make it disappear.

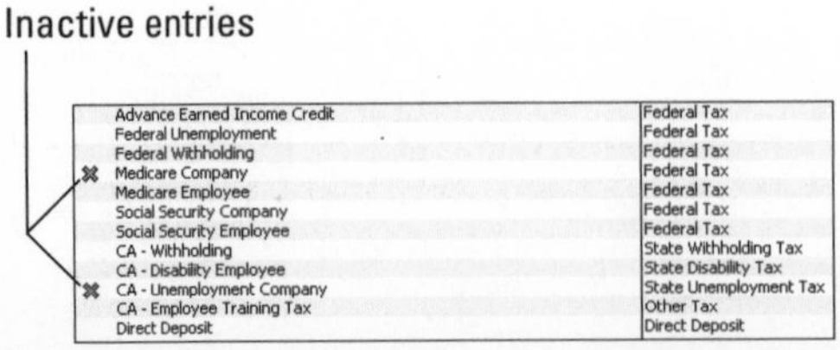

Figure 8-7: If you want to view a complete list, including the inactive entries, go to Edit ➪ Show Inactive Vendors. Inactive entries appear in the list with an X icon next to them.

Finding List Entries in Transactions

Most of the lists in QuickBooks enable you to generate a quick report that shows all transactions involving a particular list entry. This can be extremely handy for tracking certain kinds of information relevant to your business, such as whether a particular customer has given you any business in a certain time period or whether a particular inventory Item has been selling. You'll learn about the whole array of reports you can create with lists later in this chapter, under "Generating List Reports." For now, take a look at how to generate a list of transactions for a particular list entry:

1. Open the appropriate list, and select the list entry whose transactions you want to see.
2. Click the list button (for example, Vendor in the Vendor List) and choose Find in Transactions. A Find window appears, with the list entry already entered as a criterion.
3. Click Find to perform the search. A list of the transactions found appears at the bottom of the dialog box. From here, double-clicking any one of the transactions takes you to the record for that transaction.
4. If you want to see a report based on this search, click the Report button. A report appears, including totals, if applicable.
5. Click X to close the report.

Merging List Entries

You may end up with some duplicate records, especially if you have more than one person doing data entry in QuickBooks. For example, the same customer might be listed twice under slightly different names, or the same Item might appear under two different part numbers.

When this happens, the first thing to check is whether both of the entries have been used in transactions. Do this by following the steps in the preceding section, "Finding List Entries in Transactions," for both entries. If one of them has not been used, you can simply delete it. (See "Deleting List Entries" later in this chapter.)

If both entries have been used in transactions, you must merge them. When you merge two entries, you pick one that should stay and one that should go away. Then QuickBooks reassigns all the past transactions from the one that's going away to the one that's staying.

Tip

You can merge entries only in these lists: Chart of Accounts, Item, Payroll Item, Customer:Job, Vendor, Employee, and Other Names. Also, merging works only in single-user mode.

To merge two entries, follow these steps.

1. Display the desired list (from the List menu).
2. Double-click the list entry you want to get rid of. The Edit dialog box for the selected entry appears.
3. Change the name of the entry you want to remove to exactly the same name as the entry you want to keep.
4. Click OK to close the Edit dialog box. A message appears asking whether you want to merge the two entries.
5. Click Yes.

Deleting List Entries

You cannot delete list entries unless they have no transactions associated with them. If an entry has been used, you must inactivate it instead of deleting it, as discussed in the section "Making list entries inactive" earlier in this chapter.

To delete a list entry, select it and press Ctrl+D, or open the list menu and choose Delete. A dialog box appears to confirm the deletion. Click OK to confirm.

Adding, Moving, and Removing Columns in a List

QuickBooks allows you to further customize the level of detail that appears in a particular list by adding or deleting columns. To use this feature, follow these steps:

1. From the list name menu button (in the lower left corner of the list), choose Customize Columns.
2. In the Customize Columns window, select a column name on the left, and then click Add. You also can select column names on the right, and then click Delete or Move.
3. When you're finished rearranging the columns, click OK.
4. Click Default if you want to return to the preset columns for the list.

Printing a List

You can print any of your lists at any time. When you print a list, it appears more or less exactly as it does in the List window on-screen. (For more sophisticated details and formatting, see "Generating List Reports" later in this chapter.) A raw printout like this might be useful, for example, if you wanted to keep a hard copy of a list handy for employees. I have a friend who runs a lawnmower repair shop, and he prints a list of all the parts he stocks and puts a copy next to each of the cash registers.

To print a list, follow these steps.

1. Display the list you want to print.
2. Click the list button in the lower right corner of the screen and choose Print List.
3. If a dialog box appears suggesting that you use a report instead, click OK to bypass it. The Print Lists dialog box then appears as shown in Figure 8-8.

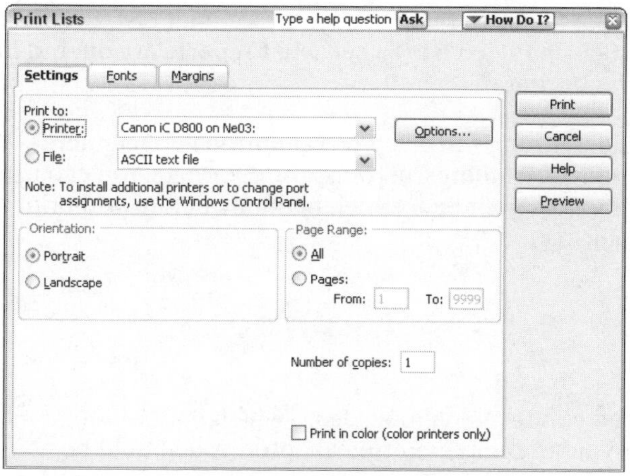

Figure 8-8: The Print Lists dialog box lets you choose some common printing options.

4. Set any print options desired and then click Print.

Displaying Different Views of Lists

You can choose to view the following types of lists in more than one way:

- ✦ Chart of Accounts and Items
- ✦ Customer:Job and Customer Type.
- ✦ Vendor Type and Job Type. By default, the hierarchical view is displayed when you first open one of these lists.

You can view lists with subentries in either hierarchal or "flat" view. The hierarchal view is the default view, where subentries are indented. With the flat view all entries are at the same level.

To see a flattened view of a list, click the list name menu button in the lower left corner of the list and choose Flat View.

To see the hierarchy of a list, choose Hierarchical View from the list name menu button in the lower left corner of the list.

Generating List Reports

Several reports are associated with each list, and you can access them from the Reports button in the list's window. The reports are different for each list; for example, the Customer:Job List includes reports such as Contact List, whereas the Item List includes reports such as Price List. To see what reports are offered for a list, simply click the Reports button.

To choose a report, select it from the list. Several buttons appear across the top of the report preview window, including Customize and Format. You can use these buttons to tailor the report to your exact specifications before you print. See Chapter 30 for more information.

Summary

This chapter introduced you to QuickBooks lists, which enable you to manage your information. Now that you've completed this chapter, you should be able to do the following:

- ✦ Display any list in its own list window
- ✦ Create, edit, and delete list entries such as vendor records, inventory Items, and payment terms
- ✦ Customize fields in a list to include extra fields for information that you need to track for your business
- ✦ Organize and merge lists to avoid duplication in your record keeping
- ✦ Print a list or generate a printed report based on it

✦ ✦ ✦

CHAPTER 9

Working with Customers and Jobs

In This Chapter

Entering new customers

Setting up jobs for customers

Managing your Customer:Job List

Changing the job status

Maintaining a job notebook

Creating job and customer reports

Using the Letter and Envelope Wizard

Customers are the heart and soul of any business. So it makes sense to court your customers and guard their good will like any other valuable resource.

One way to show customers that you care is to maintain accurate, complete records about them and about their jobs. What customer doesn't like it when you remember to send a birthday card with a discount coupon in it, or when you make a follow-up call on the three-month anniversary of their job's completion? Little touches like this can leave a customer feeling good enough to give you referrals and repeat business.

QuickBooks makes it easy to maintain good customer and job records and to pull up reports on the data that you can use to provide good customer service. This chapter gives you an insider's education on QuickBooks' "customer care" features.

The Convenient Customer Center

Use the Customer Center to access on a single screen all your customers and their transactions. You can access the customer bar either by clicking the icon on the Navigator screen or from the menu bar, as shown in Figure 9-1.

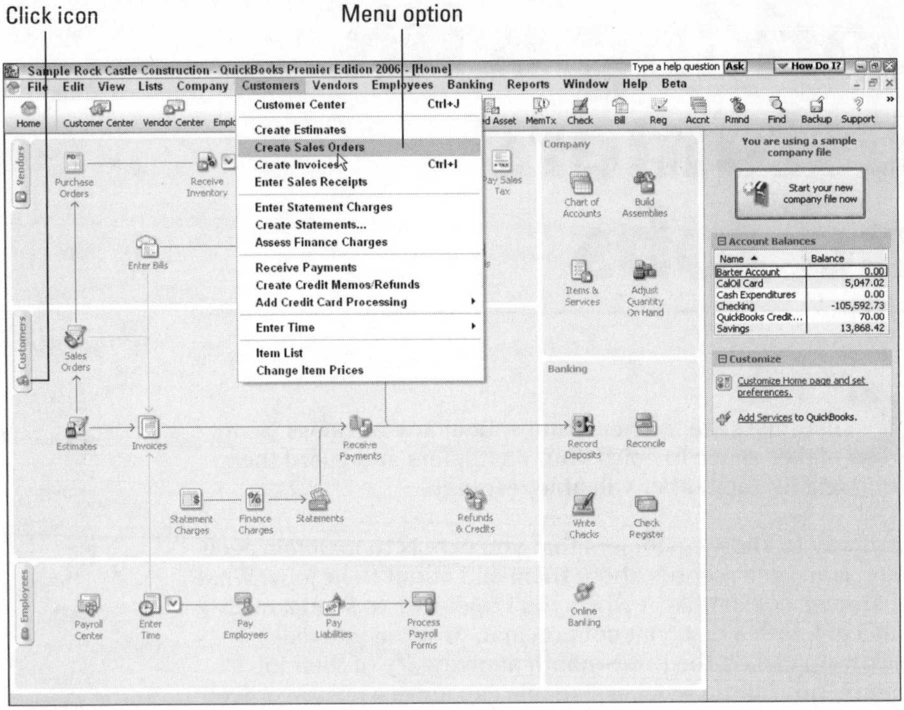

Figure 9-1: Two ways to access the Customer Center.

The Customer Center has two default views: Transaction view, shown in Figure 9-2, and Customer & Jobs view (Figure 9-3). You access the views by clicking on either the Transaction or Customer & Jobs tab in the Customer Center.

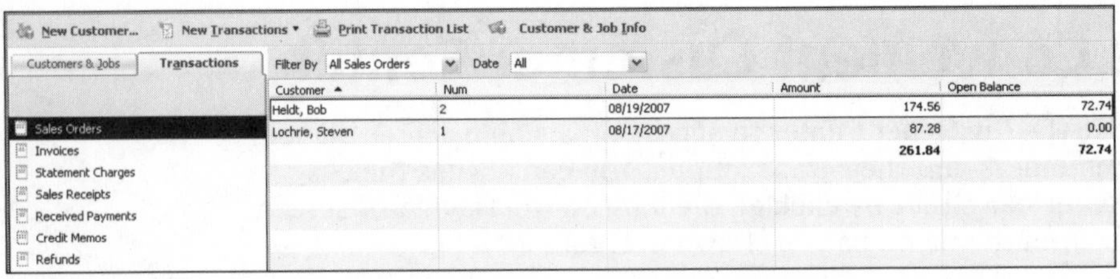

Figure 9-2: The default view of the QuickBooks Customer Center.

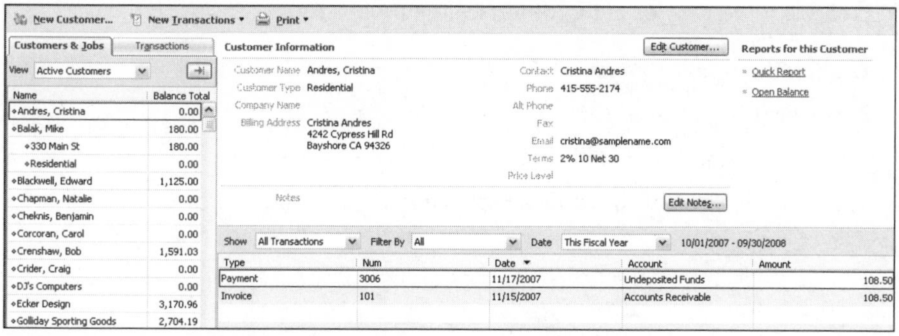

Figure 9-3: The Customers & Jobs view of the Customer Center.

Customers & Jobs tab

One default view of your Customer Center, the Transactions View (previously shown in Figure 9-2) shows detail information and a transactions list for selected customers or jobs on the right.

You can click the Customers & Jobs tab in the Customers window (previously shown in Figure 9-3) to display information about the customer or job as well as the transactions associated with that customer or job.

In QuickBooks, a *customer* is anyone who pays you for goods or services. A *job* is a specific project or scope of work that you want to track. If you do only one job for each customer, you can store job information with the rest of the information for each customer. In that case, your Customers & Jobs list will contain only entries for customers. However, if you do multiple jobs for a customer, or if you want to keep track of your income and expenses on a job-by-job basis, you can create individual job entries for your customers, as shown in Figure 9-4.

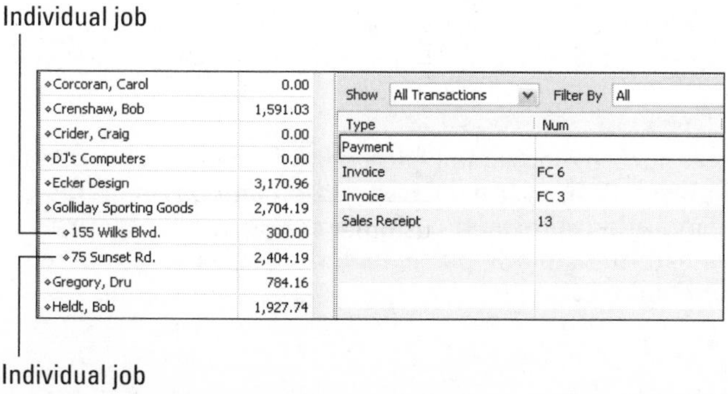

Figure 9-4: A listing showing multiple jobs for one customer.

To create a job entry for a customer, follow these steps:

1. Click Customer Center.
2. Select the customer for whom you are doing this job.
3. Right-click and choose Add Job.
4. Fill in the New Job window as shown in Figure 9-5.

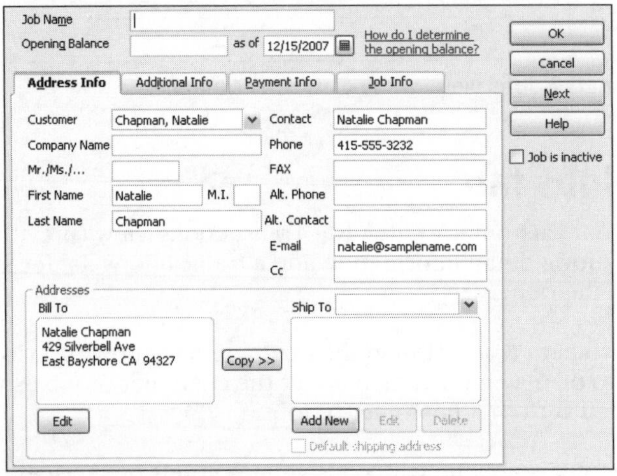

Figure 9-5: Use this window to create a new job record for a customer.

5. Check the information shown on the Address Info tab, Additional Info tab, and Payment Info tab.
6. On the Job Info tab, enter information for tracking the progress of the job.
7. Click Record.

Transactions tab

Using the Customer Center screen, shown in Figure 9-6, you can quickly find and print customer contact information, customer transaction and payment histories, current balances, notes, and other information. You can also efficiently process transactions for all your customers in one place, including sales receipts, received payments, and statement charges.

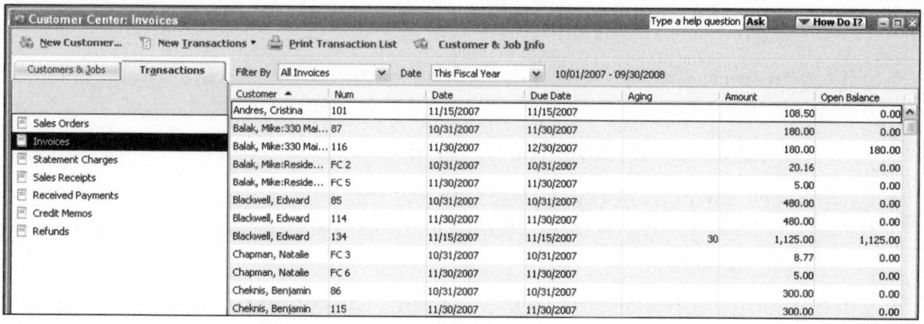

Figure 9-6: Viewing Invoice transactions by customer, using the Transactions tab of the Customer Center.

Click one of the transaction types to see a list of those transactions for all your customers. You can view, listed by customer, a list of all open sales orders, invoices, statement charges, sales receipts, received payments, credit memos, and refunds for your company.

By using the drop-down menu shown in Figure 9-7, you can filter the transactions by type and choose a date range to view.

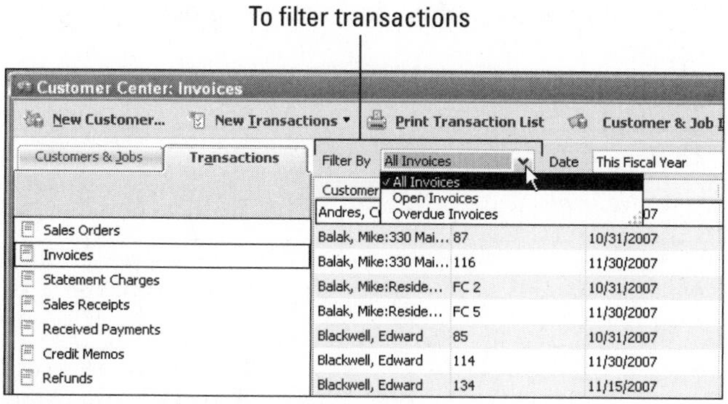

Figure 9-7: Filtering customer information.

Customer & Jobs list

QuickBooks maintains a convenient Customers & Jobs List to maintain records on the people and companies that patronize your company. If you have elected to track information on individual jobs, the job entries appear indented under the customer's name.

You can view the Customers & Jobs list in any of several useful ways:

- ✦ **All Customers:** Choose this to see both your active and inactive customers and jobs.
- ✦ **Active Customers:** Choose this to see only your active customers and jobs.
- ✦ **Customers with Open Balances:** Choose this to see only your active customers with any kind of open balance. (This option does not display any inactive customers.)
- ✦ **Custom Filter:** Choose this to search your Customers & Jobs list for specific entries.

Setting Up New Customers

Customers and jobs are list Items, similar to the many other list Items you learned to create in Chapter 8. You can set up new customers and jobs on the Customer:Job List, or you can do it on the fly as you enter transactions that involve a customer.

As you saw in Chapter 8, in some lists you can have two levels of entries. For example, in the Chart of Accounts, you can have main accounts and subaccounts. In the Customer:Job List, the customer is the main account and each of the customer's jobs is a subaccount. Figure 9-8 shows a list of customers, some of them with several jobs.

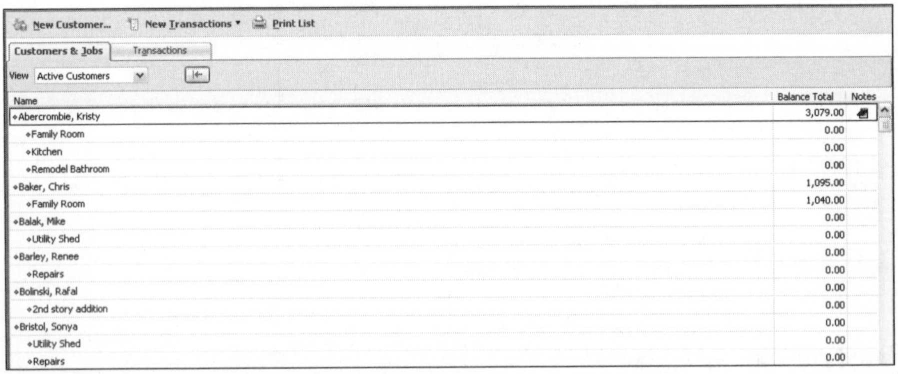

Figure 9-8: Jobs are subaccounts of customers.

A *job* in QuickBooks is a project that has a beginning and an end. Not all customers have jobs. Suppose that you own a flower shop. Miss Jones is planning a big wedding and wants you to provide all the flowers. The job begins with your initial consultation with the bride and ends when you deliver the flowers on the wedding day—a four-month period in total. This wedding is a job. In contrast, Mr. Smith drops by every month or so to buy a bouquet for his wife. This customer has no real jobs that you can track.

So, when you're setting up a new customer, you need to make a decision. Will you track individual jobs for this customer or not?

If you are sure that the customer will not have more than one project that could properly be considered a "job," or if you are not interested in tracking individual jobs, you can make a single customer entry and assign all the job information to it.

If you are starting a job for a new customer and that customer might have other jobs in the future, and you want to track the jobs separately, you set up the customer first and then the individual jobs. That way, should that customer give you repeat business, you can simply start a new job for the customer.

Tip

You can track customer information without adding a job. You do not need to add jobs to the Customers & Jobs list if your company never does more than one job or project per customer. Jobs in QuickBooks are optional. If you don't use jobs in QuickBooks, you can still associate job-related information with each customer. Click the Job Info tab when you create a new customer or when you edit the customer information in the Customer Center.

Creating a new customer record

To create a customer record, follow these steps:

1. Click Customer Center.
2. Click New Customer at the top of the list. The New Customer dialog box shown in Figure 9-9 appears.
3. Type the customer name that you want to use as its identifier in the Customer Name field. It need not be the complete name, but it must be unique.
4. If you have an outstanding balance for this customer, enter the Opening Balance and As Of information.
5. Fill in the customer's contact information. Notice that the company name and the first and last names transfer to the Bill To area automatically. You must fill in the street address, city, state, and zip code in the Bill To area, however, to complete the billing address.

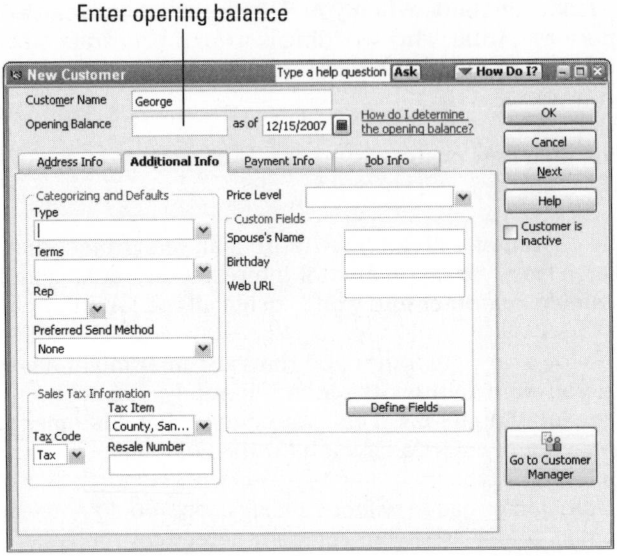

Figure 9-9: Entering information for a new customer.

6. Fill in the information in the appropriate blanks. Here's a rundown of the fields:
   - **Type:** An optional field. This one is used to categorize different types of customers (for example, business or residential) so you can create reports that show you how your business is divided between them. To create additional types, choose Add New and create a new type, as you learned in Chapter 8.
   - **Terms:** The payment terms you choose here for the customer appear on any invoice that you create for the customer. You can override them on individual invoices as needed (see Chapter 15).
   - **Rep:** If you want to track sales by employee (for example, to award commissions), choose a set of employee initials from the list here. All the initials for all the employees you have entered in the system appear on this list. If you choose Add New, you're taken to the New Employee dialog box where you can enter a new employee. See Chapter 22 for more information about employees.
   - **Preferred Send Method:** Indicate the preferred method for sending communications, such as e-mail or regular mail.
   - **Credit Limit:** If you enter a dollar amount here, QuickBooks will warn you when you are creating an invoice that will cause the customer's account to exceed the limit. For unlimited credit, leave this blank.

- **Tax Item:** You'll see this field only if Sales Tax use is turned on in your Preferences (see Chapter 12). From this drop-down list, you can choose the sales tax that the customer must pay (for example, state or county tax). To set up a new tax, choose Add New.
- **Tax Code:** Indicate the type of tax (such as sales or service tax). This check box is also visible only if Sales Tax is turned on. It's marked by default. Deselect it if the customer buys items for resale rather than for end use.
- **Resale Number:** If your customer has one, enter it here. Customers with valid resale numbers who are buying merchandise that they plan on reselling should not be charged sales tax on their purchases.

7. Click the Payment Info tab and enter the relevant account information.
8. (Optional) If you are not going to track individual jobs for the customer, click the Job Info tab and fill in any information about the customer's current job. Skip to step 5 in "Setting Up Jobs for a Customer."
9. Click OK to save your changes and close the dialog box, or click Next to save and clear the form so you can enter another customer.

Setting up payments terms for a customer

Follow these steps to set up payment terms:

1. Go to the Lists menu, choose Customer & Vendor Profile Lists, and then click Terms List as shown in Figure 9-10.

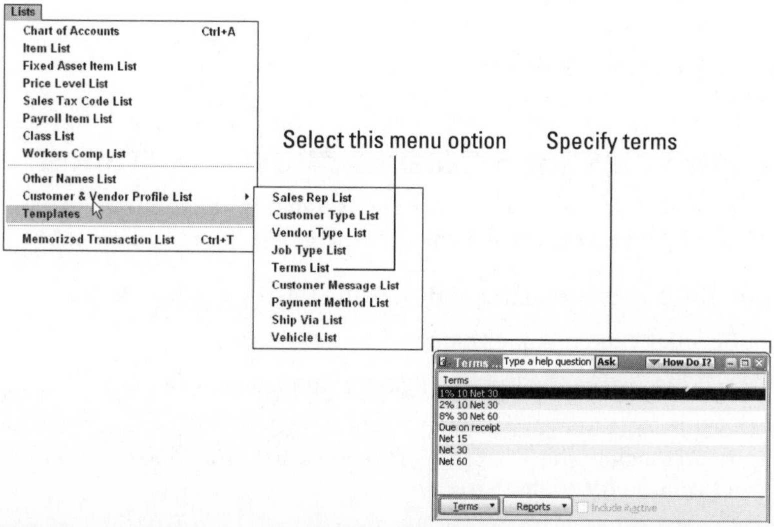

Figure 9-10: Choose payment terms for a customer from this list.

2. Click Terms at the bottom of the list and click New.
3. In the Terms field, enter a word or phrase that will help you recognize the terms when you use the Terms List (what you enter here appears on the list).
4. Indicate the type of terms that you want to use (for example Standard versus date-driven payment terms).
5. Fill in the fields shown in Figure 9-11, and click Record.

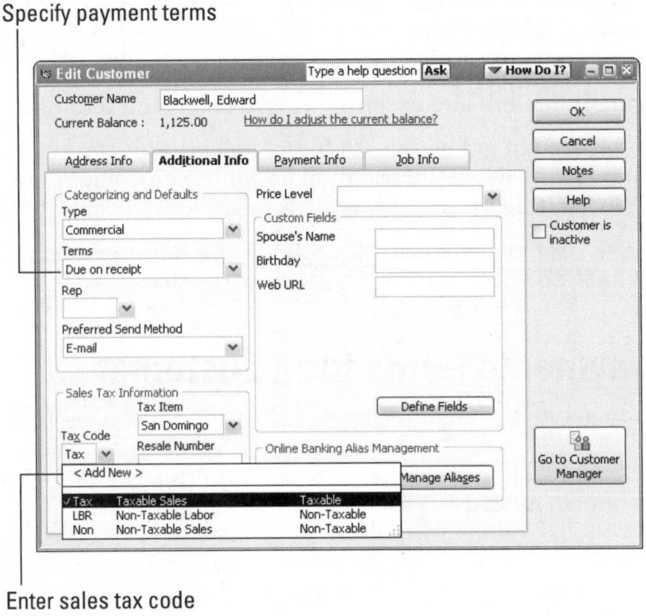

Figure 9-11: Entering payment terms.

To assign sales tax information to a customer

After you have added a customer, you can assign or change the sales tax code for the customer by following these steps:

1. Go to the Customer Center and click the Customers & Jobs tab.
2. Double-click the customer name.
3. In the Edit Customer window, click the Additional Info tab.
4. In the Sales Tax Information section of the window (previously shown in Figure 9-11), click the Tax Code drop-down list and choose the appropriate sales tax code for that customer.

   If you do not see the Tax Code drop-down list, you have not set up sales tax in QuickBooks.

5. If the customer is taxable, click the Tax Item drop-down list and choose the sales tax item with the sales tax rate that you usually charge for this customer (previously shown in Figure 9-11).

   If this customer is sometimes or always exempt from sales tax, enter the customer's tax exemption ID in the Resale Number field. For example, a transaction might sometimes be non-taxable if the customer is buying items from you for personal user and they also buy items from you for a non-profit organization for which they work.

6. Click OK.

Creating estimates for a customer

You can create professional written estimates for customers that will reflect well on your company and help you land the job.

First you must ensure the estimates feature is turned on, by following these steps:

1. Go to Edit ➪ Preferences. In the Preferences window, scroll through the list on the left and click Jobs & Estimates.
2. Click the Company Preferences tab.
3. Click Yes to the question, "Do You Create Estimates?", as shown in Figure 9-12.

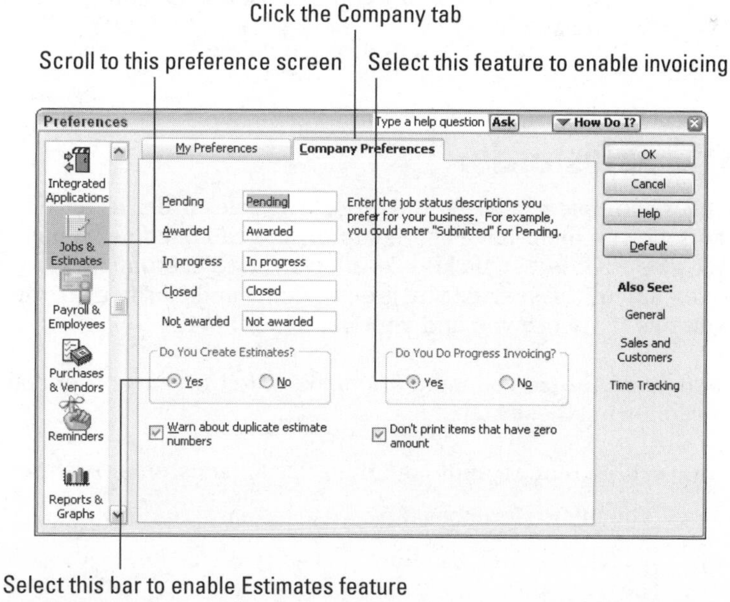

Figure 9-12: Let QuickBooks know whether you create estimates.

4. To have QuickBooks warn you when you try to record an estimate with the same number as the existing estimate, select Warn About Duplicate Estimates Numbers.
5. If you do progress invoicing, click Yes to the question, Do You Do Progress Invoicing?
6. Specify whether you want line items that have zero amounts to print on your progress invoice.
7. Click OK.

After you have activated the Estimates in the Preferences window, you can follow these steps:

1. Go to the Customers menu and select Create Estimates, or click the Estimates icon on the Navigator screen.
2. Enter the name of the client or project.
3. Enter the name of the customer or job.
4. Select a template.

   To create a proposal, for example, select the Proposal template.
5. Enter the line items.
6. Change the sales tax information, if necessary.
7. Enter the class information if you want to track this estimate by location, subsidiary, group, and so on.
8. Click Print.

Creating a sales order

The goal of every company is to get the order. The sales order form reflects the terms you and the customer have agreed upon, and can become an important legal document if a dispute arises. QuickBooks allows you to customize many aspects of this form to document the service you are providing and clarify the order fulfillment expectations that both you and your customer have.

To create sales order forms, you must first make sure the sales order feature is turned on, by following these steps:

1. Go to Edit ➪ Preferences, and open the sales and customer preferences.
2. Click the Company Preferences tab.
3. Select Enable Sales Orders, as shown in Figure 9-13.

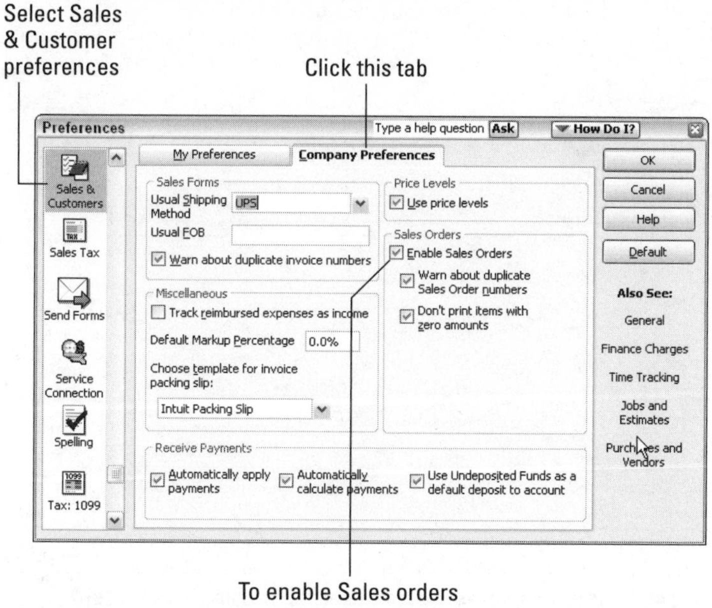

Figure 9-13: Enabling the sales order creation feature.

4. To have QuickBooks warn you when you try to record a sales order with the same number as an existing sales order, select Warn About Duplicate Sales Order Numbers (see Figure 9-13).
5. If you don't want QuickBooks to print items with zero amounts, select Don't Print Items with Zero Amounts.
6. Click OK.

After you've activated the Sales Order Preference, follow these steps to create the sales order:

1. Go to the Customers menu and select the Create Sales Orders option. The Sales Order screen shown in Figure 9-14 appears.
2. Type the name of the customer or job.
3. Select a template.
4. Enter the line items and change any sales tax information, as necessary.
5. Enter the class information if you want to track this sales order by location, subsidiary, group, and so on.
6. Click Print to print the sales order.

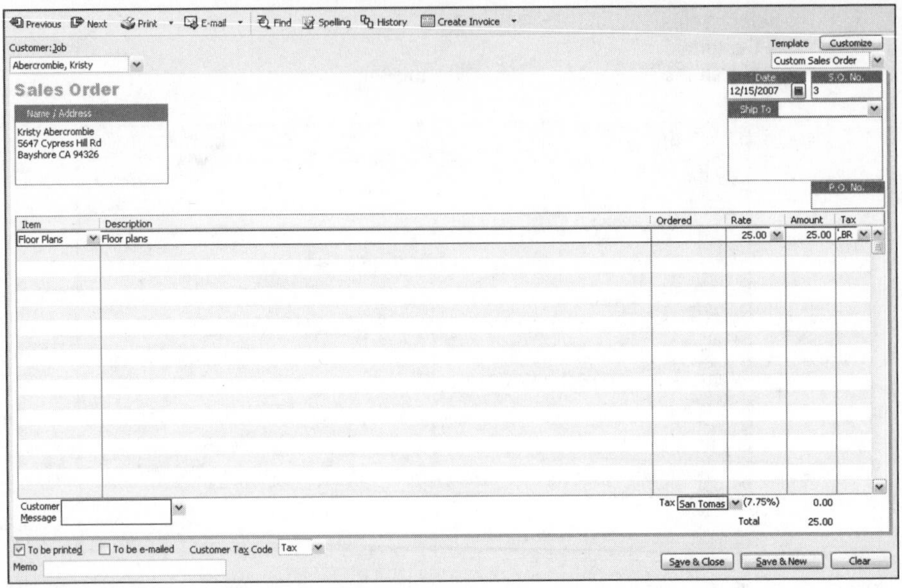

Figure 9-14: Create a customer sales order form using this screen.

Creating customer invoices

An *invoice* is the document you issue to notify a customer of a payment that is due or about to become due. Invoices inform customers of the amount they owe, and the terms according to which they are expected to pay.

Invoicing is also an important accounting event because it signals that your company has completed the work that entitles it to treat amounts reflected on the sales form as receivables and revenue. When you save an invoice, the following QuickBooks balances are automatically adjusted for you:

- ✦ The Accounts Receivable account increases by the amount of the invoice.
- ✦ The new invoice appears in the Open Invoices report.
- ✦ The items on the invoice are tracked in the Sales by Item Summary report.
- ✦ The income from the items shows in your Profit and Loss report.

To create an invoice:

1. Go to the Customers menu and select Create Invoices, or click the Create Invoices icon on the Customer section of the Navigator screen. The screen shown in Figure 9-15 appears.
2. Fill in the name of the customer or job. If you want to track the sale by location, subsidiary, or group, you must also enter the class information.

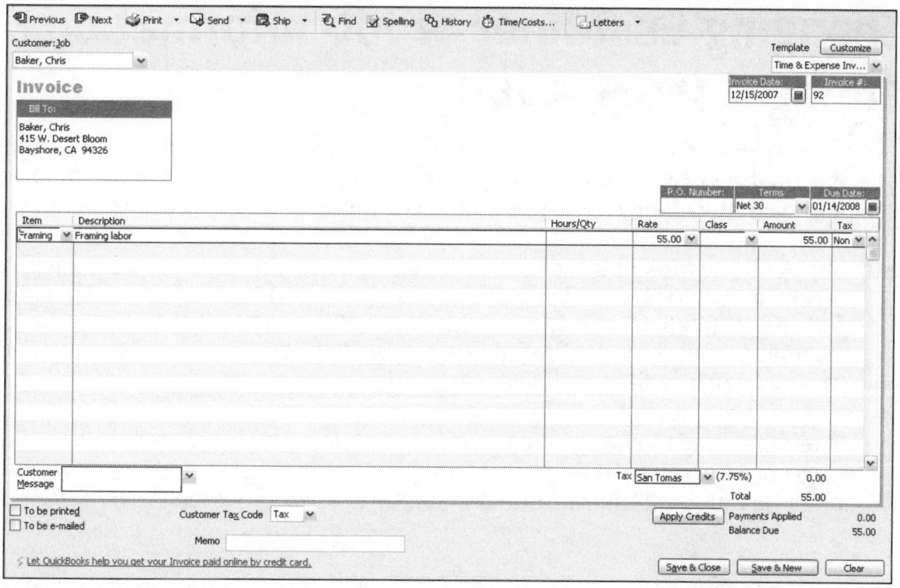

Figure 9-15: Create a customer invoice using this screen.

3. Select a template.
4. In the detail area, enter the line items.
5. Enter a message for your customer in the Customer Message field, if you want to include one.
6. Enter a memo for this sale, if you want to include one. (The memo is a reminder to you; it is not shown on the printed form.)
7. To print the invoice, click Print on the toolbar to print the invoice now, or select the To Be Printed check box to print the form later.
8. To e-mail the invoice, select the To Be E-mailed check box at the bottom of the screen to have the invoice e-mailed to the customer, or you can select the To Be Mailed through QuickBooks check box to have your invoices mailed to customers through the QuickBooks Billing Solutions mailing service, if you have signed up for it.
9. Save the invoice.

Managing Your Customer:Job List

A Customer:Job List is only as valuable as it is current. You can make corrections directly in the Customer:Job List and see the results on your reports and business forms immediately.

Changing Customer or Job Information during a Transaction

As you enter a transaction for a customer or job, you may notice that some of the information is wrong. You can quickly correct it right there on the transaction form and have the change reflected in the Customer:Job List for future use.

Suppose you are creating an invoice, and you realize that the customer's payment terms are set for Net 30 by default, when you would prefer that this customer pay you immediately on receipt of the invoice. You can make the change by choosing the new setting from the Terms drop-down list (as previously shown in Figure 9-15). Then complete the invoice as usual.

The other way to change customer or job information, of course, is to do it from the Customer:Job List. To do so, just double-click any customer or job on the list to open its Edit Customer or Edit Job dialog box, as shown in Figure 9-16.

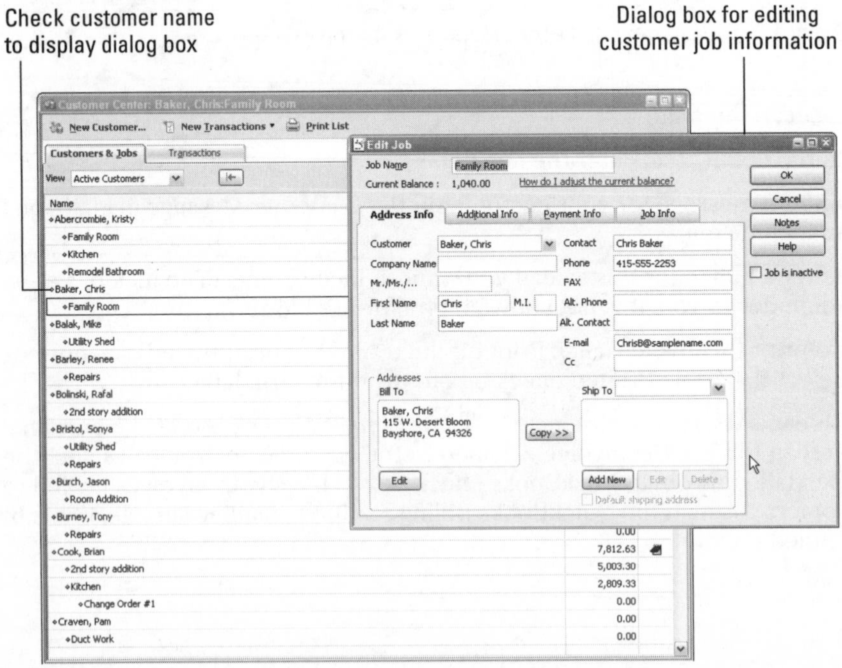

Figure 9-16: Making modifications from the Customer:Job list.

Tip You can change the customer or job name, if you want, and all the transactions that were formerly assigned to the old name will be transferred to the new name.

As you learned in Chapter 8, you can make a customer or job inactive if you don't plan on getting any more business from it. For example, if you cater a wedding and the wedding is over, you will probably not get any more business from that wedding, so you can make it inactive. This removes it from the drop-down list of customers and jobs, so you don't have to be forever tripping over it. Just select the customer or job from the list, and then click the Customer:Job button and choose Make Inactive. Or, if you are already editing the job or customer just select the Job Is Inactive or Customer Is Inactive check box.

Keeping Notes for a Customer or Job

Each customer or job you set up has its own notepad where you can keep miscellaneous notes to yourself about the customer or job. For example, if the customer has a preference for particular products or styles, you can record those preferences on the notepad.

Follow these steps to use the Customer Notes feature:

1. Click Customer Center.
2. Click the Customers & Jobs tab.
3. Select the customer or job with the note you want to create.
4. Go to the Information area and click Edit Notes.
5. (Optional) Click Date Stamp to add the current date to the note.
6. In the notepad, enter the text of the note.
7. (Optional) Add a reminder note to your To Do list. Click New To Do and enter the text of the reminder note.
8. In the Remind Me On field, enter the date you want the note to appear on your Reminders list and click OK.
9. (Optional) Click Print to print your notes.
10. Click OK.

Viewing Current Balance Information for Customers and Jobs

Follow these steps to view open balance information for a customer:

1. From the Customer Center window, right-click the name of any customer.
2. Click Customer Center.
3. Right-click the name of any customer, and select View Open Balance from the menu that appears, as shown in Figure 9-17.

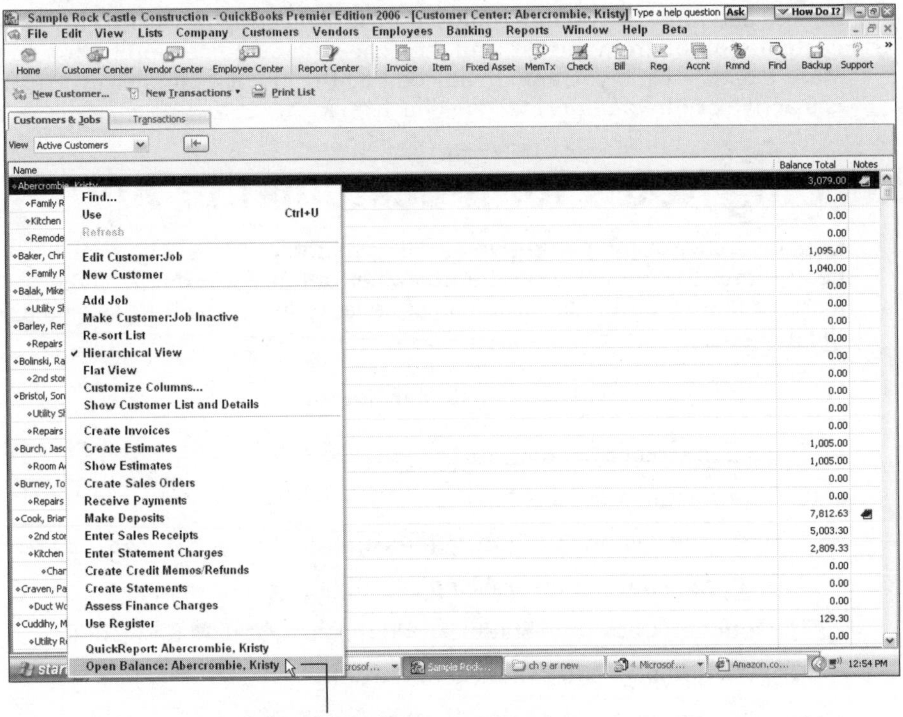

Figure 9-17: View balance information for a customer.

4. A customer balance report like the one in Figure 9-18 appears.

This type of report shows all transactions that involve that customer or job during a specified period. The report shows how much activity a particular customer or job has been getting lately. You can change which period is covered by choosing a different one from the Dates drop-down list (the default is This Month-to-date), or you can enter specific dates in the From and To boxes.

Rock Castle Construction
Customer Open Balance
All Transactions

Type	Date	Num	Memo	Due Date	Open Balance	Amount
Burch, Jason						
Room Addition						
Invoice	11/25/2007	75		12/25/2007	1,005.00	1,005.00
Total Room Addition					1,005.00	1,005.00
Total Burch, Jason					1,005.00	1,005.00
TOTAL					**1,005.00**	**1,005.00**

Figure 9-18: Open balance report for a customer.

Reports for All Customers or Jobs

The lion's share of the customer and job reports provide information on multiple customers and jobs. (I say "multiple" rather than "all" because you can customize the reports to show only certain customers or jobs. All is the default for each report.)

Figure 9-19 shows a sample Accounts Receivable Aging Summary. Reports are discussed in more detail in Chapter 30.

Rock Castle Construction
A/R Aging Summary
As of December 15, 2007

	Current	1 - 30	31 - 60	61 - 90	> 90	TOTAL
Abercrombie, Kristy						
Remodel Bathroom	3,111.28	0.00	0.00	0.00	0.00	3,111.28
Total Abercrombie, Kristy	3,111.28	0.00	0.00	0.00	0.00	3,111.28
Baker, Chris						
Family Room	1,040.00	0.00	0.00	0.00	0.00	1,040.00
Baker, Chris - Other	55.00	0.00	0.00	0.00	0.00	55.00
Total Baker, Chris	1,095.00	0.00	0.00	0.00	0.00	1,095.00
Burch, Jason						
Room Addition	1,005.00	0.00	0.00	0.00	0.00	1,005.00
Total Burch, Jason	1,005.00	0.00	0.00	0.00	0.00	1,005.00
Cook, Brian						
2nd story addition	5,003.30	0.00	0.00	0.00	0.00	5,003.30
Kitchen	2,109.33	0.00	700.00	0.00	0.00	2,809.33
Total Cook, Brian	7,112.63	0.00	700.00	0.00	0.00	7,812.63
Ecker Designs						
Office Repairs	7,694.41	0.00	0.00	0.00	0.00	7,694.41
Total Ecker Designs	7,694.41	0.00	0.00	0.00	0.00	7,694.41
Fisher, Jennifer	0.00	0.00	0.00	0.00	850.63	850.63
Jacobsen, Doug						
Kitchen	2,245.00	75.00	0.00	0.00	0.00	2,320.00
Total Jacobsen, Doug	2,245.00	75.00	0.00	0.00	0.00	2,320.00
Lew Plumbing - C	0.00	175.00	0.00	0.00	0.00	175.00
Melton, Johnny						
Dental office	-4,999.50	0.00	0.00	0.00	0.00	-4,999.50
Total Melton, Johnny	4,999.50	0.00	0.00	0.00	0.00	4,999.50

Figure 9-19: A sample A/R Aging Summary.

Writing Letters in Word Using QuickBooks Data

You can send letters to customers, employees, or vendors with QuickBooks letter templates: a set of prewritten, preformatted business letter templates. These letter templates include collection letters, thank you notes, and other routine business correspondence.

You can access these templates and create letters by following these steps:

1. Go to the Company menu, choose Prepare Letters with Envelopes as shown in Figure 9-20, and then click the type of letter you want to prepare.

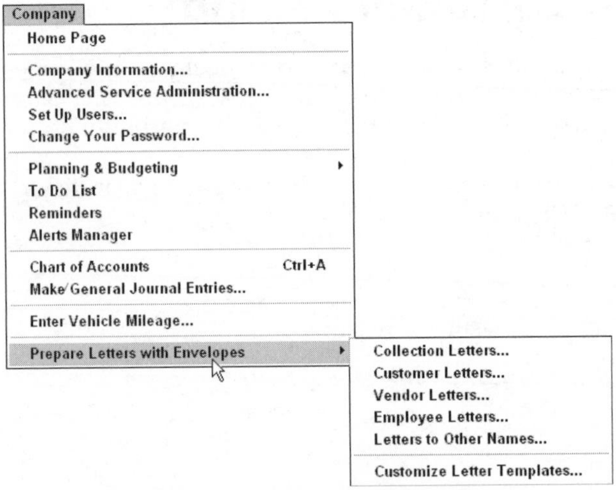

Figure 9-20: The Letters and Envelopes Wizard.

2. The Choose the Recipients page of the Template Wizard, shown in Figure 9-21, is the first screen of the Letters and Envelopes wizard. This page appears after you select your template, which allows you to specify the criteria for determining who receives the letter. (The screen shown is for a customer collection letter template.) Click Next.
3. The Review and Edit Recipients page appears. (You may also get a warning message that one or more customers have unapplied payments or credits.) Use this page to verify and edit the list of recipients based on the criteria you have specified. Click Next.

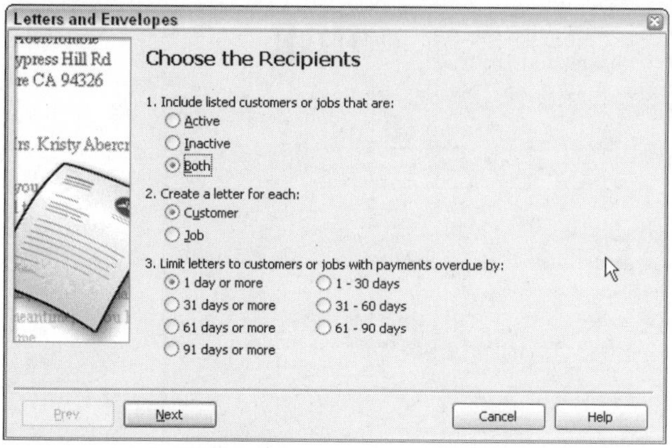

Figure 9-21: Verify the recipients from the list created based on your criteria.

4. In the Choose a Letter Template page, indicate whether you want to send a friendly collection letter or a harsh one, or whether to stick with a formal sounding tone, as shown in Figure 9-22. Click Next.

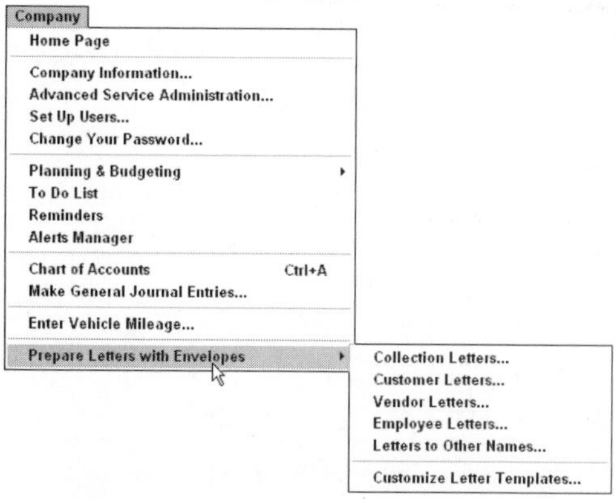

Figure 9-22: Decide on the appropriate tone for your letter.

5. The Enter a Name and Title page opens, as shown in Figure 9-23. Indicate how you want to sign your letters using the fields on the following screen, and then click Next. QuickBooks will then create customer collection letters according to your specifications, which you may save and print using Microsoft Word.

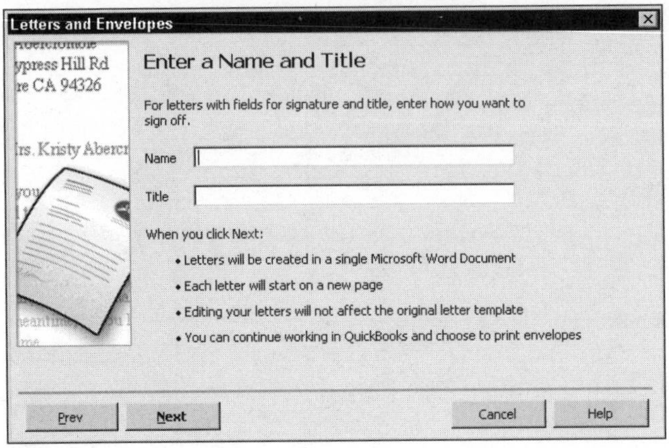

Figure 9-23: Indicate how you want to sign your letters.

6. The Print Letters and Envelopes page opens, as shown in Figure 9-24. Click Next to automatically export data for printing envelopes, and to send to the printer the letters you have created.

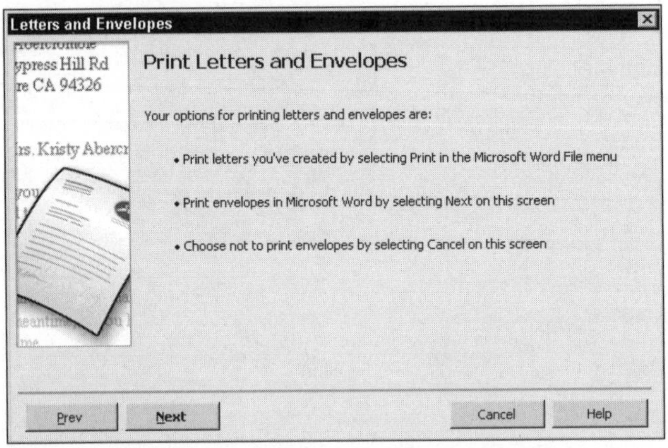

Figure 9-24: The Print Letters and Envelopes page.

7. The Envelope Options page appears (see Figure 9-25), asking you to specify options for creating envelopes. Specify the size and type of envelopes you want to create and then click OK.

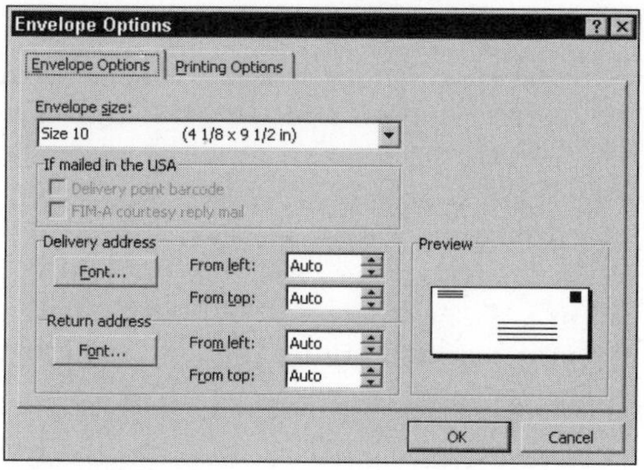

Figure 9-25: One of the Envelope printing options screens.

8. A warning screen appears telling you to check your letters and envelopes before you send them. Click Finish, and start stuffing the envelopes!

Creating Customer Letters from Scratch Using QuickBooks Pro

You can also use the integrated Word feature to create a letter from scratch or use an existing prewritten letter you have saved in Word. To do either, follow these steps:

1. Go to Customers ⇨ Customer Letters with Envelopes ⇨ Customize Letter Templates.
2. If you are creating a letter based on an existing or previously written letter, select View or edit existing letters, and then click Next.
3. Select the template to edit, and then click Next.
4. Edit the existing letter, and then save it in Word by selecting File ⇨ Save As and providing your document with a name and destination in the resulting dialog box.

Creating Customer Mailing Labels

QuickBooks provides in-program support for mailing labels. In other words, you can create them from within QuickBooks itself, without exporting anything or relying on your word processing program. To create mailing labels, follow these steps:

1. Go to File ➪ Print Forms ➪ Labels.
2. Indicate the Names, Customer type, or Vendor types for which you want to print labels, by selecting the correct options and using the drop-down menus provide.
3. (Optional) Select Print Labels for Ship to Address, Print Labels for Inactive Names, and/or Print Labels for Jobs.
4. Click OK.
5. Enter information about the label size and printer that you want to use and click the Print button.

Setting Up Your Printer for Labels

Before you print labels in QuickBooks for the first time, you need to tell the program what kind of labels you will use. This is a one-time setup; QuickBooks remembers your settings forever after. To tell QuickBooks what kinds of labels you plan to use, follow these steps:

1. Choose File ➪ Printer Setup. The Printer Setup dialog box appears.
2. Open the Form Name drop-down list and choose Label, as shown in Figure 9-26.
3. Check the settings in the Printer Name and Printer Type fields. They should already be correct; if they are not, open the drop-down list and choose the correct settings.

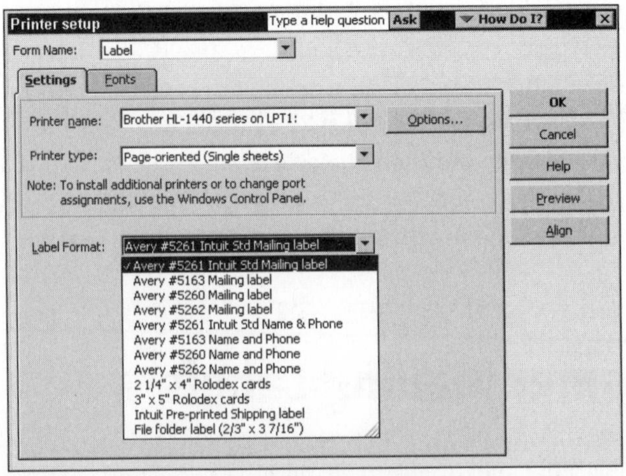

Figure 9-26: Use the Settings tab of the Printer setup dialog box to specify how you want your labels to print.

4. Look on the box of labels that you have and find the Avery number. (Even if Avery does not make the labels, they should have a four-digit number that is equivalent to the Avery numbers.) Then open the Label Format drop-down list and choose the appropriate label number.

5. Click the Fonts tab, and then click the Font button to open the Select Font dialog box.

6. Choose the Font, Font Style, Size, and Color to use, and then click OK.

Caution

Let the label size determine the font size that you use. If you are using a relatively small label and have several lines of text to put on each one, you'll want a small font size, such as 8 or 9 points. QuickBooks will not warn you if you choose a font that is so large that the text spills off the labels.

7. Click OK. Your label printing is now set up.

Tip

If you have trouble later with the labels being slightly misaligned, you may want to experiment with the Align button in the Printer Setup dialog box (previously shown in Figure 9-26). It lets you print an alignment grid that can help you precisely adjust the text placement on each label.

Summary

In this chapter, you learned about customer and job records, the most important data that you need at your fingertips for good customer service.

- You can add new customers to QuickBooks, including their contact information, credit limit, payment terms, and demographics.
- You can create multiple jobs for a customer, and track the jobs' progress with status indicators and start/end dates.
- You can make changes to a customer's or job's information while working on a transaction that involves it, or make those changes from the Customer:Job List at your leisure.
- You can keep detailed notes on specific customers and jobs to share information with other employees.
- You can create new transactions for a customer or job directly from the Customer:Job List.
- You can produce a variety of reports for specific customers and jobs or for your entire database of customers as a whole.
- You can create customized mailing lists using convenient letter and envelope wizards and templates.

✦ ✦ ✦

CHAPTER 10

Using Items to Designate Products and Pricing

✦ ✦ ✦ ✦

In This Chapter

What is an Item?

Setting up accounts for Items

Selling and buying with Items

Managing inventory purchases with Items

Reimbursable Items

Creating Service Items

Partial payments

Discounts and subtotals

Sales taxes

Other charges

Item management tools

✦ ✦ ✦ ✦

I vowed that I would never write an accounting book using widgets to illustrate a concept. But if I did, this would be the chapter because Items are the indexing system used for tracking the services and products that a business regularly sells. You can also use Items to standardize recurring calculations related to goods and services. Items add consistency to your pricing and billing procedures because each time you enter a previously listed Item, all relevant information concerning that Item is automatically accessed. QuickBooks all but forces you to make use of this organizational tool by prompting you to create a new Item each time you enter a product or service into the system that was not previously listed. With Items, it is almost impossible for a QuickBooks business to accidentally charge a client the wrong amount for one of its regular goods or services.

What Is an Item?

The term *Item* is really short for the accounting term *line item.*

A line item is the accounting term for the information about each product or service that appears on a bill and that is listed on its own line. Line items are added to arrive at a total amount billed.

In QuickBooks, an Item is anything that your company buys, sells, or resells in the course of business, such as products, shipping and handling charges, discounts, and sales tax (if applicable).

Items help you fill out the line item area of a sales or purchase form quickly. When you choose an Item from your Item list, QuickBooks fills in a description of the line item and calculates its amount for you.

QuickBooks provides 11 different types of Items. Some, such as the Service Item or the Inventory Part Item, help you record the services and products your business sells. Others, such as the Subtotal Item or Discount Item, are used to perform calculations on the amounts in a sale.

With QuickBooks, when you enter the name of each product or service from an Item list, all of the relevant information is automatically entered on the document you are completing. Items are used not only on bills but also in the preparation of invoices, purchase orders, receipts, and other sales forms. When you're completing these forms, a drop-down menu appears that enables you to insert the proper Item and associated information in the relevant fields. An invoice form with a drop-down Item menu is shown in Figure 10-1.

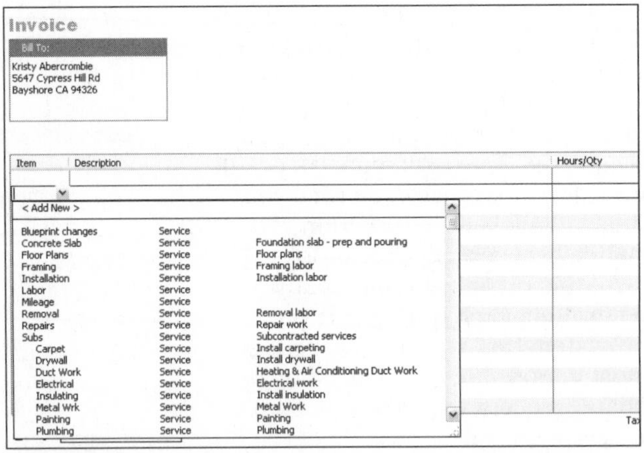

Figure 10-1: You can fill in Items from a convenient drop-down menu or add an Item to the drop-down list when you enter information on form fields associated with Items.

What is the difference between Items and lists? It helps to think of an Item as a little file of descriptive data on each product, inventory part, service, sales tax, and associated charge. Lists, on the other hand, are data-management tools used to track files maintained on Items, employees, customers, vendors, and so forth.

QuickBooks allows you to create several types of Items according to the following categories: Inventory Part, Noninventory Part, Service, Sales Tax, Discounts, Subtotal, Other Charge, and Group. Some of these Items refer to products and services, whereas other Items refer to calculations (for example, discounts, subtotals, and sales tax). When setting up any new Item, remember that it is very important to specify the type of Item that you are creating.

Your choice of Item type tells QuickBooks three things. First, it tells the program what stored pricing and descriptive information to include on sales forms and invoices. Second, it tells QuickBooks what calculations are to be performed when this Item is entered (for example, sales tax percentages). Finally, the Item type determines what types of accounts are used to track and report Item activity on the company's financial statements. For example, a product Item (such as a Noninventory Part Item) will post an entry to an income account each time it is entered. A Discount Item will post to an income account. Group Items post information to various accounts set up to track activity for individual Items within the Item group.

The Relationship of Accounts to Items

Each time you set up a new Item, QuickBooks asks you to specify an account type to track activity for that Item. It then uses the accounts you specify to track income and expenses for each Item, which is integral to your accounting system. These balances in the accounts flow through to the Profit and Loss Statement.

Tip

As you set up your Items, you should make a decision whether you want to track income derived from various types of products and services specifically or whether you want to aggregate them. Remember that you can always merge accounts and combine their balances if you have maintained separate accounts or if you decide that this type of tracking is not necessary. But it's hard to track income from various transactions recorded in a single account. Similarly, it's difficult and time-consuming to discern the exact amounts paid for specific types of expenses unless you have maintained separate accounts for each type of outlay. It is best to err on the side of creating more accounts, rather than fewer.

Remember that your reports reflect the structure and specificity of your accounts. Your reports show a separate total for each account you have created, as well as a subtotal of all sales or expenses, as shown in Figure 10-2.

9:20 AM
12/15/07
Accrual Basis

Rock Castle Construction
Sales by Item Summary
December 1 - 15, 2007

	Dec 1 - 15, 07							
	Qty	Amount		% of Sales		Avg Price	COGS		Avg COGS
Inventory									
Cabinets									
Cabinet Pulls	38	290.51		0.4%		7.65	62.30		1.64
Light Pine	2	3,598.00		4.8%		1,799.00	3,000.00		1,500.00
Total Cabinets			3,888.51		5.2%			3,062.30	
Hardware									
Doorknobs Std	11	330.00		0.4%		30.00	297.00		27.00
Lk Doorknobs	4	154.00		0.2%		38.50	141.05		35.26
Total Hardware			484.00		0.7%			438.05	

Figure 10-2: This report shows the totals derived from Item entries.

Creating New Items

QuickBooks allows you to create 11 different types of Items, as summarized in Table 10-1.

Table 10-1
Types of Items and How to Create Them

Item Type	*What to Use It For*
Service	Services you charge for or purchase from others, such as labor, consulting hours, and professional fees
Inventory Part	Goods you purchase, track as inventory, and resell
Inventory Assembly (Premier and Enterprise editions only)	Assembled goods you build or purchase, track as inventory, and resell
Noninventory Part	Goods you buy but don't track (such as office supplies)
Fixed Asset (Pro, Premier, and Enterprise editions only)	An asset you do not expect to convert to cash during one year of normal operations
Other Charge	Miscellaneous labor, material, or part charges such as delivery charges, setup fees, and service charges
Subtotal	Totals all Items above it on a form, up to the last subtotal; useful for applying a percentage discount or surcharge to many Items
Group	Useful to quickly enter a group of individual Items that you've already set up as single Items on your list
Discount	Subtracts a percentage or fixed amount from a total or subtotal; do not use this Item type for an early payment discount
Payment	Records a partial payment you received at the time of the sale; it reduces the amount owed on an invoice
Sales Tax Item	Calculates a single sales tax at a specific rate that you pay to a single tax agency
Sales Tax Group	Calculates and individually tracks two or more Sales Tax Items that apply to the same sale; the customer sees only the total sales tax

You can create Items easily in QuickBooks and there are prompts designed to ensure that you don't omit any useful information. The name or number of the new Item you create will appear on the drop-down list of Items when you are filling out a sales form or purchase order. The process differs slightly depending on whether you are creating Items for services or products.

Creating a Service Item

Creating Service Items helps you maintain uniform billing practices and adds to your professionalism. To create new Service Items, follow these steps:

1. From the Lists menu, choose Item list. A list of Items appears.
2. Click the Item menu button at the bottom of the screen. From the pop-up menu, choose New. The window shown in Figure 10-3 appears.

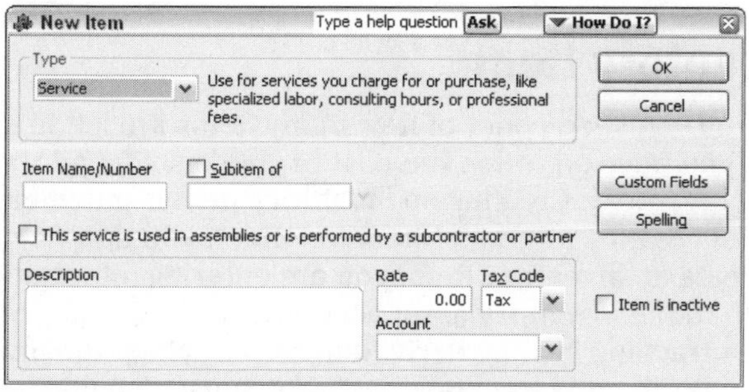

Figure 10-3: A window for creating a new Item.

3. Access the drop-down menu from the Type field of the New Item window, as shown in Figure 10-4, and choose the type of Item you want to create. You cannot change a Service Item to another Item type.

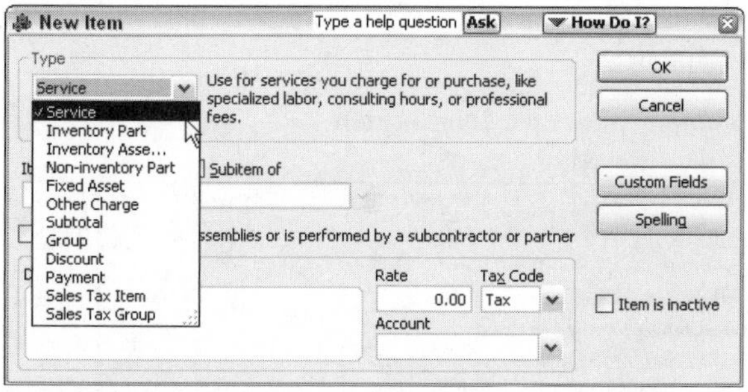

Figure 10-4: Drop-down list for selecting the new Item type.

4. Enter an Item name or number. If this Item is a subitem of an existing Service Item, select the Subitem Of check box and specify the parent Item's name.
5. Enter a description. This description will appear on the sales and purchase forms.

6. Enter a rate for the service. The amount can be either a flat fee or an hourly rate. Leave the field blank if this rate varies. If you purchase this service, enter the vendor's rate. If you sell this service, enter the rate you charge your customers.
7. (Sales only) If you don't charge sales tax for this Item, choose Non-taxable Labor or Non-taxable Sales from the Sales Tax Code field.
8. Click Custom Fields to fill in any custom fields that apply to this Item.
9. In the Account field, enter an income account for sales or an expense account for purchases.

Creating an Inventory Item

If you track inventory, you can keep count of how many Items are left in stock after a sale, how many Items you have on order, the cost of goods sold, and the total value of your remaining inventory. Creating an Inventory Item is much more complicated than the process of creating a Product Item for which you don't need to track inventory. When you create an Inventory Item, you are entering information that ultimately flows through to the inventory asset account shown on the company's Balance Sheet, as well as tracking income derived from the sale of the inventory to report on the company's Profit and Loss Statement. You must also make sure that the inventory-tracking preferences are turned on. To create an Item and track it in inventory, follow these steps:

1. Go to Edit ➪ Preferences.
2. Choose Purchases & Vendors in the scroll box that appears, as shown in Figure 10-5.

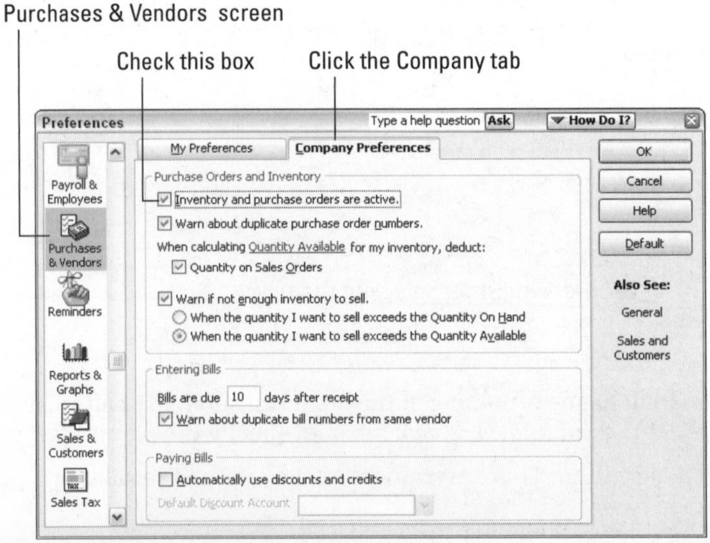

Figure 10-5: Changing Item preferences.

3. Click the Company Preferences tab.

4. Make sure that the Inventory and Purchase Orders Are Active box is checked. Click OK to save your preferences and exit the Preferences window.

5. Go to Lists ➪ Items.

6. Click the Item button and choose New. Select Inventory Part from the drop-down menu in the Type field. A window with fields for tracking inventory appears, as shown in Figure 10-6.

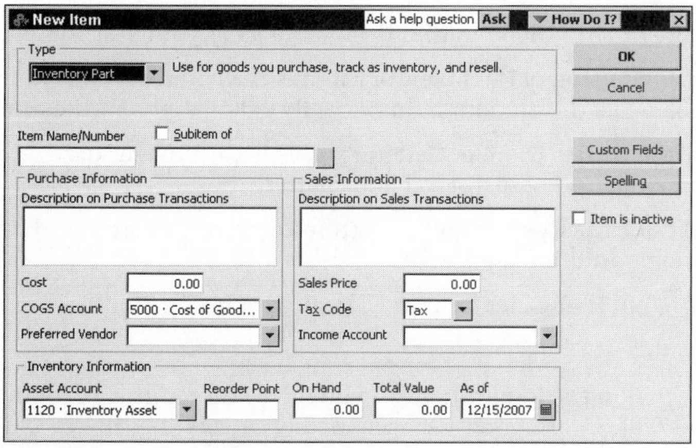

Figure 10-6: This window enables you to track both the cost of goods sold and the current value of your inventory.

7. Enter the Item name or number. QuickBooks uses the name you enter in this field on invoices, sales receipts, and purchase orders.

8. Indicate whether this is a subitem.

9. Fill in the Description on Purchase Transactions field with any information that you want to appear on purchase documents generated by the program.

10. Enter the anticipated cost per Item (you can reflect any price changes when you prepare the actual purchase order).

11. In the COGS (Cost of Goods Sold) Account field, select a different account if you do not want to use the one that appears automatically or if you want to create a special additional account for expense tracking and reporting purposes.

12. (Optional) Use the drop-down menu to enter the name of one vendor who is your regular supplier for this Inventory Item. This vendor will then appear on your Stock Status by Vendor Report, which can make your inventory reordering more efficient.

13. Enter the sales price that should automatically appear on invoices, cash sales receipts, and credit memos.

14. Indicate in the Taxable check box whether the Item is subject to sales tax.
15. In the Income Account drop-down list, specify an account for tracking income.
16. (Optional) Enter an amount in the Reorder Point box to have QuickBooks provide you with a reorder reminder when the number of pieces on hand drops below the quantity indicated.
17. Enter an asset account. This account is different from the income account that you specified in step 15, which will flow through to the Profit and Loss Statement. The asset account that you specify in this field tracks the value of the inventory to be reflected as an asset on the company's Balance Sheet.
18. Enter the quantity of the Item that is on hand as of your start date.
19. Adjust the total value of the Inventory Item shown in the Total Value field if it is not the same as the amount automatically calculated by QuickBooks.
20. Enter a date in the As Of field. Generally, this is the current date or the start date, if you are entering historical information.
21. (Optional) Click the Custom Fields button to add any customized fields that you require for additional information.
22. Click Next to enter another Item or OK to leave the screen.

You may find this 22-step procedure for entering a single Inventory Item arduous, but it is well worth it in the long run. After you have entered the foregoing information, QuickBooks will reward you by automatically calculating the cost of goods sold and the total value of the inventory on hand as of the current date.

QuickBooks automatically calculates the cost of goods sold by using the average cost of the Items in stock at the time of the sale. For example, assume that you sold two pink flamingo yard ornaments. Prior to the sale, your stock was six of the scarlet birds. Two of the birds cost you $20.00, two cost you $25.00, and two cost you $30.00. QuickBooks will compute the cost of goods sold as $50.00, or two Items having an average cost of $25.00.

QuickBooks computes the total value of inventory on hand at any given time on the average-cost basis. In theory, if you divide the value of the Inventory Items reported on your Balance Sheet by the quantity of Inventory Items that QuickBooks thinks you have on hand, this number should agree with the actual number of Inventory Items you have in stock.

However, this isn't always the case because of a factor called *shrinkage*. Shrinkage is a reduction in inventory due to events such as spoilage, theft, and damage. It is wise to take a physical count of your inventory regularly (at least annually) so that you can detect and monitor shrinkage. When you make your count, if the quantity of inventory on hand is not the same as the quantities reflected in QuickBooks, you should make a general journal entry to adjust your QuickBooks information so that it will be accurate.

Purchasing Items

QuickBooks not only streamlines the process of purchasing the inventory and supplies your business needs, but it also tells you exactly how much the company has spent on a particular type of Item at any time during the fiscal year. For example, if you want to know how much your desktop publishing company spends on disposable color printer cartridges, you would create an Item to track those cartridges and create a purchase report whenever you want to see how much you have spent on cartridges.

You can access an Item from a drop-down list of Items directly from the relevant field on the purchase order. QuickBooks fills in all of the descriptive and pricing information. It also keeps track of the number of Items that you have on order. You can even track Items received against purchase orders. A good manager can then analyze the quantity on hand and the quantity on order by pulling up a QuickReport from the Item List window to determine whether supplies will be sufficient to meet projected needs.

You can use QuickBooks to track numbers of Items that you have purchased in the past. This capability allows you to review a prior period's sales to determine whether an increase (or decrease) in sales justifies a change in inventory ordering habits. This is discussed in Chapter 30, which covers reports and graphs.

Partial Payments Items

If you receive a down payment, deposit, or other such amount at the time that your company issues an invoice or statement, you may want to create an Item for partial payments. For example, a construction company may require a deposit of 20 percent before beginning a remodeling job. An Item for partial payments would accurately subtract the down payment from the outstanding customer balance.

When you record a partial payment, the amount reflected in accounts receivable is decreased by the amount of the payment. If you receive complete payment at the time of sale, you would record the transaction as a cash sale rather than using a partial payment.

To create a special Item to reflect partial payments and deposits, follow these steps:

1. Go to Lists ⇨ Items. Click the Item button and choose New from the drop-down menu that appears.
2. In the Type field of the New Item window, choose Payment. The screen shown in Figure 10-7 appears.

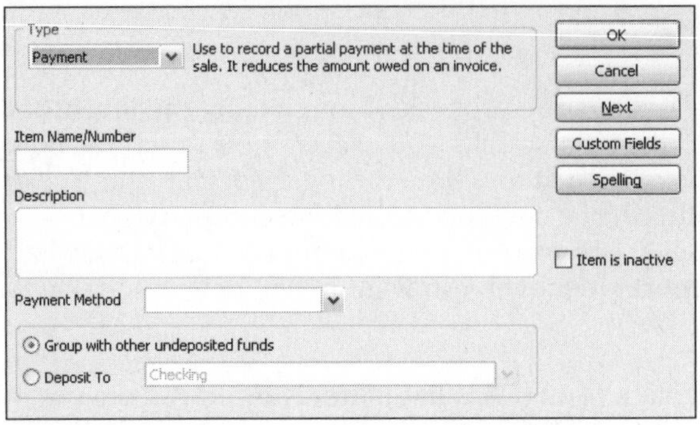

Figure 10-7: Creating a Partial Payment Item.

3. Specify a name for the Item, such as Partial Payment or Down Payment.
4. Indicate the payment method.
5. Enter any descriptive information. It is a good idea to also indicate the payment method in this field.
6. Indicate whether you want to add the amount of the payment to the Undeposited Funds account or whether you want to deposit the payment directly into a specific account using the fields shown at the bottom of the screen.
7. Add custom fields if you feel that additional information is required.
8. Click Next to enter another Item or OK to leave the window.

Tip

What if you sometimes deposit partial payments immediately and at other times hold them in the Undeposited Funds account? You may want to create two separate identical Items, one for deposits and one for the Undeposited Funds account. Similarly, if you want to track payment by different methods, set up Items for each method.

Subtotal and Discount Items

What customer doesn't love a discount? QuickBooks makes it easy to record both fixed-amount and percentage discounts. But before you can calculate and add discounts, you need to learn to create and use Subtotal Items.

Subtotal Items

Figure 10-8 shows a sample invoice using subtotals for labor and materials. You may enter up to three subtotals on an invoice. Each time you enter a subtotal, this

QuickBooks feature will operate in a slightly different manner. When you enter the first Subtotal Item, the program will add all of the line items directly above. When you enter a Subtotal Item for the second time, the program adds all Items after the first subtotal. When you enter a third Subtotal Item, QuickBooks gives you the sum of the first two subtotals. You may enter a markup or discount to the subtotaled amounts or to individual amounts.

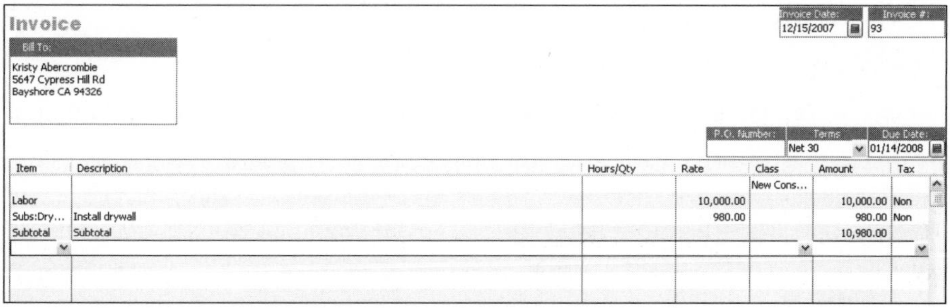

Figure 10-8: The QuickBooks Subtotal Items feature.

To create a Subtotal Item, follow these steps:

1. Go to Lists ➪ Items. Click the Item button and choose New.
2. Enter the Item name.
3. In the Type field, enter Subtotal.
4. Enter a description to appear on the customer invoice such as Labor Subtotal.
5. Click Next to enter another Item or OK to close the window.

Discount Items

Items are used to reflect discounts given to customers for any purpose other than prepayment. Prepayments are handled in a different manner and are covered in Chapter 16. Discounts may be given either in the form of a percentage of the purchase or fee or as a stated amount. You can discount a single Item or a group of products or services. Subtotal Items are used along with Discount Items when you are applying a discount to more than one Item on an invoice.

Discounting a single Item

If you give a discount that is a stated amount (for example, "$20.00 off with this coupon"), you can just type the amount of the discount on the sales form. You don't need to set up an Item. But when the description is lengthy or you want to track the expense associated with a specific discount program in a separate account, it makes sense to create a special Discount Item for a stated-amount discount.

If the discount is to be applied to a percentage of a purchase, the Item that you set up will calculate the correct amount. You can also specify whether you want the discount to be applied before or after sales tax. If the discount is applied before sales tax, it will reduce the amount of tax that the customer has to pay because the discount reduces the total amount of the taxable sale.

To create a Discount Item, follow these steps:

1. Go to Lists ⇨ Items.
2. Click the Item button and choose New.
3. In the Type field, choose Discount. The window shown in Figure 10-9 appears.

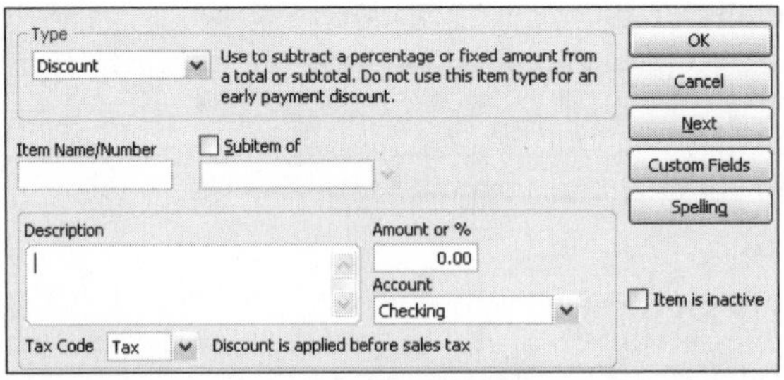

Figure 10-9: You use this window to set up either set-rate or percentage discounts.

4. In the Item Name/Number box, enter the name of the discount.
5. In the Description box, enter any information that you want to appear on the customer invoice or receipt when you use this Item.
6. In the Amount or % box, enter either the dollar amount of the discount or the percentage rate to be applied. If it varies, leave this field blank and enter the amount or percentage on each sales form directly. If you are entering a percentage, be sure to type the % sign in this field.
7. In the Account field, enter the name of the account that you want to use to track this expense.
8. Indicate in the check box at the bottom of the screen whether you want the discount to be applied before or after sales tax.

Tip

You can set up a special expense account to evaluate the effectiveness of a specific promotion or sale. For example, was it worth the expense of the full-page ad and coupon that your business ran in last Sunday's newspaper? Set up a special

Newspaper Discount account to gather useful information. To determine how much the promotion increased gross sales, simply divide the balance in the Newspaper Discount account by the percentage discount. For example, if the account balance shows $10,000 and you offered a 10 percent discount with the coupon, you'll know that gross sales increased by $100,000 as a result of the promotion.

9. Click Next to enter another Item or OK to exit the window.

Discounting multiple Items

The Subtotal Item allows you to apply a discount percentage to several Items all at the same time. When you enter a percentage Discount Item, QuickBooks computes the discount on the line directly above it. If the line above the Discount Item is a single product or service, QuickBooks applies the discount to that line item. If the line above the Discount Item is a subtotal, QuickBooks applies the discount on the subtotaled amount.

Sales Taxes

Sales taxes vary from state to state and even among localities within a state. If your business collects sales taxes, you must make sure that you have activated the sales tax preference, as discussed in Chapter 23.

You may select two different types of Items for sales tax from the New Item menu: Sales Tax Item or Sales Tax Group. You use a Sales Tax Item to calculate a single tax imposed as a set rate and paid to a single government agency. Figure 10-10 shows an example of the setup of such an Item. In contrast, a Sales Tax Group Item calculates two or more sales taxes paid to different government entities and shows the combination tax as a single line item on the customer receipt or invoice.

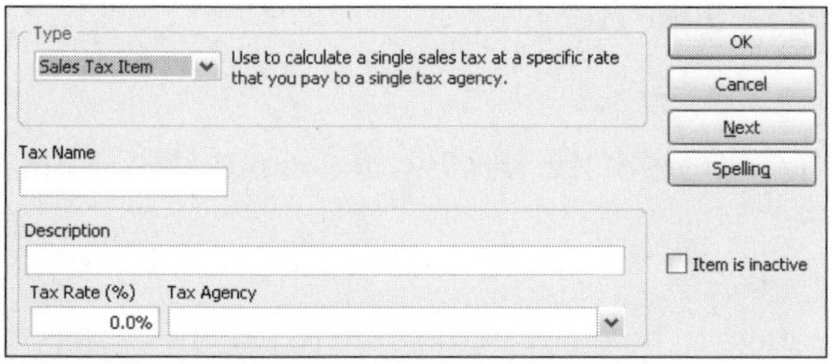

Figure 10-10: Use this window to compute a single tax payable to a single government agency.

Even if you are charging a combination of several sales taxes to your customers, they will want to know only the total percentage rate they must pay. You can use the Sales Tax Group type to display the aggregate of the taxes imposed as one rate on one line on a receipt or invoice. Figure 10-11 shows the use of the New Item window for such a purpose. Chapter 23 is devoted to the topic of sales taxes.

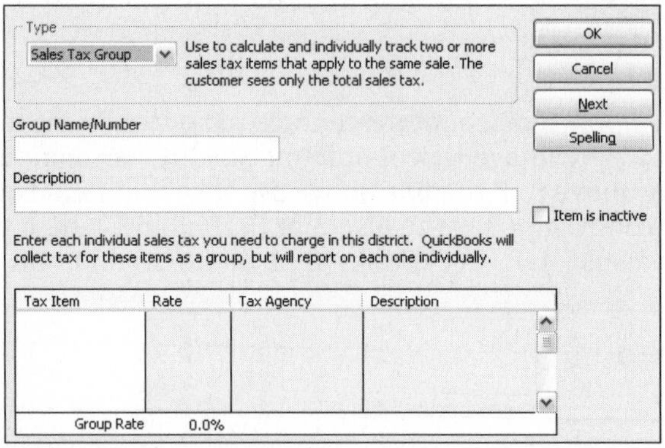

Figure 10-11: Use this window to aggregate groups of Sales Tax Items so that they appear on a single line of a sales form.

Other Charges

Examples of the kinds of Items that fall under this rather vague heading are shipping charges, delivery charges, trip charges, and miscellaneous kinds of expenses that you pass on to your customers. A rather irritating example that comes to mind is the "handling charge" that box offices and even some travel agents charge when they book tickets. (What else do they do besides "handle" tickets?) In any event, to create an Other Charge Item, follow these steps:

1. Go to Lists ➪ Items.
2. Click the Item button at the bottom of the window, and choose New from the drop-down list that appears.
3. Enter the Item name or number.
4. Enter an amount or percentage to be charged. Be sure to use the % sign if it is to be a percentage.
5. Indicate whether this Item is subject to sales tax in the Taxable check box.
6. Indicate the income account that you want to post this Item to.

7. Enter optional information about whether this Item is a subitem, any descriptive information, and any custom fields if you think additional information is needed.
8. Click Next to enter another Item or OK to close this window.

Item Management Tools

As your business grows, so will your list of Items. The topics covered in this section enable you to manage and organize your list. The basic tools for managing Items are creating groups and subitems, and editing, deleting, and inactivating Items.

The Group type

The Group type of Item allows you to bill several Items at a time on an invoice, receipt, or other customer sales form. You can elect either to have all the Items in the group appear on the sales form or to have the group appear as a single line without a detailed breakdown of the Items that make up the group.

To create a Group Item, follow these steps:

1. Go to Lists ⇨ Items.
2. Click the Item button at the bottom of the Lists window and select New from the drop-down window that appears.
3. In the Type field, select Group.
4. Indicate the group name or number in Group Name/Number field.
5. In the Description box, enter the information that you want to appear on sales forms whenever you use the Group Item.
6. Indicate whether you want to print all the Items in the group on sales forms or just the group name and information by either selecting or deselecting the Print Items in Group check box.
7. In the Item column, enter all the Items that you want to appear in the group. Using the scroll bar that appears when you click the Item field, enter each Item that you want to include in the group, including any applicable discounts. Remember to use the subtotal line if you are applying a discount to several Items within the group.
8. You may enter a quantity for each Item now or enter it on the sales form each time you use this group.
9. Click Next to enter another Item or OK to exit the window.

Use groups to add detail to your line items. The more detail you have, the more specific your reports will be.

Using subitems

The advantages to using subitems are similar to the ones for groups. When you indicate subitems under a general-category parent Item, you can generate reports showing both the subitem information and a subtotal of all Items under the parent category. For example, if I want to bill a client for legal representation in an IRS matter, I might create a parent Item called IRS Matter. Subitems might include legal research, drafting correspondence, and negotiating with the IRS agent. My reports would disclose how much I had billed for handling the entire matter, as well as detail the amounts billed to the subitem activities.

To create a parent Item, follow these steps:

1. Go to Lists ➪ Items.
2. Click the Item button at the bottom of the screen and choose New from the drop-down menu that appears.
3. Complete the Item Name/Number field, Item Type, and all other appropriate fields.
4. Click Next to enter another Item or OK to leave the screen.

To create a subitem, follow these steps:

1. Go to Lists ➪ Items.
2. Click the Item button at the bottom of the screen and choose New from the drop-down menu that appears.
3. Select the same Item type as the parent Item.
4. Complete the Item Name/Number field and all other appropriate fields.
5. Select the Subitem Of check box and enter the name of the parent Item in the field underneath the check box.
6. Click Next to enter another Item or OK to leave the screen.

Editing, deleting, and inactivating Items

You can edit an Item that you have created at any time. You can make changes to all information about the Item, but certain limitations apply to the Item Type field. You can change Service, Noninventory Part, or Other Charge Items only to another of these three categories. You cannot change any other Item type. To edit an Item, simply access the Item list from the File menu. Select the Item that you want to edit, and change the information that appears in the Item window.

Similarly, to delete an Item, select it from the Item list and click the Delete button that appears at the bottom of the Item List window.

You cannot delete an Item that is part of any Group Item or that has been used in any transaction recorded in the system. You can, however, make such Items inactive. Inactive Items do not appear on your lists or drop-down menus. To make an Item inactive, follow these steps:

1. Go to Lists ➪ Items.
2. Select the Item that you want to make inactive.
3. Click the Item button located at the bottom of the window.
4. Select Make Inactive from the drop-down menu that appears.

Making Items inactive is a good way to handle the issue of products that are out of stock or discontinued or services that are no longer offered. You may not be able to delete these Items because they appear in transactions, but you can get them off your lists and drop-down menus to avoid invoicing customers for them.

Searching for Items in a transaction

You can search all of your company's transactions for a specific Item by using the Filter function. To search transactions for a specific Item, follow these steps:

1. Go to Lists ➪ Items.
2. Click the Item button in the bottom left corner of the Item dialog box.
3. Choose Find in Transactions from the drop-down list.
4. Select Item from the Filter window that appears.
5. Indicate the type of Item you want to search for from the drop-down Item menu.
6. Click Find to generate a list of transactions involving the specified Item.

Reports about Items

QuickBooks provides many reports that break information down by the goods or services you purchase and sell. These goods and services are the Items on your Item List. These reports help you answer many important questions pertaining to the growth and profitability of your business. You can access the following types of reports from the QuickBooks Reports menus and submenus (access the submenus by clicking on the arrow next to any option in the Report menu as shown in Figure 10-12):

✦ **Sales by Item:** QuickBooks allows you to prepare reports of Sales by Item Summary and a more specific Sales by Item Detail.

✦ **Purchases by Item:** QuickBooks allows you to view summaries of Item purchases, with or without details about Item subaccounts.

✦ **Item cost estimates:** QuickBooks greatly enhances your business's capability to estimate the costs of Items and the consequent probability of jobs with four different types of reports:

- Job profitability detail and Item profitability detail — Shows you which jobs and Items are most profitable.
- Job estimates versus actuals detail — Shows you the difference between what your staff has estimated and the actual costs incurred in performing a job.
- Item profitability — Shows you a breakdown of the profits your company has made on each Item.
- Item estimates versus actuals — Allows you to compare what you estimated to be the cost of Items associated with particular jobs with what the Items actually cost.

✦ **Time tracking:** You can generate Item reports to track time by job or by Item.

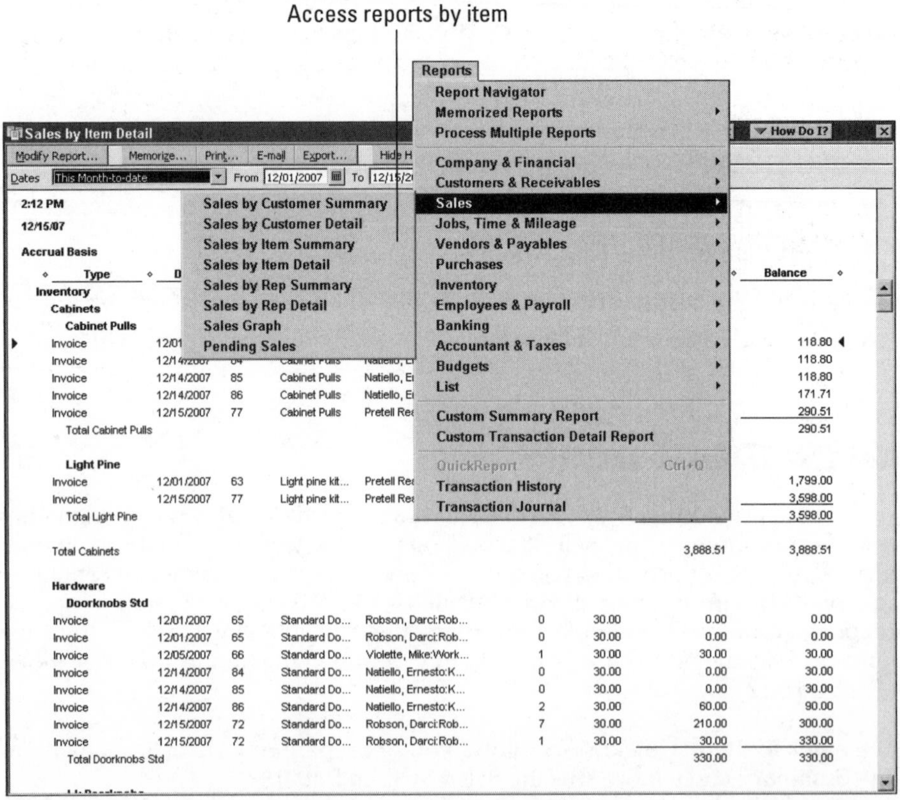

Figure 10-12: QuickBooks offers many reports that give you Item breakdowns.

Summary

An Item is an indexing tool used to "file" information about products, services, and related calculations such as discounts and sales taxes. This chapter introduced you to these Item types: Service, Inventory Part, Noninventory Part, Other Charge, Subtotal, Group, Payment, Sales Tax, and Sales Tax Group.

- ✦ You learned that each Item is associated with an account that tracks information about the Item to be reported on the company's Income Statement or Balance Sheet.
- ✦ Setting up an Inventory Item can be complex, but your efforts are rewarded by accurate information about the cost of goods sold, the current value of inventory on hand, and the correct reorder point.
- ✦ Reimbursable Items can be charged directly to specific customers and jobs, and service companies can use Items to set up different billing rates.
- ✦ Items simplify the computation of discounts, which you can apply to individual products and services or to groups of products and services using the Subtotal Item.
- ✦ You can use items to automatically calculate applicable sales taxes and display the appropriate information on customer sales forms. You can also set up Other Charge Items as you need them to record service, delivery, handling, and other miscellaneous charges.
- ✦ You can view a number of reports that disclose your company's sales and profitability on an Item-by-Item basis.

✦ ✦ ✦

CHAPTER 11

Printer Settings and Options

✦ ✦ ✦ ✦

In This Chapter

Selecting a printer to use

Setting up your printer

Specifying printing preferences for your company forms

Printing batches of checks and other documents

Troubleshooting common printer problems

✦ ✦ ✦ ✦

Your printer is an important part of your overall QuickBooks business solution. Even in this day and age of e-mail and electronic files, paper files remain an integral component of virtually all business record-keeping systems. QuickBooks allows you to generate many types of printed material — checks, invoices, address labels, financial statements, and more. This chapter tells you how to keep your printer running smoothly and operating properly, as well as how to troubleshoot common printer problems.

Choosing a Default Printer

If you're using QuickBooks on a network with more than one printer, you need to tell QuickBooks which printer to print to. You must also choose a specific printer if you have had more than one printer connected to your computer at one time or another. The reason for this is that your operating system remembers each printer that has ever been attached to your computer. Therefore, every time you install a new printer to your computer, the list of printers you can select from grows by one.

If your computer has access to more than one printer, you can select a *default printer*. The default printer is the printer used automatically when you print from QuickBooks — without your having to select one.

To specify a default printer, follow these steps:

1. From the Windows Start menu, select Printers & Faxes. The Printers window appears.
2. Find the printer you want to set as the default and right-click either its name or icon.
3. Select Set as Default Printer from the menu.

Setting Options to Print Forms

QuickBooks allows you to choose from a number of customized options when printing forms for your particular company. It is simple to select and change these options; in fact, you can change them whenever you print a form. Follow these steps to set your printer options:

1. From the File menu, choose Printer Setup. The Printer Setup dialog box appears
2. From the Form Name drop-down list, select the form you want to print, such as Invoice, as shown in Figure 11-1.

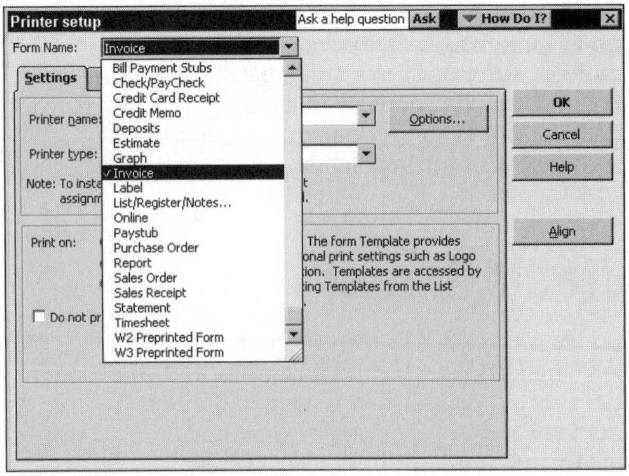

Figure 11-1: You can set your printer for specific QuickBooks forms by using this option.

3. Select the options you want to use when you print your form.
4. When you're finished setting the options, select another form. The options on the Printer Setup window change depending on which form you select. Figure 11-2 shows the options for printing invoices.
5. When you're finished setting printer options for all of your forms, click OK.

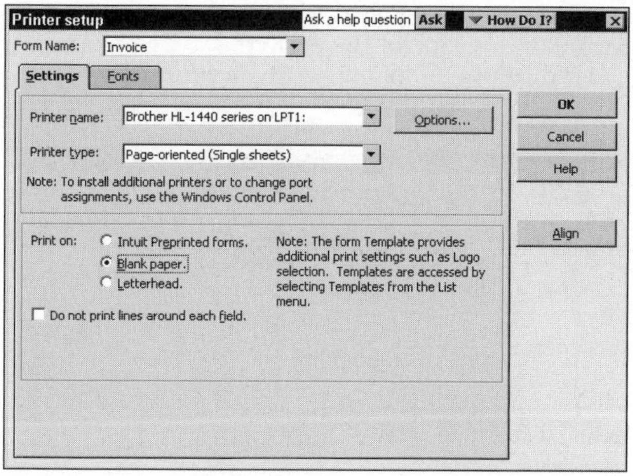

Figure 11-2: QuickBooks offers individualized options for printing each type of form.

Printing Reports and Graphs in Color

QuickBooks offers a visually appealing array of charts and graphs best viewed in color. To print graphs in color, follow these steps:

1. Display the report or graph you want to print.
2. From the Report or Graph button bar, click Print.
3. Select the Print in Color check box and then click OK.

Note

If the Print in Color check box does not appear on the screen, try clicking the Options box on the print menu and then the Paper/Quality tab on that submenu.

Printing Batches of Checks, Invoices, or Other Forms

Batch processing is a time-saving tool that allows you to print several checks, invoices or other forms all at once, instead of one at a time. This is a useful feature, but it can be a bit tricky the first few times you attempt it. Invoicing and paying bills are events that particularly lend themselves to batch processing and printing. Follow these steps to ensure your batches are not botched, and print smoothly and efficiently:

1. From the File menu, choose Print Forms and then choose the type of form you want to print. A window appears for the particular type of form you have selected. Figure 11-3 displays a window for invoice forms.

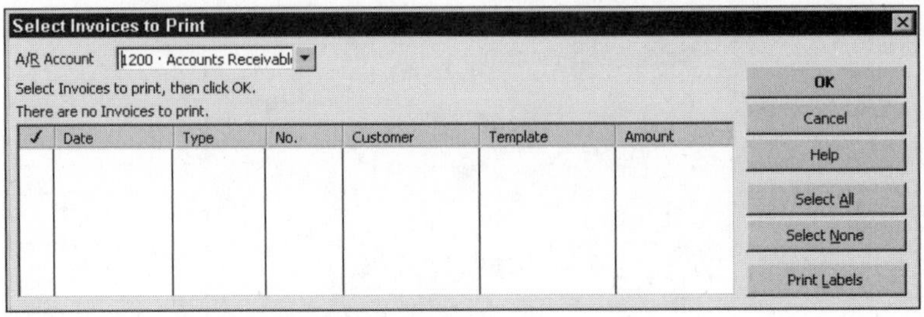

Figure 11-3: Selecting invoices to print.

2. In the Select (forms) to Print window, select the items you want to print, and click OK.
3. Review your print options and make any necessary changes to them.
4. Click Print.

Caution

If you want to print mailing labels for invoices, you must print them before you print the invoices. If you have selected several invoices for the same customer, QuickBooks prints one mailing label for that customer. If you want to print the mailing labels, click Print Mailing Labels.

Printing Labels

The ability to print labels using the information maintained in your QuickBooks customer and vendor lists is a key program feature. As with batch printing, it takes a couple seconds to set up and monitor properly. For crisp-looking labels each time you print them, follow these steps:

1. Make sure that your printer is on and that the sheets for the labels or cards are properly loaded in the printer. (You may want to try a "test run" on some blank sheets of paper the first time you try this feature.)
2. From the File menu, choose Print Forms and then choose Labels. The Select Labels to Print dialog box opens, as shown in Figure 11-4.
3. Choose the names you want to appear on the labels or cards, or the customer or vendor types you want to print.

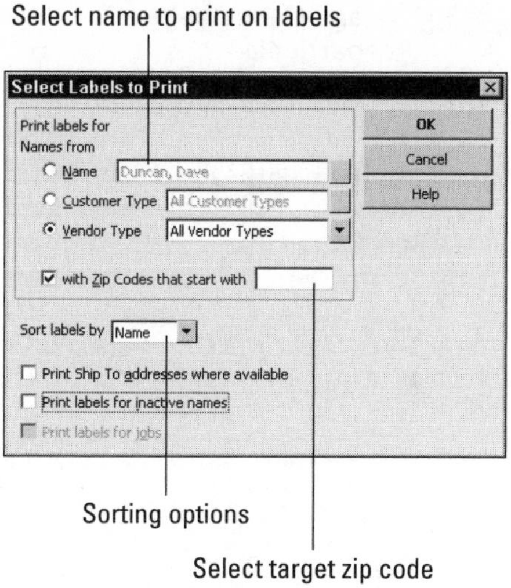

Figure 11-4: Label-printing options.

4. (Optional) You can target your mailing to a specific geographic area by specifying a particular zip code or group of zip Codes to print. To do this, select the With Zip Codes that Start With check box and enter the zip code (or partial zip code) that you want to use to limit your printing.
5. (Optional) To sort the labels or cards by zip code, from the Sort By drop-down list, choose Zip Code. Otherwise, QuickBooks sorts the labels or cards alphabetically by name.

Caution

For the zip code sort to work, the last line of addresses should contain only the city, state, zip code, and country (if necessary). The comma after the city name is optional, and the zip code can be either five or nine digits.

6. Indicate whether you want to use the customers' billing or shipping addresses in Print Ship To Addresses Where Available check box.
7. Indicate whether you want to print labels for inactive names; then click OK.
8. Check that the Label Format setting is correct, and click Print.

Paycheck Printing Issues

Processing checks on payday is a breeze with QuickBooks, so long as you keep your employee and payroll records up-to-date. You can print checks with your company logo, or display company and employee information.

Adding your logo to checks and paychecks

Adding your logo to checks is a feature that enhances the image of your business. It is simple to accomplish by following these steps:

1. Go to File ➪ Printer Setup ➪ Check/PayCheck path. Then click the Logo window, and browse for the logo image you want. Once you load a logo, the Logo option appears on the Print Checks screen.
2. In the Logo window, click File.
3. In the Open Logo File window, enter the drive, directory path, and name of the file that contains the logo. QuickBooks will copy your logo file to the same location as your company file.
4. Click OK in the Open Logo File window, and then in the Logo window.

Tip This works best for square-shaped logos.

Printing company or employee information on the check voucher

To include information about your company or specific to particular employees on your checks, follow these steps:

1. From the Edit menu, choose Preferences to open the Preferences window.
2. Scroll down to and click the Payroll & Employees icon.
3. Click the Company Preferences tab.
4. Click Printing Preferences under Paystub and Voucher Printing.
5. Select from among the printing preferences shown in Figure 11-5.

The check-printing process

Prior to printing checks, update any information for employees that may have changed since your last pay period, add your logo, and specify the company and employee information you want to appear on your checks. Then follow these steps to print your checks:

1. Load your checks in the printer. From the File menu, choose Print Forms and then choose Paychecks.

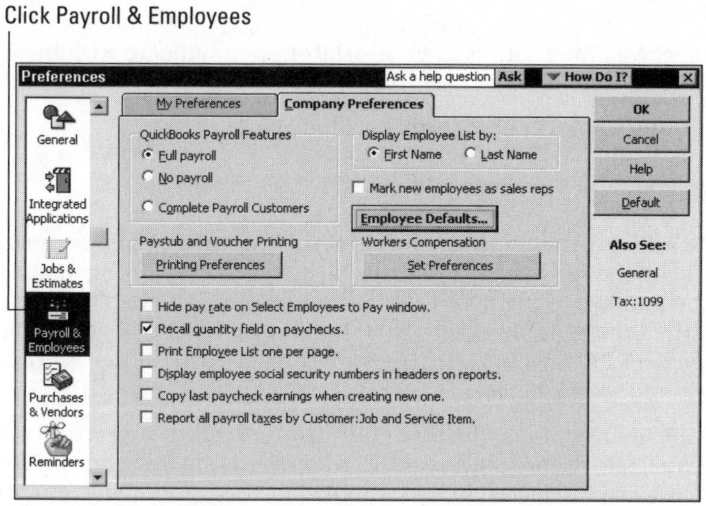

Figure 11-5: Preferences for printing employee and company information on check vouchers.

2. From the Bank Account drop-down list, choose the payroll checking account that contains the checks you want to print.
3. Verify that the number in the First Check Number field matches the first number on your checks in the printer.
4. Select the checks you want to print; click OK.
5. Click Print.

Common Printing Problems

Printing problems can be some of the most difficult to diagnose. The reason for the difficulty is the number of components. Consider this list of the components involved in printing from QuickBooks, keeping in mind that a problem with printing can be related to any one or combination of these components:

- ✦ QuickBooks software
- ✦ Your company data loaded in QuickBooks
- ✦ Operating system
- ✦ Fonts loaded on your computer

- Your printer
- The driver software that helps your printer communicate with the operating system
- Toner, printer cable, or any peripheral hardware

Here are some common problems and possible solutions:

- **Your operating system reports an error in connecting to your printer or to LPT1:** This message usually indicates an easy-to-solve problem. It appears when you attempt to print, but there is no printer attached to your computer. Be sure the printer cable is snugly attached to the back of your computer, or, if you are working on a network, be sure the network printer is connected. Also be sure the printer is on.
- **Poor print quality:** It may be that your printer cannot support the font you chose, especially if the font is exotic. Your operating system tries to simulate the font you have selected in QuickBooks for the printer, and sometimes this simulation does not work properly. Also, check your printer's toner to see if it needs replacement. Last, check with the manufacturer of your printer (easy to do over the Internet) to see if an updated driver is available for your operating system.
- **An "Out of Memory" message appears:** If your report contains many different size and format options, you could run out of memory as you print the file. You can address this problem by reducing the number of fonts used in the report or by increasing the memory in your computer or printer. Also, you can address this problem by ensuring that no other applications are running when you run the report.
- **Missing text at borders:** If the text near the edges of a report or graph is missing or cut off, the margins may be too small, or you may have specified margins that are beyond the printable area of your printer. If the text within a form you have designed is cut off, the field may be too small. The selected font you are using may be too complex for the print area. From the File menu, choose Printer Setup. In the Printer Setup window, choose the appropriate Font area and select another font, and/or reduce the font size. Disable any font controllers, such as Adobe Type Manager.
- **Missing lines on forms:** Lines may be missing when you're printing on either blank or letterhead paper and you selected the Print Lines Around Each Field option. If some of the vertical lines are missing from the boxes, you need to change the horizontal alignment for the form. If the left side is missing, increase the horizontal alignment. If the right side is missing, decrease the horizontal alignment.

Summary

This chapter outlined the customized printing features available in QuickBooks and how to optimize your printer to take advantage of them.

- You have several options for customizing your company's printed forms.
- Batch printing is a great time saving feature.
- Labels can easily be printed from information maintained in QuickBooks lists.

✦ ✦ ✦

Preferences and Data Management

PART

III

In This Part

CHAPTER 12

Setting QuickBooks Preferences

✦ ✦ ✦ ✦

In This Chapter

Learning the difference between My Preferences and Company Preferences

Figuring out how to change any Preference

Restoring QuickBooks' default Preferences

Getting to know the different Preference options

QuickBooks makes very few assumptions about the way companies conduct business. For example, QuickBooks can adapt to the way you pay and send invoices, how and when you pay your employees, how you prepare your cash flow statements, and the nuances of various state regulations.

This flexibility is harnessed through the QuickBooks set of Preferences. QuickBooks allows you to set dozens of options and elements to support your business and practices. This chapter discusses the Preferences you can set to make QuickBooks work best for you.

QuickBooks has so many Preferences that it is impossible to cover all of them in this chapter. Fortunately, many QuickBooks Preferences require little or no explanation to set and use effectively.

Changing Preferences

Changing QuickBooks Preferences is easy. Besides understanding what Preferences do, there is very little to learn. This section demonstrates the difference between the two different types of Preferences, how to change a Preference, and how to restore a Preference to QuickBooks' default settings.

You can access dozens of Preferences in QuickBooks from the Preferences dialog box. Specific Preferences are available according to the program area to which they pertain. You can access Preferences for different program areas by using the scrollbar on the left side of the Preferences dialog box. To access dozens of Preferences in QuickBooks, follow these steps:

1. Go to Edit ➪ Preferences. A Preferences dialog box, such as the one shown in Figure 12-1, appears.

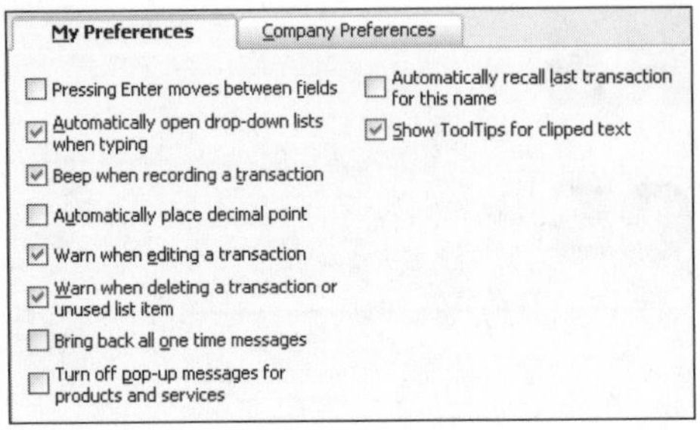

Figure 12-1: All Preferences are changed from this dialog box, which changes based on the icons accessed and whether you select the My Preferences or Company Preferences tab.

2. Scroll to the type of Preferences you want to access using the scroll bar on the left of the Preferences dialog box.

What Preferences Does QuickBooks Offer?

QuickBooks offers hundreds of Preferences that are organized by program area. It's helpful to have an overview of the Preferences features you can use to customize QuickBooks to meet the needs of your company. Some of the following Preferences are discussed later in this chapter:

✦ **Accounting:** Allows you to use account numbers, specify which subaccounts to show on your chart of accounts, use class tracking, maintain an audit trail of transactions affecting an account, automatically assign general journal entry numbers to accounts, warn when you are posting a transaction to Retained Earnings, and set a password or establish a closing date.

✦ **Checking:** Allows you to print account names on vouchers, change the check date when it is printed, start with the payee field on each check, display warnings about duplicate check numbers, autofill payee account numbers in the memo portion of checks, set default accounts to use, and activate online banking payee aliasing.

✦ **Desktop View:** Allows you to select options for customizing the appearance of your QuickBooks desktop.

✦ **Finance Charge:** You can specify your annual interest rate, minimum finance charge, and grace period; specify a finance charge account to debit; indicate how to assess overdue finance charges; and mark finance charge invoices "to be printed."

- **General:** These Preferences allow you to specify additional warnings or sounds you may want to accompany transactions and indicate the format for displaying numbers in QuickBooks fields.
- **Integrated Applications:** You can specify what other computer applications can access your QuickBooks files, and manage all applications that interact with QuickBooks (such as QuickBooks Fixed Asset Manager and specifying whether you are creating estimates, progress invoicing, and so on).
- **Jobs & Estimates:** Specify information maintained on employees and jobs in progress.
- **Payroll & Employees:** Allows you to customize options pertaining to the preparation of your payroll.
- **Purchasers and Vendors:** Includes options for purchase orders and inventory and entering and paying bills.
- **Reminders:** Includes options for displaying and creating reminders.
- **Reports and Graphs:** Allows you to specify the information and appearance of your reports and graphs.
- **Sales and Customers:** Includes information pertaining to shipping and recording payments, sales forms, payments, price levels, and so forth.
- **Sales Tax:** Allows you to specify how sales tax is recorded.
- **Send Forms:** You can create customized messages for forms from this Preferences dialog box.
- **Service Connection:** Specify how you want to access optional fee-based QuickBooks services.
- **Spelling:** Customize spell checking and other editing options.
- **Tax: 1099** Optimize your tax tracking feature.
- **Time Tracking:** Allows you to specify how you want to track time and maintain time records by selecting a first day of the workweek.

Other Preferences, such as the ones for finance charges, charts and graphs, Missing Send Forms, Service Connections, and Spelling Preferences, are self-explanatory.

Understanding Company Preferences versus My Preferences

Each Preference in QuickBooks comes under one of two categories: Company Preferences or My Preferences.

When you change a *Company Preference*, the change is made for all users of the application. For example, if you change the Bills Are Due after *n* Days option from 10 days to 15 days, all invoices sent out and all reports run by any user of the application immediately reflect the new 15-day value. Because Company Preferences are set for all users of the application, no users may be logged on to the system when a Company Preference is set. You can log off users by switching QuickBooks to single-user mode.

Other Preferences are known as *My Preferences*. My Preferences options do not apply to all users of the QuickBooks application, only to the person setting the Preference. An example of a My Preferences option is whether pressing Enter moves the cursor to the next field. Any menu or icon bar customizations are also My Preferences options.

Note Preferences are either companywide or personal. A Preference cannot be both. As you move through the sets of Preferences (for example, accounting Preferences, finance charge Preferences, general Preferences), you will find that certain sets do not allow you to set any personal Preferences. Certain sets of Preferences are only applicable to the entire organization using the QuickBooks application.

For example, you can set general user Preferences in the General section of the Preferences dialog box by clicking the General icon (previously shown in Figure 12-1) and then the My Preferences tab. Figure 12-2 shows the Desktop View Preferences. You switch between My Preferences and Company Preferences by clicking the appropriate tab.

```
┌─────────────────────────────────────────────────────────────────┐
│  My Preferences │ Company Preferences │                          │
│                                                                   │
│  Select the features that you want to show on the Home page.      │
│  ┌─ Customers ──────────────────┐  ┌─ Vendors ──────────────┐    │
│  │ ☑ Invoices  *                │  │ ☑ Enter Bills and Pay  │    │
│  │ ☑ Sales Receipts             │  │   Bills  *             │    │
│  │ ☑ Statements and Statement   │  │                        │    │
│  │   Charges                    │  │                        │    │
│  └──────────────────────────────┘  └────────────────────────┘    │
│                                                                   │
│       * How do I remove this feature icon from the Home page?     │
│  ┌─ Related Preferences ─────────────────────────────────────┐   │
│  │ To show or hide feature icons on the Home page, you need   │   │
│  │ to turn the features on or off. Click a feature name below │   │
│  │ to view its preferences.                                   │   │
│  │                                                            │   │
│  │      Estimates     (on)    Inventory      (on)             │   │
│  │      Sales Tax     (on)    Payroll        (on)             │   │
│  │      Sales Orders  (on)    Time Tracking  (on)             │   │
│  │                                                            │   │
│  │ To return to these preferences, click the Desktop View     │   │
│  │ icon on the left.                                          │   │
│  └────────────────────────────────────────────────────────────┘  │
└─────────────────────────────────────────────────────────────────┘
```

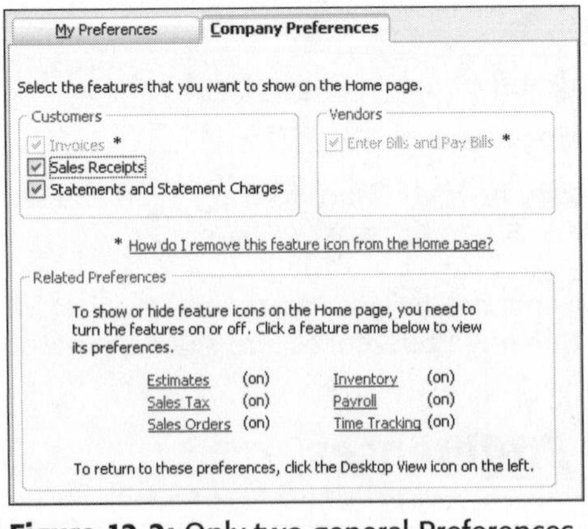

Figure 12-2: Only two general Preferences are used for the entire company.

QuickBooks does not allow you to save more than one set of personal Preferences on a workstation. If your employees share a computer, you may want to agree on a set of Preferences for that computer. Otherwise, individual users will have to reset their Preferences each time.

Changing a preference

QuickBooks makes it easy to change more than 100 individual Preference options from one central area. You change a Preference by selecting the check box or button next to it. QuickBooks organizes Preferences into groups, both of which are discussed later in this chapter. To change Preferences, follow these steps:

1. Choose Edit ➪ Preferences. The Preferences dialog box appears (previously shown in Figure 12-1).

   Note If you plan to change any Company Preferences, all users (other than you) must be logged off of the system and QuickBooks must be set to single-user mode. To configure QuickBooks for single-user use, open the File menu. If the third choice is Switch to Multi-User Mode, QuickBooks is already configured for single-user use. Otherwise, choose Switch to Single-User Mode. A message appears when QuickBooks is ready for single-user use. Click OK.

2. Choose the QuickBooks functional category containing the Preferences you want to change from the list of Preference categories at the left of the window. Use the scroll bar to move to sets not visible in the list.
3. Choose the Company Preferences tab to set Preferences that affect all users, or choose the My Preferences tab to set personal Preferences.

   Note It's easy to switch between Company Preferences and My Preferences — simply click the tab for the desired category.

4. Change the appropriate Preferences. Preferences are presented a number of different ways, such as check boxes, option buttons, scroll boxes, and more. You can find detailed information on most of the Preferences in the "Reviewing Preference Options" section later in this chapter.
5. Return to the list of QuickBooks categories if you want to change other Preferences. If you switch to a different category of Preferences, QuickBooks prompts you to save your changes first. Answer Yes to save changes, answer No to discard the changes you made on the last Preferences screen, or choose Cancel to return to the Preferences you were just working on.
6. When you are finished setting Preferences, choose OK. If you do not want to save the changes you made, choose Cancel. You are returned to the QuickBooks desktop.

Restoring defaults

You can return all the Preferences to the settings that were in place when you installed the application — that is, to the default settings. To do so, choose Edit ➪ Preferences ➪ Preferences. When the Preferences dialog box appears, choose the Default button. This will restore all Preferences, both My Preferences and Company Preferences, to the default values (previously shown in Figure 12-1).

Reviewing Preference Options

Many of the Preferences you set in QuickBooks are easy to understand, such as whether you want the system to beep when recording a transaction, or determining whether your company charges sales tax. Many of the Preferences, though, while they may seem easy to understand, have an impact on other areas. For example, if you change options in the Checking category, you impact how QuickBooks works when you write checks.

This section explains the different types of Preferences you can set in QuickBooks. Each of the following sections corresponds to an item on the list box, which displays icons for the different categories of Preferences.

Accounting Preferences

QuickBooks lets you specify whether you use an account number with accounts you establish. This account number would complement the name you specify for the account. For example, you might have account name 3800 Accts Receivables. When you select the Use Account Numbers Option, QuickBooks will require that you enter an account number every time you create a new account. That account number appears in any reports or lists in which the account is shown. Figure 12-3 shows the Preferences dialog box opened to the accounting Preferences where you select this option.

If you choose to use account numbers, you may also specify that only the lowest-level accounts be shown when you enter transactions. This makes sense because you cannot enter transactions at a parent level. You specify this option by choosing the Show Lowest Subaccount Only option.

There are three other accounting-related Preferences to review, which allow you to specify the following:

✦ Whether an account must be selected when a transaction is created (otherwise, these transactions are assigned to an uncategorized section on reports).

✦ Whether to use class tracking, which allows you to create high-level categories of transactions such as New Projects or Budget; and whether every transaction should be captured in an audit trail file.

✦ Whether you want to activate any other accounting Preferences such as automatically assigning general ledger entry numbers, warning when a posting affects Retained Earnings, specifying a closing date, and requiring a password.

Remember that all of the accounting Preferences are applicable to the entire company. There is no accounting-specific My Preferences.

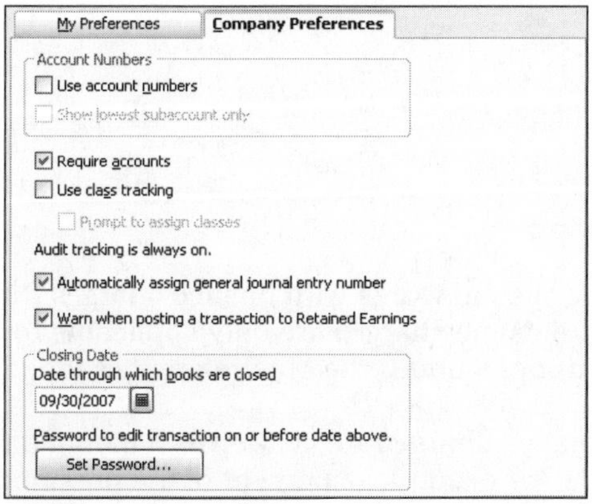

Figure 12-3: Accounting Preferences are limited to the Company Preferences type.

Checking Preferences

A number of Preferences (all Company Preferences) help you customize how check-writing works in QuickBooks. You can specify whether account names appear printed on vouchers; whether the date on a check should be changed to the date the check is printed (which is relevant only if you write checks one or more days before you actually print them); whether the payee is the first piece of information you supply when writing a check; and whether QuickBooks should warn you if you manually enter a check number when you write the check and the number has already been used on another check. The Checking Preference Company tab window is shown in Figure 12-4.

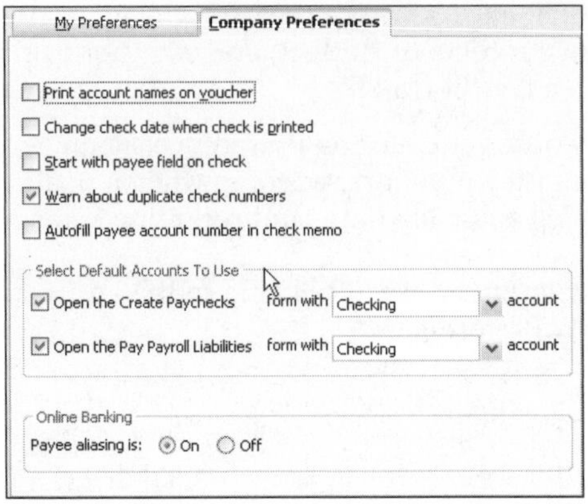

Figure 12-4: The Checking Preferences window.

Finance charge Preferences

QuickBooks lets you customize how the system works with finance charges that you might apply to customer accounts. Finance charges are only applicable to the entire company, so you won't find any options under the My Preferences tab.

QuickBooks lets you enter an annual finance charge rate, as well as a minimum amount. The minimum finance charge is, for example, 2 percent of the outstanding balance, or $5, whichever is greater. You may also specify a grace period, which indicates the maximum number of days after a purchase in which the finance charge is not calculated.

In addition, you can specify the account to which finance charges are applied. To specify the account, choose an account from the Finance Charge Account by clicking the down arrow on the box. If an appropriate account does not appear in the list, you can create a new one and a separate account to assess overdue finance charges.

To create a new account from the Finance Charge Preferences screen, follow these steps:

1. Choose Add New from the Finance Charge drop-down list. The New Account dialog box shown in Figure 12-5 appears.
2. Enter information about the new account in the fields provided, and then click OK. The account you added appears as the selected account for tracking finance charges.

Cross-Reference

For more information on adding new accounts, refer to Chapter 6.

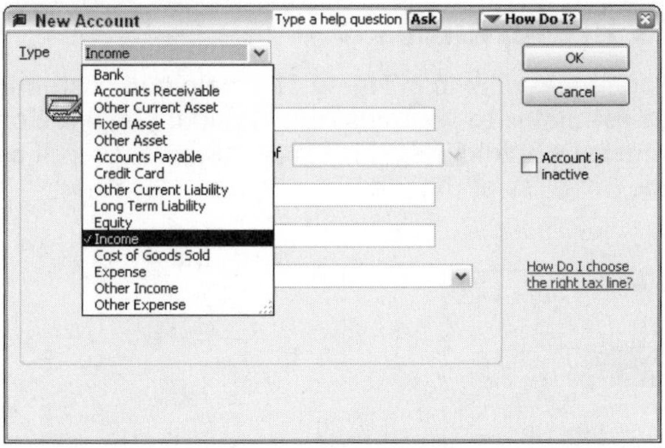

Figure 12-5: QuickBooks allows you to add a new account to track finance charges.

General Preferences

Most of the general Preferences are on the My Preferences tab. These Preferences reflect the individual tastes of the user. For example, you can specify whether the decimal point automatically appears before you enter decimal values and whether a beep sounds after you complete entering a transaction. Figure 12-6 shows the general Preferences you can set. In addition, there are two companywide Preferences you can set on the Company Preferences tab. You can specify whether minutes are shown as actual minutes or as a percentage of hours, as well as whether name information is updated when a transaction is saved.

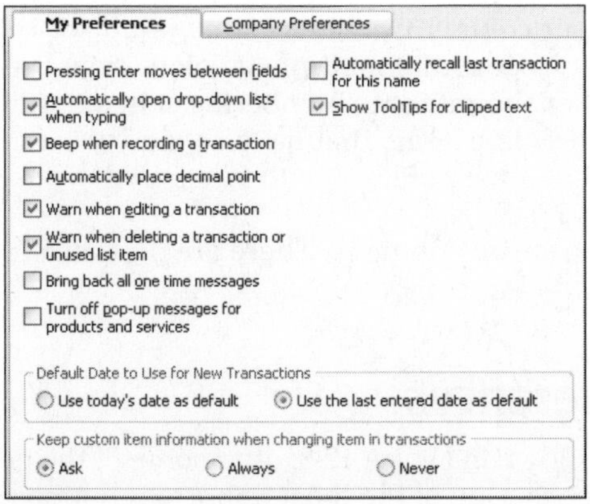

Figure 12-6: Using the My Preferences tab, you can define a number of general Preferences that reflect your personal tastes.

Jobs & Estimates Preferences

The Jobs & Estimates Preferences shown in Figure 12-7 help you customize QuickBooks if you supply estimates to your customers and if you work on longer jobs that may require numerous invoices as the job progresses, as well as if you have the need to track the progress of the job.

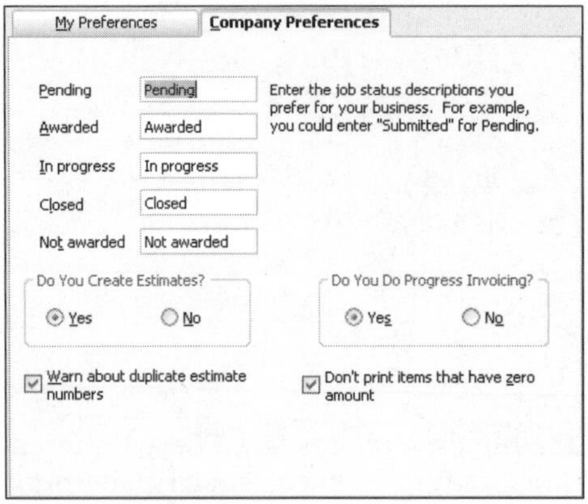

Figure 12-7: Enter Preferences for job status and invoicing.

The Jobs & Estimates Preferences allow you to supply your own labels for the different statuses of a job. You can supply the label that QuickBooks uses in reports for the Pending, Awarded, In Progress, Closed, and Not Awarded phases of a job.

In addition, you can specify whether your company creates estimates. If so, and if you generate progressive invoices (that is, generate multiple invoices from the same estimate), you may specify whether the estimate numbering scheme will allow duplicates, and whether to suppress line items that have a value of 0 in reports, estimates, and invoices.

Each of these Preferences applies to the entire company. There are no such Preferences applicable to single users.

Payroll & Employees Preferences

The Payroll & Employees Preferences, shown in Figure 12-8, offer some of the greatest opportunities to customize QuickBooks. One of the most important options determines to what level, if at all, you use QuickBooks payroll management features.

If you choose Payroll Reports Only, you can still enter and manage payroll-related expenses, but you lose the capability to generate W-2s, W-3s, and Forms 940 and 941, as well as to write and print payroll checks. These capabilities are granted by choosing the Full Payroll Features in the Preferences dialog box.

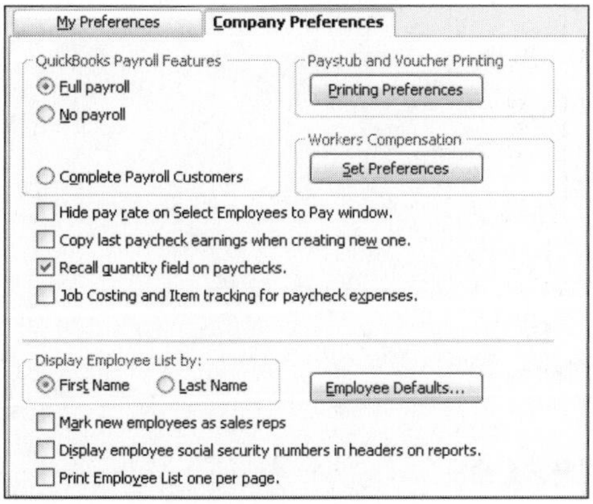

Figure 12-8: Payroll Preferences.

Many of the options presented on the Company Preferences tab of the Payroll & Employees category are self-explanatory; a majority relate only to printing. The Preferences dialog box also gives you access to employee templates.

Cross-Reference

Creating and managing employee templates are discussed in Chapter 22.

Reminders Preferences

One of QuickBooks' best features is its capability to remind you of certain events and tasks that you must perform, such as printing checks and depositing money. On the Company Preferences tab (see Figure 12-9), you can specify for each reminder item whether you want to see a summary reminder, such as one that reminds you that there are checks to print; whether you want to see a list of detailed reminders, such as a list of all the checks due to be printed; or whether you want to be reminded at all. In addition, for certain events and tasks, you can specify how many days in advance you are to be reminded.

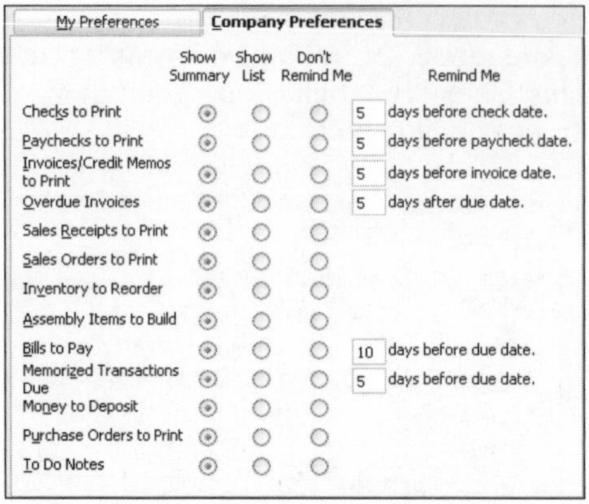

Figure 12-9: QuickBooks enables you to customize when reminders occur.

Sales & Customers Preferences

The Sales & Customers category of Preferences, shown in Figure 12-10, helps you customize QuickBooks for retail-type activities. You can define shipping methods, and then specify the default shipping method. To add a shipping method, click the Usual Shipping Method drop-down list and then choose Add New from the list. Then enter the shipping method and choose OK. When you define a shipping method, you may also mark the method as inactive. This allows you to maintain a history for a particular shipping method, but no longer use it.

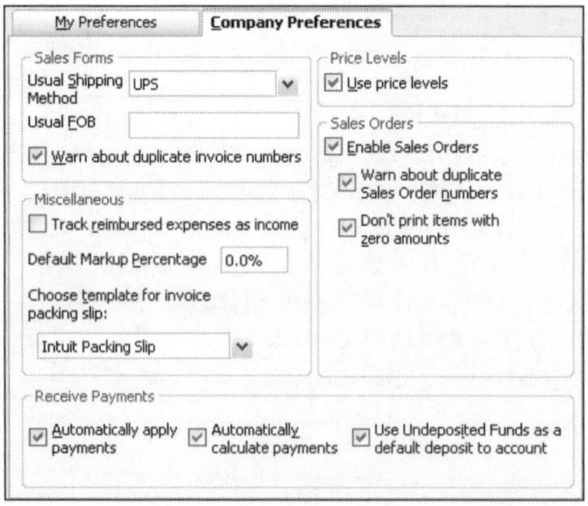

Figure 12-10: Sales and Customers Preferences.

In addition, you can define a default markup percentage and a Usual FOB term. QuickBooks can also automatically warn you when you create an invoice with a number that already exists. It can also be set to automatically apply any payment received for a customer and/or job against the oldest invoice (otherwise you must manually specify how to apply a payment). QuickBooks can also keep track of reimbursed expenses in a special income account if you want.

Sales Tax Preferences

The Sales Tax Preferences category allows you to specify whether you charge sales tax. When you answer Yes, a number of other options become available. You specify the frequency at which you pay sales tax (monthly, quarterly, or annually), whether tax is charged to your customer at the date of the invoice or when payment is received, and whether the letter *T* should appear on invoices beside taxable items.

Tax: 1099 Preferences

Tax Preferences are applicable to the entire company, so you can find them on the Company Preferences tab in the Preferences dialog box. The Tax: 1099 Preferences, shown in Figure 12-11, enable you to specify whether you file the 1099-Misc form and, if so, which account stores the expense for each 1099 category. You must create an account for each category you use when you file the 1099. If the account has been created already, you can select it from a list. That list appears when you click the Account field for any 1099 category. If the account does not exist, you can create it by choosing Add New from the list. In addition, you may also override the default threshold provided by QuickBooks. Click the threshold field for the 1099 category you want to change, and then click and drag over the existing value and enter the new value.

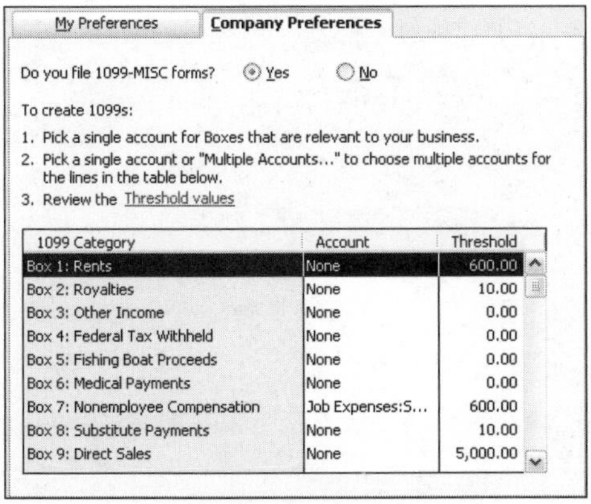

Figure 12-11: 1099 Preferences.

Time Tracking Preferences

With the Time Tracking Preferences you define whether you track specific time activities in your QuickBooks application, as well as specify the first day of the workweek. If you bill hours to customers and track employee hours in QuickBooks, then you must choose Yes for the Do You Track Time option. There are no My Preferences for time tracking.

Cross-Reference

Time tracking is discussed in greater detail in Chapter 20.

Summary

In this chapter, you learned how to customize QuickBooks to your liking. There are dozens of settings covering all aspects of QuickBooks, from how addresses appear on checks to the default markup percentage for items you sell.

- To change a QuickBooks Preference, choose Edit ⇨ Preferences from the menu.
- Switch between the Company Preferences tab and the My Preferences tab to see whether the options apply only to you or to all users.
- To restore all Preferences to their default value, choose Edit ⇨ Preferences from the menu and then choose the Default button.

✦ ✦ ✦

CHAPTER 13

Data Management and Security

In This Chapter

Determining a strategy for backing up QuickBooks data

Using the QuickBooks backup facilities

Importing and exporting Excel data into and out of QuickBooks

Understanding why and how to condense QuickBooks data

Configuring QuickBooks for multiple users

Defining security for users

Some of the most critical tasks required to maintain a healthy and productive QuickBooks application have nothing to do with entering invoices, generating financial reports, or anything related to debits and credits. Critical to an effective and successful QuickBooks application is the integrity and well being of your data. The financial data you enter and report is of no value if it is lost or becomes corrupted, if unauthorized users change critical data, or if your QuickBooks application becomes so large that the system becomes unusable. It's important to ensure these types of events do not occur.

This chapter covers QuickBooks data backups, setting user access rights, and periodically archiving old financial data. In addition, there may be times when you need to load external data into QuickBooks, such as payroll information, or extract data from QuickBooks for use in another application. That subject is also covered in this chapter.

Backing Up Data

Your financial data is the most important data your company maintains — your financial data is more critical than your client lists, a purchased list of leads, or even competitive information. Think for a moment. What information would be the most difficult to recreate if it were lost? You can probably generate a client list without too much effort, and it is probably easy to regenerate a list of sales leads, but can you imagine having to re-create six months worth of invoices or cash balances? For this reason, backing up your QuickBooks data is the most important task after entering the data itself.

Why, though, should you care about backing up data? What could happen to the data you enter in QuickBooks? Here are some of the calamities that could destroy your QuickBooks financial data:

- ✦ The hard drive where the QuickBooks company data file is stored becomes corrupted or simply stops working, destroying not only your QuickBooks application, but all other data and applications loaded on that hard drive.
- ✦ A temp you hired to enter invoices mistakenly deletes every invoice that has ever been entered in the application.
- ✦ Your PC contracts a virus that periodically erases data.
- ✦ Your company suffers a computer loss as a result of a fire, flood, or other disaster.

QuickBooks provides an easy-to-use backup feature. Taking advantage of this feature can help you survive the misfortunes in the preceding list. In this section, you learn how to use QuickBooks' built-in backup feature. You will learn how to prepare to back up your data, how to reliably back up your QuickBooks data, and how to develop a sound backup strategy.

Options for backing up your data

I strongly recommend you back up your QuickBooks company files daily. To access the Back Up window, go to File ➪ Back Up. QuickBooks offers you the following back-up options:

- ✦ **Back up manually to a CD drive or other local media:** To back up your QuickBooks company file to a CD, you must have a read-writable CD drive and software for writing to a recordable CD. A read-writable CD drive is called a CD-R or CD-RW drive. This type of CD drive allows you to write to a recordable CD, otherwise known as "burning a CD." To learn more about backing up to a CD, check the QuickBooks Help database for instructions for your particular operating system.
- ✦ **Schedule backups to occur when you close your company file or at regular intervals:** As discussed later in this chapter, you can schedule automatic backups that take place when you close your company file and you can schedule backups that take place at regular intervals (even when you're away from your desk).
- ✦ **Automate your backup routine using the Online Backup service:** For more information, click Tell Me More in the QuickBooks Backup window.

Preparing to back up

Although the backup feature in QuickBooks is simple to use, there are a few things you must do to prepare for a backup:

- ✦ You must be in single-user mode to back up your data. To set your system to this mode, go to File ➪ Switch to Single-User Mode.

Note If you do not see this menu option but instead see File ➪ Switch to Multi-User Mode, then you are already in single-user mode.

- ✦ Determine which drive or media (floppy disk, tape, network drive, CD-ROM) you will back up to.
- ✦ Determine whether there is sufficient free space to accommodate the backup.

Determining space requirements for the backup

Before beginning the backup process, you must be sure you have sufficient free space on the target media to accommodate the backed up file. The backup process creates a compressed version of the original data. This means, in effect, that after backing up you will have two versions of your QuickBooks data, one live and one compressed. The compressed version is your backup, and that version should be stored in a safe place apart from your live application.

Because the backed-up version of your QuickBooks data is smaller than the live version, you need less room to store the backup than the space occupied by your live data. You must ensure, however, that you have enough space to accommodate the compressed file or the backup process will fail. This requirement applies even if you back up QuickBooks data to floppy disks. QuickBooks automatically prompts you to insert a new disk if the backup spans more than one disk, but you should be sure you have enough disks to accommodate the entire backup.

You should reserve approximately 10 percent of the space occupied by the live version of your data. To determine the space occupied by your live data, open the QuickBooks program and go to File ➪ Open Company. Find the name of your company in the dialog box that appears. Select the file containing your company and right-click to display the menu shown in Figure 13-1; then select Properties.

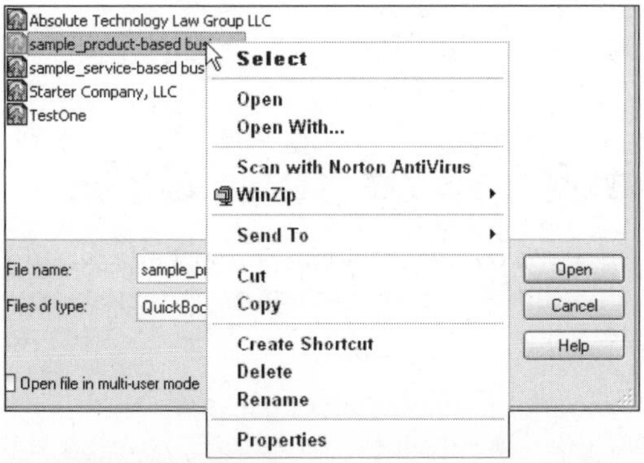

Figure 13-1: Locate your QuickBooks company file in this dialog box.

The Properties dialog box shown in Figure 13-2 appears, which displays the size of the QuickBooks file. In this case, the file is 9.81MB. To exit the Properties dialog box and continue opening the company file, click the X in the upper right-hand corner.

Be sure to monitor the size of your live data on a regular basis, as well as the empty space available on your backup target media. Ensure that you always have sufficient room for the backup. Chances are the one occasion when a backup wasn't completed properly because there was insufficient space will be the one occasion when you really need a backup copy of your data.

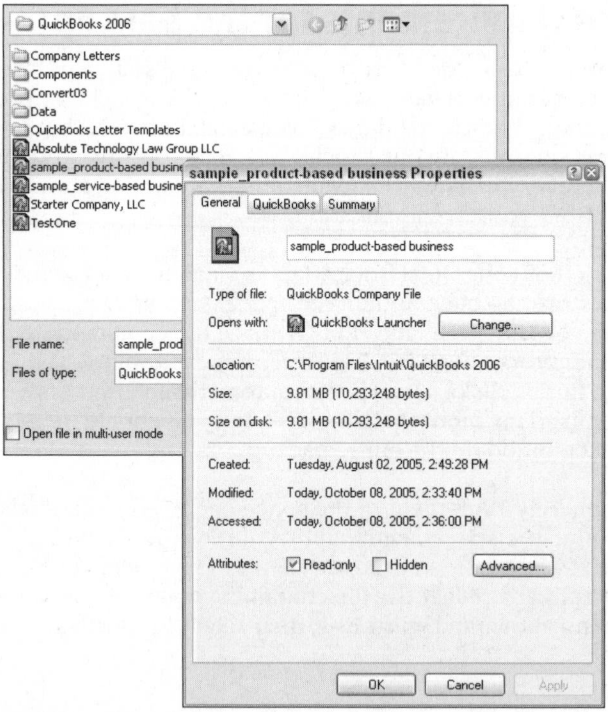

Figure 13-2: The Properties dialog box shows your file size.

Scheduling Regular Backups of Your Data

With QuickBooks you can schedule backups to take place automatically when you close your company file, or you can schedule backups for regular intervals when you know you'll be away from your desk.

Caution You must be in single-user mode to perform either type of backup.

Creating a backup strategy

A question typically raised by users new to backing up critical information is "How often should I back up my data?" The answer is usually related to the frequency with which the data is changed. The more often you change or enter new data in QuickBooks, the more often you should back it up. For example, if you make only a few changes to your data every week, then perhaps backing up every week is sufficient. If you work with QuickBooks every day, entering transactions, invoices, and perhaps downloading balances from your financial institution, then making daily backups should be part of your strategy. This might suggest that the finest granularity for your backups might be daily, but there is nothing to stop you from backing up your QuickBooks data periodically during the day, especially if you have just completed entering a large number of transactions.

You can create any backup routine, but the routine you create should have two characteristics. The routine should be easy to implement, and it should provide you with the greatest protection of your data. Considering these goals, you may want to consider regular backups — daily or weekly — in which you rotate the target media through a predetermined cycle. This means, for example, that if you conduct daily backups, at the end of the week you would have backups for each day of the week, Monday through Friday. When you restart the cycle, perhaps each Monday, you would reuse the target media from the previous cycle, in this case, a week. You can easily apply this system to any frequency you choose. You might also choose to conduct regular backups on a greater frequency than the rotating media system and store the target media offsite. For example, in addition to weekly backups, you might also make monthly backups in which the target media is stored at an offsite storage facility.

Scheduling automatic backups

Configure QuickBooks to initiate backups when you close your company files. Once scheduled, these backups take place by themselves, automatically, and without human intervention, as often as you specify.

To configure QuickBooks to schedule automatic backups, follow these steps:

1. From the File menu, choose Back Up.
2. Click the Schedule a Backup tab to open the Schedule a Backup dialog box, shown in Figure 13-3.
3. Select the Automatically Backup When Closing a Data File check box, and then specify how often you want your data file automatically backed up. (For example, to back up your data file every fifth time you close it, type **5** in the field provided.)
4. Click OK.

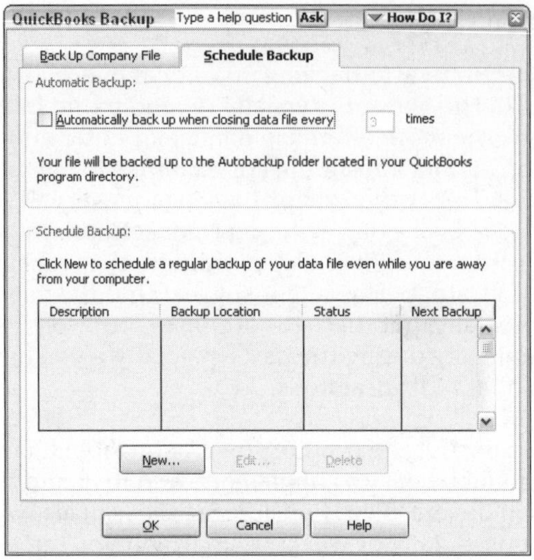

Figure 13-3: Scheduling automatic backups.

Scheduling regular backups

QuickBooks allows you to schedule backups to take place at regular intervals. You may want to key backups to take place at key intervals in your business cycle. Each time your data file is backed up as scheduled, the new backup replaces the oldest one.

Caution

For the backup to take place, the computer you use to run QuickBooks must be on, but the data file you want to back up *cannot* be in use (you can be working in a different data file, though). Be sure to schedule your backups accordingly.

Follow these steps to schedule backups at regular intervals:

1. From the File menu, choose Back Up. Click the Schedule a Backup tab.
2. Click New under Schedule backup to display the Schedule Backup window.
3. Type a description for your scheduled backup. This description will appear in the backup list on the Schedule a Backup tab.
4. Specify a location for your scheduled backup. If necessary, click Browse and navigate to the desired location.

   (Optional) If you want to keep more than one backup, select Number of Backups to Keep and specify how many. For example, if you want to keep three backups, click the Number of Backups to Keep check box and type **3** in the field provided.
5. If you want to keep all backups, make sure Number of Backups to Keep is unchecked.

6. Select the time and day you want your backup to run. (You can select as many days in a week as you want. You can also select whether you want the backup to run every week, every two weeks, and so on, up to every five weeks.)

7. (Optional) Set a password.

Note

The first time you try this procedure in QuickBooks, you may need a user name and password for Windows in order to run the scheduled backup.

8. Click OK.

Restoring Data

Restoring data probably seems like a task that you will never want to have to undertake. Having to restore means, naturally, that you have lost data. Keep in mind, though, that there is a significantly more unpleasant alternative to restoring data, and that alternative is having no backup to restore and having to recreate all your data. So, having to restore data isn't necessarily the worst thing that could happen to you.

When you restore data, you do not necessarily have to overwrite your existing live data. You can create a new file for your company from the backup. This gives you the opportunity to create a new file based on your backup and then compare it to the current version. This way, you can study the changes reflected in your backup before committing to it.

The process of restoring data may be slightly different, depending on whether you've backed up your data on a local drive or have used an online backup service.

Restoring a local backup

Backups are useful only if you can retrieve the data you've backed up. Follow these steps to restore your local backup so you can get back to business-as-usual after a data glitch:

1. If the backup copy is on a removable disk, put the disk in your disk drive. If the backup copy is on several disks, insert the first disk in the disk drive.
2. From the File menu, choose Restore Company Backup to open the Restore Company Backup dialog box shown in Figure 13-4.
3. In the upper section of the window, click Disk; then click Browse to select the location and filename of the backup file.
4. In the lower section, click Browse to select or change the location and filename to which you want to restore your backup file.
5. Click Restore. This uncompresses your backup file and creates a new company file using data from the backup.

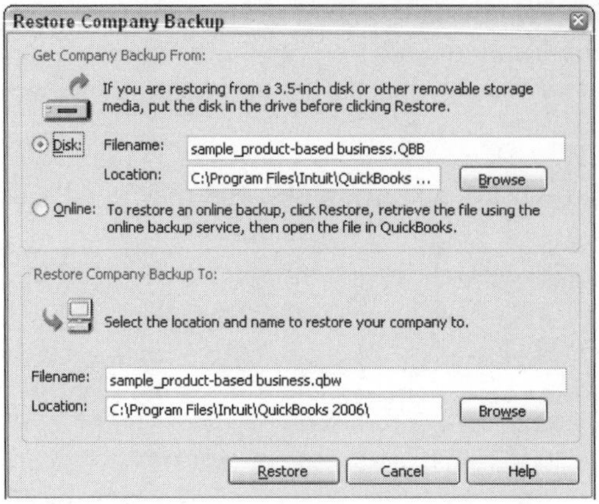

Figure 13-4: Restoring data that has been backed up.

Restoring data backed up with an online service

If you backed up your company file using the online backup service, you must restore it through that same service. To do so, follow these steps:

1. From the File menu, choose Restore.
2. Select Online to restore a company file that you backed up using the Online Backup service.
3. Click Restore and then follow the on-screen directions until you have retrieved the file.
4. From the File menu, select Open Company.
5. Select the file you have retrieved and click Open.

If you are restoring data because of peculiar behavior in your existing QuickBooks company data file, or because the existing company data file is corrupted, do not restore with that file as the target. Instead, create a new file with the same name as your existing company file in a different folder. After the backup file is restored, test the new file. If QuickBooks behaves properly, and if the new company file does not seem to be corrupted and has all of the data you expect, then (and only then) delete the file that was in use before you restored from backup.

Importing Data from Excel

Many companies store financial data in Excel. QuickBooks allows four types of data to be imported: Customer, Vendor, Item, and Account Information. The Excel data must be specially formatted using these column headers.

Preparing Excel data for export

You must format Excel data by type before exporting it to QuickBooks, as follows:

✦ **Customer:** Use the headings and follow the guidelines shown in Table 13-1 to prepare Excel customer data to import to QuickBooks.

Table 13-1
Customer Data

JOB OR CUSTOMER NAME (REQUIRED)	Enter the name of the Customer (and Job, if needed) as it appears in QuickBooks. Example: Kristy Abercrombie: Bathroom Remodel. Note: If you're importing a child (or sub) entry for a parent (or main) entry, the parent entry must already exist in order for the child entry to be imported correctly.
OPENING BALANCE	No "$". Enter the opening balance. You cannot enter an opening balance for an existing customer, only for a new one.
OPENING BALANCE AS OF	Enter a date. The date must be entered as MMDDYYYY. You cannot set an opening balance "as of" date for an existing customer, only for a new one.
COMPANY NAME	Enter a company name, maximum 41 characters long.
SALUTATION	Enter a salutation, such as **Mr.**, **Mrs.**, or **Dr.**
FIRST NAME	Enter the customer's first name.
MIDDLE INITIAL	Enter the customer's middle initial.
LAST NAME	Enter the customer's last name.
CONTACT	Enter the contact name for the customer.
PHONE	Enter the customer's phone number.
FAX	Enter the customer's FAX number.
ALTERNATE PHONE	Enter the customer's alternate phone number.
ALTERNATE CONTACT	Enter the alternate contact name for the customer.
EMAIL	Enter the customer's e-mail address.
BILLING ADDRESS 1 through BILLING ADDRESS 5	Enter the customer's billing address. Maximum length for each field: 41 characters.
SHIPPING ADDRESS 1 through SHIPPING ADDRESS 5	Enter the customer's billing address. Maximum length for each field: 41 characters.

Continued

Table 13-1 *(continued)*	
CUSTOMER TYPE	Enter a QuickBooks customer type.
TERMS	Enter a QuickBooks term.
SALES REP	Enter a QuickBooks sales rep.
PREFERRED SEND METHOD	Enter a QuickBooks preferred send method. Example: E-mail.
TAX CODE	Enter a three-character tax code. To view your tax codes, from the Lists menu, choose Sales Tax Code List.
TAX ITEM	Enter a QuickBooks tax item.
RESALE NUMBER	Enter a resale number.
PRICE LEVEL	Enter a QuickBooks price level.
ACCOUNT NUMBER	Enter an account number, which can contain both letters and numbers.
CREDIT LIMIT	Enter a credit limit.
PREFERRED PAYMENT METHOD	Enter a preferred payment method. To view your choices, from the Lists menu, choose Customer & Vendor Profile Lists and then Payment Method List.
CREDIT CARD	Enter the customer's credit card number, appended with a single quotation mark (').
CREDIT CARD EXPIRATION MONTH	Enter the month as two digits. Example: Enter May as **05**.
CREDIT CARD EXPIRATION YEAR	Enter the year as four digits.
NAME ON CARD	Enter a name.
CREDIT CARD ADDRESS	Enter an address.
CREDIT CARD ZIP CODE	Enter a Zip code.
JOB STATUS	Enter a job status. To view your choices, from the Edit menu, choose Preferences, select Jobs & Estimates in the scroll box, and click the Company Preferences tab.
JOB START DATE	Enter the start date.
JOB PROJECTED END	Enter the projected completion date.
JOB END DATE	Enter the actual end date.
JOB DESCRIPTION	Enter information about the job.
JOB TYPE	Enter a job type. To view your choices, from the Lists menu, choose Customer & Vendor Profile Lists and then Job Type List.
IS INACTIVE	Enter **Yes**, or **No**, **Active**, or **Not-Active**.
NOTE	Enter a note about the customer.

✦ **Vendor:** Use the column headings and follow the guidelines shown in Table 13-2 to prepare Excel vendor data to import to QuickBooks.

Table 13-2
Vendor Data Types

NAME (REQUIRED)	The name of the vendor.
OPENING BALANCE	No $. Opening balances can be set for new vendors only, not existing vendors.
OPENING BALANCE AS OF	Enter a date. The date must be entered as MMDDYYYY. You cannot set an opening balance "as of" date for an existing vendor, only for a new vendor.
COMPANY NAME	Enter a company name, maximum 41 characters long.
SALUTATION	Enter a salutation.
FIRST NAME	Enter the vendor's first name.
MIDDLE INITIAL	Enter the vendor's middle initial.
LAST NAME	Enter the vendor's last name.
ADDRESS 1 through ADDRESS 5	Enter address information; each field can contain a maximum of 41 characters.
CONTACT	Enter the contact name for the vendor.
PHONE	Enter the vendor's phone number.
FAX	The vendor's FAX number.
ALTERNATE PHONE	Enter the vendor's alternate phone number.
ALTERNATE CONTACT	Enter the alternate contact name for the vendor.
EMAIL	Enter the vendor's e-mail address.
PRINT ON CHECK AS	Enter the vendor's name as you'd like it to print on a check. Maximum length: 41 characters.
ACCOUNT NUMBER	Enter the vendor's account number.
VENDOR TYPE	Enter one of the QuickBooks vendor types.
TERMS	Enter one of the QuickBooks terms.
CREDIT LIMIT	Enter the vendor's credit limit.
TAX ID	Enter the vendor's Tax ID number. Maximum length: 9 characters.
VENDOR ELIGIBLE FOR 1099	**Yes** or **No**.
IS INACTIVE	**Yes** or **No**; **Active** or **Not-Active**.
NOTE	Enter a note or to-do for your customer.

✦ **Item:** Use column headings and follow the guidelines shown in Table 13-3 to prepare Excel account data to import to QuickBooks.

Table 13-3
Account Data Types

TYPE (REQUIRED)	The type of account: Accounts payable Accounts receivable Bank Credit card Equity Other expense Other income Expense Fixed asset Income Long-term liability Other asset Other current asset Other current liability
NUMBER	The account number of the account.
NAME (REQUIRED)	The name of an account in your chart of accounts. Note: If you're importing a child (or sub) entry for a parent (or main) entry, the parent entry must already exist in order for the child entry to be imported correctly.
DESCRIPTION	A brief description of the account.
BANK ACCT. NO./ CARD NO./NOTE	The account number of the account.
OPENING BALANCE	The opening balance of the account.
AS OF (DATE)	A date.
REMIND ME TO ORDER CHECKS	When you use the check number you enter here, you'll be reminded to order checks.
TRACK REIMBURSED EXPENSES	Enter **Yes** or **No**.
INCOME ACCOUNT FOR REIMB. EXPENSES	Enter the name of the income account that you use to track the above reimbursed expenses.
IS INACTIVE	Enter **Yes**, **No**, **Active**, or **Not-Active**.
TAX LINE	Specify the tax return form and line of the tax return with which you want this data associated.

✦ **Account Information:** Use the column headings and follow the guidelines shown in Table 13-4 to prepare Excel customer data to import to QuickBooks.

Table 13-4
Item Type Excel Data

TYPE (REQUIRED)	Enter a QuickBooks item type.
NAME (REQUIRED)	Enter the name of the item. If you're importing a child (or sub) entry for a parent (or main) entry, the parent entry must already exist in order for the child entry to be imported correctly.
IS REIMBURSABLE CHARGE	Enter **Yes** or **No**. If the charge is for services performed by someone else, the item type should be **Service Item**. If the charge is for a reimbursable expense, the item type should be **Other charge**.
DESCRIPTION/DESCRIPTON ON SALES TRANSACTION	Enter the description of the item.
TAX CODE	Enter a three-character tax code. To view your tax codes, from the Lists menu, choose Sales Tax Code List.
ACCOUNT/INCOME ACCOUNT (REQUIRED)	Enter an account name.
EXPENSE/COGS ACCOUNT	Enter an expense account name from your chart of accounts. To view the Chart of Accounts, from the Lists menu, choose Chart of Accounts.
ASSET ACCOUNT	Enter an asset account name from your chart of accounts. To view the Chart of Accounts, from the Lists menu, choose Chart of Accounts.
DEPOSIT TO (ACCOUNT)	Enter a bank account name from your chart of accounts. To view the Chart of Accounts, from the Lists menu, choose Chart of Accounts.
DESCRIPTION ON PURCHASE TRANSACTIONS	Enter a text description.
ON HAND	Enter an amount.
COST	Enter an amount.
PREFERRED VENDOR	Enter a vendor's name.
TAX AGENCY	Enter the name of a tax agency from the Vendor list. To view it, from the Lists menu, choose Vendor List.

Continued

Table 13-4 *(continued)*

PRICE/AMOUNT or %/RATE	Enter a price or rate. Keep in mind that you can't use percentages when setting a price for inventory items or items whose expense will be passed on to the customer. In those cases, use dollar amounts.
IS INACTIVE	Enter **Yes**, or **No**, **Active**, or **Not-Active**.
REORDER POINT	When your inventory item reaches this number, QuickBooks will remind you to reorder the item.
TOTAL VALUE	This is for inventory items only. QuickBooks calculates this amount for you by multiplying the number of items on hand by the cost of each item. If you want, you can manually enter a different number.
AS OF (DATE)	Enter a date.
PAYMENT METHOD	Enter a QuickBooks payment method.

Caution

If you are importing an Excel file, you must have Microsoft Excel version 97, 2000, 2002, or 2003.

Mapping the data from your Excel file to QuickBooks

Mapping allows you to specify how you want the information in your Excel file to be imported into QuickBooks. This process allows you to control how each column of information from your spreadsheet appears in QuickBooks.

You can create, edit, and delete mappings. When doing so, you need to map certain required fields in order to save a mapping. Mapping other fields is optional.

To create a new mapping, follow these steps:

1. From the File menu, choose Utilities ➪ Import; then choose Excel Files. The Import a File dialog box appears, as shown in Figure 13-5. Select the Excel file you want to import.
2. Select a sheet. If your worksheet contains only one page, select Sheet 1.
3. From the Choose a Mapping drop-down list, select Add New. Give your new mapping a name in the dialog box that appears.
4. Select an Import type.
5. In the QuickBooks column, select the row of information you want to map.
6. In the Import Data column, using the drop-down button, select which column in the import file should be mapped to the QuickBooks column.
7. Repeat this process until the mapping is complete.

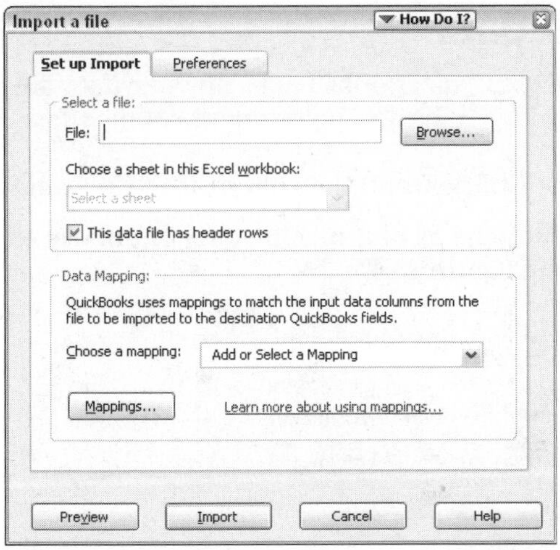

Figure 13-5: Importing data into QuickBooks from an Excel database.

8. Click Save.
9. Click Preview to preview the data you have mapped.
10. From the In Preview Data Show: drop-down list, choose whether you want to see all the data or only the errors. If you select "all data," records that will be imported successfully are marked as "OK." Records that will not be imported successfully are marked as "Error." Additionally, fields that have no corresponding data mapping with show "EMPTY."

Cleaning Up Data

I would like to think that your company would grow and become increasingly prosperous. I would also like to think that this book contributed to that success.

Why clean up data?

As your business grows, it is likely that your QuickBooks application will grow, too. You will add more transactions to your ledger, more lines of accounts receivable data, and more transactions from across your different bank accounts. To create detailed reports, file taxes, and track spending, you need the details of individual transactions.

However, as time passes, you may no longer need these details and all this extra data taking up space. Cleaning up your company data file summarizes the transactions for which you no longer need the details. If you later need to check the details of a transaction, you can restore one of your earlier backup copies or open one of the archive files.

Steps for cleaning up data

Before starting the clean-up process, QuickBooks backs up your data file and creates an archive of your company file. To clean up your data, follow these steps:

1. Go to the File menu, choose Utilities, and then click Clean Up Company Data.
2. Choose to remove all transactions as of a specific date or choose to remove all transactions., as shown in Figure 13-6.

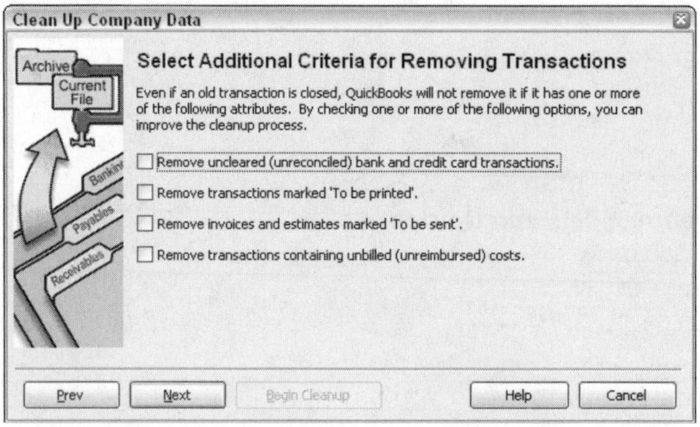

Figure 13-6: QuickBooks offers several clean-up options.

3. Click Next to go to the next screen, shown in Figure 13-7. Choose the items to be removed and click Next.

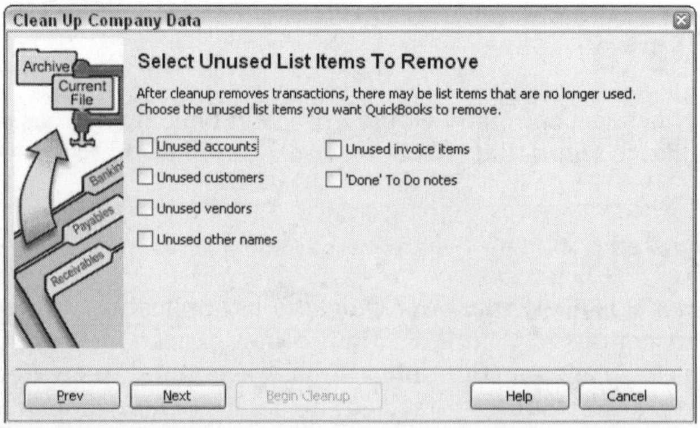

Figure 13-7: Choose items to be removed during the clean-up process on this screen.

4. Click Begin Cleanup when you are sure you want to proceed.

   QuickBooks displays a message stating that it will make a backup file before it removes the transactions. The backup file ensures that you will still have a record of the details of any transactions that QuickBooks deletes from your company file.

5. Click OK to close the message window, and then click Create Back Up.

What happens when you clean up your files?

Only transactions prior to the ending date that you specify during the clean-up process are affected. For example, if your ending date is 12/31/05, all transactions dated 1/1/06 and later remain unchanged in your company file.

Of the transactions dated on or before the ending date, QuickBooks deletes and summarizes only those that have no effect on transactions dated after the ending date.

QuickBooks creates a summary of general journal transactions for the transactions it deletes from your file. You can spot the summary transactions, except for transactions that affect the value of your inventory, by looking for GENJRNL in the Type field of your registers.

There is usually one GENJRNL transaction for each month in which QuickBooks deleted transactions. The transaction amount is the total of the transactions that QuickBooks deleted for the month. For a given month, the register may also show other transactions that QuickBooks did not delete. These are transactions that could be affected by transactions you have yet to enter.

QuickBooks removes all inventory transactions until it finds one that cannot be removed. Any inventory transactions falling after the date of the unremovable transaction will not be removed. Upon finding a transaction that cannot be removed, QuickBooks creates an inventory adjustment reflecting the average cost of items on that date.

Managing Security

If other people work with your financial data in QuickBooks, you may want to establish a security system. This means you can give certain users specific access to certain areas of QuickBooks. For example, if one person in your organization is responsible for accounts receivable, you might allow that person to access only the accounts receivable reports in the system; that person would be unable to see any other parts of the QuickBooks application, such as employee records or cash balances. QuickBooks provides the functionality to help you restrict users' access to areas of the system for which they have no responsibility. Here is the operational model for security in QuickBooks:

- The Administrator of the system creates a user ID and password for each user of the QuickBooks application.
- The Administrator determines what tasks each user should and should not have the rights to accomplish and then assigns those task rights to the appropriate user ID.
- The Administrator provides to each user his or her user ID and password.
- Users log on with the ID and password provided to them and have access only to the functional areas specified for them.

In this section, you learn how to implement and manage security in your QuickBooks application, including each step in the preceding model.

Reviewing the role of the Administrator

In this chapter, there are a number of references to the Administrator. The QuickBooks Administrator is responsible for maintaining the security of QuickBooks and the data associated with it. Many times, the Administrator is also the person who spends the greatest amount of time using QuickBooks, knows QuickBooks the best, most likely is the most computer savvy person in the organization, and probably is the person who installed QuickBooks. As you can tell, you need to specifically identify the Administrator; there probably is a person who is playing the role of the Administrator already. If not, you should designate an Administrator. Every organization in which more than one person uses QuickBooks should designate an Administrator.

Tip In the single-user version of QuickBooks, the single user is the Administrator.

The responsibilities of the QuickBooks Administrator are as follows:

- Create a user ID and password for each user of the application.
- Assign security access for users.

In addition, there are a number of QuickBooks tasks that only the Administrator may complete, including:

- Cleaning up data
- Importing and exporting data
- Using the Interview feature to create a new company
- Backing up data

Reviewing security options

QuickBooks provides a flexible security model. This means that you can specifically define what tasks in QuickBooks each user is allowed to complete. For example, the person who manages accounts receivable (A/R) for your organization, perhaps on a part-time basis, might only have access to A/R reports; that person might not have access to the accounts payable (A/P) reports, purchasing, sensitive financial reports, or your customer list. QuickBooks makes it easy to define a security profile for your users by grouping most functions into logical categories. For example, you can specify that some users have access to checking and credit card functions but not to sales and accounts receivable reports and transactions, and you can do this in just two steps.

The following list describes the options available for securing QuickBooks. The list includes the logical categories just mentioned. For each category of access, you specify whether a user has complete access, no access, or a subset of access rights. This subset is unique to each category. Before adding a user to QuickBooks, review this list and determine what tasks the user will be required to complete. Then assign the appropriate rights for the following categories:

- **Sales and Accounts Receivable:** You may provide a user full access to sales and A/R. For example, you may allow them to enter invoices, create estimates, and enter cash transactions. You may also decide to not allow access to sales and A/R, or access to just certain areas of sales and A/R. You can provide a user the right to create A/R transactions and also run A/R reports; or create transactions, run reports, and also create reports.
- **Purchases and Accounts Payable:** You may provide a user full access to purchases and A/P so that they can enter and pay bills and enter purchase orders. You may deny access to purchases and A/P information, or only allow access to certain purchasing and A/P tasks. You can provide a user the right to create A/P transactions; or create A/P transactions and also run A/P reports; or create transactions, run reports, and also create reports.
- **Checking and Credit Cards:** You may provide a user full access to checking and credit cards, allowing them to write checks, print checks, void checks, mark checks as cleared, enter credit card transactions, enter and pay bills, or enter purchase orders. You can also deny a user's rights to all of these tasks. Last, you can provide a user a subset of these rights.
- **Time Tracking:** You can set access rights to time-tracking activities, such as entering time sheets and running time reports. You can also provide a user with a subset of these rights.
- **Certain Accounting Activities:** You can set access right to some of the most sensitive activities related to your business, such as the transferring of funds, entering and posting journals, and downloading and posting online transactions. You can also provide a user with a subset of these rights.

✦ **Sensitive Financial Reports:** You may set access rights for creating, viewing, printing, and modifying confidential financial reports, such as profit and loss reports, balance sheets, and budgets and plans. Lastly, you can provide a user with a subset of these rights, allowing someone, for example, to create reports only, or to both create and print reports.

✦ **Change or Delete Transactions:** You can specify whether a user has the right to change or delete transactions in areas to which they have access such as A/R. Providing a user the access to delete or change these transactions gives the user the ability to make significant changes to your ledger. On the other hand, if a user with no rights to change or delete the transactions makes a mistake, that user has no ability to correct it.

✦ **Change or Delete Transactions Recorded before Closing Date Transactions:** You can specify whether a user has the right to change or delete transactions with a date previous to the closing date in areas to which they have access such as A/R.

Adding users to QuickBooks

To take advantage of QuickBooks' capability to allow multiple users to perform different tasks in the application, you must add users to the application. This means that you must add a user ID for each user, specify a password, and then define the new user's access rights. QuickBooks requires a few preliminary steps before you actually add the first user. You must first:

1. Switch QuickBooks to multi-user mode. (Go to File ⇨ Switch to multi-user mode.)
2. Create the Administrator ID and password.

You have the opportunity take a look at the two preliminary steps in the next two sections. Then, you will be walked through the steps required to add a user to QuickBooks.

Multi-user mode

By default, QuickBooks is not configured for multiple users. This means that only one user at a time can open the QuickBooks company data file. To allow multiple users access to QuickBooks, as well as to secure the QuickBooks application, you must install and configure QuickBooks for multi-user use. Certain tasks, though, require the application to be set in single-user mode. These tasks include condensing data and backing up data. QuickBooks makes it easy to switch between single-user and multi-user modes.

To switch QuickBooks to multiple user use, open the File menu. If the second choice reads Switch to Single-user Mode, then QuickBooks is already set for multiple user use. Otherwise, choose Switch to Multi-user Mode. A message appears when QuickBooks is ready for multiple user use. Click OK. Switching to multi-user mode has an effect on your application; that is, for as long as the application is in multi-user mode, users must supply a user name and password to open the company data file. It makes sense to add access rights for a few users as soon as you switch to multi-user mode, if you haven't done so already.

To switch QuickBooks to single-user use, open the File menu. If the second choice reads Switch to Multi-user Mode, then QuickBooks is already set for single-user use. Otherwise, choose Switch to Single-user Mode. A message appears when QuickBooks is ready for single user use. Click OK.

Creating the Administrator ID and password

Before any security work is allowed in QuickBooks, the Administrator must have a user ID and a password. Before you can add users, QuickBooks forces you to supply this information, if you haven't done so already. The prompts to supply this information appear automatically under these two conditions:

✦ When you answer Yes to the prompt to add users to QuickBooks, which appears after you switch to multi-user mode for the first time

✦ When you choose Company Menu ➪ Set Up Users

The prompts appear in the Set Up QuickBooks Administrator dialog box (see Figure 13-8). Enter the name of the Administrator in the Administrator's Name box. Do not use a proper name, such as Don or Sandy, because another person may take over the role of the Administrator. Instead, use a name such as Admin, which is the default, or Administrator. You may use up to 29 alphanumeric characters.

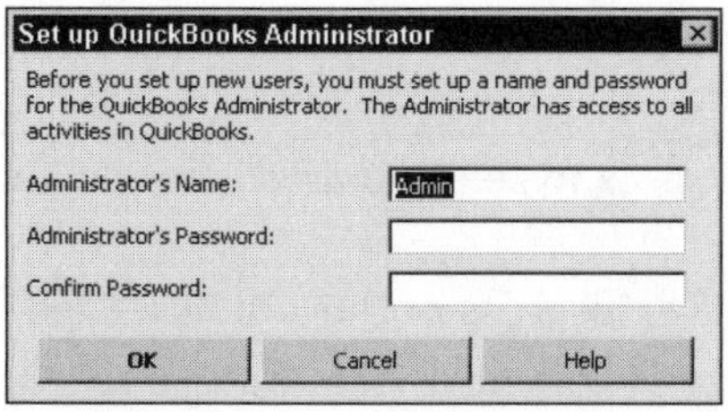

Figure 13-8: This dialog box prompts you for an Administrator logon name, as well as a password.

Enter a password in the password field. It is not a requirement to use a password, but not doing so means any user can access QuickBooks as the Administrator and gain unrestricted access to the application. You may use a maximum of 16 alphanumeric characters. After you have entered your password, re-enter it in the Confirm Password field. Doing so associates the user ID with the password.

Steps for adding a QuickBooks user

The following steps walk you through the process of adding a QuickBooks user:

Note Only an Administrator can add a new user.

1. From the Company menu, choose Users, then Setup Users and Roles. The Set Up Quick Books Administrator dialog box appears for the administrator to enter their name and password.
2. Select the User List tab, and then click New. The User List dialog box appears.
3. Click the Add User button.
4. Enter the name of the person in the User Name field, as shown in Figure 13-9.

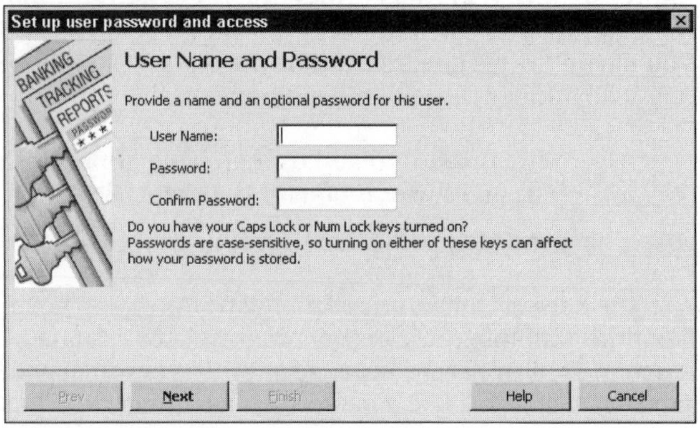

Figure 13-9: Entering a new user.

5. Enter a password first in the Password field and then in the Confirm Password field. Click Next.
6. Choose whether this person will have access to selected areas of QuickBooks or all areas of QuickBooks. Click Next.
7. If you want to grant the new user access to all areas of QuickBooks, click Yes to confirm that you want this person to have full access. Then click Finish to complete the setup process.
8. If you are selecting the areas the user has access to, make your selections on each screen that appears. Click Next to go to the next screen.
9. When the last screen appears, review the table that summarizes the access rights you granted. If you need to make a change, click Prev to return to the appropriate screen.
10. Click Finish to complete the setup process.

Changing User Access and Deleting Users

There may come a time when you want to change the access rights assigned for a user, or perhaps even delete the user. There also may come a time when you just want to view the user's currently assigned rights. The following options are available from the New Users dialog box, which is available to Administrators only and appears when you choose Company Menu ➪ Choose Users ➪ Setup Users and Roles:

✦ To change the rights assigned to a user, choose the user and then choose Edit User. The process described in the "Steps for adding a QuickBooks user" section begins.

✦ To delete a user, click the name and choose Delete User.

✦ To view a user's access rights, choose the name of the user and then choose View User.

Changing a password

There may come a time when you or one of the users of your QuickBooks application may need to change a password. In fact, it is probably a good policy to require users to change their password on a regular basis, perhaps every one to three months. Follow these steps to change a password:

1. Be sure QuickBooks is in multi-user mode. Next, choose Company Menu ➪ Users ➪ Set Up Users.
2. The Change Password dialog box appears. Enter the existing password in the Enter Old Password box, and then enter and reenter the new password.
3. Click OK.

Summary

Though not specifically a part of the financial process, managing the data in your QuickBooks application is a critical task. You must take the time to back up data, condense it, manage the security that protects it, and complete the chores of loading and extracting data when you need to.

✦ When your application becomes so large that performance is affected, condense data to remove all of the detail as of a date that you specify. QuickBooks creates a closing transaction that captures the balance as of the date you specify.

✦ To add multiple users to your QuickBooks application, you must switch to multi-user mode. In multi-user mode, you define which users have the security rights to see certain data and complete certain tasks.

✦ You can import data about customers, items, sales, and vendors into QuickBooks from Excel, if you follow specific formatting conventions.

✦ Back up data on a regular basis. Establish a formal backup procedure and then secure the backed up media in a safe, offsite location.

✦ ✦ ✦

CHAPTER 14

Recording Sales Transactions and Creating Sales Forms

✦ ✦ ✦ ✦

In This Chapter

Overview of sales forms

Recording and tracking customer sales

Extending customer credit: statements versus invoices

Issuing invoices

Billing customers with statements

Sales tax

Nonposting transactions: finance charges and packing slips

Tools for managing and editing sales forms

✦ ✦ ✦ ✦

Most businesses have identifiable transaction cycles, which define the steps they take in servicing customers, recording customer transactions, and realizing revenue from customer-related activities. These changes are reflected on invoices, sales, credit memos, purchase orders, statements, and estimates. In the aggregate, these forms are referred to as sales forms in QuickBooks, regardless of whether you provide goods or services to your customers. Sales forms document the important communications you have with your customers during the course of a transaction and are critical to your accounting records as well as your relationship with your customers.

How QuickBooks Helps You with Each Customer Transaction Cycle

In QuickBooks, the steps in the customer transaction cycle are approximated on the Customer section of the Navigator screen, shown in Figure 14-1. Icons on the screen represent significant accounting events in each customer transaction, such as providing customers with estimates, creating invoices, and receiving payments.

Estimates are the first step in the customer transaction cycle for companies that provide them. The estimate feature is available only in the Pro, Premier, and Enterprise Solutions editions.

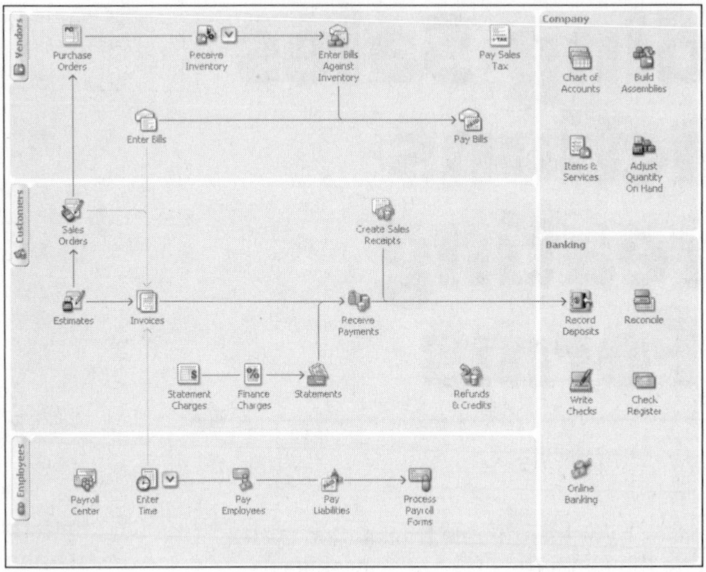

Figure 14-1: Icons in the Customer section of the Navigator screen represent events in the customer transaction cycle.

An *estimate* is a document that establishes certain expectations between you and the customer within an agreed-upon range of certainty. Estimates differ from final bills because they are not intended to reflect the final amount that will be billed, only to inform the customer of an approximation of this amount.

To create an estimate, you must first make sure the QuickBooks estimate feature is turned on. Only the administrator can do this. To activate the estimates feature, perform the following steps:

1. From the Edit menu, choose Preferences. Select Jobs & Estimates in the scroll box, and then click the Company Preferences tab. The Preferences dialog box shown in Figure 14-2 appears.
2. Click Yes in response to Do You Create Estimates?
3. To have QuickBooks warn you when you try to record an estimate with the same number as an existing estimate, select the Warn about Duplicate Estimate Numbers check box.
4. If you do progress invoicing, do the following:
   - Make sure Yes is selected in response to Do You Do Progress Invoicing?
   - Specify whether you want line items that have zero amounts to print on your progress invoice.
5. Click OK.

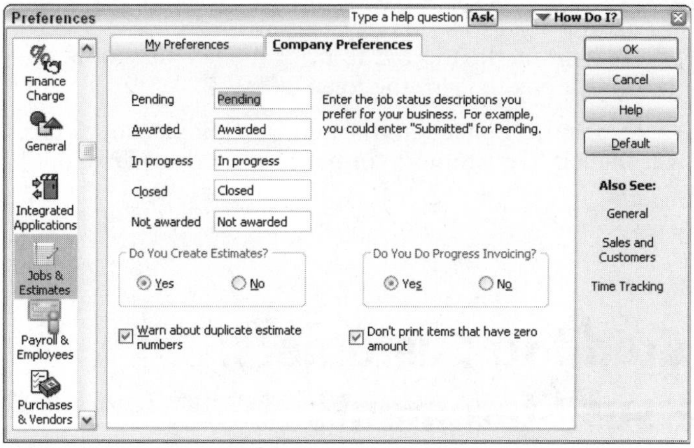

Figure 14-2: The Jobs & Estimates Preferences dialog box.

To create a customer estimate, follow these steps:

1. Make sure the estimates feature is turned on.
2. From the Customers menu, choose Create Estimates. The Proposal window shown in Figure 14-3 appears.

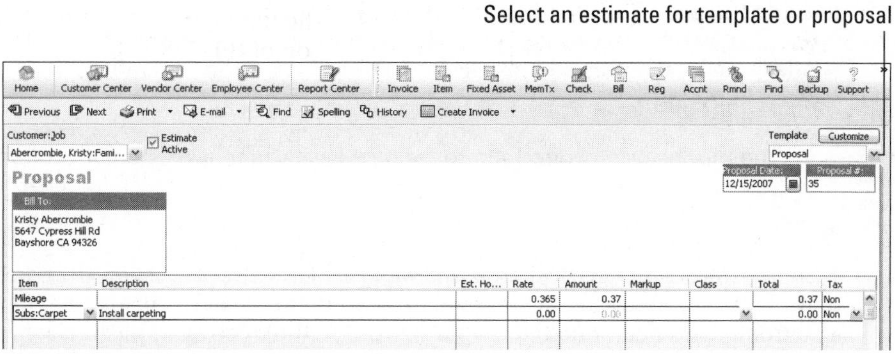

Figure 14-3: Creating estimates.

3. Enter the name of the client or project (Customer:Job).
4. Enter the name of the customer or job by selecting it from the Customer:Job drop-down list or by selecting Add New.
5. Select a template. You can select Custom Change Order, Custom Estimate, Proposal, Quote, or Retail Estimate from the drop-down template menu.
6. Enter the line items.

7. Apply sales tax (if applicable).
8. (Optional) Click Print on the toolbar to print the estimate now, or select the To Be Printed check box to print the form later.
9. (Optional) Select the To Be Mailed through QuickBooks check box to have your invoices mailed to customers through a service (Deluxe Billing or Basic Billing).
10. Click Print.

Extending Credit to Customers: Invoices versus Statements

Whenever a customer does not pay for goods or services at the time of delivery, you are extending some form of credit to the customer. The transaction itself is referred to as a *credit sale*, and it takes place in two steps: delivery (or performance) and payment. When your company provides goods or services to the customer, you may specify the terms of payment on an invoice, on a statement, or in a separate written contract.

It is important to grasp the distinction between invoices and statements. Invoices reflect the price and quantity of goods or services that you sell on a given date and which may be delivered in the future. For example, a vendor selling supplies may provide the goods at the time the invoice is issued, or the supplier may place an order to a warehouse for inventory to be delivered to customers at a future date. Similarly, a contractor may invoice a customer for a remodeling job to be performed in the future.

Cross-Reference

You may use an invoice form to create a legally binding customer contract, as discussed in Chapter 33.

A billing statement (just called a *statement* by QuickBooks) is another document that identifies charges to a customer. A statement always reflects past charges that a customer has accumulated over a period of time. For example, a law firm might issue a statement for services performed in the past month. QuickBooks presumes that you use invoices, rather than statements, when sales taxes or discounts are applied. Service companies such as doctors, dentists, and consultants primarily use statements because sales taxes are not generally imposed on such services.

You might also opt to use a combination of invoices and statements for billing your customers. For example, you may issue an invoice at the outset of the transaction to memorialize contractual terms — quantity, price, time and place of delivery, and payment. You may follow up by sending the customer reminder statements as to invoiced items provided in the past. QuickBooks automatically tracks the information necessary to create reminder statements. Table 14-1 provides a useful summary of considerations for deciding whether you should use invoices or statements.

Table 14-2
When to Use an Invoice versus a Statement

Requirement	*Use Invoice*	*Use Statement*
Need detailed records of items sold	X	
Charge sales tax	X	
Apply item discounts	X	
Bill at time of sale	X	
Bill at completion of job		X
Bill at regular intervals regardless of completion		X
Have mostly ongoing customer relationships		X
Have many non-repeat customers	X	
Bill for hourly services only		X

Creating Invoices

Invoices document credit sales and are issued either at the time a customer places an order or at the time goods and services are provided. For example, a contractor might invoice a client at the time a remodeling job is requested. In turn, the paint store might invoice its contractor or client for 10 gallons of paint picked up in the course of doing a job. Invoiced transactions differ from cash sales in that payment does not always occur at the time of delivery. Invoiced transactions require separate accounting entries for delivery and payment.

Creating an invoice is a very important accounting event that impacts your QuickBooks accounts and financial statements in the following four ways:

- The Accounts Receivable account increases by the amount of the invoice.
- The new invoice appears in the Open Invoices report.
- The items on the invoice are tracked in the Sales by Item Summary report.
- The income from the items shows in your Profit and Loss Statement.

Tip

QuickBooks Help contains a four-minute tutorial on creating a database. You can locate the tutorial by going to Help ⇨ QuickBooks Help and searching the index under the topic "Creating an Invoice."

To create an invoice, follow these steps:

1. From the Customers menu, choose Create Invoices, and then select the name of the customer.
2. Fill in the name of the customer or job.

   If the customer you choose has outstanding estimates (as the example shows), you must choose an estimate. This allows QuickBooks to raise questions about progress billing with a second menu as shown in Figure 14-4. To close this menu, click Cancel. QuickBooks asks you to update the progress of your billing (see Figure 14-5). The screen shown in Figure 14-6 appears.
3. Select a template for the invoice form from the drop-down menu.
4. In the detail area, enter the line items.
5. Apply sales tax (if applicable).
6. (Optional) Enter a message for your customer in the Customer Message field from the list that is provided.
7. (Optional) Enter a memo for this sale. The memo is displayed on the screen, on sales reports, and on reminder statements.
8. (Optional) Click Print on the toolbar to print the invoice now, or select the To Be Printed check box to print the form later.

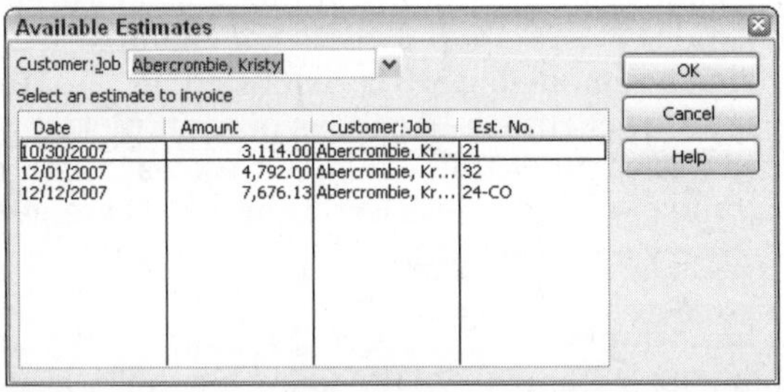

Figure 14-4: QuickBooks prompts you to relate your billing to outstanding estimates, when appropriate.

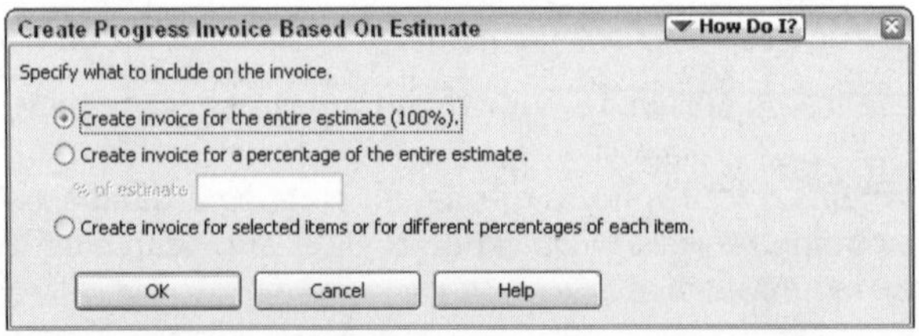

Figure 14-5: QuickBooks asks you to update the progress of your billing.

Select a template

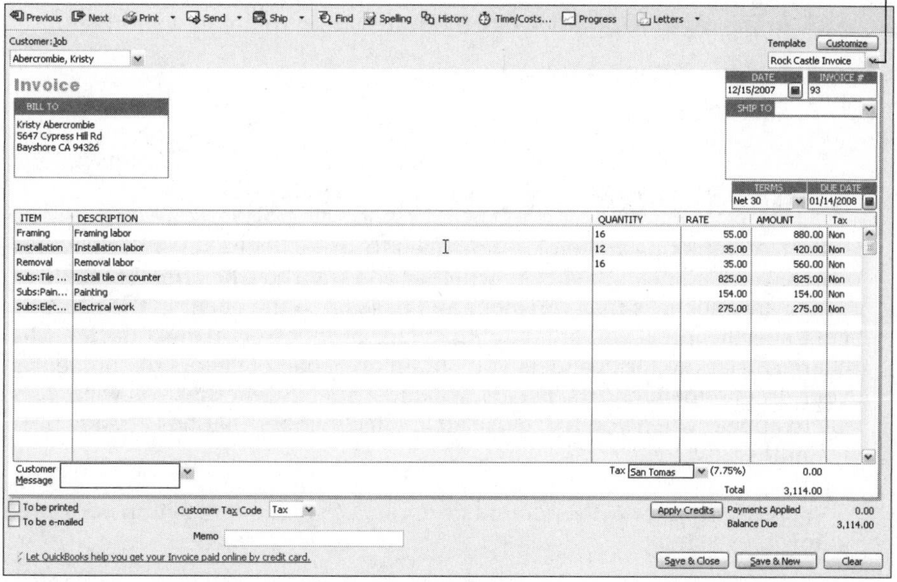

Figure 14-6: Use this screen to create your invoice.

9. (Optional) Select the To Be E-Mailed check box to have the invoice e-mailed to the customer.
10. (Optional) Select the To Be Mailed through QuickBooks check box to have your invoices mailed to customers through a service (Deluxe Billing or Basic Billing).
11. Save the invoice.
12. Click Save & Close or Save & New to create another invoice.

Editing customer and sales transactions

You can edit the information that appears on invoices and sales receipts. The procedure varies slightly depending on whether you have deposited or undeposited funds.

To edit a prior sales transaction, follow these steps:

1. From the Lists menu, choose Chart of Accounts.
2. Double-click the account that you want to edit. In the account register, perform one of the following actions:
   - For an invoice, double-click Accounts Receivable.
   - For a sales receipt (if you have not deposited the payment), double-click Undeposited Funds. Scroll to find transactions of type RCPT.

- For a sales receipt (if you have deposited the payment), open the register for the account where you deposited the payment.

3. In the register, double-click the transaction that you want to edit.
4. Edit the form as necessary.
5. Save the changes.

Setting the correct invoice preferences

Prior to completing an invoice, you need to specify your sales and customers preferences. You also need to specify whether you want to track reimbursable expenses, which are expenses that you incur and pass on to the client in the course of performing a specific job. If you are reimbursed for products, you must decide whether to charge a markup for products you obtain on behalf of clients to compensate you for your procurement efforts. Finally, you must specify whether you want a special warning to appear when you try to use an invoice number that has already been assigned to another invoice.

To access the Sales & Customers Preferences screen and set up your preferences, follow these steps:

1. Go to Edit ➪ Preferences. Click the Sales & Customer icon on the scroll bar and then click the Company Preferences tab. The Sales & Customer Preferences screen appears as shown in Figure 14-7.

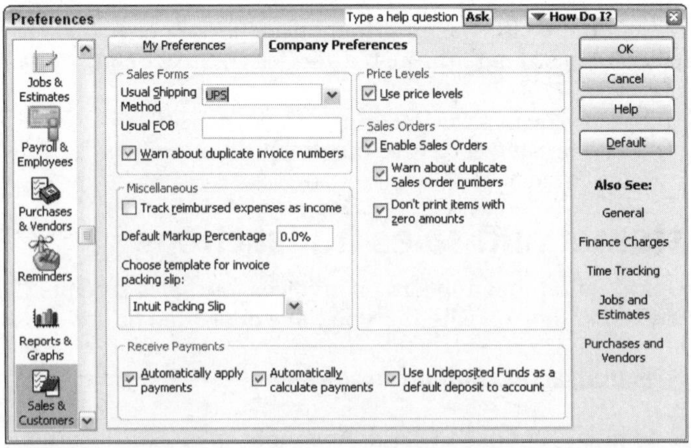

Figure 14-7: You can specify shipping methods, track reimbursed expenses, and enter a default markup percentage when these options are applicable to your business.

2. If you aren't using the product invoice, skip to step 3. If you are, indicate your usual shipping method. You may select a method from the drop-down list or enter a new one.
3. Indicate at what point legal ownership of the goods shifts from seller to buyer using the FOB field.
4. Indicate whether you want the system to warn you about duplicate invoice numbers.
5. Check the Track Reimbursed Expenses as Income check box if you want this option; otherwise, leave it blank.
6. Enter a default markup percentage if your company customarily charges a markup on reimbursed products or services.
7. (Optional) Select additional options.
8. Click OK to save your changes.

Billing Clients with Statements

Some businesses bill customers on a regular and periodic basis. Law firms and consulting firms are a good example. Generally, these professional service firms issue monthly statements for all time spent on client matters during the previous month. Another example is a health club, which bills members for monthly dues and amenities such as meals or equipment rental fees. To bill customers by statement, you need to learn how to enter statement charges and how to generate and print statements.

Entering statement charges

You enter statement charges in a Customer register. The Customer register displays all accounts receivable transactions for a specific customer or job. You enter each item as a separate charge on a statement and appears as a separate register entry. To enter a statement charge, follow these steps:

1. From the Navigator screen (home page) click the Customer icon, and then click the Customers & Jobs tab. Go to Lists ➪ Customer:Job List. The Customer:Job List appears as shown in Figure 14-8.
2. Choose the customer and job you want to charge from the list.
3. Click the New Transactions menu button at the bottom and select Enter Statement Charges from the drop-down list. A register window appears as shown in Figure 14-9.
4. Go to the end of the register by scrolling down and clicking in the blank field after the last entry. The register appears with the date in the first blank line highlighted.

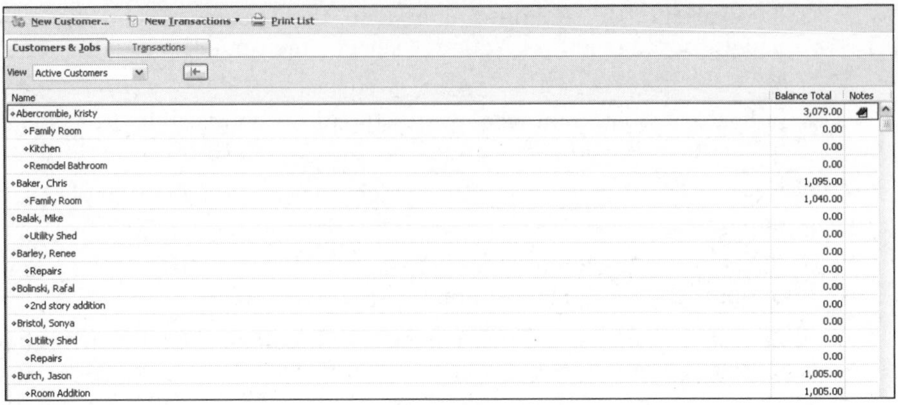

Figure 14-8: Use the Customer:Job List to locate customers to whom you want to issue statements.

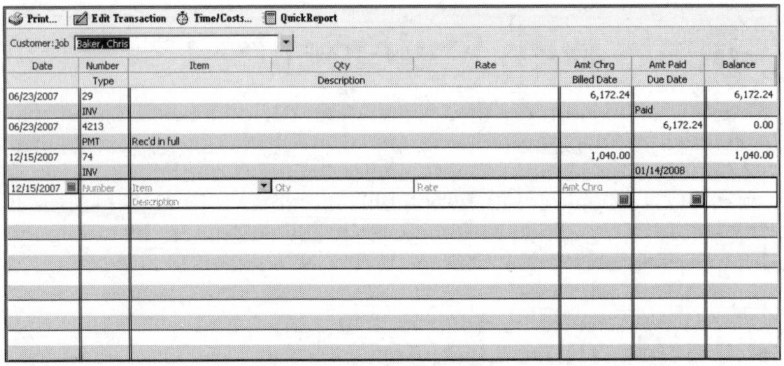

Figure 14-9: Use Customer registers to enter statement charges.

5. Enter the date of the charge if not the current date (QuickBooks fills in the current date by default).
6. Enter the charge number (if applicable).
7. Enter the Item and Quantity. QuickBooks will automatically complete the Rate, Description, and Charge fields based on previously stored information about the Item.
8. Click Record to record the charge and post it to the Customer register.

If you enter statement charges for reimbursable job costs or time, follow these steps:

1. From the Navigator screen (home page) click the Customer icon, then click the Customers & Jobs tab. Choose the customer you want to charge from the list.
2. Go to Edit ➪ Use Register. Click the Time/Costs button to enter the charge for all job costs previously charged, including Items, Time, and Other Expenses and Mileage previously assigned.
3. Indicate whether you want to use the current date to reflect each reimbursed expense or the actual date from the table of each charge.
4. Click OK to add the reimbursed expenses to the Customer:Job register.
5. Click Record to finish.

Creating and printing a customer statement

In addition to reflecting all charges to a specific customer or job, the Customer register discloses which ones have been billed and the date of the billing. Additionally, QuickBooks automatically determines when payment is due based on the payment terms you have previously entered on the statement.

To create and print a statement, follow these steps:

1. Go to Customers ➪ Create Statements. The window shown in Figure 14-10 appears.

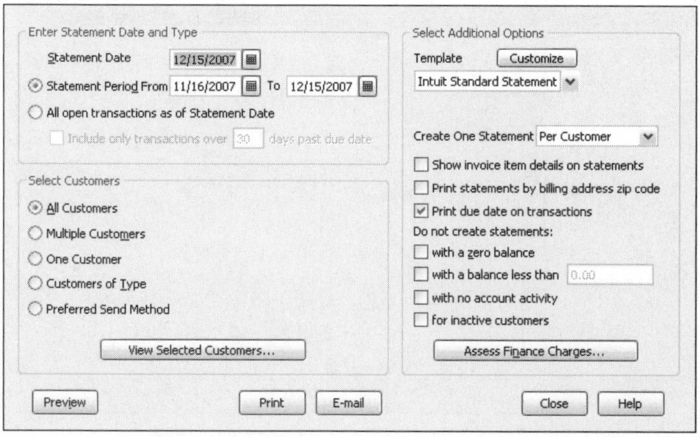

Figure 14-10: Create and print statements from this window.

2. Enter the date for this statement if different from the last date in the date range.
3. Enter the date range in the appropriate fields (by default, QuickBooks prints statements from the date of the last statement printed).
4. Indicate whether you want to prepare an invoice for all open transactions or just those transactions falling within a specific date range.
5. In the Create One Statement field, indicate whether your want to create one statement per customer or per job.
6. Indicate whether you want to print invoice details on your statements.
7. Indicate whether you want to print statements by billing address or zip code, and whether you want to print the due date on your invoices by selecting the appropriate check boxes.
8. Indicate whether you want to suppress statements with a balance less than a certain amount or with no customer activity.
9. If you want to assess finance charges, click the Assess Finance Charges button to access the dialog box shown in Figure 14-11. Identify the customers for whom you want to assess finance charges by clicking in the Assess column, and then click Assess Charges to exit the dialog box. If customers have unapplied finance charges, a box pops up informing you of that fact and suggesting that you apply payments before creating the statement.

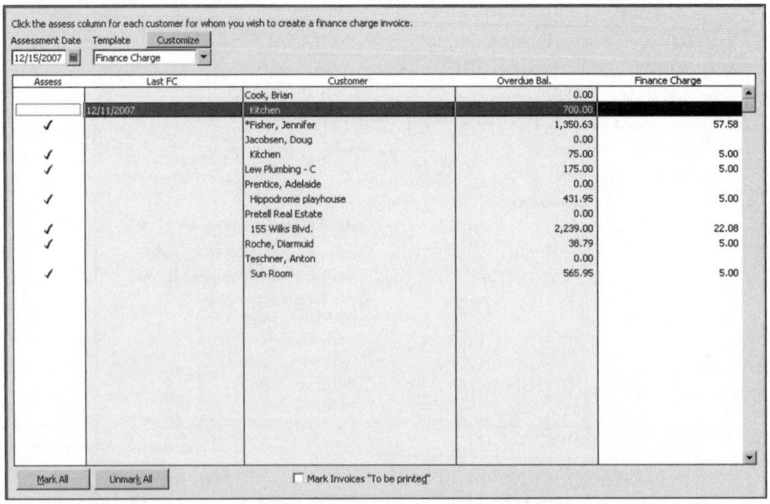

Figure 14-11: Use this dialog box to assess finance charges.

10. Choose the printer name and type and the paper type, and select whether to print lines around each field. Indicate the number of copies.

11. Click Print.

Cash versus accrual accounting in sales transactions

In Chapter 7, you learned that a transaction in which a customer pays for goods or services at the time of delivery or performance is called a *cash sale*. Delivery and payment occur simultaneously; there is no need to send bills or maintain accounts receivable. A receipt issued at the time of sale documents the entire transaction. Payment may be in the form of cash, check, or credit card.

In contrast, a credit sale is a two-step transaction. Delivery of goods or services is the first step, and payment is the second step. An invoice or statement reflects the delivery or performance.

Cross-Reference Payments are recorded at a later date, as discussed in Chapter 17.

It is important not to confuse the term *cash sale* with the terms *cash-basis accounting* and *accrual accounting*, which were introduced in Chapter 4. Cash sale describes how a single transaction is handled. On the other hand, cash-basis accounting identifies the method by which a company reports all of its transactions on its Profit and Loss Statement. As you may recall from Chapter 4, cash-basis companies do not recognize a transaction until a payment (for example, cash) is actually made or received by the company. In contrast, an accrual-based accounting system recognizes a transaction at the time a legal right or obligation to payment arises.

Both cash-basis and accrual accounting systems recognize cash sales, but only an accrual-based accounting system recognizes all types of credit sales. For example, cash-basis and accrual systems treat the issuance of an invoice in dramatically different ways. An *invoice* is a form used to document a sale for which payment will occur at a later date. An invoice documents both a company's legal obligation to provide goods and/or services and its legal right to a payment. Issuance of an invoice is a recognizable accounting event for accrual companies, but it is not necessarily a recognizable accounting event for cash-based accounting systems. Accrual systems recognize and record an accounting event as having occurred at the time the rights to payment and delivery arose. Cash-based companies recognize an accounting event only to the extent that there has been a reduction in inventory or a payment along with the issuance of the invoice. Table 14-2 summarizes how cash and accrual accounting systems recognize cash sales, invoices, and statements.

Table 14-2
Cash versus Accrual Recognition

	Cash	*Accrual*
Cash sale	Y	Y
Invoice	N	Y
Statement	N	N

In accounting, regardless of whether the term cash is used to describe an entire accounting system or a single event, it is used synonymously with payment by credit card or check. These forms of payment — cash, credit card, and check — are referred to as *cash equivalents*. For accounting purposes, the dollar value and legal rights associated with cash equivalents are assumed to be identical to the value and rights associated with payment in actual dollars.

Recording and Tracking Customer Payments

QuickBooks allows you to easily record all types of customer payments and quickly allocate them to one or more invoices, including payments for sales that have not previously been invoiced. The Receive Payments window, shown in Figure 14-12, allows you to enter specific information about each payment.

To enter a customer payment, follow these steps:

1. Go to Customers ➪ Receive Payments (or click the Receive Payments icon on your Customer Navigator screen). The Receive Payments window shown in Figure 14-12 appears.
2. Select an option for the Received From field from the drop-down list, or choose Add New from the Received From drop-down list to set up a new job if you are tracking by the job. After you select the customer, a list of unpaid invoices appears in the window.
3. Enter the amount and select a payment method from the drop-down menu. QuickBooks allows you to select cash, check, barter, or credit card methods of payment.

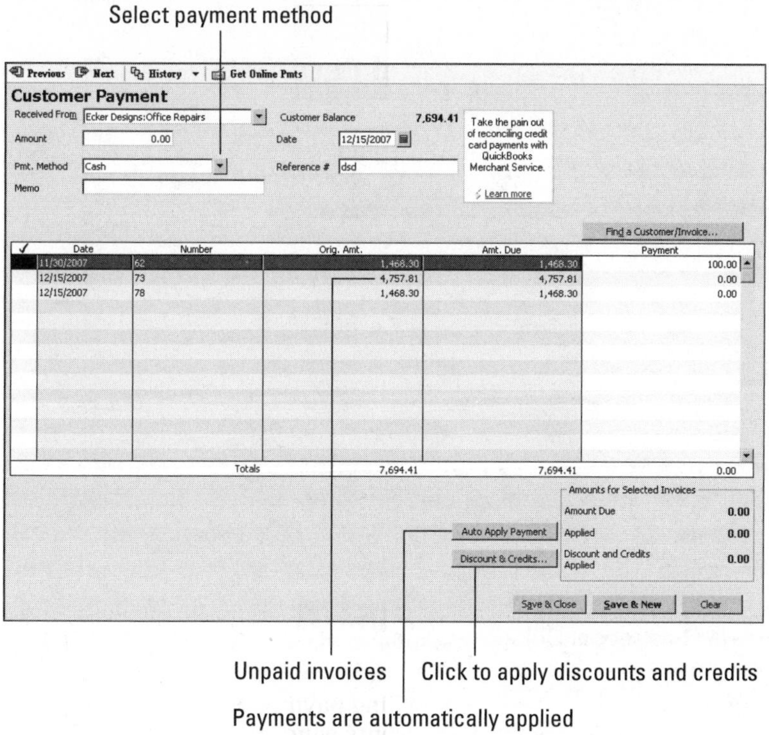

Figure 14-12: Use this window to record customer payments.

4. Select each invoice you want to pay, one at a time, and indicate the amount of the payment to be applied to each invoice in the Payment column. The payment will automatically be applied if the Auto Apply Payment button is displayed. To reverse the transaction, click the Auto Apply button to display the Un-Apply Payment button, as shown in Figure 14-13.
5. Click Auto Apply Payment if you want to apply the payment to each outstanding invoice.
6. Enter the date in the Date field. Today's date is filled in as the default.
7. If your company uses a reference number for its internal billing purposes, enter it in the Reference # field.

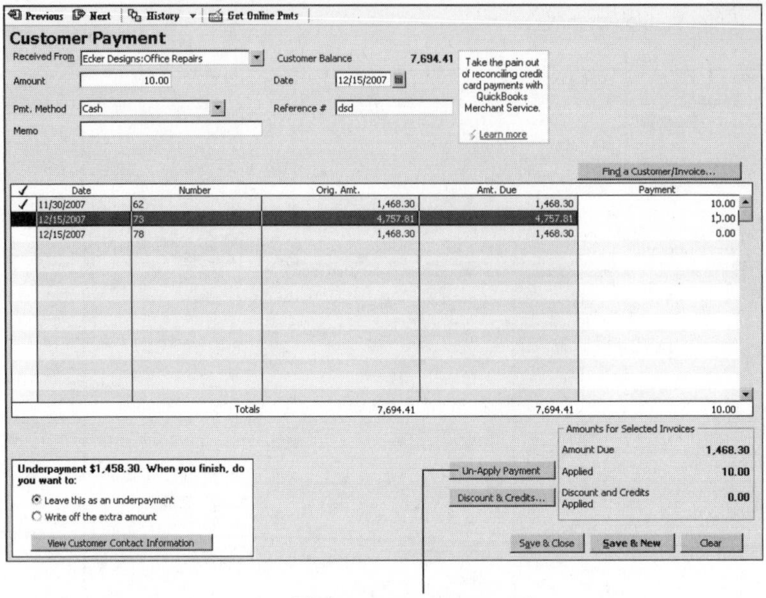

Figure 14-13: This special QuickBooks window is used to record information about payments received.

8. If your company offers discounts, click the Discounts & Credits button and enter the information in the dialog box that appears.
9. Click Save & Close. QuickBooks records the customer payments and adjusts the accounts receivable and outstanding invoice balances accordingly.

What if you have an overage or shortage in cash receipts on a given day when you compare the number of items sold to the amount of money you should have taken in for the items? To track these annoying but inevitable discrepancies, set up a special Item and corresponding income account for each of them — one Item called Cash Overages and one called Cash Shortages.

Caution

Chapter 10 mentioned that whenever you create an Item, you must specify a corresponding income or expense account to track the Item. If you are creating a new account, you must establish it before setting up the Item. Both the overages and shortages accounts will be set up as income accounts, but you will enter only negative amounts in the shortages accounts.

To set up an account for overages and shortages, follow these steps:

1. From the Lists menu, select Chart of Accounts.
2. From the Account menu button, choose New.
3. Create an Income account called Discrepancies. Click OK.
4. Create two new income subaccounts — Overages and Shortages — for the Discrepancies account, following step 2 above.

To set up overage and shortage items, follow these steps:

1. From the Lists menu, choose Item List.
2. From the Item menu button, choose New.
3. Create a noninventory part Item called Overages, and assign it to your Overages subaccount.
4. Decide whether you want to mark this Item as taxable. If marked as taxable, this amount appears on your sales tax liability report. Click Next.
5. Create a noninventory part Item called Shortages, and assign it to your Shortages subaccount.
6. Decide whether you want to mark this Item as taxable. If marked as taxable, this amount appears on your sales tax liability report.
7. Click OK.

Activating Sales Taxes

This section discusses how to set your preferences for how QuickBooks handles sales taxes.

Cross-Reference

Sales taxes are specifically addressed in Chapter 23. If you have difficulty answering any of the questions required to activate the appropriate preferences at this point or aren't even sure which preferences are activated, go to Chapter 23 for an explanation.

To activate the sales tax preference, follow these steps:

1. Go to Edit ➪ Preferences. The screen shown in Figure 14-14 appears.
2. Select the Sales Tax icon from the scroll box on the left and click the Company Preferences tab.
3. In response to the questions that appear on the screen, indicate whether you charge sales tax, how often you pay sales tax to the appropriate government agency, and whether you show sales tax obligations as a liability on your books on a cash basis (as of payment date) or an accrual basis (invoice date).

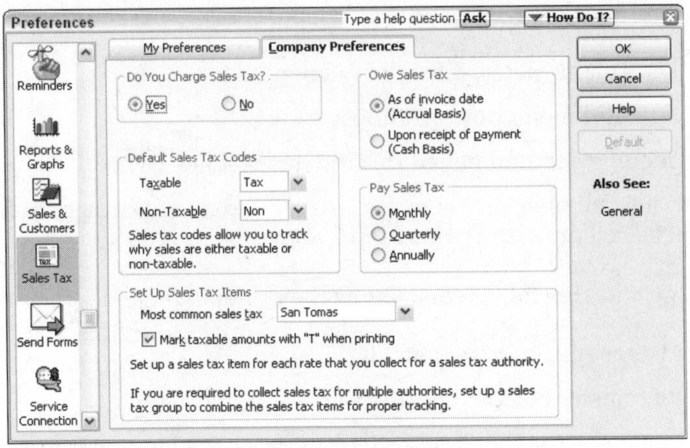

Figure 14-14: Use this screen to set up the sales tax preferences that appear on all customer sales forms.

4. In the Most Common Sales Tax drop-down menu, indicate the locality in which your company most often does business. This will be the default used for computing sales tax.
5. Indicate in the check box at the bottom of the screen whether you want to print a T next to each taxable Item on an invoice or sales form. (This is probably most useful on the service invoice in which you enter both products subject to sales tax and services that are not.)
6. Click OK to save your changes and exit this window.

Note

QuickBooks allows you to specify special preferences for reporting and collecting sales tax from the screen previously shown in Figure 14-14.

Finance Charges

Finance charges are another preference item that you must activate prior to issuing invoices and statements. You need to decide on an appropriate interest rate and on a minimum assessment. You also need to make a customer-relations decision about whether to allow a grace period before assessing finance charges on late payments or not. Later, when you review your accounts receivable aging information, as discussed in Chapter 16, you can decide for each delinquent customer whether you want to print a special invoice assessing finance charges.

To direct QuickBooks to calculate finance charges, follow these steps:

1. Choose Edit ➪ Preferences. The Preferences dialog box opens.

2. Select the Finance Charge icon on the left side of the screen to open the window shown in Figure 14-15. If the icon is not visible, use the scroll bar to scroll down until it appears. Click the Company Preferences tab.

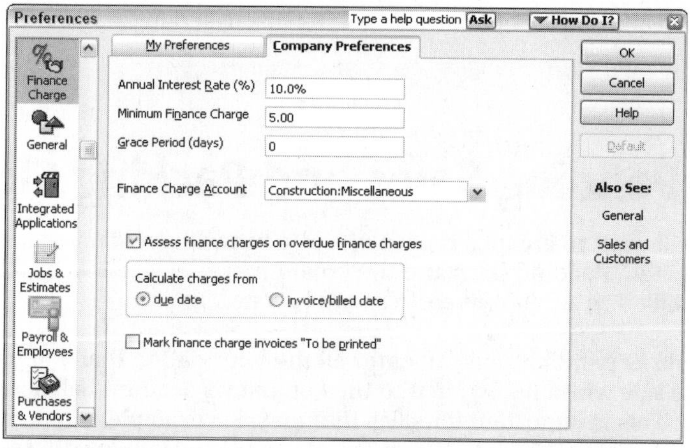

Figure 14-15: Use this window to set your company's finance charge preferences, which are determined by your company's policies and practices regarding late payments.

3. Enter the annual interest rate percentage that you want QuickBooks to use (this amount is prorated monthly). If you want to charge a flat amount as a late fee (for example, $5.00 every 30 days), enter a 0 in this field and proceed to the next step.

4. Enter a dollar amount in the Minimum Finance Charge field if you want to assess a flat amount rather than a percentage each billing period. Also, enter a dollar amount here if you want to assess a finance charge that will either be an actual amount or a minimum amount that you specify.

5. If you allow a grace period, enter the appropriate number of days in the Grace Period field.

6. In the Finance Charge Account field, select or create an expense account to which you want finance charges to be posted.

7. Indicate whether you want QuickBooks to assess finance charges on overdue finance charges.

Note

Some states have usury laws that prohibit you from assessing finance charges on overdue finance charges and that may also limit the total rate of interest that you may charge on consumer obligations.

8. Indicate whether you want to calculate finance charges from the date the invoice was issued or the date that payment was due. Most businesses do the latter.

9. The purpose of the check box labeled Mark Finance Charge Invoices 'To be printed" is to indicate whether you want the default to be to print a finance charge invoice for this customer. If you think that it is more likely than not that you'll decide to print a finance charge invoice, check this box. You can always change your mind when you review your accounts receivable aging information and assess finance charges, as discussed in Chapter 16.
10. Click OK to save your changes.

Recording Pending Sales and Packing Slips

At times, you will want to create a record of a sale but will not want account balances to be affected. Pending sales and the creation of special packing slips for goods that are billed to a different address are two examples.

If you mark a sale as pending, you can enter all the information that you want to retain about the sale without posting it to the company's account balances, registers, or reports. This is important for sales that may, for example, require third-party approval or a government permit. To mark a sale as pending, follow these steps:

1. Complete the invoice as usual without recording it.
2. Go to Edit ➪ Mark Invoice Pending. QuickBooks prominently displays "Pending" on the sales form that appears on your screen, as shown in Figure 14-16.
3. Add an appropriate message in the Memo area to indicate that the sale is pending on the printed form.
4. Click OK or Next to save the information about the transaction without posting it to any accounts.

If you deliver products to one address and send the invoice to another, such as a main office, it may be convenient for you to know how to create a special "packing slip" invoice to be included with the delivered goods. To create a packing slip, follow these steps:

1. Go to Customers ➪ Create Invoices.
2. From the drop-down form menu, select New.
3. In the Template drop-down menu, choose Customize from the drop-down list.
4. Select New and enter **Packing Slip** as the title of the new template.
5. Complete all the required information on the new template; clear the rate and amount information so that no amounts are posted to the company's accounts, and click OK.
6. Save or print the form as you would with any other sales form.

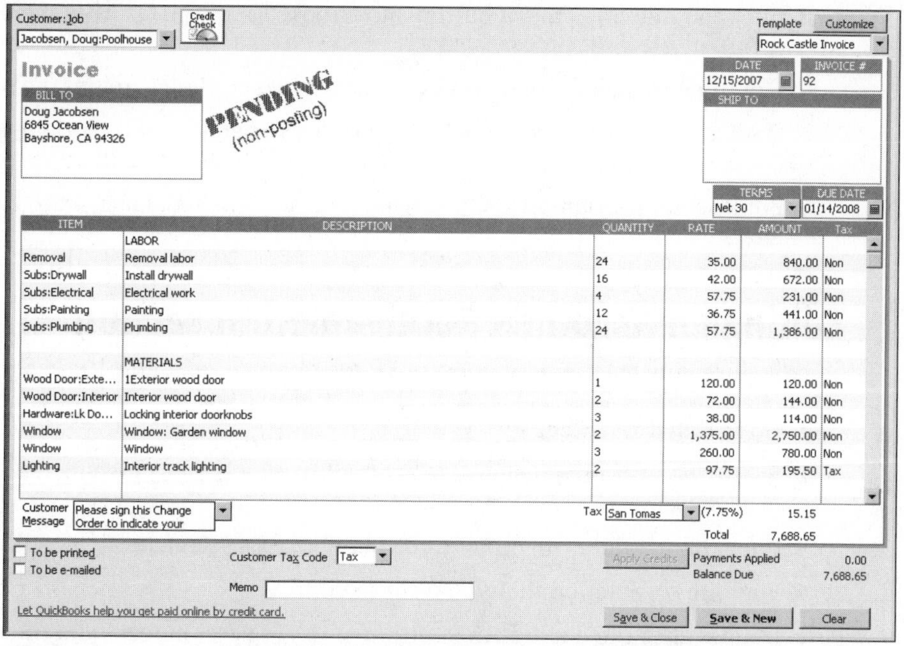

Figure 14-16: This window shows a pending sale; only the notation that appears in the Memo field will appear on the printed form.

Creating other custom template forms is discussed in Chapter 15, but it is useful to learn about packing slips in this section along with pending sales because both forms contain information that is not posted to existing account balances.

Tools for Managing and Editing Sales Forms

QuickBooks allows for the inevitable human error or change of heart by making it surprisingly easy for you to edit, delete, and void sales.

Editing a cash sale

Here's how to edit a cash sale transaction:

1. Go to Edit ➪ Use Register.
2. Select either Undeposited Funds or the bank account to which you previously deposited funds received from the transaction that you are editing.

3. Click the Activities menu button and choose Use Register from the drop-down menu.
4. Find the transaction that you want to edit by scrolling through the register.
5. Double-click the entry at the bottom of the register screen, and the Receive Payments window for the transaction that you chose to edit appears.
6. Edit the appropriate fields, and when you are finished, click OK to save your changes.

Editing an Accounts Receivable transaction

To edit a previously entered invoice or statement charge, follow these steps:

1. Go to Edit ➪ Use Register.
2. Select the Accounts Receivable account to which the transaction was posted originally.
3. Click the Activities menu button and choose Use Register.
4. Find the transaction that you want to edit.
5. Double-click the entry at the bottom of the register screen, and the original invoice or statement for the transaction that you chose to edit appears.
6. Edit the appropriate fields, and when you are finished, click OK to save your changes.

Deleting and voiding sales

When you delete a sale, all records of the transaction are wiped out — forever. To delete a transaction, simply display the invoice and select Delete from the Edit menu.

But it's probably better to be safe rather than sorry when you find that you have to reenter a lot of information that you need after all. You may want to consider voiding erroneous sales rather than deleting them entirely. This will maintain a complete record of all transactions. To void a sale, follow these steps:

1. Select the sale that you want to void.
2. Go to Edit ➪ Void Invoice. QuickBooks changes all the amounts to 0 and enters VOID in the Memo field.
3. Click OK.

Caution It is almost as hard to reverse a VOID as to recall a deleted transaction. Handle with care.

Summary

QuickBooks generates three basic types of sales forms for documenting customer transactions: receipts, invoices, and statements. Issuing a customer receipt memorializes a cash sale. In contrast, credit-sale customers receive an invoice or statement. Sales forms are used to maintain a complete record of all customer transactions and to post correct information to income and asset accounts. The information entered on the sales form is ultimately reflected on the company's Profit and Loss Statement and Balance Sheet.

- Use the Receive Payments window to record sales for which payment is made at the time of delivery by any cash-equivalent form — currency, credit card, or check.
- You can modify the Receive Payments window to summarize an aggregate of transactions (such as daily sales) if you have a high-volume business.
- Some businesses find it advantageous to transact only cash sales because there is no need to maintain accounts receivable to track balances owed to the business.
- Invoices or statements memorialize credit sales. Invoices reflect customer charges for services performed at the time the invoice is issued or at a later date. Statements reflect charges for past services.
- There are three types of standard invoice forms: the product invoice, the professional invoice, and the service invoice.
- Pending sales and packing slips are sales forms that do not post any information to accounts and do not affect any account balances.
- You can edit, modify, and delete invoices.

✦ ✦ ✦

PART

IV

Managing Your Business with QuickBooks

✦ ✦ ✦ ✦

In This Part

✦ ✦ ✦ ✦

CHAPTER 15

Customizing Sales Forms

✦ ✦ ✦ ✦

In This Chapter

Why customize sales forms?

How to work with templates

Choosing which fields appear

Changing the fonts

Inserting your company logo

Working with the layout designer

✦ ✦ ✦ ✦

QuickBooks' sales forms (invoices, sales, credit memos, purchase orders, statements, and estimates) are adequate without any special customization, but some would say they're a bit austere. The plain lines and tiny text do not create a vibrant visual image. That's why most businesses take the time to dress up the sales forms and make them more compatible with the company attitude, whether that attitude is relaxed cheerfulness or sophisticated good taste.

Why Customize Sales Forms?

The biggest reason to customize your sales forms is image. Each time you present a sales form to a customer, that customer gets an impression of your company. What image do you want to convey to your customers? It's probably not "we're a generic, right-out-of-the-box kind of outfit." You want invoices, statements, and estimates that are special. Take a look at Figure 15-1 (a generic QuickBooks invoice) and Figure 15-2 (a customized one). Which one has the more distinctive image?

As you may remember from Chapter 14, you can choose different templates when creating invoices and statements by opening the Customize Template drop-down list and selecting Customize.

You may also want to customize sales forms to add extra fields or to remove ones that you don't use.

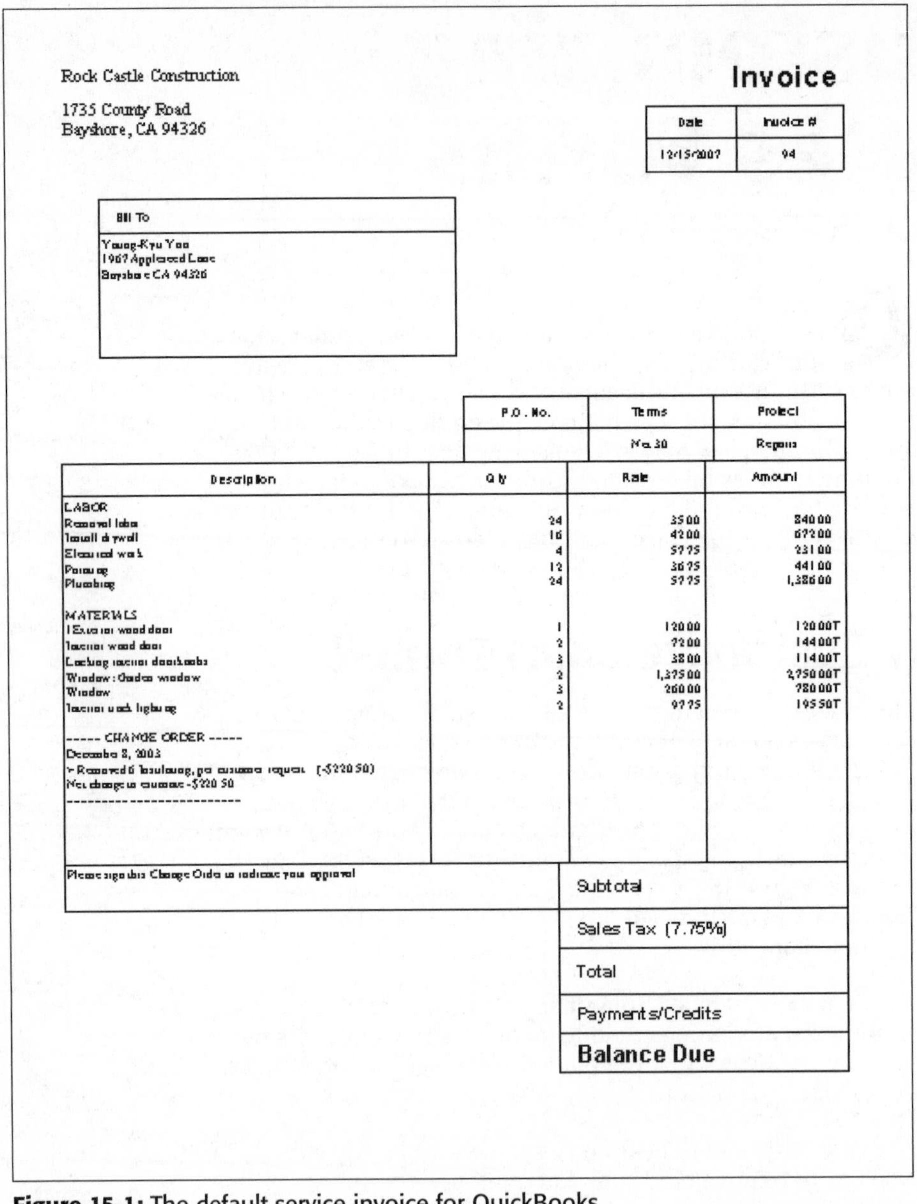

Figure 15-1: The default service invoice for QuickBooks.

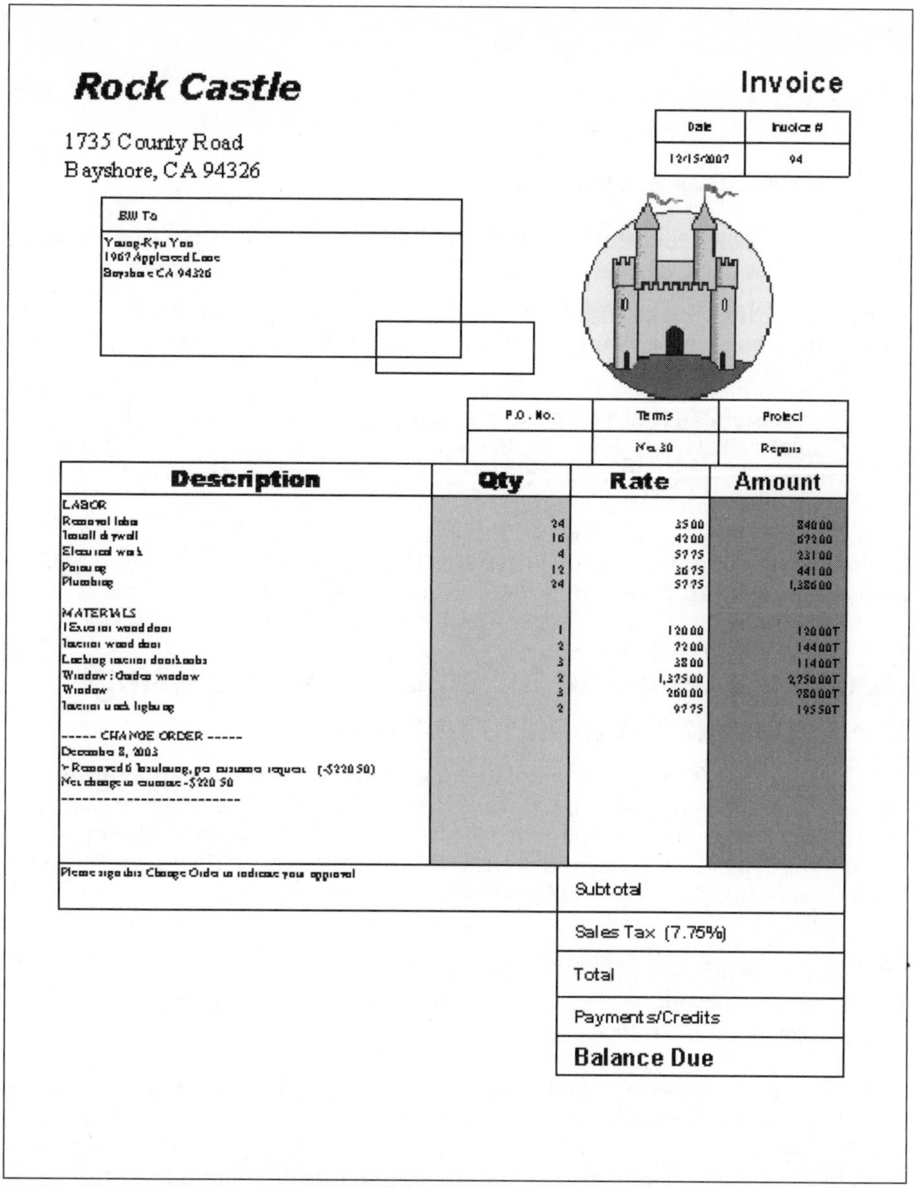

Figure 15-2: A custom-created invoice that uses a graphic and some different fonts.

Working with Template Files

When you create any kind of sales form, its format is based on a template. The template specifies all formatting — from font size to field placement.

There are three classes of templates:

- **Intuit invoice templates:** These special templates, recognizable by the "Intuit" in their names, can be customized in only a very limited way.
- **Other QuickBooks-supplied templates:** Other templates that come with QuickBooks (for example, Custom Statement) allow for more customization than Intuit invoice templates.
- **New templates that you create:** You can create your own templates based on either of the two types of premade templates just described. Templates that you create yourself can be customized normally, regardless of the type of template on which they are based.

You can create or edit templates from the Templates list or on-the-fly as you prepare a sales form. The following sections discuss both methods.

Opening a template for editing and accessing the Customize Template options

There are two ways to open a template for editing. You can start either from the sales form or from the Templates list. Both methods are equally good; it all depends on the situation. If you are working on sales forms when it occurs to you to customize one of them, the former method is best. On the other hand, if you are setting up all the forms for your company at once, you may prefer the latter.

Opening a template from the sales form

To customize a template as you are filling out a sales form (for example, an invoice or a purchase order), follow these steps:

1. From the sales form, open the Customize Template drop-down list and choose Customize. The Customize Template dialog box appears (see Figure 15-3).

2. In the Select a Template box, scroll to the template that you want to customize and then click Edit. If you selected an Intuit invoice template, you'll get a warning box explaining that your editing options are limited — click OK.

   The template's Customize dialog box appears.

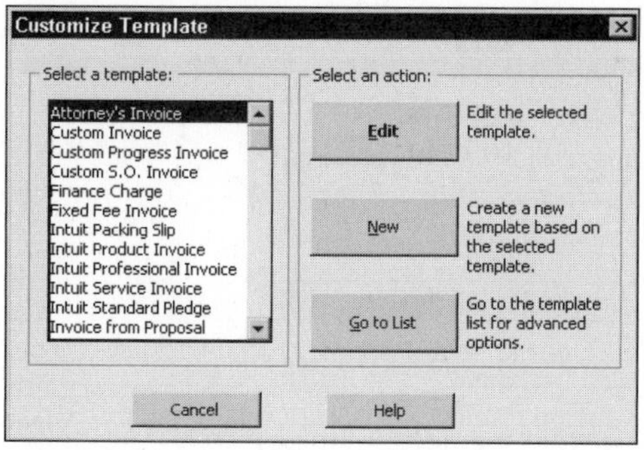

Figure 15-3: The Customize Template dialog box allows you to choose a template to customize.

Opening a template from the Templates list

The second method is to choose a template to edit from the Templates list. You can make limited modifications to an existing template. However, if you want to modify more than fonts, and certain limited fields, you must create a Custom Template. (Refer to Chapter 8 for more information about lists.) To edit a template from the Templates list, follow these steps:

1. Choose Lists ➪ Templates to open the list of templates.

   Tip: If the template you want to customize does not appear, you can't use this method. Instead, you must either use the steps in the preceding method or create a new template of that type (as described in the next section, "Creating a new template").

2. Highlight the template you want to edit.
3. Click the Templates menu button to open its drop-down list and choose Edit (see Figure 15-4). The template's Customize dialog box appears and you can start to edit text and change some limited options, such as whether the company name and address appear on the invoice.
4. Click the Templates button and then choose Edit.

Creating a new template

When you create a new template, you make a copy of an existing one and modify the copy. You then have complete freedom to modify the copy—you can add or delete fields, move things around, use the Layout Designer—the whole works.

You can create a new template either from the sales form or from the Templates list. Both methods have their fans—try each and see which you prefer.

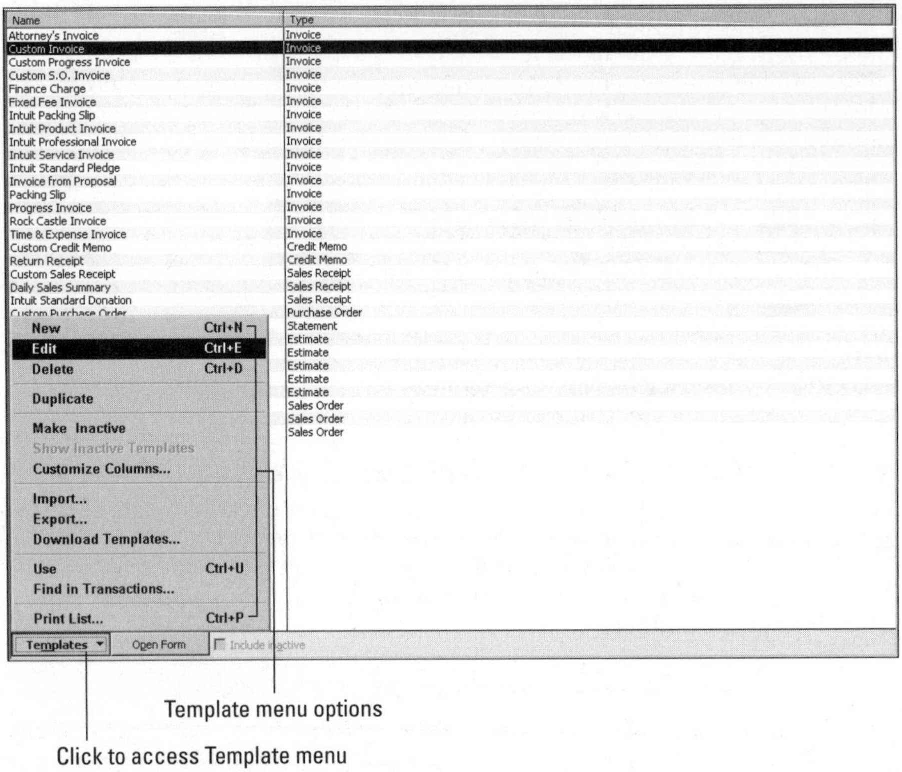

Figure 15-4: Select a template from this list.

Creating a new template from the sales form

To create a new template while working on a sales form (such as an invoice or estimate), follow these steps:

1. On the sales form, open the Custom Template drop-down list and choose Customize. The Customize Template dialog box appears (shown previously in Figure 15-3).
2. Click the template that you want to base the new one on and then click New. The Customize dialog box appears.
3. Type a name for the new template in the Template Name field at the top of the dialog box.
4. Make your changes to the template, as explained in later sections of this chapter.

Creating a new template from the Templates list

If you want to customize all the forms in QuickBooks in one sitting to ensure a consistent look and feel, this method is the one you want. You can set up all sales forms — invoices, cash sales, credit memos, purchase orders, statements, and estimates — without having to use the Activities menu to visit each form.

1. Choose Lists ➪ Templates to open the Templates list.
2. Click the Templates button to open the drop-down list and then choose New. The Select Template Type dialog box appears, asking which type of template you want (see Figure 15-5).

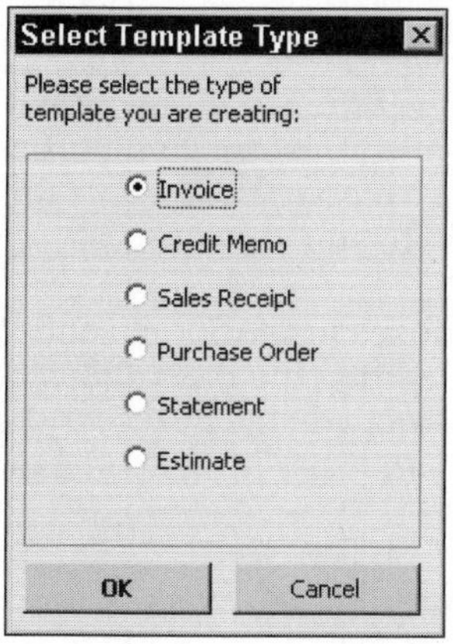

Figure 15-5: This dialog box allows you to choose the sales form for which you want to create a template.

3. Click the option button for the type you want and then click OK. A Customize dialog box for that template type opens.
4. Type a name for the new template in the Template Name field at the top of the dialog box.
5. Edit the template as explained later in this chapter.

Using the Customize Dialog Box

The Customize dialog box contains dozens of options for editing and creating templates to convey the visual image you want. One of the primary functions of the Customize dialog box for a template is to choose which elements appear on the form. There are eight tabs. Each tab allows you to customize how headers, fields, columns, and footers appear.

When customizing elements on a form, there are two settings for each: Screen and Print. You may want certain fields to appear on the screen so that you can enter information for accounting purposes, but you don't want those fields to print on the customer's copy. Item is a prime example. The code you use for the Item is not significant to the customer — the customer wants to see only the description associated with it and so the Item code does not need to appear on the printout. For you, however, viewing the Item code on each invoice line on-screen is critical.

Tip If you mess up the fields to the point where you just want to start over, click the Default button in the Customize dialog box to return all fields to the original settings of the template on which the one you are working is based.

Choosing header fields

On the Header tab, you'll find the fields that belong at the top of the form. Figure 15-6 shows the Customize dialog box for a template called Custom Invoice. Its header tab contains the fields Default Title, Date, Invoice Number, Bill To, and Ship To. These fields vary depending on the type of template you are editing.

You can turn each field on or off with the check boxes in the Screen and Print columns. You can also reword the field labels by editing the ones shown in the Default Title column. For example, on a credit memo, you might prefer the Credit Number field to be labeled CR# for consistency with other forms you use.

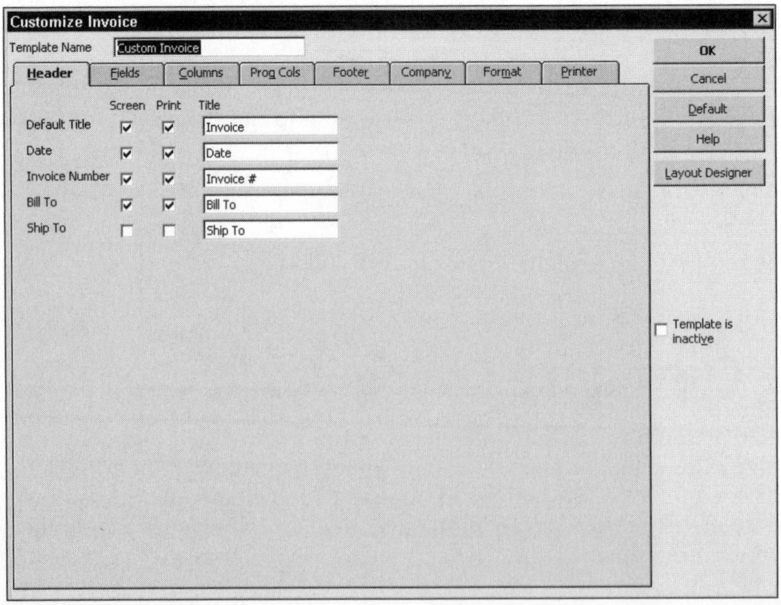

Figure 15-6: You can customize which fields appear in your form's header through this dialog box.

Two other items that traditionally appear in the header are your own company's name and address. These don't appear on-screen because you already know them, but they do appear on the printouts because the customer needs to know whom the sales form is from. If you have a good reason to do so, such as because you are using preprinted invoice paper, you can turn off their display on the Company tab by deselecting the Print Company Name and Print Company Address check boxes.

Choosing other fields at the top of the form

The Fields tab contains a list of other fields that you may want to appear at the top of your form. The list varies somewhat depending on the form you are working with (invoices, for example, have different fields from purchase orders).

Like the header fields, you can turn them on or off for both screen and printing, and you can customize their titles. See Figure 15-7.

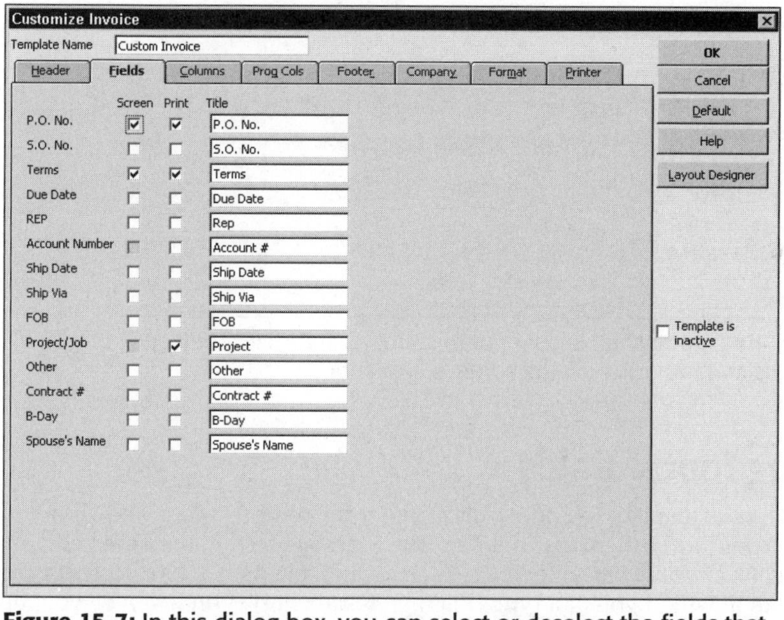

Figure 15-7: In this dialog box, you can select or deselect the fields that you think would be helpful to include on your form.

Tip

Make sure that you do not turn off the screen display of a field that contains important accounting information. Notice in Figure 15-7 that the Project/Job field's Screen check box is gray, which means that you can't deselect it. That's for your own protection because QuickBooks requires that every invoice be assigned to a particular job. If there are other fields that you watch closely as part of your business management, make sure those fields remain on-screen.

Setting the column layout

Next, you need to decide what fields belong in the columns on the form, and in what order. As Figure 15-8 shows, the Columns tab contains an extra bit of customization for each line. You can specify an order number for each field, which determines the field's position from left to right.

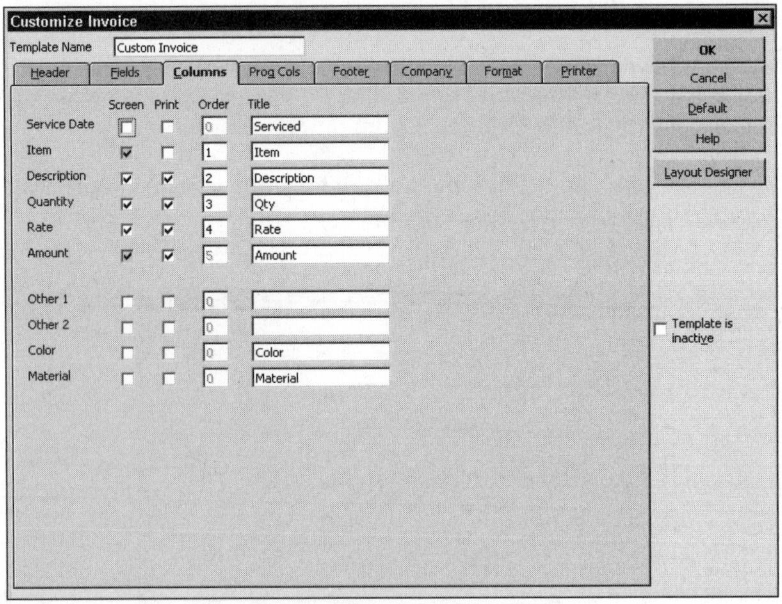

Figure 15-8: The Columns tab allows you to choose which fields belong in the columns and the order in which they are to appear.

Choosing footer fields

Footer fields work just like header fields. The footer options tab is shown in Figure 15-9. Your footer includes the total, the message to the customer, and any special "long text" you want to include, such as a disclaimer. There's a text box on the Footer tab in which you can type this text. For example, on invoices you might want to say something about the finance charges you will apply if the invoice is late: "Finance charges of 2% per month will be applied to accounts that are more than 30 days overdue as of the first of each month."

Company Information tab

The Company Information tab, shown in Figure 15-10, allows you to design the template to display or suppress specific information about the company that you are billing to be printed on the form. You can include a phone number, fax number, e-mail address, and the like.

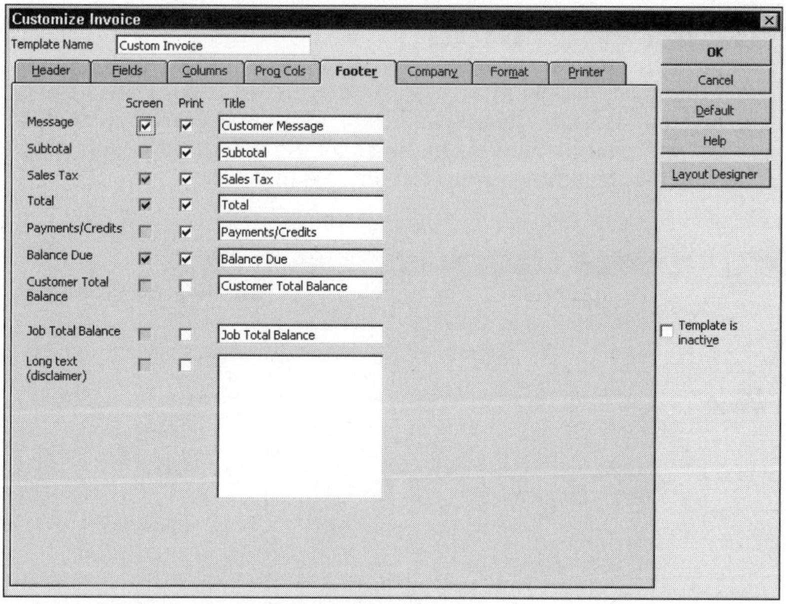

Figure 15-9: Options for editing footers.

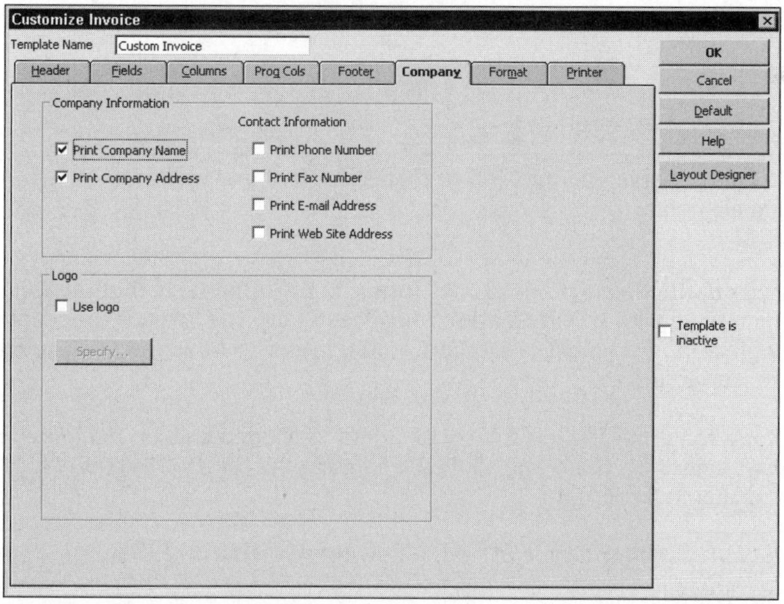

Figure 15-10: Decide which information about the company to include on the customized template form.

Selecting Different Fonts

Under the Format tab is a Fonts section, as shown in Figure 15-11. It lists the types of text on the form, such as Title, Labels, and Data. Most of the text types on the list include many fields; for example, Labels includes all the field labels. QuickBooks offers a single setting for the whole group to ensure consistency.

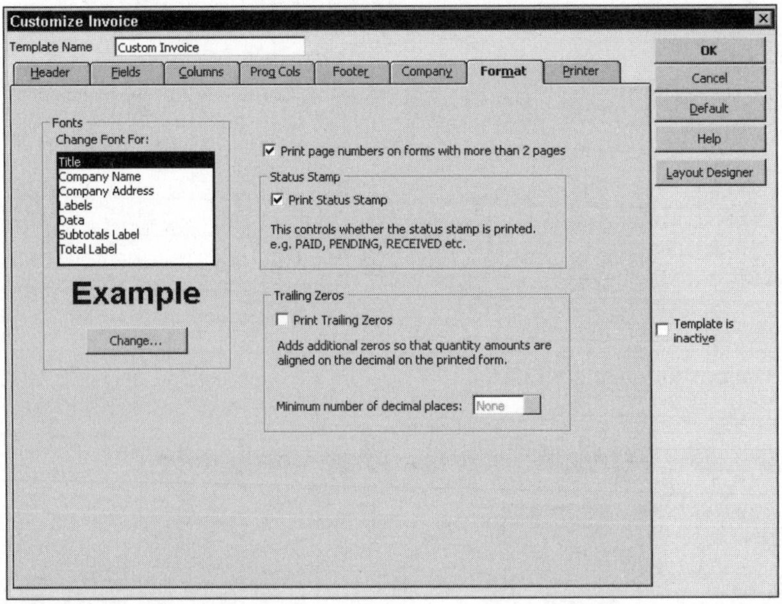

Figure 15-11: The Format tab permits you to change the font that is used for certain form elements.

One of the faults of the default QuickBooks forms, in my opinion, is that the fonts are too small. If you have a lot of information to squeeze onto the form, it is acceptable. But most people don't and most customers would prefer to have the text appear in a larger, more readable size.

Tip

Don't worry about making text too big to fit into its allotted area on the form. You can always adjust the size of the allotted area using the Layout Designer, which is explained later in this chapter.

To change the font used for a type of text, follow these steps:

1. On the Format tab's Fonts list, choose the type of text you want to change (for example, Labels).

2. Click the Change button. The Example box appears, as shown in Figure 15-12.

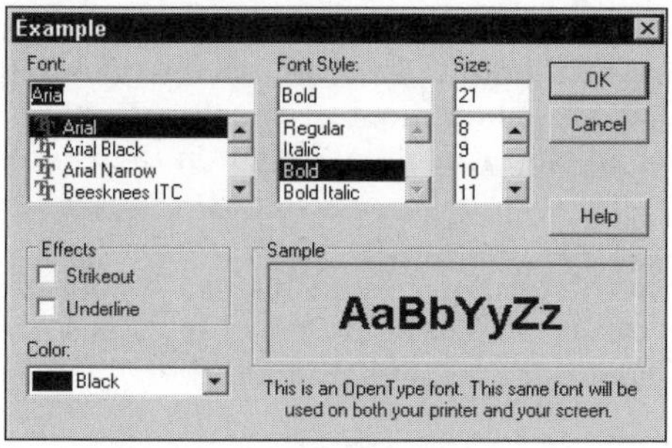

Figure 15-12: The Example box shows the effect of changing the font properties of specific form elements.

3. Use the dialog box controls to choose the correct Font, Size, Font Style, Effects, and Color. For example, you might increase the Font Size by a few points. Then click OK.
4. Examine the sample text on the Format tab. If it doesn't look right, repeat steps 2 and 3 until it's right.
5. Repeat steps 1 to 4 for each form element.

Setting Up Your Printer

The Printer tab options, shown in Figure 15-13, allow you to use the printer settings that have already been established for existing templates, or to modify the printer settings for the template you have just created.

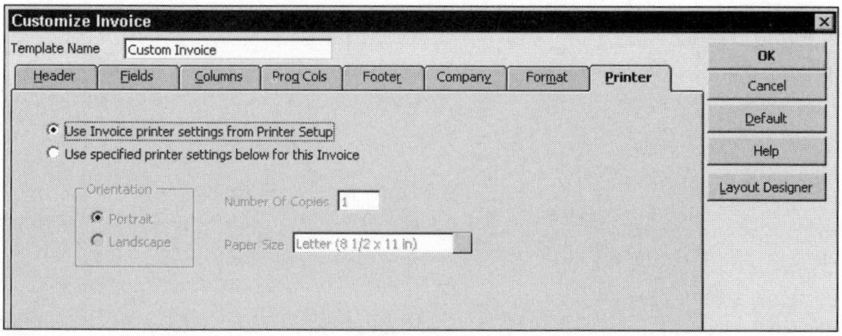

Figure 15-13: You may need to modify your printer settings for a custom template.

Adding a Logo

If you want to include your company logo on your forms (smart idea!), you must first have the logo scanned or created in a computer drawing program. It needs to be contained in a graphics file on your PC before you can use it in QuickBooks. Many copy shops offer scanning services, as do most professional artists who create logos. After you have the logo as an electronic file, save it in the QuickBooks folder on your hard disk.

QuickBooks accepts graphics only in the bitmap (.bmp) format. If your graphic is in any other format, you will have to convert it. There are many graphics programs that enable you to open a file in one format and save it in another. Paint Shop Pro, which is shareware, works well.

To include your logo on a form, follow these steps:

1. Go to Lists ➪ Templates. A list of existing templates appears.
2. Double-click the template to which you want to add a logo (or click the Templates menu button and select Edit). A Customize Invoice dialog box appears as shown in Figure 15-14.

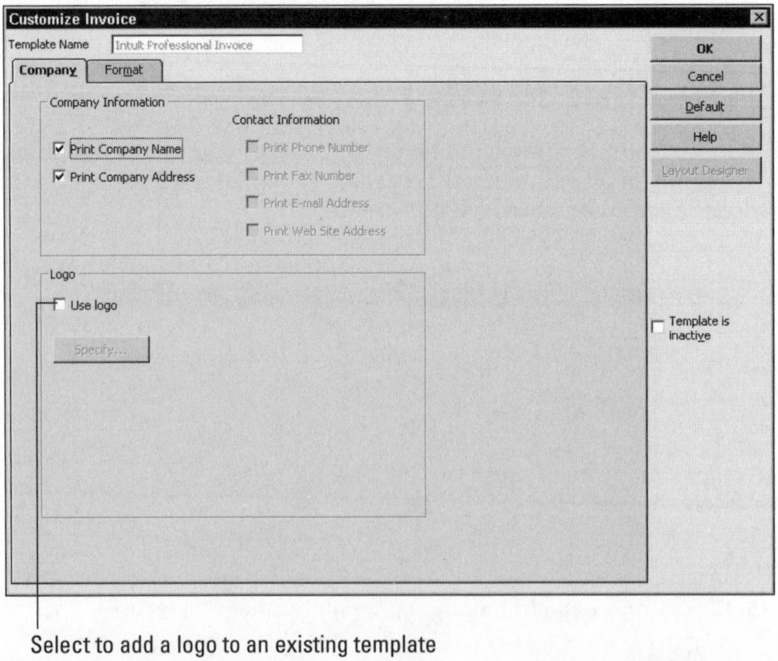

Figure 15-14: This Customize dialog box contains limited options for modifying an existing template.

3. Open the template for customization, as you learned earlier, and click the Customize button to access the Company tab in the Customize dialog box.
4. Click the Use Logo check box. The Select Image dialog box appears.
5. Click the File button to choose the file you want. The Open Logo File dialog box appears. Select the template file to which you want to add a logo from the drop-down menu.
6. Select the logo. (Change drives and folders if needed.) Click OK. Your logo appears in the Logo dialog box.
7. Click OK to accept the logo. Continue customizing your form as needed.

Previewing Your Changes

When you have made your modifications to a template, you should check it out to make sure that the changes look the way you want them to. The best way to do this is with an actual sales form in Print Preview. You can also use the Layout Designer to see your changes, as you'll learn in the following section, but Print Preview is better because it shows a real-life use rather than a sample.

To preview a custom template, follow these steps:

1. Close any customization dialog boxes that are still open by clicking OK to accept your changes.
2. Open the sales form you want to check out (for example, Create Invoices or Create Credit Memos/Refunds).
3. At the top of the form, open the Custom Template drop-down list and choose your new or modified template.
4. Click the Print button and select Preview from the drop-down menu. Your new form appears in Print Preview.

Using the Layout Designer

The Layout Designer is a special paste-up grid that gives you precise control over your template. You can adjust the placement of fields, change field size, change the font used in a particular field, and much more.

Tip The Layout Designer is not available for Intuit invoice templates, which allow only font size changes and the addition of a logo.

To open the Layout Designer, just click the Layout Designer button from the Customize dialog box as you are customizing a template. The Layout Designer shows every element on your template form, placed on a dotted layout grid (see Figure 15-15).

Moving and resizing boxes

Notice in Figure 15-15 that the box where the date appears has a dark border around it with little black squares in the corners. These squares are called *sizing handles*. Whatever box you click becomes selected and its sizing handles appear. All objects in the Layout Designer appear in boxes. Even the grid of columns is composed of boxes. Look at it closely—the boxes are placed close together, so they appear to be a single box with lines drawn to create separate compartments within it.

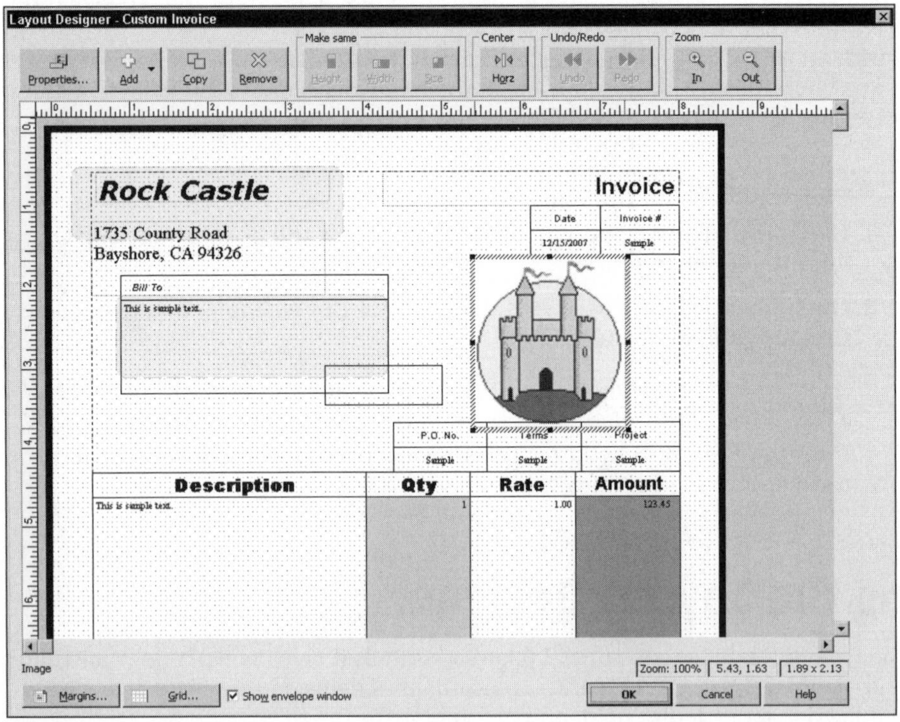

Figure 15-15: The dotted layout grid in Layout Designer can help you position fields precisely.

You can drag these handles to resize the box. Just position the mouse pointer over a handle, so that the mouse pointer turns into a double-headed arrow. Then, hold down the left mouse button and drag to resize. You can resize any box by dragging its handles.

You can also move any box on the Layout Designer. To do so, position the mouse pointer over the middle of the box so that the mouse pointer turns into a four-headed arrow. Then, hold down the left mouse button and drag to move the box.

Some boxes need to stay together. For example, the box where the date appears needs to stay with the box above it that says DATE. To select more than one box to move at once, hold down the Shift key as you click each box that you want to select. Then, drag all the boxes as a group.

Tip

If you make a mistake, click the Undo button at the top of the Layout Designer window. You can undo as many actions as you need.

Making several boxes the same size

If you want to make more than one box the same size, you can save time with the Make Same controls. Here's how it works:

1. Make one box the size you want it (both height and width).
2. Select all of the other boxes that you want to be that same size. Hold down the Shift key while selecting the other boxes.
3. While still holding down the Shift key, click the box that's already the right size. Make sure you choose it last, after all the others.
4. Click the Height, Width, or Size button to resize the boxes to be the size of the correct one. The Height and Width buttons resize in one dimension only; the Size button resizes in both dimensions at once.

Setting object properties

Many of the objects on the Design Layout have properties. Properties vary depending on the object but may include font and font size, box border lines (left, right, top, and/or bottom), horizontal alignment (centered, left, or right), and vertical alignment (top, bottom, or centered).

To view a box's properties right-click a box. A Properties dialog box appears. These dialog boxes normally have two tabs: Text, where you set font and alignment, and Border, where you turn on or off the border on each side of the box individually. Figure 15-16 shows the Properties dialog box for a box containing text.

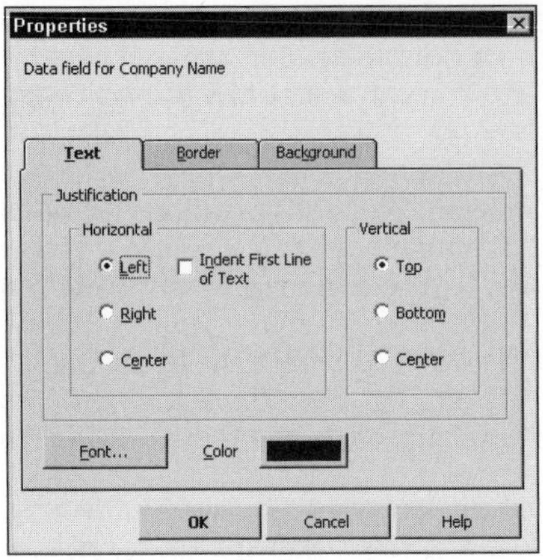

Figure 15-16: Use the Properties dialog box to change a box's text attributes, alignment, and border and to access a dialog box that allows you to change the font.

Setting page margins

To set the margins for the printed form, click the Margins button at the bottom of the screen. The Margins dialog box opens, where you can change the Top, Bottom, Left, and Right margin settings (see Figure 15-17).

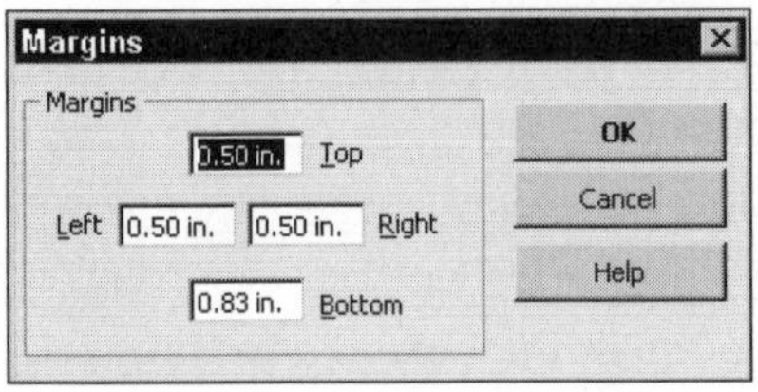

Figure 15-17: The Margins dialog box controls the margin settings for the form.

Note that the Margin settings do not control the objects on the form. They control only the placement of the margin guideline around the edge of the form on-screen in the Layout Designer, so you can see where the margins should be. You must manually move any objects inward that fall outside your margin guidelines.

Fitting addresses for use with window envelopes

If you use window envelopes to mail sales forms to customers, you'll appreciate this feature. The Layout Designer can show you exactly where the windows will be, so you can move the fields on the form accordingly.

To see shaded boxes for the windows, click the Show Envelope Window check box (previously shown in Figure 15-15).

Zooming in and out

Want a closer view of a particular area? Just click the In button to zoom in for greater detail. Use the Out button to step back and see the bigger picture. Zooming in can help you position elements more precisely because you can see an object's relationship to surrounding objects more clearly. Zooming out can give you a view of the form as a whole.

Adjusting the grid sensitivity

The *grid* is the mesh of little dots on the background. By default, objects "snap to" this grid, so you can line boxes up evenly without too much trouble.

To adjust the grid, click the Grid button at the bottom of the screen to display the Grid and Snap Settings dialog box (see Figure 15-18).

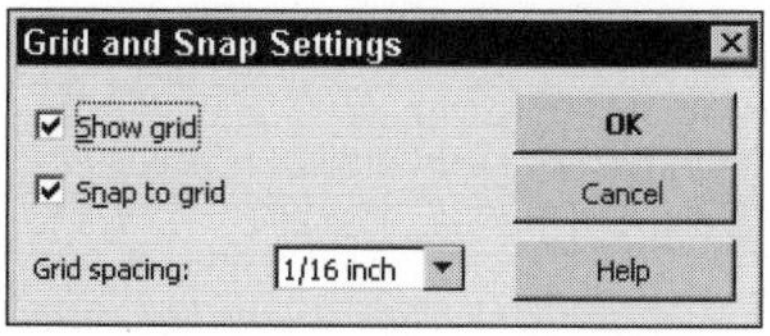

Figure 15-18: By using the Grid and Snap Settings dialog box, you can adjust the way the grid looks and works in Layout Designer.

From this screen, you can do the following:

- ✦ Select or deselect the Show Grid check box to control whether the dots appear on-screen. (They don't appear, of course, on printed copies.) Most people prefer to see the grid, but some find it distracting.
- ✦ Select or deselect the Snap to Grid check box to control whether objects align with the grid dots when you move them around.
- ✦ Choose a different spacing from the Grid Spacing drop-down list to choose how far apart the dots are spaced.

If you are having trouble getting things to align with one another, try setting the dots farther apart. If the dots won't allow you to position something where you want it, make the dots closer together, or deselect the Snap to Grid check box.

Summary

This chapter taught you how to use your business forms to project a professional image by customizing them to create your own distinctive look. By creating your own custom forms, you send the message to your customer that your company is conscientious and professional. In this chapter, you learned the following:

- Each sales form has one or more templates. You can create new templates or modify existing ones.
- You can create new templates from the sales forms or from the Templates list.
- The Customize dialog box for a template controls which elements appear on the form, such as payment terms, shipping method, and company name.
- You can control what fonts are used for each element of a sales form. Often, increasing the size of the fonts used on a form makes it more readable; QuickBooks' default fonts are rather small.
- The Layout Designer opens your form on a layout grid. You can drag each element to place it anywhere on the form you like.

✦ ✦ ✦

CHAPTER 16

Accounts Receivables and Deposits

✦ ✦ ✦ ✦

In This Chapter

Receiving payments

Issuing refunds

Handling a bounced check

Writing off bad debts

Making deposits

Creating deposit reports

Aging accounts receivable

Improving your collection ratio

Properly handling barter transactions

✦ ✦ ✦ ✦

This chapter deals with accounts receivable (A/R), which means the money that you will be receiving. Whenever you issue an invoice (as you learned in Chapter 14), you create an A/R entry in QuickBooks. QuickBooks keeps track of your A/R entries and remembers how many days it has been since you issued each invoice. (The process of tracking outstanding invoices is called aging, and I talk about it later in the chapter.) You can create reports in QuickBooks that track A/R aging, so you can see who needs to be reminded to pay.

When you receive a payment, you apply it to one or more of the customer's invoices, reducing or eliminating the amount that the customer owes you. If you don't receive the payment, well, the latter part of this chapter talks about strategies for encouraging customers to pay.

Receiving Payments

The two most critical events in your customer billing cycle are invoicing and receiving payment from customers. (Invoices are discussed in Chapter 14.) The exact amount of time that passes between invoicing and receiving payment depends on your customers' reliability and on the payment terms negotiated with them (such as Net 30 or Due on Receipt). When you do receive the payment, you need to record it in QuickBooks to credit the customer's account.

The most convenient way to access information about customer transactions is from the Customers Navigator screen shown in Figure 16-1. The icons are logically organized to correspond to the typical phases of a customer sale cycle.

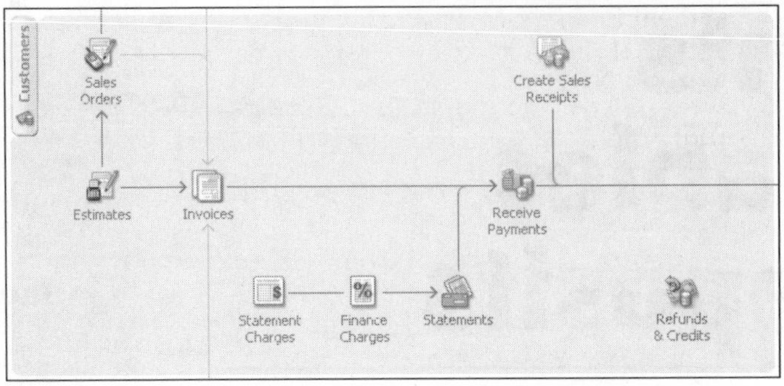

Figure 16-1: The Customers section of the Navigator screen.

To receive a payment, follow these steps:

1. Go to Customers ➪ Receive Payments, or click the Receive Payments icon (see Figure 16-1). The Receive Payments window shown in Figure 16-2 appears.

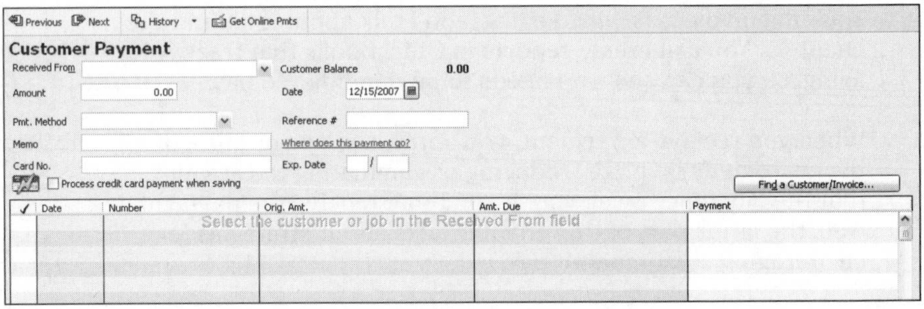

Figure 16-2: You use this special QuickBooks window to record information about a cash sale.

2. Select a payment method from the drop-down menu. QuickBooks allows you to select cash, check, barter, or credit card methods of payment.

3. Select an option for the Received From field from the drop-down list, or choose Add New from the Customer:Job drop-down list to set up a new job if you are tracking by the job. After you select the customer, a list of unpaid invoices appears in the window.

4. Select each invoice you want to pay, one at a time, and indicate the amount of the payment to be applied to each invoice in the Payment column. If the Auto Apply Payment button is displayed (as shown previously in Figure 16-2), the payment will automatically be applied. To reverse the transaction, click the Auto Apply Payment button to display the Un-Apply Payment button.

5. Click Auto Apply Payment if you want to apply the payment to each outstanding invoice. Enter the date in the Date field. Today's date is filled in as the default.
6. If your company uses a reference number for its internal billing purposes, enter it in the Reference Number field.
7. If your company offers discounts, click the Discount & Credits button. To set up multiple templates for cash sales, choose the template you want to use from the Template drop-down list. (See Chapter 22 for details.)
8. Click Save & Close. QuickBooks records the customer payments, and adjusts the accounts receivable and outstanding invoice balances accordingly.

Correcting misapplied or incorrect payments

If you have multiple jobs for customers, it is easy to misapply a payment. Suppose that Mr. Jones had three jobs for you. Instead of applying his payment to the correct job, you apply it to Mr. Jones himself (that is, to no job in particular). This won't do because Mr. Jones himself will show a credit while his invoices that pertain to the certain job appear past due. Payments may also have been applied to the wrong invoices for a job or entered for the wrong amount.

To correct a misapplied payment, using the register QuickBooks maintains for each customer and job, follow these steps:

1. To open the register for an individual customer or job, click Customer Center and then click the Customers & Jobs tab. Right-click the customer or job and choose Use Register.

Note

If the account is an income or expense account, a QuickReport appears instead of a register. Income and expense accounts do not have registers in QuickBooks.

2. Locate the payment that was applied incorrectly within the window shown in Figure 16-3, and double-click the transaction. The Receive Payments window appears as shown in Figure 16-4.

Select customer for whom a misapplied payment was recorded.

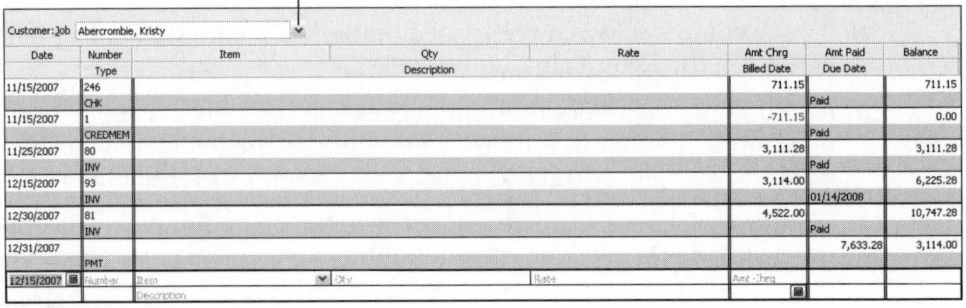

Figure 16-3: Customer or job register.

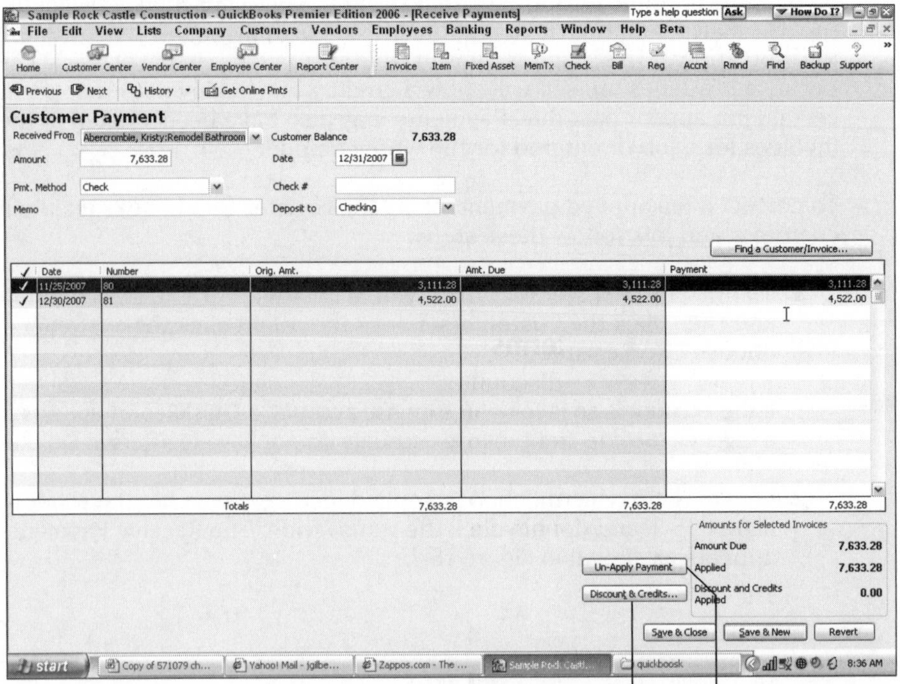

Click to access dialog box for discounts and credits

Click to un-apply payment

Figure 16-4: The details for the selected payment.

3. Enter the correct amount of the payment (or 0 if no payment) and click the Un-Apply Payment button.
4. Click OK. QuickBooks adjusts all affected account balances.
5. Follow the steps you learned in "Receiving Payments" earlier in this chapter to record the correct amount of payment.

Entering a discount for early payment

Many businesses like to reward prompt-paying customers with a discount. Payment terms such as 2% 10 Net 30 encourage prompt payment by offering a discount (2 percent, for example) for payment within 10 days.

When you enter payment terms for a customer, such as 2% 10 Net 30, those terms appear on any invoices issued for the customer. However, if you want to actually award the discount to the customer, you must do it manually. QuickBooks does not assume that the discount is automatically awarded, even if the payment is being recorded within the allotted time since the invoice was issued.

Tip

You apply discounts as you are entering the customer's payment. (That's the logical time to do it, because you have the payment in hand and you are certain that the customer deserves the discount.) Even if the customer has sent you the full amount owed, you can still give a discount. QuickBooks will hold the credit until the customer has another invoice to apply it to, or until you send a refund check.

Setting up payment terms

To offer and calculate a discount for early payment, you need to establish policies regarding payment terms for your customers and let QuickBooks know what they are. To set up payment terms, follow these steps:

1. From the Lists menu, choose Customer & Vendor Profile Lists; then choose Terms List. A list of payment terms offered by your company appears, as shown in Figure 16-5.

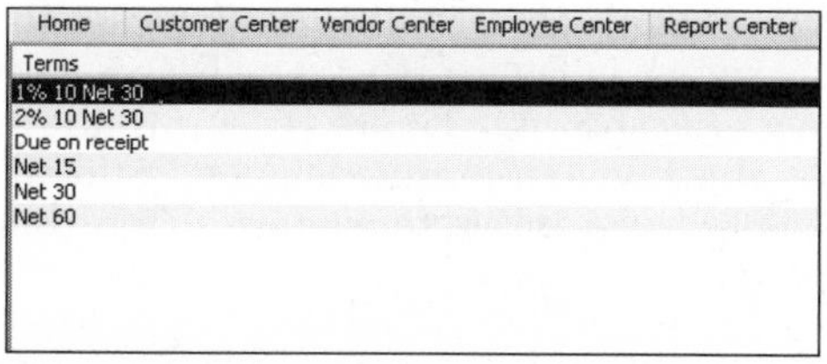

Figure 16-5: QuickBooks maintains a list of payment terms offered by your company.

2. From the Terms list, select and double-click the terms you want to edit. An Edit Terms window, like the one shown in Figure 16-6, appears.

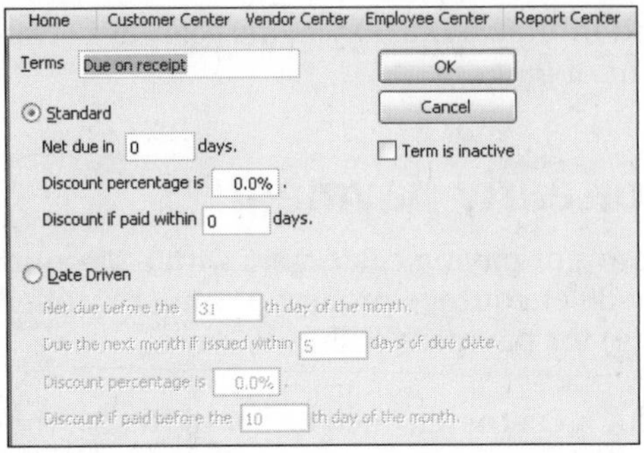

Figure 16-6: Modify payment terms to reflect your company's policies.

3. In the Terms field, enter a word or phrase that will help you recognize the type of terms you are offering.
4. Indicate the type of terms that you want to use (standard versus date-driven payment terms).
5. Record the payment terms.

Applying an early-payment discount

Use the following procedure *only* for early-payment discounts:

Note

If you want to give a discount for some other reason (for example, a coupon), use a discount item on the invoice instead (see Chapter 14).

1. Go to Customers ➪ Receive Payments (or click the Receive Payments icon on the Customer section of the Navigator screen). The Receive Payments dialog box opens.
2. While entering a payment as discussed earlier in this chapter, click the Credits & Discounts button (previously shown in Figure 16-4). The Discount and Credits Information dialog box appears (as shown in Figure 16-7) with the suggested discount calculated based on the payment terms assigned to the invoice and whether the payment is being received within those terms (for example, within 10 days for 2% 10 Net 30).

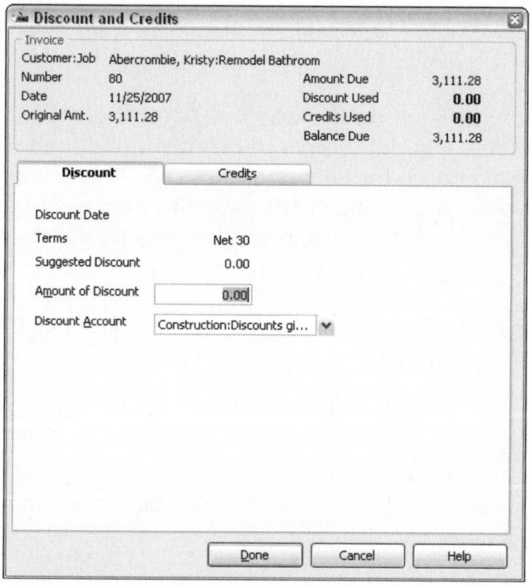

Figure 16-7: QuickBooks suggests the amount of the discount, which you can accept or override.

QuickBooks calculates a suggested discount amount based on your payment terms, as shown in Figure 16-7, with the customer and the payment date. You can enter any discount amount you choose; you don't have to use the suggested amount. However, the amount of the discount cannot be higher than the original invoice.

3. Enter the name of the expense account you use to track discounts (for example, Discount Expense).

4. Click Done to record the discount. Save the payment.

Note

Even if the customer has sent you a payment for the full amount of the invoice (or statement charges), you can apply a discount. QuickBooks holds any credit amount in accounts receivable until you apply it to an invoice or issue a refund check.

Assessing finance charges for late payments

In the name of "goodwill," some companies prefer not to assess finance charges to customers. Often, these companies are selling themselves short. Who suffers when your customers don't pay promptly? You do! Cheerfully putting up with slow payments doesn't endear you to customers; rather, it may cause them to think that slow payment is acceptable and part of the routine.

Cross-Reference

For more information regarding how to set up finance charges on your invoices, refer to Chapter 14.

After you've got your finance charges set up the way you want them, you're ready to apply them to overdue invoices. You don't have to do this individually for each customer; you can do it in one big batch for all customers. The charges are then applied to each customer's account, and you can either print finance charge invoices or allow the charges to appear on the customers' next statements. To assess finance charges, follow these steps:

1. Choose Customers ➪ Assess Finance Charges. The Assess Finance Charges dialog box appears (see Figure 16-8).

Click the assess column for each customer for whom you wish to create a finance charge invoice.

Assessment Date Template [Customize]

12/15/2007 ■ Finance Charge ▾

Assess	Last FC	Customer	Overdue Bal.	Finance Charge
		Cook, Brian	0.00	
✓	12/11/2007	Kitchen	700.00	5.00
✓		*Fisher, Jennifer	1,350.63	57.58
		Jacobsen, Doug	0.00	
✓		Kitchen	75.00	5.00
✓		Lew Plumbing - C	175.00	5.00
		Prentice, Adelaide	0.00	
✓		Hippodrome playhouse	431.95	5.00
		Pretell Real Estate	0.00	
✓		155 Wilks Blvd.	2,239.00	22.08
✓		Roche, Diarmuid	38.79	5.00
		Teschner, Anton	0.00	
✓		Sun Room	565.95	5.00

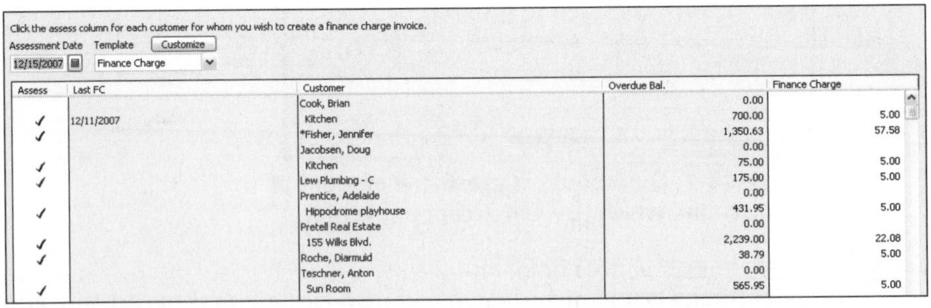

Figure 16-8: You use this dialog box to choose which customers to assess finance charges against.

2. If you see a warning box about one or more customers having unapplied payments, click OK to go on. Such customers will appear with an asterisk beside their names. You may want to hold off on assessing finance charges for such customers until you have investigated why the payment has not been applied.

3. In the Assessment Date field, enter the date on which the finance charges should appear on the statements. For example, you might assess charges as of the first of the month.

4. In the Customize drop-down menu, choose the template to use for the invoices that assess finance charges. (QuickBooks provides one called Finance Charge that works well; there is no need to change it in most cases.)

5. Click to add or remove check marks in the Assess column next to each customer as needed. You might want to give a good customer a break, for example, if the customer is hardly ever late and is only a few days late on the current invoice. Use the Collection History button to examine the customer's payment record. Use the Mark All or Unmark All button to change all of them at once.

6. Change any finance charge amounts if needed in the Finance Charge column.

Tip

If the finance charges are wrong, click the Settings button to go to the Preferences dialog box and change the settings to match your needs, as explained in Chapter 14.

7. If you are going to print finance charge invoices, select the Mark Invoices To Be Printed check box. If you use statements instead, leave this deselected.
8. Click Assess Charges. QuickBooks applies the finance charges to the customer accounts.

Processing a Refund or Return

Occasionally you may need to give a customer a refund. Depending on your policies and the customer's wishes, you can either leave the credit in the customer's account, to be applied against future invoices, or issue a refund check.

Start by creating a credit memo for the customer by following these steps:

1. From the Customers menu, choose Create Credit Memos/Refunds. The Create Credit Memos/Refunds window appears, as shown in Figure 16-9.
2. In the Customer:Job field, choose the customer and job for which you are creating the credit memo or refund check. If you have created more than one job for the customer, be sure to assign the credit memo to the correct job. You can apply the credit memo only to the same job for which it was created.

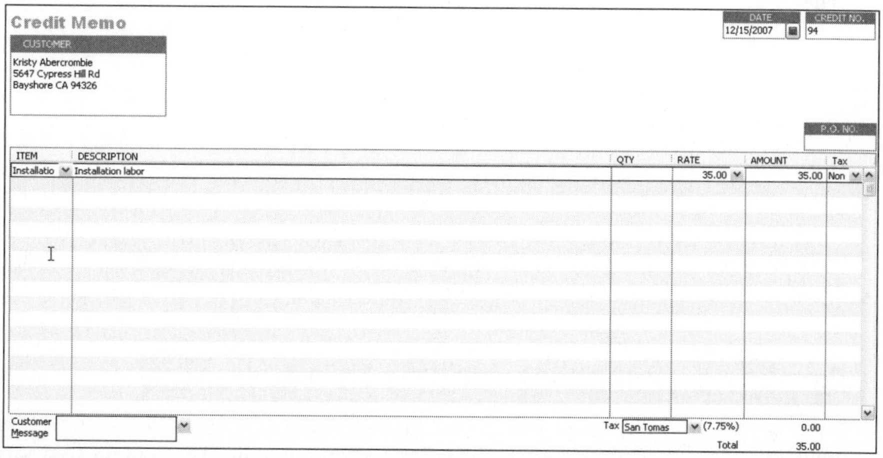

Figure 16-9: A credit memo is like a reverse invoice. You enter the materials being returned or the services being refunded.

3. Select a template.
4. From the Account drop-down list, choose which A/R account to use. This field appears only when you have more than one A/R account (most companies have only one).
5. Enter the items being returned in the line item area. Use the same information that was on the original invoice or billing statement. QuickBooks decreases the income accounts of the invoice items by the amount of the return.
6. (Optional) In the Customer Message field, choose a message from the drop-down list, or enter a new message to your customer.
7. (Optional) Enter a memo for this transaction. The memo does not print on the credit memo, but it does appear in the A/R register and in the customer register.
8. (Optional) Print the credit memo.
9. Save the credit memo. The dialog box shown in Figure 16-10 appears, asking you whether you want to retain the credit as an available credit, give a refund, or apply the credit to an open invoice. QuickBooks enters a negative amount in your A/R register for the credit memo.
10. If you now owe the customer money, click Check Refund to create a refund check.

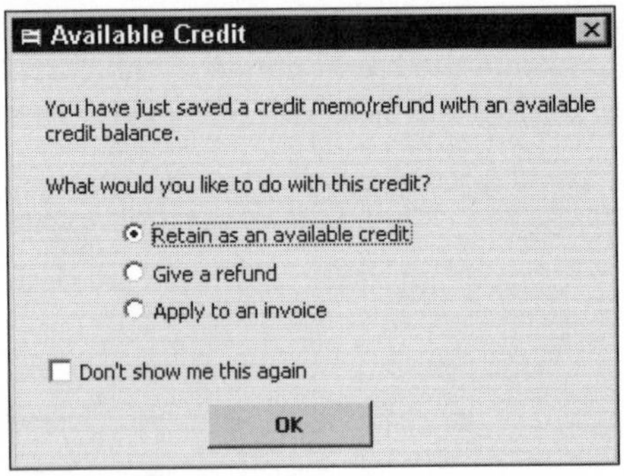

Figure 16-10: These options are presented to you every time you save a credit memo.

To view your credit memo, choose Activities ⇨ Create Credit Memos/Refunds. A Create Credit Memos/Refunds screen appears, as previously shown in Figure 16-9.

Applying customer credits to an invoice

If you process a refund or return but do not issue an immediate refund check to the customer, the customer's account will contain a credit. This credit just sits there until you tell QuickBooks what to do with it.

One of the most common ways to "spend" a customer credit is to apply it to one of the customer's other outstanding invoices. To do this, follow these steps:

1. Choose Customers ➪ Receive Payments. The Receive Payments screen appears.
2. Select the customer and job from the Received From list.
3. Click Discounts & Credits, and then the Credits tab. A summary of all applied and unapplied credits for the customer appears as shown in Figure 16-11.
4. Select the credit that you want to apply, and click Done. A credit appears on the invoice.
5. Click Save & Close to accept the payment and close the window.

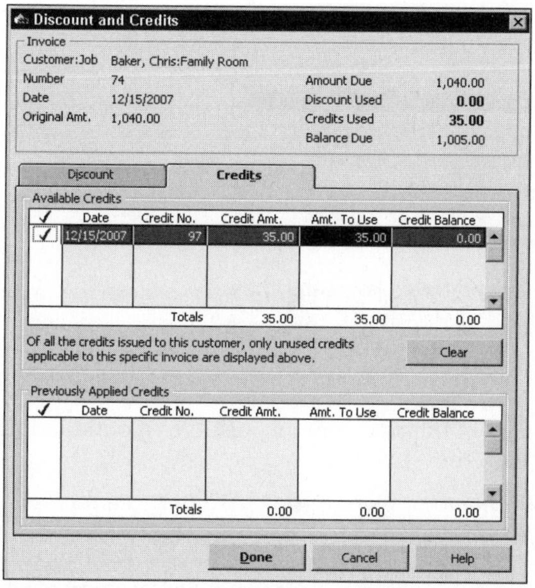

Figure 16-11: QuickBooks tracks all applied and unapplied credits and allows you to apply them to outstanding customer invoices at the appropriate time.

Editing or deleting a credit memo

To edit a credit memo you've previously issued to a customer, follow these steps:

1. Find the credit memo in the Customer or A/R register. Select the credit memo in the register. The credit memo transaction will be of the type CREDMEM.

2. From the Edit menu, choose Edit Credit Memo.
3. Edit and save the credit memo.

Handling overpayments, down payments, and prepayments

Depending on your business, you may sometimes (or always) request a down payment or prepayment from a customer. Occasionally a customer may overpay on an invoice. To handle overpayments and down payments, follow these steps:

1. Enter the payment in the Amount field of the Receive Payments window, as shown in Figure 16-12. If the payment is more than the outstanding invoices, the Payment Credit dialog box shown in Figure 16-12 appears.

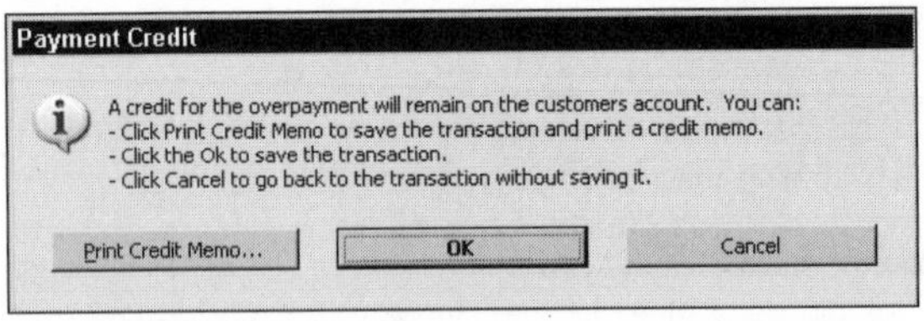

Figure 16-12: When the amount paid is greater than the amount on the invoice, this Payment Credit dialog box appears.

2. Click OK to apply as much of the payment as possible to outstanding invoices and create a record of the credit balance.
3. (Optional) Print a credit memo to give to the customer as a receipt for the down payment or overpayment.

Note The credit memo is for your customer only. It does not become part of your financial records in QuickBooks.

4. Save the payment.

Handling a Bounced Check

Unfortunately, almost all businesses receive a bad check now and then. When you get one, you'll need to inform QuickBooks that the customer's bill is no longer paid, at least until you can recover the money. Bounced checks are actually quite a lot of work to enter in QuickBooks because they involve making a correction to the customer's records plus, in some cases, tacking on a service charge.

When you receive notification from the bank that a check has bounced, you may want to try putting it through again — perhaps the customer's account balance dipped temporarily and the funds are available now.

If that doesn't work, you need to record the bounced check in QuickBooks. This is a multistep process. You need to record the service charge that the bank charged you as a debit to your bank account; then, you reissue the customer invoice and bill the customer for both the original amount and the service charges.

Set up QuickBooks to track bad checks

If you have not done it yet, now is a good time to set up a special Item in QuickBooks for bad-check handling. This is a one-time process. To set up the special Item to track bad checks, start with the Items List (Lists ➪ Items List) and create two Items.

To create the two new Items needed to record a bad check and the bad-check charges you assess, follow these steps:

1. Go to Lists ➪ Items List. Click the Items menu button, and choose New.
2. Create an Other Charge Item and call it **Bad Check**.
3. In the Amount field, leave a 0 amount.
4. From the Tax Code list, choose None.
5. In the Account field, choose your bank account. Click Next.
6. Create a second Other Charge Item and call it **Bad Chk Chrg** for the service charge you assess customers for bounced checks. Use this item when you reinvoice the customer to recover the service charge.
7. In the Amount field, leave a 0 amount.
8. From the Tax Code list, choose None.
9. In the Account field, choose an income account, such as Returned Check Charges. If the account doesn't exist, set it up now.
10. Click OK.

Now that you've created the Items you need for handling bounced checks, your next step is to enter the bad-check charges in your checking account, which you do in the following section. (You use the new accounts you set up a bit later in the process.)

Recording bank charges for a bounced check

Unfortunately, most banks will charge you some sort of fee when they must charge your account for the bad check of one of your customers. Not only is this an unwanted cost, it is extra work to account for the bad-check fee. To record your bank's service charges for a bad check, follow these steps:

1. Go to Banking ⇨ Use Register, and then select the account and click OK. Click a blank transaction.
2. In the blank transaction, enter the charge as **NSF Fee**, using the QuickBooks QuickAdd feature to create this new Item, if necessary. (Also remember to delete the check number for this transaction.)
3. Enter the bank charge amount in the Payment column.
4. In the account field, enter your Returned Check Charges account, enter a memo if necessary, and then click Record.

Recording a credit memo to back out the original sale and write off a bad debt

After determining whether you are likely to collect on the check in the future, you may want to back out the original sale that you recorded. This may give a truer picture of your company's actual performance and sales. To back out a transaction, follow these steps:

1. From the Customers menu, choose Create Credit Memo/Refunds.
2. Enter all of the Items from the original Invoice or Sales Receipt. Include the Sales Rep and Sales Tax if applicable.
3. Enter the Bad Check Other Charge Item as a negative amount.

Note: The amount entered must match the total of all the Items on the credit memo and result in a credit memo with a 0 total.

Recharging the customer and applying a bad-check charge

Next, you reinvoice the customer. Rather than charging the customer for the same Item again, you charge the customer for the Bad Check Item that you set up earlier in this section. That Bad Check Item automatically enters a debit in your checking account, compensating for the fact that the bounced check did not get deposited. You can also charge the customer for an additional Item, the Bad Chk Chrg Item that you also set up earlier. Using this Item, you can make the customer pay your bank service charge, plus an additional charge to compensate you for your time and trouble. Follow these steps:

1. Choose Customers ➪ Create Invoices, and start a new invoice for the customer. For the date, enter the date on which the bank reversed the deposit.
2. For the first Item, choose the Bad Check Item you set up earlier. In the Amount field, enter the amount of the original check.
3. Next, enter a Bad Chk Chrg Item. For the amount, enter the bank service charge you paid plus any additional charge you want to tack on ($20 is an acceptable amount to charge).
4. In the Terms field, set the invoice terms to Due on Receipt, if it is not already set for that.
5. (Optional) Enter the original invoice's invoice number for your own reference in the Memo field.
6. (Optional) Print the invoice now by clicking Print, or click the To Be Printed check box to print it later. If you see a message about buying preprinted forms, click OK to move past it.
7. Click OK to close the window.

Making Deposits

When you receive payments, you can either record them as deposits directly into an account or group them with other undeposited funds for later deposit. The former is certainly less work, but it is not quite truthful — the money is not actually deposited until you physically make the trip to the bank. The latter, while it requires an extra step in QuickBooks to record the deposits, involves more meticulous record keeping and eliminates any possibility of confusion over whether "deposited" funds have actually been taken to the bank or not.

Depositing money from sales

Your undeposited funds wait in a special account by that name in QuickBooks for you to take them to the bank. Follow these steps to make the transfer from your QuickBooks' Undeposited Funds account to your checking account (or other bank account where you deposit funds):

Note

Using the Undeposited Funds account also makes reconciling your checkbook easier. Without it, every check shows as a separate deposit when, in reality, you received and posted a bunch of individual checks and then took the total to the bank.

1. Choose Banking ➪ Make Deposits. If you have any payments to deposit, the Payments to Deposit window appears (see Figure 16-13).

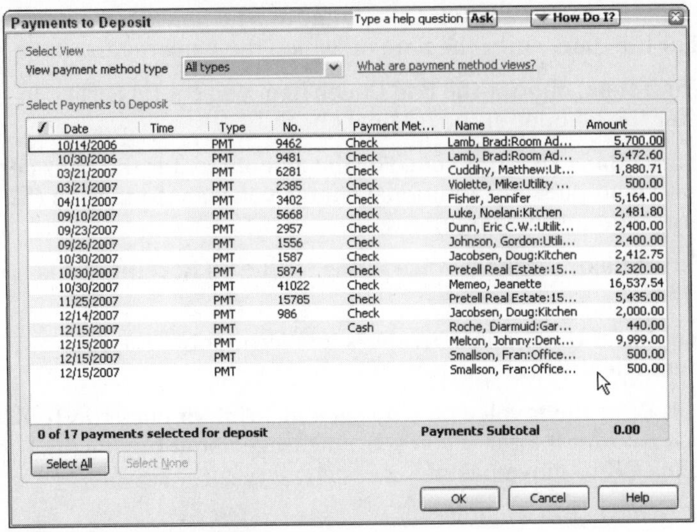

Figure 16-13: All undeposited payment money appears in the Payments to Deposit window.

Tip

If you do not have any undeposited funds, the Make Deposits window appears instead. You can click the Previous button from that screen to view a list of the payments that were deposited in the last deposit you made.

2. Click the check mark column to place a check mark next to each payment that you want to deposit. Or, to select all the listed payments, click the Select All button.
3. Click Next. The Make Deposits window appears with the selected payments listed (see Figure 16-14).

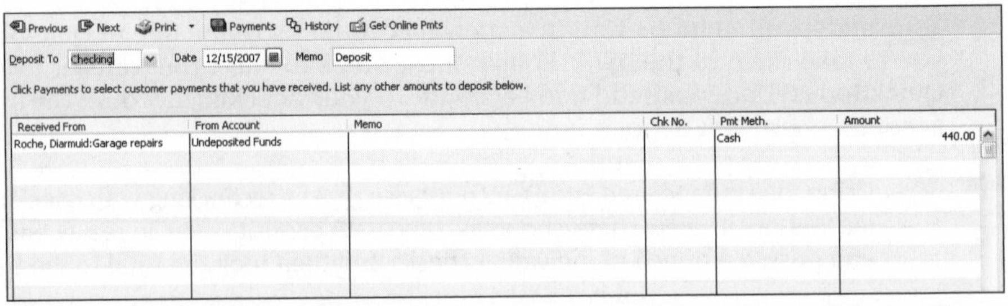

Figure 16-14: Confirm that you want to deposit these payments, and choose the account in which to deposit them.

4. Click OK in the Payments to Deposit window.

Tip

You can reopen the Payments to Deposit window by clicking the Payments button in the Make Deposits window.

5. Choose the appropriate bank account from the Deposit To drop-down list (for example, Checking).
6. Confirm that the date in the Date field is correct.
7. (Optional) Add a memo describing the transaction or anything notable about it.
8. Click the OK button.

You may sometimes want to deposit some payments to one bank account and some payments to another. No problem — just choose only the ones you want to go into the first bank account in step 2, and then choose that account in step 4. Then repeat the entire procedure, choosing the payments for the second deposit in step 2 and the other bank account in step 4.

Depositing other money

Sometimes you may have extra money to deposit that does not correspond to a particular payment. Perhaps you got an unexpected refund or rebate (remember that $20 you got for sending in 12 proof-of-purchase seals for those ink cartridges?). To deposit that money, make a manual entry at the bottom of the Make Deposits screen, as follows:

1. Choose Banking ⇨ Make Deposits.
2. Click below the last Item on the Make Deposits list to start a new line.
3. In the Received From field, open the drop-down list and choose the person or vendor that you received the payment from, if known. If not, choose some generic name such as Other Deposit. (Create a new Other Name Item for it if you have to.)
4. In the From Account field, enter the account where you want QuickBooks to track the money. (Use Other Income if there's no particular account appropriate for it.)
5. Enter information about the money in the Memo field if appropriate. This could include a check number, a payment method, or a note about the source of the money (such as Ink Cartridge Rebate).
6. Enter the amount of the extra deposit in the Amount field.
7. Finish the deposit normally by clicking Save & Close.

Editing or deleting a deposit

To edit a deposit after you have already made it, you must edit the register for the Undeposited Funds account. The Undeposited Funds account acts as a holding account, similar to holding money in a drawer until you make a deposit to your financial institution. When you delete a payment from QuickBooks, you need to start by editing the original transaction that flowed through the Undeposited Funds account. Follow these steps:

1. Go to Lists ➪ Chart of Accounts and open the Undeposited Funds register, by double-clicking on this account. (This account appears near the top of the Chart of Accounts, grouped with other asset accounts.)
2. In the register, select the deposit that contains the payment you want to edit or delete as shown in Figure 16-15.
3. Click the Edit Transactions button.
4. In the Make Deposits window, select the line containing the payment you want to edit or delete.

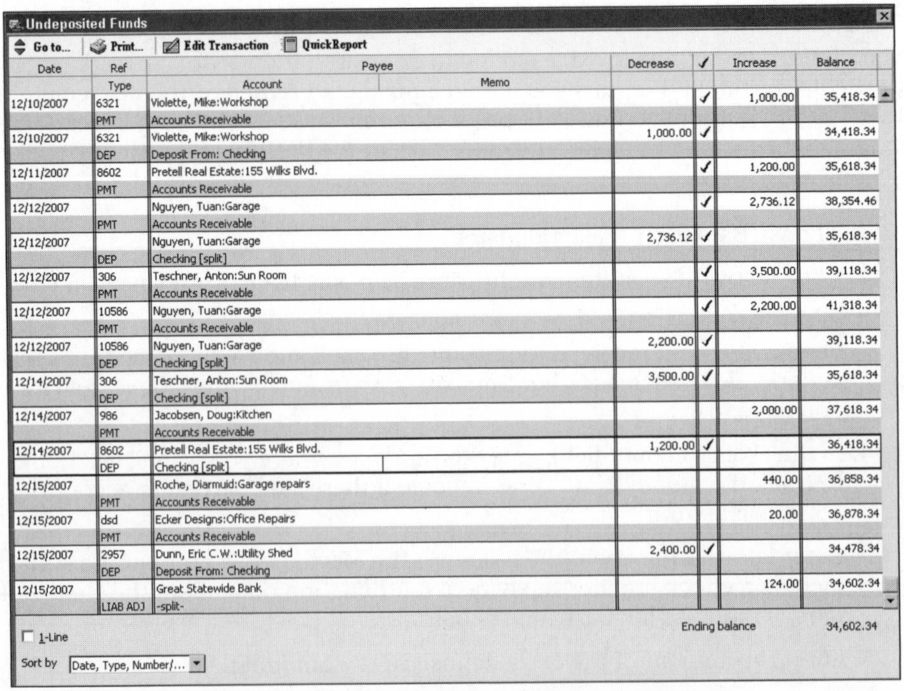

Undeposited Funds
Go to... Print... Edit Transaction QuickReport
Date Ref Payee Decrease ✓ Increase Balance
Type Account Memo
12/10/2007 6321 Violette, Mike:Workshop ✓ 1,000.00 35,418.34
PMT Accounts Receivable
12/10/2007 6321 Violette, Mike:Workshop 1,000.00 ✓ 34,418.34
DEP Deposit From: Checking
12/11/2007 8602 Pretell Real Estate:155 Wilks Blvd. ✓ 1,200.00 35,618.34
PMT Accounts Receivable
12/12/2007 Nguyen, Tuan:Garage ✓ 2,736.12 38,354.46
PMT Accounts Receivable
12/12/2007 Nguyen, Tuan:Garage 2,736.12 ✓ 35,618.34
DEP Checking [split]
12/12/2007 306 Teschner, Anton:Sun Room ✓ 3,500.00 39,118.34
PMT Accounts Receivable
12/12/2007 10586 Nguyen, Tuan:Garage ✓ 2,200.00 41,318.34
PMT Accounts Receivable
12/12/2007 10586 Nguyen, Tuan:Garage 2,200.00 ✓ 39,118.34
DEP Checking [split]
12/14/2007 306 Teschner, Anton:Sun Room 3,500.00 ✓ 35,618.34
DEP Checking [split]
12/14/2007 986 Jacobsen, Doug:Kitchen 2,000.00 37,618.34
PMT Accounts Receivable
12/14/2007 8602 Pretell Real Estate:155 Wilks Blvd. 1,200.00 ✓ 36,418.34
DEP Checking [split]
12/15/2007 Roche, Diarmuid:Garage repairs 440.00 36,858.34
PMT Accounts Receivable
12/15/2007 dsd Ecker Designs:Office Repairs 20.00 36,878.34
PMT Accounts Receivable
12/15/2007 2957 Dunn, Eric C.W.:Utility Shed 2,400.00 ✓ 34,478.34
DEP Deposit From: Checking
12/15/2007 Great Statewide Bank 124.00 34,602.34
LIAB ADJ -split-
1-Line
Ending balance 34,602.34
Sort by Date, Type, Number/...

Figure 16-15: Edit deposits using the Undeposited Funds register.

5. From the Edit menu, choose Delete Deposit. QuickBooks deletes the payment from the deposit. The payment still exists in your QuickBooks records — it's just undeposited. QuickBooks puts the money back into Undeposited Funds.
6. Save the deposit. Clicking Save & Close or Save & New in the Make Deposits window records the deposit without the payment you've just deleted.
7. Edit or delete the original payment transaction.
8. After editing a payment, you can redeposit it using the Make Deposits window.

Generating Deposit Reports

QuickBooks provides several reports that help you keep track of your deposits. You can print a simple Deposit Summary or a complex Deposit Detail record that summarizes deposits by customer and job (or by any other category that you specify).

Printing a Deposit Summary

The simplest deposit report is a Deposit Summary, which is a list of all the payments in the deposit. It's not really a report — it's just a printout of what's on your Make Deposits list. It shows the check number, the payment method, from whom the check was received, the memo, and the amount, and it provides a grand total for the deposit. It's handy for reference in filling out your bank deposit slip, for example. To print it, simply click the Print button at the top of the Make Deposits window (shown previously in Figure 16-14). Tired of filling out deposit slips? You can save time at the bank by using preprinted deposit slips that you can purchase from Intuit. These work directly with QuickBooks, so you do not have to handwrite your bank deposit slip each time. (Intuit guarantees that any bank accepts its slips.) Call 800-433-8810 or visit `http://www.intuitmarket.com`.

Creating a Deposit Detail report

The Deposit Detail report shows all the payments deposited during a certain period of time, grouped by customer. Unlike the Make Deposit list, which shows only one deposit, this report summarizes information from all deposits. You can use it to see how much money you have received and deposited from a particular customer and to see how much money you have deposited in total.

To create the report, choose Banking ➪ Reports ➪ Banking ➪ Deposit Detail. It appears in a preview window, as shown in Figure 16-16. You can customize it to show different dates, customers, formatting — the works. See Chapter 30 for details.

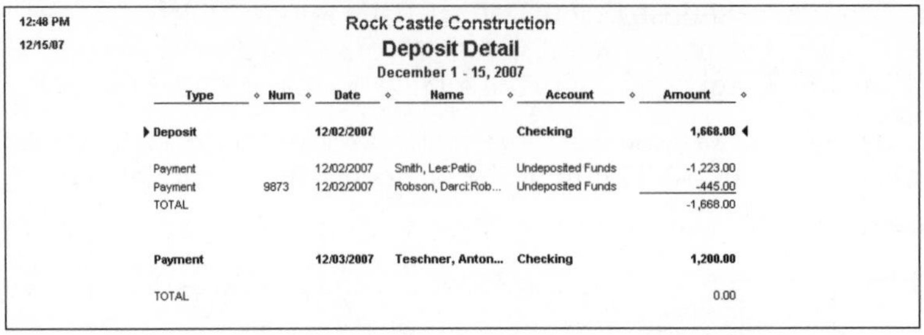
12:48 PM
12/15/07

Rock Castle Construction
Deposit Detail
December 1 - 15, 2007

Type	Num	Date	Name	Account	Amount
Deposit		**12/02/2007**		**Checking**	**1,668.00**
Payment		12/02/2007	Smith, Lee:Patio	Undeposited Funds	-1,223.00
Payment	9873	12/02/2007	Robson, Darci:Rob...	Undeposited Funds	-445.00
TOTAL					-1,668.00
Payment		**12/03/2007**	**Teschner, Anton...**	**Checking**	**1,200.00**
TOTAL					0.00

Figure 16-16: The Deposit Detail report provides detailed information about which customer accounts made up what portion of your deposits.

Aging Accounts Receivable

Aging means keeping track of outstanding invoices and unpaid bills. A/R aging refers specifically to the money that others owe you, which is the subject of this chapter. Accounts payable (A/P) aging is discussed in Chapter 17.

One of the biggest mistakes a business owner can make is to not consider A/R aging in business decisions. To continue to work for a customer who has not paid you in 90 days isn't good financial management, nor is passively waiting an extra 30 days for each payment from a customer without sending a reminder. Late receivables are money that you don't have in your pocket!

QuickBooks offers several very helpful reports that show you exactly what is due and what is overdue. You should review these reports frequently (at least every month) and take action based on what you find.

Viewing Accounts Receivable reports

Any of the A/R reports can be viewed from the Reports ➪ Customers & Receivables menu and can be customized as explained in Chapter 30.

Many of the reports break receivables into aging categories: Current, 1–30 (days past due), 31–60, 61–90, and >90. You can take action on accounts based on these categories. For example, you might create a mail-merge letter, as you learned in Chapter 9, to send to all customers who have a balance that is past due by more than 60 days.

To view the various A/R reports available in QuickBooks, go to Reports ➪ Customers & Receivables as shown in Figure 16-17.

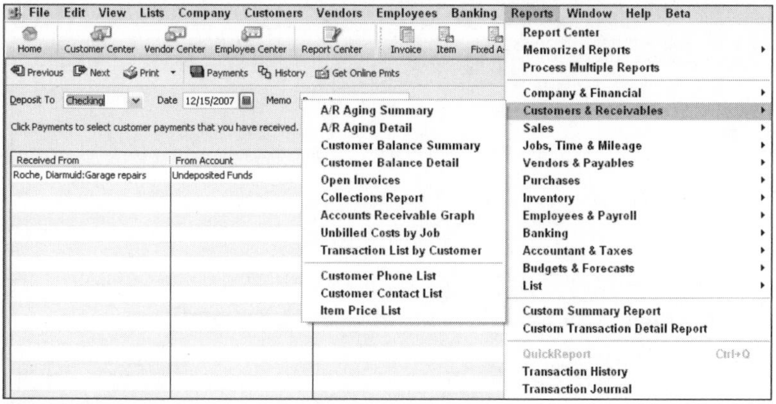

Figure 16-17: QuickBooks offers a wide array of reports to help you track your A/R activity.

The A/R reports available in QuickBooks are as follows:

✦ **A/R Aging Summary:** This report lists all customers and jobs and shows how much they have due in each aging category. It shows at a glance which customers are tardy and by how much.

✦ **A/R Aging Detail:** This report lists every outstanding invoice, grouped by category. For example, it first lists all the current invoices, then those past due by 1–30 days, then those past due by 31–60 days, and so on. It gives you a picture of how much income is overdue in each category.

✦ **Customer Balance Summary:** This report shows each customer who has an outstanding balance and what the balance is. It's not all that helpful for A/R aging because this report doesn't tell you whether an amount is current or 90 days past due. However, you can double-click an amount to open a mini-report that lists all the invoices regarded as open invoices.

✦ **Customer Balance Detail:** This report is the same as the Customer Balance Summary except that each invoice is listed. Unlike similar reports, this one does not show aging numbers, so it is not the best choice for tracking A/R.

✦ **Collections Report:** This report shows all the invoices with at least one day of aging, grouped by customer, with the customer contact information (address and phone number) included so that you can easily contact the customer to inquire about the payment.

✦ **Accounts Receivable Graph:** This report gives you a visual, graphical representation of your accounts receivable, as shown in Figure 16-18.

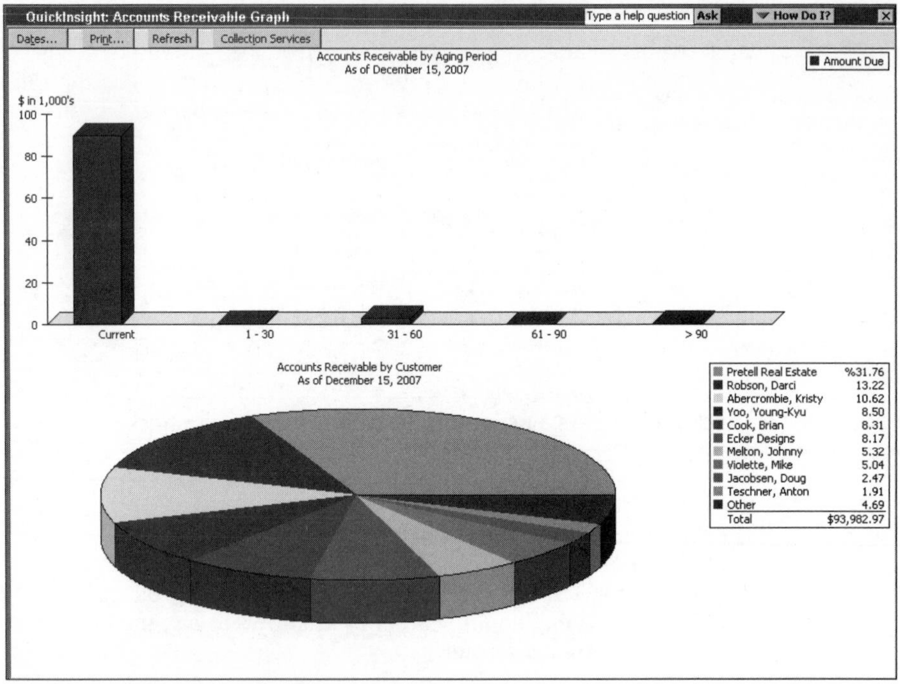

Figure 16-18: An Accounts Receivable graph.

✦ **Unbilled Costs by Job:** This report is not really an A/R report so much as it is an invoicing reminder. It lists all expenses you have incurred on specific jobs for which you have not charged the customer.

✦ **Transaction List by Customer:** This report lists all customers and their transactions with your company during the relevant time-period identified on the report.

Tip

On almost all QuickBooks reports, whenever the mouse pointer is a magnifying glass with a Z in the middle, you can use QuickZoom to zoom in on a detail. QuickZoom opens a separate report with more information about the line or total that you clicked on.

Taking action on overdue accounts

Armed with your aging information, you can make business decisions to ensure your continued financial success. This section gives you some ideas for collecting the money owed to you — and improving your overall collection ratio — while preserving customer goodwill whenever possible.

Use the QuickBooks Write Letters feature

After you've done the work and are waiting for the payment, it's important to keep in contact with the customer. The more personal contact you have with them, the guiltier they may feel about not paying you.

Tip

The new Write Letters feature in QuickBooks provides an array of effective collection letters that can be sent to customers that you select from your customer list. Chapter 9 discusses this feature in detail.

Most businesses make a habit of sending out collection letters to all overdue accounts. These are effective because they remind the customer that you are still waiting without being intrusive. You will want at least two levels of letter — the first one friendly, the second one with some teeth. Such letters often spur customers into making payment. You may even want to place phone calls to seriously delinquent customers.

Screen out bad customers

A customer who doesn't pay you is not a customer worth having. But what about a slow-paying customer? If a customer regularly provides a significant amount of business and always pays eventually, you may decide that you want to keep his or her business, even if you have to wait 60 days or more for payments.

Another option is to place certain customers on a cash-only plan, where payment is due in full on receipt of the product or service. You can send a polite letter to such customers explaining the change in policy. If you don't want to make the customer feel like he or she is being singled out, you can mask the insult by making up customer "classes" and saying that all accounts in this customer's particular class are being made cash-only. A letter similar to this one would do:

> Dear <Customer>:
>
> Our company is able to give you the best in service at a very low price because our profit margin is extremely thin. We pass along our savings to you. Because of this, when customer accounts go unpaid for more than 30 days, our company's finances are severely strained.
>
> To ensure our continued solvency, we have been forced to convert all of our Class 12 residential and commercial customers to Due on Receipt terms. Technicians performing your service will be collecting payment at the end of each session. No credit will be extended.
>
> We hope that our top-notch service and low prices will continue to keep your business and that this new policy will not cause undue hardship for your organization.
>
> Sincerely,
>
> <Your Name>

Negotiate partial payments

You should always be willing to take partial payments over time. A customer who pays you $25 a week is at least making a good-faith effort; taking the customer to court would eat up time and money and might not result in a better payment schedule.

If a customer requests more time to make payments, get the payment plan in writing. Prepare a schedule of payments, including the amounts and dates due, and charge interest on the outstanding balance. Include a note saying that the entire amount is payable immediately if the customer misses or is late on any payments. Ask the customer to sign the schedule to show his or her agreement. That way, if you do end up going to court, you have a binding contract.

Cross-Reference

See Chapter 33 for more information on using QuickBooks to create customer contracts.

Courts and collection agencies

If you cannot get the money by friendly warnings and negotiation, you have two options: small-claims court or collection agencies. Neither is particularly appealing.

Small-claims courts are slightly different in each state, but in most states, you can sue for up to $5,000. You have to appear in court a few times, and there is usually a filing fee of up to $200. You may also have to pay to have the subpoena served to the customer. Small-claims court can eat up a lot of your valuable business time, with trips to the courthouse, consultations with lawyers, and time spent organizing written evidence. For a few hundred dollars, it may not be worth the trouble.

You can find collection agencies in the phone book for any city; additionally, QuickBooks offers collection services. These organizations specialize in recovering money from customers who won't pay. They generally have a minimum number of accounts you must give them to work on, and a minimum balance level for the accounts. A collection agency is usually not willing to take on a single customer account for collection; they want you to establish a relationship with them through multiple accounts. Some smaller agencies may be more flexible. A collection agency typically takes a percentage of the recovered amount as its fee.

Tip

For information about QuickBooks collection agency services, click the Collection Services button that appears at the top of any A/R report window.

With a small amount due from a single customer, it is often best to just write it off as a bad debt. The fees involved in pursuing the other remedies make them impractical.

For large balances on single accounts, litigation is the best bet even though you have to pay attorney fees and court costs.

Note

When writing customer contracts, try to include a clause stating that the customer will pay any legal fees incurred in collecting past-due amounts from them. Such a clause may not hold up in small-claims court, but it gives you a better shot at recovering some of your costs than if you had no contract.

For medium or large groups of past-due accounts, a collection agency is the way to go because you save the time involved in tracking the money down yourself.

Improve your future collection ratio

Many businesses can improve their accounts receivable collection dramatically just by following a few simple guidelines:

- **Bill promptly.** Send a bill within 10 days of a job's completion. If you wait 60 days to bill, clients get the idea that you are not particularly eager to be paid, and they may put off (and possibly forget) the payment. They may also forget what a benefit to them your services were, and be less cheerful about paying.
- **Review your A/R aging information frequently**, as explained earlier in this chapter, and take the appropriate actions based on your review. Don't be afraid to insist on money that is due you.
- **Consider dropping habitually delinquent accounts.** If a customer has to be prodded to pay you each time, the customer may be more trouble than he or she is worth. Don't be afraid to be choosy about who you work for.
- **Require a down payment or deposit when accepting a job.** Money up front "commits" the customer to the project and puts the customer in the correct frame of mind for paying you promptly in the future.
- **Have the customer review and sign invoices.** When you present an invoice to the client in person, have two copies handy. Ask the client to sign both copies. Keep one copy for your records and give the client one copy from which to pay you. Signing something makes a client feel more committed to it. Also, if you have to take the client to court to recover the money, the fact that the client signed the invoice means that the client agreed to the charges and is obligated to pay.

Handling Barter (Noncash) Payments

According to the Internal Revenue Code, a special kind of transaction, known as a *barter*, occurs when any two persons agree to a reciprocal exchange of goods or services and carry out that exchange without using money. In a barter transaction between persons who are dealing with each other at arm's length, it is a fundamental principle that each of those persons considers that the value of whatever is received is at least equal to the value of whatever is given up in exchange.

QuickBooks requires you to create both a barter bank account and a barter payment Item before entering barter transactions. To create a barter bank account, follow these steps:

1. From the Lists menu, choose Chart of Accounts.
2. From the Accounts menu button, choose New.
3. In the Type field, choose Bank.
4. In the Name field, enter Barter (or something similar).
5. Click OK.

To create a barter payment Item, follow these steps:

1. From the Lists menu, choose Items List.
2. From the Items menu button, choose New.
3. From the Type field, select Payment.
4. In the Name field, enter a name like Barter Pay.
5. For Payment Method, create a new method by choosing Add New from the drop-down menu. A payment window appears.
6. Set up for deposit directly into your barter bank account by selecting the Deposit option and selecting the barter bank account from the drop-down menu.
7. Click OK.

To enter a barter transaction, follow these steps:

1. Create the invoice by entering the Items that represent the services or products this customer received.
2. On the next blank line of the invoice, enter your barter payment Item.
3. (Optional) In the Description area, add information about the barter arrangements.
4. The amount of the invoice must equal the fair market value of the trade.
5. Save the invoice.

Summary

Accounts receivables are the lifeline of your business. To ensure success, you must induce your customers to pay you promptly and take action to minimize the losses from customers who do not. This chapter taught you how to process payment transactions when they arrive and how to deposit those funds in the bank. You also learned about tracking your A/R aging and how to pursue delinquent accounts. You learned the following in this chapter:

- To apply a customer payment to an outstanding invoice by using the Customers ➪ Receive Payments command. Make sure you apply the payment to the correct job for the customer.
- To give a customer a refund or process a return by using Customers ➪ Create Credit Memos/Refunds.
- To process a bounced check by subtracting any bank charges from your checking account and then recharging the customer by using Bad Check and Bad Chk Chrg Items instead of the original invoice Items. You can set up these Bad Check Items in your Item List yourself if they do not already exist.
- To track A/R aging by creating an aging report. There are many A/R reports that come with QuickBooks. You can access them from the Reports ➪ Customers & Receivables menu.
- To handle the bulk of your collections difficulties yourself by developing a series of progressively more serious collection letters and sending them to delinquent customers. You might also investigate local collection agency services and legal remedies.
- To record barter transactions.

✦ ✦ ✦

CHAPTER 17

Purchase Orders and Accounts Payable

✦ ✦ ✦ ✦

In This Chapter

Creating purchase orders

Entering bills to be paid

Paying bills

Memorizing transactions

Setting payment reminders

✦ ✦ ✦ ✦

Every business has expenses. Your business expenses may include inventory, fixed assets, supplies, services, or subcontractors. In addition to carefully tracking these expenses in QuickBooks so that you can view and analyze them, you need to save paper receipts to document the transactions you've recorded for the IRS. Hopefully, you'll never be audited, but maintaining good QuickBooks records and holding on to your receipts should ensure that you will emerge unscathed in the event that you are.

Tools for Tracking Expenses

QuickBooks is a complete and integrated accounting system that tracks and cross-tracks your expenses in a variety of ways that facilitate accurate reporting. The following are the main tracking tools and expense accounting features in QuickBooks:

✦ **Accounts:** During the Interview (covered in Chapter 2), you will set up expense accounts to track various categories of expenses that will ultimately offset revenue to determine your profit or loss for an accounting period.

✦ **Classes:** Classes provide a way for you to logically track income and expenses for various activities and segments in your company You can learn more about tracking expenses with classes in Chapter 28.

✦ **Customer and job:** QuickBooks allows you to track expenses separately for each customer and job as previously discussed in Chapter 9.

- **Tax tracking:** QuickBooks allows you to track and associate expenses with specific lines on your income tax form. You activate this feature during the Interview discussed in Chapter 2.
- **Purchase orders:** Purchase orders help you track inventory, supplies, and services that you sell and use in your business. (A purchase order is often referred to as a *PO*.)

Entering Purchase Orders

You use purchase orders to maintain a record of orders for goods and services placed and authorized by your business. As goods are delivered or services are performed or delivered, they are matched against outstanding purchase orders. There are several good reasons for your business to use purchase orders:

- If you maintain inventory records in QuickBooks, purchase orders provide essential records about what you have ordered and when you can expect to receive it.
- The use of purchase orders prevents duplication in the ordering process; without a purchase order, an employee might notice that you are out of something and place an order for something that has already been ordered.
- Purchase orders help show how much money you have committed to purchases that you have not yet received invoices for. If you don't use purchase orders, your QuickBooks system will not show that the money is earmarked for anything until the invoice arrives and is entered.

You can create a QuickBooks purchase order by following these steps:

1. Go to Vendors ⇨ Create Purchase Orders or click the Purchase Orders icon in the Vendors section of the Navigator screen (which is also the Home screen). The Create Purchase Orders window shown in Figure 17-1 appears.
2. Select a vendor from the Vendor drop-down list, or add a new vendor to the list if necessary.
3. Select the Item ordered from the Item drop-down list, or add a new Item to the list if necessary.
4. Enter the quantity and rate (cost) of each Item in the appropriate column. QuickBooks automatically calculates the total amounts. Verify the information in the Date and Ship To fields.

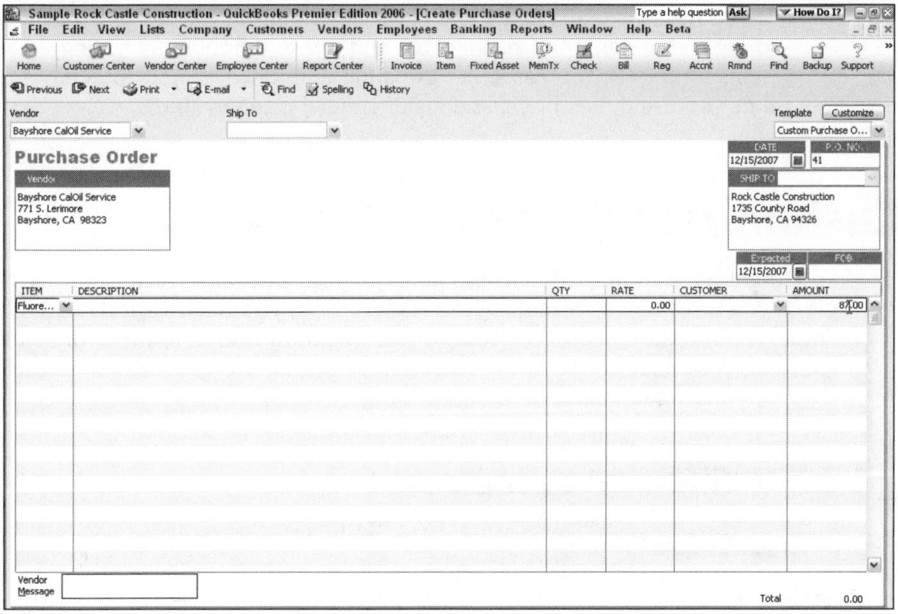

Figure 17-1: Create a new purchase order by using this window.

5. (Optional) If your business keeps track of FOB, enter it in the FOB field.

Tip

FOB stands for Free On Board, which refers to the terms regarding the transportation of the merchandise. It has no effect on the bookkeeping in QuickBooks. You can use it to indicate where the merchandise is being shipped from, if you find that information useful.

6. If you want to ship goods directly to a customer, select the customer address from the Ship To drop-down list. Otherwise, QuickBooks will assume, by default, that you want the goods shipped directly to you. (This optional drop-shipping address is a new feature unique to the latest version of the software.)
7. To record the purchase order, click the Save & Close or Save & New button.

Tip

You can edit a purchase order you have previously prepared by clicking the Previous button.

You cannot include sales tax on your purchase order, but when the invoice arrives, you can indicate on the Enter Bills screen what portion of the invoice's total was sales tax. You learn more about this in the section "Entering Bills" later in this chapter.

Tip

Set up miscellaneous Items and Items describing categories of goods and services to keep your Items list manageable and to avoid frequently having to create new Items on-the-fly. You can enter the applicable price on your purchase order each time you use these miscellaneous or general category Items.

Customizing Purchase Orders

You might want to add some extra fields to your purchase order template. For example, if you have multiple employees issuing POs, you may want to add a field for the employee initials. QuickBooks allows you to add or omit a number of fields from your standard purchase order form. You can use one of the other fields in the Customize Template dialog box shown in Figure 17-2.

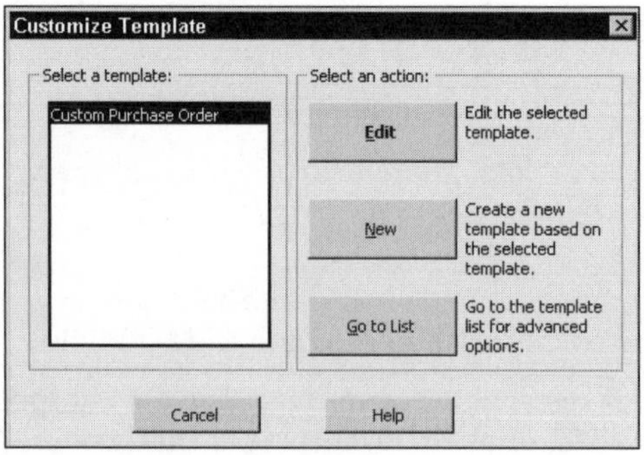

Figure 17-2: You can customize and edit your purchase orders.

To customize your purchase order, follow these steps:

1. Click the Customize button in the upper right-hand corner of the Purchase Order window (previously shown in Figure 17-1). The Customize Template dialog box appears (as previously shown in Figure 17-2).
2. Click Edit. The Customize Purchase Order dialog box appears, as shown in Figure 17-3.

Cross-Reference

See Chapter 15 for full details on customizing templates.

Tip

You can also modify fonts and layouts and add a logo.

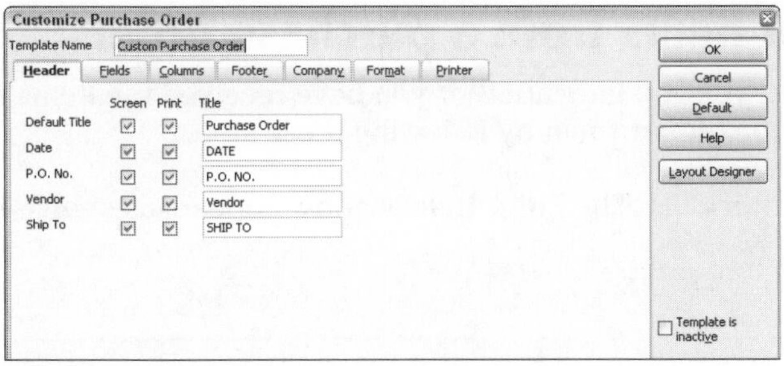

Figure 17-3: Options for editing purchase orders.

Entering Bills

Usually you receive a bill along with a shipment of merchandise or when a service is performed. Sometimes, however, you may receive the service or merchandise first and the bill for it later.

Tip

In QuickBooks, *bills* are invoices that you receive from someone else. Do not confuse them with *invoices*, which are bills that you send to receive payment.

When you receive a bill, you have two choices. You can pay it immediately, or you can schedule it for payment later. If you want to pay a bill immediately, you do not have to enter it as a bill. You can simply write a check from the Write Checks window, as explained in Chapter 25. If you have issued a purchase order when you write the check to the vendor, you are asked whether you want to apply the payment to the PO.

On the other hand, if you want to schedule the payment for later, use the Enter Bills window. Then later, when it's time to pay the bill, you use the Pay Bills window, as described later in this chapter.

When do you pay the bill that you've entered? It depends on the bill's terms. Just as you specify terms on the invoices you send out (see Chapter 15), so do other businesses. The bills you receive will probably include terms such as Net 30, 2% 10 Net 30, Due on Receipt, or some other designation. It's important to locate the terms on the bill and enter them into QuickBooks as you enter the bill.

Caution

Some businesses make it a policy of taking advantage of any discount offered for quick payment. In other words, if an invoice's terms are 2% 10 Net 30, they will make sure to pay that invoice within 10 days in order to get the 2% discount. Other businesses pay bills once a month, without exception, and it is not worth the small discount to disrupt their system. You must choose for yourself what works best for your business.

Entering a bill for Items from a purchase order

If you use purchase orders, you can indicate that you have received the Items at the same time that you enter the bill for them by following these steps:

1. Choose Vendors ➪ Enter Bills. The Enter Bills window appears as shown in Figure 17-4.

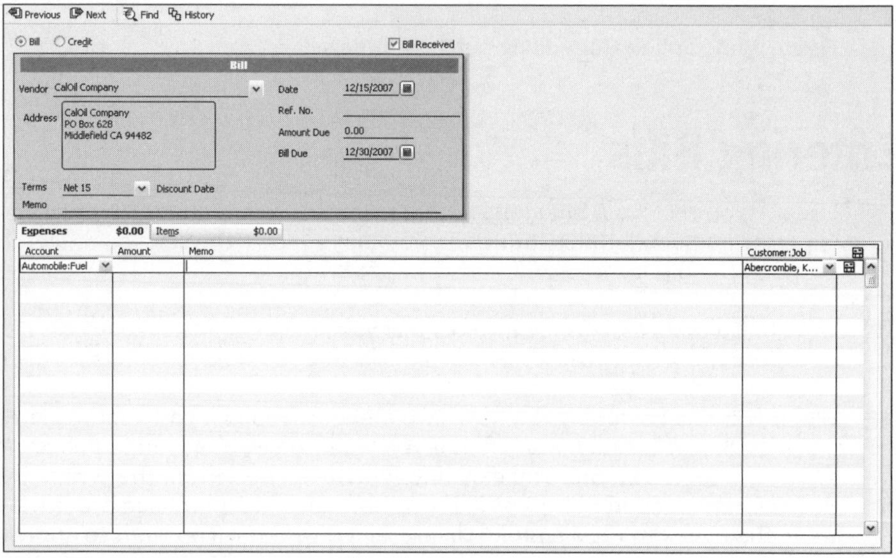

Figure 17-4: Enter bills by using this window.

2. Choose the vendor from the Vendor drop-down list. (The vendor will already be on this list because you had to choose a vendor when you created the PO.)
3. A box appears stating that there are open POs for this vendor. Click Yes to indicate that you want to receive against them.
4. The Open Purchase Orders dialog box then appears. Click to place a check mark next to each PO you want to use and then click OK. The vendor's name and address now appear in the Enter Bills window, and the Items from the POs appear on the Items tab at the bottom.
5. Check the date in the Date field, and if necessary, change it to match the date on the bill.

Caution

Do not change the amount in the Amount Due field. It was transferred from the PO. If it does not match the bill you received, you can make adjustments, as you learn later in these steps.

6. Put the bill number in the Ref. No. field.
7. Choose the terms from the Terms drop-down list. Add new terms using Add New if necessary.
8. If necessary, change the Bill Due date. By default, it is calculated from the Net amount in the terms. If you want to pay a bill that is 2% 10 Net 30, for example, you will want to manually set the Bill Due date for 10 days from today, instead of the 30 days it fills in for you.
9. (Optional) Enter a note in the Memo field if you find it helpful.
10. Click the Item tab and select each received Item.
11. On the Item tab, confirm that all the Items listed are on the bill. If an Item came from the PO but isn't on the bill you received, remove it by clicking its line and then choosing Edit ➪ Delete Line.
12. You are done if the amount shown in the Amount Due line matches the amount of the actual bill. Click Save & Close or Save & New. If the amounts do not match, go to step 13.
13. Click the Expenses tab, and enter any additional charges from the bill (such as shipping charges or sales tax). Choose the appropriate expense account for each additional line from the Account column's drop-down list.

Tip

Make sure that when you're choosing an account for sales tax, you do not use your Sales Tax Payable account. That account is for storing money that you have collected from your own customers before you send it to your tax collection authority in your state or locality. Instead, use the appropriate subaccount under Taxes, such as State, Local, or Federal.

If you are buying the Item for resale but the vendor has charged you sales tax, contact the vendor and inform them that your purchase should be tax-free. You may need to send them documentation to back up your claim.

14. Check the Amount Due field. It should reflect the additional charges you have entered. If it does not, click the Recalculate button.
15. Click OK to record the bill, or click Next to record it and start another one.

Entering a bill without an associated purchase order

If you do not use purchase orders, or if a particular bill is not associated with one, you must enter the bill "from scratch." No Items will be available for transfer from a PO, so you must enter all Items from the bill.

Follow these steps to enter a new bill:

1. Choose Vendors ⇨ Enter Bills. The Enter Bills window appears (previously shown in Figure 17-4).
2. Click the Bill Received check box.
3. Choose the vendor from the Vendor drop-down list, or create a new vendor with Add New if necessary.

Cross-Reference

See Chapter 8 for detailed instructions on creating new vendors.

4. Check the date in the Date field, and change it if necessary to match the date on the bill.
5. Put the bill number in the Ref. No. field.

Note

You do not have to enter anything in the Amount Due field because QuickBooks will calculate it based on the Items and expenses you assign to the bill.

6. Choose the terms from the Terms drop-down list. Add new terms using Add New if necessary.
7. Change the Bill Due date if necessary. By default, QuickBooks calculates this from the Net amount in the terms. If you want to pay a bill that is 2% 10 Net 30, for example, manually set the Bill Due date for 10 days from today, instead of the 30 days it fills in for you.
8. (Optional) Enter a note in the Memo field if you find it helpful.
9. If you are receiving any Items (that is, merchandise that you want to track as inventory), click the Item tab and enter each Item as a separate line. Make sure that the quantities and prices match up with the bill you received.
10. Click the Expenses tab and enter any remaining Items from the bill that do not qualify as "items." These could include services, shipping charges, taxes, and installation charges.

Note

If you are receiving Items that you do not track as inventory in QuickBooks, you can safely enter them as expenses rather than Items. For example, if you received a case of paper towels for use in your office's kitchen, it would be considered an expense rather than an Item.

11. Check the amount in the Amount Due field. If it does not match the bill amount, click the Recalculate button. If it still does not match, check the bill to see what you may have missed entering.

12. When the Amount Due amount matches the bill, click Save & Close to enter it, or click Save & New to enter it and start another bill.

Receiving and paying for Items at the same time

If you pay for Items as soon as you receive them, you can pay by check or credit card or pay online immediately, debiting the correct account when you make your payment. Here's how:

- To pay for Items with a check, go to the Banking menu and select Write Checks.
- To pay for Items with a credit card, go to the Banking menu and choose Record Credit Card Charges, and then choose Enter Credit Card Charges.
- To pay for Items with an online payment, go to the Banking menu and select Write Checks. In the Write Checks window, select the check box for online payment.
- To pay for Items with cash, go to the Banking menu and select Write Checks. Choose your petty cash account from the drop-down list in the Bank Account field.

Receiving Items that arrive ahead of the bill

If Items for which you have created a purchase order arrive ahead of the bill and/or invoice, you can either create an Item receipt and pay for them when the invoice comes or pay for them immediately using the instructions in the previous section.

To record and account for the Items when you receive them, follow these steps:

1. Go to Vendors ⇨ Receive Items. The Create Item Receipts window appears, as shown in Figure 17-5.
2. Choose the vendor from whom you received the Items.
3. Click Yes in the Open POs Exist window.
4. In the Open Purchase Orders window, select each PO that contains the Items you're receiving, and then click OK.
5. In the Create Item Receipts window, make any necessary changes to the line items, such as changing the quantity or cost (or deleting an Item completely from the detail area).
6. Save the Item receipt.

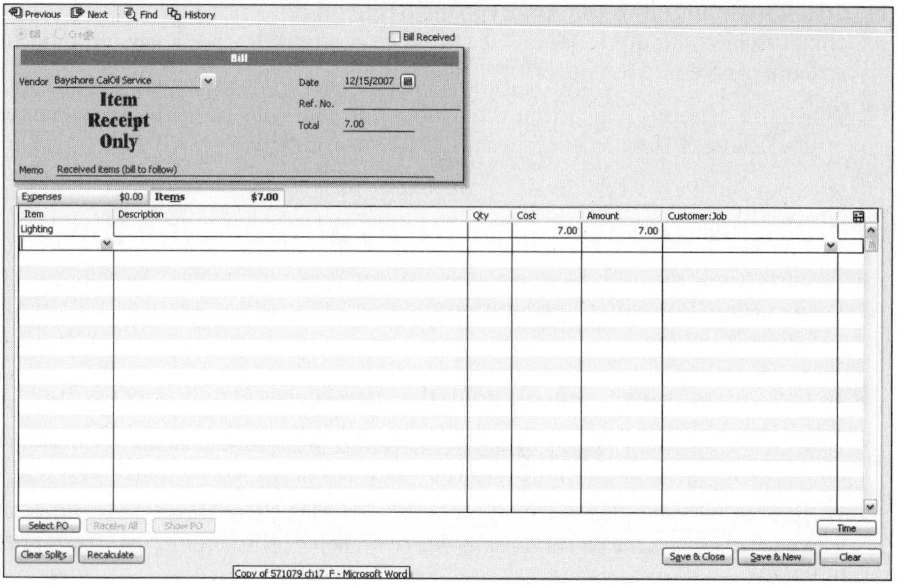

Figure 17-5: Create Item receipts by using this window.

Entering the bill when you receive it

To enter a bill when you receive it, follow these steps:

1. From the Vendors menu, choose Enter Bill for Received Items. The Select Item Receipt window appears, as shown in Figure 17-6.

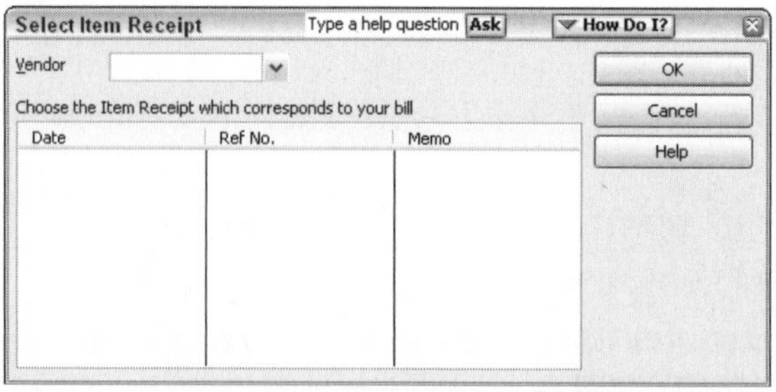

Figure 17-6: You use this window to enter bills when they arrive.

2. In the Select Item Receipt window, enter the vendor name in the Vendor field and press Tab.
3. Click the Item receipt associated with this bill, and then click OK. QuickBooks changes the Item receipt to a bill.
4. If necessary, change the date shown on the bill (the date shown is the date you entered on the Item receipt).
5. Complete the Ref. No., Terms, and Memo fields as necessary.
6. In the detail area of the bill, correct any costs or amounts if necessary.
7. (Optional) Enter any additional expenses, such as freight charges or sales tax.
8. Save the bill.

Receiving Items that arrive with a bill

A common scenario is that goods will arrive with a bill and packing slip. When this is the case, follow these steps:

1. From the Vendor menu, go to Receive Items & Enter Bills to display the Enter Bills window.
2. In the Vendor field, choose the vendor from whom you ordered the Items. At the prompt about receiving against a purchase order for this vendor, click Yes to display the Open Purchase Orders window.
3. In the Open Purchase Orders window, select one or more purchase orders that you are receiving against, and click OK.
4. On the Items tab in the Enter Bills window, verify that the number of Items shown equals the number of Items received.
5. If necessary, edit the quantities to match the shipment.
6. Verify that the costs on the Items tab match the costs on the bill.
7. If necessary, edit the costs to match the bill.
8. To enter shipping charges or taxes not associated with any one Item, click the Expenses tab. In the detail area, enter each charge and associate it with its correct expense account.
9. Verify that the Amount Due field matches the amount of the bill.
10. (Optional) Change the date of the bill.
11. Complete the Ref. No., Terms, and Memo fields as necessary.
12. Save the bill.

Billing a customer for a charge

Sometimes you may want to pass along a charge to one of your customers. For example, if it costs you $100 to rent some equipment for a construction job, you will want to add that cost to the invoice that you send to your customer.

Caution

Don't confuse passing on a charge with selling the customer a product. When you buy a product and then sell it to a customer, you typically mark it up so that you make some profit. When you pass along a cost, you charge the customer only the amount that you were charged.

To pass along a charge on a customer invoice, follow these steps:

1. Go to Customers ➪ Create Invoices and create an invoice for the customer as you normally would.

   See Chapter 15 for more information regarding how to create a customer invoice.

2. Click the appropriate button for Items, Expenses, Time, or Mileage to be added to the invoice form.
3. Click the Time/Costs button at the top of the screen, as shown in Figure 17-7. Choose Billable Time and Costs. The Choose Billable Time and Costs window appears.

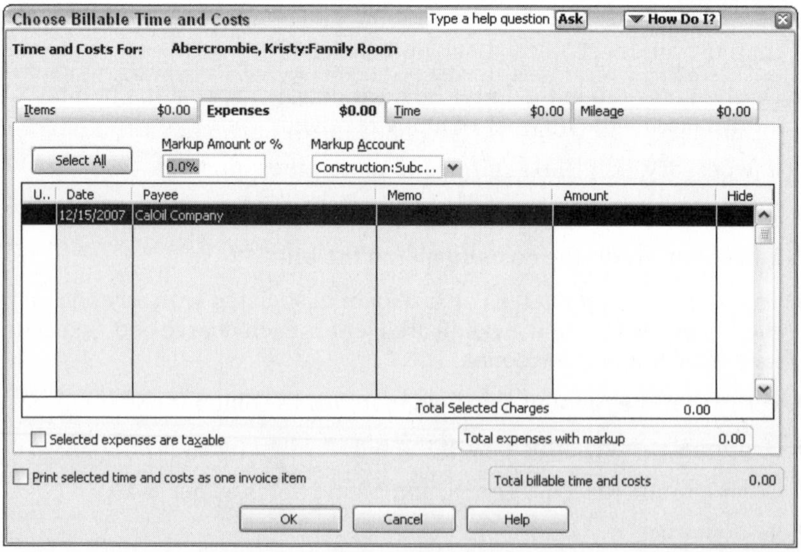

Figure 17-7: You can enter time and costs directly on a customer invoice.

4. Click the Item tab if it is not already displayed.
5. Click the Use column to place a check mark next to the Items to be assigned to that invoice (see Figure 17-8).

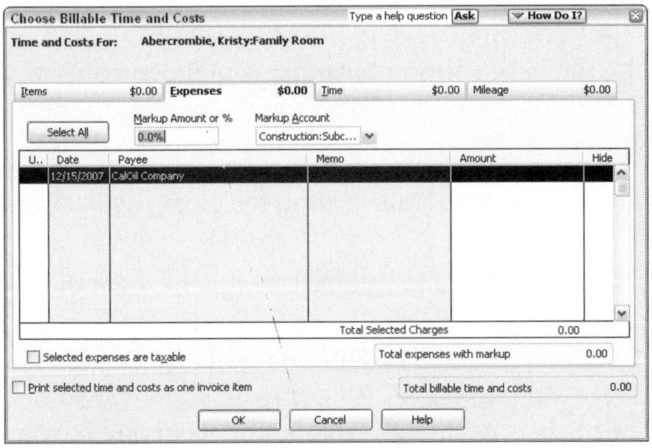

Figure 17-8: Choose which Items should be added to the invoice by placing a check mark next to the Item in the Use column.

6. Click OK. The expense is transferred to the invoice.
7. Complete the invoice normally.

Cross-Reference

For more information about assigning costs to customer invoices, see Chapter 20.

Working with Memorized Bills

Almost every business has bills that they have to pay on a regular basis, such as power, water, and telephone bills. When you memorize a bill with the QuickBooks Memorize feature, you can call up the details whenever you need to pay it again, so you don't have to look up the information each time. The details you can memorize include your account number, the payee's name and address, the usual amount, and more. You can also have QuickBooks remind you when it's time to enter the bill again.

Note

You aren't limited to just memorizing bills to be paid. You can memorize any kind of transaction: checks, invoices, and so forth. The procedure for memorizing them is the same as shown in the following section for a bill.

Memorizing a bill

To memorize a bill, enter the bill as you normally would on the Enter Bills window. When you're done, before you click Save & Close or Save & New, choose Edit ➪ Memorize Bill. The Memorize Transaction dialog box appears (see Figure 17-9).

After naming the transaction, your first task in the Memorize Transaction dialog box is to choose one of the following option buttons, which control how you want to be reminded:

- **Remind Me:** When it's time to enter the bill again, QuickBooks displays a notice in your Reminders window. This is good for most regularly recurring payments.
- **Don't Remind Me:** Nothing special happens. Use this for bills that occur only sporadically, at no particular interval.
- **Automatically Enter:** When it's time to enter the bill again, QuickBooks automatically makes an entry in your Enter Bills screen, so that the bill shows up as needing to be paid. This is especially helpful for recurring payments for which you don't get a monthly bill (for example, monthly insurance payments).

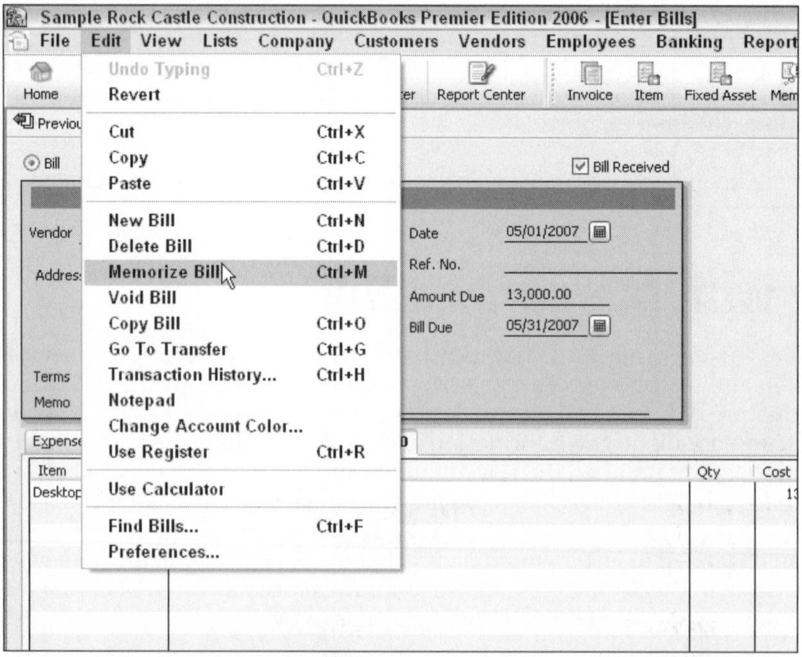

Figure 17-9: Memorize a bill so that you can recall its details whenever you need to pay the same payee again.

If you chose Don't Remind Me, you're done. Click OK.

If you chose Remind Me or Automatically Enter, open the How Often drop-down list and choose a frequency (Weekly, Monthly, and so on). Then, enter the starting date for the recurrence in the Next Date field.

If you chose Remind Me, you're now done. Click OK. But if you chose Automatically Enter, there are more things to do. In the Number Remaining field, enter the number of automatic bill entries you want to schedule into the future. For example, to schedule a year's worth of monthlies, enter 12. You can enter some extra lead time in the Days In Advance To Enter box if you want. Then click OK.

Tip

If you use transaction groups, a fourth option is available in the dialog box: With Transactions in Group. You can group certain transactions together and process them all at once (for example, enter all your recurring utility bills at once). To create groups of memorized transactions, choose Lists ➪ Memorized Transaction List, and choose New Group from the Memorized Transactions menu button. For more information, see the QuickBooks Help system.

Recalling a memorized bill

To enter a memorized bill, follow these steps:

1. Choose Lists ➪ Memorized Transaction List. Or, if a memorized bill that is due appears on your Reminders list, double-click it.
2. On the list of memorized transactions, double-click the bill you want to enter. It opens in the Enter Bills window.
3. If necessary, change the date to today's date.
4. Click Save & Close. The bill is entered.

This procedure works for all memorized transactions, not just bills. When you double-click a memorized transaction, the window opens where you can create that new transaction. Just change the date if needed, click Save & Close, and QuickBooks enters your transaction. Now isn't that better than reentering all that information?

Paying Bills and Taking Discounts

When it is time to pay a bill, it appears on your Reminders list, under the heading Bills to Pay. You may choose to pay bills when they appear on this list, or you may decide to pay bills at a specific time each week or month (for example, the second and fourth Fridays of every month).

To pay bills, follow these steps:

1. Choose Vendors ➪ Pay Bills. The Pay Bills window appears, listing all the bills that are currently due (see Figure 17-10).

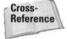

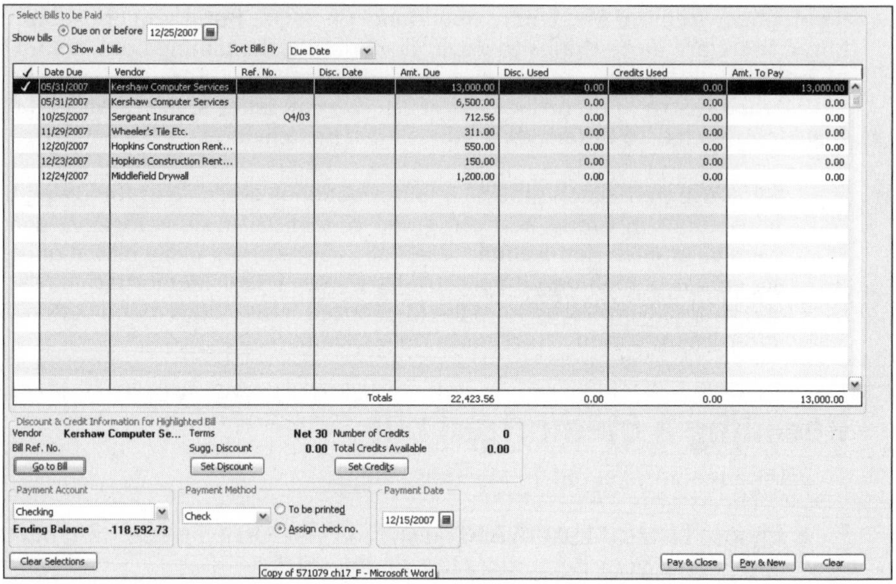

Figure 17-10: In the Pay Bills window, you can choose which bills to pay and how to pay them.

2. In the Payment Account box, choose a payment method: Online Payment, Check, or Credit Card. You can pay some bills one way and some another, but you must go through these steps a separate time for each method.

Cross-Reference

See Chapter 26 for more information about online banking if you plan to use the Online Payment option in step 2.

3. If you chose Check in step 2, select or deselect the To Be Printed check box as necessary, depending on whether you use QuickBooks to print checks (as explained in Chapter 25). If you chose Credit Card, choose the credit card account from the Payment Account drop-down list.
4. By default, QuickBooks shows all bills that are due as of today. To show a different set of bills, enter a different date in the Show Bills Due On or Before box. To show all bills, even the ones that are not due yet, click Show All Bills.
5. Click to place a check mark next to each bill that you want to pay by the payment method currently selected, or click the Select All Bills button to place a check mark next to them all.

6. Click Pay & Close or Pay & New.
7. If you want to pay other bills using another payment method, repeat these steps.

Your bills are now "paid." Well, not quite yet. QuickBooks thinks that the bills are paid, but you must make sure that QuickBooks' view matches reality. If you are using checks, you need to either print the checks (use File ⇨ Print Forms ⇨ Checks) or handwrite and mail the checks. If you are using a credit card, you must make arrangements to make the payments. If you are using online bill paying, you must connect to the online service and pay the bills, as described in Chapter 26.

Note You can pay less than the invoice amount by editing the Amt to Pay field.

Editing Payments

Sometimes you might need to edit payments after entering them to correct mistakes you made during entry. Maybe you added an extra zero to the end of a check amount, or perhaps you assigned a payment to the wrong vendor. To edit a payment after you've recorded it, you must use the Accounts Payable register. Follow these steps:

1. Choose Lists ⇨ Chart of Accounts. The Chart of Accounts window appears.
2. Double-click the Accounts Payable line. The Accounts Payable register appears.
3. Click the bill or payment to edit and click Edit Transaction.
4. Make your changes.

Cross-Reference See Chapter 19 for more information on working with account registers.

5. Click Record to save your changes.
6. Close the register.

Deleting Bills and Payments

When you delete a bill or payment, QuickBooks is smart enough to balance things out for you. For example, suppose you enter a bill and then enter a payment for it. If you delete the payment and leave the bill, the bill simply goes back to being unpaid. If you delete the bill and leave the payment, QuickBooks shows the payment you made as a credit you have with that vendor, because you made a payment when none was due.

Some people prefer to void rather than delete bills and payments. Voiding zeros out the dollar impact of the transaction but leaves it in place, so you will see it and remember that you voided it. QuickBooks will do either.

To delete or void a payment or bill, follow these steps:

1. Choose Lists ➪ Chart of Accounts. The Chart of Accounts window appears.
2. Double-click the Accounts Payable line. The Accounts Payable register appears, as shown in Figure 17-11.

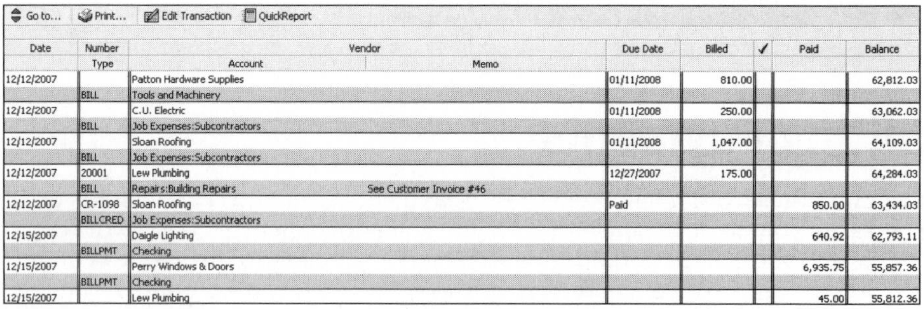

Go to... Print... Edit Transaction QuickReport
Date Number Type Vendor Account Memo Due Date Billed ✓ Paid Balance
12/12/2007 BILL Patton Hardware Supplies Tools and Machinery 01/11/2008 810.00 62,812.03
12/12/2007 BILL C.U. Electric Job Expenses:Subcontractors 01/11/2008 250.00 63,062.03
12/12/2007 BILL Sloan Roofing Job Expenses:Subcontractors 01/11/2008 1,047.00 64,109.03
12/12/2007 20001 BILL Lew Plumbing Repairs:Building Repairs See Customer Invoice #46 12/27/2007 175.00 64,284.03
12/12/2007 CR-1098 BILLCRED Sloan Roofing Job Expenses:Subcontractors Paid 850.00 63,434.03
12/15/2007 BILLPMT Daigle Lighting Checking 640.92 62,793.11
12/15/2007 BILLPMT Perry Windows & Doors Checking 6,935.75 55,857.36
12/15/2007 Lew Plumbing 45.00 55,812.36

Figure 17-11: Edit payments by using the Accounts Payable register.

3. Click the bill or payment to delete or void.
4. Open the Edit menu and choose Void Bill (or Void Bill Pmt) or Delete Bill (or Delete Bill Pmt).
5. At the confirmation dialog box, click Record.

Receiving Credits from Vendors

QuickBooks enables you to enter credits to your accounts with your vendors. You might use this, for example, to credit yourself for material you returned or services that were not satisfactory.

You enter a vendor credit the same way you enter a bill, with one small change. Notice in Figure 17-12 that the Enter Bills window has a Credit option button at the top. Click it before entering the transaction to make it a credit rather than a bill. The title changes to Credit, and any amounts you enter here will be "negative charges," or credits.

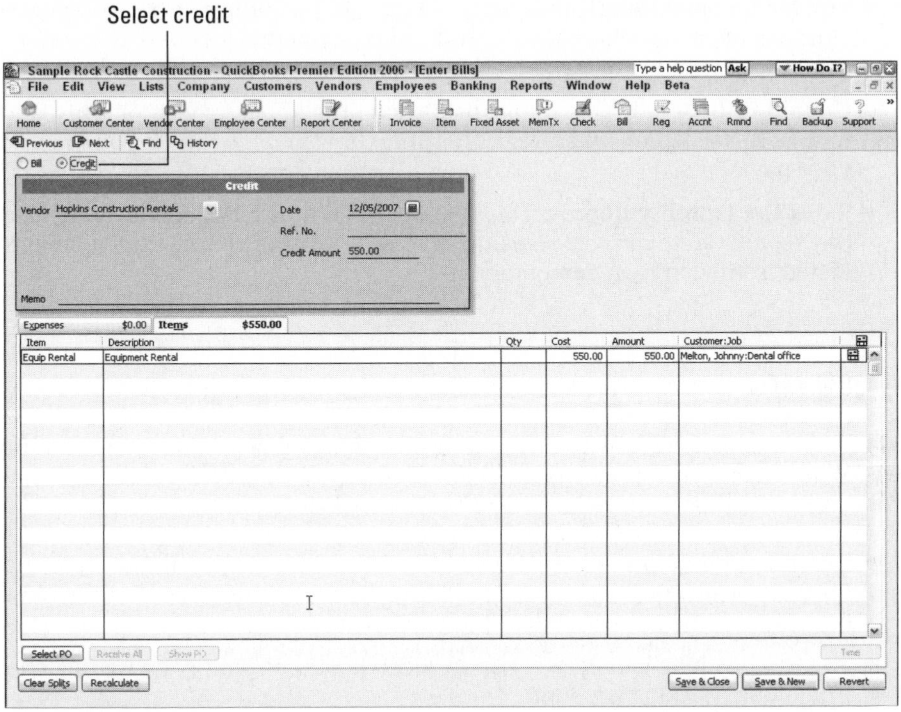

Figure 17-12: Entering a credit is just like entering a bill, except that you choose the Credit option button.

Reviewing Accounts Payable Reports

QuickBooks has a complete suite of accounts payable (A/P) reports to help you track who needs to be paid and when. Choose Reports ⇨ Vendors & Payables to open a submenu that lists the available reports. (See Chapter 29 for full details on managing reports.) A few of the most useful reports are listed here:

- **A/_P Aging Summary:** This report shows how many days overdue you are in paying vendors. The amounts you owe are broken down into Current, 1–30 days overdue, 31–60 days overdue, and so on.
- **A/_P Aging Detail:** This report is the same as the Aging Summary except that it lists each bill in each category. This is helpful for seeing which invoices are the most overdue.
- **Vendor Balance Summary:** This report shows at a glance how much you owe each vendor. It shows all vendors, even those with a 0 balance.

✦ **Vendor Balance Detail:** This report shows all recent transactions for each vendor's account, including both bills and payments. It shows all vendors, even those with a 0 balance.

✦ **Unpaid Bills Detail:** This report lists each unpaid bill by vendor. This is helpful to see whom you owe, rather than how much overdue you are in your payments.

✦ **Sales Tax Liability Report:** This report shows how much money you need to pay to your state or local sales tax authority. This is money that you have collected from your own customers.

Summary

This chapter explained how to buy and pay for things that you need for your business. Whether it's inventory you need or office supplies, QuickBooks' purchase order and billing system can keep excellent records for you.

✦ Purchase orders provide written documentation of each purchase you make for your business. If you use purchase orders, you can generate a QuickBooks report to see what is on order at any given time.

✦ You can pay bills immediately upon receiving them, simply by writing checks from your checking account.

✦ If you don't want to pay a bill immediately upon receiving it, you can enter it in the Receive Payments window to be scheduled for later payment.

✦ If you pay the same bills frequently, you can save time by memorizing one instance and then recalling it each time you need to enter that bill again.

✦ QuickBooks will remind you when bills are due, and you can use the Pay Bills feature to pay them. You can take a discount for early payment if appropriate.

✦ ✦ ✦

CHAPTER 18

Working with Inventory

In This Chapter

- Inventory accounts
- Using QuickBooks inventory tracking
- Receiving your inventory
- Viewing the inventory register
- Adjustments to inventory accounts
- Accounting for returned Items

Inventory is an enigmatic asset. Large inventory accounts on a Balance Sheet are usually perceived as an indication of a company's capability to make a future profit. But a huge inventory balance can also signal other things, such as poor management and an incapability to convert the inventory to cash by selling it off. It can also mean that the inventory is overvalued — that market factors have driven the cost of finished goods below what they were when the inventory acquisitions were first recorded. Accounting for inventory involves both keeping an accurate count of what you have and addressing changes in valuation.

The Definition of Inventory

Almost all businesses, even service businesses, maintain some form of inventory asset account.

Accounting Jargon

Inventory is defined as asset Items held for sale in the ordinary course of business or for use in the production of goods to be sold.

Manufacturing and retail companies usually maintain more active and varied inventory accounts than service companies. Law firms and consulting firms, for example, maintain few or limited inventory accounts. Other types of service companies, such as construction companies, require extensive inventory, such as building materials and fixtures, to perform their services. An inventory Item can be a type of asset; for example, a building contractor may maintain an inventory of vacant lots. But in all cases, inventory is intended to be sold in either its existing form or as a component of a manufactured product. Inventory transactions affect asset, income, and expense accounts.

What Types of Inventory Does QuickBooks Track?

QuickBooks does not track all types of inventory. Before you proceed, make sure that you can answer "Yes" to all of the following questions in this checklist:

- ✦ Is your inventory *not* made up of one-of-a-kind, unique Items (such as artwork or antiques)?
- ✦ Is your inventory tracking based on what you pay (the purchase price) of each Item?
- ✦ Do you sell the inventory Items you are tracking, rather than use them in the course of your business?
- ✦ Do you keep Items in stock rather than order for each job?
- ✦ Are you willing to track your inventory based on the average-cost method, which assigns a value based on the average cost you have paid for identical Items of inventory you maintain?

QuickBooks inventory tracking is probably not appropriate for you if any of the following are true:

- ✦ You stock unique Items, such as antiques.
- ✦ Your inventory includes Items you rent or lease out, or you sell Items on consignment.
- ✦ You need to maintain inventory using a method rather than using the average-cost method (such as first-in, first-out; or last-in, last-out).
- ✦ You fill a lot of back orders rather than maintain an inventory for future orders.
- ✦ You have a manufacturing business.

Note

If you have a manufacturing business, purchase QuickBooks Premier, which allows you to track in your inventory products that you create from different raw materials.

Inventory Accounts

Your QuickBooks accounting system uses three types of accounts to keep track of what happens with your inventory: asset, income, and expense. As you may remember from Chapter 4, each type of account has its unique characteristics and special place on the company's financial statements.

Cross-Reference

If you don't already know about the three types of accounts, this is a good time to take a look at the material in Chapter 4.

Inventory asset accounts

This section summarizes the classic accounting equation for computing the number of Items (ending balance) in an inventory asset account. QuickBooks enters the opening inventory balance in the system during your initial company setup. QuickBooks subsequently increases the balance by purchases and decreases it by sales and shrinkage.

Accounting Jargon

Shrinkage refers to losses due to theft, damage, and unexplained differences between an actual inventory count and what you show on your books.

An actual count of inventory Items on hand is referred to as a *physical inventory*, and it is a good practice to conduct one periodically. QuickBooks then multiplies the number of Items in ending inventory by the average cost per Item to derive the dollar value of the inventory account.

QuickBooks uses the following equation for the value of the inventory asset account:

> Beginning Inventory Balance + Purchases – Sales – Shrinkage = Total Number of Items in Inventory Asset AccountMltiAverage Cost Per Item

QuickBooks shows inventory as a current asset on a company's Balance Sheet. It's categorized as current because you expect it to be sold and converted to cash within the current business cycle. Assets excluded from the definition of inventory include property, buildings, and equipment, because they are not held for sale. The faster a business "turns over" or sells its inventory, and the more frequently it does so, the more profit it shows, as discussed in Chapter 28.

When you establish inventory accounts, it is good practice to set up inventory as a parent asset account and to set up various subaccounts to separately reflect and track individual inventory Items. (Chapter 6 tells you how to do this.) The subaccounts give you a specific count and breakdown of your inventory assets, but QuickBooks displays only the parent inventory account on the company's Balance Sheet. With a click of your mouse, you can view a register or create a subaccount report that contains details of all the transactions involving a specific Item. This is the best way to weed out unprofitable Items whose disappointing performance might otherwise escape your notice.

Figure 18-1 shows the current asset portion of the Balance Sheet for the QuickBooks Pro sample company, reflecting inventory as a single line (Inventory Asset).

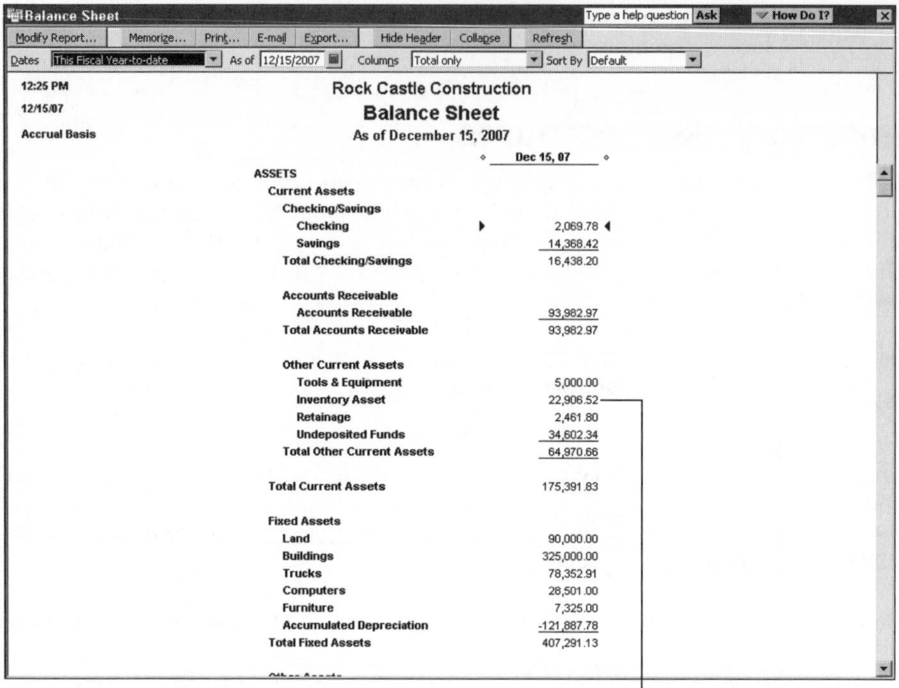

Rock Castle Construction
Balance Sheet
As of December 15, 2007

	Dec 15, 07
ASSETS	
Current Assets	
Checking/Savings	
Checking	2,069.78
Savings	14,368.42
Total Checking/Savings	16,438.20
Accounts Receivable	
Accounts Receivable	93,982.97
Total Accounts Receivable	93,982.97
Other Current Assets	
Tools & Equipment	5,000.00
Inventory Asset	22,906.52
Retainage	2,461.80
Undeposited Funds	34,602.34
Total Other Current Assets	64,970.66
Total Current Assets	175,391.83
Fixed Assets	
Land	90,000.00
Buildings	325,000.00
Trucks	78,352.91
Computers	28,501.00
Furniture	7,325.00
Accumulated Depreciation	-121,887.78
Total Fixed Assets	407,291.13

Inventory is usually shown as a single line item on a balance sheet

Figure 18-1: QuickBooks typically represents inventory as a single line on a company's Balance Sheet.

Expense account: Cost of Goods Sold

The Cost of Goods Sold account (also referred to as the COGS Account by QuickBooks) is a special inventory expense account that QuickBooks automatically creates when you first set up your company. Every time a sale occurs, QuickBooks calculates the cost of the Item sold to the company and decreases the value of the inventory account by a corresponding amount. The cost of goods sold appears on the Profit and Loss Statement, shown in Figure 18-2, as a reduction of income to arrive at the company's gross profit.

Income accounts

When a sale of inventory occurs, the accounting system recognizes both an increase in a sales or service income account and an increase in either a cash equivalent or receivables account. You may record sales revenue in a single account for all Items sold, or use parent and subaccounts to keep a record of inventory derived from different products or services.

12:30 PM
12/15/07
Accrual Basis

Rock Castle Construction
Profit & Loss
December 1 - 15, 2007

		Dec 1 - 15, 07
Ordinary Income/Expense		
Income		
Construction		
Labor	17,111.00	
Materials	38,931.51	
Miscellaneous	2,232.03	
Subcontractors	27,408.01	
Total Construction		85,682.55
Total Income		85,682.55
Cost of Goods Sold		
Cost of Goods Sold		4,982.30
Total COGS		4,982.30
Gross Profit		80,700.25
Expense		
Automobile		
Fuel	71.02	
Total Automobile		71.02
Bank Service Charges		10.00
Freight & Delivery		104.60
Insurance		
Disability Insurance	150.00	
Liability Insurance	1,050.00	
Work Comp	825.00	
Total Insurance		2,025.00

Figure 18-2: QuickBooks deducts the cost of goods sold from income to derive the gross profit for Rock Castle Construction Company.

Tip

If you are unsure whether it is advantageous to track income from each type of Item sold, err on the side of creating more subaccounts than you may need. You can always combine the income account balances at a later date with a few mouse clicks, as discussed in Chapter 10. But QuickBooks does not have a procedure for retroactively creating separate accounts should you later decide that you do need this information.

QuickBooks reports sales revenue on the Profit and Loss Statement. QuickBooks allows you to maintain classes to track different profit-making activities conducted by your company separately. Chapter 28 discusses classes.

Using the QuickBooks Inventory-Tracking Features

QuickBooks has a staggering array of inventory-tracking features, and it handles complex accounting transactions by automatically taking relevant information from sales forms and purchase orders. To take advantage of this truly amazing accounting technology, you only need to set up appropriate Items and accounts and activate the proper program preferences.

Creating a new Item

In Chapter 7, you learned how to set up Items for every product or service that your company sells. You learned that there are various Item types — including Inventory Part Items and Noninventory Part Items. When you select the Inventory Part type for an Item, the New Item screen presents you with the relevant information fields, as shown in Figure 18-3.

Figure 18-3: Use the New Item window to create a new Inventory Part Item.

Cross-Reference

Refer to Chapter 10 if you want step-by-step guidance on setting up a new Item. It is helpful to take another look at this window after reading the information earlier in this chapter about how inventory transactions affect asset, income, and expense accounts. You'll have a lot more insight as to why you need to specify asset- and income-tracking accounts in the New Item window and how to do so.

Activating inventory preferences

Because not all companies maintain or track inventory, you must let QuickBooks know that your company happens to be one that does. You already made the choice to track inventory during the initial setup interview. If you haven't done so, you can activate the inventory-tracking preferences now by following these steps:

1. Go to Edit ⇨ Preferences.
2. Select the Purchases and Vendors icon from the scroll box on the left side of the screen.
3. Click the Company Preferences tab. Click the Inventory and Purchase Orders Are Active check box to select it (place a check mark in it), as shown in Figure 18-4.

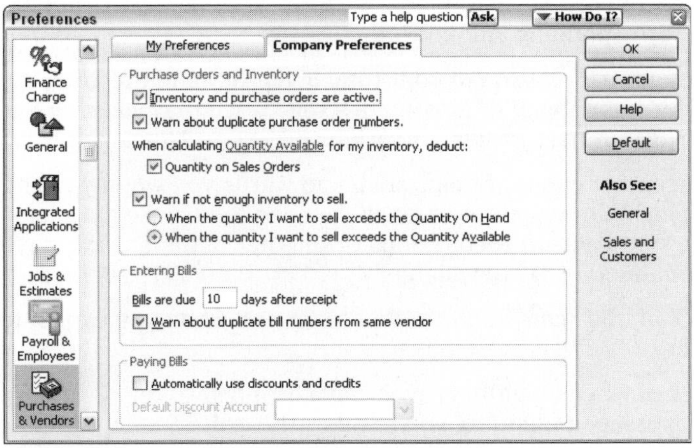

Figure 18-4: Activating inventory preferences.

4. Indicate whether you want the system to display a warning if you attempt to sell more Items than you presently have in your inventory by selecting or deselecting the Warn If Not Enough Inventory to Sell check box.
5. Indicate whether you want the system to warn you about duplicate purchase order numbers to avoid a situation where you either inadvertently place a duplicate order or create confusion by assigning two transactions to the same purchase order number.
6. Let the system know how many days after receipt bills are due so that it can generate an appropriate reminder.
7. Indicate whether you want the system to warn you about duplicate bill numbers so that you don't inadvertently pay a vendor twice for the same merchandise.
8. Indicate whether you want to automatically use discounts and credits when paying bills, and if so, against what default discount account.
9. Click OK to activate and save the preferences you selected.

Overview of automatic inventory-tracking features

After you set the stage by creating your inventory Items and activating inventory preferences, QuickBooks performs its impressive repertoire of complex inventory-tracking and valuation tasks behind the scenes. All you need to do is complete a simple invoice or purchase order form. The system does all of the following, discreetly and quietly, without bothering you a bit:

✦ Tracks the cost of goods sold for each inventory Item for which you have set up a special Cost of Goods Sold account.

✦ Reduces the appropriate inventory asset account by the number of Items sold, as reflected on the customer sales form, and increases your sales revenue by a corresponding amount.

✦ Tracks changes in the value of your total inventory and the average cost of each Item by maintaining a "moving" average price that takes into account your differing purchase prices for various orders and lots.

✦ Keeps an accurate count of Items sold, and warns you when you enter a sale for more Items than you have in stock. You can then make a decision as to whether to sell "back-ordered" goods or tell the customer that the Item has been discontinued or is unavailable.

✦ Keeps track of how many Items are on order and when you expect to receive them.

✦ Keeps track of when inventory levels have dropped to the reorder point, and displays a message reminding you to place the order.

✦ Maintains a separate register for each inventory account that reflects all transactions affecting the account balance.

After you set up Items and indicate preferences, all the features discussed in this section are automatically activated. All you need to do is enter customer sales on the QuickBooks sales forms introduced in Chapter 14. QuickBooks Pro offers additional job order costing features, which you learn about in Chapter 20.

Inventory Valuation

QuickBooks uses the *average-cost method* to value inventory. Other generally accepted accounting methods exist for purposes of valuing inventory, such as first-in, first-out (FIFO) and last-in, first-out (LIFO), but QuickBooks does not accommodate these methods.

In keeping with the average-cost method, QuickBooks automatically recalculates the average cost of each Item in stock every time you get a new shipment. Here's how it works: Suppose you own a T-shirt shop and you receive two shipments of identical novelty shirts bearing the same vaguely offensive one-liner. (In other words, the goods are indistinguishable and interchangeable for purposes of this example.)

QuickBooks adds the Items on hand to each shipment of newly delivered Items and computes the average cost as shown in Table 18-1.

Table 18-1
Using the Average-Cost-Basis Method to Arrive at an Inventory Account Balance

Average Cost per Item	*Number of Items*	*Average Cost*	*Total Value of Inventory*	*Average Cost of Inventory per Item*
Beginning Inventory	10	$10.00	$100.00	$10.00
Add: Purchases from Shipment #1	100	$12.00	$1,200.00	$11.81 ($1,300.00/110)
Add: Purchases from Shipment #2	100	$15.00	$1,500.00	$13.33 ($2,800.00/210)
Total (210 _ $13.33)	210	N/A	$2,799.30	

Receiving Inventory

Receipt of inventory is an important accounting event. *You must properly record it in order to maintain accurate totals and correct valuation.* Inventory receipts are accounted for in one of three ways, depending on when payment occurs in relation to receipt of the goods. In the first accounting scenario, you receive the goods and pay for them simultaneously. In the second scenario, you receive the goods and get a bill for them at a later date. The third and final scenario is based on your paying for goods you haven't yet received.

Scenario 1: Paying for goods at the time of receipt

This is a called a *cash transaction* because you are paying for the goods at the time you receive them with cash or its equivalent — a credit card or check. Delivery and payment occur in a single transaction, so the vendor is not extending you any credit. To pay by check and update your inventory accounts, follow these steps:

1. Go to Banking ⇨ Write Checks.
2. Select the name of the bank account from which you want to issue the check.
3. Enter the name of the vendor in the Pay to the Order Of field.
4. Enter the date of the check (if different from the current date) and any memo information you wish to appear on the check.

5. Click the Items tab.
6. If a purchase order exists for these Items, QuickBooks prompts you to receive against the open purchase order as soon as you select a vendor name. Indicate the quantity and cost of the Items you are receiving if they are different from what the purchase order shows. Or, if there is no purchase order for the Items, enter the Items and their cost in the bottom portion of the screen as shown in Figure 18-5.

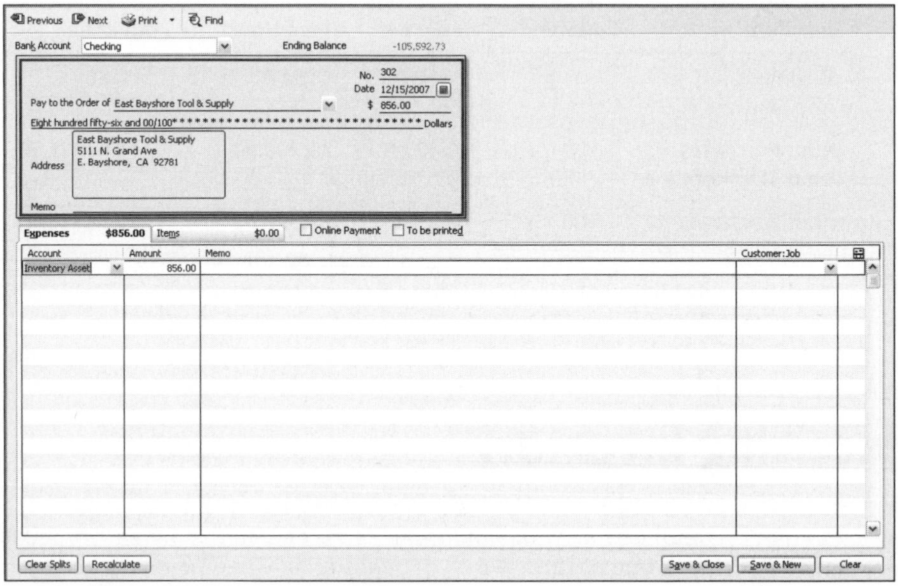

Figure 18-5: Paying for inventory by check.

7. If you are charging a specific Customer:Job, enter it next to the Item.
8. If there are expenses such as shipping or tax that are not associated with a specific Item, click the Expenses tab and enter them in the appropriate fields
9. Enter the amount of the check or click the Recalculate button to automatically calculate the check amount based on the Items and expenses that you entered. If you enter an amount on the check that does not agree with the Items and expenses listed, a message displays that tells you the transaction is not in balance and asks you to make sure the amounts in the detail area agree with the amount being paid.
10. Click the Print button to print this check now, or select the To Be Printed check box to include this check as part of a batch of checks to be printed later.

If you are paying for inventory Items by credit card, follow these steps:

1. Go to Banking ➪ Record Credit Card Charges ➪ Enter Credit Card Charges.
2. Make sure that the credit card you want to use appears in the Credit Card field.
3. Enter the name of the vendor in the Purchased From field.
4. Click Charge or Credit.
5. Enter the date and reference number of the transaction.
6. Click the Items tab.
7. If a purchase order exists for these Items, QuickBooks prompts you to receive against the open purchase order as soon as you select a vendor name. Indicate the quantity and cost of the Items you are receiving if they are different from what the purchase order shows. Or, if there is no purchase order for the Items, enter the Items and their cost in the bottom portion of the screen as shown in Figure 18-6.

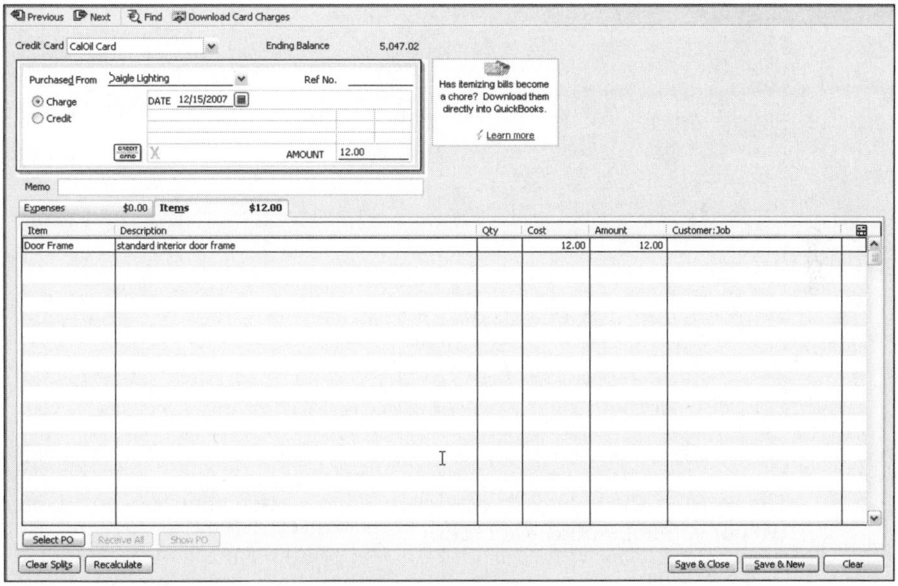

Figure 18-6: Paying for inventory by credit card.

8. If you are charging a specific Customer:Job, enter it next to the Item.
9. If there are expenses such as shipping or tax that are not associated with a specific Item, click the Expenses tab and enter them in the fields displayed.

When you pay for Items at the time of purchase by credit card or check and follow the steps outlined above, QuickBooks automatically updates your inventory quantity and cost of goods sold. It also keeps track of which goods have been received against a purchase order and how many are still outstanding.

Scenario 2: You receive the goods and get a bill later

This is probably the most common business scenario. Most vendors deliver the goods on credit — provided yours is sound. To record a transaction reflecting billing subsequent to delivery, follow these steps:

1. Go to Vendors ➪ Receive Items. The Enter Bills window shown in Figure 18-7 appears.

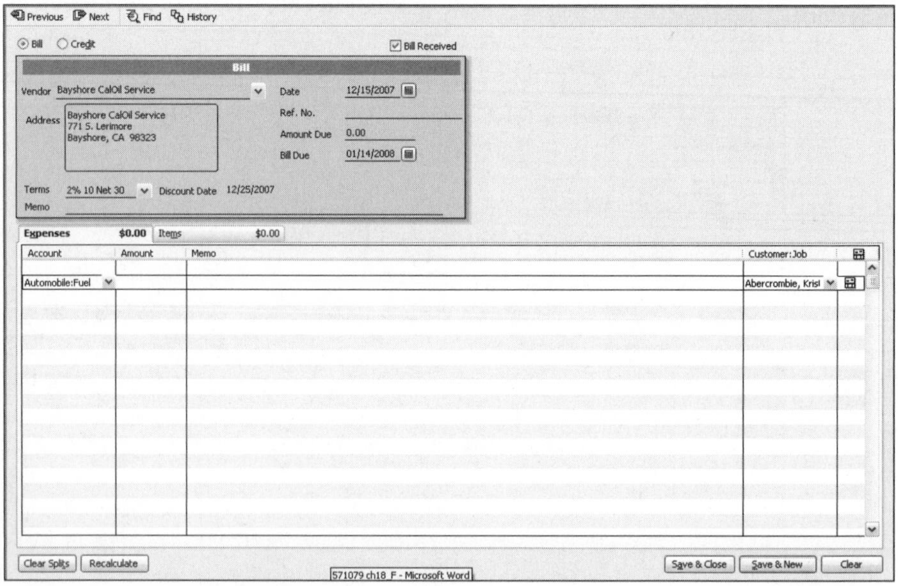

Figure 18-7: The Enter Bills window used to receive Items can be adapted for use with or without a purchase order.

2. Select a vendor from the drop-down list or set up a new one when prompted. If you enter a vendor for whom the system shows outstanding purchase orders, you must respond to the message asking whether you want to receive against open purchase orders. (If you select No when this option is presented, you can later click the Show PO button to receive against a purchase.) Edit the purchase order as necessary, or enter the Items that you are receiving in the Item field.

3. Click Save & Close to record the receipt of Items.

Tip

You may also want to advise the user to verify the date, amount, and reference number of the Items received in case you want to match this Item receipt against a future invoice.

When you receive the bill at a later date, follow these steps:

1. Go to Vendors ➪ Enter Bills. The Enter Bills window shown in Figure 18-8 appears. A list of prior Item receipts appears in the Memo field when you select a vendor.
2. Select a vendor from the drop-down list or add a new one when prompted.
3. Click the Items tab and select the Item to which the bill applies from the drop-down list.
4. Correct any information that is not accurate in the Item fields.
5. Click the Expenses tab, and add any additional charges, such as freight or shipping, in these fields.
6. Enter the amount due, or click Recalculate to have QuickBooks calculate the total of all Items and expenses entered in the fields at the bottom of the screen.
7. Click Save & New to enter another bill or Save & Close to save the changes that you entered on this one.

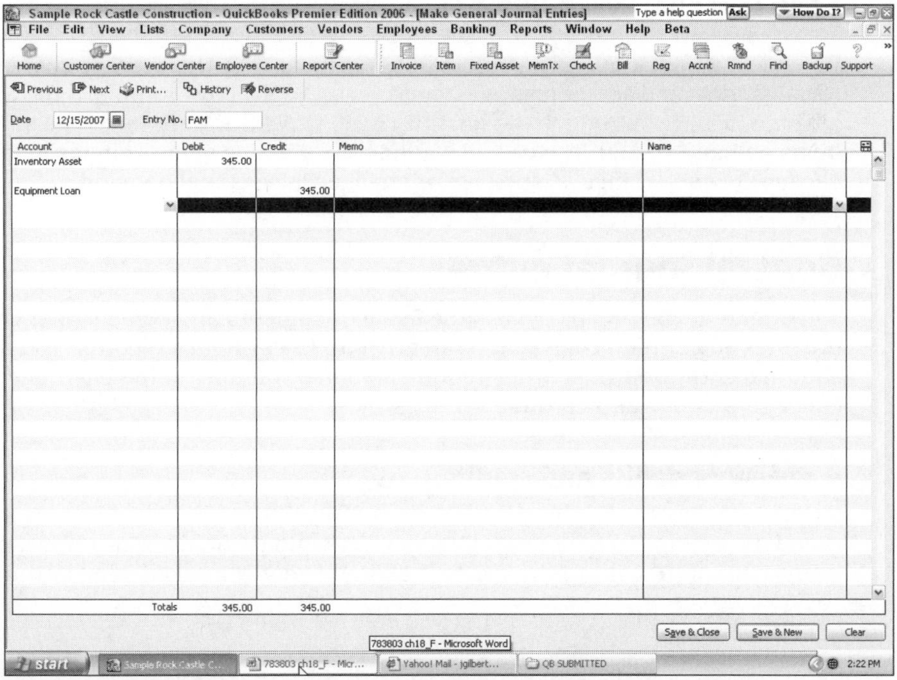

Figure 18-8: The window used to make General Journal entries.

QuickBooks automatically recalculates the amount and value of inventory on hand and the average cost of each Item. It also increases your accounts payable by the amounts shown on the form.

Scenario 3: You pay for goods you have not received

To record this type of transaction, you need to create a purchase order for the goods. You also need to create a special asset account called something like "Prepaid Inventory." See Chapter 17 for the steps to create a purchase order and Chapter 6 for instructions on adding a new account. After you create the purchase order and new account, follow the steps in Scenario 2, and enter the cash or credit card payment for the outstanding purchase order.

Adjustments to Inventory

Although QuickBooks automatically adjusts the quantity on hand and value of your inventory each time you enter a transaction, there are some things that the system just can't know about unless you tell it. You must make special entries to record loss and shrinkage. You can make these adjustments in one of two ways. If you are an experienced accountant, or just comfortable with debits and credits, you may find it simplest to make an entry in the General Journal. You can use the special Adjust Quantity/Value on Hand window discussed as a second alternative.

When you adjust a quantity, QuickBooks assumes that the average cost of the Item remains the same and adjusts the value accordingly. For example, if the average cost is $10 and you reduce the quantity by 2, QuickBooks reduces the value of the Items on hand by $20. You can also adjust the average value of Items in inventory because of such things as spoilage or changes in seasonal demand.

General Journal entries

Sometimes it's helpful to bypass the usual documents and screens that QuickBooks provides and enter a transaction directly into the system's records. You do this via a journal entry. Journal entries require an understanding of the basic accounting concept of debits and credits.

A review of debits and credits

Inventory transactions affect the balances of a company's asset, income, and expense accounts. It helps to understand the flow and impact of inventory transactions by giving a bit of thought to the concept of double-entry bookkeeping introduced in

Chapter 4. That chapter stated that every transaction is recorded as a journal entry: a debit to one account and an offsetting credit to another account. Asset and expense accounts are debited to reflect an increase. Revenue, liability, and equity accounts are credited to reflect an increase and debited to reflect a decrease, as shown in Table 18-2.

Table 18-2
Increase and Decrease of Account Balances by Journal Entries

Item	*Debit*	*Credit*
Asset	Increase	Decrease
Liability	Decrease	Increase
Equity	Decrease	Increase
Income	Decrease	Increase
Expense	Increase	Decrease

If there is an increase or decrease in one inventory-related account, there must be an offsetting increase or decrease in another inventory-related account. For example, if you decrease (credit) an inventory asset account, there is a corresponding increase (debit) to the expense account called Cost of Goods Sold. Accountants traditionally record journal entries using a two-column format, one for debits and one for credits (hence the term *double-entry bookkeeping*). Credits are shown in the rightmost column, and debits to the left. The journal entry debiting the Cost of Goods Sold account and crediting an inventory account looks like this:

Debit	*Credit*
Cost of Goods Sold $100.00	Inventory Asset $100.00

Entering an adjustment in the General Journal

How do you know which accounts to debit and credit in the General Journal? Fortunately, most of the time, you don't have to know. QuickBooks makes sure that accounts are appropriately debited and credited. But you need to understand them thoroughly when you make a direct entry to the General Journal window.

One adjustment you might want to make directly is to reflect inventory shrinkage (loss or damage). There are no sales forms to specifically record this event. Recording this event requires both a reduction (credit) to the inventory asset account and an increase in a corresponding expense account. Let's call the expense account "damage expense" for the purposes of this example. To make an adjustment for damaged inventory directly to the General Journal, which will be displayed in the inventory account register, follow these steps:

1. Go to Company ➪ Make General Journal Entries. The General Journal Entries window (previously shown in Figure 18-8) appears.
2. Indicate the date you want to use for the entry—either the current date or the actual date of the loss.
3. In the lower portion of the screen, indicate the accounts that you want to debit and credit.
4. Click Save & New to record another transaction or Save & Close to save this one and exit the window. QuickBooks posts the adjustment you made to the appropriate accounts and registers.

Other common examples of inventory adjustments that you may want to make using the General Journal include shortages, valuation changes, and usage overruns.

The Quantity/Value On Hand window

If the preceding discussion of debits and credits boggles your mind, QuickBooks offers you an alternative that doesn't require you to know as much about them. This procedure is limited—it allows you to make an adjustment only for a reduction in the quantity of your inventory. You cannot, for example, reflect an increase in the value or a reduction due to simple market factors rather than due to a loss in the number of Items. To make a simple adjustment that reduces the quantity of your inventory, follow these steps:

Note This process can be performed only when QuickBooks is in single-user mode. To make sure you are in single-user mode, go to the File menu and make sure the option Switch to Multi-User Mode appears as an option. If the Switch to Single User Mode option appears instead, select it to enter the single-user mode.

1. From the Vendors menu, choose Inventory Activities, and then choose Adjust Quantity/Value On Hand. The window shown in Figure 18-9 appears.
2. (Optional) Change the Adjustment date if appropriate, and enter a Ref. No.

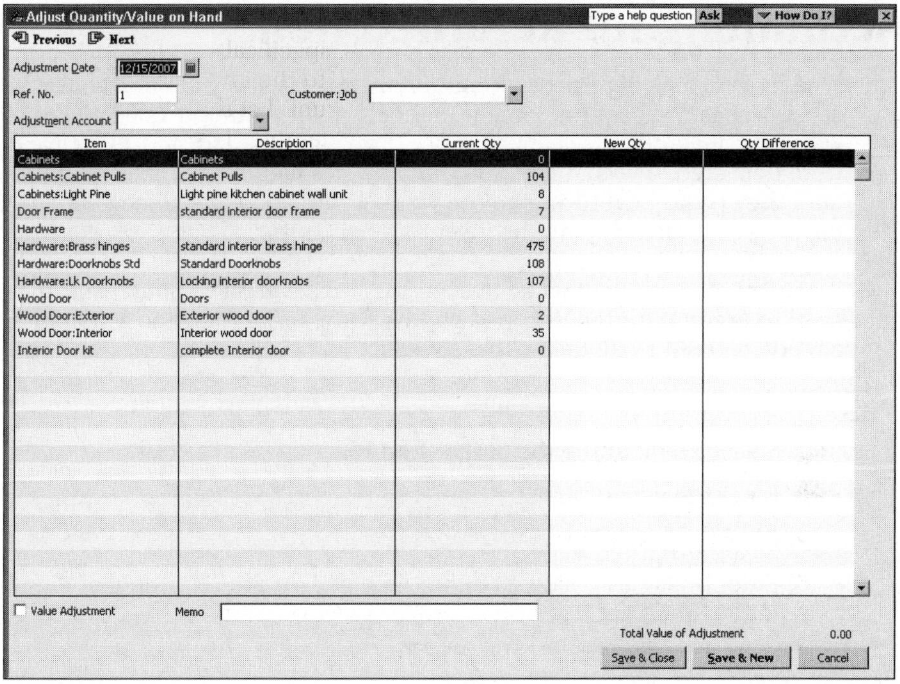

Figure 18-9: You make adjustments to inventory using the Adjust Quantity/Value On Hand window.

3. Enter the name of the Adjustment account where you track inventory loss and shortages.
4. Change the Customer:Job and class, if necessary.
5. For each inventory Item whose quantity has changed, enter either the new quantity or the quantity difference.
6. If you are disassembling an inventory assembly Item, select the assembly Item and each component Item in the list. (Assembly Items are listed alphabetically after all inventory parts in the Adjust Quantity/Value On Hand window.) Decrease the number of assembly units in inventory and increase the number of component Items to match.
7. (Optional) Click the Value Adjustment check box at the bottom and edit the value of the inventory.
8. Save the inventory adjustment.

Accounting for Returned Items

Whenever I think of returned Items, I remember a story about a cousin who worked as a purchasing agent for a major hotel chain and ordered 1,000 pieces of silverware. The inventory code on an order form was misread, and 1,000 live chickens were delivered. It wasn't her fault, but she still had to deal with the squawking mess until they could be returned to the vendor. And someone somewhere had to make the proper adjustments to the inventory accounts.

It may not be your fault when live animals arrive in place of utensils, but you still need to account for the returned goods. To record a return to a vendor after you've already entered a bill, follow these steps:

1. Go to Vendors ⇨ Enter Bills.
2. Select Credit at the top of the window.
3. Enter the vendor name.
4. Click the Items tab.
5. Enter the Items (that you either received, or are returning, or did not receive in the first place).
6. Click Save & Close.

Inventory Reports

QuickBooks offers a number of inventory reports, which you can access from the Reports ⇨ Inventory menu, as shown in Figure 18-10.

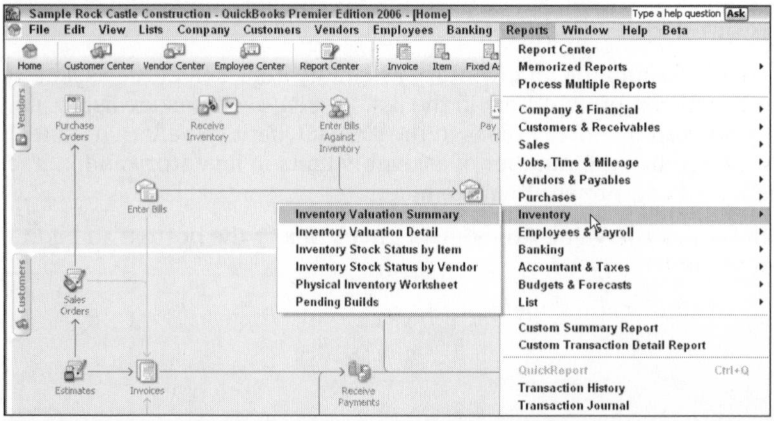

Figure 18-10: QuickBooks offers a number of useful inventory-tracking reports.

These reports include the following:

- ✦ **Inventory Valuation Summary:** Tells you the current value of your inventory, by Item.
- ✦ **Inventory Valuation Detail:** Identifies which transactions have affected the value of your inventory.
- ✦ **Inventory Stock Status by Item:** Tells you what inventory you currently have in stock, by Item.
- ✦ **Inventory Stock Status by Vendor:** Lists by vendor all of the inventory you have on hand.
- ✦ **Physical Inventory Worksheet:** Provides the worksheet shown in Figure 18-11 to assist you in taking a physical inventory to account for inventory shrinkage caused by theft, breakage, error, or other factors.
- ✦ **Pending Builds:** This report lists all build transactions currently marked as pending. For each pending build, the report shows the date of the build, the build reference number, the name of the assembly Item, the quantity to build as entered in the build form, and any memo information from the build form. You can display each pending build form by clicking the transaction's line entry in the report.

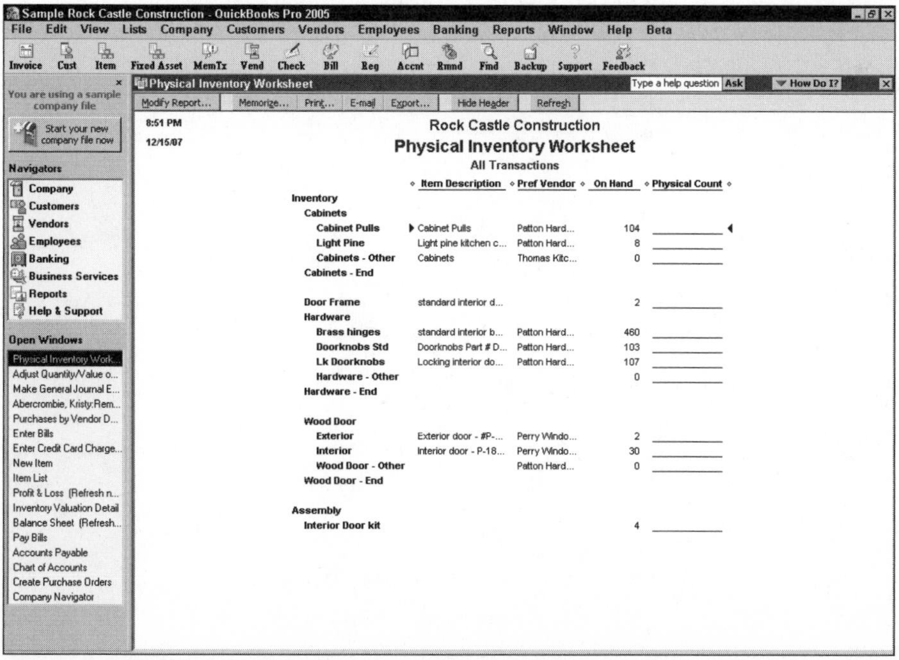

Figure 18-11: The Physical Inventory Worksheet assists you in conducting a physical inventory to identify shrinkage.

Summary

For many businesses, the inventory account values reflected on their Balance Sheet represent their profit-making potential, so it's important to accurately track inventory Items purchased, sold, lost, damaged, returned, and revalued because of market fluctuations.

- Inventory Items are held for sale or production of goods for sale to customers in the ordinary course of business.
- Inventory transactions affect asset, expense, and Balance Sheet accounts.
- QuickBooks values inventory using the average-cost-of-goods-sold method of accounting as goods are received.
- QuickBooks accounts for receipt of goods in three different ways, depending on whether payment occurred at the time of receipt, goods were received prior to issuance of a bill, or the payment was made prior to receipt of the goods.
- The inventory register for each Item discloses all transactions affecting the account balance. The ending register balance is the current value of the inventory Item.
- QuickBooks has several useful inventory-tracking reports, including a worksheet to help you in conducting periodic physical inventories.

✦ ✦ ✦

CHAPTER 19

Reviewing Registers and Reconciling Accounts

✦ ✦ ✦ ✦

In This Chapter

What's in a register?

Entering and editing transactions

How to enter split transactions

Moving, voiding, and deleting transactions

Reconciling your checking account

✦ ✦ ✦ ✦

Your financial statements tell the world how your business is doing — and give you an annual dose of objectivity about your company's performance. Registers, on the other hand, are meant for insiders only. They provide a roadmap that shows how your company arrived at each asset, liability, and equity account balance. And you can change the route by editing individual transactions directly from the register. This chapter tells you how to view and modify register account balances and how to reconcile your cash accounts register to the records maintained by the bank.

What's in a Register?

QuickBooks maintains a register for each asset, liability, and equity account.

Accounting Jargon As you may recall from Chapter 4, asset and liability accounts are on the Balance Sheet and hence are sometimes referred to as Balance Sheet accounts.

A QuickBooks register is comparable to the register you maintain for your checking account. As in your check register, each transaction is entered on its own line. The ending balance shown in the register is equal to the current balance in the asset account.

Viewing the Accounts Receivable register for the company

You can open a register from a window that you are working in by simply going to the Activities menu and choosing Use Register. Different registers appear depending on which window you are currently using. For example, if you are entering an invoice, you can access the Accounts Receivable (A/R) register from the Activities menu. If you are in the Pay Bills window, you can view the Accounts Payable (A/P) register.

Registers for all company accounts are accessible from the Chart of Accounts list. Remember that registers are available only for Balance Sheet accounts — assets, liabilities, and equity. To open a register from the Chart of Accounts list, follow these steps:

1. Go to Lists ➪ Chart of Accounts.
2. Select a Balance Sheet account (asset, liability, or equity).
3. Double-click the selected account (or click the Activities menu button and select Use Register). The register for that account appears.

A sample Accounts Receivable register for Rock Castle Construction is shown in Figure 19-1.

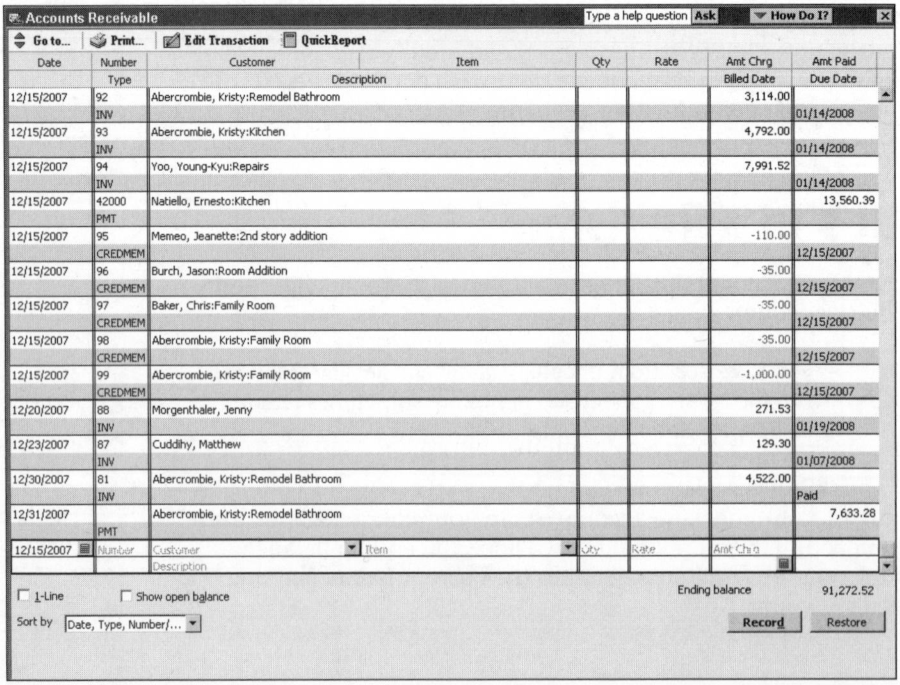

Figure 19-1: This is the A/R register for the hypothetical Rock Castle Construction Company.

Sometimes it is convenient to view transactions in less detail by having them shown on a single line. If you want the register to appear this way, select the 1-Line check box that appears at the bottom of the screen.

Registers for QuickBooks checking accounts contain a special column to the right of the check amount to let you know whether the check has cleared. A check mark indicates that it has cleared. Additionally, checking registers contain special symbols to denote online banking transactions. For example, a lightning bolt in the check mark column indicates that transactions have been matched to your QuickStatement.

Cross-Reference

Special checking register symbols are discussed in further detail in Chapter 25.

Locating a specific transaction in the company's Accounts Receivable register

You can also locate a specific transaction if you know the payee, vendor, customer, amount, transaction number, check number, or what's in the text of the Memo field. You can search for transactions located in one open register at a time. To find a specific transaction from an open register, follow these steps:

1. From the A/R register, click the Go To button located at the upper left corner of the screen. The dialog box shown in Figure 19-2 appears.

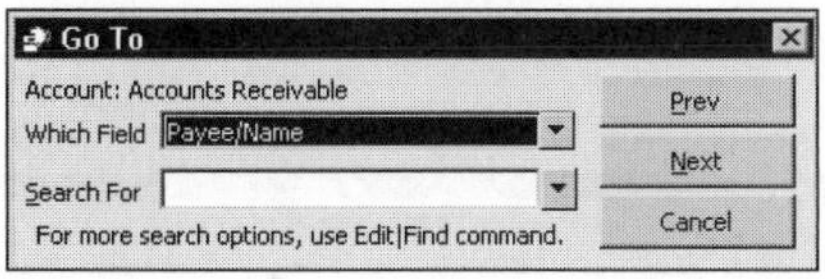

Figure 19-2: Enter your search request in the fields appearing in this window to locate a specific transaction.

2. In the field labeled Which Field, enter a search criterion from the drop-down list (for example, Payee/Name, Number/Ref, Memo, or Amount).
3. In the Search For field, enter the specific name or number pertaining to your selection in the previous step. When you click Next or Prev, QuickBooks displays the first transaction that meets the search criteria.
4. Click Next to search forward chronologically or Prev to search backward.

Viewing the Accounts Receivable register for a particular customer or job

It is also convenient, at times, to view the A/R register for a particular customer. To view the register, follow these steps:

1. Go to Lists ➪ Customer:Job List. The Customer:Job List appears as shown in Figure 19-3.
2. Click the name of the customer whose register you want to access.
3. Click the Activities button at the bottom of the screen, and select Use Register. An A/R register for the particular customer appears, as shown in Figure 19-4.

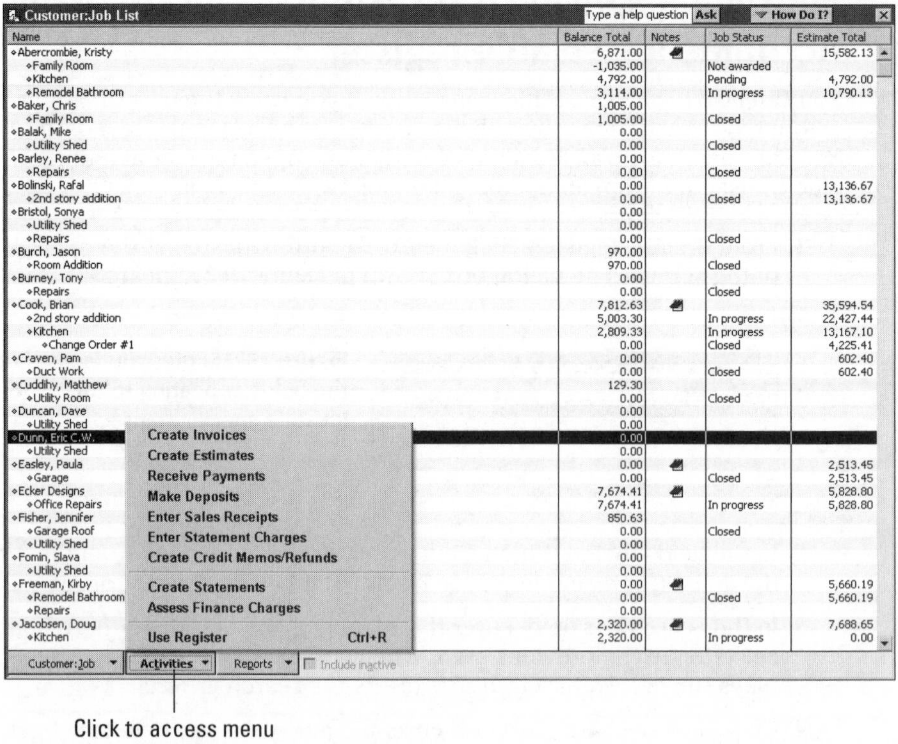

Figure 19-3: Use the Activities menu to view a register for the selected customer.

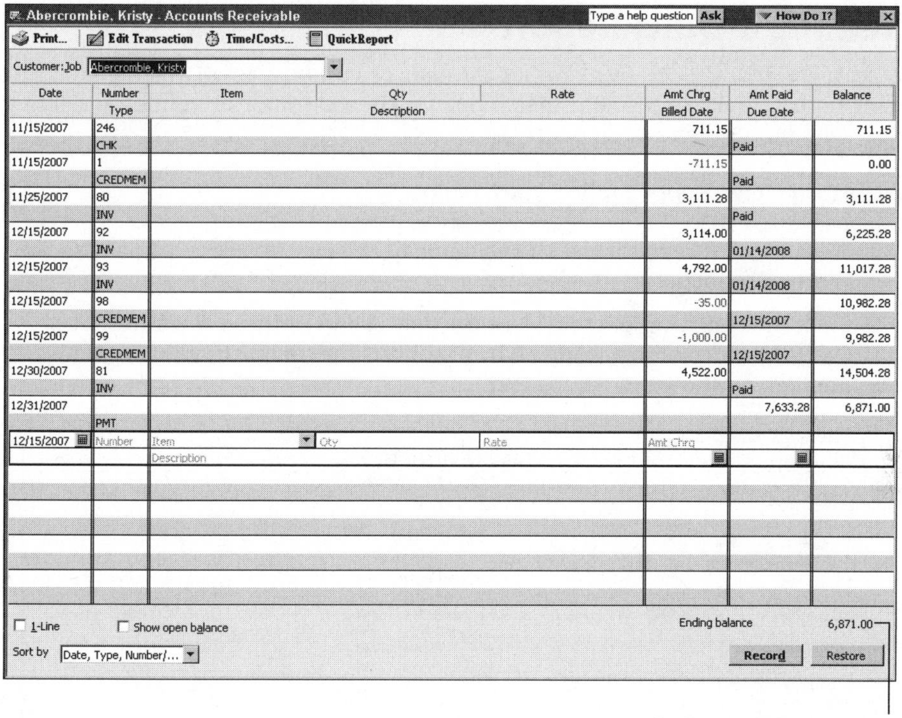

Figure 19-4: A sample savings account register for a particular customer.

Scrolling through a register

You can scroll through the register using the arrows on the right side of the screen. This is convenient for smaller registers but gets cumbersome as the transaction history lengthens over time. If you need to maneuver through a lengthy register to find a specific transaction, try some of these keyboard shortcut techniques:

- ✦ Move up or down one transaction: up or down arrows
- ✦ Move up or down an entire screen: PgUp or PgDn
- ✦ Move back or ahead one month: Ctrl+PgUp or Ctrl+PgDn
- ✦ Go to the beginning of a register: Home
- ✦ Go to the end of a register: End

Creating a QuickReport

You can create a QuickReport for a customer or vendor shown in a register. The QuickReport summarizes all transactions for the customer or vendor and lets you know which ones have been paid.

To create a Quick Report, follow these steps:

1. From the A/R register, select the name of the customer for whom you want to create a report.
2. Click the QuickReport button at the center top of the A/R window. A QuickReport, summarizing all transactions for the particular customer, appears as shown in Figure 19-5.

11:17 AM
12/15/07
Accrual Basis

Rock Castle Construction
Register QuickReport
All Transactions

Type	Date	Num	Memo	Account	Paid	Open Balance	Amount
Abercrombie, Kristy							
Remodel Bathroom							
Check	11/15/2007	246		Accounts Receiva...	Paid		711.15
Credit Memo	11/15/2007	1		Accounts Receiva...	Paid		-711.15
Invoice	11/25/2007	80		Accounts Receiva...	Paid		3,111.28
Invoice	12/15/2007	92		Accounts Receiva...	Unpaid	3,114.00	3,114.00
Invoice	12/30/2007	81		Accounts Receiva...	Paid		4,522.00
Payment	12/31/2007			Accounts Receiva...	Paid		-7,633.28
Total Remodel Bathroom						3,114.00	3,114.00
Total Abercrombie, Kristy						3,114.00	3,114.00
TOTAL						**3,114.00**	**3,114.00**

Figure 19-5: This QuickReport summarizes all transactions, the payment history, and the outstanding customer balance for this customer, Kristy Abercrombie.

Printing from a register

You can print all or a portion of any QuickBooks register. To print from a register, follow these steps:

1. Go to Lists ➪ Chart of Accounts.
2. Double-click the Balance Sheet account for which you want to print a register.
3. Go to File ➪ Print Register. The dialog box shown in Figure 19-6 appears.
4. In the From and To fields, enter a date range for the transactions you want to print.
5. Select the Show Splits Detail check box if you want additional transaction detail about payments split between more than one invoice to appear.

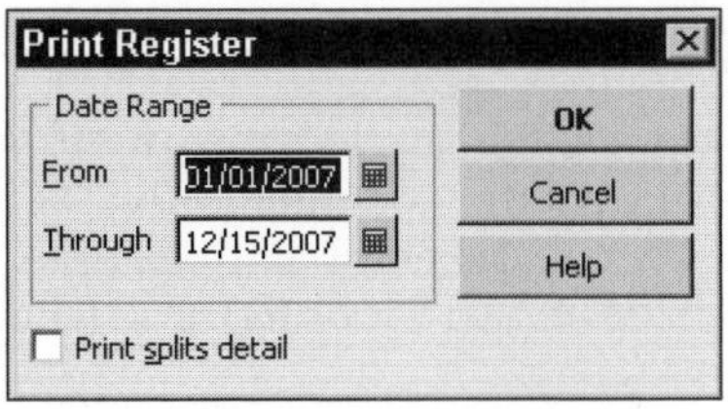

Figure 19-6: Indicate the time period and amount of detail for the transactions that you want to print in the Print Register dialog box.

6. Click OK. QuickBooks displays the Print Lists window shown in Figure 19-7. Indicate in this window whether you want to print the register now or store it in a file.
7. Click Print.

Cross-Reference

For more information about printing options, see Chapter 11.

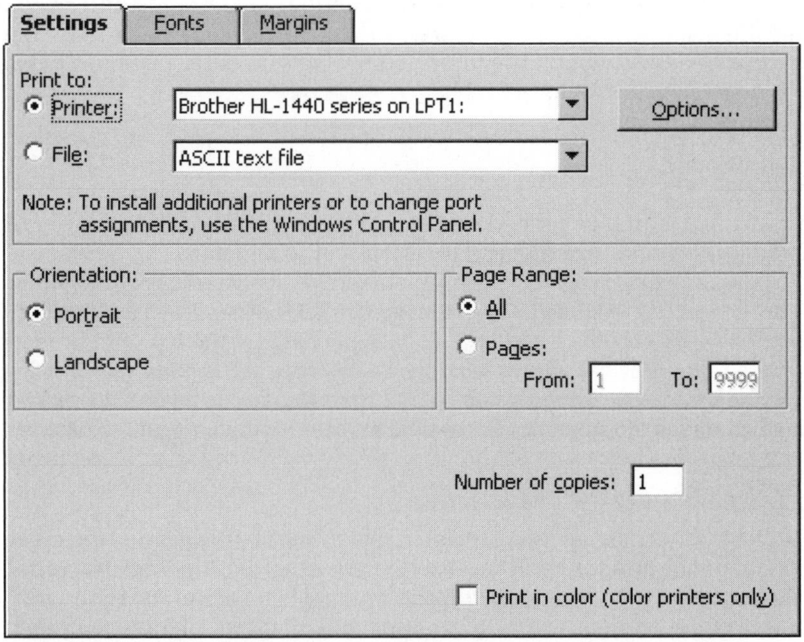

Figure 19-7: Indicate whether you want to print your register to a file or to a printer using this window.

Entering and changing transactions

QuickBooks not only allows you to view a transaction history directly from the register window but also lets you view the underlying documentation for all listed transactions. To see this information, double-click the entry. For example, double-click an invoice transaction listed in the register to take a look at the original invoice.

New transactions

At times, you may find it faster and more convenient to enter transactions that affect an asset account directly into the register. This may be the case, for example, if you have multiple receivables and payment transactions to enter for a single customer and you are in a hurry to update the customer's outstanding balance. To enter a new transaction directly into the register, follow these steps:

1. Click the current date shown on the last line of the register, in the lower left corner.
2. Fill in the register fields to record the transaction. These fields differ depending on which account register you are working in. You may be prompted to set up new Items or accounts if the information that you enter does not already appear on a QuickBooks list.
3. Click Record. QuickBooks automatically updates the register and all affected account balances.

If you enter a transaction that precedes the current date, QuickBooks moves the transaction to its correct chronological location on the register.

Tip

If you want to record more detail than the register fields allow, select the transaction that you have just recorded and click Edit. Depending on the type of transaction you entered, you may get a form window, or you may get another register. If you are entering a transaction directly into the Accounts Receivable register, for example, clicking Edit opens the Accounts Receivable register for the particular customer.

Editing previously entered transactions

Unlike an ordinary checking account register, QuickBooks allows you to view the underlying documentation for each transaction directly from the register window. And you can change history. You can edit the original transaction so that a different amount is immediately reflected on the register, and all other affected accounts are adjusted accordingly. To edit a previously entered transaction, follow these steps:

1. Select the transaction that you want to change in the register and double-click it. The original transaction window appears.
2. Edit the transaction to reflect any changes that you want to make.
3. Click Save & Close. All affected account and register balances from the date of the original transaction are adjusted.

Moving, Voiding, and Deleting Transactions

What good is the ability to review a complete list of transactions affecting an account balance if you can't fix the occasional inevitable error that you may spot? QuickBooks makes it easy to correct and modify register balances.

Moving a register entry

A common accounting error is to record the right transaction in the wrong account. QuickBooks recognizes this age-old accounting dilemma and allows you to move the information without reentering it. You can cut and paste transactions among registers of similar account types (for example, bank register transactions can be pasted to other bank registers, but not to A/R registers). To move a transaction from one account register to another, follow these steps:

1. Go to Lists ➪ Chart of Accounts and click the account in which you erroneously entered the transaction.
2. Go to Activities ➪ Use Register. The account register appears.
3. Select the transaction that you want to move.
4. Go to Edit ➪ Copy. (The wording of the menu option varies depending on the type of register you are in. For example, it may say something similar to "Copy Check.")
5. Go to Lists ➪ Chart of Accounts and open the register to which you want to post the transaction. Click the space after the last entry.
6. Go to Edit ➪ Record.
7. Go back to the original register and delete the incorrect transaction now that you have safely created a record of it in another register.

Voiding and deleting transactions

If you are absolutely sure that you don't need any detail about a transaction, and you don't want the detail cluttering your system, you can delete it by following these steps:

1. Select the transaction that you'd like to delete from the account register.
2. Go to Edit ➪ Delete.
3. Click OK to confirm that you are absolutely positive that you never want to see this transaction again.

If you are not absolutely sure you want to purge a transaction, it is better to be safe than sorry. Voiding a transaction enables you to keep a record of it. To void a transaction, follow these steps:

1. Select the transaction that you'd like to void from the account register.
2. Go to Edit ➪ Void.
3. Click Record. The entry appears in your register.

Reconciling Your Check Register

When you first set up a company, you need to reconcile the bank account statements to the opening balance information you have entered.

Cross-Reference

See Chapter 7 for more information on entering historical transactions.

There are two types of troublesome transactions that stand between you and a perfectly reconciled checking account balance. First, you must properly account for transactions that occurred prior to your start date but which won't show up on your account statement until after the start date (for example, that uncashed check that the vendor misplaced). You also need to make an adjustment for any difference between what you entered into the system and what was actually in the account according to the bank — taking into account service charges, interest, and so forth. The basic accounting equation for reconciling a checkbook to a bank statement is shown here:

> Balance per Checking Account Register + Interest + Deposits That Have Not Yet Posted – Service Charges + Checks That Have Not Cleared = Balance per Bank Statement

Reconciling Your Checking Account

QuickBooks provides a special window to simplify the process of reconciling your checking account. The fields in this window ensure that you include all transactions that could account for any differences between the two balances. To accomplish the reconciliation process, perform these steps:

1. Go to Banking ➪ Reconcile. The window shown in Figure 19-8 appears.
2. Select the account that you want to reconcile in the Account field.
3. Enter the Statement Date and the ending balance from your bank statement in the Ending Balance field.
4. Enter the service charge and interest earned in the designated fields, and click Continue.

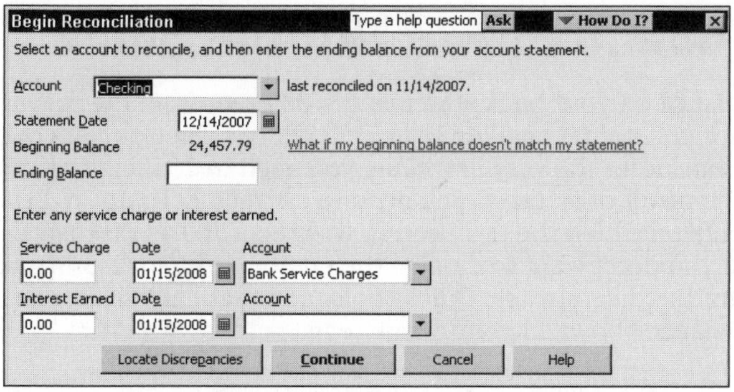

Figure 19-8: This window enables you to enter information about all transactions that could account for any difference in your register and statement balances.

5. Scroll through the transactions shown in the window and place a check mark next to each transaction that has cleared the bank by clicking in the leftmost column. Click again to deselect the transaction. (A cleared transaction is one that has been processed by the bank.)
6. Add to the register any transactions that appear on your bank statement but which are not shown on your QuickBooks screen by opening the register and editing it as discussed previously in this chapter.
7. Correct any errors or incorrect entries in your QuickBooks register by opening the register and editing it as discussed previously in this chapter.
8. Click Reconcile Now to complete the reconciliation; a new dialog box appears.
9. Click Enter Adjustment to have QuickBooks make an adjusting entry directly to your Checking Account register or click Cancel if you want to track down the reason for the difference on your own. Here's a checklist of possible errors that might account for the discrepancy:
   - Forgot to record checks
   - Double-entered checks
   - Wrong amounts; transposed numbers
   - Erroneously cleared check or failed to mark check as cleared
   - Entered a deposit as a payment or payment as a deposit
   - Entered a transaction in a wrong account
   - Bank error

When you have completed the process just detailed, you can print a report of your last reconciliation by clicking the Last Report button. QuickBooks stores only your most recent reconciliation, overwriting the report each time that you perform a reconciliation.

If Opening Balances Are Not the Same

If the opening balance on your bank statement is different from the previously reconciled balance, or if you are reconciling your QuickBooks Checking Account register to your bank statement for the very first time, you need to do one of two things. If the discrepancy is the result of an error, you need to correct it. To do so, bring up the original documents on which the transaction was recorded as discussed earlier in this chapter. If you don't want to change the customer history, or if you cannot find the reason for the discrepancy, QuickBooks automatically makes an adjustment to the opening balance shown in your check register.

Summary

Registers are roadmaps telling you how a specific account balance got from its beginning balance to its ending balance. They are generally used to provide summary information rather than to record day-to-day activities, although you can enter and edit transactions directly from a register.

- You can access registers for any Balance Sheet account. Balance Sheet accounts are asset, liability, and equity accounts (except for retained earnings).
- You can access registers directly from the Chart of Accounts list, from a transaction window in which you are currently working, or from the Balance Sheet.
- You can enter, edit, and modify transactions by accessing the appropriate task window directly from the register screen. When you change a previously entered transaction, QuickBooks automatically updates all affected account balances and the register.
- Voiding a transaction, as opposed to deleting it, allows you to maintain complete records. You can also move, edit, and delete transactions.
- You can use QuickBooks to reconcile the balance in the Checking Account register as shown on the system with the balance shown on the company's bank statement.
- When reconciling a Checking Account register balance to a bank statement, you must adjust for transactions that have not cleared, interest, service charges, and errors. QuickBooks gives you the option of having the system make an adjusting entry to the register for any discrepancy that you cannot track down.
- QuickBooks automatically updates your reconciliation reports and overwrites the old report, unless you save the old report by printing it to a file.

✦ ✦ ✦

CHAPTER 20

QuickBooks Pro: Estimates and Time Tracking

✦ ✦ ✦ ✦

In This Chapter

Developing estimates

Creating an invoice from an estimate

Tracking employee time

Billing customers for employee time

Working with QuickBooks Pro in multi-user mode

✦ ✦ ✦ ✦

With QuickBooks Pro, you can create estimates to bid on jobs, and if you get the bid, you can quickly convert an estimate into an invoice. You can also track employee time spent on jobs, either with employee time cards in QuickBooks or with a special Timer. Then, you can charge customers for the time on their invoices.

QuickBooks Pro also allows you to use the program in multi-user mode, so several users can provide input into a common QuickBooks company file. For example, sales clerks at several terminals can create new invoices and purchase orders at the same time.

Developing Estimates

An estimate is much like an invoice. It has most of the same fields. The difference is its purpose. An *invoice* bills a customer for what you have already done, and an *estimate* is an offer to do something. If the customer accepts your estimate, you can quickly convert it to an invoice.

The main difference between an invoice and an estimate form is that the default estimate form contains several fields that are used only on-screen — they do not print. These are fields for you to calculate how much to bid the job at. For example, an estimate can show that you buy doorknobs at $27 apiece, and you can decide what markup to assign to them (for example, 11 percent, or $3). When you print the estimate for the customer, it shows doorknobs at $30 each, with no mention of your wholesale cost. Figure 20-1 shows the Create Estimates window.

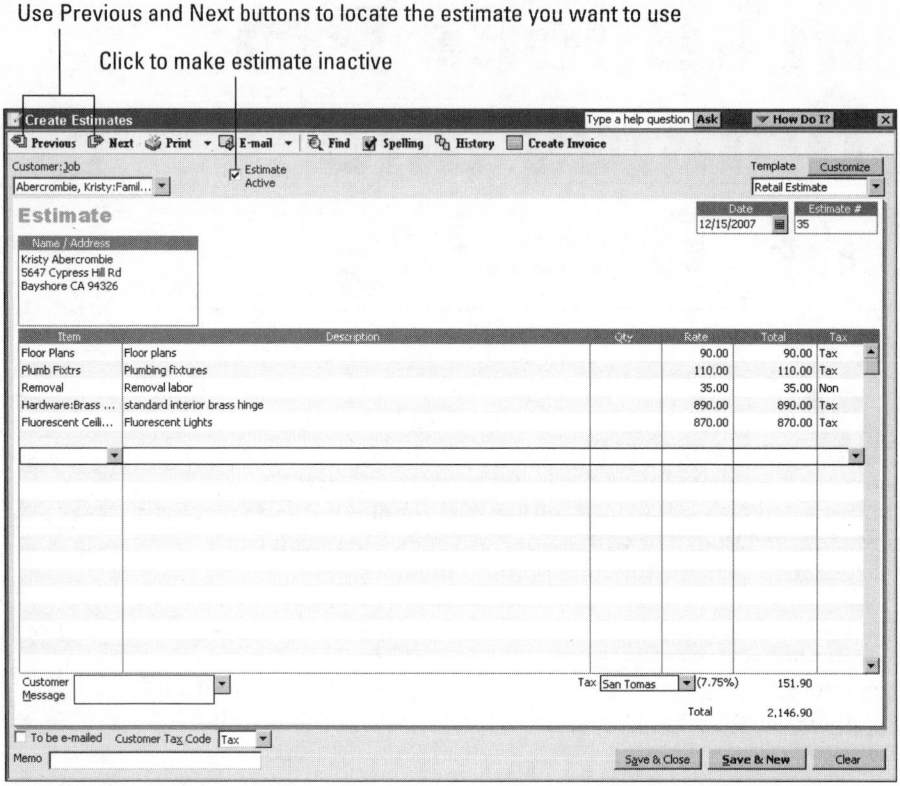

Figure 20-1: The on-screen version of an estimate includes nonprinting fields for your use in calculating the bid.

Before you can create estimates, you must turn the Estimates feature on. Open the Activities menu. If there is a Create Estimates command on it, then the feature is on. If not, choose File ➪ Preferences. Click the Jobs & Estimates icon and then the Company Preferences tab. Click Yes under Do You Create Estimates?. Then click OK.

To create an estimate, follow these steps:

1. Choose Customers ➪ Create Estimates. The Create Estimates window opens (previously shown in Figure 20-1).
2. In the Customer:Job field, choose the customer or job from the drop-down list or create a new one with Add New.

Tip

If you're bidding a job for an existing customer, you may want to create a new job in QuickBooks to separate this estimate from other jobs you have done for the customer. Then, if you get the bid, you will have a new job ready to roll. See Chapter 9 for details about setting up customers and jobs.

3. (Optional) If you have created your own estimate templates, choose the template you want from the Template drop-down list.

Cross-Reference

See Chapter 15 for information about customizing templates.

4. Open the drop-down list on the first empty line of the Item column, and choose the first Item for the estimate. Information for it is filled in automatically in the other columns.

5. Confirm or change the information in the other columns, as follows:

   - If necessary, change the Description to something the customer will understand and recognize. For example, for your own internal purposes, you might list a long model number for a doorknob, but all the customer needs to know is "Brass Doorknob."
   - In the Qty field, fill in the quantity the customer needs.
   - In the Rate field, your wholesale cost for the item may already appear, if you set it up when you set up your Items in Chapter 18. Change it if necessary.
   - The Total field, which displays the Qty multiplied by the Cost, is automatically calculated. You can't change it.
   - The Markup field may already contain a markup (a dollar amount or a percentage) if you set it up with the Item in Chapter 18. Change it if necessary.
   - The total is calculated automatically, but you can override it if necessary. If you change the total, the Markup field's entry changes to show the amount of markup between your cost and the amount you are charging.
   - The Tax column marks taxable items. There may already be a Tax notation there if you set the item up as taxable in Chapter 18. Click that column to place or remove the Tax notation as needed.

6. Repeat steps 4 and 5 for each item you want to add to the estimate.

7. Choose a tax rate from the Tax drop-down list if applicable.

8. (Optional) Choose a message from the Customer Message drop-down list.

9. (Optional) Select the To Be E-Mailed check box if you want the estimate to be e-mailed to the customer.

10. (Optional) Select a tax code from the drop-down menu.

11. (Optional) To print the estimate now, click the Print button.

12. Click OK to enter the estimate.

Customizing estimates

There are several minor changes you may want to make to the estimate template. The default estimate shows a message at the bottom of the form that says, "This estimate is good for 30 days." You may want to change that to a different time period (such as 15 or 60 days). The default estimate also uses a rather small font; you may want to make it larger. You might also want to add a field for employee initials, to keep track of which employee issued the estimate.

To customize the estimate template, follow these steps:

1. Click the Customize button in the upper right corner of the Estimate window, and then click New (or open the Template drop-down list and choose Customize).

   The Customize Estimate window appears, as shown in Figure 20-2.

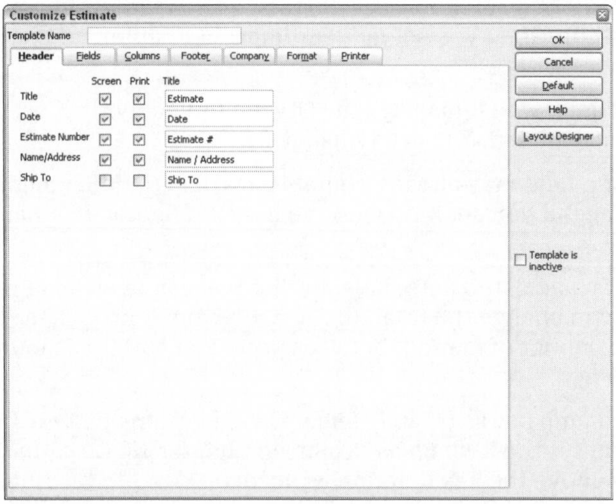

Figure 20-2: Customize estimate forms using this window.

2. Choose the estimate template name in the Templates window.
3. Click the Templates menu button, and choose Edit.
4. Follow the procedures described in Chapter 15 to customize the form.

Creating multiple estimates for a single customer

QuickBooks allows only one estimate per job. If you already have an estimate for a particular customer and job, when you choose it from the Customer:Job drop-down list in step 2 of the preceding exercise, the old estimate appears. You must modify or delete it; you can't create an additional one.

Sometimes, however, you may need more than one estimate per job. Suppose that Mr. Smith wants a new deck, but he isn't sure what size he wants. He wants you to give him estimates for two different sizes so that he can compare the costs. To do this in QuickBooks, create a separate job for each estimate you want to create. Give the jobs similar names so that it's clear they are related. For example, you might have Deck Option1 and Deck Option2.

To create multiple estimates for a customer or job, make sure the estimates feature is turned on (go to Edit ➪ Preferences ➪ Jobs & Estimates ➪ Company Preferences) and then follow these steps:

1. From the Customers menu, choose Create Estimates.
2. Enter the name of the client or project (Customer:Job).
3. Enter the name of the customer or job.
4. Select a template from the drop-down menu.
5. To create a proposal, select the Proposal template from the drop-down menu.
6. Enter the line items for each job. Each estimate will be marked Active. You can change the status later.
7. When the customer accepts one or all of the estimates for a job, but you want to keep a record of the estimates, change the status of each job to Closed.

   Changing the status to Closed allows you to keep a record of the estimates and allows you to condense data in the future. Only closed jobs can be condensed.

Note If you create invoices from estimates, creating an invoice for one of multiple estimates for the same job requires you to choose one of the active estimates and then create the invoice directly from that estimate form.

When the customer accepts one of the estimates, you can either delete the unaccepted estimates or mark their status as Inactive. Deselect the Estimate Active check box and choose Edit ➪ Delete Estimate from the Create Estimates window (previously shown in Figure 20-1).

Cross-Reference See Chapter 9 for information about setting the status of a job.

Creating an Invoice from an Estimate

After the customer accepts your estimate and you perform the job or deliver the merchandise, you're ready to create an invoice. Rather than start from scratch and try to remember what prices you quoted, you should let QuickBooks turn the estimate into an invoice for you. This ensures that you do not charge the customer more than you originally estimated and that you don't leave out any billable items that you promised and delivered.

Tip

Instead of using the following procedure, you can create an invoice for the Customer:Job you want to bill. QuickBooks will point out that an estimate exists and ask if you wish to bill from it.

To convert an estimate into an invoice, follow these steps:

1. Display the estimate. To do so, choose Customers ➪ Create Estimates, and locate the estimate for the customer and job that you want to display using the Previous and Next icons until you arrive at the estimate you want.
2. Click the Create Invoice button. The invoice appears. (If you have set up QuickBooks to do progress invoicing, an extra dialog box appears first; see the section that follows these steps for the details.)
3. Make any changes needed to the invoice.
4. (Optional) Print the invoice now by clicking the Print button, or make sure that the To Be Printed check box is marked to print it later.
5. Click Save & Close.

Creating a progress invoice from an estimate

A progress invoice bills the customer for a portion of the estimate. You might want to create multiple invoices for a single estimate, for example, if you require a customer to pay 25 percent of the job cost up front, another 25 percent when the job is half done, and the balance when the job is finished.

You can also use progress invoices to bill for only certain estimate items. For example, you might bill the client only for the merchandise that has been received and wait to bill for inventory that is back-ordered.

To set up QuickBooks for progress invoicing, choose Edit ➪ Preferences and click the Jobs & Estimates icon and the Company Preferences tab. Click Yes under Do You Do Progress Invoicing? and then click OK, as shown in Figure 20-3.

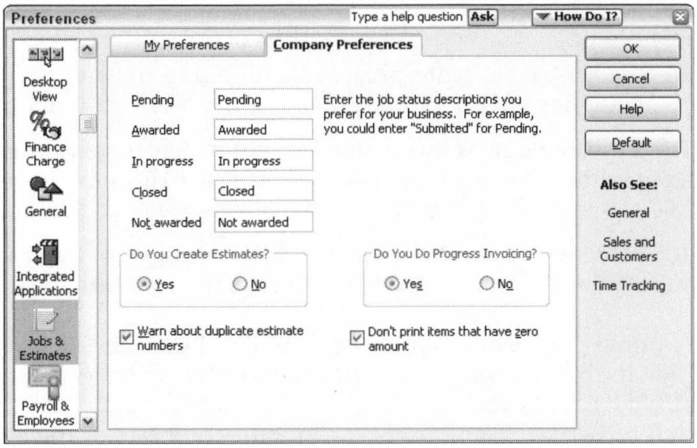

Figure 20-3: Setting preferences for progress invoicing.

After setting the preferences to do progress invoicing, follow these steps:

1. From the Customers menu, choose Create Estimates.
2. Find the estimate using the Previous & Next arrow buttons.
3. Click Create Invoice at the top of the Create Estimates window.
4. Indicate how you want QuickBooks to set up the invoice, and then click OK.
5. If you choose to invoice for selected items, or for a different percentage of each item, specify the amounts or percentages to put on the invoice, and then click OK.

After turning progress invoicing on, when you click the Create Invoice button on the estimate, a Create Progress Invoice Based on Estimate dialog box appears (see Figure 20-4).

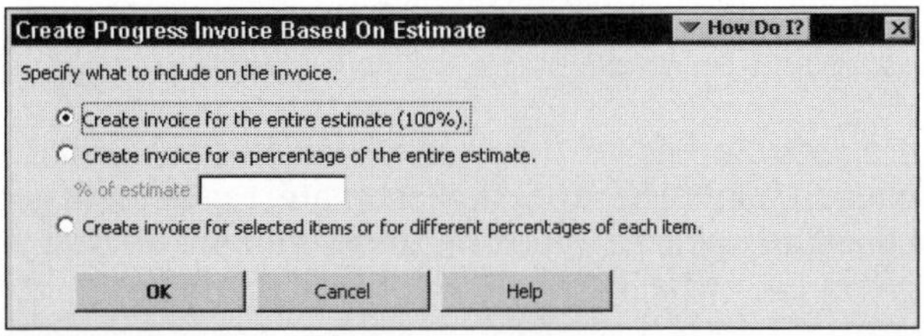

Figure 20-4: You get this extra dialog box when creating invoices from estimates if you have chosen to use progress invoices in QuickBooks' preferences.

From there, choose one of the following:

- ✦ **Create Invoice for the Entire Estimate:** Select this option to transfer the entire estimate to an invoice now, and then complete the invoice normally.
- ✦ **Create Invoice for a Percentage of the Entire Estimate:** Select this option and then enter a percentage to create an invoice for part of this job (for example, 50%).
- ✦ **Create Invoice for Selected Items or for Different Percentages of Each Item:** Select this option to bill for certain individual Items on the estimate.

If you choose the last option, the Specify Invoice Amounts for Items on Estimate dialog box appears. Click the Show Quantity and Rate and/or Show Percentage check boxes to choose which fields you will work with in this box. Figure 20-5 shows the box with both turned on. Enter either the quantity and rate or the percentage for each Item to be included on the invoice. To include all of an Item, choose 100% or the entire estimate quantity, and then click OK.

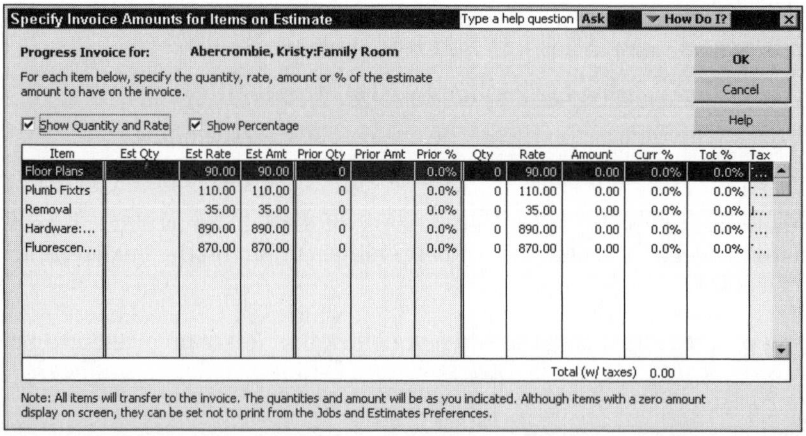

Figure 20-5: Choose which Items and what quantities of each Item should be transferred to the invoice.

Notice in Figure 20-5 that there are columns for Prior Qty, Prior Amount, and Prior %. When you create subsequent invoices from this estimate, the amounts of the Items that have already been used on invoices appear in these columns so that you do not invoice for more of an Item than what originally appeared on the estimate.

When the invoice is created, a warning box appears advising you that some zero-quantity Items are on the invoice. Click OK to move past it. If you don't want those zero-quantity Items to print, make sure that you have set up QuickBooks to suppress them. (Choose Edit ➪ Preferences and click the Jobs & Estimates icon and the Company Preferences tab. Make sure that the Don't Print Items That Have Zero Amount check box is marked.)

Determining whether estimates are active

If you create a lot of estimates, it's easy to lose track of which ones are active and which have either had invoices created for them or are no longer pending. To view a list of active and inactive estimates, follow these steps:

1. From the Navigator (Home) screen, click the Customers icon or select Customer Center from the menu.
2. Click the Transactions tab. Click Estimates on the left side of the screen, and filter your list by selecting either Open Estimates or All Estimates from the drop-down list, as shown in Figure 20-6.

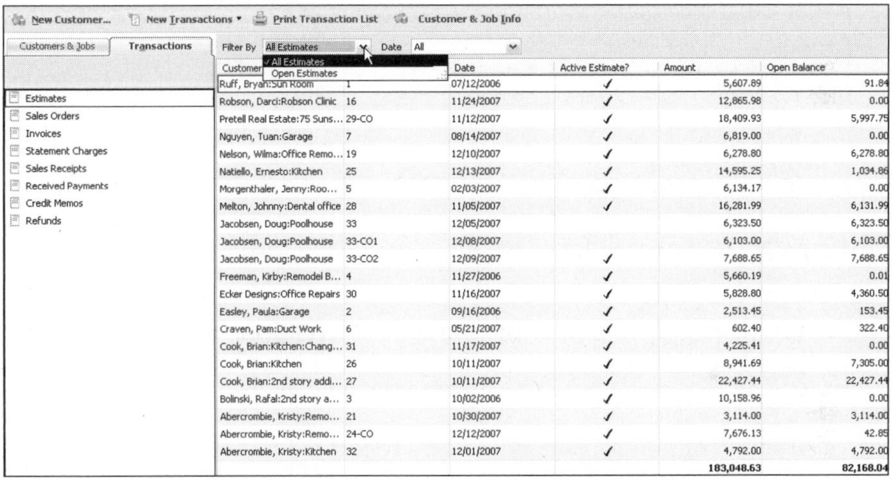

Figure 20-6: Viewing a listing of active and inactive estimates.

Checking Your Actual Job Cost against the Estimate

QuickBooks offers several project reports that help you see how well you are doing on jobs in relation to your original estimates. You can access them by selecting Reports ➪ Jobs, Time & Mileage as shown in Figure 20-7.

Project reports fall into three categories: Job, Item, and Time. The Job reports show how profitable individual jobs have been overall, taking both merchandise and time into consideration. The Item reports show the profitability of individual Items sold; they report the original costs of the Items versus how much you sold them for. The Time reports show how much time has been spent by a particular job, customer, item, or employee.

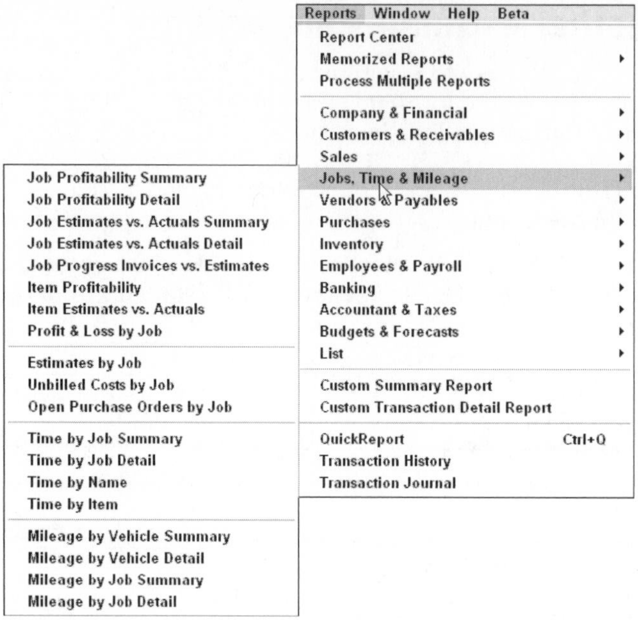

Figure 20-7: Viewing estimate reports.

The most helpful reports of these are the Job reports, because they provide information about whether you are achieving your profitability goals on a job-by-job basis. The reports you can use include the following:

✦ **Job Profitability Summary:** This report is just like the Job Estimates vs. Actuals Summary report, except that it is missing the columns for the estimates. It shows only the actual costs, actual revenues, and difference (profits).

✦ **Job Profitability Detail:** This report is just like Job Estimates vs. Actuals Detail, except that it lacks the Estimates column.

✦ **Job Estimates vs. Actuals Summary:** This report summarizes your cost and income by job. It shows your estimated cost, your actual cost, and the revenue (profit) made.

✦ **Job Estimates vs. Actuals Detail:** Same as the preceding report, except that it lists all Items for all invoices. When you choose this report, a dialog box appears asking for a particular customer and job. You can run this report for only one job at a time.

✦ **Job Progress Invoices vs. Estimates:** This report compares the original estimate with any progress invoices you have created based on it. It also reports a percentage of progress made on the job, which is helpful for knowing how much more you have to do on a job before it is complete.

Tracking Employee Time

There are two benefits of tracking employee time in QuickBooks. One is that it makes your payroll a snap. If you've set up your employee information correctly (see Chapter 22), all you need to tell QuickBooks is how many hours an employee has worked and it can calculate the amount of pay due. The other benefit is that you can charge employee time directly to customers and jobs. For example, if you had an employee spend three hours installing a part for Smith Construction, you can place the charge for the employee's time on their invoice with a couple of mouse clicks.

Tracking time in QuickBooks also makes it easy to see how much time was spent on a job so that you can more accurately bid similar jobs in the future. There are a variety of reports that show time spent, which you look at later in this chapter.

QuickBooks Pro options for tracking time

Before you begin exploring the Time Tracking feature, you need to make sure that QuickBooks' preferences are set up for using time tracking. To set your preferences, follow these steps:

1. From the Edit menu, choose Preferences.
2. From the scroll box, select Time Tracking.
3. Click the Company Preferences tab.
4. Click Yes under Do You Track Time? as shown in Figure 20-8.
5. (Optional) From the drop-down list, choose the day you want to be the first day of your workweek for the weekly timesheet.
6. Click OK.

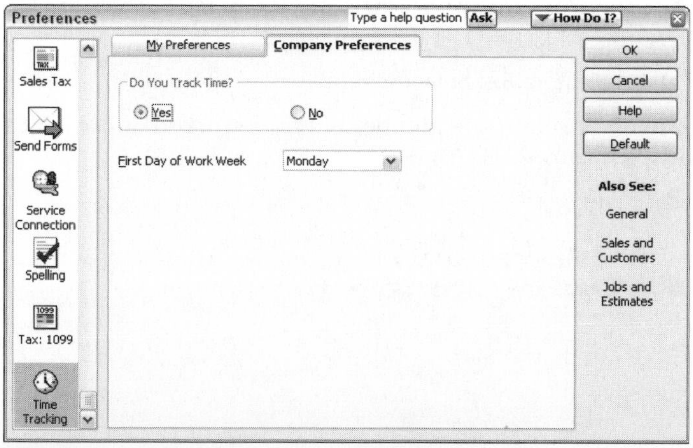

Figure 20-8: Activating time-tracking preferences.

Two ways to track time

You can enter employee time in one of two ways: you can either enter single activities as they occur (and use the internal stopwatch feature) or work with weekly timesheets. You can switch freely between the two methods as much as you want because both store the same information in the same accounts. They're just two ways of looking at the same fields.

Entering single activities is a good method if you are using QuickBooks only to bill customers and not to process payroll from the hours entered, or if you enter time for only one employee, day, and job at one time. Entering an activity makes a notation that the customer received something valuable from your company (service) so that you can later charge the customer for it.

Entering time on a weekly timesheet is good if you typically enter all of an employee's hours in QuickBooks for an entire week (or day) at one time. People who use QuickBooks to process payroll like this method because it shows at a glance the total number of hours entered for that employee for the week. This way, if you know that the employee worked 40 hours but only 20 hours appear on the sheet, you know there has been an entry error.

Entering single activities

When an employee performs a service for a customer, you may want to record that information right away in QuickBooks. You do so by using the Enter Single Activity window.

To access the Enter Single Activity window, follow these steps:

1. From the Employees menu, choose Enter Time, and then choose Time/Enter Single Activity.
2. Enter the date the work was performed and the name of the person who performed the work.
3. Enter the Customer:Job and Service Item.
4. In the Duration field, enter the number of hours worked on this date and this job, as shown in Figure 20-9.
5. Click Save & Close.

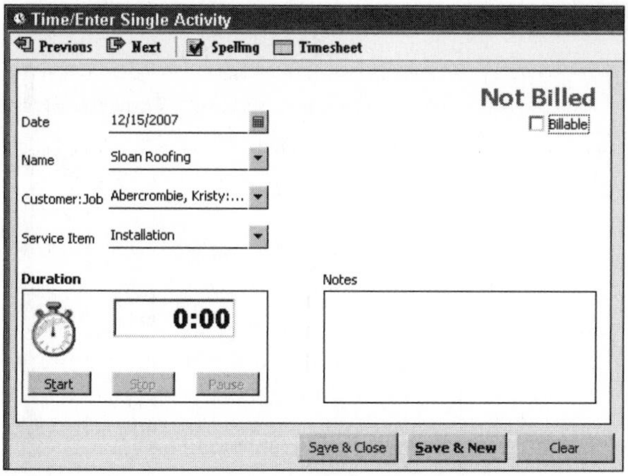

Figure 20-9: The Enter Single Activity window.

The drawback to this method is that you can enter only one day's worth of hours at a time for that employee and job. If the employee worked eight hours a day for four days, you must make four entries. With a weekly timesheet (discussed in the next section), you can enter an entire week's hours on the same sheet. Also, you can't see that employee's other hours for the week as you are entering a single activity, so you can't tell whether the employee worked more or less than the employee's normal hours.

Using the internal stopwatch feature

QuickBooks also provides an internal stopwatch feature for you to track single activity time. To use this feature, follow these steps:

1. Click Start to begin timing.
2. Click Pause when necessary to stop timing temporarily.
3. Click Stop to end timing.

Filling out weekly timesheets

The weekly timesheet is a big-picture way of recording employee time. I prefer it, as do most people who use QuickBooks for payroll, because I can make sure that each employee is working a full 40 hours of work each week, and I can assign extra activities to employees who do not seem to have enough to do. A blank weekly timesheet form appears in Figure 20-10.

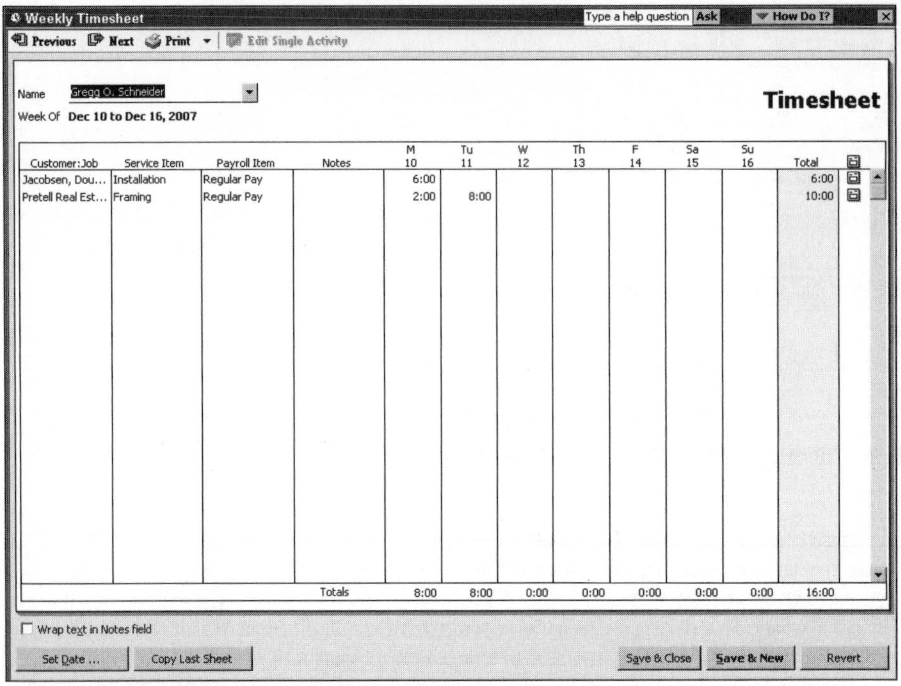

Figure 20-10: A weekly timesheet filled out for an employee.

To track time by filling out weekly timesheets, follow these steps:

1. Enable time tracking to fill in a timesheet.
2. From the Employees menu or the Customers menu, choose Enter Time and then choose Use Weekly Timesheet to display a weekly timesheet like the one shown in Figure 20-11.
3. Enter the name of the person who performed the work (or select it from the drop-down menu provided) and press Tab.
4. If there is existing time data for this person for this week, QuickBooks displays it. You can edit the entries.
5. If necessary, change the date range of the week displayed.
6. To change to the previous week, click Previous; to change to the next week, click Next. To change to any other week, click Set Date and enter a date in the week you want to display.

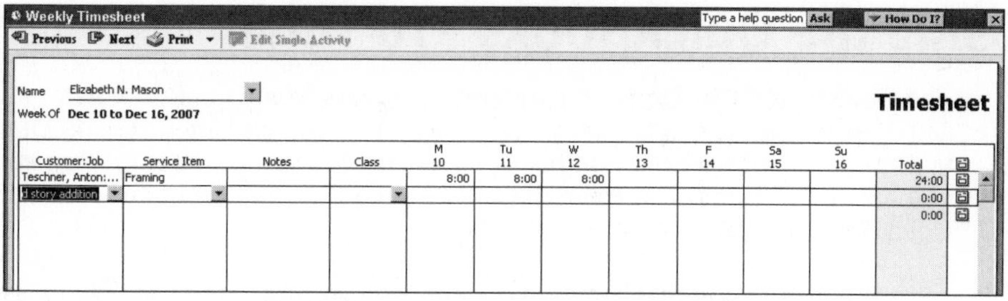

Figure 20-11: A weekly timesheet for employee Elizabeth Mason.

7. Enter the Customer:Job and Service Item.
8. If the employee earns overtime, make sure you have set up the employee's earnings Items correctly in the employee record. Otherwise, the overtime rate might not calculate correctly on paychecks.
9. (Workers' Compensation only) In the WC Code field, enter or change the workers' compensation code, if necessary.
10. (Optional) In the Notes field, enter any additional information about this activity.
11. (Optional) If you want the text in the notes to wrap, select the check box to allow text to wrap in the Notes field.
12. (Optional) In the Class field, enter the name of the class you want to associate with this activity.
13. For each day of the week that work was performed, enter the number of hours worked in the appropriate date column. You can also enter the range of hours worked, such as 8–5.
14. (Optional) Click the check box to wrap notes in the Notes field if you prefer to wrap text in this column so that you can read the entire contents of a note. If the check box is not checked, notes will be truncated to fit the column width.
15. Continue on additional lines, if necessary, to record time spent on other jobs, time spent doing other services, or time associated with other payroll Items.
16. Save the timesheet.

Using the QuickBooks Pro Timer

The QuickBooks Pro Timer is a separate program from QuickBooks Pro itself. You can distribute it free to as many people as you want, and each person can use it to track his or her own hours on his or her own PC. Then, each employee can send you his or her Timer files (on a disk or by e-mail) and you can import them into QuickBooks Pro for use on timesheets.

Note

This feature is available only in the Pro, Premier, and Enterprise Solutions editions.

If you are distributing the QuickBooks Pro Timer to employees who do not use QuickBooks, you might want to give them the steps provided in the next section so that they will have some instructions on how to set up and use Timer.

Overview: Using Timer for the First Time

The first time you use Timer, some extra setup steps are required. You must export your QuickBooks lists to an export file and then import that information into Timer. You must also set up a Timer file.

QuickBooks users need to do the following:

1. Add names of all persons whose time you want to track to the appropriate QuickBooks lists (Employee, Vendor, or Other Name).
2. For employees whose time you'll transfer to payroll, set up payroll information and select the check box for transferring time data.
3. Set up customers and jobs for which time will be tracked.
4. Create an IIF file of lists exported from QuickBooks for use with the Timer.

Timer users need to do the following:

1. Install the Timer.
2. Set up a data file in the Timer.
3. Import the IIF file of QuickBooks lists into the Timer.

Exporting lists for Timer from QuickBooks Pro

Timer relies on lists of customers and employees that it takes from QuickBooks Pro. It can't retrieve the information automatically from QuickBooks, however. You must export the information from within QuickBooks and then import it from within Timer.

To export the needed lists from QuickBooks, follow these steps:

1. From the File menu, choose Timer, and then choose Export Lists for Timer.
2. If you're exporting the lists to a floppy disk or CD, insert the disk or CD in the appropriate drive.
3. Accept the default or indicate another filename and location for the data file.
4. If you change the filename, keep the .IIF extension. The Timer uses this extension to locate your data file.
5. If you inserted a disk or CD, choose the appropriate drive from the Save In drop-down list.
6. Click Save.

Setting up the Timer file and importing information

The QuickBooks Timer is included on your QuickBooks Pro, Premier, or Enterprise Solutions CD-ROM. You can make copies of the Timer to give to others. Follow these steps to create Timer install disks to give to others.

1. Label three formatted floppy disks or CDs as follows: Timer Install Disk #1, Timer Install Disk #2, and Timer Install Disk #3.
2. Insert the QuickBooks Pro, Premier, or Enterprise CD-ROM in your floppy disk or CD drive.
3. From your Windows Start menu, choose the QuickBooks program group; then, choose Create Timer Install Disks.
4. Follow the on-screen instructions to create the Timer install disks.

After you have installed the Timer program on a computer, the computer is ready to read a Timer file and import time data. To import this data from a Timer file, follow these steps:

1. From the File menu, choose Timer and then choose Import Activities from Timer.
2. If you're importing the activities from a floppy disk or CD, insert the disk or CD in the appropriate drive.
3. Enter the filename and location of the .IIF file that contains the activity data.
4. If the file is on a floppy disk, choose the drive where you inserted the disk from the Look In drop-down list.
5. Click Open.

Charging Billable Time and Costs to Invoices

As mentioned earlier in this chapter, there are two benefits to entering employee time activities. One is to process payroll, which is discussed in Chapter 21. The other is to bill customers for the time spent.

When working on an invoice (see Chapter 16), you may have noticed the Time/Costs button on the right edge of the form. Click it to open the Choose Billable Time and Costs dialog box.

You can use this dialog box to assign costs for Items, expenses, and time to the customer's invoice, but here you're most interested in the time, so click the Time tab. The hours spent by each employee on the job appear, as shown in Figure 20-12.

Click to place a check mark next to each line you want to transfer to the invoice, or click Select All to mark them all at once. By default, each line appears separately on the invoice; you can condense them into one line by marking the Print Selected Time and Costs as One Invoice Item check box. When you do this, all times with the same Service Item are combined. Items with different Service Item settings continue to appear separately.

Rock Castle Construction

Time by Job Detail

December 1 - 15, 2007

Date	Name	Billing Stat...	Duration
Baker, Chris:Family Room			
Floor Plans			
12/15/2007	State Board...	Unbilled	0:01
Total Floor Plans			0:01
Total Baker, Chris:Family Room			0:01
Cook, Brian:2nd story addition			
Framing			
12/04/2007	Gregg O. Sc...	Unbilled	4:00
Total Framing			4:00
Installation			
12/07/2007	Dan T. Miller	Unbilled	8:00
12/08/2007	Dan T. Miller	Unbilled	8:00
12/09/2007	Dan T. Miller	Unbilled	8:00
Total Installation			24:00

Figure 20-12: Every billable hour of employee time that was attributed to this job appears on the list.

When you're finished, click OK. QuickBooks appends the times to the invoice, in a group, and a subtotal line adds them.

Viewing Time-Tracking Reports

Choose Reports ⇨ Jobs, Time & Mileage and look at the bottom of the submenu to see a list of these four time-tracking reports:

- ✦ **Time by Job Summary:** This report can help you see how many hours your company as a whole is spending on each project.
- ✦ **Time by Name:** This report shows the tracked time broken down by employee. It can tell you at a glance which projects each employee is spending the bulk of his or her time on.
- ✦ **Time by Job Detail:** This report shows the hours worked on each job broken down into various phases or components of the total job, as shown in Figure 20-13.
- ✦ **Time by Item:** This report shows the hours charged to various Service Items. You can see how much of your business comes from certain service activities such as repair or installation.

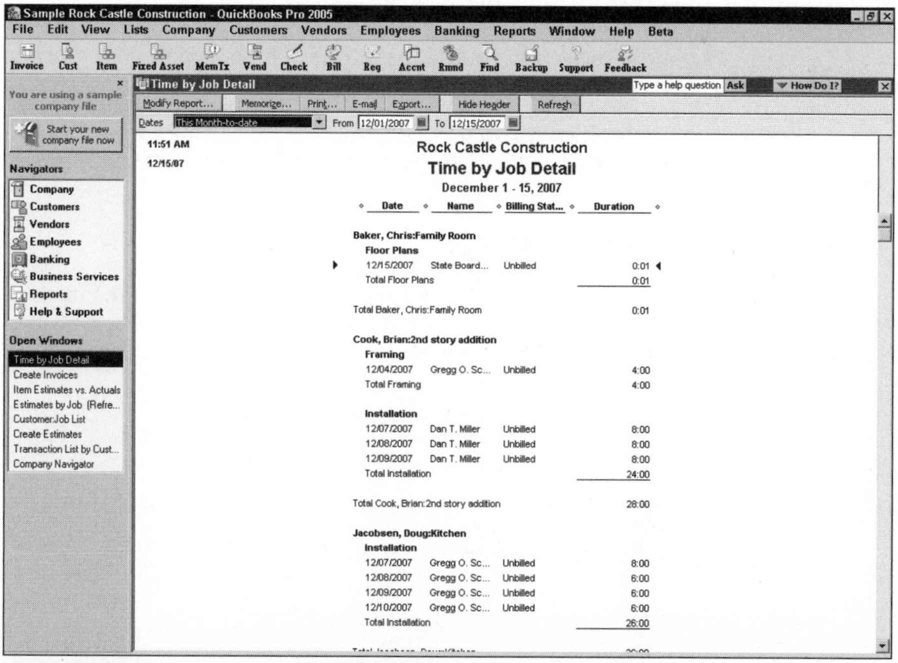

Figure 20-13: A Time by Job Detail report.

Working in Multi-User Mode

Multi-user mode is new in QuickBooks Pro 6.0. It enables up to five people to access the same QuickBooks company file simultaneously. For example, you could store your QuickBooks company file on your network server, and then up to five employees connected to the network could work with the file at the same time. This can be useful when several employees need to use the QuickBooks file simultaneously, such as at a sales counter, where there are multiple clerks taking walk-up customer orders, or in internal sales, where there are multiple operators taking orders via phone.

You can also use multi-user mode on a single PC to control access to sensitive data. When you enable multi-user access, you can set up user profiles and assign passwords to them. This can, for example, keep your data entry clerks from having access to your payroll records, or keep nonemployees out of your system.

Switching to multi-user mode

To enable multi-user mode to access the file from multiple PCs, start from the server PC — that is, the one that will be considered the "administrator." The first time you switch to multi-user mode and set up users, you're logged on as the administrator. The administrator has the ability to set and change passwords and to assign access rights to other users.

To work in multi-user mode, follow these steps:

1. Choose File ⇨ Switch to Multi-User Mode. The company file closes and then reopens in multi-user mode.
2. If this is the first time you have used multi-user mode, you are prompted to set up new users. Click Yes to begin doing so, and then read the next section.

Setting up new users

To set up new users, start from the User List. When you click Yes in step 2 of the preceding steps, you end up there, or you can choose Company ⇨ Set Up Users to get there. Once you are at the User List, follow these steps:

1. From the Company menu, choose Set Up Users.
2. The User List window appears. Click Add User.
3. Enter the name of the person you want to add in the User Name field.
4. Enter a password first in the Password field and then in the Confirm Password field.
5. Click Next to finish adding the new user.

Cross-Reference The process of adding new users and assigning roles to them is discussed in more detail in Chapter 13.

Summary

This chapter explained the bonus features that come with the Pro version of QuickBooks. You learned about creating estimates, working with time tracking and job costing, and operating in multi-user mode.

- To create estimates, use the Customers ⇨ Create Estimates command. You can customize the estimate template as needed, as you learned to do for other sales forms.
- You can include discounts on estimates as sales incentives by adding the Discount Item to the estimate.
- You can create an invoice from an estimate by clicking the Create Invoice button on the estimate form.
- To create a partial invoice based on progress made toward the complete estimate, you must turn on progress invoicing in the Company Preferences.
- You can check your actual job cost against the estimate to manage profitability using a number of QuickBooks Pro reports.
- You can track employee time spent on jobs or on overhead with the Time Tracking feature. You can then charge the billable time to your customer invoices.
- Teach employees how to use Timer to track their own time so that you can save some administrative time by importing their tracking files into QuickBooks.
- You can set up QuickBooks to work in multi-user mode so that more than one user can access your QuickBooks company file simultaneously. To manage the security of the system, you can create user profiles and assign passwords.

✦ ✦ ✦

CHAPTER 21

Payroll Taxes and Items

✦ ✦ ✦ ✦

In This Chapter

✦ ✦ ✦ ✦

An employee paycheck is probably one of the most complicated routine documents a business generates — an amalgamation of overlapping computations and specialized functions that make you wonder how anybody ever got paid before the advent of computers. You could send your payroll off to an outside service. However, with the convenience of delegating comes a loss of control over this vital aspect of your business. This chapter introduces you to the essential concepts and convenient QuickBooks features that enable you to take charge every payday.

Payroll Decisions You Must Make at the Outset

QuickBooks tracks a lot of payroll information, and these features are very easy to activate and set to meet the needs of your business. But a few of the questions require careful thought at the outset to avoid wasting time re-entering data as the result of a future change. It's a good idea to consider the following issues before you sit down at your QuickBooks screen:

- **How often will you pay your employees?** QuickBooks uses this information to calculate the number of pay periods in the year and to prompt you with appropriate reminders when necessary.
- **In which states do you file payroll taxes? For each, what is your state taxpayer identification number?** Generally, you are responsible for filing taxes in each state in which your company maintains employees or payroll. QuickBooks can also track any local taxes to which your company might be subject in various states.

Most states require your company to obtain a state taxpayer identification number that is used by the state for tracking returns, payments, and filings. If your company is to begin filing as a new taxpayer in a particular state, you can obtain this number by contacting the state's Department of Revenue (which you can locate by calling directory assistance in the capital city of the state). Multi-state filing issues can arise when a company has employees who maintain out-of-state home offices.

✦ **What is your state unemployment tax rate (SUI)?** This is a tax imposed for the purpose of paying unemployment compensation to the state's displaced workforce. It is set up in QuickBooks as a separate tax rate Item as discussed later in this chapter. Many states condition employers' rates on how many of their employees have successfully filed for unemployment benefits in the past.

Tip

Publications are available from most states' Department of Revenue that tell you how these unemployment tax rates are determined. These publications may also clue you in as to when employees are eligible for benefits as opposed to having been fired for a reason that makes them ineligible for benefits (such as not showing up for work or stealing from the company). To keep their SUI rates as low as possible, many employers routinely challenge unemployment claims made by employees who do not meet the legal criteria.

✦ **If applicable for your state, what is your state disability tax rate (SDI)? Which local taxes do you withhold?** Not all states impose this tax. When it is applicable, it is imposed as a separate tax, and it is set up in QuickBooks as a separate tax rate Item. Again, it is helpful to consult publications from your state's Department of Revenue and/or a tax advisor who practices in that jurisdiction for tips about making your company eligible for the lowest rate available.

✦ **Do you qualify for the federal unemployment (FUTA) tax credit?** In most states, employers can take a credit against federal unemployment taxes for the state unemployment taxes paid. Again, you'll need to check with your accountant or the IRS on a state-by-state basis.

✦ **By what method do you compensate your employees? Hourly? Salary? Commission?** After you specify the compensation methods, QuickBooks asks you to supply additional information for each option that you choose. Your answers are used to set up salary, hourly, and commission Payroll Items, as discussed later in this chapter.

✦ **What deductions do you withhold from net (after tax) pay?** Examples of what QuickBooks is looking for here include employee-paid insurance and 401(k) and other retirement plans, to name a few. QuickBooks sets up a special Item for each one you specify.

✦ **What additions, if any, do you apply to employee paychecks (for example, bonuses, tips, reimbursements)?**

- **What contribution amounts does the company pay? Company-paid taxes, miscellaneous expenses, insurance?** Again, QuickBooks sets up a special Item for each one.
- **What are the beginning balances in the company's payroll accounts from the beginning of the calendar year to the start date (for example, payments made and liabilities accrued)?** It's important to enter these amounts for each employee so that correct year-to-date amounts appear on paychecks and correct balances are reported for payroll and payroll tax liability reports.

You may not be able to complete the interview in a single sitting. You may need to check with your accountant, your lawyer, the owner of the business, or the local Department of Revenue, or read further on in this chapter. QuickBooks recognizes that the interview asks for a lot of information and allows you to exit the interview at any time. When you reenter the interview, you'll find yourself at the exact point where you left off.

Tip It is a good practice not to file for a tax identification number unless you are sure your company is required to have one. Once a number is obtained, the state tax system is alerted to look for returns and, in some states, may even assess taxes and penalties based on assumptions about the company's payroll.

Setting Up Payroll and Employee Preferences

You use the Payroll & Employees Preferences window, shown in Figure 21-1, to activate payroll features that determine what appears on employee paychecks.

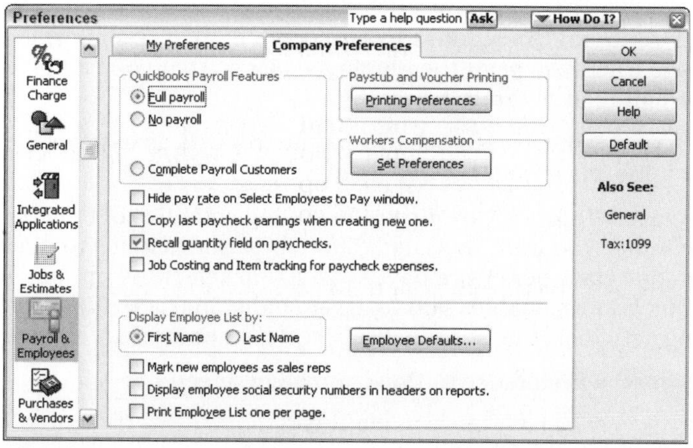

Figure 21-1: Set and activate payroll preferences from this dialog box.

The choices that appear in the Preferences window depend on which other aspects of the program have been activated. For example, questions about payroll class tracking appear in this window only if the class-tracking feature has been activated. To access the Preferences window, follow these steps:

1. Go to Edit ➪ Preferences. Scroll to the Payroll & Employees icon, and click the Company Preferences tab. You are presented with payroll preference options, as previously shown in Figure 21-1.
2. Indicate whether you want to activate one of the following:
   - Full payroll
   - No payroll
   - Complete payroll customers

   If you do not select the Full Payroll option, some options appearing in the Preferences window are dimmed. This means that you cannot access them.
3. Indicate whether you want to sort the company's employee list by first name or last name.
4. Select from among the various printing preferences for paychecks by clicking the Printing Preferences button. The options are self-explanatory.
5. Select whether to hide or show the hourly rates or salaries in the Select Employees to Pay window by selecting or deselecting the Hide Pay Rate on Select Employees to Pay Window check box. (You might not want the employee who is preparing the paychecks to see what everyone is making.)
6. Select whether you want QuickBooks to recall (prefill) the quantity entered on the employee's last paycheck for additions, deductions, and contributions. You can edit these amounts on-screen for any occasional variations.
7. Indicate whether you want QuickBooks to print each employee's information on a separate page when you print the Employee List so that you can place a copy of the information in separate paper files.
8. Indicate whether you want QuickBooks to generate reports as to payroll expenses for each job, class, and Service Item.
9. If you are using classes to track various profit-making activities of the company, indicate whether you want to assign different earnings Items to different classes or assign one class per entire paycheck. If you select the option Earnings Item, QuickBooks enables you to assign individual activities to various profit-making activities. Classes are discussed further in Chapter 28.
10. Click OK to activate the Preference options you have selected.

Who Is an Employee?

Before you begin entering payroll information for everyone who provides services to your business, it's a good idea to give some thought to a common payroll issue that can potentially save your company some money. When is a worker classified as an employee and when is that same individual an independent contractor? The answer to this question determines whether the business must withhold payroll taxes and is financially responsible for the employer-matching portion. Obviously, it is to the company's advantage to classify workers as independent contractors whenever it is appropriate to do so. But, as discussed in Chapter 3, the penalties for erroneous classification and failure to withhold dictate some caution.

You'll want to check with your accountant before making a decision — but you may want to know something about the IRS criteria so that you can ask the right questions. Generally, the IRS applies two basic methods to determine whether someone is an independent contractor or an employee: the common-law test and rules of the IRS Safe Harbor law.

According to the common-law test, a worker is an employee if the employer has the right to control the method and the result of work — what an employee does, how they do it, and when they do it. Some of the questions considered in applying the common-law test include the following:

- Does the employer specify hours of work, place of performance, and how something is to be accomplished?
- Does the employer provide a place for the worker to perform their responsibilities and the tools and implements with which they are expected to perform them?
- Is there a continuous, full-time relationship?
- Does the worker perform the services for one company or individual, as opposed to multiple companies or individuals?

If you answered yes to any of the foregoing questions, under the common-law test, you are probably required to withhold from the worker's wages. The Safe Harbor law consists of IRS regulations and practices that make it reasonable to assume that a certain type of worker can be classified as an independent contractor. Your tax advisor may be able to make you aware of specific IRS rulings or may feel that you have an argument that there is long-standing industry practice you may rely on in treating certain workers as independent contractors.

Note

The IRS uses one standard to classify workers, whereas the U.S. Department of Labor Wage and Hour division relies on more stringent criteria. The Department of Labor generally presumes all workers are employees unless the company can prove otherwise. This has implications for determining whether workers are subject to federal minimum-wage requirements.

Federal Taxation Overview

The basic federal payroll tax forms are the W-4 form, the W-2, Form 941, and Form 940. QuickBooks tracks the information required, and calculates and prints each form.

W-4 forms

We all have an obligation to pay our federal income taxes during the year, as incurred. Employees must have 90 percent of their liability withheld by the end of the calendar year. An employee may claim exemption from tax withholding only if he or she was not obligated to pay taxes for the prior year. The amount of federal taxes you must withhold is a function of your employees' federal taxable wages, marital status, number of withholding allowances claimed, the pay period, and the federal income tax withholding tables. The W-4 form, filled out by the employee, contains the necessary information as to marital status and personal withholding allowances. All employees are required to complete and sign a W-4.

W-2 forms and 1099 forms

Employers are required to issue a W-2 form to all employees at the close of the taxable year. The W-2 form contains information as to wages, tips, taxes withheld, retirement plan contributions, reimbursed amounts, and other items either paid to employees or withheld from their wages.

QuickBooks tracks amounts required to be reported on W-2 forms when you set up individual Payroll Items. Both the employee and the Social Security Administration must be provided with a copy of the form. Employees must be mailed copies by January 31 for the prior year. The Social Security Administration must be sent a copy by February 28 following the close of the tax year.

You use 1099 forms to report amounts paid for services to individuals who are nonemployees and who are paid more than $600 during the tax year. The company may be required to file a 1099 for amounts it pays to corporations, partnerships, or other business entities. As with the W-2, recipients of such must be furnished with a copy of the 1099 reporting amounts for the prior year postmarked January 31.

W-5 forms

Low-income individuals who meet certain criteria are eligible for the earned income credit. The income limitation to qualify for the credit is $25,760 if the taxpayer has a dependent child. The limit is $29,290 if the employee has more than one dependent child, and it is $9,770 if the taxpayer has no dependent children. More information is provided in the instructions for preparing Schedule EIC included with the IRS individual income tax return Form 1040.

This credit can be claimed on the employee's individual tax return at the end of the year or can be used to offset required withholding amounts. If the credit is used as an offset, the employee is required to file a W-5 form.

Forms 940 and 941

Form 941 must be filed by all employers who withhold income tax, social security tax, or both from their employees' wages. Employers must report both the amount of tax withheld from employees' paychecks and their share of the tax. Form 941 is filed quarterly. QuickBooks tracks the necessary information and prepares this form.

Form 940 is an annual form used to report and pay federal unemployment taxes. QuickBooks also calculates and prints this form for your company.

Payroll Item Lists and Item Types

When you set up your payroll using the EasyStep Interview, QuickBooks automatically creates Payroll Items for earnings; federal, state, and local taxes; commissions; and certain additions and deductions. All these Payroll Items appear on your Payroll Item List. The list is organized by type, with Wage Items appearing at the top. To view the Payroll Item List for your company, simply go to the Lists menu and choose Payroll Items List. Figure 21-2 shows a sample Payroll Item List.

Item Name	Type
Salary	Yearly Salary
Sick Salary	Yearly Salary
Vacation Salary	Yearly Salary
Overtime Rate	Hourly Wage
Regular Pay	Hourly Wage
Sick Hourly	Hourly Wage
Vacation Hourly	Hourly Wage
Bonus	Addition
Mileage Reimb.	Addition
Health Insurance	Deduction
Workers Compensation	Company Contribution
Advance Earned Income Credit	Federal Tax

Figure 21-2: A sample Payroll Item List.

There are eight types of Payroll Items that QuickBooks automatically creates or that you can set up on your own:

✦ **Federal Tax Withholding Items:** These Items are added during the initial interview and cannot be edited or changed. (That's why there's no section in this chapter on setting them up.)

- **Wage Payroll Items:** Hourly Wage and Salary Payroll Items are automatically set up by QuickBooks and added to the Item List as you answer the questions pertaining to how your company compensates employees — for example, hourly, salary, and commission. You may need to set up additional types of Items for your company on-the-fly as you add different compensation classifications.
- **State and Local Tax Items:** QuickBooks sets up these Items in response to your answers in the EasyStep Interview, but you may need to add more Items to track additional states. You can also request Payroll Tax Items for more than one state during the Interview.
- **State Disability Insurance:** Some states collect disability insurance premiums from employers. If your state is one of them, you need to set up an additional Item for tracking purposes.
- **Payroll Addition Items:** Payroll Addition Items include bonuses, tips, awards, reimbursements for travel and other expenses, taxable noncash fringe benefits, and advance EIC payments. You need to set these up for your company.
- **Payroll Deduction Items:** These include some taxable fringe benefits, deductions for 401(k) and other retirement plans, cafeteria plans and flexible spending plans, medical savings accounts, garnished wages, employee charitable donations, and employee-paid insurance contributions. You can set up most of these Items as you recognize the need for them.
- **Commissions:** This type of compensation must be set up as a special Commission Item.
- **Company Contribution Items:** These Items include employer contributions to retirement plans, company-paid insurance premiums, miscellaneous employer-paid taxes, and company-paid amounts that you can set up at any time. Many of these Items have corresponding Deduction Items that account for the employee-paid portion of the benefits.

Setting Up Wage Items

There are two categories of Wage Items: Salary Wage Items and Hourly Wage Items. Generally, you establish one of these Item types each time you create a different salary category — for example, executive salaries, driver salaries, and administrative wages. The main reason for creating different Salary and Wage Item types is so that you can track the expenses in different accounts. For example, administrative salaries might be charged to administrative expense, salesperson salaries might be charged to a sales expense account, and so on. You do not indicate the hourly salary amounts for each of the employees. You do this when you set up the individual employee templates, as demonstrated in the next chapter.

To set up a new Salary Payroll Item or Hourly Payroll Item, follow these steps:

1. Go to Lists ➪ Payroll Items. The Payroll Item List window appears. (The Items in the list may vary depending on what choices were made during the payroll setup.)
2. Click the Payroll Item menu button that appears in the lower left corner of the window and choose New from the pop-up menu, as shown in Figure 21-3.

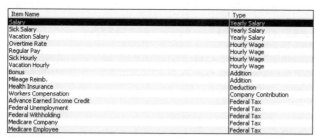

Figure 21-3: Adding a new Payroll Item.

The Add New Payroll Item dialog box appears, with the initial screen shown in Figure 21-4, followed by subsequent screens requesting information.

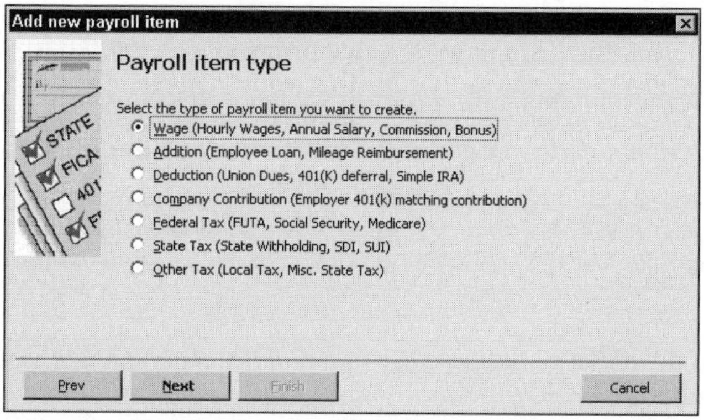

Figure 21-4: Select Custom Setup for a series of screens to guide you through the Payroll Item setup process.

3. Click Wage, and click Next.
4. Indicate whether you want to create an Hourly Wage Item, an Annual Salary Item, a Commission Item, or a Bonus Item, and click Next.

5. Follow the on-screen instructions for setting up the following types of hourly wages: Regular Pay, Overtime Pay, Sick Pay, and Vacation Pay. Click Next.
6. Enter a name for the Item, and click Next.
7. Indicate the account you want to use for tracking this Item from the drop-down list (for example, Payroll Expenses).
8. Click Finish. The new Wage Item appears on your Payroll Items List.

State and Local Payroll Tax Items

You must create a separate Item for each state and local income tax your company is required to withhold. QuickBooks tracks the liabilities separately for each state so that you can pay them accordingly.

State payroll taxes

To set up a State Payroll Withholding Tax Item, follow these steps:

1. Go to Lists ⇨ Payroll Item List. Click the Payroll Item menu button that appears in the bottom left corner of the window, and choose New from the pop-up menu. The Add Payroll Item dialog box appears.
2. Select State Tax as your Item type, and click Next.
3. Select a state from the drop-down list that appears.
4. Select the Withholding tax option for type of tax. Click Next.
5. Indicate an Item name (for example, WI Withholding). Click Next.

   Note

   For withholding tax, QuickBooks automatically creates a name consisting of the state and the word ***Withholding.*** QuickBooks is also aware of which states have no income tax (like Nevada) and will not allow you to set up a withholding item for that state.

6. Use the drop-down list to indicate the name of the state agency to which taxes are paid, your state tax ID number (if applicable), and the liability account to be used for tracking this Item. Click Next.
7. Check off the Items that are subject to withholding tax. Click Finish.

Local Tax Items

QuickBooks sets up some Local Tax Items for New York, Ohio, Indiana, and Michigan residents, but for the most part, you need to set these up yourself. To add a Local Tax Item, follow these steps:

1. Go to Lists ➪ Payroll Item List. Click the Payroll Item menu button that appears in the lower left corner of the window and choose New from the pop-up menu.
2. Click Next. Select Other Tax from the list of Item types. Click Next.
3. The screen shown in Figure 21-5 appears, asking you to select a tax name from the drop-down menu. If your local tax does not appear on the menu, select User-Defined Tax. Also, before you leave this screen, specify whether the company or the employee is responsible for paying the tax. Click Next.

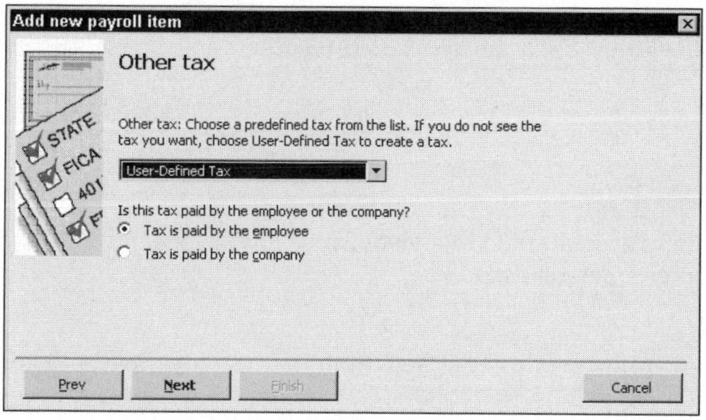

Figure 21-5: Selecting user-defined tax.

4. Indicate an Item name (for example, Sample Town Withholding) on the next screen. Click Next.
5. Indicate the name of the agency to which taxes are paid, your company's identification number (if any), and the liability account to be used for tracking this Item. If you indicated that this is a company-paid Item, you are also prompted to indicate an expense account. Click Next.
6. Specify the descriptive classification to be used for the income tax–reporting form to which you want your liability to be tracked. Click Next.
7. On the screens that follow, indicate whether the tax is computed as a percentage of the paycheck, a percentage of hours, or neither. (Neither applies when the tax is based on a percent of net or gross pay or when the tax is a flat amount.) Click Next after answering the questions to progress to the next screen.
8. Indicate whether you want the system to automatically enter a default amount for most employees. If the number varies with employees or is computed based on a rate computation for each employee, leave this field blank. Also, indicate whether the tax is subject to an annual limit, which is the maximum amount to be paid by any employee. Enter the limit in the appropriate field, as

illustrated in Figure 21-6. After you enter this limit, QuickBooks displays a warning if you attempt to withhold in excess of that amount. Click Next.

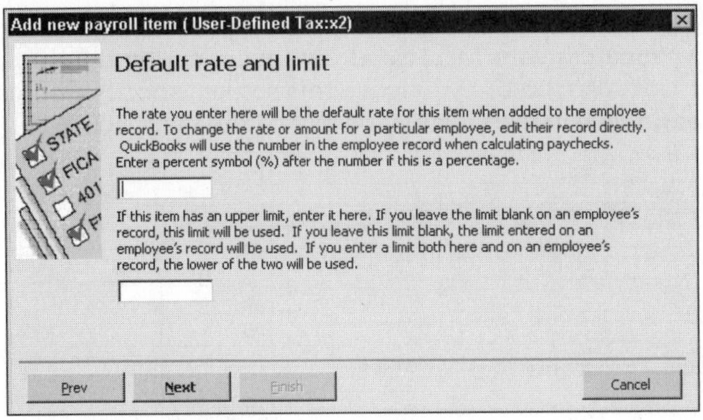

Figure 21-6: If the amount paid by most of your employees is the same, enter a default amount.

9. QuickBooks prompts you to specify which Items are subject to the rate. Click Finish when you are done.

State disability insurance

Only a few states collect disability insurance premiums from employers, but if you are in one of those lucky jurisdictions, you'll need to know how to deal with this. You actually need to set up two Items for this purpose: one to pay the company expense and one to collect it from your employees.

To set up the State Disability Insurance Items, follow these steps:

1. Go to Lists ⇨ Payroll Item List. Click the Payroll Item button that appears in the bottom left corner of the window, and choose New from the pop-up menu.
2. Select State Tax from the list of Item types and choose State Disability Tax from the list of options that appears. Click Next. (This option is grayed out or dimmed if not applicable to the state chosen.)
3. Enter the name of the state agency that collects the tax, your company's identification number if you have one, and the name of the liability account in which you plan to track this expense.
4. Indicate which Payroll Items are considered in computing the tax amount. Click Finish.

Payroll Deduction Items

Deductions can be computed based on gross wages, number of hours, or some other formula. Some deductions are subject to annual limitations. The following is a list of common payroll deductions:

- 401(k) plans
- Cafeteria plans
- Employee charitable contributions
- Employee-paid insurance
- Flexible spending plans
- Garnished wages
- Loan repayments
- Retirement plan contributions
- Simple plans
- Taxable noncash fringe benefits
- Tips (if the employee keeps the tips but reports the amounts to the employer)
- Union dues

To set up common Payroll Deduction Items, do the following:

1. Go to Lists ⇨ Payroll Item List. Click the Payroll Item button that appears in the lower left corner of the window, and choose New from the pop-up menu.
2. Select Deduction from the list of Item types. Click Next.
3. Enter the name you want to assign to the Item (for example, Loan or 401(k) Plan) and click Next.
4. If applicable, enter the agency to which the liability is paid and any applicable identification number. Enter the name of the account that you want to use for tracking or liability. Click Next.
5. Indicate the line of your company's tax-reporting form to which this Item is tracked if you want QuickBooks to do this. Click Next.
6. Indicate which taxes apply to the deduction. When you select a tax using the screen shown in Figure 21-7, QuickBooks decreases the wage base on which taxes are calculated by the amount of this Item. Click Next.
7. Indicate which Items should be calculated after wages have been reduced by deductions, as shown in Figure 21-7. Click Next.

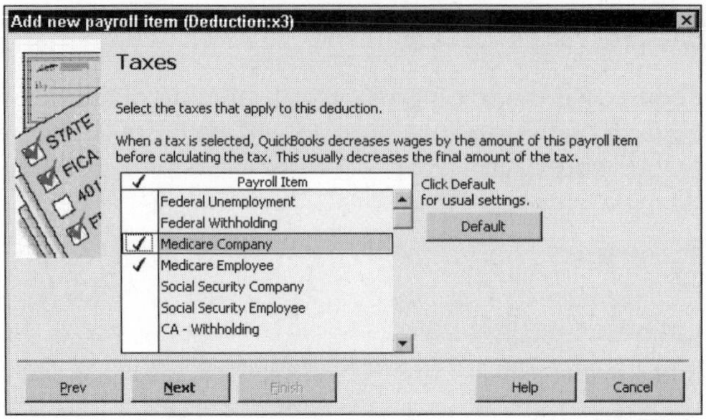

Figure 21-7: Indicate whether the Item is deducted before or after taxes.

8. On the screens that follow, indicate whether the tax is computed as a percentage of net or gross pay, as a set amount, or as a dollar rate times a quantity (for instance, $5.00 per thousand). Click Next to proceed through the screens that ask you for this information.
9. Indicate whether you want the system to automatically enter a default amount for most employees. If the number varies with employees or is computed based on a rate computation for each employee, leave this field blank. Also, indicate whether the tax is subject to an annual limit, which is the maximum amount to be paid by any employee. Enter the limit in the appropriate field. After you enter this limit, QuickBooks displays a warning if you attempt to withhold in excess of that amount.
10. Click Next. If you told QuickBooks that this deduction is based on a percentage of pay, you are prompted to provide the additional information as to whether the deduction is computed based on the same rate for all employees. If it is not, leave the field blank. You are also asked to enter any annual limit to which the deduction is subject.
11. Click Finish.

Tip

If you set up a 401(k) or Simple Deduction Item, you must set up a corresponding Item for the company contribution amount. Contribution Items are discussed later in this chapter.

Payroll Addition Items

As with Deduction Items, the Item setup screens prompt you to specify how the Item should be tracked on tax forms and the appropriate annual limitations and percentages. The following is a list of common Payroll Addition Items:

- Advanced earned income credit payments
- Awards
- Bonuses
- Employer contributions to medical assistance and medical savings accounts
- Expense reimbursements
- Moving expense reimbursements
- One-time compensation payment or distribution
- Reimbursement for qualified adoption expenses
- Supplemental wages
- Tips
- Travel advances

To set up a Payroll Addition Item, follow these steps:

1. Go to Lists ➪ Payroll Item List. Click the Payroll Item button that appears in the lower left corner of the window, and choose New from the pop-up menu.
2. Select Addition from the list of Item types. Click Next.
3. Enter a name for the Addition Item, and click Next.
4. Select an account for tracking this expense from the drop-down menu.
5. Indicate which taxes apply to the deduction, and click Next. When you select a tax, QuickBooks decreases the wage based on which taxes are calculated by the amount of this Item (previously shown in Figure 21-7).
6. On the screens that follow, indicate whether the tax is computed as a percentage of net or gross pay, as a set amount, or as a dollar rate times a quantity (for instance, $5.00 per thousand). Click Next to proceed through the screens that ask you for this information.
7. Indicate whether you want the system to automatically enter a default amount for most employees. If the number varies with employees or is computed based on a rate computation for each employee, leave this field blank. Also, indicate whether the tax is subject to an annual limit, which is the maximum amount to be paid by any employee. Enter the limit in the appropriate field. After you enter this limit, QuickBooks displays a warning if you attempt to withhold in excess of that amount.
8. Click Next. If you told QuickBooks that this deduction is based on a percentage of pay, you are prompted to provide the additional information as to whether the deduction is computed based on the same rate for all employees. If it is not, leave the field blank. You are also asked to enter any annual limit to which the deduction is subject.
9. Click Finish.

Company Contribution Items

This category of Items includes company-paid amounts on which taxes are not withheld. Within this category are the following:

- ✦ Company-paid expenses
- ✦ Employer-contributed amounts to 401(k) and other retirement plans
- ✦ Employer-paid portion of state and local taxes
- ✦ Health and life insurance benefits not subject to federal taxation

To set up a Company Contribution Item, do the following:

1. Go to Lists ➪ Payroll Item List. Click the Payroll Item button that appears in the lower left corner of the window, and choose New from the pop-up menu.
2. Select Company Contribution. Click Next.
3. Enter the name that you want to give this Item in the field specified. Indicate whether you want to track this expense by job by selecting or deselecting the indicated box. Click Next.
4. Specify the agency to which the liability is paid and your identification number, if applicable. You must also choose both an expense and a liability account for tracking the company obligations. As the screen explains, this type of Item is both an expense that the company must meet and a liability when amounts are accumulated but not paid. Click Next.
5. Indicate which taxes the Contribution Item is subject to. QuickBooks selects several likely tax fields based on the Tax Tracking Type chosen. Click Next.
6. On the screens that follow, indicate whether the tax is computed as a percentage, as a set amount, or as a dollar rate times a quantity (for example, $5.00 per thousand). Click Next to progress through the screens.
7. If you indicated that the Contribution Item is computed based on a percentage, you are prompted to specify whether the percentage is based on gross pay or on some other quantity. Indicate whether you want the system to automatically enter a default amount for most employees. If the number varies with employees or is computed based on a rate computation for each employee, leave this field blank. Also, indicate whether the Contribution Item is subject to an annual limitation.
8. Click Finish.

Commission Items

You can create custom Commission Items to reflect any type of performance-based compensation that your company pays. QuickBooks tracks taxes and prints the correct year-end amount on the W-2 forms. To create a Commission Item, follow these steps:

1. Go to Lists ⇨ Payroll Items. Click the Payroll Item button that appears in the lower left corner of the window and choose New from the pop-up menu.
2. Select Commission. Click Next.
3. Enter the name you want to give this Item in the field specified. Indicate whether you want to track this expense by job by selecting or deselecting the indicated box. Click Next.
4. Indicate the name of the expense account that you want to use to track this Item. Click Next.
5. Indicate whether you want the system to automatically enter a default amount for most employees. If the number varies with employees or is computed based on a different rate computation for each employee, leave this field blank.
6. Click Finish.

Editing and Deleting Payroll Items, and Making Them Inactive

When you edit a Payroll Item, the change can affect all future paychecks. Previously recorded transactions are affected by any changes made to the name of the Item, the tax-tracking information, and the accounts to which the Item is charged. Calculations and amounts shown on previously written checks are not altered. To edit an existing Payroll Item, follow these steps:

1. Go to Lists ⇨ Payroll Items. Select the Item you want to change by clicking it in the list of Payroll Items.
2. Click the Payroll Item button that appears in the lower left corner of the window and choose Edit from the pop-up menu.
3. The Item Setup information screens appear in the same order as if you were setting up a new Item. Correct the information appearing in any of the fields as you progress through them. Click Next to progress to the next screen.
4. When you have completed all the screens, click Finish to save the changes.

You can also delete certain Payroll Items. You cannot delete any Items that you have used in employee templates or records, or even on an employee paycheck. In other words, if you want to delete an Item, you have to delete it from every place it appears on the system. To delete a Payroll Item, do the following:

1. Go to Lists ➪ Payroll Items, and select the Item you intend to delete.
2. Select Delete from the pop-up menu that appears, as shown in Figure 21-8.
3. Click OK.

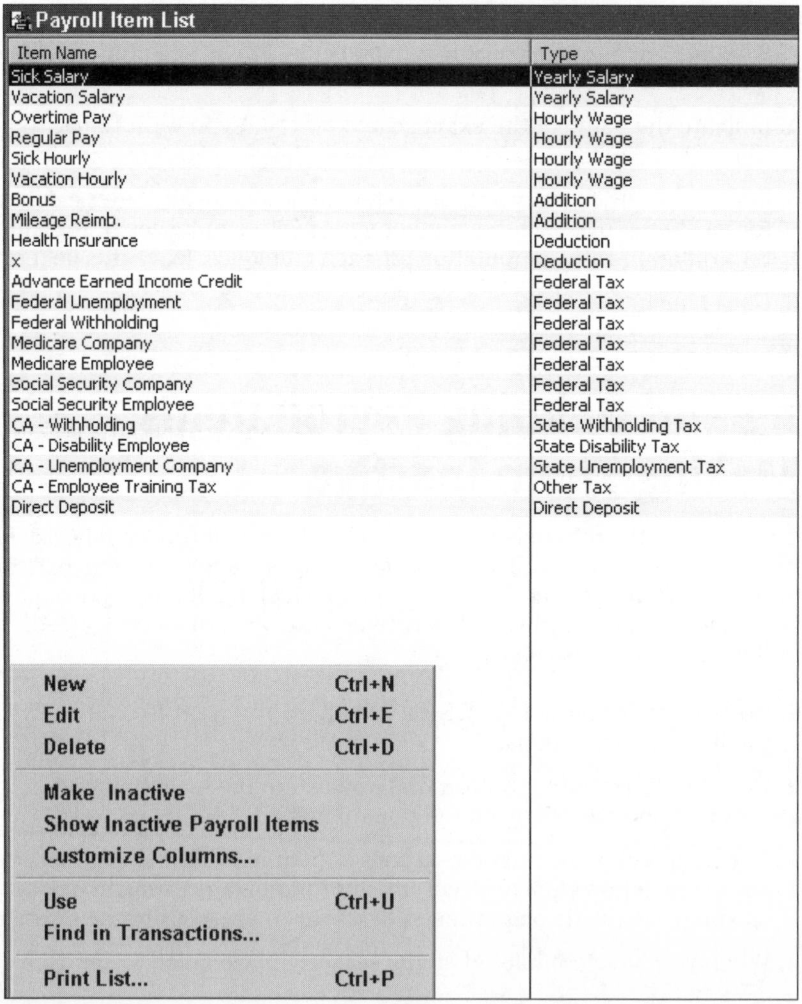

Figure 21-8: You can delete an unused Item with a click of your mouse.

You can't delete a Payroll Item previously used on templates, reports, or checks, but you can make it inactive. If you make an Item inactive, it won't appear on your lists unless you select the Show All option on the Payroll Item List.

To make a Payroll Item inactive, follow these steps:

1. Go to Lists ➪ Payroll Items, and select the Payroll Item you want to hide.
2. Click the Item button and choose Make Inactive from the pop-up list that appears (previously shown in Figure 21-8).

To view all Payroll Items, even the inactive ones, do the following:

1. Go to Lists ➪ Payroll Items.
2. Select Show All. All Payroll Items appear on the list. A special X icon is used to identify those Items that are inactive, as shown in Figure 21-9.

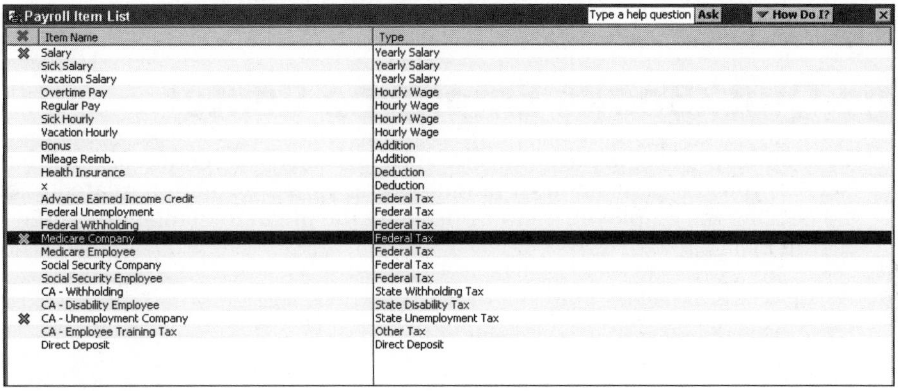

Figure 21-9: The X icon is used to designate inactive Payroll Items.

QuickBooks Payroll Services for an Additional Fee

QuickBooks offers several payroll-processing services for an additional fee. You can sign up for these services by going to Employees ➪ Payroll Setup. QuickBooks presents you with a series of interview screens such as the one shown in Figure 21-10, including screens with information and questions to help you choose among the various fee-based payroll-processing plans offered by QuickBooks.

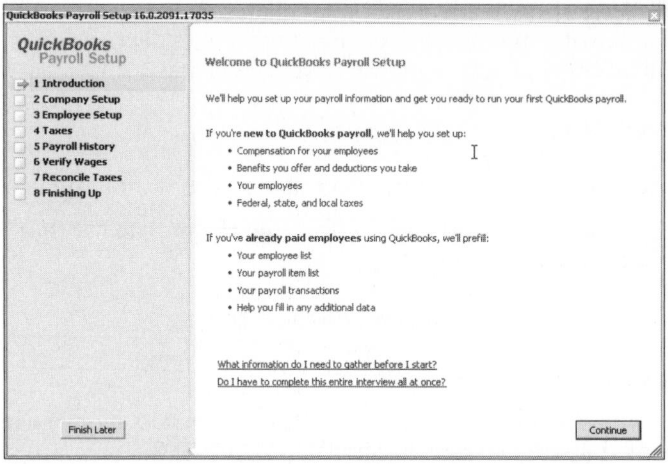

Figure 21-10: An interview is available to help you decide among various payroll-processing services offered by QuickBooks for an additional fee.

The QuickBooks Employee Center

In addition to using menus and icons on the Employee section of the Navigator screen, you can perform most functions and view information related to employees by clicking the Employee Center option on the menu to display the screen shown in Figure 21-11.

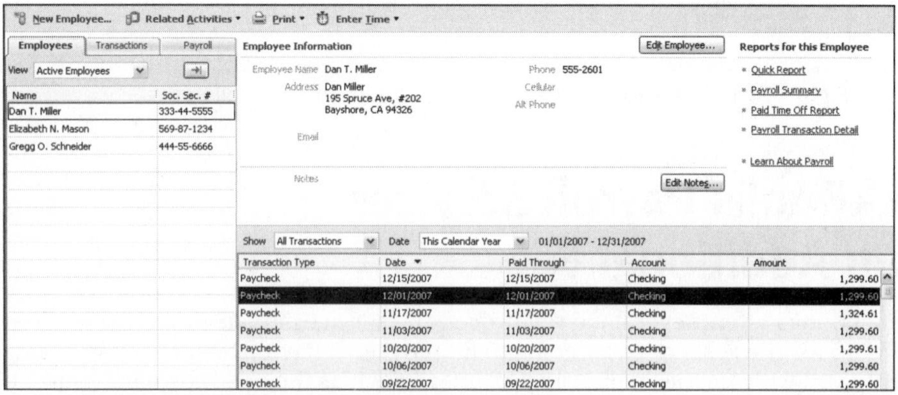

Figure 21-11: The Employee Center screen.

The three different views, accessed from the tabs on this screen, are as follows:

✦ **Employees:** Using this tab (shown in Figure 21-11), you can view a list of your current employees and click a listing to view their paycheck information.

✦ **Transactions:** The view from this tab allows you to see a listing of all employee paychecks for a period you designate, as well as lists of adjustments and other payroll-related liabilities.

✦ **Payroll:** You can pay employees, set deposit frequencies and process payroll forms directly from this screen, shown in Figure 21-12.

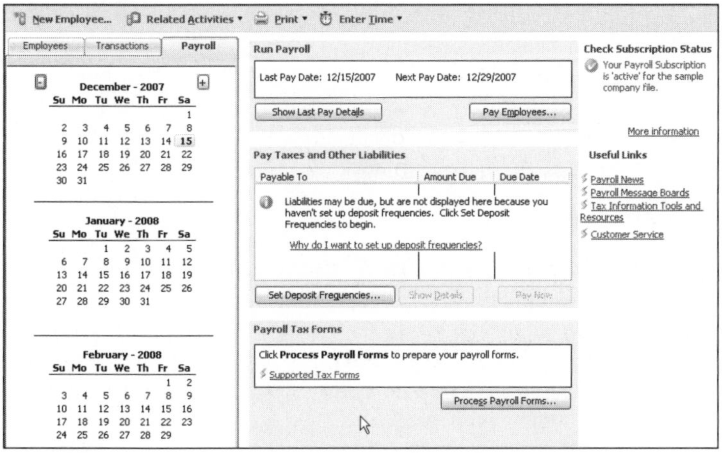

Figure 21-12: The Payroll tab of the Employee Center Screen.

Summary

Employee paychecks are surprisingly intricate documents, often involving multiple Wage, Tax, Addition, Deduction, and Contribution Items. QuickBooks streamlines the process by enabling you to set up Items for recurring types of payroll entries.

✦ The EasyStep Interview is highly recommended for setting up your payroll initially. Many of the Payroll Items your company needs are automatically set up during the interview process.

✦ Pay attention to the legal difference between an employee and an independent contractor. You do not need to withhold taxes for workers that meet the legal criteria for independent contractor status.

- There are four basic tax forms filed by every business that maintains payroll: the W-4, the W-2, Form 940, and Form 941. Employers are also required to file a W-5 form for any employees claiming the advance payment of the earned income credit.
- All Payroll Items appear on a special Payroll Items List. There are eight categories of Payroll Items: Wage, Commission, Addition, Deduction, Company Contribution, Federal Tax, State Tax, and Other Tax.

✦ ✦ ✦

Payroll and Taxes

PART

V

✦ ✦ ✦ ✦

In This Part

✦ ✦ ✦ ✦

22

CHAPTER

Maintaining Employee Information and Keeping Your Employee List Up-to-Date

✦ ✦ ✦ ✦

In This Chapter

The QuickBooks Employee Defaults feature

Setting up individual employees

Entering year-to-date payroll information

Maintaining an Employee List

✦ ✦ ✦ ✦

It is necessary for you to read this chapter even if your company sends its payroll to an outside service. This chapter is for any business that deals with that all-important human element — the employees. This chapter teaches you how to set up and maintain an Employee List, which contains necessary personnel information about each worker who crosses your threshold. (Unfortunately, I can't help you figure out how to make everyone get along, show up, or stop surfing the Internet on company time.)

Employees versus Independent Contractors

Although the services they perform for your company may be the same, there is a vast difference between accounting for workers who are classified by the IRS as employees and those who are considered independent contractors. Chapter 21 delved into this topic in detail and summarized the IRS criteria.

Basically, if a worker is an employee, your business must withhold payroll taxes and is financially responsible for the employer-matching portion of Social Security. Obviously, it is to the company's advantage to classify workers as independent contractors whenever it is appropriate to do so. But, as discussed in Chapter 3, the penalties for erroneous classification and failure to withhold dictate some caution.

In QuickBooks, the process for adding employees and independent contractors is slightly different. Both procedures are discussed in this section.

Adding Employees

Employees are workers for whom you withhold taxes. You can designate employees as inactive if they have not yet started, are on a leave of absence, are suspended, or have been terminated. You can also customize the information you maintain for each employee. QuickBooks helps you maintain accurate personal information for each employee. Just follow these steps:

1. Click the Employee Center, and click the Employees tab, as shown in Figure 22-1. Choose Active Employees or All Employees from the drop-down menu.

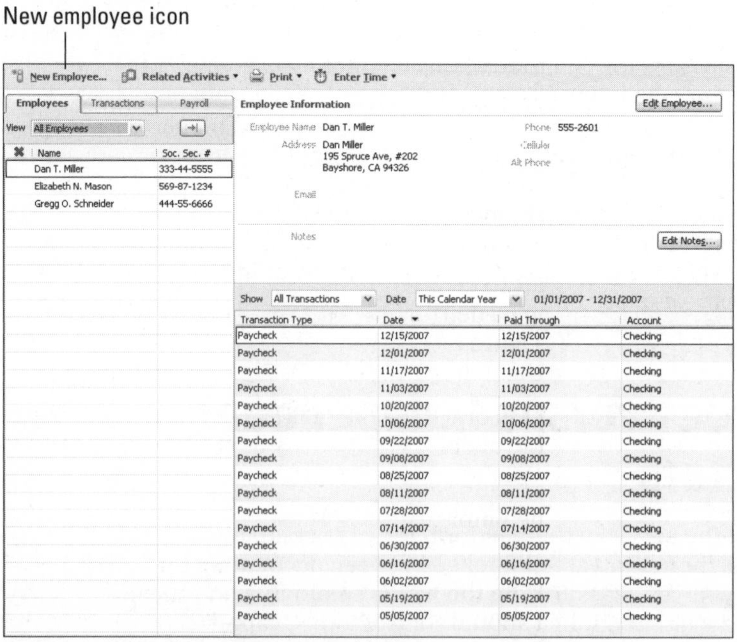

Figure 22-1: A sample Employee List.

2. Click the New Employee icon in the upper left hand corner, and choose New. The dialog box shown in Figure 22-2 appears.

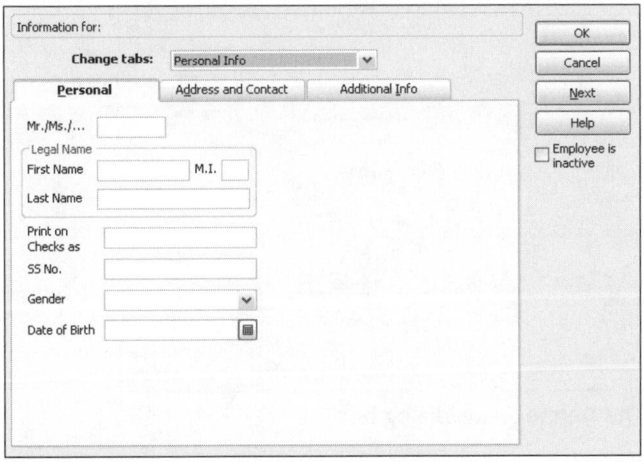

Figure 22-2: Enter employee information by using this dialog box.

3. Complete the Personal, Address and Contact, and Additional Info tabs. (You can export the information you enter in these fields use it in a form letter.)
4. (Optional) To the right of the dialog box, just below the Help button, select the Employee Is Inactive check box. If you check this box, the employee's paycheck will not be processed with the rest of your payroll and the employee will not be displayed on your Employee List.
5. On the Additional Info tab, enter any information you want to store for this employee.
6. (Optional) If you want to customize the information maintained on your employees by adding or deleting information fields, click the Define Fields button as shown in Figure 22-3. In the Define Fields dialog box (shown in Figure 22-4), set up the defined fields as desired and click OK.
7. Fill in any custom fields or click Define Fields to add custom fields that track employee information, such as a spouse name, and click OK when finished.
8. From the Change Tabs drop-down list, choose Employment Info, and fill out the information in the Employment tab.
9. If you are using QuickBooks to manage your payroll, choose Payroll and Compensation Info from the Change Tabs drop-down list and fill out the Payroll Info tab. You should also complete information for other options, such as including the pay rate, pay period, tax (W-4) information, and vacation and sick pay setup as appropriate for your business.

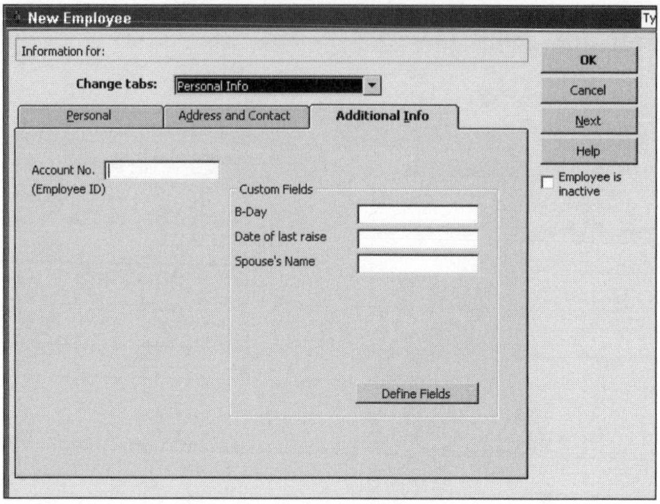

Figure 22-3: The Define Fields dialog box.

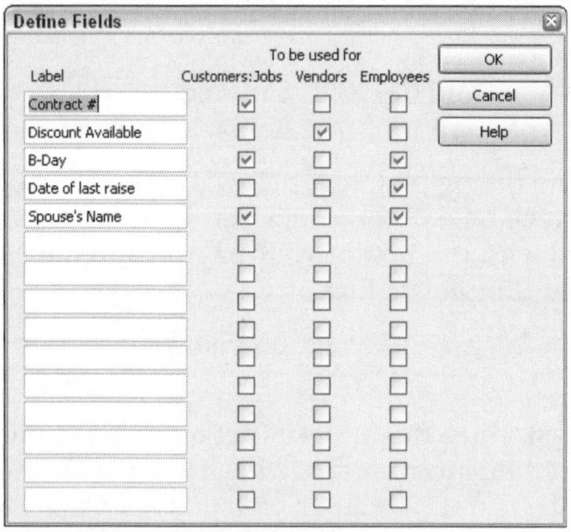

Figure 22-4: Setting up defined fields to maintain employee information.

10. If you want to add another employee to the list, click Next.

11. When you have finished adding employees, click OK to close the window.

Types of QuickBooks Employees

QuickBooks defines the following four types of employees:

✦ **Regular:** According to the IRS, "anyone who performs services for you is your employee if you can control what will be done and how it will be done." Most people on your payroll are probably regular employees, for purposes of withholding taxes and computing benefits.

✦ **Statutory:** Some employees that do not fit the preceding IRS definition for "regular employees" are considered statutory employees. Examples of statutory employees include commission salespeople, truck drivers, and certain types of domestic service workers. When you choose Statutory, QuickBooks marks the Stat. Emp. Check box on the W-2 form for the employees of this type.

✦ **Officer:** These are the corporate officers in a company that sit on its Board of Directors. They include the Chief Executive Officer (CEO) and Chief Financial Officer (CFO).

✦ **Owner:** These are the people who own a company. Because of government requirements, QuickBooks does not do payroll for owners. Owners or partners are paid with "regular" checks (using Write Checks), not paychecks.

For more information on these categories and how they affect tax treatment, you can download IRS Publication 15, Circular E, Employer's Tax Guide, at `www.IRS.org`.

Employee Defaults

The Employee Defaults feature in QuickBooks allows you to enter payroll information that most employees have in common, such as deductions for taxes, health insurance, or union dues. This default feature saves you time, because you need enter this information only once. When you are setting up the payroll record for a new employee, QuickBooks automatically fills in the information you entered into the default setup. If you need to, you can customize any of the prefilled information for each employee.

Setting up tax defaults

To set up Employee Defaults for federal, state, and other tax information, follow these steps:

1. Click Employee Center.

2. Click Related Activities at the top of the list and click Employee Defaults, as shown in Figure 22-5.

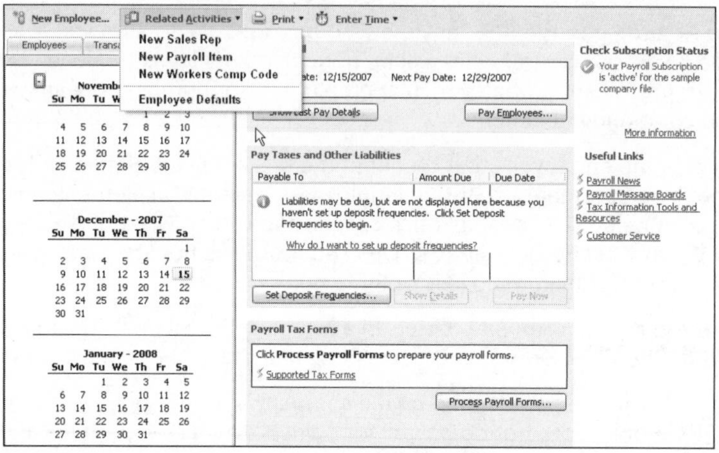

Figure 22-5: Locating the Employee Defaults screen.

3. In the first line of the Additions, Deductions, and Company Contributions table, click a payroll item from the Item Name drop-down list, as shown in Figure 22-6.

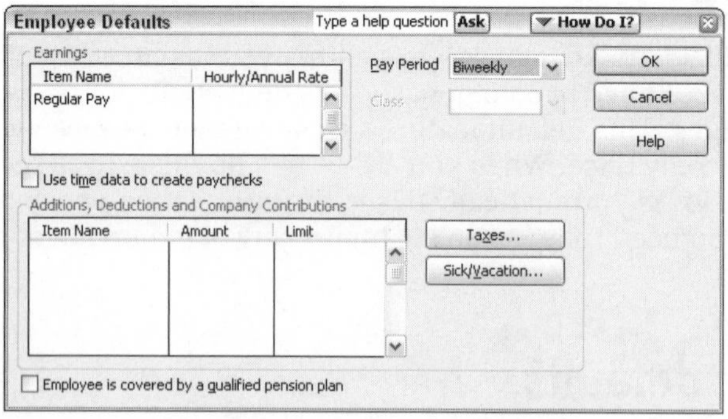

Figure 22-6: Setting up employee defaults.

If the amount and limit are different for each employee, leave them blank. You can customize the amount and limit for each employee when you set up your employee records.

4. If the payroll item you want is not listed, choose Add New from the drop-down list.
5. Enter other payroll items on additional lines of the table, as needed.

   If any payroll item is based on a percentage of gross pay, the order in which you enter it in the table is important.
6. Click OK to record the employee default setup.

To set up Employee Defaults for federal, state, and other tax information, follow these steps:

1. Click Employee Center.
2. Click Related Activities at the top of the list and click Employee Defaults (previously shown in Figure 22-5).
3. Click the Taxes button.
4. In the Taxes Defaults window, click the Federal tab and select whether you will be, by default, withholding Medicare, Social Security, and unemployment taxes and whether you want QuickBooks to determine eligibility for the earned income credit as shown in Figure 22-7. When you are finished, click the State tab.

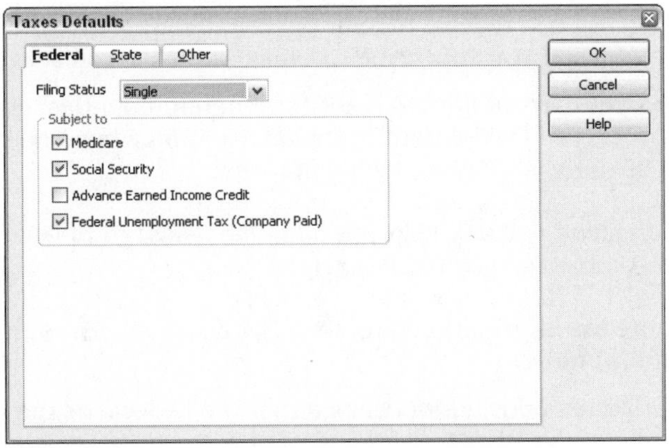

Figure 22-7: Setting up federal tax preferences.

5. In the State Worked section, choose the state where most (or all) of your employees work from the State drop-down list.

   Depending on the state you select, QuickBooks displays the SUI and SDI check boxes.

6. If your employees are subject to state unemployment insurance, either company-paid or withheld, select the SUI check box. If your employees are subject to state disability insurance, select the SDI check box.

7. In the State Subject to Withholding section, choose the state where most (or all) of your employees are subject to state withholding from the State drop-down list.

Note

If you have not set up payroll items for the corresponding SUI, SDI, and Withholding state you specify here, you will not be able to set that state up as a default

8. On the Federal tab of the Taxes window, select the federal taxes that apply to most (or all) of your employees.

9. Make sure that you select all taxes your company has to pay, regardless of whether they are withheld or are a company expense.

10. To enter local and other taxes, click the Other tab.

11. In the Item Name drop-down list, choose the tax you want to apply. Fill in the fields for this tax only if the information applies to most (or all) of your employees:

    - If you are not asked for the tax rate, QuickBooks already has the rate in its tax tables. You can receive regular payroll updates, which include current tax tables, if you subscribe to QuickBooks Payroll services.
    - If your employees are subject to taxes for different counties, cities, or school districts, you can customize the information when you set up the payroll tax information for each employee.

Tip

For additional information that will help you fill in the fields, go to `www.intuit.com/quickbooks/products/tax/localtax.html`.

12. If you have no more tax information to enter, click OK to return to the Employee Defaults window.

13. To continue entering tax information, click either the Federal or the Other tab.

Setting up defaults for benefits and other adjustments

To set up defaults for benefits, such as sick pay and vacation pay rates, additions, deductions, and contributions, follow these steps:

1. Click Employee Center.
2. Click Related Activities at the top of the list and click Employee Defaults (as previously shown in Figure 22-5.)
3. In the first line of the Additions, Deductions, and Company Contributions table, choose a Payroll Item from the Item Name drop-down list, as shown in Figure 22-8.

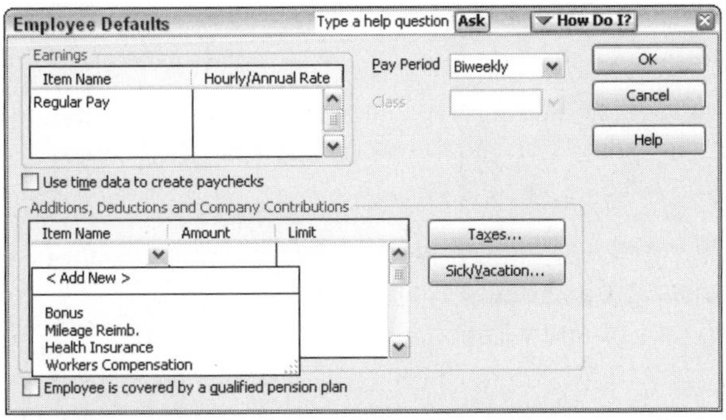

Figure 22-8: Setting up Employee Defaults for additions, deductions, and company contributions.

If the amount and limit are different for each employee, leave them blank. You can customize the amount and limit for each employee when you set up your employee records.

4. If the Payroll Item you want is not listed, choose Add New from the drop-down list.
5. Enter other Payroll Items on additional lines of the table, as needed.

   If any Payroll Item is based on a percentage of gross pay, the order in which you enter them in the table is important because it can affect the calculation.

6. Click OK to record the employee default setup.

Setting up sick and vacation time employee defaults

If most of your employees accrue sick and vacation hours at the same rate, you can use the QuickBooks default feature to calculate sick and vacation accruals. To set up these defaults, follow these steps:

1. Click Employee Center.
2. Click Related Activities at the top of the list and click Employee Defaults (as previously shown in Figure 22-5).
3. Click the Sick/Vacation button. The dialog box shown in Figure 22-9 appears.

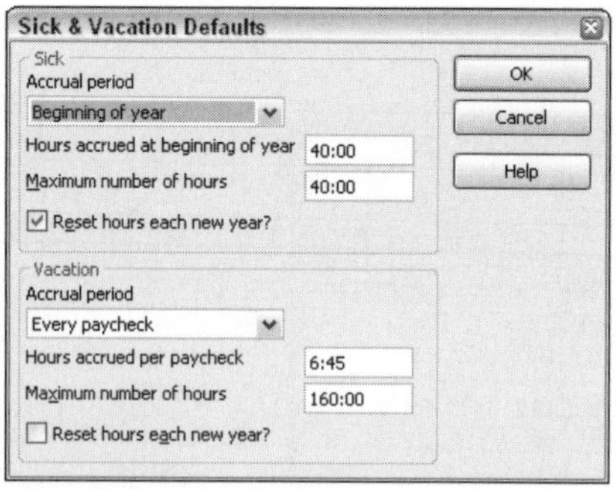

Figure 22-9: Setting up sick and vacation pay defaults.

4. In the top half of the Sick & Vacation Defaults window, choose an accrual period for sick time.
5. In the Hours Accrued at the Beginning of Year field, enter the number of sick hours that accrue during the accrual period you selected.
6. (Optional) In the Maximum Number of Hours field, enter the maximum number of sick hours that employees may ever accrue.
7. If you want sick hours to reset to 0 when a new calendar year begins, select the Reset Hours Each New Year? check box.
8. To specify accrual information for vacation hours, repeat steps 4 through 7 for the Vacation section of the window.
9. Click OK to record your selections.

Setting up wage and salary defaults

Setting up wage and salary defaults can streamline some of the most tedious aspects of your bookkeeping. Wages, salaries, and related liabilities occur with regularity and reflect human variables that make transactions tricky to standardize. Nevertheless, QuickBooks offers several efficient features that identify and handle common elements of payroll transactions, while allowing you to account for variations with predetermined user-friendly procedures.

Tip Make sure you have set up the necessary Payroll Items to use this feature. Chapter 21 tells you how to do this.

Caution Don't enter an hourly rate or an annual salary unless you pay most employees at the same rate or salary.

Caution Don't enter overtime, sick, or vacation Payroll Items in the Earnings section. If you do, QuickBooks displays them on all paychecks for all employees.

Follow these steps to set up wage and salary defaults:

1. Click Employee Center.
2. Click Related Activities at the top of the list and click Employee Defaults (as previously shown in Figure 22-5).
3. Fill in the Earnings section of the Employee Defaults window.
4. In the Pay Period field, choose the pay period that applies to most or all employees from the drop-down list, as shown in Figure 22-10.

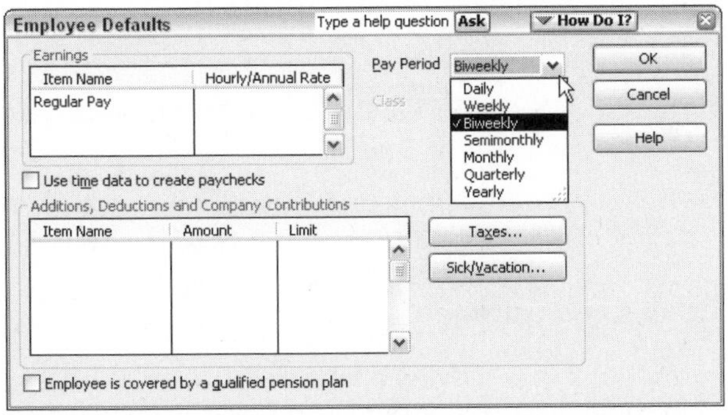

Figure 22-10: Setting up wage and salary defaults for employees paid at the same rate.

5. (Optional for those who track payroll expenses by class) If you want to assign most of your employees to the same class, choose a class type from the drop-down list. For example, you can use classes to group employees by location or by department.
6. (Optional) Select the Use Time Data to Create Paychecks check box if you want employees' hours from your time data to prefill paychecks.

Entering Information for Individual Employees

Although it is convenient to use defaults if you have a number of employees, there are times when you want to enter information for an individual employee. This section tells you how to do so.

Entering basic payroll data for one employee

To enter individual payroll information for an employee, follow these steps:

1. Go to the Employees tab in the Employee Center, and click the New Employee icon in the upper left hand corner. The screen shown in Figure 22-11 appears.

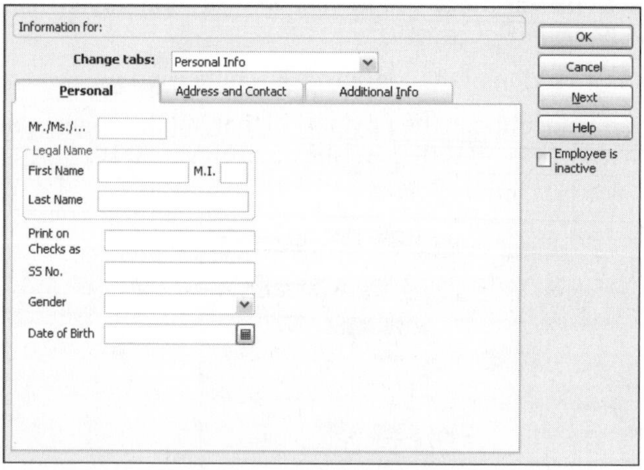

Figure 22-11: Setting up a new employee.

2. After entering the personal information for the employee, as discussed at the beginning of this chapter, select Payroll and Compensation Info from the drop-down menu in the Change Tabs field.
3. In the Earnings section, enter the appropriate hourly or fixed salary Items. (Do not enter Items for sick pay or vacation pay in this window.)

4. Make sure that the correct pay period is reflected in the Pay Period field.
5. If you track payroll expenses by class, enter the correct class name. The class drop-down box appears under Pay Period only if Use Class Tracking is checked in the Accounting Preferences.
6. Select the Use Time Data to Create Paychecks check box if you want to use the employee's time data hours when creating paychecks.

Entering taxes for an individual employee

To set up taxes for an employee, follow these steps:

1. In the New Employee window, click the Change Tabs drop-down list and select Payroll and Compensation Inf, and then click the Taxes button.
2. Enter the appropriate Federal Tax Items using the fields accessed by the tabs.
3. Click the State tab, and select the correct State Tax Items using the fields and drop-down menu.
4. To record and save all of the tax information that you have entered and to exit the employee withholding tax setup window, click OK.

Entering sick and vacation time for one employee

To enter sick or vacation time for an individual employee, follow these steps:

1. Click the Change Tabs drop-down and select Payroll and Compensation Info. Then click on the Sick/Vacation button (previously shown in Figure 22-11).
2. Enter the number of sick and vacation hours that the employee has available as of the current date. Adjust these numbers for hours used or added as the result of "comp" time or some other company policy.
3. Indicate how many hours are accrued each year or each pay period according to company policy.
4. Indicate the maximum number of hours that the employee can accrue each period, if the company sets a limit.
5. Specify whether sick and vacation hours can be accumulated from one year to the next by selecting or deselecting the Reset Hours Each New Year? check box
6. Click OK to save and record the information you entered in this window.

Entering individualized payroll adjustments

The previous chapter introduced you to the various types of adjustments that appear on employee paychecks — commissions, additions, deductions, and company contributions. To enter these adjustments for an individual employee, follow these steps:

1. Use the Additions, Deductions, and Company Contributions table located at the bottom of the New Employee window's Payroll Info tab to enter each desired Payroll Item from a convenient drop-down list. If the Item does not appear on the drop-down list, you can set it up now.
2. If the Payroll Tax Item amount is the same with every paycheck, enter the figure in the Amount column. If the amount varies with each paycheck, leave this column blank.
3. If the Item is subject to an annual limit, enter this figure in the Limit column.
4. Repeat steps 1 to 3 to add Payroll Items. You can add up to 10 additional Payroll Items for each employee.
5. Click OK to record and save the information that you entered in this window.

Entering Year-to-Date Payroll Information

If your QuickBooks start date is after January 1, you need to enter additional information for all employees after you complete the new setup. You must compile and enter year-to-date summaries of the following information:

- ✦ Wages, commissions, bonuses, and other compensation
- ✦ Each federal, state, and local tax withheld
- ✦ Each addition and deduction amount
- ✦ Each company contribution amount

This information is necessary to print correct year-to-date amounts on checks and to prepare W-2s, IRS Forms 940 and 941, and any required state and local withholding reporting forms.

You also need to enter any outstanding liabilities as of December 31 of the prior year for payroll withholding, deduction, and company contribution amounts. These liabilities may be the result of prior years' payroll transactions, but they are liabilities that carry forward to the current year and are paid in the current year.

Cross-Reference

You must also enter any payroll transactions that have occurred between the company's start date and today. Chapter 7 tells you how to enter these after-the-start-date transactions.

Entering Year-to-Date Information

To display the Prior Payments of Taxes and Liabilities window, follow these steps:

1. From the Employees menu, choose Payroll Service Activities and then Payroll Set Up.
2. In the Payroll Setup window, choose Set Up Year-to-Date Amounts.
3. The Interview screen appears. Answer the questions on this Interview screen, and on the screen that follows, set up your payroll.
4. In the Payment Date field, enter the date you made the liability payment.
5. In the For Period Ending field, enter the end date for the payments you are summarizing. When you process tax forms for a particular tax period, QuickBooks uses this date to determine the amount of tax you have paid. For example, if you are entering a tax payment you made on 9/10/01 for tax you owed as of 8/31/01, enter 8/31/01.
6. In the Item Name field, choose a Payroll Item. In the Amount field, enter the amount that you paid for that Item during the time period.
7. On additional lines, choose Payroll Items for other liabilities and enter the amount that you paid for each.
8. (Optional) To summarize payments for another period or for another group of Payroll Items, click Next Payment. Change the date to the end date for the new period and fill in the window.
9. To close this window, click Done.

Maintaining the Employee List

Employee turnover is as inevitable as rain on the day you wash your car. And so are changes in company policies that affect payroll. For this reason, the savvy QuickBooks user will want to stay current on the procedures that help keep the Employee List and company payroll information accurate and up-to-date.

Editing and deleting employees

Relationships and housing change, and when that happens, you need to change the information that you maintain for an employee. To edit employee information, follow these steps:

1. Go to Employees ➪ Employee Center and click the Employees tab.
2. Click the Edit Employee button in the upper right portion of the screen.
3. Click the Employee button in the lower right corner of the Employee List and choose Edit from the pop-up menu (previously shown in Figure 22-1).
4. Edit the information about the employee as it appears on the information screens.
5. Click OK to save the changes that you made.

To delete an employee, follow these steps:

1. Go to Employees ➪ Employee Center and click the Employees tab.
2. Select the employee that you want to delete.
3. Click the Employee button and select Delete from the pop-up menu (previously shown in Figure 22-1).
4. Click OK.

Making employees inactive

This is a good feature to remember when you have an employee that takes an extended leave of absence, such as a maternity leave. To make an employee inactive, follow these steps:

1. Go to Employees ➪ Employee Center and click the Employees tab.
2. Select the employee that you want to make inactive, and click the Edit Employee button. Select Make Inactive from the pop-up menu.

When you make an employee inactive, the employee does not appear on any lists or drop-down menus unless you select the Show All button at the top of the Employee List window (previously shown in Figure 22-1). When you do this, the special hand icon appears next to all inactive employees.

Keeping notes about employees

You can maintain notes, such as "Do not rehire" or "Up for review and raise," about employees directly in your QuickBooks system. To use the convenient "notepad" provided for this purpose, follow these steps:

1. Go to the Employees tab in the Employee Center, and click the Edit Notes button.
2. Select the employee you want to annotate.
3. Click the Employee menu button at the bottom of the list window. Choose Notepad from the pop-up menu.
4. Enter your notes on the notepad. Figure 22-12 shows an example. You can edit, delete, or print your notepad entries. (Some personnel issues just can't be summed up on a single line of a standard form.)

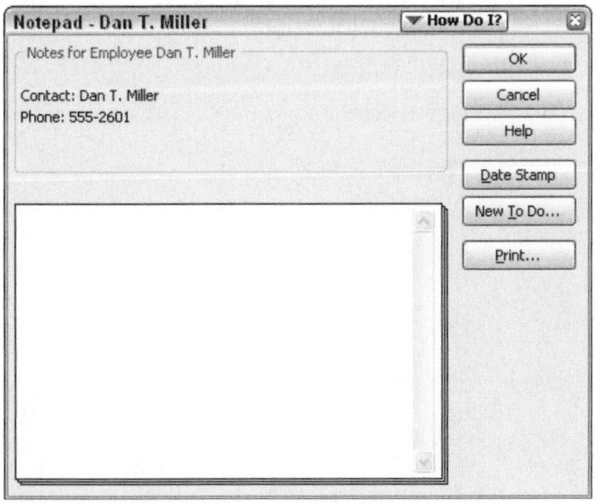

Figure 22-12: Use the notepad shown here to annotate your personnel files.

5. Click OK.

Summary

This chapter discussed setting up payroll records for individual employees. It also discussed topics related to maintaining an accurate Employee List.

- ✦ There are two methods of entering employee information: the QuickBooks default feature and setting up each employee file individually from scratch.
- ✦ The default method allows you to specify default information that will be pre-filled each time you enter a new employee. This approach works well if you have many employees for whom similar payroll entries are required.
- ✦ For correct totals to be reflected on employee paychecks, W-2 forms, IRS Forms 940 and 941, and state reporting forms, you must enter accurate year-to-date payroll information.

✦ You must enter payroll data and transactions from the QuickBooks start date through the current date.

✦ You can edit, delete, and hide employee information. You can also maintain notes about employees using QuickBooks' convenient notepad.

✦ ✦ ✦

CHAPTER 23

Sales Taxes

✦ ✦ ✦ ✦

In This Chapter

Accounting for sales taxes

Setting sales tax preferences

Sales Tax Items

Charging your customers

Viewing your sales tax liability

Paying your sales tax obligations

✦ ✦ ✦ ✦

There's a certain irony to the collection and remittance of sales taxes. Sales taxes are someone else's financial obligation — your customers'. But even though they are imposed on the purchaser, it is the company's obligation to collect them. These amounts are ultimately reflected as a current liability on the business's Balance Sheet.

Whereas sales taxes are computed on a straightforward fixed-percentage basis, the overall process of accounting for them is a little more complicated. This chapter discusses the accounting basics, setting up Sales Tax Items, and reviewing and reporting your obligations.

Accounting for Sales Taxes

Sales taxes involve three major accounting events for a business: charging the customer, recording the company's liability, and paying the appropriate tax agency. QuickBooks documents these events by recording the liability on customer receipts and invoices, by generating Sales Tax Liability Reports, and by recording reports in the Sales Tax Payable register.

You can expedite the process of setting up your QuickBooks accounting system for collection and payment of sales taxes if you have the following information at your disposal:

- ✦ A list of all of the municipal, county, and state authorities for which your company must charge sales tax (generally, this is any jurisdiction where your company solicits customers and does business)
- ✦ The applicable tax rates for each obligation imposed
- ✦ A list of nontaxable transactions for each applicable jurisdiction
- ✦ Information as to whether the company pays sales taxes monthly, quarterly, or annually (depends on specific factors such as the taxing locality and the amount of your obligation)

At first glance, collection of sales tax seems like a relatively straightforward type of transaction—you compute the applicable percentage on each nonservice item. But you can encounter some gray areas. For example, what are the obligations of a mail-order business? Or a business that does not actively solicit out-of-state customers but receives orders based on its national reputation?

Tip

If you find yourself facing these types of issues, it's probably worthwhile to consult with a tax advisor who is familiar with sales tax issues and the concept of *nexus*. Nexus is a legal term pertaining to whether a business has a sufficient presence in a particular state so as to make it obligated to pay taxes in that state. This issue can require some research, but ignoring it can be devastating to the future of your business. If you need to be persuaded, take a look at the section on tax penalties at the end of Chapter 3.

What about services companies? Services are generally exempt from sales taxes, but the status of some transactions is not obvious. If I purchase a pair of earrings with ear piercing, is it a sale or a service? Can the shop avoid the imposition of a sales tax by charging for the piercing and throwing in the earrings for free? That's the type of question you should discuss with a tax expert who is knowledgeable about the ins and outs of tax law. An interesting bit of trivia: The following benevolent states don't allow localities to impose their own sales taxes:

Connecticut	Massachusetts
Delaware	Michigan
District of Columbia	Mississippi
Hawaii	New Jersey
Indiana	Rhode Island
Maine	Vermont
Maryland	West Virginia

After you tackle the thorny legal issues, accounting for sales taxes is simply a matter of performing a few new variations of familiar system tasks—activating preferences and setting up Items.

Setting Sales Tax Preferences

You need to initiate the sales tax collection features of the program by activating the right preferences. You may have already done this during your initial company setup when prompted by the EasyStep Interview. If you didn't, here's how to do it now:

1. Go to Edit ➪ Preferences. Scroll to the Sales Tax icon on the left side of the screen and click it.

2. Click the Company Preferences tab. The Preferences screen shown in Figure 23-1 appears.

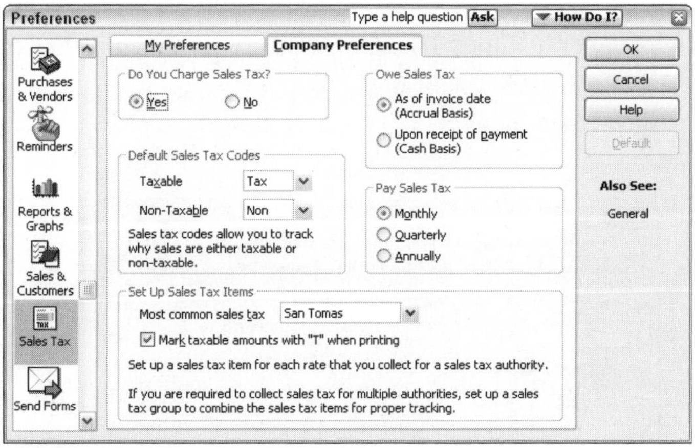

Figure 23-1: Sales tax preferences are set by using this screen.

3. Answer Yes to Do You Charge Sales Tax?

4. (Optional) Use the default sales tax code fields if you want to track why certain types of transactions are nontaxable. (For example, labor is not generally subject to sales tax.)

5. In response to Owe Sales Tax, specify whether the company owes sales tax at the time the customer is invoiced or at the time the customer pays. This preference is really asking you whether the company keeps its books on the cash or accrual basis, and whether you want your sales tax reports to be generated on a different basis. (If you can't remember what these terms mean, review Chapter 4 or refresh your recollection by going to the Glossary.)

6. Indicate whether you pay sales taxes to government agencies monthly, quarterly, or annually. QuickBooks uses this preference solely to determine how your sales tax reports are prepared and when you receive reminders to pay. You can make payments at any time regardless of the option that you specify here. Your actual payment obligations depend on the regulations of the taxing jurisdiction.

Tip

QuickBooks rises to the occasion if you keep your books using one method — cash or accrual — and your taxing jurisdiction requires payment on another. For example, your company might keep its books on the cash basis, but the taxing jurisdiction might recognize a liability at the time the customer is invoiced. No problem. You can change the option specified in step 5 as often as you need to.

7. In the Most Common Sales Tax field, choose the Sales Tax Item (or Sales Tax Group Item) that you will use most often. This field determines the default information that QuickBooks will automatically enter on customer sales forms. If you have not set up your Sales Tax Item or Sales Tax Group Item, you can do so now or set this preference later. (The next section of this chapter discusses setting up Sales Tax Items.)
8. If you check the box to mark taxable amounts with a T when printing, QuickBooks prints the notation tax next to each taxable item listed on a customer invoice form, as shown in Figure 23-2.
9. Click OK to save your changes.

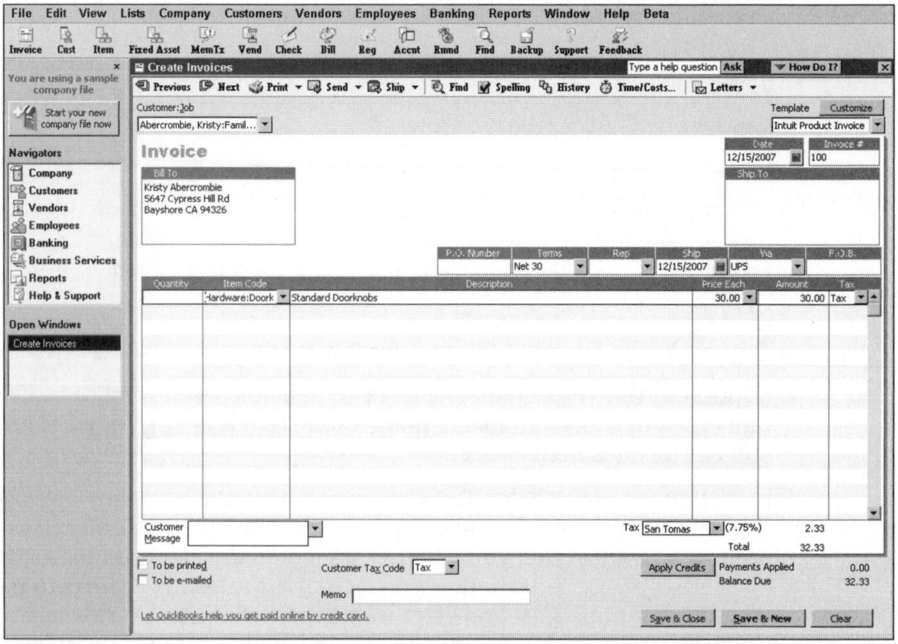

Figure 23-2: Customer invoices indicate whether an Item is taxable.

Sales Tax Items

You set up and use Sales Tax Items in two ways: as individual Items and as groups of Items. Single Sales Tax Items are set up to calculate taxes imposed by a single entity. Sales Tax Group Items are composed of several individual Sales Tax Items assigned a single name so that you can have QuickBooks calculate and enter them all at one time on a customer sales form as a single amount. For example, if your jurisdiction imposes state, city, and county sales taxes, you probably want to show the total of all sales taxes as one Item on the invoice. (Your customers probably don't care about a breakdown; they just want to know the total amount they owe.)

You can set up individual state, county, and city Sales Tax Items under a Group Item designation. When you enter the Group Item, QuickBooks calculates all individual Sales Tax Items and shows their sum as a single amount on the sales form.

Setting up single Items

You need to create an Item for each tax your company collects (unless it is an isolated event that you enter directly on a sales form — for example, a one-time sale by a Wisconsin company made at an Alaskan Trade Show). Whenever you enter the Item on a sales form, QuickBooks automatically calculates the rate and enters any stored descriptive information.

To create an Item for each tax obligation that the company must report, follow these steps:

1. Go to Lists ⇨ Item List. Click the Item menu button and select New from the pop-up menu that appears.
2. For Item Type, choose Sales Tax Item from the drop-down menu shown in Figure 23-3.

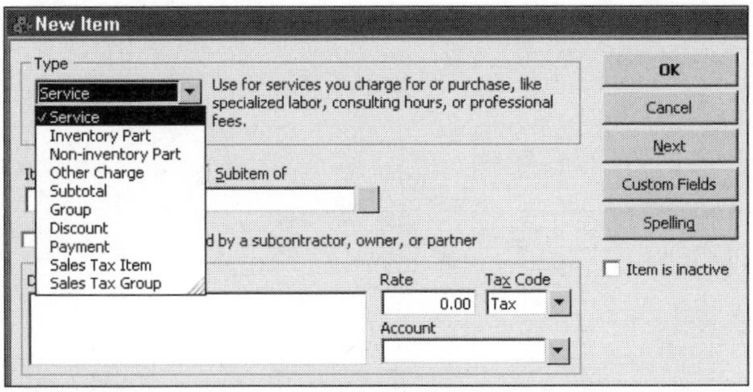

Figure 23-3: Use this New Item dialog box to set up a Sales Tax Item for each individual tax that is imposed.

3. Enter the tax name in the Tax Name field. QuickBooks uses this name on any future sales tax reports you create.
4. Enter the description that you want to appear on your customer invoices and receipts in the Description field.
5. Enter a tax rate in the Tax Rate % menu field. QuickBooks assumes that the number you enter in this field is a percentage.
6. Enter the name of the government agency to which the tax is paid in the Tax Agency field.
7. Click Next to enter another Item or OK to leave this dialog box.

Creating Sales Tax Group Items

Generally, even if you are charging a combination of several sales taxes to your customers, they will want to know only the total percentage rate they must pay. To accommodate this desire for simplicity, QuickBooks enables you to create a Sales Tax Group Item so that you can display the aggregate of the imposed taxes as one rate on one line on a receipt or invoice. To create a Sales Tax Group Item, perform these steps:

1. Go to Lists ➪ Item List. Click the Item menu button at the bottom of the window and choose New from the pop-up list that appears.
2. In the Type field drop-down menu, select Sales Tax Group. The New Item window shown in Figure 23-4 appears.

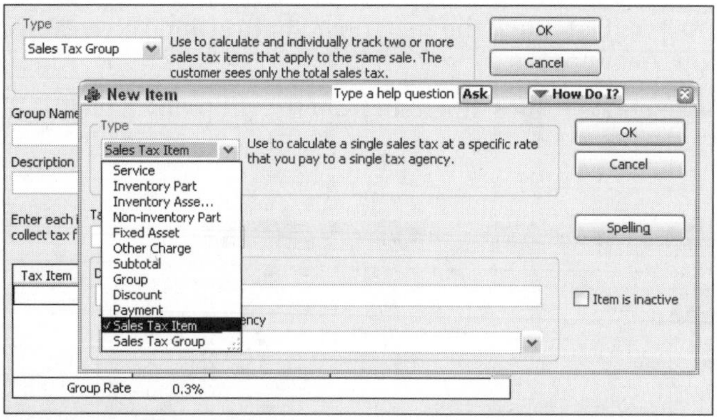

Figure 23-4: The New Item window enables you to create a Sales Tax Group.

3. Choose an identifying name or number for the group of taxes and enter it in the Group Name/Number field.
4. Enter the information that you want to appear on your invoices, receipts, and other customer sales forms in the Description field.
5. In the Tax Item column, enter the name of each tax to be included in the group. If you have previously set up each tax as an Item, simply enter the Item name and press Tab. QuickBooks will add the Item to the group list, along with the relevant rate, taxing authority, and descriptive information, or you can select Add New. If you have not previously entered each tax, when you press Tab, QuickBooks displays the dialog box shown in Figure 23-5.

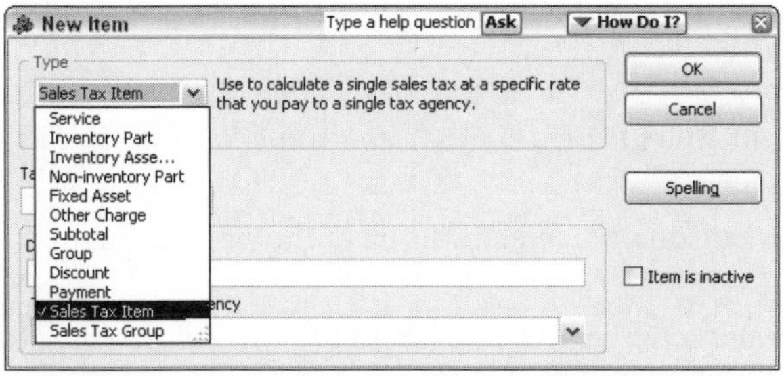

Figure 23-5: If you select Add New and click Set Up when this message appears, a window that enables you to set up a single Sales Tax Item to be included within the group appears.

6. When you are finished entering information about all of the taxes that will make up the group, click OK to add the new group to your Item list and exit the window.

Cross-Reference

You can edit Sales Tax Items, delete them, or make them inactive so that they are still available but do not appear on your drop-down lists. To learn more about doing this, review the "Item Management Tools" section of Chapter 10.

Charging Your Customers

You can't charge sales tax to all of the people all of the time. Some customers are tax-exempt, such as certain not-for-profit organizations. And to make matters even more confusing, some customers are tax-exempt some of the time but not all of the time. For example, a regular customer may be charged sales tax when purchasing business supplies from your company. But that same customer is a tax-exempt customer when the same products are purchased in the customer's capacity as a Brownie leader, because the Girl Scouts of America is a recognized tax-exempt organization.

Designating Items as taxable or nontaxable

Not only does taxable status vary from customer to customer, but it also can vary depending on the particular Item you sell. Most of the time, products are taxable and services are not. Items purchased for resale rather than end-use generally are not subject to tax. Thus, you have to know not only who is purchasing the Item but also something about their intended use of the Item.

You can rely on QuickBooks to mark items as taxable or nontaxable. Simply follow these steps:

1. Go to Lists ➪ Item List. Select the Item that you want to designate as taxable or nontaxable.
2. Click the Item menu button and select Edit from the pop-up menu. The Edit Item window shown appears.
3. Use the drop-down menu in the Tax Code field to indicate whether the Item is subject to sales tax, as shown in Figure 23-6.

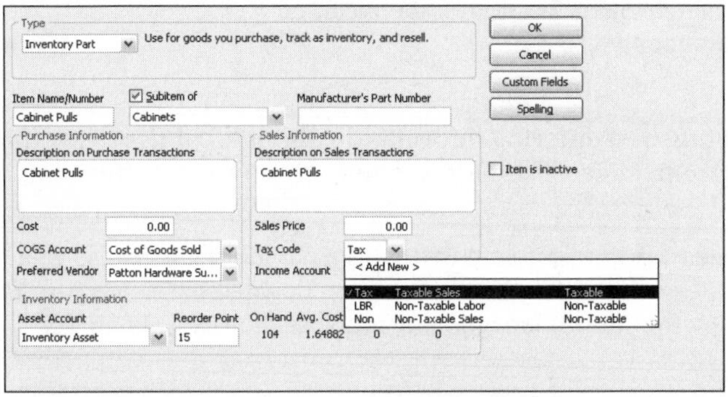

Figure 23-6: You can designate Items as taxable or nontaxable at any time by using the check box provided in the Edit Item window.

4. Click OK.

Cross-Reference You can set up Discount Items to apply any discounts before or after sales tax, as company policy and tax regulations may dictate. See Chapter 10 for more information.

Calculating tax on sales forms

Once you have figured out your tax rates and the taxable status of your Items and customers, it's unbelievably easy to apply this information to a specific sale. Calculation of sales tax is automatic when you follow these steps:

1. Complete the fields in your customer receipt or invoice as you normally would.
2. Select the applicable Item or Group Item using the drop-down menu as provided in the Tax field of the sales form previously shown in Figure 23-6.
3. Continue preparing your customer invoice, as shown in Figure 23-7.

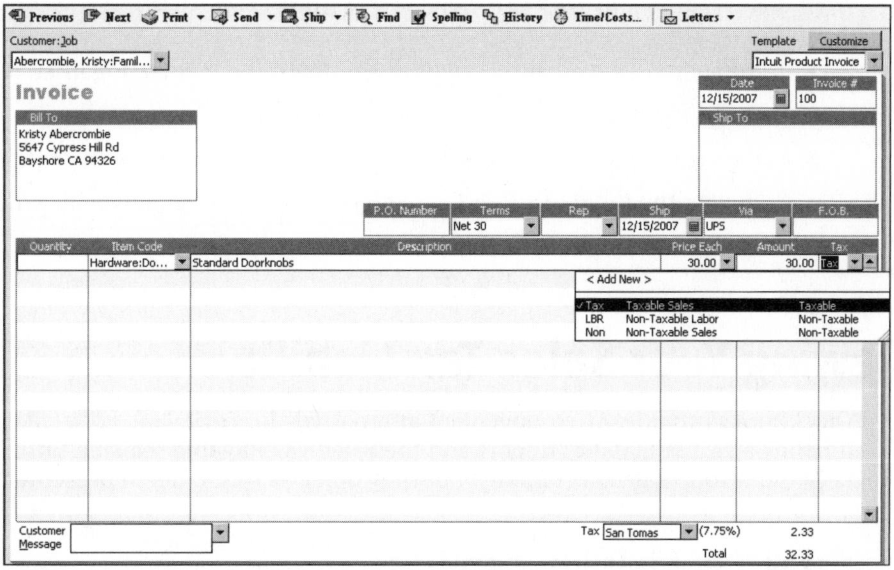

Figure 23-7: QuickBooks applies to the current invoice the Item or Group Item you specify.

Tip

If you want to apply sales tax to some items on an invoice but not to others, consider using the Subtotal Item discussed in Chapter 10. Sales tax will be calculated on taxable Items shown above the subtotal line but will not include Items shown below the line.

Applying different tax rates to items on the same invoice

You may have a situation where Items are taxed at different rates on a single invoice. Or perhaps some items, such as cigarettes, are taxed at a special additional rate. To apply different rates to different Items, follow these steps:

1. Enter all Items taxed at the first rate on the invoice together.
2. Add a Subtotal Item directly below the list of Items taxed at the first rate.
3. Add a tax line below the subtotal of the group of Items taxed at the first rate.
4. Repeat steps 1 to 3 for each group of Items taxed at a different rate.
5. Enter 0% in the Tax field, because you have already calculated all of the sales taxes using the line items added in step 3.
6. Complete the Customer:Job field and other fields as you usually would.
7. Click OK to calculate each of the subtotaled groups at the appropriate tax rates.

If you have some Items that are subject to an additional tax rate, follow these steps:

1. Enter all Items taxed at the additional rate on the invoice together.
2. Subtotal the Items subject to the additional rate.
3. Enter the tax Item set up to reflect the additional tax below the subtotal line.
4. Complete the Customer:Job field and other fields as you usually would.
5. Click OK.

Viewing Your Sales Tax Liability

QuickBooks provides two convenient alternatives for reviewing your sales tax liability: the Sales Tax Liability Report and the Sales Tax Payable register. Both formats show your total sales tax liability, but they differ as to the detail presented.

Sales Tax Liability Reports

The report format has an advantage over the register because it summarizes the amount you owe to each taxing authority, as well as the total of your nontaxable sales. All liabilities are displayed on an accrual basis unless you specify otherwise when you set up your sales tax preferences, as discussed earlier in this chapter. A sample Sales Tax Liability Report is shown in Figure 23-8.

7:07 PM
12/15/07
Accrual Basis

Rock Castle Construction
Sales Tax Liability
November 2007

	Total Sales		Non-Taxable Sales		Taxable Sales		Tax Rate	Tax Collected		Sales Tax As of No
City of East Bayshore										
East Bayshore	0.00		0.00		0.00		0.3%	0.00		69.68
Total City of East Bayshore		0.00		0.00		0.00			0.00	
State Board of Equalization										
Out of State	0.00		0.00		0.00		0.0%	0.00		0.00
San Domingo	23,483.50		16,675.00		6,808.50		7.5%	510.64		510.64
San Tomas	26,524.25		18,938.25		7,586.00		7.75%	587.91		5,015.87
State Board of Equalization - Other	0.00		0.00		0.00			0.00		0.00
Total State Board of Equalization		50,007.75		35,613.25		14,394.50			1,098.55	
TOTAL		**50,007.75**		**35,613.25**		**14,394.50**			**1,098.55**	

Figure 23-8: QuickBooks displays your liability to each taxing authority on an accrual basis.

To view the Sales Tax Liability Report, go to Reports ➪ Vendors & Payable and then choose Sale Tax Liability Report.

Sales Tax Payable registers

The Sales Tax Payable register is a chronological history of all transactions affecting sales tax liability—taxable sales, payments, and adjustments. Figure 23-9 shows a sample Sales Tax Payable register.

When you enter a customer sales form that shows more than one rate, QuickBooks records each rate calculation as a separate transaction in the register. You can view a separate report summarizing the transactions reportable to each tax agency by clicking the QuickReport button. To view your company's Sales Tax Payable register, follow these steps:

1. Go to Lists ➪ Chart of Accounts, and click the Sales Tax Payable liability account.
2. Click the Activities menu button and select Use Register.

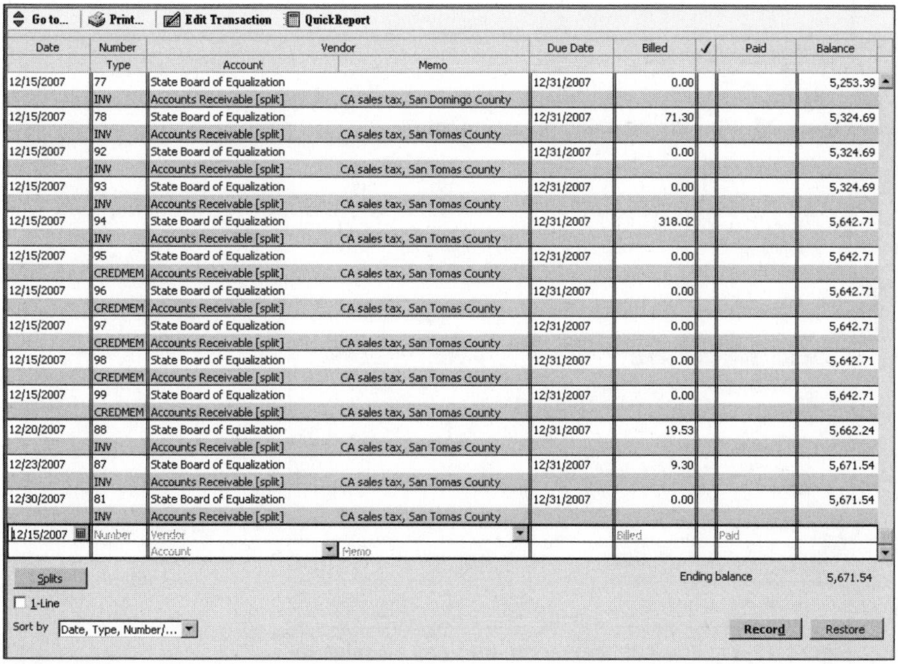

Date	Number / Type	Vendor / Account	Memo	Due Date	Billed	✓	Paid	Balance
12/15/2007	77 / INV	State Board of Equalization / Accounts Receivable [split]	CA sales tax, San Domingo County	12/31/2007	0.00			5,253.39
12/15/2007	78 / INV	State Board of Equalization / Accounts Receivable [split]	CA sales tax, San Tomas County	12/31/2007	71.30			5,324.69
12/15/2007	92 / INV	State Board of Equalization / Accounts Receivable [split]	CA sales tax, San Tomas County	12/31/2007	0.00			5,324.69
12/15/2007	93 / INV	State Board of Equalization / Accounts Receivable [split]	CA sales tax, San Tomas County	12/31/2007	0.00			5,324.69
12/15/2007	94 / INV	State Board of Equalization / Accounts Receivable [split]	CA sales tax, San Tomas County	12/31/2007	318.02			5,642.71
12/15/2007	95 / CREDMEM	State Board of Equalization / Accounts Receivable [split]	CA sales tax, San Tomas County	12/31/2007	0.00			5,642.71
12/15/2007	96 / CREDMEM	State Board of Equalization / Accounts Receivable [split]	CA sales tax, San Tomas County	12/31/2007	0.00			5,642.71
12/15/2007	97 / CREDMEM	State Board of Equalization / Accounts Receivable [split]	CA sales tax, San Tomas County	12/31/2007	0.00			5,642.71
12/15/2007	98 / CREDMEM	State Board of Equalization / Accounts Receivable [split]	CA sales tax, San Tomas County	12/31/2007	0.00			5,642.71
12/15/2007	99 / CREDMEM	State Board of Equalization / Accounts Receivable [split]	CA sales tax, San Tomas County	12/31/2007	0.00			5,642.71
12/20/2007	88 / INV	State Board of Equalization / Accounts Receivable [split]	CA sales tax, San Tomas County	12/31/2007	19.53			5,662.24
12/23/2007	87 / INV	State Board of Equalization / Accounts Receivable [split]	CA sales tax, San Tomas County	12/31/2007	9.30			5,671.54
12/30/2007	81 / INV	State Board of Equalization / Accounts Receivable [split]	CA sales tax, San Tomas County	12/31/2007	0.00			5,671.54

Figure 23-9: The Sales Tax Payable register provides more detail on tax transactions than does the Sale Tax Liability Report.

Paying Your Sales Tax Obligations

The last step in the tax cycle is writing the check. Then you start accumulating liabilities all over again, for the next period. A special Pay Sales Tax window is available to expedite the process of settling accounts with the various taxing authorities. To pay what you owe, follow these steps:

1. Go to the Vendors Center screen and click the Sales Tax Payments link on the left side of the screen, as shown in Figure 23-10: ➪ Sales Tax ➪ Pay Sales Tax (or click the Pay Sales Tax icon on the Taxes and Vendors navigator screen).

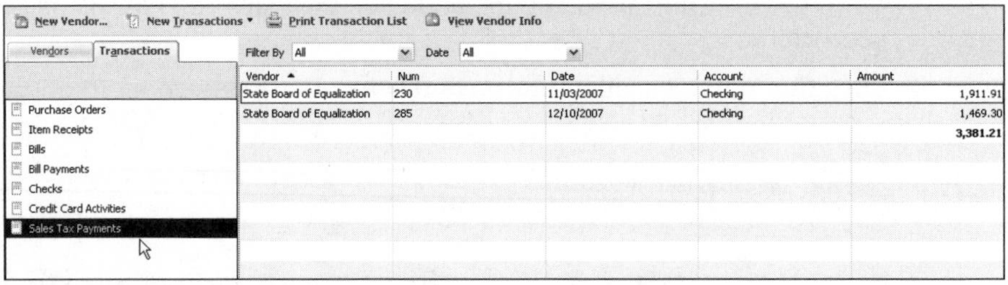

Figure 23-10: Making sales tax payments.

2. In the Pay From Account drop-down list in the upper right corner (shown in Figure 23-11), scroll to the account from which you want to make the payment.

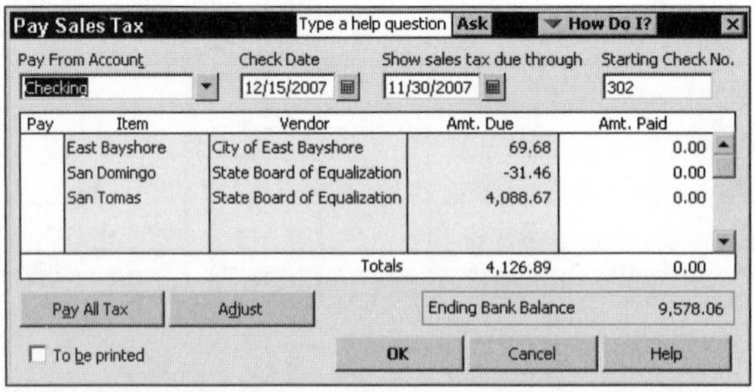

Figure 23-11: You can view, edit, and pay all sales tax obligations from this window.

3. In the Show Sales Tax Due Through field, QuickBooks enters the date of the last sales tax month, quarter, or year depending on what you specified in the Preferences section as your payment frequency.
4. Place check marks in the Pay column for the Items you want to pay in the Vendor column.
5. Edit the amount of the payment for any of the tax agencies if necessary.
6. Click OK to have QuickBooks write checks to each agency as indicated and update your Sales Tax Liability Report and Sales Tax Payable register to reflect the payment.

Summary

Paying sales taxes is more than applying a set rate to the total of Items sold. Your company may be subject to the jurisdiction of several state and local taxing authorities. In this chapter, you learned everything necessary to keep track of this liability that belongs to your customers but is tracked by your business.

- Sales taxes are a current liability equal to the amount owed by your non-tax-exempt customers for taxable Item sales.
- Services generally are not subject to sales tax, nor are Items purchased for resale. But there are gray areas and exceptions to determining the status of some customers and Items. It is best to consult a tax advisor if you are in doubt.
- You must activate sales tax preferences and create a separate Item representing each tax rate to which the business's customers may be subject.
- You can review your sales tax liability at any time with the Sales Tax Liability Report and Sales Tax Payable register. The register provides details about each transaction, whereas the report provides a breakdown of your obligation to each taxing authority.
- The Pay Sales Tax window enables you to easily calculate, edit, and pay your sales tax. QuickBooks automatically updates the appropriate accounts, registers, and reports when a sales tax payment is made.

✦ ✦ ✦

CHAPTER 24

Tax Forms and Tax Payments

In This Chapter

Associating account totals with income tax forms

Generating income tax reports and summaries

Payroll tax forms

1099 Misc forms

Paying payroll tax liabilities

QuickBooks is not an income tax program, but it does its part toward tax simplification. QuickBooks tracks the information that you need to prepare income and payroll tax forms. You can also train the system to associate certain totals with specific lines on the returns and tax forms.

Associating Account Totals with Income Tax Forms

If you used the EasyStep Interview to set up your company as discussed in Chapter 5, you were asked to provide the company's tax year and the income tax form that your company uses to report its liability. Chapter 3 mentioned that the form used for reporting tax liability is based on the type of business entity. Chapter 3 also gives you a rundown of the various types of legal entities — sole proprietorship, partnership, corporation, and limited liability corporation. Refer to Chapter 3 now if you are having an identity crisis as to which type of tax form your company should use.

If you are not familiar with the type of form your company uses, or if you have questions as to how to complete it, you need to consult with an accountant. There's no way around it. Once you have reviewed the form and are comfortable with the information requested, you can go ahead and associate account information with the various lines on the tax form by following these steps:

1. Go to Lists ⇨ Chart of Accounts. Select the account that you want to have associated with a specific line on the tax-reporting form (or add a new account).
2. Click the Account menu button at the bottom of the screen, and select Edit from the pop-up menu. The Edit Account window appears.

3. Use the Tax Line drop-down list (shown in Figure 24-1) to associate the account with the correct tax line. If the account does not appear on the tax form, select Not Tax Related.

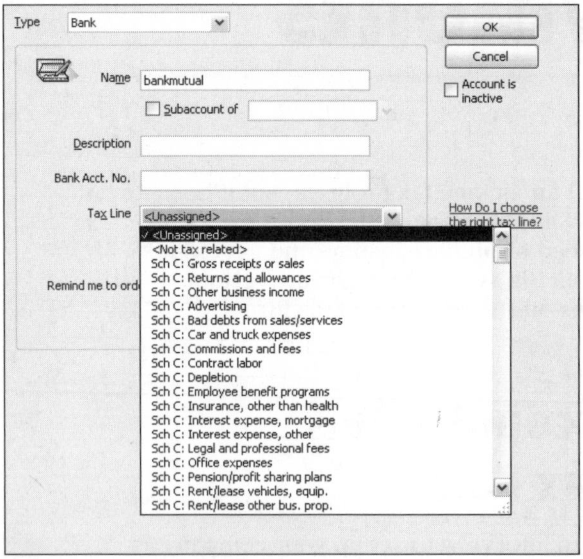

Figure 24-1: Associating an account with a tax form line.

Cross-Reference

If tax lines are not showing in the Edit Account window, you need to select a tax form for the company as discussed in Chapter 5.

If you would like to prepare the tax return for your new business but feel that you are not quite up to the task, you might consider having an accountant prepare it the first year. You'll then have a sample return to help you figure out how to report various types of revenue and expenses in subsequent years.

Generating Income Tax Reports and Summaries

QuickBooks generates three different types of income tax reports: the Income Tax Summary, the Income Tax Detail, and the Income Tax Preparation reports. To access them, go to Reports ➪ Accountant & Taxes, and then select the type of report you want from the submenu.

The Income Tax Summary discloses the total cumulative year-to-date amount associated with each line of the company's tax form as shown in Figure 24-2.

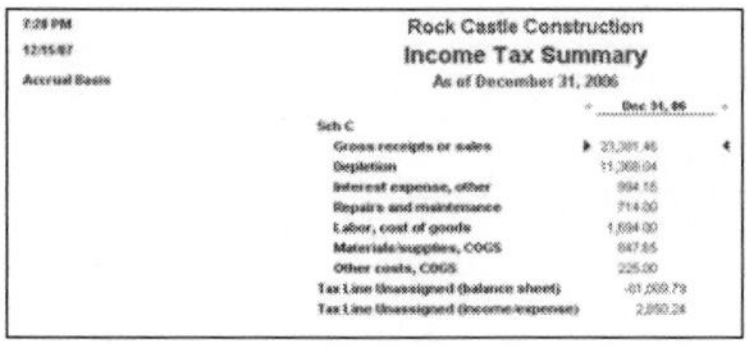

7:28 PM
12/15/07
Accrual Basis

Rock Castle Construction
Income Tax Summary
As of December 31, 2006

	Dec 31, 06
Sch C	
Gross receipts or sales	23,381.46
Depletion	11,368.04
Interest expense, other	994.15
Repairs and maintenance	714.00
Labor, cost of goods	1,894.00
Materials/supplies, COGS	847.85
Other costs, COGS	225.00
Tax Line Unassigned (balance sheet)	-61,069.79
Tax Line Unassigned (income/expense)	2,050.24

Figure 24-2: The Income Tax Summary shows you the total amount assigned to each line on the tax form.

The Income Tax Detail report shows the actual transactions associated with each tax line for the tax form, as shown in Figure 24-3. The Income Tax Preparation report lists each account in your Chart of Accounts and indicates what type of account it is and the line on your income tax return with which it is associated.

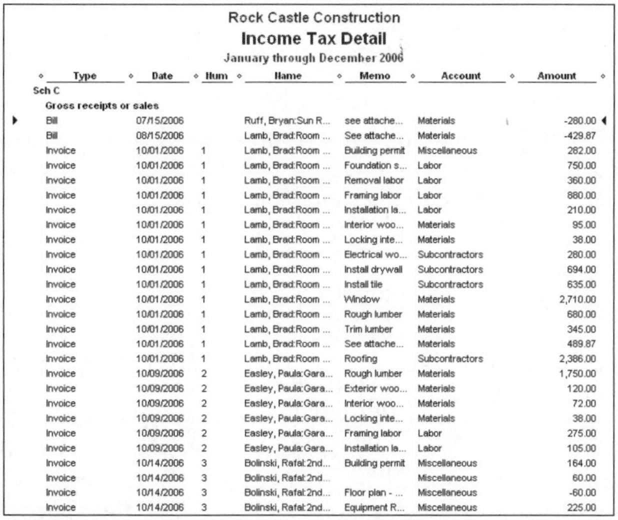

Rock Castle Construction
Income Tax Detail
January through December 2006

Type	Date	Num	Name	Memo	Account	Amount
Sch C						
Gross receipts or sales						
Bill	07/15/2006		Ruff, Bryan:Sun R...	see attache...	Materials	-280.00
Bill	08/15/2006		Lamb, Brad:Room ...	See attache...	Materials	-429.87
Invoice	10/01/2006	1	Lamb, Brad:Room ...	Building permit	Miscellaneous	282.00
Invoice	10/01/2006	1	Lamb, Brad:Room ...	Foundation s...	Labor	750.00
Invoice	10/01/2006	1	Lamb, Brad:Room ...	Removal labor	Labor	360.00
Invoice	10/01/2006	1	Lamb, Brad:Room ...	Framing labor	Labor	880.00
Invoice	10/01/2006	1	Lamb, Brad:Room ...	Installation la...	Labor	210.00
Invoice	10/01/2006	1	Lamb, Brad:Room ...	Interior woo...	Materials	95.00
Invoice	10/01/2006	1	Lamb, Brad:Room ...	Locking inte...	Materials	38.00
Invoice	10/01/2006	1	Lamb, Brad:Room ...	Electrical wo...	Subcontractors	280.00
Invoice	10/01/2006	1	Lamb, Brad:Room ...	Install drywall	Subcontractors	694.00
Invoice	10/01/2006	1	Lamb, Brad:Room ...	Install tile	Subcontractors	635.00
Invoice	10/01/2006	1	Lamb, Brad:Room ...	Window	Materials	2,710.00
Invoice	10/01/2006	1	Lamb, Brad:Room ...	Rough lumber	Materials	680.00
Invoice	10/01/2006	1	Lamb, Brad:Room ...	Trim lumber	Materials	345.00
Invoice	10/01/2006	1	Lamb, Brad:Room ...	See attache...	Materials	489.87
Invoice	10/01/2006	1	Lamb, Brad:Room ...	Roofing	Subcontractors	2,386.00
Invoice	10/09/2006	2	Easley, Paula:Gara...	Rough lumber	Materials	1,750.00
Invoice	10/09/2006	2	Easley, Paula:Gara...	Exterior woo...	Materials	120.00
Invoice	10/09/2006	2	Easley, Paula:Gara...	Interior woo...	Materials	72.00
Invoice	10/09/2006	2	Easley, Paula:Gara...	Locking inte...	Materials	38.00
Invoice	10/09/2006	2	Easley, Paula:Gara...	Framing labor	Labor	275.00
Invoice	10/09/2006	2	Easley, Paula:Gara...	Installation la...	Labor	105.00
Invoice	10/14/2006	3	Bolinski, Rafal:2nd...	Building permit	Miscellaneous	164.00
Invoice	10/14/2006	3	Bolinski, Rafal:2nd...		Miscellaneous	60.00
Invoice	10/14/2006	3	Bolinski, Rafal:2nd...	Floor plan - ...	Miscellaneous	-60.00
Invoice	10/14/2006	3	Bolinski, Rafal:2nd...	Equipment R...	Miscellaneous	225.00

Figure 24-3: The Income Tax Detail report provides information about specific transactions associated with each tax line.

Figure 24-4 shows a sample Income Tax Preparation report.

Tip You can use the QuickZoom on the Tax Line Unassigned line to view a list of all accounts that are not associated with a specific tax line.

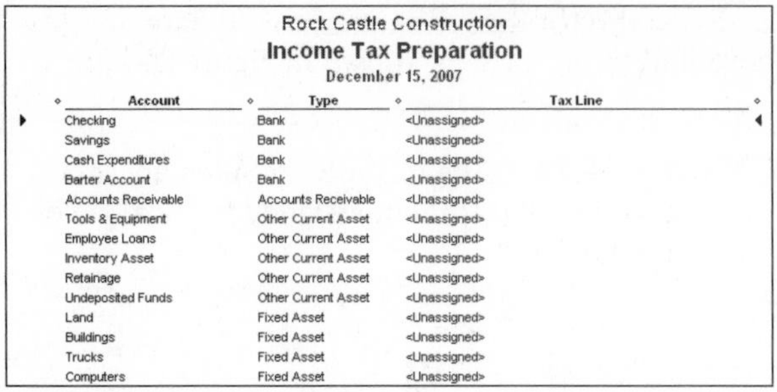

Rock Castle Construction
Income Tax Preparation
December 15, 2007

Account	Type	Tax Line
Checking	Bank	<Unassigned>
Savings	Bank	<Unassigned>
Cash Expenditures	Bank	<Unassigned>
Barter Account	Bank	<Unassigned>
Accounts Receivable	Accounts Receivable	<Unassigned>
Tools & Equipment	Other Current Asset	<Unassigned>
Employee Loans	Other Current Asset	<Unassigned>
Inventory Asset	Other Current Asset	<Unassigned>
Retainage	Other Current Asset	<Unassigned>
Undeposited Funds	Other Current Asset	<Unassigned>
Land	Fixed Asset	<Unassigned>
Buildings	Fixed Asset	<Unassigned>
Trucks	Fixed Asset	<Unassigned>
Computers	Fixed Asset	<Unassigned>

Figure 24-4: The Income Tax Preparation report shows the tax form lines with which each account is associated.

Payroll Tax Forms

You can use QuickBooks to create and print Form 941 (Employer's Quarterly Federal Tax Return) and Form 940 (Employer's Federal Unemployment Tax Return). QuickBooks calculates the amounts reported on these forms using the numbers from the W-2 forms.

Tip

To be sure that you have the most up-to-date payroll tax reporting forms, subscribe to the QuickBooks tax table update service. You'll find information on how to do this enclosed with the program disk, or you can call Intuit at 800-771-7248.

W-2 and W-3 forms

An employer is required to submit the W-2 form to both the Social Security Administration (SSA) and the employee. The company is required to report wages, additions, deductions, commissions, company contributions, FICA taxes, and the advanced earned income credit. Generally, an employer must provide W-2 forms to employees no later than January 31 after the close of the tax year and to the SSA no later than February 28. The SSA transmits the tax information on the return to the IRS. The employer is also required to submit a copy of each W-2 to the appropriate state revenue agency.

The W-3 form summarizes the information from all employee forms. An employer must file it with the SSA on February 28 following the close of the tax year.

Reviewing W-2 forms

Before you print W-2 forms, you should review them. You can edit the forms to adjust for anything that hasn't been tracked on the paychecks but needs to be reported on the form. To preview and edit a W-2 form before printing, follow these steps:

1. Go to Employees ➪ Process Payroll Forms. The Select Form Type dialog box appears, as shown in Figure 24-5.

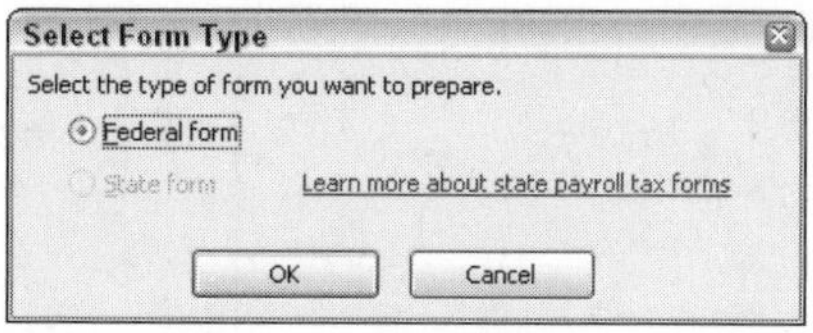

Figure 24-5: Select Federal in this dialog box.

2. Select Federal Form and click OK. The Select a Form dialog box appears.
3. Select Annual Form W-2–Wage and Tax Statement, as shown in Figure 24-6, and click OK.

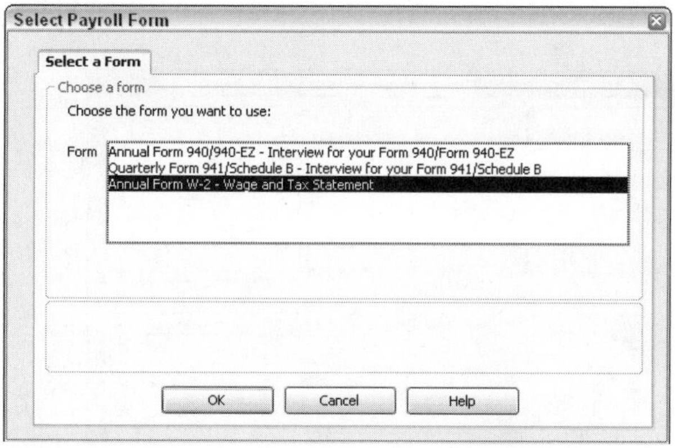

Figure 24-6: Select Annual Form W-2–Wage and Tax Statement.

4. In the screen that appears (shown in Figure 24-7), indicate the names of the employees whose W-2s you want to review by placing a check mark to the left of their names.
5. Place a check mark by the names of the employees whose forms you want to review.
6. Make sure that the tax year that appears in the upper left corner is correct.

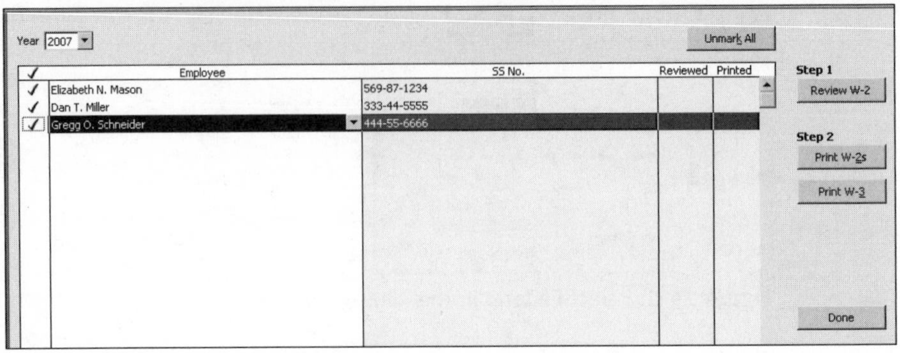

Figure 24-7: Indicate the names of the employees whose W-2s you want to review by placing a check mark to the left of their names.

7. Click the Review W-2 button. A W-2 form similar to the one shown in Figure 24-8 appears.

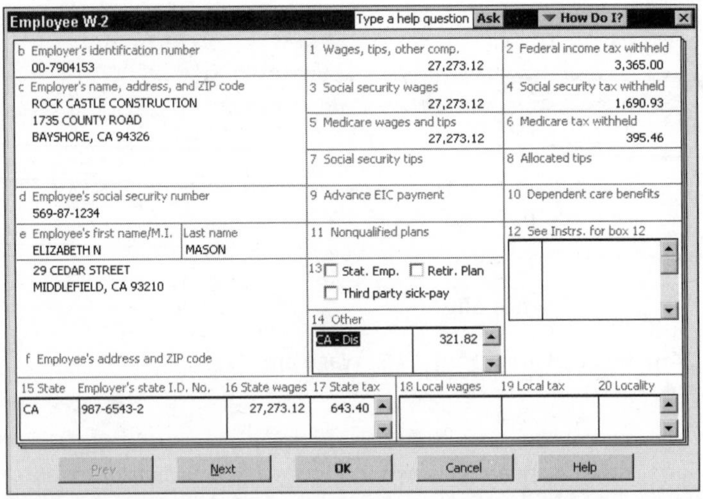

Figure 24-8: The on-screen W-2 form resembles the paper form.

8. To edit any of the numeric fields on the form, double-click the amount, and an edit window such as the one shown in Figure 24-9 appears.

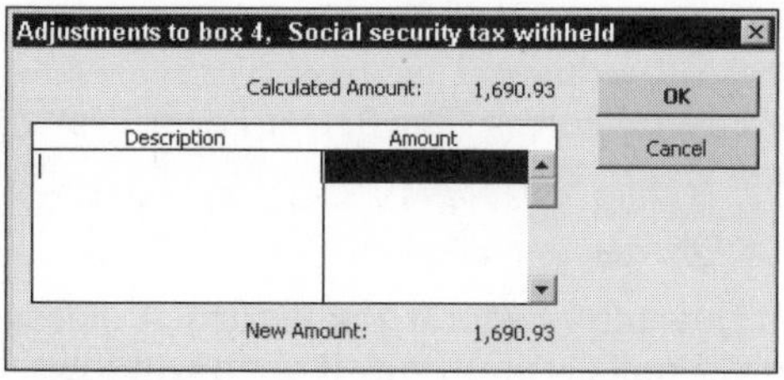

Figure 24-9: You can edit incorrect amounts when you double-click the incorrect field.

9. Click OK to approve and save your changes.
10. Repeat steps 4 to 7 for each remaining employee.
11. Click OK to leave the window after you have completed the last W-2 form.

Printing W-2 forms

To prepare W-2 forms using QuickBooks, you must first order the blank forms specially printed for use with computers. You can contact Intuit at 800-433-8810 for this purpose. Basically, you will need to follow the directions that come with the forms, depending on whether you have a continuous or sheetfed printer.

To direct QuickBooks to print W-2 forms, follow these steps:

1. Go to File ➪ Printer Setup. Choose W-2 Preprinted Form from the drop-down list. The Printer Setup window appears.
2. Choose the printer name and type.
3. If the printed form is not aligned properly, click the Align button to adjust the alignment.
4. Click OK to save the W-2 printer setup and to exit the window.

Form 941 (employer's quarterly federal tax return)

Use Form 941 to report the amounts the company withholds from employee paychecks for income, social security, and Medicare taxes.

Note

To use this feature you must purchase use the fee-based QuickBooks payroll service.

To generate Form 941, follow these steps:

1. Go to Employees ➪ Process_Payroll Forms. The Select Form Type dialog box appears (previously shown in Figure 24-5).
2. Select Federal Form and click OK.
3. Select Form 941–Employer's Quarterly Federal Tax Return. A message appears, telling you that QuickBooks is shutting all open windows, as shown in Figure 24-10. A special Payroll Tax Form window opens.

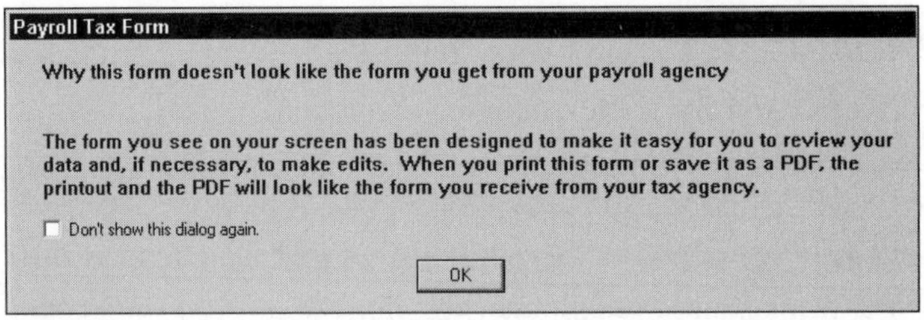

Figure 24-10: This message appears in the Payroll Tax Form window.

4. Another message appears telling you that the form that appears on your screen does not look like the government form because it is designed for easy on-screen review and editing, as shown in Figure 24-11.
5. Click OK, and a message prompts you to make any necessary adjustments to the numbers shown on the form. You can view or edit Form 941 on-screen. If you select Preview, you will have the opportunity to view an on-screen version of the form.
6. Click Done to save your data and close the window.

Editing your Form 941

Not all data on the Form 941 can be edited. If you want to edit a blank field, type the new information directly into the field. The new data is shown in blue on-screen. (It does not print in blue.) To edit a field that was prefilled with data from QuickBooks, follow these steps:

1. Right-click in the field and choose Override.
2. Type the new data in the override box, and press Tab.
3. The new data appears in the field. It is red on the screen, to indicate that you manually overrode the data that was exported from QuickBooks. (It will not be red when you print the form.)

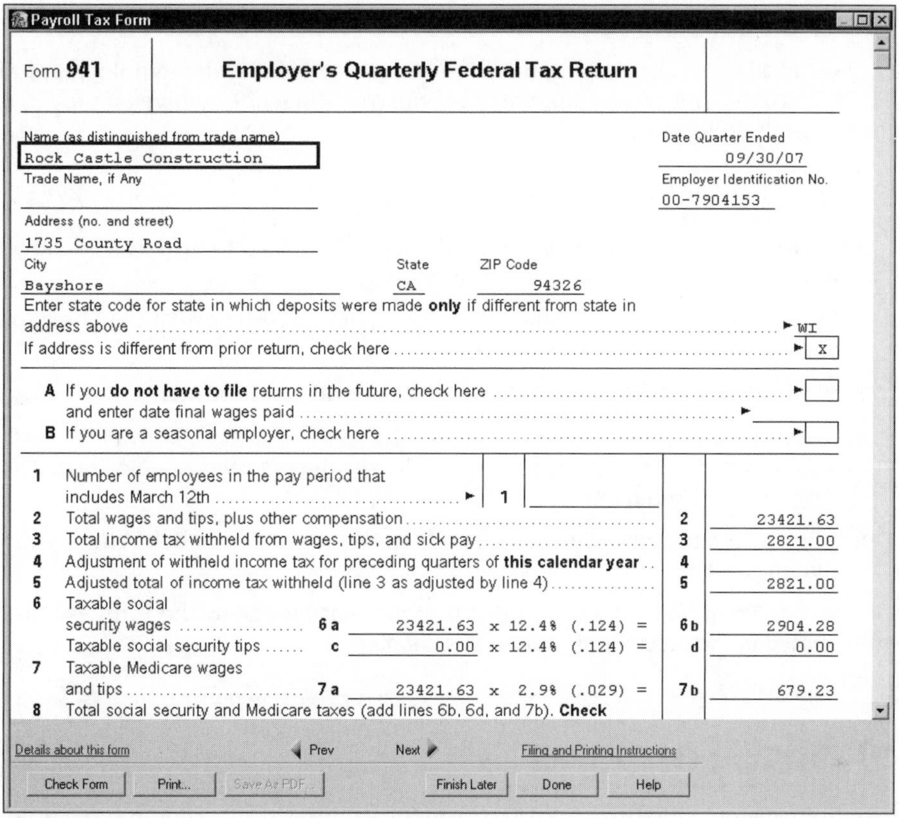

Figure 24-11: The Payroll Tax Form window.

Tip

You can undo an override by right-clicking in the field and choosing Cancel Override.

Data you cannot edit

You cannot edit the following types of data on a payroll tax form:

✦ **Filing period:** You cannot change the filing period that you specified when you created the form. To create a form for a different filing period, close your existing form and create a new one.

✦ **Totals:** You cannot change any field that is a sum of other fields on the form. QuickBooks calculates these automatically, based on the values in the other fields. To change a total, change one of the fields it was calculated from.

✦ **Employer Identification Numbers or Social Security numbers:** You must edit the appropriate Company or Employee data to change these.

Form 940 (employer's federal income tax return)

Use Form 940 to report the amount of the employer's federal unemployment tax (FUTA) liability. This is an employer-paid tax that does not involve employee withholding or contributions.

To generate Form 940, follow these steps:

1. Go to Employees ⇨ Process Payroll Forms. The Select Form Type dialog box appears (previously shown in Figure 24-5).
2. Select Federal Form and click OK. The Select Payroll Form dialog box appears (previously shown in Figure 24-6).
3. Select Form 941 Employer's Quarterly Federal Tax Return.
4. After making any necessary adjustments to the numbers shown on the form, you may preview or print the Form 940 by clicking the Preview Form 940 or Print Form 940 button.
5. Click Leave to save your data and close the window, or click Print if you would like to print the form.

Tip To edit Form 940, follow the same procedure as for editing the Form 941, as discussed in the previous section of this chapter.

1099 Misc Forms

An employer must file the 1099 Misc form for each person to whom the employer pays at least $600 for rents or services. Generally, the business is not required to issue a 1099 to a corporate or partnership entity.

Use the 1099 Form Preferences option to associate amounts with various 1099 categories reflected on the forms. To activate these preferences and tracking features, follow these steps:

1. Go to Edit ⇨ Preferences. Click the Company Preferences tab.
2. Select the Tax: 1099 icon from the scroll box at the left.
3. Click Yes to indicate that the company does file 1099 forms. The Company Preferences tab of the Preferences dialog box appears, as shown in Figure 24-12.
4. The left column lists all the boxes that appear on the 1099 form. Use the drop-down list of accounts to the right of this column to associate accounts with the boxes on the 1099 form. If you need to associate more than one account with a 1099 category, choose Multiple Accounts from the drop-down list.

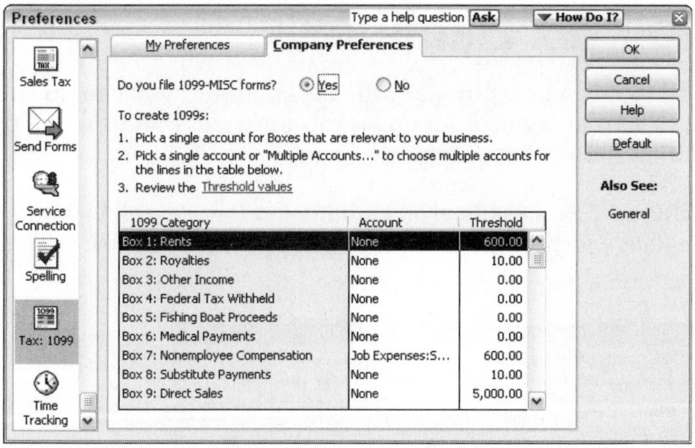

Figure 24-12: Edit 1099 preferences from this screen.

5. Click the Threshold column to change the minimum amounts that are reported on the 1099 form.
6. Click OK to save the changes and leave the screen.

Reviewing and Printing 1099 Forms

Before you print a 1099 form, you can preview and verify the information on the 1099 Report. To view the report, follow these steps:

1. Go to Reports ➪ Vendors & Payables ➪ 1099 Summary. A report summarizing all 1099 vendors and amounts appears.
2. Check the report for any missing vendors or accounts.
   - **To correct missing accounts:** Return to the Preferences window discussed in the previous section and add the account.
   - **To correct missing vendors:** Go to Lists ➪ Vendors. Click the Edit button and the Additional Info tab. Select the Vendor Eligible for 1099 box.
   - **To correct any amounts shown:** Double-click the amount to view a 1099 Detail Report of all transactions affecting that total. Check for erroneous or omitted transactions.
3. Exit the Report window by clicking the X in the upper right corner when you have completed your review.

Paying Payroll Tax Liabilities

When that inevitable time comes to pay your tax liabilities, you can do so using the convenient QuickBooks window set up for this purpose. To review and pay the company's liabilities, follow these steps:

1. Go to Employees ➪ Process Payroll Liabilities ➪ Pay Payroll Liabilities. The Select Date Range for Liabilities dialog box appears, as shown in Figure 24-13.

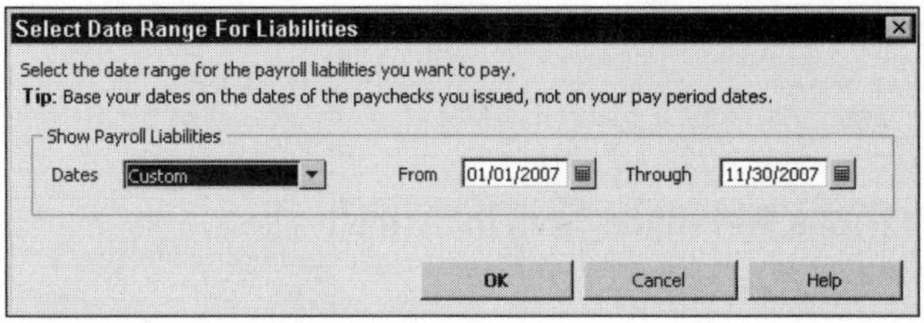

Figure 24-13: Pay payroll liabilities by using this dialog box.

2. Set the date range for the liabilities you want to pay.
3. Click OK. The screen shown in Figure 24-14 appears.

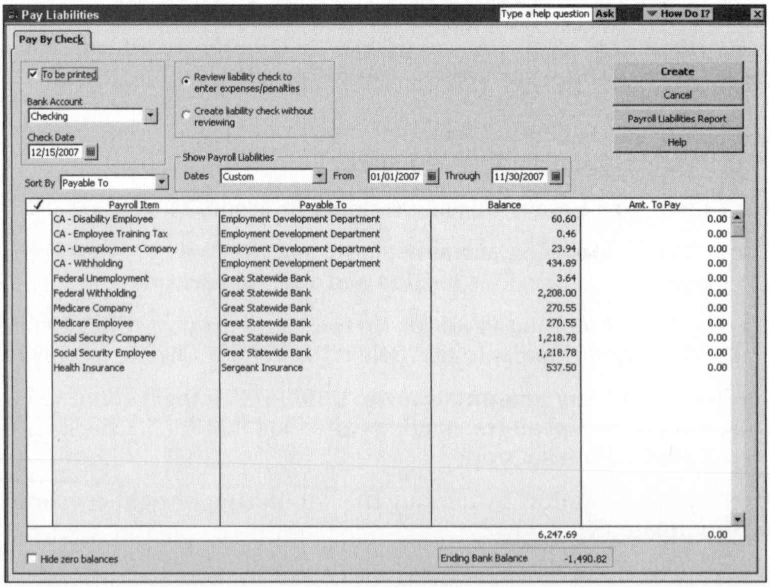

Figure 24-14: Use this window to review and pay company liabilities.

4. Indicate whether you plan to print the checks or write them by hand.
5. Select the To Be Printed check box if you print your own checks.
6. Choose the bank account from which to pay your liabilities.
7. In the Check Date field, enter the date to appear on your liability payment checks.
8. Choose whether to review each check individually or to create them without reviewing them.
9. Verify the date range shown in the Show Payroll Liabilities fields.
10. Select the liabilities you want to pay now.
11. To have QuickBooks display only liabilities where you have balances to pay, select the Hide Zero Balances check box.
12. (Optional) To pay less than the full amount due for a selected liability, enter the amount in the Amt. To Pay field.
13. Click Create. QuickBooks writes the checks you specified.
14. If you selected more than one liability payable to the same vendor, QuickBooks creates a single check for all the liabilities. If you selected to review your checks in step 8, review your checks now.

Summary

This chapter showed you how QuickBooks streamlines the preparation of tax forms and the payment of tax liabilities in several important ways.

- QuickBooks allows you to associate each account listed on your Chart of Accounts with the appropriate line of the company's income tax reporting form or to indicate that an account is not tax related.
- You can generate an Income Tax Summary and Income Tax Detail report to view the year-to-date totals for each associated line on the tax forms.
- QuickBooks prepares a full range of payroll tax reporting forms: W-2, W-3, 940, 941, and 1099 Misc forms.
- QuickBooks provides a single window for reviewing and paying payroll tax liabilities and allows you to adjust totals and print checks directly from a single window.

✦ ✦ ✦

CHAPTER 25

Check Writing and Expense Recording

✦ ✦ ✦ ✦

In This Chapter

Establishing QuickBooks check writing and processing preferences

Entering information on QuickBooks checks

Specifying line item detail about a check

Tracking the Items you use a check to purchase

Making changes to a check already written

Printing a check

✦ ✦ ✦ ✦

Check writing may be the primary reason why your organization acquired QuickBooks. You can use QuickBooks to prepare the payments for persons and vendors you pay. Typically, the format of the payment is a check. When you write a check in QuickBooks, you enter the name of the person to pay, the amount to pay, and the date. QuickBooks automatically keeps a running total of checks you write, it makes sure you don't enter a bogus date, and once you have written a check to a person, you no longer have to enter his or her name — you simply select it from a list. After you write checks in QuickBooks, you can load special printer checks into your printer so that QuickBooks can generate the paper checks that you send in the mail.

Setting Up Check Preferences

Before writing any checks in QuickBooks, you should establish company-wide settings for check writing. You do this by setting QuickBooks preferences. QuickBooks offers you both personal preferences and company preferences.

You set both of these types of preferences from the Preferences dialog box. To display the Preferences dialog box, choose Edit ➪ Preferences and use the scroll bar on the left to select the Checking icon. Click either the My Preferences or Company Preferences tab. Figure 25-1 shows the personal Preferences for checking.

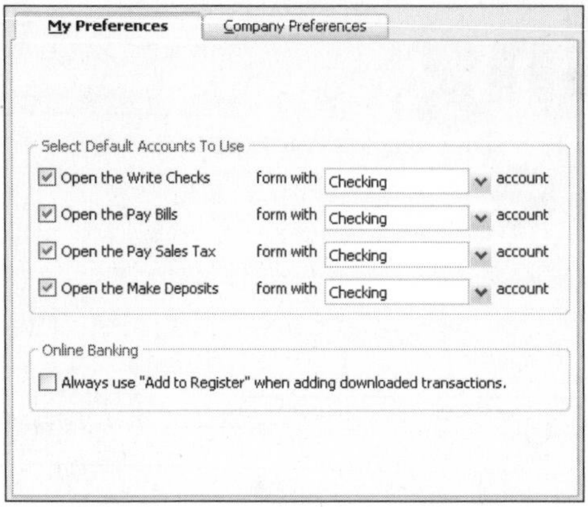

Figure 25-1: Checking personal Preferences.

Figure 25-2 shows the Company Preferences.

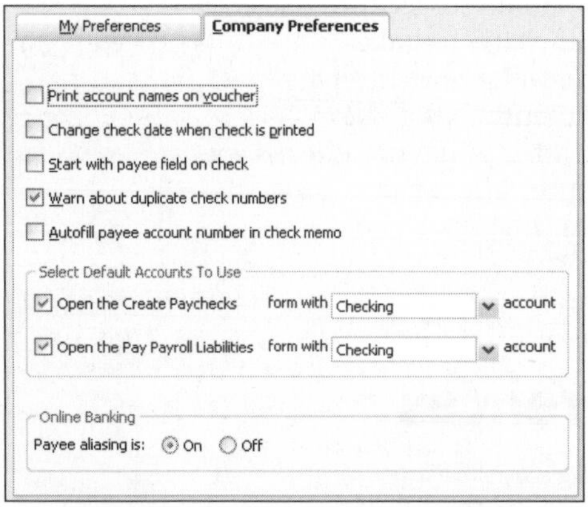

Figure 25-2: Checking Company Preferences.

Personal Preferences accessed via the My Preferences tab primarily indicate the default account to use for various activities, such as writing checks, paying bills, paying sales tax, and making deposits.

The Company Preferences include the following:

✦ **Account names printed on vouchers:** You can specify whether the name you have assigned to an account appears on the check voucher.

✦ **Check date update:** You can specify whether the date on a check should be changed to the date the check is printed, which is relevant only if you write checks one or more fixed days before you actually print them.

✦ **Payee first:** You may define whether the payee is the first piece of information you supply when writing a check.

✦ **Duplicate check number warning:** QuickBooks can warn you if you manually enter a check number that has already been used on another check.

✦ **Autofill payee:** Let QuickBooks know if you want to automatically fill in the payee's account number.

✦ **Default accounts:** You can set the default accounts to use when creating paychecks or paying payroll liabilities.

Writing Checks

Typically, you do not physically write checks in QuickBooks. Instead, you enter information about payments to be made to individuals and to organizations, such as the name of the person to whom you are making the payment, the amount to be paid, when they are paid, from which account the funds are to be drawn, how to categorize the payment, and more. QuickBooks then either generates information to be passed to your financial institution so that the payment may be made electronically or stores the information so that it can print to checks you load into your printer.

Writing a check in QuickBooks requires a number of steps, and because of the range of features in QuickBooks, these steps can go in several directions. This section breaks down the process of writing a check into a few sets of steps. Here, you learn how to enter the basic information every check needs, how to categorize the amount you are paying via the check into one or more expense categories, and how to inspect the check and then move on to writing the next one.

Entering the basic information

The first set of steps to review for writing checks is related to the basic information you enter on every check. Follow these steps whenever you want to write a check in QuickBooks:

1. Choose Banking ⇨ Write Checks. The Write Checks window appears, as shown in Figure 25-3.

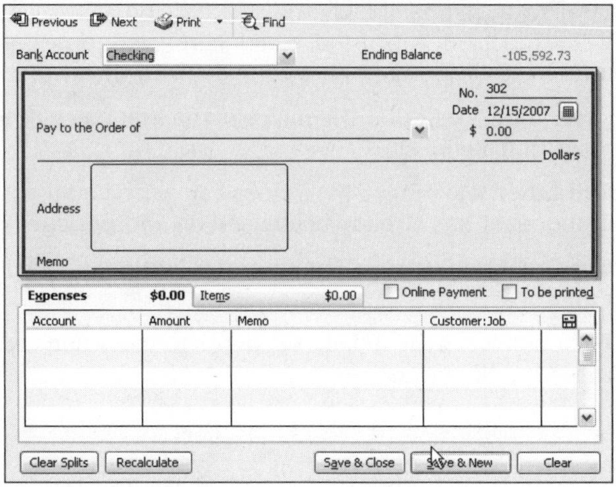

Figure 25-3: The Write Checks window.

2. Select the bank account you want to use from the Bank Account drop-down list, or click Add New to create a new account. If you click Add New, the New Account dialog box appears. Enter information about the new account and then choose OK. Be sure that you choose an account that has been enabled for online access if you wish to pay the bill electronically.
3. Specify a payee for the check. For detailed information about specifying a payee, read the next section. Otherwise, skip to the "Entering expense detail" section.
4. If open purchase orders exist for the payee, you will be prompted about whether you want to apply the check to them.
5. Enter the amount of the check in the $ field. If you leave this field blank, the amounts you enter in the detail area of the check will automatically be totaled and displayed here.
6. Complete the Address and Memo fields as needed.
7. Enter the date that you want to appear on the check in the Date field. To choose a date from a graphical calendar, click the button beside the Date field. If the check is for an online payment (meaning that you have selected the Online Payment option described in step 3), QuickBooks automatically inserts a date no earlier than the fifth day from the date of the writing. For example, if you are paying a large, established vendor that sends and receives many payments electronically, the date may be only two days after the current date. If the payee you specified is a small vendor or even a private person, the date QuickBooks selects may be four or five days after the current date.

8. One of the checking preferences available to the QuickBooks Administrator automatically displays a payee's account number whenever you write a check to a particular payee. Use this number or edit it appropriately.

9. To edit Items from your purchase order or to enter new Items, click the Items tab. In the detail area, enter the purchased Item and associate it with the appropriate customer job.

10. To enter shipping charges, taxes, and other expenses not associated with any one Item, click the Expenses tab. In the detail area, enter each charge and associate it with its correct expense account. More information is provided about entering expense information in a later section of this chapter.

11. If the check will be paid electronically, click the Online Payment check box. Notice that when you select the Online Payment option, the following events occur:

    - The check number changes to the word SEND. This occurs because the number of the check is generated electronically when you connect to your financial institution.
    - The Transmit Memo option appears. If you select this option, a notation, such as the invoice numbers covered by the check, is printed on a voucher that accompanies the check. When you select this option, the check and voucher must be printed and sent (by your financial institution) rather than paid electronically.

12. For the time being, ignore the To Be Printed option. When you move to the next check to print or you close the Print window, QuickBooks automatically selects this option, indicating that this check is pending to be printed.

13. You can enter dates in the Date field when you write checks very quickly. For example, to enter the first day of the month, click the Date field and press **M**. To enter the first day of the year, press **Y**. To increment or decrement the current date in the field, press the + or the - key. Pressing **T** enters today's date, pressing **H** gives the last day of the current month, and pressing **R** generates the last day of the year.

14. Save the check.

Specifying the payee

The next step in writing a check is specifying to whom the check should be paid. One of the great benefits of using QuickBooks is that you enter the name of a payee only the first time you specify the name as a payee. QuickBooks remembers the name, so the subsequent times when you want to pay that payee, you select that payee's name from a list.

The first time you specify a particular payee's name, QuickBooks requires you to provide some information about the payee, such as whether the payee is a vendor, customer, or other. Given these special features related to specifying the payee, the steps in this section involve more than selecting a name from a list. Follow these steps to add a new payee to the list, as well as select existing payees:

1. To specify a payee, click the Pay to the Order Of field and enter the name of the vendor to whom the check should be written. As you enter the letters of the name of the recipient of the check, QuickBooks tries to match an existing recipient name with the letters that you enter. To select an existing recipient, click the arrow button at the end of the Pay to the Order Of field.
2. Leave the Pay to the Order Of field by either pressing the Tab key or clicking elsewhere on the screen. When you do so, QuickBooks checks to see whether the name already exists in the application. If the name does exist, QuickBooks fills in the rest of the check with information it already knows about the recipient, such as the street address, city, state, and zip code. You may edit this information. (Figure 25-3 showed a check that was automatically filled in by QuickBooks.) If QuickBooks does not recognize the name you entered, the Name Not Found dialog box appears, as shown in Figure 25-4.

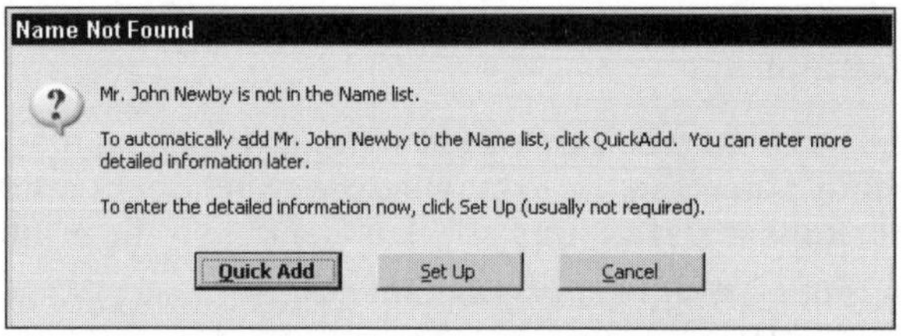

Figure 25-4: A prompt to add a new payee.

3. To add a new payee, click the Quick Add button in the Name Not Found dialog box (see Figure 25-4) if you want to simply write the check to this payee and not add detailed information to any Customer, Vendor, Employee, or other QuickBooks lists. The Select Name Type dialog box shown in Figure 25-5 appears if you click either Quick Add or Set Up.

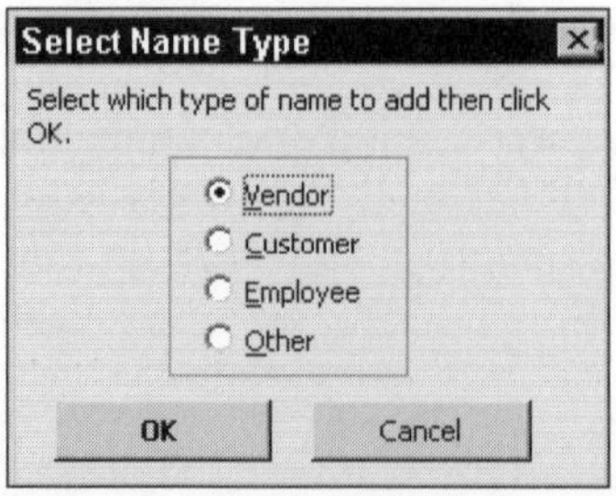

Figure 25-5: Indicate the type of new payee you are adding so that the payee information will appear in the appropriate QuickBooks list.

4. If you select Set Up, the New Vendor dialog box appears, as shown in Figure 25-6, which allows you to enter the payee information to be added to and maintained in your QuickBooks Customer, Vendor, Employee, or other list. (You can also add a new vendor by going to the Vendor Center screen and clicking the New Vendor icon.)

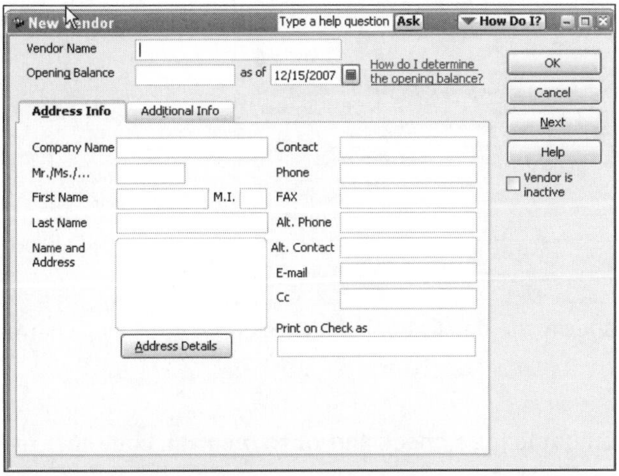

Figure 25-6: Use this dialog box to enter information about the payee to be maintained on the appropriate QuickBooks Vendor, Customer, Employee, or other list.

Entering expense detail

QuickBooks enables you to assign the value of checks you write to specific accounts. This gives you the capability to report against many accounts, such as to develop a detailed Profit and Loss Statement. An example might be assigning the check you write to the landlord of your building to the Rent account.

It is also likely that a check you write may cover many types of expenses. For example, a check to a consulting firm may cover a number of different projects and services. Or a check you wrote to the landlord may include not only rent money but also the payment for new plants for the office.

You can use the Expenses tab at the bottom of the Checks window to assign the value of the check to one or more expense accounts. In addition, you can record the customer on whose behalf the check may have been written. This might be the case if you incur an expense (for which you are using the check) and you want to record the customer in order for the customer to reimburse your company. Figure 25-7 shows a check with a number of expense line items defined with detail.

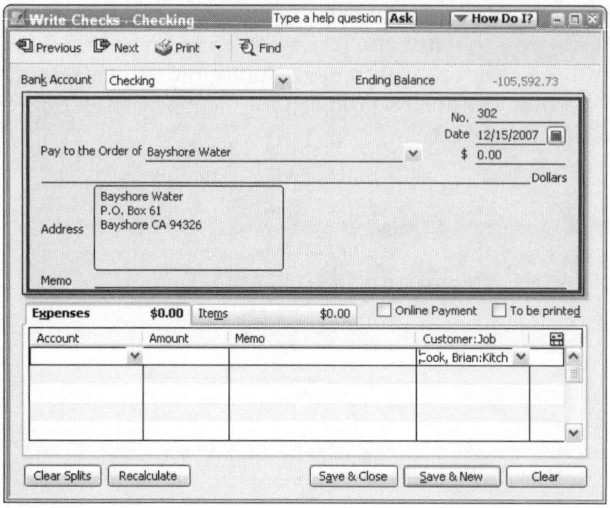

Figure 25-7: You can specify the details behind a check you write.

To specify expense accounts for a check and/or to record a customer or job, follow these steps:

1. Click the Expenses tab.
2. Click the Account column. An arrow button appears.
3. Click the arrow and then select which account to assign either the entire value of the check or a portion of the entire amount, if you will be assigning the check to more than one expense account.
4. Press Tab to move to the Amount field or simply click the Amount field. Enter the amount you want to assign to the expense account you just specified.
5. If you want to make a notation about this line item, move to the Memo field and enter the note.
6. Click the Customer:Job field to associate the expense line item with a specific customer.
7. Click the arrow to display the list of all customers and select the customer.
8. Repeat steps 4 to 7 until you have completely allocated the total amount of the check to one or more line items. You cannot save the check if the total of all expense line items does not match the value of the check.

Entering Item detail

Oftentimes, a check you write in QuickBooks is for specific Items for your company. For example, you might write a particularly large check to a supply company or a store for a large number of Items. Your only record of the Items purchased with the check is the receipt. With QuickBooks, you can specify per check the Items you purchased with the check. These items are the same Items that you defined in your QuickBooks application. This relationship to Items you track in your application is very useful. If an Item defined in your application is flagged as an inventory Item, specifying Items you purchase with a check automatically updates your inventory count of that Item. For more detailed information on Items, refer to Chapter 10.

In addition, you can record the customer for whom the Item was purchased in order for the customer to reimburse your company. Figure 25-8 shows a check with an Item detail.

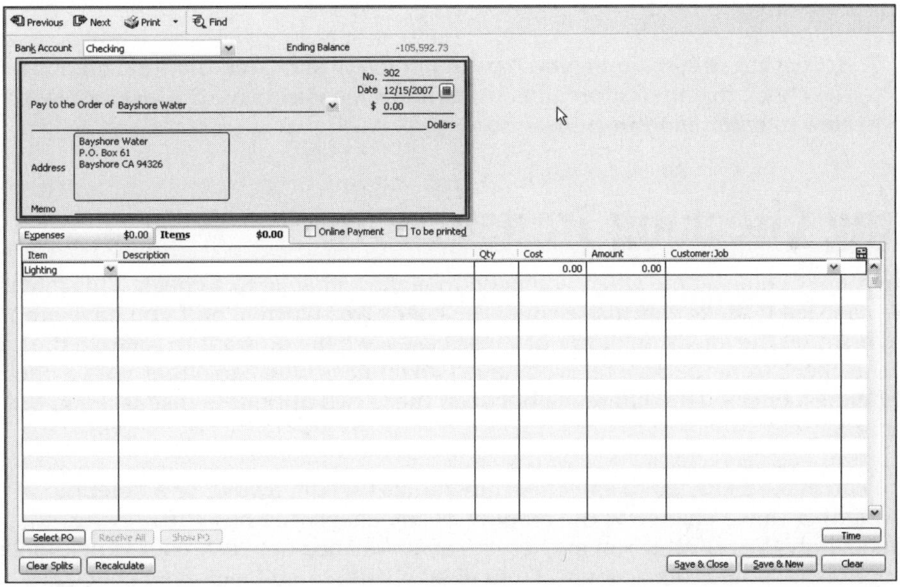

Figure 25-8: You can specify detail about the Items you used the check to purchase.

To enter detail about the Items you used the check to purchase, follow these steps:

1. Click the Items tab at the bottom of the Write Checks window.
2. Click the Item column, and an arrow for a drop-down menu appears. Click the button to select the first Item to record. If the Item you wish to record does not appear in the list, choose Add New from the list, which appears as the first entry on the list. For help in adding Items, refer to Chapter 10.
3. After you have entered the Item, press Tab to move to the Description field. Enter any description you wish for the Item (such as how the Item will be used).
4. Next, enter the quantity and the cost of each Item in the appropriate fields. The amount is automatically calculated. If you know only the amount and quantity, enter those values and the cost is automatically calculated.
5. Click the Customer:Job field to associate the Item with a specific customer.
6. Click the arrow to display the list of all customers, and then select the customer.
7. Repeat these steps until you have completely allocated the total amount of the check to one or more line items, and then click Save & Close or Save & New to enter another transaction.

Editing Checking Transactions

There may come a time when you need to make a change to a check. This might be the case if a mistake was made when the check was written, or if you have stopped payment on the check. In either of these cases, when you want to remove the value of the check from the register, you have two choices: you can either void a check or delete a check. The difference between these two options is discussed in this section.

You can make a change to any check, including an edit, a void, or a deletion. Remember that a change to the amount of any check that has already cleared affects only the register. You may create an imbalance between your QuickBooks account and your bank account if you delete, void, or edit a cleared check.

To make any other changes to a check, such as to the date or expense category, you can edit the check by following these steps:

1. Go to Banking ⇨ Use Register, and select Checking Account. A checking account register window appears, such as the one shown in Figure 25-9.

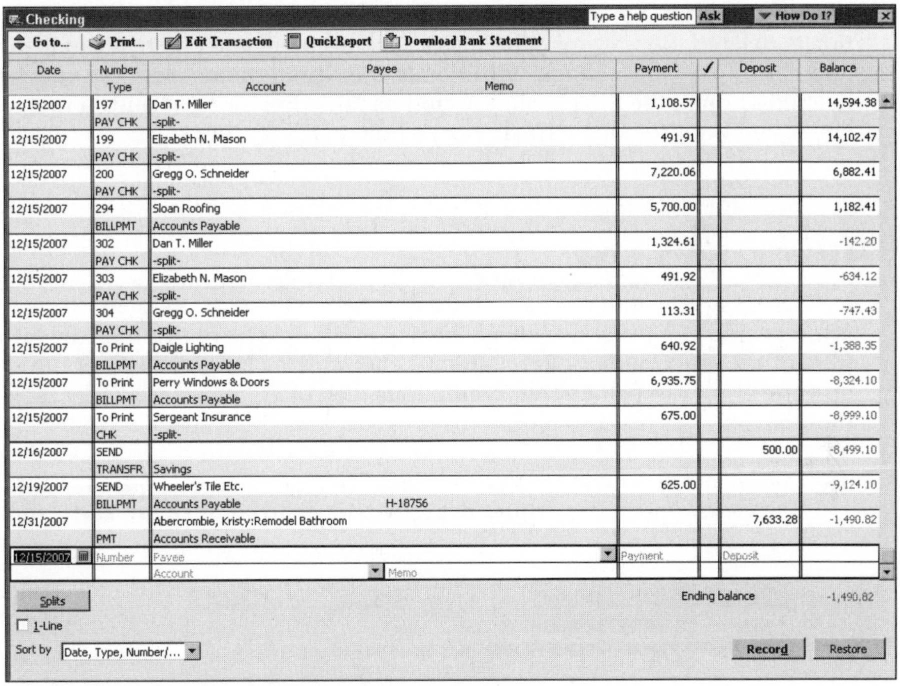

Figure 25-9: A sample checking account register.

2. Select and click the check that you want to edit, or open the Bill Payments Check window and use the Prev or Next button to move to the check you want to edit. Make the required changes to the check and choose Save & Close. You may also use the Prev or Next button to move to another check that you may want to edit.

Voiding and Deleting Check Transactions

When you void a check, the check (specifically, the register Item) is not deleted. Only the amount of the check is zeroed. To void a check, follow these steps:

1. Select the transaction you want to void.
2. From the Edit menu, choose Void (the name of the transaction appears on the menu).
3. Click Record.

Deleting a check is more significant. When you delete a check, the entire transaction is deleted. Be wary of deleting a check because you create a gap in your check numbers. To delete a check, either open the register and select the check to be deleted or open the Check window and use the Prev or Next button to move to the check you want to delete. Next choose Edit ➪ Delete Check.

Printing Checks

QuickBooks prints checks using both continuous-feed printers and page-oriented printers. You can purchase check forms for either type of printer from Intuit or from other vendors that offer standard check forms for your printer type. To set up your printer to print either continuous-feed or page-oriented checks, follow these steps:

1. Go to File ➪ Printer Setup and select Check/PayCheck from the Form Name drop-down list. The Printer Setup window shown in Figure 25-10 appears.

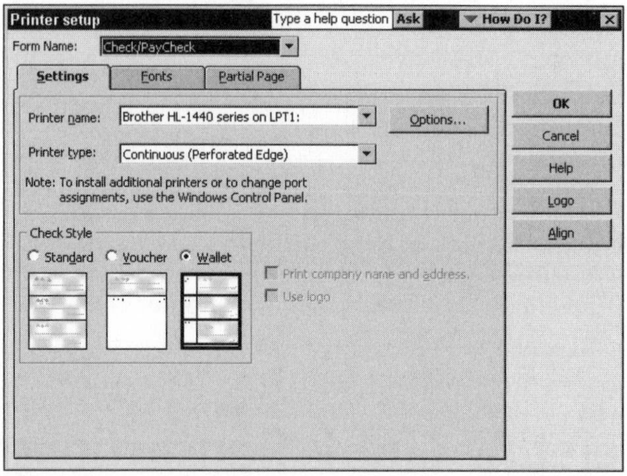

Figure 25-10: The Printer Setup window.

2. Select the type of printer you are using from the drop-down menu.
3. Select the type of check format you want to use.
4. Click OK.

To print multiple checks, follow these steps:

1. Go to File ➪ Print Forms ➪ Checks. The Select Checks to Print window appears, as shown in Figure 25-11.

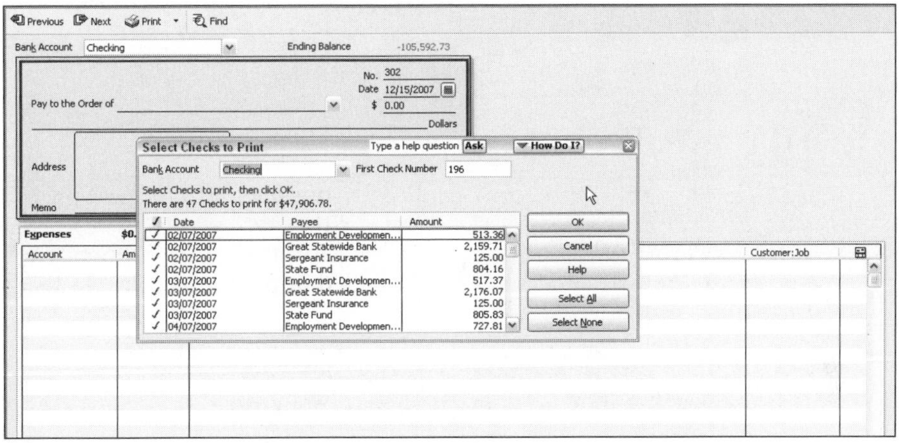

Figure 25-11: Select the checks you want to print from this window.

2. In the Print Checks window, choose the options you want and click OK.

Note

To print employee paychecks, select the Employee Paychecks window from the Employee Navigator screen, and use the Print Employee Paychecks window.

Summary

QuickBooks lets you write checks as if your checkbook were open and a pen were in your hand. The difference between QuickBooks and this manual method is that QuickBooks does the math for you, ensures that you correctly spell payee names, and records every check you write in QuickBooks in the QuickBooks register.

- ✦ To access the window where you write checks, choose Banking ➪ Write Checks.
- ✦ Enter information about the Items you use a single check to purchase at the bottom of the Check Writing window. This enables you to store detail about the transaction, even if several Items or services were purchased with the check.
- ✦ To print checks after you have completed writing them, use the correct settings for continuous-feed or page-oriented printers.

✦ ✦ ✦

PART

VI

Banking and Credit Card Transactions

In This Part

CHAPTER 26

Online Banking and Bill Payment

In This Chapter

Understanding the benefits and features of online banking

Establishing an online account with your financial institution

Reviewing typical online banking tasks and functions

Reconciling an online account

QuickBooks' online banking features, although requiring a little more time to learn, present so many advantages for a company that it would be foolish not to examine how online banking can help.

With online banking, companies do not have to worry about printing checks, or addressing or stamping envelopes. Instead, bills are paid electronically. In addition, you can download statements at any time, day or night, which provides companies with much quicker updates than provided by the once-per-month statements that financial institutions mail. Last, online banking allows you to check the balance of any account at any time. This way, for those occasions when cash flow is tight, you can get an immediate update of your balance and cleared transactions.

Introducing Online Banking

Online banking represents a brave new world for many companies. The switch from a manual method of executing financial functions to an online method usually represents a significant change in process and habits for most organizations. With this change in process come certain emotions and reactions. Many users of online banking experience a loss in confidence or sense a loss of control when they cannot reconcile their accounts against a printed statement. Others feel uneasy if they cannot pay a bill without a printed check. Some simply have concerns over transmitting financial information over telephone lines. The anxiety associated with executing traditional tasks over the Internet usually disappears quickly when the time- and money-saving benefits are realized. Also, Internet security has progressed to the point where the benefits of online banking outweigh the small risk in exchanging financial information over the Internet.

In this section, you learn about the time- and money-saving benefits to be gained from online banking. This section helps you determine whether online banking is suitable for your company. If it is, this chapter has all the details you need to establish an online account to begin banking over the Internet.

Using online banking

Online banking gives you the capability to execute the four most typical financial functions directly from your office at any time of the day or night:

- ✦ Check balances of checking and savings accounts
- ✦ Make payments
- ✦ Transfer funds between accounts
- ✦ Update the register with new and cleared transactions

You can take advantage of any one, any combination, or all of these uses. For example, if you want to use online banking just to update your register, you may continue to write or print checks manually. Or, you can choose to download transactions to closely monitor cleared transactions but still reconcile your register manually. Before you decide which features of online banking to use, however, review the following descriptions of each online financial task.

Getting set up for online banking

Online banking has a number of requirements. The overall requirement for online banking is a connection to the Internet. Participating financial institutions offer online banking service through QuickBooks. Online banking requires access to the Internet either directly using a LAN or via an Internet service provider (ISP).

You can open an online banking account with any bank that offers online banking services. If you use more than one bank, you may apply for and use multiple online banking accounts.

Fees for online banking vary and are determined by the bank. Contact the banking institution directly, and consider comparing fees for online banking services.

Applying for online banking

You can access a list of institutions from which online banking services are available by going to Banking ➪ Online Banking ➪ Available Financial Institutions. This service offers information about services offered by various institutions and provides links for you to contact them directly, as shown in Figure 26-1.

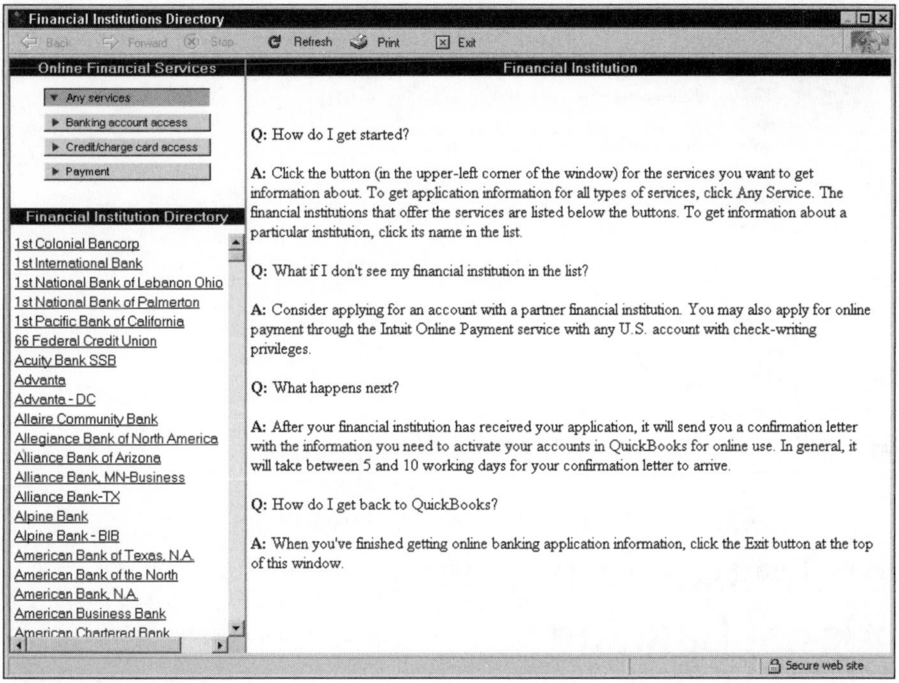

Figure 26-1: You can research institutions that provide online banking services directly from QuickBooks.

After comparing fees and services offered by various institutions, you are ready to apply for banking services. You can apply for online banking services using the QuickBooks program. You will need to apply separately to each financial institution where you want to use the online banking services. Follow these steps:

1. From the Banking menu, choose Online Banking ➪ Setup Account for Online Access. The screen shown in Figure 26-2 appears.
2. Click Apply Now and answer the questions on the screens that appear, to connect to the Financial Institutions list on the Internet.
3. If you're looking for a particular service, select that service by clicking one of the choices in the Online Financial Services list. The list of financial institutions will change to reflect the ones that provide the service you selected.
4. Select your financial institution. You are instructed to apply either by phone or on their Web site (where you'll receive additional instructions from your financial institution for completing your application).

Figure 26-2: Apply for online banking services by using this window.

Online Transactions versus Traditional Banking

When you bank online, there are some differences compared with the traditional style of banking:

✦ **Reconciling accounts:** You still reconcile your accounts as you always do; however, because your online banking data is in a convenient electronic format, you can reconcile your accounts whenever you want to instead of waiting for a statement.

✦ **Transferring funds:** You cannot use online banking to transfer funds between accounts, but you can use QuickBooks' functions to accomplish the same thing. Simply make an online payment payable to yourself at the institution where you want the funds deposited. The payment is drawn from the account from which you want funds transferred and has the same effect as an account-to-account transfer.

✦ **Twenty-four-hour access:** An advantage of online banking is that most institutions offer 24-hour access, which is a real plus if you travel across time zones for your business.

✦ **Vendors and online payments:** Many vendors accept online payments; however, if a particular vendor does not, your online banking service has the capability to cut them a paper check. This saves you time.

✦ **Posting transactions:** A particular advantage of online banking is that most transactions post immediately. This allows you to keep up-to-the-hour books.

Downloading Online Banking Transactions

You can enjoy the convenience of banking 24 hours a day, with the ability to download recent transactions from financial institutions round the clock. More important, QuickBooks allows you to reconcile downloaded transactions with your records with amazing efficiency.

Follow these steps to download transactions:

1. Go to Banking ➪ Online Banking ➪ Online Banking Center to display the Online Banking Center window shown in Figure 26-3.
2. Send online requests to download transactions that have occurred since the last time you downloaded transactions if you have not already done so (for example, select Get New QuickStatement for Account: Checking).
3. After the download finishes, select an account from the Items Received From Financial Institution list and click the View button on the left to see a QuickStatement of the transactions downloaded from that account, such as the one shown in Figure 26-4.

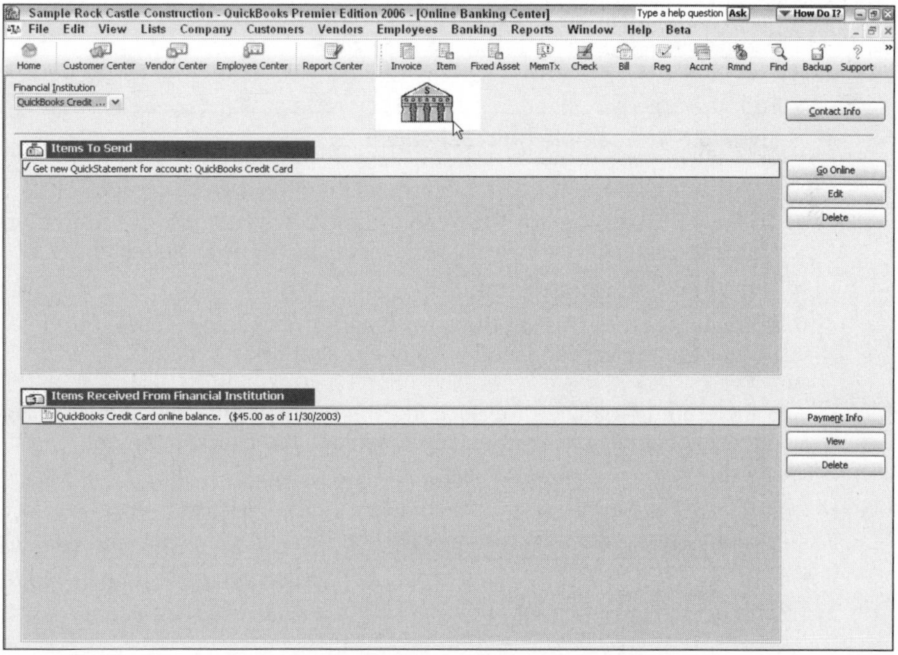

Figure 26-3: The QuickBooks Online Banking Center window.

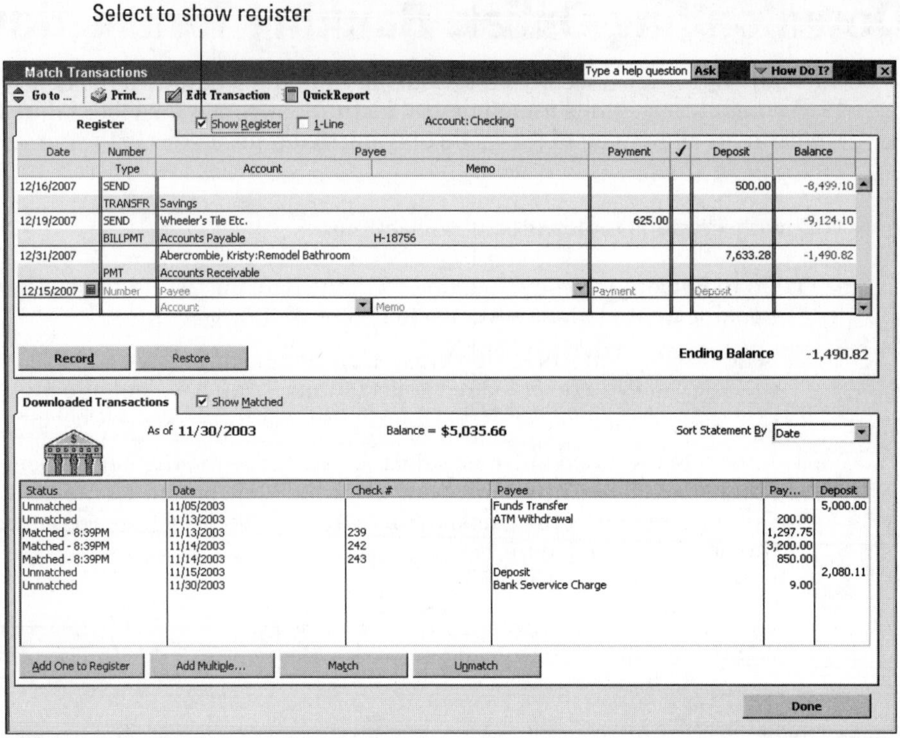

Figure 26-4: A sample QuickStatement.

4. To view the register for the account and have QuickBooks match your QuickStatement to your register, select the Show Register check box in the Match Transactions window.
5. You may correct transactions for which the QuickStatement and your register do not match as discussed in the next section.

Note

If there are unmatched transactions, the warning message shown in Figure 26-5 appears on your screen when you download the QuickStatement.

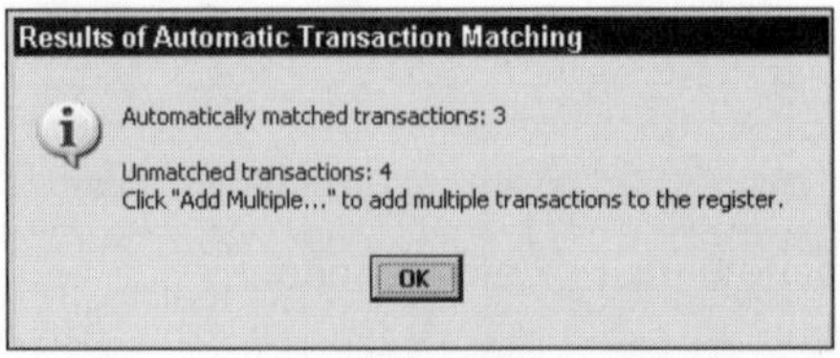

Figure 26-5: This message warns you when you have unmatched transactions.

Account Reconciliation and Reports

Perhaps the best aspect of QuickBooks' online banking feature is its capability to reconcile your local register. With QuickBooks' online banking features, you can update your register every day, marking transactions that have cleared and logging new transactions that you may not have entered locally. This saves you from the tedious monthly process of reviewing the printed account statement provided by your financial institution against the register you keep at the office. In effect, you reconcile your register automatically every time you download transactions.

As checks clear and other transactions are posted to your account, a database for each of your accounts is also updated. You do not actually see this database. Your financial institution provides access to this database when you sign up for online banking. When you connect to the Internet with QuickBooks and choose to download the latest statement for a particular account, QuickBooks compares the register you maintain in QuickBooks to your online database, noting any new transactions as well as any discrepancies between otherwise matched transactions. An example of this scenario might be a transaction listed in both sources with the same check number, although with a different amount value. QuickBooks works most efficiently when there are no discrepancies between your online account and your register. It automatically detects matching transactions and then marks them as cleared in your local register.

The only significant work involved in online banking is reconciling the online account to the account you maintain at your computer via the register. In this process, a small statement detailing the activity in your account since the last time you completed this process is downloaded to your computer. This small statement is known as a *QuickStatement*. QuickBooks automatically attempts to match transactions it has downloaded with uncleared transactions in your local register. This process is the equivalent to the month-end reconciliation process you normally endure if you do not use online banking. The advantage to the reconciliation process when you bank online is that the process occurs almost instantaneously as you transact business during the month and that the matching and verification of register transactions to bank-recorded transactions is handled by QuickBooks, not you.

Matching downloaded transactions to your register

Although the process for matching transactions in your register to transactions that have cleared through your financial institution is largely automated, there is still a process (though relatively simple) that you must follow. To reconcile your account, follow the steps in the "Downloading Online Banking Transactions" section, earlier in this chapter. Next, from the Online Banking Center window, click the View button to display the QuickStatement window. You will see transactions in your online account listed at the top of the dialog box, and your register appears at the bottom.

New transactions cleared at the financial institution that match transactions in your register show a Matched status. Also, the matching transaction in the register is marked as cleared. You may want to consider printing the QuickStatement and then storing the hard copy in a binder. It is impossible to review the QuickStatement when you complete the updates of your registers. If any questions arise, such as who has been paid, how much, and from what account, the answers will be available in printed form. For mismatched transactions, you may have some work to complete. The following section helps you manage mismatched transactions.

Correcting a mismatched or missing entry

There are three conditions in which a mismatch exists between the downloaded QuickStatement and your register:

- A transaction appears in the register but not in the QuickStatement.
- A transaction appears in the QuickStatement but not in the register.
- A transaction appears in both the QuickStatement and the register, but the amount, date, or payee does not match. You can recognize this condition by the Unmatched status that appears in the first column for the transaction in the QuickStatement.

When you encounter any of these conditions, you must make an adjustment to your register in order to keep the register in balance with your bank account, with transactions cleared by your financial institution.

If a transaction appears in the register but not in the QuickStatement, either the transaction has not cleared with your financial institution or the transaction in the register is in error and QuickBooks cannot match it to a downloaded transaction. In this case, either wait for the transaction to clear, or be sure that the transaction in the register doesn't contain errors such that QuickBooks cannot identify it.

If a transaction appears in the QuickStatement but not in the register, add the transaction by choosing the transaction from the QuickStatement and clicking the Add button. This is usually the case if you have forgotten to enter a transaction in your QuickBooks register, or if there is an automatic or unexpected charge from your financial institution.

If a transaction appears in both the QuickStatement and the register, but the amount, date, or payee does not match, you must edit the register transaction. To do so, make the change to the transaction in the Account Reconciliation window and click Record. To make the change to the transaction in the Write Checks window, choose the transaction and click Edit. The Write Checks window appears with the transaction selected. Make any appropriate edits so that the transaction matches the cleared bank transaction and click OK. You are returned to the Account Reconciliation window with the change that you made reflected in the QuickStatement and its status changed to Matched.

Summary

QuickBooks enables you to conduct all your banking functions with your financial institution electronically.

- ✦ You can pay vendors and others electronically, eliminating the need to handwrite or print checks.
- ✦ You can download statements from your financial institution on a round-the-clock basis.
- ✦ QuickBooks' convenient QuickStatement and reconciliation features allow you to reconcile your accounts accurately, efficiently, and as often as you like, even daily.

✦ ✦ ✦

CHAPTER 27

Recording Credit Card Transactions

✦ ✦ ✦ ✦

In This Chapter

Creating accounts in QuickBooks to track your credit card transactions and associated expenses

Entering credit card transactions

Deleting or voiding a credit card transaction

✦ ✦ ✦ ✦

Most companies today supplement their various cash accounts with one or more credit card accounts. Banks or financial institutions, gas companies, or other vendors might issue these credit card accounts. Many companies provide a credit card to those employees who work in the field. In QuickBooks, you can maintain information about your credit card accounts. You can maintain your periodic balance, if you carry one, as well as information about the individual transactions you create with the card every month. In addition, you can track the individual items or professional services you use your card to purchase. This is helpful if you want to report on specific expense types, such as office supplies or computer hardware and software.

Creating a Credit Card Account

Before you can enter credit card transactions, you must create a Credit Card account in QuickBooks. This account tracks all the activity for that card. You create a separate Credit Card account in QuickBooks for every credit card account you maintain with a financial institution or vendor. You need not create a separate account in QuickBooks for each card in use at your company, only for each credit card account. These accounts include not only the traditional card accounts provided by financial institutions but also the credit cards issued by service station companies, wholesale stores, and more.

Another point to remember is that the Credit Card account you create in QuickBooks is separate from the account maintained by the company that provided the card. Though you probably already have an account with a credit card company, you still must enter information into QuickBooks. Certain companies — for example, American Express — provide access to your credit card account online, so you can download your statement to reconcile your account in QuickBooks with the account maintained by the institution that provided the card.

The steps to create a Credit Card account in QuickBooks are easy to follow, but there is a caveat: the account must already exist with the company providing the card. You cannot create the account in QuickBooks unless you are able to provide information supplied by the company that granted you the card. So, open the credit card account first, and then enter the supporting information into QuickBooks.

To create a Credit Card account in QuickBooks, follow these steps:

1. Choose Lists ➪ Chart of Accounts.
2. The Chart of Accounts window appears (see Figure 27-1). Click the Menu button, and then select New.

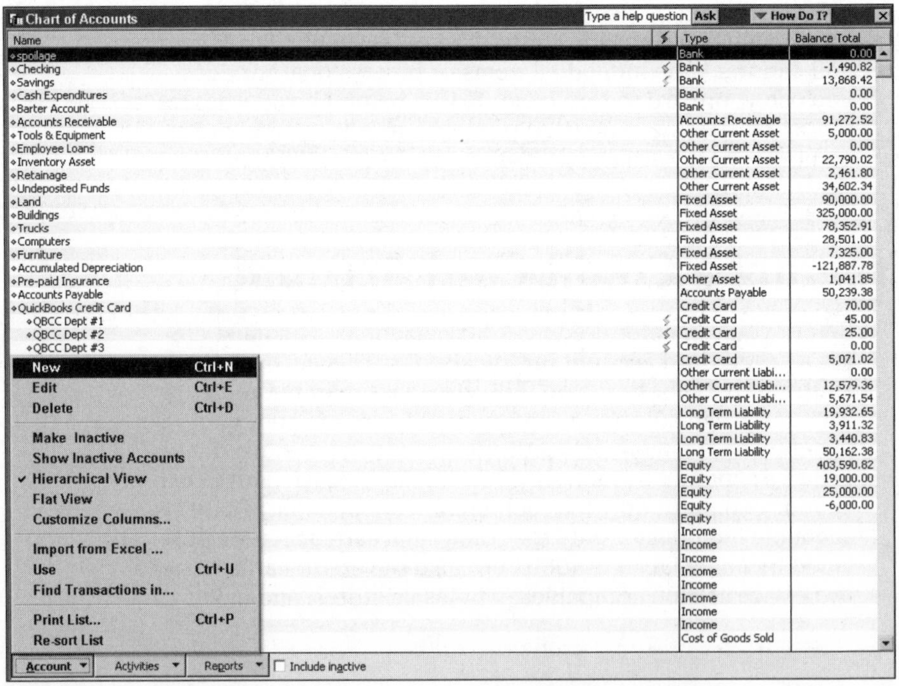

Figure 27-1: View all accounts from the Chart of Accounts window.

3. The New Account window appears as shown in Figure 27-2. Choose Credit Card from the Type drop-down list. If you have chosen to use account numbers, assign a number in the Number field at this time.

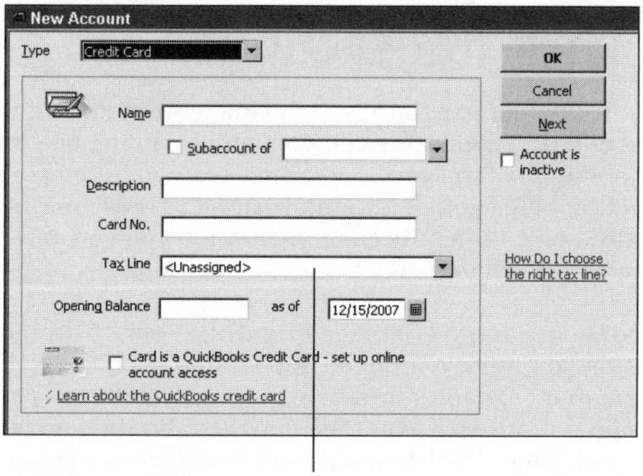

Credit card expenses can be associated with a tax schedule

Figure 27-2: Use this window to create a new Credit Card account.

4. In the Name field, enter a name by which you can identify the Credit Card account. You will have the opportunity to enter both a description and an account number for the credit card, so enter a name that you can recognize when the name is presented in a list of all accounts you create in QuickBooks.
5. In the Description field, enter any text you want to use to help describe the Credit Card account. You may enter extra information in the field, such as the date when the account was opened, the interest rate, the credit limit, or other terms of the account.
6. In the Card No. field, enter the account number provided by the company that issued the card.
7. If you plan to report the expense from this Credit Card account on a specific tax schedule, choose that schedule from the list in the Tax Line field (previously shown in Figure 27-2).
8. Enter the balance, if one exists, in the Opening Balance field, and then enter the date that the balance is effective in the As Of field. Indicate whether you want to set up online account access. To choose a date from a graphical calendar, choose the button adjacent to the As Of field.
9. To save the new account, click the OK button. To discard the information you entered about the Credit Card account, click Cancel. To create a new Credit Card account and save the existing Credit Card account, click Next.

As you will learn later, you can create a Credit Card account either in advance of recording credit card transactions or directly from the credit card transaction window. In either case, you can follow the steps presented here to create the account.

Entering Credit Card Transactions

By entering transactions in QuickBooks as they are made, you can monitor your cash flow status near the end of the month when you might pay the bill. In addition, the detail you can enter about all of the goods and services you purchase with a single credit card transaction helps you determine where and how your business is spending its money. Finally, considering the ease with which you can enter credit card transactions in QuickBooks, there really is no reason not to.

There is an old adage about data entry: "Garbage in, garbage out." This means that the value of the information you retrieve from an application such as QuickBooks is only as good as the information you enter into it. Regarding QuickBooks and credit card transactions, if you do not properly enter information about your transactions, the expense reports you run will have little value. Follow the steps in the next few sections to properly enter credit card transactions.

Entering the basic credit card transaction information

The first set of steps for entering credit card transactions is related to the basic information you need to supply for every transaction. Follow these steps whenever you want to record a credit card transaction in QuickBooks:

1. Go to Lists ⇨ Chart of Accounts to open the Chart of Accounts window.
2. From the Chart of Accounts window, click the Activities button and select Enter Credit Card Charges, as shown in Figure 27-3.
3. The Enter Credit Card Charges window appears, as shown in Figure 27-4. Select the appropriate Credit Card account by clicking the down arrow button in the Credit Card field. If the Credit Card account you want to use for this account does not exist, you can create the account without leaving the check-writing area of QuickBooks. To do so, choose Add New from the list of accounts, which is the first option in the list. The New Account dialog box appears. Enter information about the new account and then click OK.
4. Enter the date of the credit card transaction in the DATE field. To choose a date from a graphical calendar, click the button beside the DATE field.
5. Specify the vendor for the credit card transaction in the Purchased From field. For detailed information about specifying the transaction payee, read the following section. Otherwise, skip to the section "Entering the amount, type, and reference number."

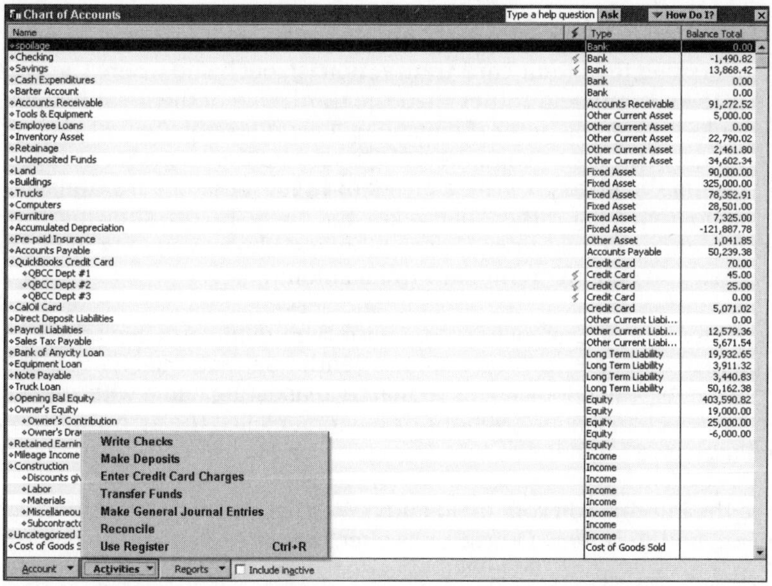

Figure 27-3: The access window to enter credit card charges.

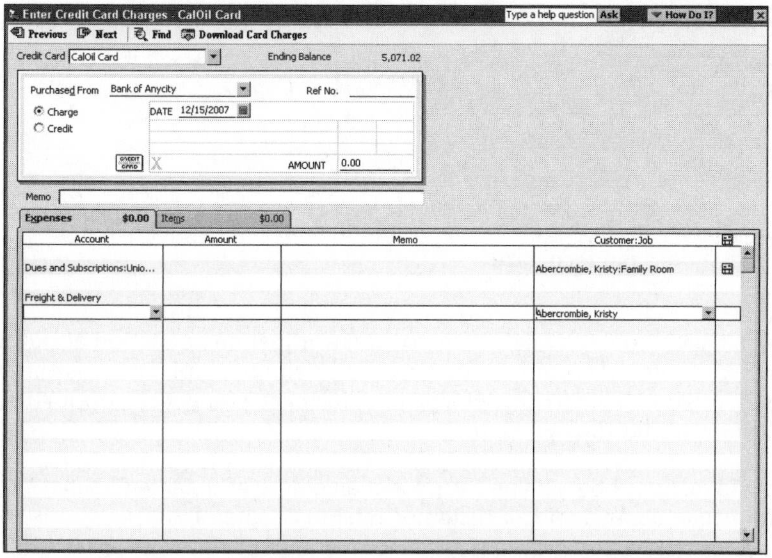

Figure 27-4: Use this window to enter credit card transactions.

Specifying where the card was used

The next step in creating the credit card transaction is specifying where the card was used. This is the second field rather than the third. One of the great benefits of using QuickBooks is that you enter the name of a vendor only the first time you specify that vendor. QuickBooks remembers the name, so the subsequent times you need to specify a name, such as to write a check or to log a credit card transaction, you select the name from a list rather than rekey the name. Before showing you how to add a new vendor or customer, this section first shows you how to use an existing name when you enter a credit card transaction.

To specify the person or company where you used the credit card, click the Purchased From field and enter the name of the vendor or customer. As you enter the letters of the name, QuickBooks tries to match an existing name with the letters that you enter. To select an existing vendor or customer, click the arrow button at the end of the Purchased From field.

When you leave the Purchased From dialog box by either pressing the Tab key or clicking elsewhere on the screen, QuickBooks checks to see whether the name already exists in the application. If QuickBooks does not recognize the name you entered, the Name Not Found dialog box shown in Figure 27-5 appears.

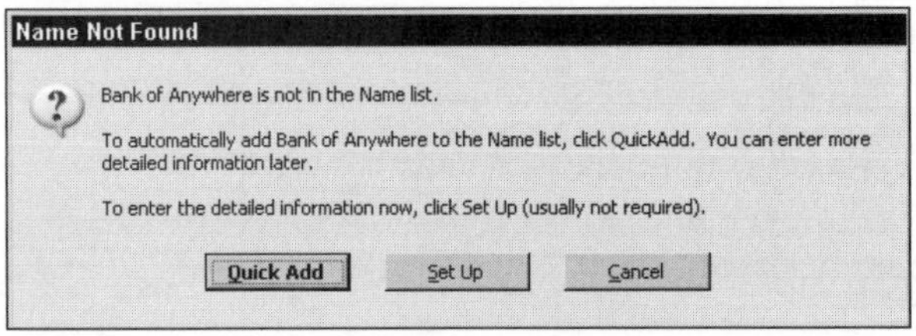

Figure 27-5: QuickBooks prompts you to supply information about a payee that it does not recognize.

You may choose Quick Add, in which case you answer just one question about the new name you have entered (whether the name is a vendor, employee, customer, or something else), or you may choose Set Up, in which case you get the opportunity to enter more detail about the new name.

Cross-Reference

For more information about adding a vendor or an employee, refer to Chapter 7. For more information about adding a customer, refer to Chapter 9.

Entering the amount, type, and reference number

Perhaps the most important information you specify for the credit card transaction is the amount. To enter the amount, follow these steps:

1. Click the Amount field and enter the amount of the transaction.

2. If the transaction represents a refund or a rebate, click the Credit option.
3. Enter the reference number (Ref No.) associated with the transaction. All credit card transactions record a unique reference or transaction number. You can find the reference number on your receipt.

Assigning expense to specific accounts

With QuickBooks, you can assign the value of credit card transactions you make to specific accounts. This gives you the capability to create reports detailing all of your expenses, even if the expenses were paid for by a single transaction, as in the case of a credit card.

A credit card transaction may cover many different types of expenses. For example, you might use a bank credit card to pay for many different types of products and services at a local consulting company, such as the cost of new computers, as well as the consulting to implement the network with the new computers.

You can use the Expenses tab at the bottom of the Enter Credit Card Charges window to assign the value of a card transaction to one or more expense accounts. In addition, you can record the name of a customer if you purchased an item for which a customer must reimburse your company.

Figure 27-6 shows a transaction with several expense line items defined with detail.

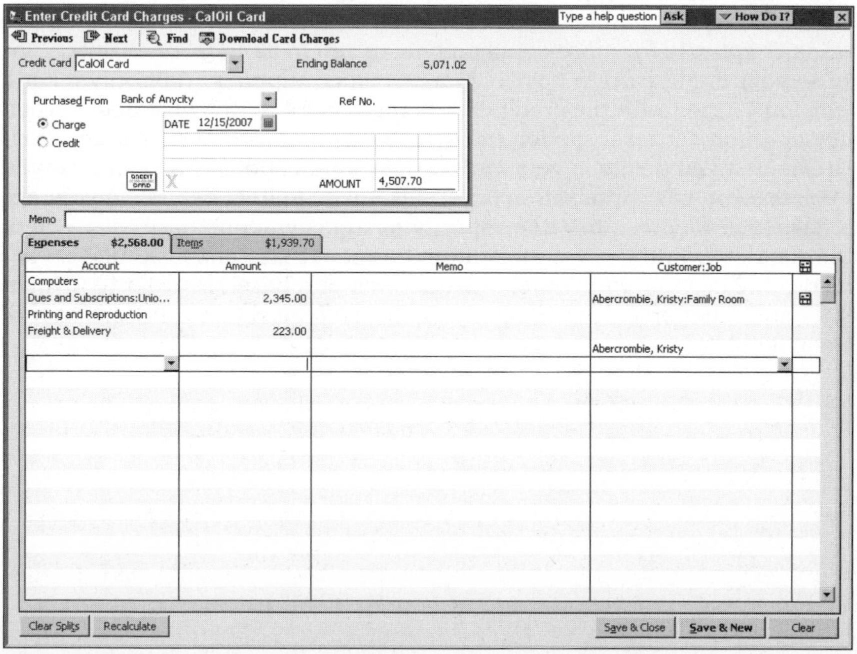

Figure 27-6: You can specify the details behind a credit card transaction you make.

Follow these steps to assign your credit card transaction to one or more accounts and/or to record a customer or job:

1. Click the Expenses tab. Then, click the Account column. An arrow button appears. Click the arrow and select the account to which you want to assign either the entire value of the credit card transaction or a portion of the entire value, if the transaction will be assigned to more than one expense account.
2. Press Tab to move to the Amount field, or simply click the Amount field. Enter the amount you want to assign to the expense account you just specified.
3. If you want to make a notation about this line item, move to the Memo field and then enter the note.
4. Click the Customer:Job field to associate the expense line item with a specific customer. Click the arrow to display the list of all customers, and then select the customer.
5. Repeat steps 2 through 4 until you have completely allocated the total amount to one or more line items. Note that you cannot save the transaction if the total of all expense line items does not match the value of the credit card transaction.

Entering Item detail

Oftentimes a credit card transaction you make (and then record in QuickBooks) is for a recurring type of purchase your company makes, which can be set up as an Item. (See Chapter 10 for more detail on how to set up Items.) For example, you might use your credit card to buy software or office supplies. Your only record of the items purchased with the credit card is the receipt. With QuickBooks, you can specify per credit card transaction the items you purchased. These items are the same Items that you define in your QuickBooks application. This relationship to Items you track in your application is very useful. If an Item defined in your application is flagged as an inventory Item, specifying items you purchase with a credit card automatically updates your inventory count of that Item. In addition, you can also record the customer for which the item was purchased in order to invoice the customer and reimburse your company. Figure 27-7 shows a credit card transaction with Item detail.

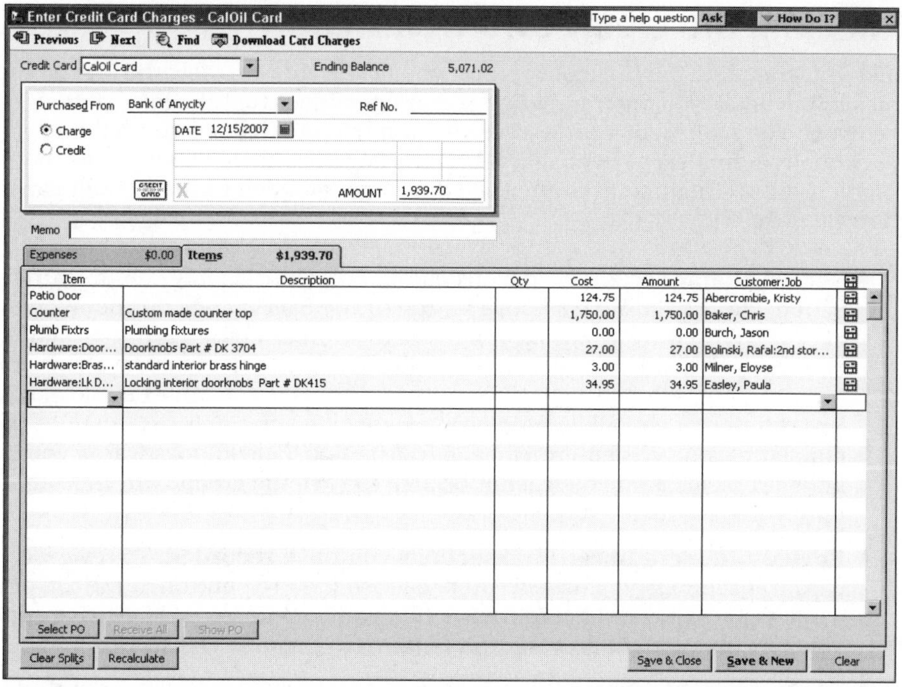

Figure 27-7: You can specify detail about the items you used the credit card to purchase.

Follow these steps to enter detail about the items you used the credit card to purchase:

1. Click the Item column, and an arrow button appears. Click the button to select the first item to record. If the item you wish to record does not appear in the list, choose Add New from the list, which appears as the first Item on the list. (For help in adding Items, refer to Chapter 10.)
2. Press Tab to move to the Description field. Enter any description you wish for the Item (perhaps how the Item will be used).
3. Enter the quantity and the cost of each Item in the appropriate fields. The amount is automatically calculated. If you know only the amount and quantity, enter those values, and the cost is automatically calculated.
4. Click the Customer:Job field to associate the Item with a specific customer. Click the arrow to display the list of all customers and select the customer.
5. Repeat the steps 2 through 4 until you have completely allocated the total amount of the credit card transaction to one or more line items.

Finishing the credit card transaction

After you complete the preceding steps, you may want to review the credit card transaction detail you entered. When you are confident that the information is correct, you may record another credit card transaction or move to other QuickBooks activities, or even take a break. The following list shows how to complete most common tasks after you have completed entering a credit card charge:

✦ **Record another credit card transaction:** To record another credit card transaction, choose the Save & Close button or the Save & New button. When you click the Save & New button, you move to another credit card transaction; any changes you made to the current credit card transaction are saved, provided there are no problems with the credit card transaction. An example of a problem is if the total of all Item details you specified on the Items tab does not equal the value you entered for the transaction. QuickBooks warns you if it finds problems, and you will not be able to save the credit card transaction until you have rectified them.

✦ **Review other credit card transactions you have recorded:** To review credit card transactions you have written, choose the Prev button at the top of the window until the credit card transaction you are interested in viewing appears. You may also use the Next button to move to the next transaction.

✦ **To clear a transaction you have started to enter:** Click the Clear button to get rid of all of the information.

Changing or Deleting a Credit Card Transaction

You may need to change a credit card transaction you entered. This might be the case if you made a mistake when entering the transaction or if a change has been made to your account.

There may also be an occasion when you need to zero the balance of the transaction you entered. In this case, you have two choices: you can either void the transaction or delete it completely. The difference between these two options is explained later in this section. For now, keep in mind that you can make a change to any credit card transaction, including an edit, a void, or a deletion. Remember that a change to any credit card transaction affects only the register. You may create an imbalance between your QuickBooks account and your Credit Card account if you do not make proper changes to your QuickBooks register.

Changing a credit card transaction

To make changes to a credit card transaction, such as the date or expense category, you can edit the credit card transaction. To edit a credit card transaction, either open the register and select the transaction to be changed, or open the credit card transactions window and then, using the Prev or Next buttons, move to the credit card transaction to be edited. Make the required changes to the credit card transaction and click OK. You may also use the Prev or Next key to move to another credit card transaction you may want to edit.

Voiding a credit card transaction

When you void a credit card transaction, it (specifically, the register Item) is not deleted. Only the amount of the credit card transaction is zeroed. To void a credit card transaction, either open the register and select the credit card transaction to be voided, or open the credit card transaction window and then, using the Prev or Next button, move to the transaction to be voided. Next, choose Edit ⇨ Void Credit Card Charge.

Deleting a credit card transaction

Deleting a credit card transaction is more significant than voiding one. When you delete a credit card transaction, the entire transaction is gone. Be wary of deleting a credit card transaction because you easily lose all of the detail associated with the transaction. To delete a credit card transaction, either open the register and select the credit card transaction to be deleted, or open the credit card transaction window and then, using the Prev or Next button, move to the credit card transaction to be deleted. Next, choose Edit ⇨ Delete Credit Card Charge.

Summary

You can use QuickBooks to store detailed information about the credit card transactions made by your company. You can track interest charged to your account, as well as maintain a list of the individual items and services purchased with each transaction.

- ✦ Update your list of company Items with new items purchased via your credit card by entering that item detail when you record the credit card transaction, including the individual price of the item.
- ✦ If you purchase an item or service with your credit card for a specific job or customer, specify that job or customer so that you can be sure you are reimbursed for the expense.

✦ ✦ ✦

CHAPTER 28

Analyzing Your Company's Profitability and Financial Strength

✦ ✦ ✦ ✦

In This Chapter

Using classes to track income-producing activities

Analyzing information by job

Ratios to analyze business performance

IRS hobby loss rules

✦ ✦ ✦ ✦

This chapter may be the biggest eye-opener in the whole book. Proceed only if you are a realist — if you really want to know how your business is doing. Here, you learn how to use classes to determine which activities conducted by your business are most profitable and, alas, which ones are simply not financially justified. You will also learn to take the totals from your Balance Sheet and plug them into revealing ratio formats that allow you to analyze the business's actual value and profitability with cold, clairvoyant objectivity.

Using Classes to Track Income-Producing Activities

Classes enable you to determine the profitability of various activities, departments, or projects within your business — without spinning them off as separate entities. For example, if you are a farmer, you might want to know whether it is more financially worthwhile to breed pigs or sheep. If you are a real estate developer, you might want to know whether strip malls or office buildings are more profitable. A litigation attorney might want to set up classes to track types of cases.

What are classes?

In QuickBooks, classes give you a way to classify your transactions. You can use QuickBooks classes to classify your income and expenses by department, business office or location, separate properties you own, or any other meaningful breakdown of the business you do.

For example, if you had a restaurant with three locations, you might create a separate class for each location. At the end of an accounting period, you could create separate reports for each restaurant location.

The classes you create appear on your Class list. The Use Class Tracking preference in the Accounting Preferences window adds a Class field to windows where you enter invoices, checks, bills, credit card charges, or other transactions.

You have already been introduced to Customer:Jobs. Unlike jobs, which track income and expenses for a single project, classes enable you to track profitability of categories of activities on a company-wide basis. For example, you can track either of the following:

✦ Performance of a department within your business

✦ Economic viability of various business locations

Profitability of categories of types of clients or jobs

Class tracking is a Preference Item. When it is activated, QuickBooks adds a special Class field to the windows used for entering checks, credit card charges, bills, register transactions, purchase orders, sales forms, and payroll transactions, as well as revenue and expense tracking.

At the end of a fiscal period, you can create a class report to show all income and expenses attributable to each of your classes, as derived from each of the preceding transactions.

Activating the preference option

When you turn on class tracking, the necessary tracking option fields appear on all relevant transaction-recording screens. To activate the class-tracking preference, follow these steps:

1. Go to Edit ➪ Preferences.
2. Using the scroll bar on the left side of the screen, click the Accounting icon.

3. Click the Company Preferences tab.

4. Select the Use Class Tracking box, as shown in Figure 28-1.

5. Click OK.

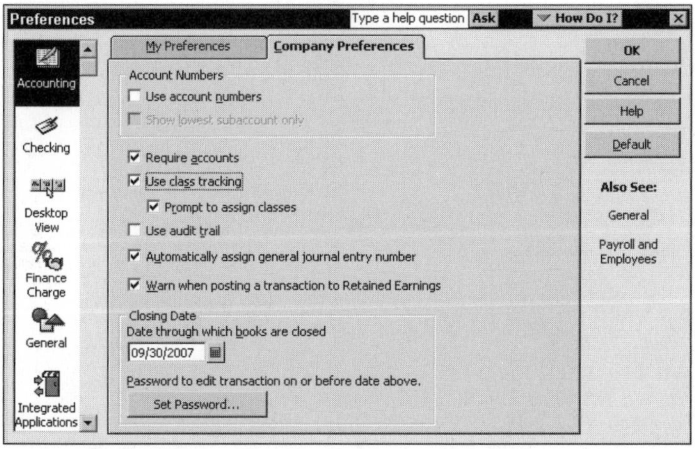

Figure 28-1: To activate class tracking, select the box labeled Use Class Tracking.

Setting up classes

After you activate the class preference option, you can create the classes you want to use for tracking purposes. You can set up subclasses within classes. For example, if you are interested in the profitability of a parent class of Beauty Products, you might set up subclasses for Hair Care, Skin Care, and so forth. The more subclasses you set up, the more detail is available in the reports.

When class tracking is turned on in the Accounting Preferences window, QuickBooks adds a Class field to the windows where you enter transactions. You can fill in this field by choosing a class from your Class list.

To set up classes and subclasses, follow these steps:

1. From the Lists menu, choose Class List. A Class list appears as shown in Figure 28-2.

Note

The Class list shows up only when you have checked the preference to use class tracking.

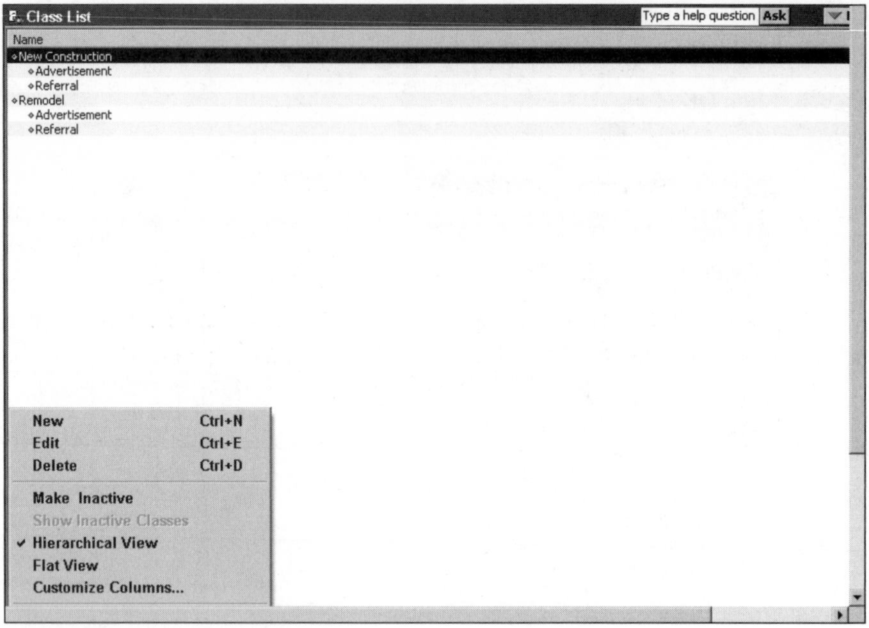

Figure 28-2: A sample Class list.

2. Click the Class menu button at the bottom of the screen and choose New from the pop-up menu that appears. The dialog box shown in Figure 28-3 appears.

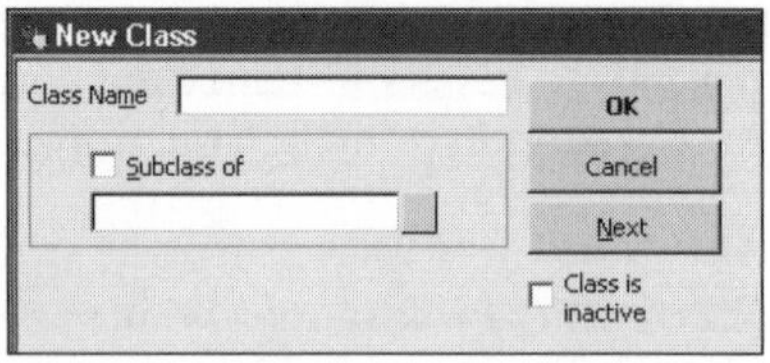

Figure 28-3: Use this dialog box to enter the name of the class and any applicable subclass.

3. Enter a name for the class.
4. If you want the class to be a subclass of another class, select the Subclass Of check box and enter the name of the parent class.
5. Record the class, and click OK.

You can also manage and update your list of classes by editing, deleting, and making classes inactive. You can delete only classes that have not been used in any transactions. If you want to delete a transaction used in previous transactions, you must delete or edit any transactions referencing the class designated for obliteration. To delete a class, follow these steps:

1. Go to Lists ➪ Class List.
2. Select the name of the class you want to delete.
3. Click the Class button and select Delete from the pop-up menu that appears.
4. Click OK.

You may want to delete a class that is obsolete but can't do so because it was used in prior transactions. If you do not want it to be mistakenly used in the future (for example, it represents a discontinued product or service), you can make it inactive. If you make a class inactive, it won't appear on your drop-down list. If you find a later use for it, you can easily reactivate it or set your screen to show inactive as well as active files.

To make a class inactive, follow these steps:

1. Go to Lists ➪ Class List.
2. Select the class you want to make inactive.
3. Click the Class menu button and then choose Make Inactive from the drop-down menu that appears.

To view inactive classes or to reactivate them, follow these steps:

1. Go to Lists ➪ Class List.
2. Click the Class button located at the bottom of the screen.
3. Select Show Inactive Classes from the pop-up menu that appears.
4. An X icon appears next to inactive classes as shown in Figure 28-4. Reactivate them by clicking the icon or by clicking the Class menu button and selecting Make Active from the pop-up menu.

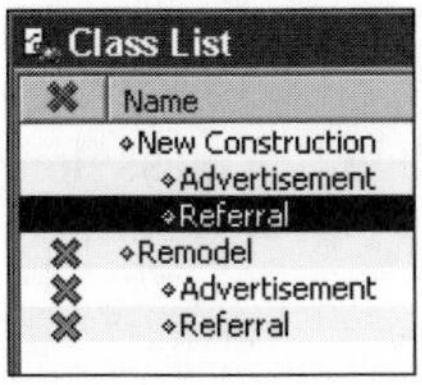

Figure 28-4: The special X icon denotes inactive classes.

Assigning classes to Items on employee paychecks

You can use QuickBooks to track payroll expenses by class in two ways. One method is to assign all the expenses on a paycheck (for example, wages, withholding amounts, company contributions, additions, and so on) to the class. Alternatively, you can assign specific amounts by class. For example, you might want to attribute hourly wages and withholding to the class, but not retirement plan contributions. Or you might decide that all expenses associated with keeping a particular employee on your payroll are attributable to that class. You must decide which payroll expenses should be used in calculating the profitability for the class.

You use the Payroll Preference window for tracking payroll check amounts by class, whether you opt to include all amounts shown on the check or designate expenses on an Item-by-Item basis. To track employee payroll expenses by class, follow these steps:

1. Go to Edit ➪ Preferences. Select Payroll & Employees from the scroll box to access the screen shown in Figure 28-5.

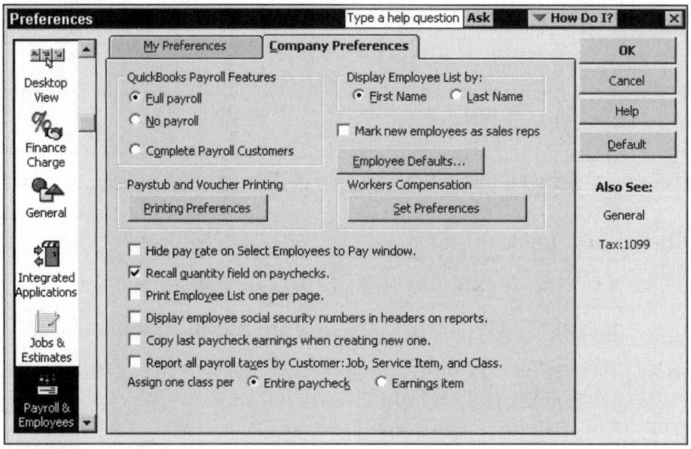

Figure 28-5: Use this window to assign either all or selected payroll expenses to a class.

2. Click the Company Preferences tab. Choose to assign one class per entire paycheck or per earnings item.
3. Click OK to save your changes.

Caution You can't use the Entire Paycheck option for employees who are set up in the QuickBooks Pro time-tracking option.

Tip You can use the Preview Paycheck window to assign specific classes to Payroll Items listed in the earning section of the window prior to printing a paycheck.

Tracking classes on sales forms, registers, and purchase orders

If you previously activated class tracking, the Class field is automatically displayed on sales forms, registers, and purchase order forms, as shown in Figures 28-6, 28-7, and 28-8.

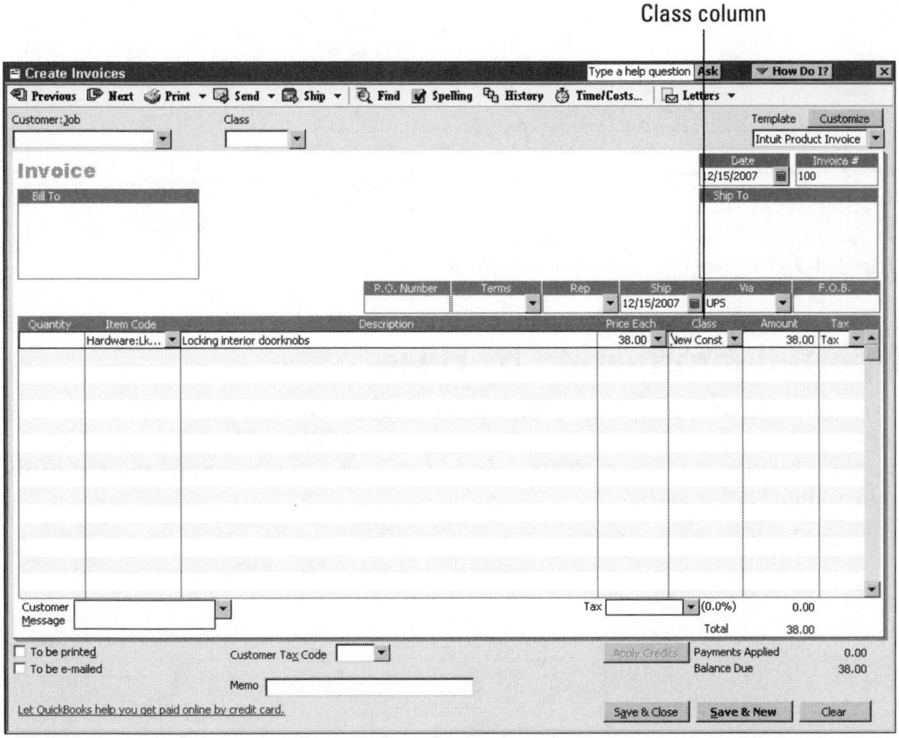

Figure 28-6: Class-tracking fields appear on sales forms when the preference is activated.

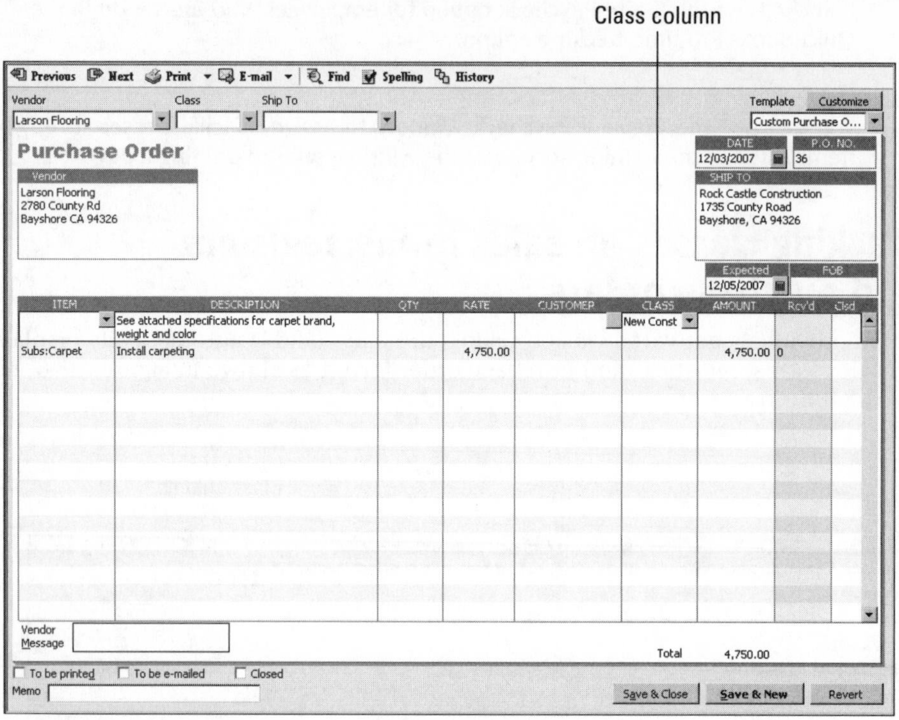

Figure 28-7: You can use class tracking for all purchase orders.

Reported information by class

To view a Profit and Loss Statement that discloses information about revenue and expenses for each class, such as the one shown in Figure 28-9, go to Reports ➪ Company & Financial. Select Profit & Loss by Class from the supplemental drop-down menu that appears.

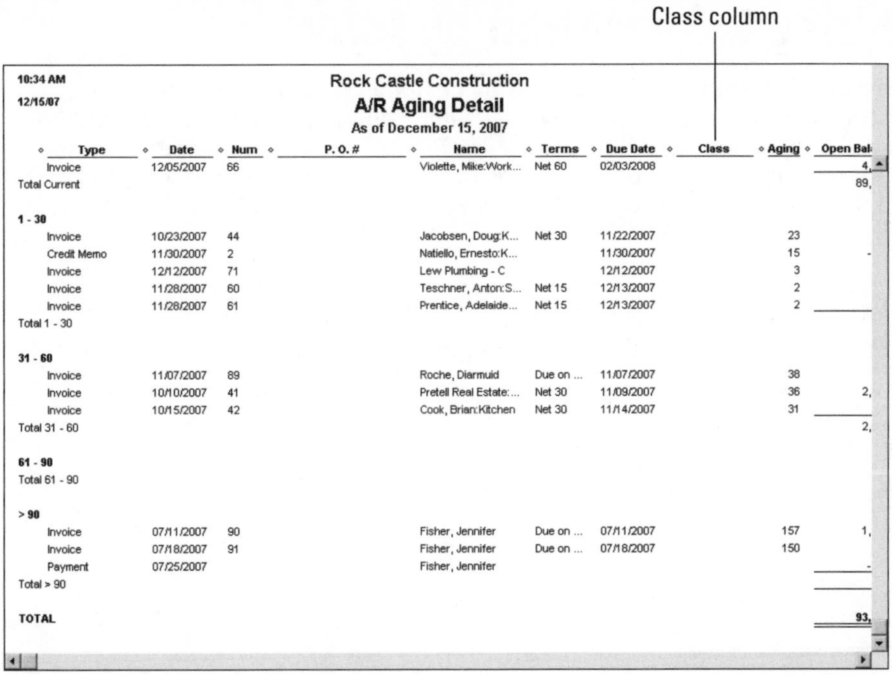

10:34 AM
12/15/07

Rock Castle Construction
A/R Aging Detail
As of December 15, 2007

Type	Date	Num	P. O. #	Name	Terms	Due Date	Class	Aging	Open Bal
Invoice	12/05/2007	66		Violette, Mike:Work...	Net 60	02/03/2008			4,
Total Current									89,
1 - 30									
Invoice	10/23/2007	44		Jacobsen, Doug:K...	Net 30	11/22/2007		23	
Credit Memo	11/30/2007	2		Natiello, Ernesto:K...		11/30/2007		15	-
Invoice	12/12/2007	71		Lew Plumbing - C		12/12/2007		3	
Invoice	11/28/2007	60		Teschner, Anton:S...	Net 15	12/13/2007		2	
Invoice	11/28/2007	61		Prentice, Adelaide...	Net 15	12/13/2007		2	
Total 1 - 30									
31 - 60									
Invoice	11/07/2007	89		Roche, Diarmuid	Due on ...	11/07/2007		38	
Invoice	10/10/2007	41		Pretell Real Estate:...	Net 30	11/09/2007		36	2,
Invoice	10/15/2007	42		Cook, Brian:Kitchen	Net 30	11/14/2007		31	
Total 31 - 60									2,
61 - 90									
Total 61 - 90									
> 90									
Invoice	07/11/2007	90		Fisher, Jennifer	Due on ...	07/11/2007		157	1,
Invoice	07/18/2007	91		Fisher, Jennifer	Due on ...	07/18/2007		150	
Payment	07/25/2007			Fisher, Jennifer					-
Total > 90									
TOTAL									93,

Figure 28-8: A class-tracking option is available on the Accounts Receivable register for transactions that are entered directly.

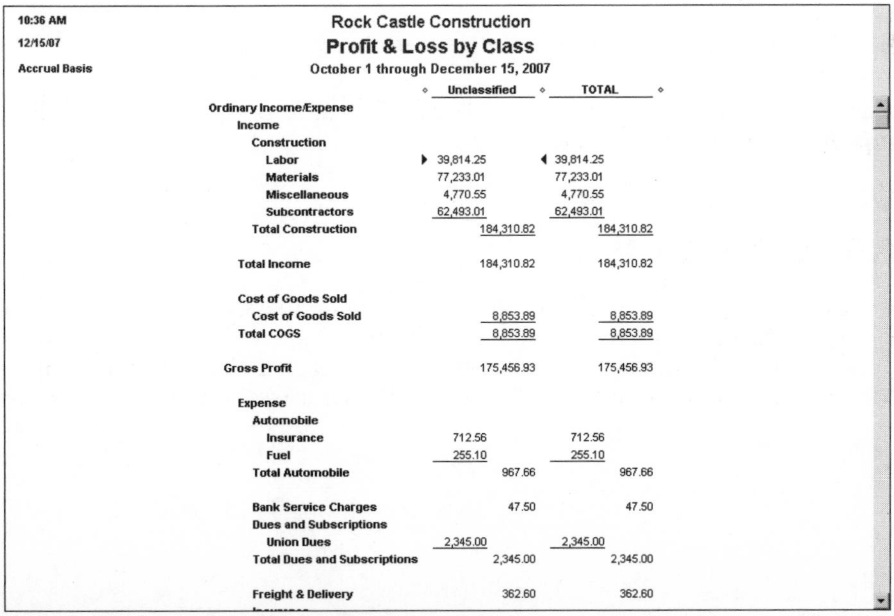

10:36 AM
12/15/07
Accrual Basis

Rock Castle Construction
Profit & Loss by Class
October 1 through December 15, 2007

	Unclassified		TOTAL	
Ordinary Income/Expense				
Income				
Construction				
Labor	39,814.25		39,814.25	
Materials	77,233.01		77,233.01	
Miscellaneous	4,770.55		4,770.55	
Subcontractors	62,493.01		62,493.01	
Total Construction		184,310.82		184,310.82
Total Income		184,310.82		184,310.82
Cost of Goods Sold				
Cost of Goods Sold		8,853.89		8,853.89
Total COGS		8,853.89		8,853.89
Gross Profit		175,456.93		175,456.93
Expense				
Automobile				
Insurance	712.56		712.56	
Fuel	255.10		255.10	
Total Automobile		967.66		967.66
Bank Service Charges		47.50		47.50
Dues and Subscriptions				
Union Dues	2,345.00		2,345.00	
Total Dues and Subscriptions		2,345.00		2,345.00
Freight & Delivery		362.60		362.60

Figure 28-9: Profit and loss shown by class.

Analyzing Information by Jobs

You can track a number of expenses by customer or job. Simply select the Customer:Job from the drop-down list when completing sales forms, purchase orders, and paychecks. You can also create and view reports about specific Customer:Jobs, as shown in Figure 28-10. Go to Reports ⇨ Company & Financial and then select Profit & Loss by Job from the supplemental drop-down menu that appears.

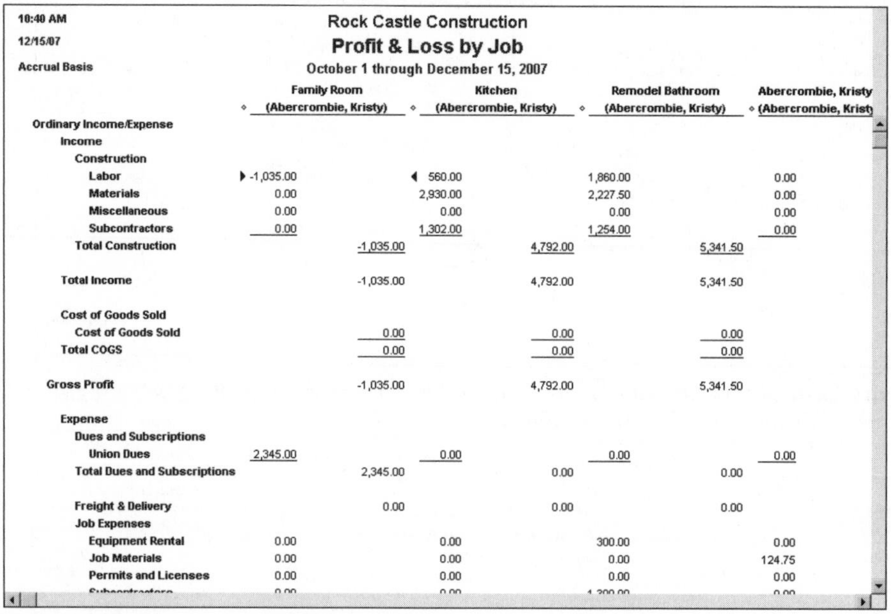

10:40 AM
12/15/07
Accrual Basis

Rock Castle Construction
Profit & Loss by Job
October 1 through December 15, 2007

	Family Room (Abercrombie, Kristy)		Kitchen (Abercrombie, Kristy)		Remodel Bathroom (Abercrombie, Kristy)		Abercrombie, Kristy (Abercrombie, Kristy
Ordinary Income/Expense							
Income							
Construction							
Labor	-1,035.00		560.00		1,860.00		0.00
Materials	0.00		2,930.00		2,227.50		0.00
Miscellaneous	0.00		0.00		0.00		0.00
Subcontractors	0.00		1,302.00		1,254.00		0.00
Total Construction		-1,035.00		4,792.00		5,341.50	
Total Income		-1,035.00		4,792.00		5,341.50	
Cost of Goods Sold							
Cost of Goods Sold		0.00		0.00		0.00	
Total COGS		0.00		0.00		0.00	
Gross Profit		-1,035.00		4,792.00		5,341.50	
Expense							
Dues and Subscriptions							
Union Dues	2,345.00		0.00		0.00		0.00
Total Dues and Subscriptions		2,345.00		0.00		0.00	
Freight & Delivery		0.00		0.00		0.00	
Job Expenses							
Equipment Rental	0.00		0.00		300.00		0.00
Job Materials	0.00		0.00		0.00		124.75
Permits and Licenses	0.00		0.00		0.00		0.00
Subcontractors	0.00		0.00		1,300.00		0.00

Figure 28-10: Profit and loss shown by job.

Ratios to Live By

You may view your Balance Sheet (your statement of financial position) and Profit and Loss Statements as informative but uninspiring lists of account balances. You may be unmoved by the logic and simplicity of the basic Balance Sheet equation introduced in Chapter 4: Assets – Liabilities = Owner's Equity. But this section will change how you view the financial statements for your company—and that of any other company—forever. The ratios introduced in this section show you how to take seemingly discrete and self-contained account balances and use them to reveal the financial strengths and weaknesses of the company.

Ratios force you to examine your venture objectively. They help you anticipate future problem areas and cash flow problems before they arise. You may have a vague sense that money has been tight lately, but these underutilized management tools help you zero in on the problem. Before you can embark on this journey of financial self-discovery, you need to pull up a copy of your company's Balance Sheet and Profit and Loss Statement.

To access the Balance Sheet, go to Reports ➪ Company & Financial ➪ Balance Sheet. Figure 28-11 shows a sample Balance Sheet.

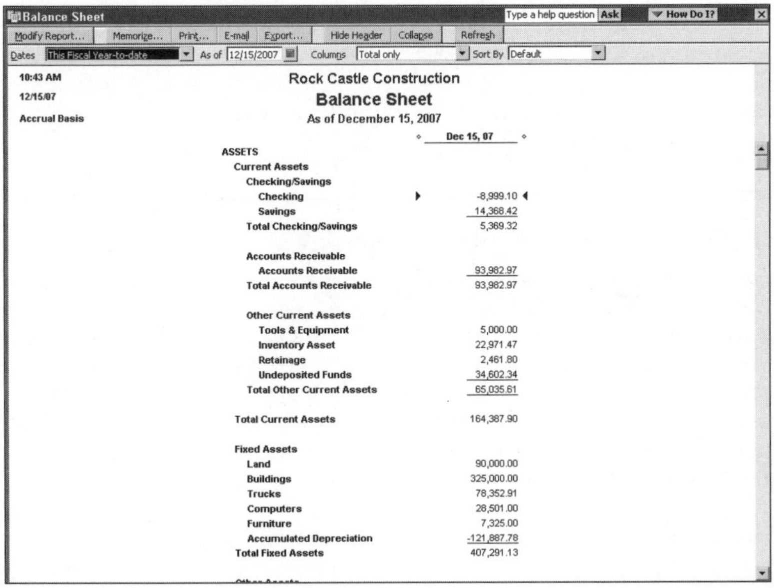

	Dec 15, 07
ASSETS	
Current Assets	
Checking/Savings	
Checking	-8,999.10
Savings	14,368.42
Total Checking/Savings	5,369.32
Accounts Receivable	
Accounts Receivable	93,982.97
Total Accounts Receivable	93,982.97
Other Current Assets	
Tools & Equipment	5,000.00
Inventory Asset	22,971.47
Retainage	2,461.80
Undeposited Funds	34,602.34
Total Other Current Assets	65,035.61
Total Current Assets	164,387.90
Fixed Assets	
Land	90,000.00
Buildings	325,000.00
Trucks	78,352.91
Computers	28,501.00
Furniture	7,325.00
Accumulated Depreciation	-121,887.78
Total Fixed Assets	407,291.13

Figure 28-11: A standard Balance Sheet.

To view the Profit and Loss Statement, go to Report ➪ Company & Financial ➪ Profit & Loss Standard. Figure 28-12 shows a sample Profit and Loss Statement.

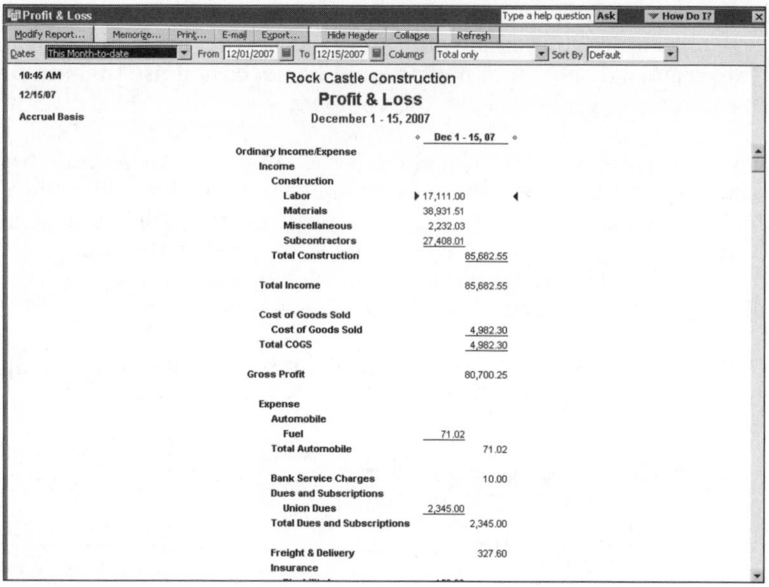

Figure 28-12: A Profit and Loss Statement.

Working capital: How much money do you have to run your business?

The amount of money that you have to run your business is called *working capital.* To calculate working capital, subtract the total of the company's current liabilities from its current assets. (You obtain this information from your company's Balance Sheet, as shown in Figure 28-13.) In other words, Working Capital = Current Assets – Current Liabilities. If this number is a negative, the company is likely to have a problem meeting its current obligations.

Accounting Jargon

You may remember from Chapter 4 that current assets are either cash equivalents or assets expected to be reduced to cash equivalents within one year. Current liabilities must be paid within one year.

Let's gauge the working capital of Larry's Landscaping. Its current assets are shown at $164,387.90. The total amount of the company's other current liabilities is $18,222.07. Subtracting current assets from current liabilities discloses working capital in the amount of $37,273.75. This is the amount of money that Larry's Landscaping has available to run its business and initiate new ventures after paying its current bills.

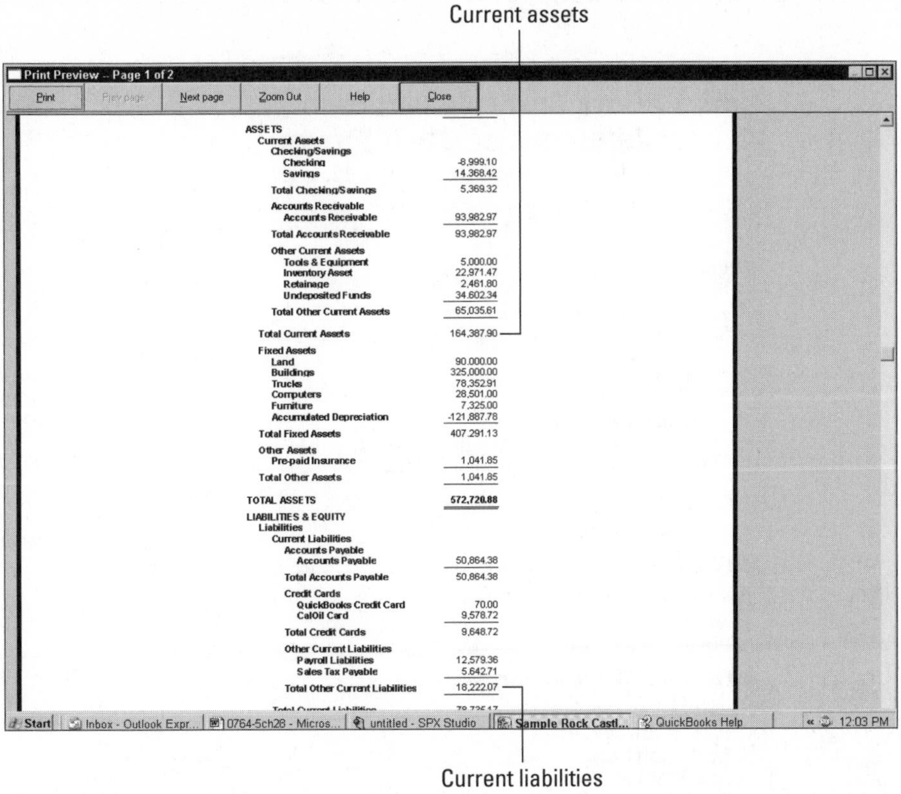

ASSETS	
Current Assets	
Checking/Savings	
Checking	-8,999.10
Savings	14,368.42
Total Checking/Savings	5,369.32
Accounts Receivable	
Accounts Receivable	93,982.97
Total Accounts Receivable	93,982.97
Other Current Assets	
Tools & Equipment	5,000.00
Inventory Asset	22,971.47
Retainage	2,461.80
Undeposited Funds	34,602.34
Total Other Current Assets	65,035.61
Total Current Assets	164,387.90
Fixed Assets	
Land	90,000.00
Buildings	325,000.00
Trucks	78,352.91
Computers	28,501.00
Furniture	7,325.00
Accumulated Depreciation	-121,887.78
Total Fixed Assets	407,291.13
Other Assets	
Pre-paid Insurance	1,041.85
Total Other Assets	1,041.85
TOTAL ASSETS	572,720.88
LIABILITIES & EQUITY	
Liabilities	
Current Liabilities	
Accounts Payable	
Accounts Payable	50,864.38
Total Accounts Payable	50,864.38
Credit Cards	
QuickBooks Credit Card	70.00
CalOil Card	9,578.72
Total Credit Cards	9,648.72
Other Current Liabilities	
Payroll Liabilities	12,579.36
Sales Tax Payable	5,642.71
Total Other Current Liabilities	18,222.07

Figure 28-13: Your company's Balance Sheet provides you with the information you need to calculate your working capital.

How is your company's cash flow?

QuickBooks enables you to view a Statement of Cash Flows Report, an option not available with previous versions of the program. This type of report, shown in Figure 28-14, enables you to gauge your present sources of cash and how they are being used in your business.

You can rely on the working capital calculation as a measure of available funds only to the extent that your receivables are collectible. So, it is a good idea to evaluate your working capital in connection with the Accounts Receivable aging summary generated by QuickBooks. To view the aging summary, go to Reports ⇨ Customers & Receivables and then select Aging Summary from the supplemental menu.

Rock Castle Construction
Statement of Cash Flows
October 1 through December 15, 2007

	Oct 1 - Dec 15, 07
OPERATING ACTIVITIES	
Net Income	32,081.78
Adjustments to reconcile Net Income to net cash provided by operations:	
Accounts Receivable	-61,234.21
Inventory Asset	-18,579.59
Retainage	-2,461.80
Accounts Payable	28,206.10
QuickBooks Credit Card:QBCC Dept #1	45.00
QuickBooks Credit Card:QBCC Dept #2	25.00
CalOil Card	4,512.84
Payroll Liabilities	8,797.37
Sales Tax Payable	1,005.67
Net cash provided by Operating Activities	-7,601.84
INVESTING ACTIVITIES	
Trucks	-44,500.00
Pre-paid Insurance	2,322.66
Net cash provided by Investing Activities	-42,177.34
FINANCING ACTIVITIES	
Bank of Anycity Loan	-868.42
Equipment Loan	3,911.32
Note Payable	-17,059.17
Truck Loan	43,013.06
Opening Bal Equity	-11,697.50
Owner's Equity:Owner's Draw	-6,000.00
Retained Earnings	8,863.39
Net cash provided by Financing Activities	20,162.68
Net cash increase for period	-29,616.50
Cash at beginning of period	69,588.16
Cash at end of period	**39,971.66**

Figure 28-14: The Statement of Cash Flows identifies sources and uses of cash for your company for the specified period.

Your company's current ratio

Sure, things look good on paper. But how easily is your business able to meet its day-to-day obligations?

The *current ratio* measures the company's capability to meet its short-term obligations and thus is a good indicator of how your business is functioning.

The current ratio is the ratio of current assets to current liabilities — in other words, current assets divided by current liabilities. It can also be expressed as a fraction, with the assets as the numerator and the current liabilities as the denominator. The higher the ratio, the better. By most standards, a ratio of 1:1 is considered barely adequate. A ratio of 2:1 is pretty comfortable, and 3:1 is excellent. For example, if a company has assets of $600,000.00 divided by liabilities of $200,000.00, this means that the company has $3.00 in assets to pay off each $1.00 in obligations. Its current ratio is 3:1. This is a fairly good ratio.

If your business had to suddenly shut down – for example, because of a fire, flood, or alien invasion – could you pay your bills? The so-called *quick ratio* provides an answer of sorts.

To calculate the quick ratio, divide the company's cash and marketable securities by its current liabilities. The quick ratio for the Rock Castle Construction Company, according to its Balance Sheet, is 0.56:1 (56%) — substantially less than 1:1. This means that the company would have only 56 cents of readily available cash to pay every dollar of debt in an emergency. This is not so good!

The turnover ratio: How well are your company's products selling?

This next ratio is a *must* for retail and manufacturing businesses, or any business that has a lot invested in inventory. If you are in this category, you need to know how much revenue your business assets are producing.

The *turnover ratio* tells you how much revenue your assets are producing and provides a basis for comparing the strength of the company's sale cycle from year to year. Its real value is to compare your company with itself at different time periods, as long as they are identical. It can also be valuable in comparing your company to a competitor or to industry averages.

To calculate the turnover ratio, divide the company's net revenues by its total assets. The ratio tells you the level of sales that the company's assets are producing at a given time.

Debt-to-equity ratio: Does your business have too much debt?

Business debt is not always a bad thing — if the rate of return on the debt exceeds what you have to pay for the money. But how much is too much?

To find out, calculate the company's *debt-to-equity ratio* and *debt-to-asset ratio*. The goals are to have the lowest possible ratios and to see a downward trend over the years.

Lenders, in making a determination whether to extend credit, often use some variation of these ratios. Again, the standard QuickBooks Balance Sheet provides you with all of the information that you need to calculate the ratios. The debt-to-equity ratio for the Rock Castle Construction Company is about 1:1, as derived by dividing its total liabilities by its equity. Its debt-to-asset ratio is about 2:1, which is the total of its debt divided by its assets.

Return on investment: Is the business profitable?

This is really the heart of the matter, isn't it? No legitimate business exists for any other purpose.

There are three simple ratios that you can use to help you answer this all-important question: net profit, gross profit, and return on investment (ROI). For all these ratios, the higher the better — and be sure to look for that healthy upward trend from year to year.

The *net profit margin* is calculated by dividing net income by net sales. This figure tells you the portion of your net sales or service revenue that your company actually gets to keep.

The *gross profit margin* is equal to the company's gross profit divided by its net revenues. It tells you what proportion of each dollar of net sales revenue is actually profit. A low ratio may indicate too much administrative, salary, and overhead costs — costs unrelated to producing the actual product the company sells.

The *ROI ratio* enables the owners of the business to evaluate their return on their investment in the business. It is calculated by dividing net income by the owner's equity. For example, assume a company's Balance Sheet discloses an owner's equity of $9,000.00 and its Income Statement reveals net income of $9,540.00. This means that the owner's ROI is an amazing 106%. You can't earn that in a passbook account!

IRS Hobby Loss Rules

The ratios in the previous section elucidated the point that cash flow isn't everything. Profit and return on investment are important, but low debt-to-equity ratios or a steady downward trend can also signal financial strength, especially for a new venture with high start-up costs.

But beware. If your healthy, low-debt sole proprietorship or subchapter S corporation does not show a profit for three of five consecutive years, you may not be able to deduct losses generated by the business on your income tax return. The IRS may reclassify the venture as a "hobby." You can file a special Form 5213 to suspend the IRS presumption until your business has been in existence for seven years.

If your business is reclassified as a hobby, you can deduct business expenses only to the extent of business income. And even then, the deductions are subject to the 2 percent floor generally applicable to miscellaneous itemized deductions.

Summary

Numbers don't lie, but they can certainly obscure. For example, high salaries and reported profits can hide a sickly debt-to-equity ratio.

- You can identify unprofitable activities, departments, and ventures by tracking income and expenses by class.
- Ratios enable you to interpret the information reported on the Balance Sheet and Income Statement to determine a company's capability to expand, its ability to meet its obligations, and its profitability.
- If your sole proprietorship or subchapter S corporation shows a tax loss for three out of five consecutive years, the IRS may limit deductibility of losses by reclassifying the venture as a hobby.

✦ ✦ ✦

PART

VII

Analyzing Business Performance

✦ ✦ ✦ ✦

In This Part

✦ ✦ ✦ ✦

CHAPTER 29

Accounting for Fixed Assets and Other Advanced Balance Sheet Topics

✦ ✦ ✦ ✦

In This Chapter

Depreciation

Selling a fixed asset

Accounting for borrowed funds

Recording capital contributions

Recording distributions to owners

✦ ✦ ✦ ✦

By now, you know that your Balance Sheet provides a snapshot of what the company is worth to its owners: Assets – Liabilities = Owner's Equity. This chapter goes beyond the Balance Sheet basics to explore some of the more complicated transactions involving assets and liabilities. Acquiring or selling a fixed asset, accounting for borrowed funds, and recording capital contributions and distributions are all events that are unrelated to the normal income-producing activities of a business. This chapter discusses the correct method for recording them and analyzes their impact on the Balance Sheet.

Depreciation

As you may recall from Chapter 4, assets are classified as either current or fixed. Classification is based on whether the assets are expected to be converted to cash within the current business cycle.

Current assets are cash equivalents and assets expected to be converted to cash within one year. *Fixed assets* are not converted to cash in the normal course of business — rather, they are used by the business to perform its revenue-generating activities. Examples of fixed assets include equipment and buildings.

Because the useful life of a fixed asset extends beyond one year, both generally accepted accounting principles, known as GAAP, and the Internal Revenue Code dictate that the expense associated with it is recognized over several years. For example, if you buy an embroidery machine for your monogramming business, the machine is expected to last for seven years.

Accounting Jargon

Each year the remaining *useful life* of the machine is diminished by one year. The reduction in the useful life of the fixed asset, due to wear or obsolescence, is called *depreciation.* In the monogramming business example, the company recognizes one-seventh of the expense of the equipment each year until the equipment has been "fully depreciated."

Accumulated depreciation refers to the total amount of depreciation recognized for an asset as of the current date. It is generally tracked in a special accumulated depreciation account established for each asset. The value of a fixed asset at any given time on a company's books is equal to the original costs of the asset less the accumulated depreciation recorded for it.

Accounting Jargon

This amount is sometimes referred to as the *carrying value* of the asset.

Figure 29-1 shows how a fixed asset, trucks, is reflected on the Rock Castle Construction Company's Balance Sheet.

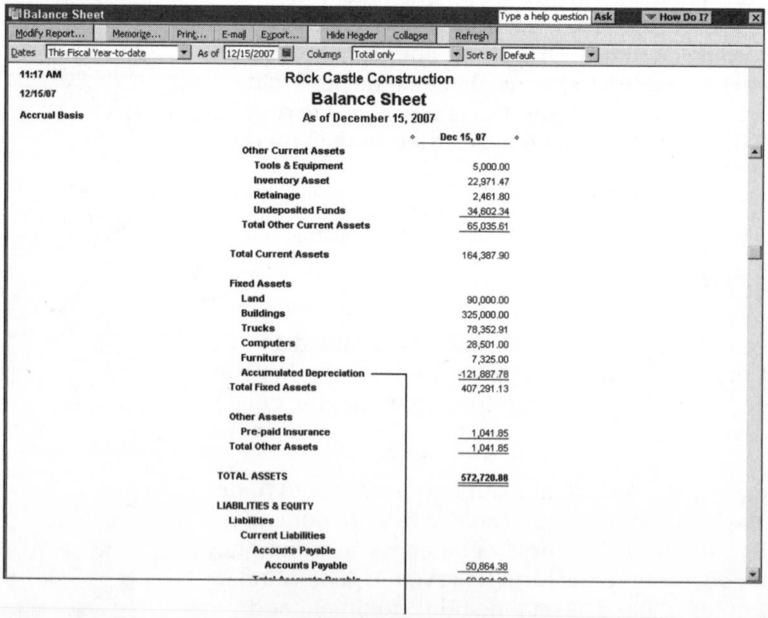

	Dec 15, 07
Other Current Assets	
Tools & Equipment	5,000.00
Inventory Asset	22,971.47
Retainage	2,461.80
Undeposited Funds	34,602.34
Total Other Current Assets	65,035.61
Total Current Assets	164,387.90
Fixed Assets	
Land	90,000.00
Buildings	325,000.00
Trucks	78,352.91
Computers	28,501.00
Furniture	7,325.00
Accumulated Depreciation	-121,887.78
Total Fixed Assets	407,291.13
Other Assets	
Pre-paid Insurance	1,041.85
Total Other Assets	1,041.85
TOTAL ASSETS	572,720.88
LIABILITIES & EQUITY	
Liabilities	
Current Liabilities	
Accounts Payable	
Accounts Payable	50,864.38

Accumulated depreciation account

Figure 29-1: The Balance Sheet reflects the value of a fixed asset as the original cost minus accumulated depreciation.

Proper valuation of fixed assets on a company's Balance Sheet involves tracking costs, accumulated depreciation, and depreciation expense.

Accounting for fixed assets and depreciation

When accounting for acquisition of a new fixed asset, it is recommended that you set up a parent account bearing the name of the fixed asset and add cost and accumulated depreciation subaccounts. The procedure to recognize cost and depreciation differs depending on whether the asset is acquired before or after the company's QuickBooks start date.

Setting up fixed asset, cost, and depreciation accounts

You may recall from Chapter 4 how a fixed asset is represented on the Balance Sheet. The asset is shown at its original cost less accumulated depreciation. The assets may also be presented as parent accounts and subaccounts. Take a look at how the accounts corresponding to the Balance Sheet presentation are set up.

To set up a fixed-asset parent account, follow these steps:

1. Go to Lists ⇨ Chart of Accounts to open the Chart of Accounts window.
2. Click the Account menu button at the lower left corner of the window. Choose New from the drop-down menu that appears. The New Account screen shown in Figure 29-2 appears.

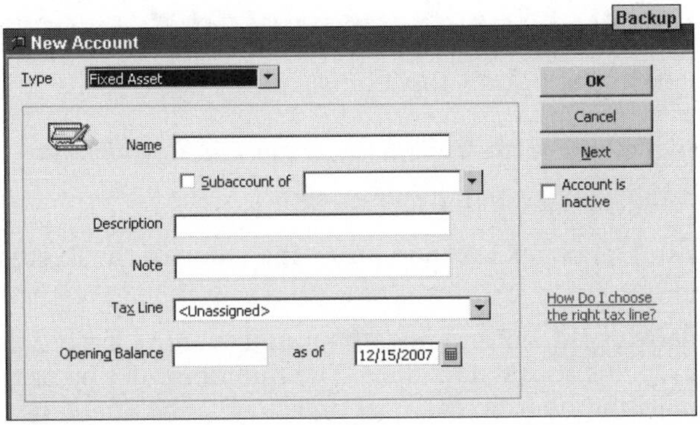

Figure 29-2: You use the New Account window to create fixed-asset accounts.

3. Using the drop-down menu in the Type field, enter Fixed Asset. Indicate whether the account is a subaccount in the check box provided.
4. Enter the name of the asset.
5. (Optional) Enter information in the Description and Note fields to help you track the asset.
6. In the Tax Line field, indicate a tax line to associate with this asset, or select Unassigned from the drop-down list. Do not enter any opening balance for the account, and verify the date in the As Of field.
7. Click Next so that you can proceed to create the subaccounts from this window.

To set up the cost subaccount in the previously opened New Account window, follow these steps:

1. In the Type field, enter Fixed Asset.
2. In the Name field, enter Cost.
3. Select the Subaccount Of check box and enter the name of the fixed-asset parent account.
4. Enter the original cost of the asset in the Opening Balance field if you purchased the asset prior to your QuickBooks start date. If you are acquiring the asset after your QuickBooks start date, leave this field at 0 for now.
5. Enter the date of purchase in the As Of field.
6. Click Next so that you can proceed to create the accumulated depreciation subaccount from this window.

Setting up an account for accumulated depreciation

To set up an accumulated depreciation subaccount, follow these steps:

1. Using the drop-down menu in the Type field, enter Fixed Asset.
2. In the Name field, enter Accumulated Depreciation.
3. Select the Subaccount Of check box and enter the name of the fixed-asset parent account.
4. In the Opening Balance field, enter a negative number if the asset was purchased before your QuickBooks start date. The number must be negative because it will be subtracted from the cost on the Balance Sheet. If you are purchasing the asset after your QuickBooks start date, leave the opening balance at 0.
5. Click Next so that you can proceed to create the depreciation expense subaccount from this window.

To create the depreciation expense subaccount, follow these steps:

1. In the Type field, enter Expense.
2. Enter a name for the account, such as **Depreciation Expense**.
3. In the Tax Line field, choose a tax line with which to associate this account or leave it designated as Unassigned.
4. Click OK to leave this window.

Acquiring fixed assets after the QuickBooks start date

If you acquire a new asset after your QuickBooks start date, you can enter the purchase transaction in the register of the account (for example, cash, credit, or accounts payable) that you used to purchase the asset. The register for the fixed-asset account is shown in Figure 29-3. In the Account field of the register, enter the name of the cost account that you created to show the original cost of the transaction.

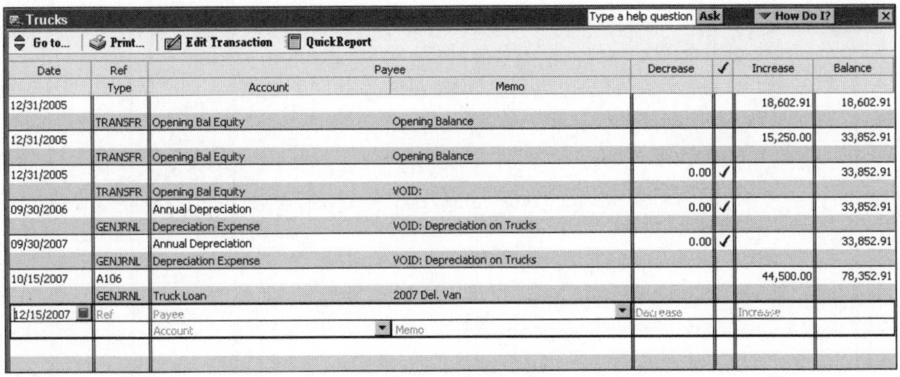

Figure 29-3: The register of a fixed-asset account.

Recording depreciation expense

There are several methods for calculating depreciation. The Internal Revenue Code sanctions certain methods depending on the type of asset. The methods used determine how many years it takes to fully depreciate the asset. The shorter the time period for depreciating the asset, the greater the expense and the less income that is reported to the IRS. Consult with your tax advisor to determine the depreciation method and the amount of the deduction to which you are entitled each year.

To record depreciation expense, follow these steps:

1. From the Lists menu, choose Chart of Accounts. Double-click the subaccount that tracks accumulated depreciation for the asset you're depreciating (for example, the Accumulated Depreciation account for a truck as shown in Figure 29-4).
2. Enter the transaction at the bottom of the register.
3. Enter the depreciation amount as a decrease in the register.
4. In the Account field, enter the expense account that you set up to track depreciation.
5. Record the entry.

   If you use a fixed-asset Item to track this asset, you can edit your fixed-asset Item and record that you've entered this depreciation transaction in the Notes field.

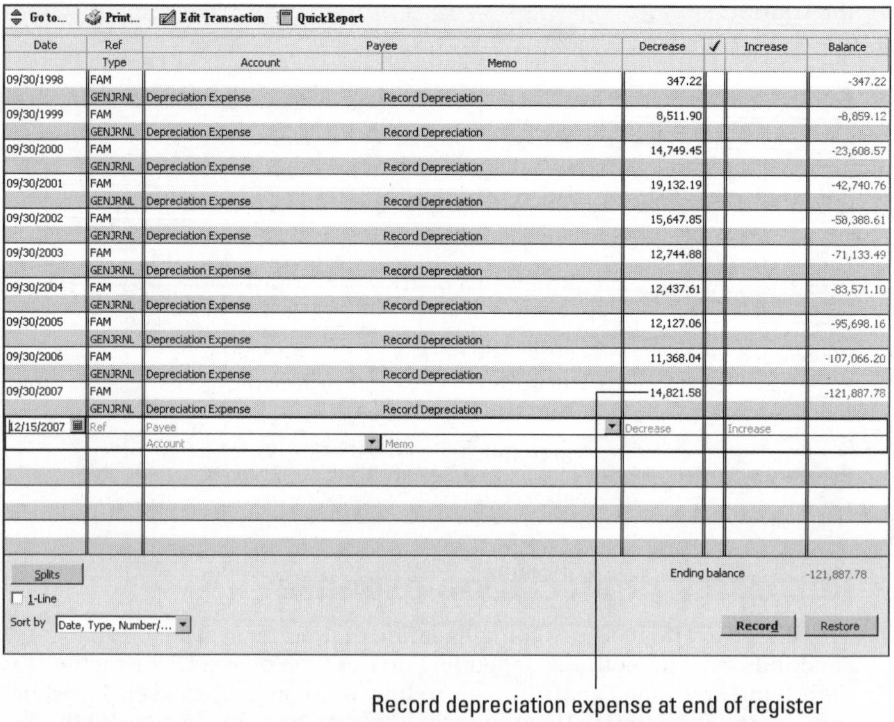

Go to... Print... Edit Transaction QuickReport
Date | Ref / Type | Payee / Account | Memo | Decrease | ✓ | Increase | Balance
09/30/1998 FAM GENJRNL Depreciation Expense Record Depreciation 347.22 -347.22
09/30/1999 FAM GENJRNL Depreciation Expense Record Depreciation 8,511.90 -8,859.12
09/30/2000 FAM GENJRNL Depreciation Expense Record Depreciation 14,749.45 -23,608.57
09/30/2001 FAM GENJRNL Depreciation Expense Record Depreciation 19,132.19 -42,740.76
09/30/2002 FAM GENJRNL Depreciation Expense Record Depreciation 15,647.85 -58,388.61
09/30/2003 FAM GENJRNL Depreciation Expense Record Depreciation 12,744.88 -71,133.49
09/30/2004 FAM GENJRNL Depreciation Expense Record Depreciation 12,437.61 -83,571.10
09/30/2005 FAM GENJRNL Depreciation Expense Record Depreciation 12,127.06 -95,698.16
09/30/2006 FAM GENJRNL Depreciation Expense Record Depreciation 11,368.04 -107,066.20
09/30/2007 FAM GENJRNL Depreciation Expense Record Depreciation 14,821.58 -121,887.78
12/15/2007 Ref Payee Decrease Increase
Account Memo
Splits
1-Line
Sort by Date, Type, Number/...
Ending balance -121,887.78
Record
Restore
Record depreciation expense at end of register

Figure 29-4: Record the depreciation expense in the Accumulated Depreciation account register for a fixed asset.

Selling a fixed asset

The sale of a fixed asset is an accounting event outside of the normal course of business. This transaction produces gain or loss, as opposed to income or loss from the operations of the business.

Accounting Jargon

When you sell a fixed asset, you must recognize either a capital gain or a capital loss. If you sell an asset for more than the original cost less accumulated depreciation, you recognize a *capital gain.* Selling an asset for less than its carrying value results in a *capital loss.*

To record the sale of an asset, follow these steps:

1. From the Company menu, choose Make General Journal Entries. The window shown in Figure 29-5 appears.

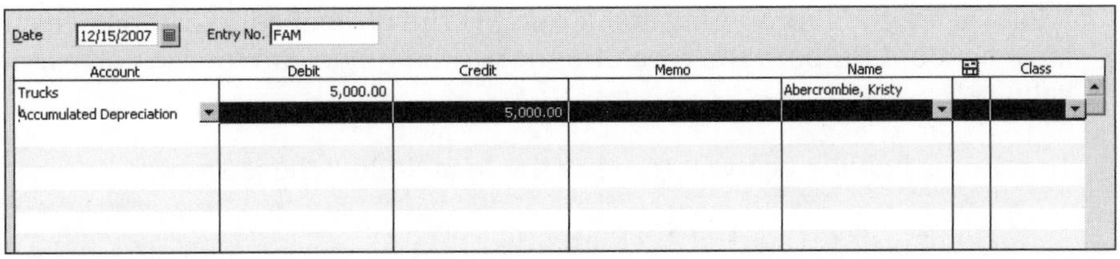

Figure 29-5: Enter journal entries to record the sale of fixed assets and adjust accumulated depreciation using this window.

2. From the Account drop-down list, choose the fixed-asset account or subaccount where you track the cost or starting value of the asset.
3. In the Credit field, enter the cost (or starting value) if you track depreciation in a separate asset account. Otherwise, enter the current book value of the asset as obtained from the QuickReport.
4. (Optional) In the Name field, enter the name of the asset.
5. If you track accumulated depreciation in a separate subaccount, follow these steps:
   a. In the Account column, choose the fixed-asset subaccount where you track the accumulated depreciation of the asset.
   b. In the Debit column, enter the total accumulated depreciation of the asset that you obtained from the QuickReport.
   c. (Optional) In the Name column, choose the name of the asset.
6. To enter the sales price of the asset, follow these steps:
   a. In the Account column, choose the bank account in which you deposited the money from the sale.

   b. In the Debit column, enter the actual amount that you deposited. This amount may be higher or lower than the current book value.
   c. (Optional) In the Name column, choose the name of the asset.
   d. Press Tab so that QuickBooks fills in the difference in the Debit or Credit field of the next line.
7. Enter the net gain or loss.
8. Save the entry using one of these options:
   - Click Save & Close to save the transaction and close the window.
   - Click Save & New to save the transaction and enter a new one.

Accounting for Borrowed Funds

A loan is another accounting event outside the normal course of business. You must account for both the receipt of borrowed funds and for the corresponding liability.

To set up a liability account to track the loan, follow these steps:

1. Go to Lists ➪ Chart of Accounts.
2. Click the Account button and choose New from the drop-down list.
3. In the Type field, enter Other Current Liability or Long-Term Liability depending on the term of the loan. The window shown in Figure 29-6 appears.

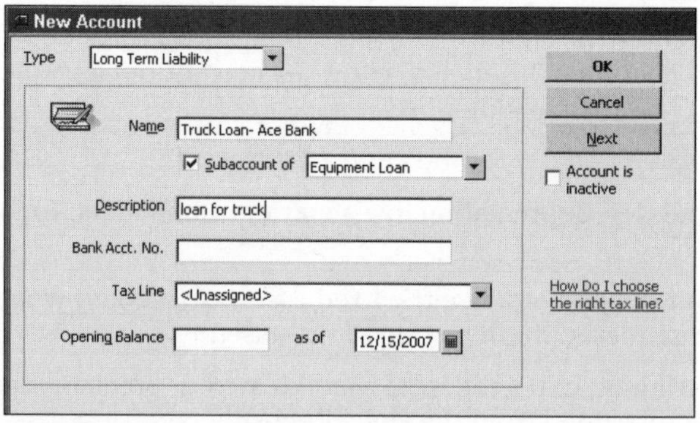

Figure 29-6: Use this window to set up the liability account to track a loan.

4. In the Tax Line field, associate a tax line with the account or indicate that it is Unassigned.

5. Enter the appropriate information in the Name, Subaccount Of, Description, and Bank Acct. No. fields.

6. If this is a new loan, enter **0** as the opening balance. If it is an account that was established prior to your QuickBooks start date and you are entering historical data, enter the current balance and the name for the loan account. You may also enter a description, if you wish.

To recognize receipt of the loan proceeds, follow these steps:

1. From the Chart of Accounts window, click the Activities menu button and select Make Deposits from the pop-up window. The window shown in Figure 29-7 appears.

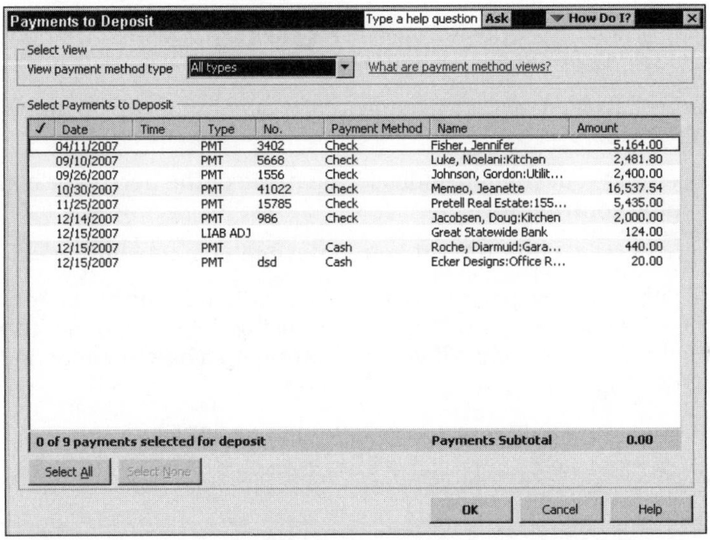

Figure 29-7: Use this window to record the receipt of loan proceeds.

2. Select the payment to deposit from the Payments to Deposit window, and click OK. The Make Deposits window appears.

3. Select the account into which you want to deposit the funds, and verify the transaction date (the current date appears by default).

4. In the Received From column, note from whom the amount was received.

5. In the Amount column, enter the amount of the loan.

6. In the From Account field, enter the name of the account that you created to track the loan.

7. Click Save & Close or Save & New.

Recording Capital Contributions

It takes money to make money, and generally it takes lots of capital to start a business. Usually these startup funds come from owners who receive an equity interest in the company.

Amounts contributed by the owners are called *capital contributions.*

To record capital contributions, follow these steps:

1. From the Chart of Accounts window, click the Activities menu button and select Make Deposits from the pop-up menu.
2. Select the payment to deposit from the Payments to Deposit window, and click Next. The Make Deposits window appears.
3. In the Deposit To field, enter the name of the account in which you will deposit the funds.
4. In the Received From column, indicate the name of the person or entity making the capital contribution.
5. In the Amount field, enter the amount of the capital contribution.
6. Enter the appropriate equity account to be credited in the From Account field. You may either choose an existing account using the scroll bar in this field or set up a new equity account. (If you are setting up a new account, indicate Equity as the Type.)
7. Fill in the payment method and check number as appropriate.
8. Click Save & Close or Save & New.

Recording Distributions to Owners

A distribution of capital to the owner of a company reduces the owner's equity account. Do not confuse a distribution of capital with payment of a salary. These are two different types of accounting transactions.

A distribution to the owners that is not attributable to salaries or wages is commonly referred to as a *draw.* A draw reduces the balance in the equity account. You must establish an account to track the draw and the transaction itself.

To set up an account to track draws, follow these steps:

1. Go to Lists ➪ Chart of Accounts.
2. Click the Account menu button and choose New from the pop-up menu.
3. Enter Equity in the Type field.

4. Enter a descriptive name for the account such as **Owner's Draws**.
5. (Optional) Enter any appropriate information in the Subaccount Of, Description, Note, and Tax Line fields.
6. Enter the opening balance for this account and complete the As Of date field if applicable.
7. Click OK.

To record an owner's draw, follow these steps:

1. From the Chart of Accounts window, click the Activities menu button and select Write Checks from the pop-up menu.
2. Select Bank Account and make the check payable to the owner receiving the distribution.
3. In the Account field, enter the name of the equity account you have set up to track owner's draws.
4. Enter the amount of the draw.
5. Click Save & Close or Save & New.

Summary

This chapter explored a series of Balance Sheet–related topics that are unrelated to the normal revenue-generating activities of the business. These topics require some knowledge of accounting principles, and hence they were labeled as "advanced."

✦ Depreciation refers to the process of expensing the cost of an asset over several years. The period over which the asset is depreciated reflects its normal, useful life.

✦ Borrowed funds are accounted for as an increase in cash and as a corresponding long- or short-term liability.

✦ The sale of a fixed asset results in a capital gain or loss. All asset accounts pertaining to the sold item (for example, cost and accumulated depreciation) must be reduced to zero.

✦ Contributed capital is a form of owner's equity and requires special accounting treatment.

✦ Withdrawals of capital by the owners (draws) also have a direct effect on the balances reflected in the equity accounts.

✦ ✦ ✦

CHAPTER 30

Reports and Graphs

Q uickBooks generates over 50 types of reports, and each report is a useful compilation of data derived from transactions that entered into the system. Reports range from summaries of transactions affecting a particular Item to complete financial statements disclosing the overall financial performance and value of a business.

In This Chapter

Standard reports and QuickReports

Report and graph preferences

The Report button bar

Memorizing and recalling report settings

Zooming in on reports and graphs

Tips for creating and reading graphs

A Tour of Reports

QuickBooks generates both standard reports and QuickReports. *Standard reports* provide a global view of some aspect of the business's value or performance. A *QuickReport* enables you to view transactions for a particular customer, vendor, or Item.

The standard reports submenus

Examples of standard reports include the Balance Sheet, a Profit and Loss Statement, a Sales Report, and an Accounts Receivable Aging Summary. All of these involve the compilation of information from accounts involving various customers, vendors, and Items. You generate these standard reports using the Reports menu and submenus, as shown in Figure 30-1. This chapter contains figures of the major submenus so that you can familiarize yourself with the basic structure of the submenus and more easily locate the reports you need, which are automatically available in QuickBooks whenever you decide to access them.

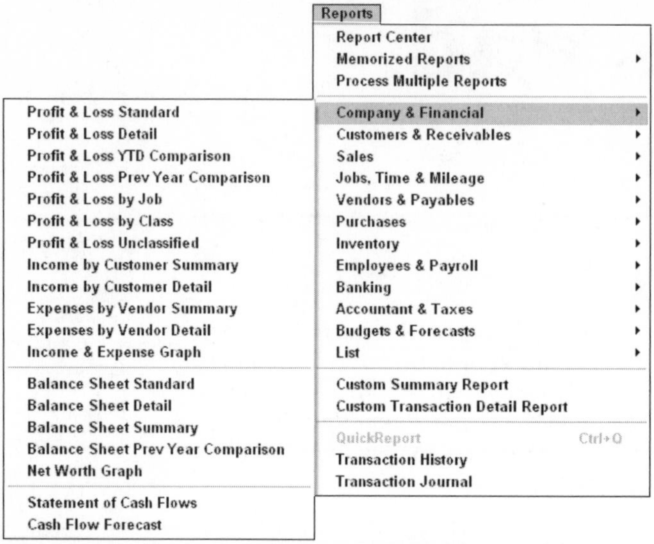

Figure 30-1: You can access dozens of reports and graphs from the toolbar.

You access Profit and Loss (P&L) reports from the Company & Financial submenu (see Figure 30-1). These reports include the following:

- ✦ Profit & Loss Standard
- ✦ Profit & Loss Detail
- ✦ Profit & Loss YTD Comparison
- ✦ Profit & Loss Prev Year Comparison
- ✦ Profit & Loss by Job
- ✦ Profit & Loss by Class
- ✦ Profit & Loss Unclassified
- ✦ Income by Customer Summary
- ✦ Income by Customer Detail
- ✦ Expenses by Vendor Summary
- ✦ Expenses by Vendor Detail

You also access Balance Sheet reports from the Company & Financial submenu (see Figure 30-1). Balance sheet reports include the following:

- Standard
- Detail
- Summary
- Prev Year Comparison

You can access information about your accounts receivable, customer balances, and collections from the Customers & Receivables submenu as shown in Figure 30-2.

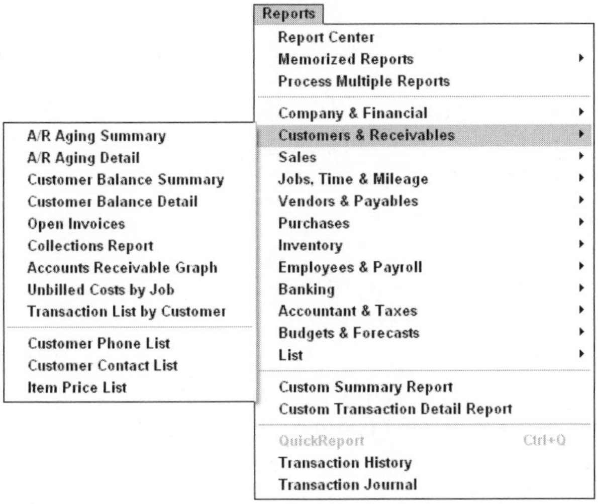

Figure 30-2: The Customers & Receivables submenu.

The reports available on this submenu are as follows:

- Accounts Receivable (A/R) Aging Summary
- A/R Aging Detail
- Customer Balance Summary
- Customer Balance Detail
- Open Invoices
- Collections Report
- Unbilled Costs by Job
- Transaction List by Customer

You can access Sales reports from the Sales submenu shown in Figure 30-3.

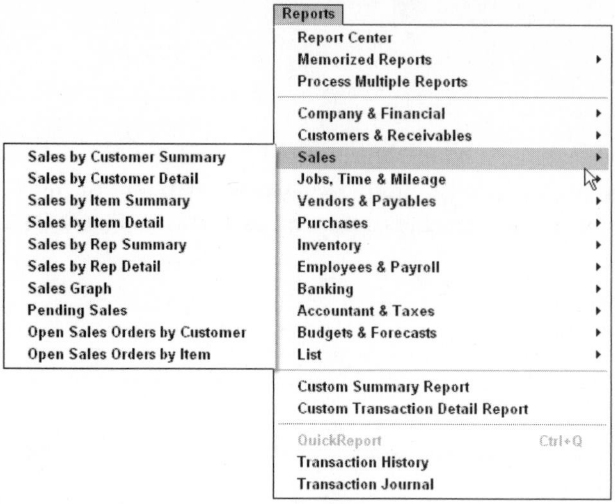

Figure 30-3: The Sales submenu.

The reports available on this submenu are as follows:

- ✦ Sales by Customer Summary
- ✦ Sales by Customer Detail
- ✦ Sales by Item Summary
- ✦ Sales by Rep Summary
- ✦ Sales by Item Detail
- ✦ Sales by Rep Detail
- ✦ Pending Sales
- ✦ Open Sales Orders by Customer
- ✦ Open Sales Orders by Item

You can access the following Accounts Payable (A/P) and Vendor reports from the Vendors & Payables submenu shown in Figure 30-4.

The reports available on this submenu are as follows:

- ✦ A/P Aging Summary
- ✦ A/P Aging Detail
- ✦ Vendor Balance Summary
- ✦ Vendor Balance Detail
- ✦ Unpaid Bills Detail
- ✦ Transaction List by Vendor

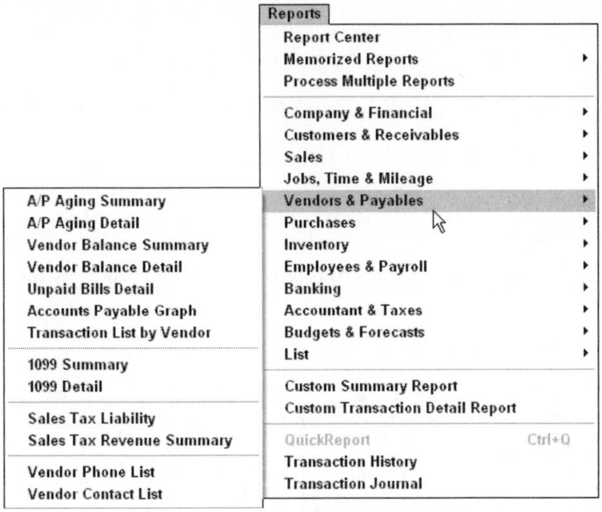

Figure 30-4: The Vendors & Payables submenu.

You can get reports about your purchases in a variety of ways from the Purchases submenu, shown in Figure 30-5.

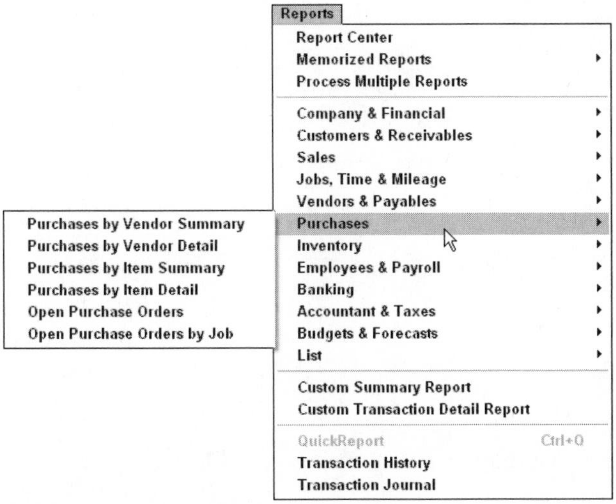

Figure 30-5: The Purchases submenu.

This submenu gives you access to the following reports:

- Purchases by Vendor Summary
- Purchases by Vendor Detail
- Purchases by Item Summary
- Purchases by Item Detail
- Open Purchase Orders
- Open Purchase Orders by Job

You can access various reports about your inventory from the Inventory submenu shown in Figure 30-6.

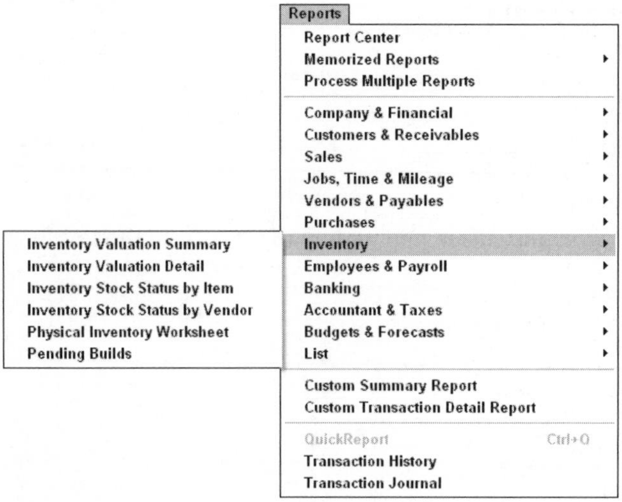

Figure 30-6: The Inventory submenu.

You can access the following from this submenu:

- Inventory Valuation Summary
- Inventory Valuation Detail
- Inventory Stock Status by Item
- Inventory Stock Status by Vendor
- Physical Inventory Worksheet
- Pending Builds

Reports that help you track and manage employees

Payroll and employee management can be time-consuming functions, complicated by a full range of daily human variables. QuickBooks offers you the following reports:

- ✦ Payroll Summary
- ✦ Payroll Item Detail
- ✦ Payroll Detail Review
- ✦ Employee Earnings Summary
- ✦ Employee State Taxes Detail
- ✦ Payroll Transactions by Payee
- ✦ Payroll Transaction Detail
- ✦ Payroll Liability Balances

You access these reports from the Employees & Payroll submenu shown in Figure 30-7.

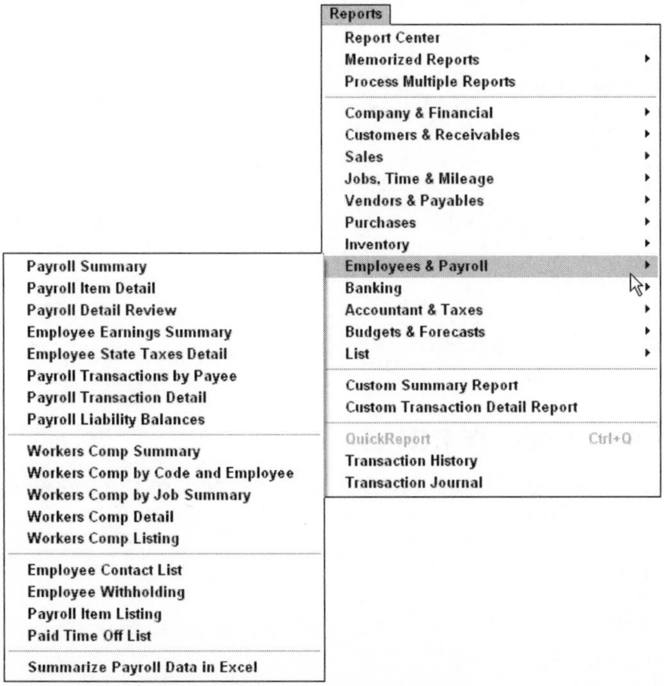

Figure 30-7: Employee and Payroll reports.

Banking and reconciliation reports

QuickBooks provides you with the following banking and reconciliation reports:

✦ Deposit Detail

✦ Check Detail

✦ Missing Checks

✦ Reconciliation Discrepancy

✦ Previous Reconciliation

You access these reports from the Banking Report submenu shown in Figure 30-8.

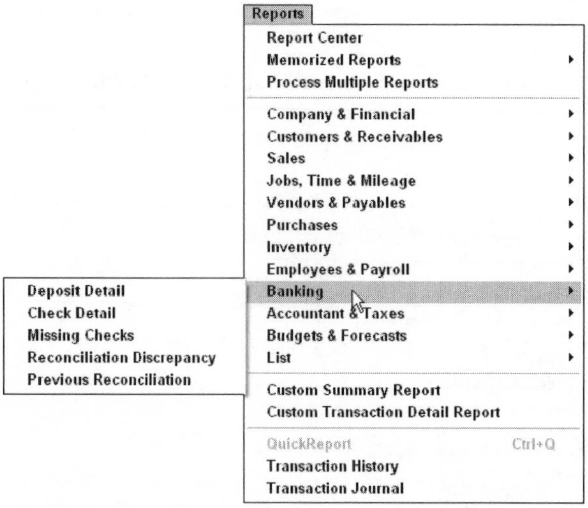

Figure 30-8: Banking and Reconciliation reports.

Jobs, time, and mileage reports

If you have QuickBooks Pro or QuickBooks Premier, you can access the following reports:

✦ Job Profitability Summary

✦ Job Profitability Detail

✦ Job Estimates vs. Actuals Summary

✦ Job Estimates vs. Actuals Detail

✦ Job Progress Invoices vs. Estimates

✦ Item Profitability
✦ Item Estimates vs. Actuals
✦ Profit & Loss by Job
✦ Estimates by Job
✦ Unbilled Costs by Job
✦ Open Purchase Orders by Job
✦ Time by Job Summary
✦ Time by Job Detail
✦ Time by Name
✦ Time by Item
✦ Mileage by Vehicle Summary
✦ Mileage by Vehicle Detail
✦ Mileage by Job Summary
✦ Mileage by Job Detail

These reports are available on the Jobs, Time & Mileage submenu, shown in Figure 30-9.

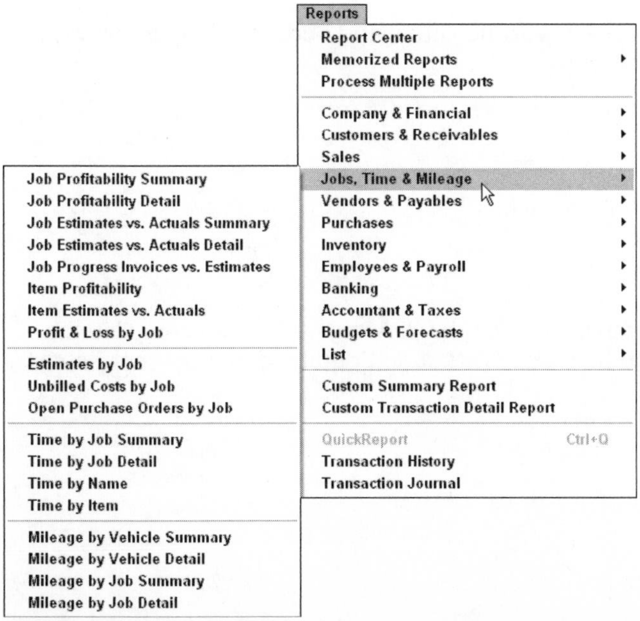

Figure 30-9: The Jobs, Time & Mileage submenu.

Accountant and taxes

The Accountant & Taxes submenu contains the following reports designed to help you track account balances and perform essential accounting functions:

- Trial Balance
- General Ledger
- Transaction Detail by Account
- Journal
- Audit Trail
- Voided/Deleted Transactions
- Voided/Deleted Transactions History
- Transactions List by Date
- Account Listing
- Fixed Asset Listing
- Income Tax Preparation
- Income Tax Summary

Budgets

QuickBooks presents and compares the actual and budgeted data to provide you with the following types of reports:

- Budget Overview
- Budget vs. Actual
- Profit & Loss Budget Performance

Lists

The List submenu offers you access to the following useful data compilations and QuickBooks organizational features that don't quite fit on the other Report submenus:

- Account Listing
- Item Price List
- Item Listing
- Payroll Item Listing
- Customer Phone List

- Customer Contact List
- Vendor Phone List
- Vendor Contact List
- Employee Contact List
- Other Names Phone List
- Other Names Contact List
- Terms Listing
- To Do Notes
- Memorized Transaction Listing

Generating QuickReports

A QuickReport provides you with a list of transactions involving one specific Item, vendor, or customer. You can generate QuickReports in two ways: from the Lists menu or directly from a form. To create a QuickReport from a Customer:Job, Vendor, or Item List, follow these steps:

1. Click the Quick Report link on the Vendors tab of the Vendor Center page, shown in Figure 30-10.

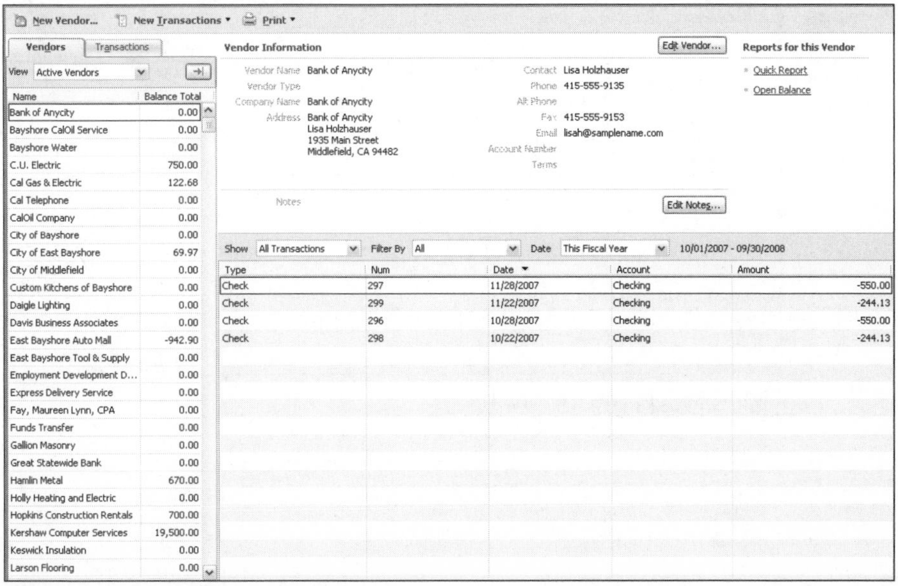

Figure 30-10: Generating a QuickReport.

2. Go to the Customer Center screen and click the Quick Report icon in the upper left hand corner.
3. Select the customer, Item, or vendor for which you want to generate a QuickReport.
4. (For Items only) Click the Reports menu button at the bottom of the window as shown in Figure 30-11.
5. Select QuickReport from the pop-up menu. A report such as the one shown in Figure 30-12 appears.

You can also create a QuickReport while you are preparing or viewing any form that has a name field by clicking the customer or vendor name and then going to Reports ➪ QuickReport.

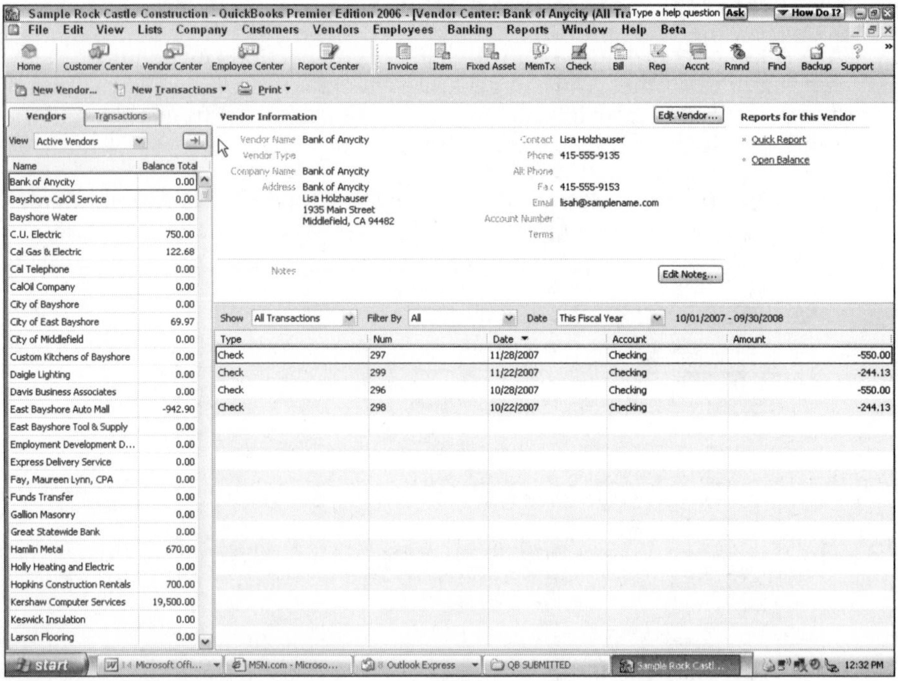

Figure 30-11: The Reports menu.

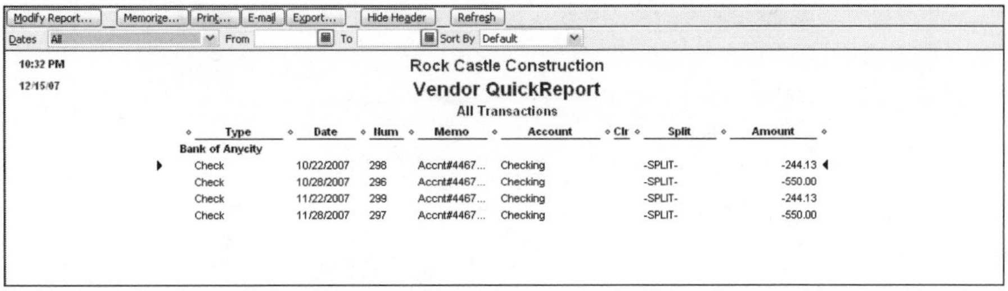

Figure 30-12: A sample Vendor QuickReport.

Report Terminology

QuickBooks reports are of two main types:

✦ **Summary reports:** These summarize amounts and do not list specific transactions. You can display this type of report in either the cash or the accrual basis.

✦ **Transaction detail report:** This type of report summarizes the detail associated with individual transactions. Accrual-basis transaction detail reports show a single amount for each transaction, because revenue and obligations are recognized at the time the transaction is initiated. Cash-basis transaction detail reports show two amounts for each transaction, because the initiation of the transaction is recorded separately from payment.

Cross-Reference

Review Chapter 4 for a comprehensive explanation of cash-basis versus accrual-basis accounting.

Report and Graph Preferences

The report and graph preferences that you select determine both how QuickBooks calculates the amounts that appear on reports and how QuickBooks displays them. To access the report and graphs Preferences window, go to Edit ➪ Preferences. Select the Reports & Graphs icon from the scroll box on the left and then click the My Preferences or Company Preferences tab to access the windows shown in Figures 30-13 and 30-14.

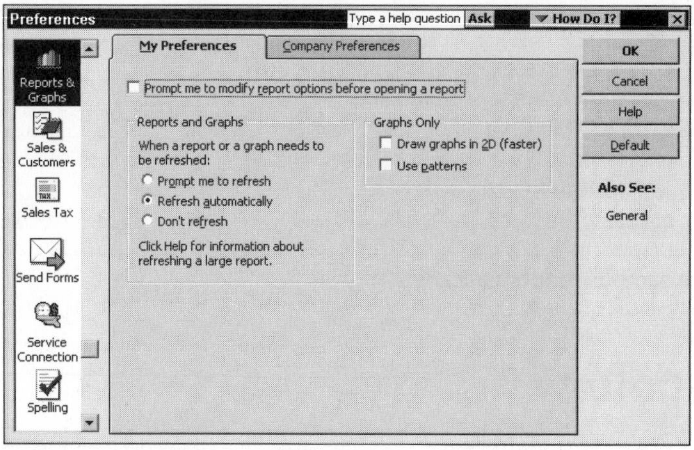

Figure 30-13: Preferences for updating (refreshing) information on reports and graphs.

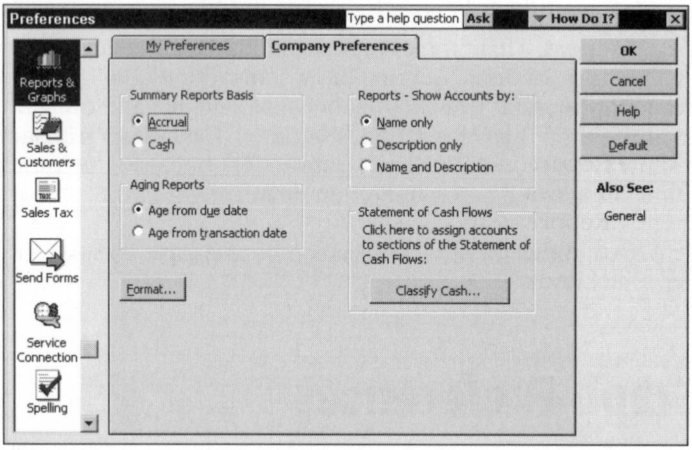

Figure 30-14: Report and graph preferences for cash versus accrual and aging.

Refreshing information on reports and graphs

This option, which appears on the My Preferences tab (previously shown in Figure 30-13), allows you to specify whether you want QuickBooks to automatically update (refresh) information on reports as you perform new transactions. You have the option of automatically updating the reports, receiving a prompt to refresh, or not updating the reports.

Cash versus accrual

The Cash and Accrual options are available on the Company Preferences tab previously shown in Figure 30-14. Regardless of which preference you select, you can customize individual reports as you generate them. If you select Accrual, QuickBooks automatically displays income and expenses as of the date the transaction is initiated by a bill, invoice, or statement. If you select Cash, summary reports reflect income as of the date payment is received and expenses as of the date paid.

This preference affects only summary reports. It does not affect transaction reports, which are always displayed on an accrual basis. Transaction detail reports are automatically displayed on an accrual basis regardless of the preference setting, but you can customize them to display on a cash basis.

Aging options

You are given the option of displaying aging reports in two ways. You can display reports that begin aging transactions either as of the date that they are due or from the date that the transaction is initiated. This option determines when QuickBooks starts counting the days reflected on the aging reports.

Modify Reports window

All reports have a Modify Report button in the upper left corner of the Report screen. Click this button to access the powerful Modify Report dialog box (see Figure 30-15). The Modify Report options in this dialog box vary with the type of Report. The options shown in the dialog box allow you to change the appearance and data contained in QuickBooks reports.

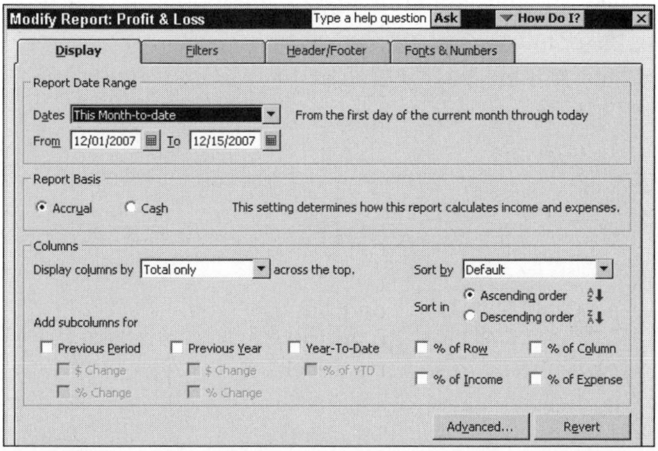

Figure 30-15: The Modify Report dialog box includes a number of options to help you determine how your report will appear.

The four tabs in the Modify Report dialog box are as follows:

✦ **Display:** Includes options for the date range, whether a cash basis or an accrual basis is used for the report, how columns and subcolumns in the report are displayed and organized, and how data is sorted (see Figure 30-15).

✦ **Filters:** The filtering options, shown in Figure 30-16, allow you to specify the type of data included in the report and which accounts are to be searched for the relevant data.

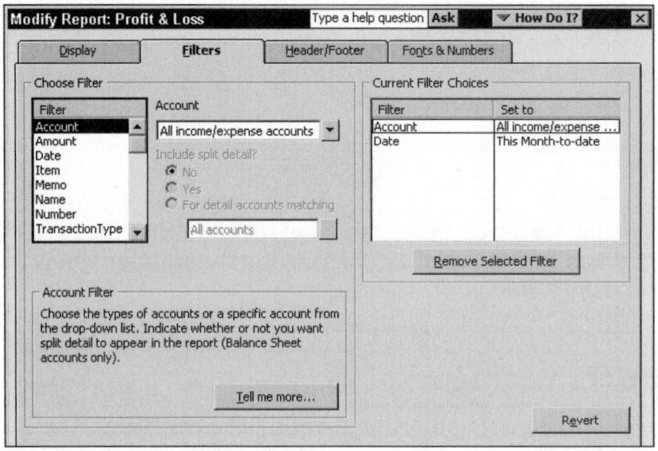

Figure 30-16: QuickBooks allows you to filter selective data to appear on your reports.

✦ **Header/Footer:** Options under this tab, shown in Figure 30-17, allow you to specify the appearance and format of the header and footer on your report.

✦ **Fonts & Numbers:** This tab, shown in Figure 30-18, contains additional options for displaying the fonts and numerical detail of your report.

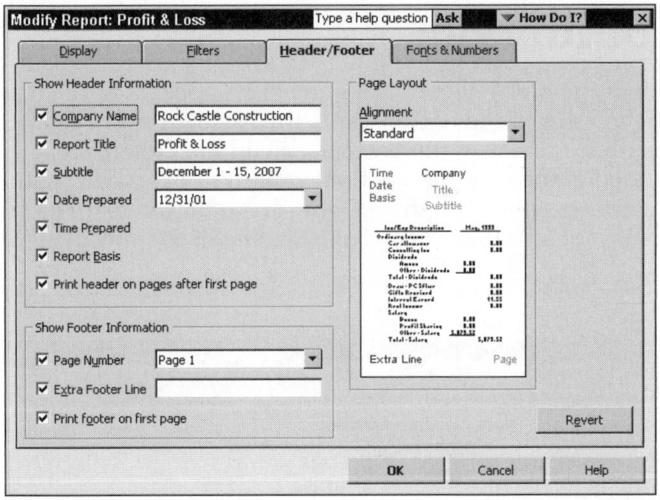

Figure 30-17: Specify the contents and appearance of headers and footers that appear on your reports.

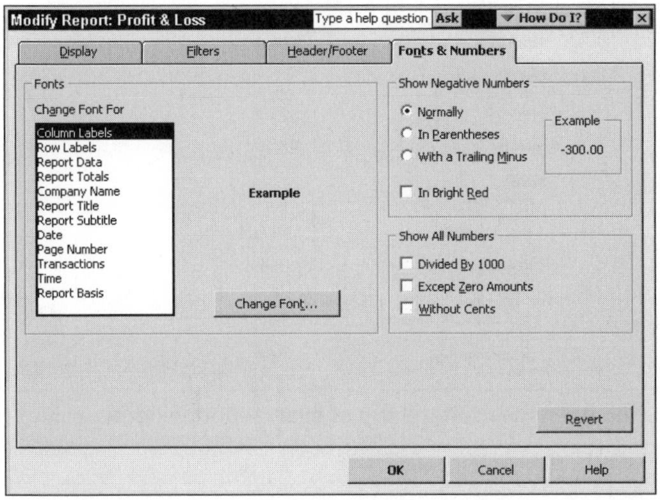

Figure 30-18: Customize fonts and numerical detail displayed on your reports.

The Report Button Bar

A button bar, such as the one depicted in Figure 30-19, appears at the top of every report screen. The top row of the button bar is the same for every report. The bottom row varies by report. Many of the buttons call up the Preferences windows discussed and illustrated in the previous section. Table 30-1 is a partial list of button bar functions that always appear on the top row of the button bar. The second row of the button bar may include date range fields and fields for specifying what columns appear.

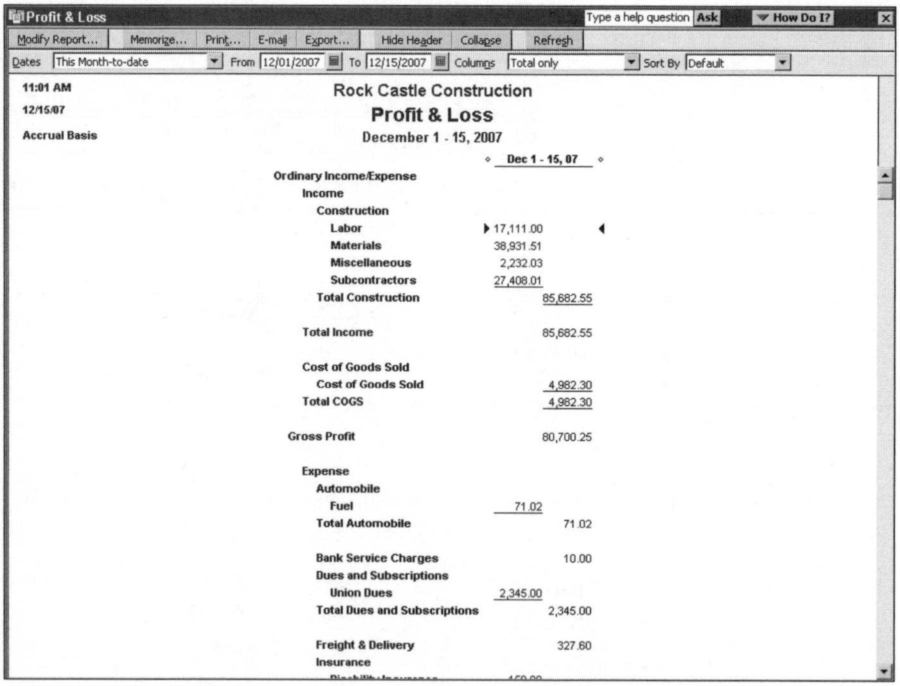

Figure 30-19: A button bar appears at the top of every report window.

Table 30-1 **Standard Report Button Bar Functions**	
Button	***Function***
Modify Report	Brings up the Modify Report window (see Figures 3-14 to 3-17)
Memorize	Enables you to memorize the settings for a report as discussed in the next section
Print	Allows you to print a report or save it to a file from the screen

Button	Function
E-mail	E-mails a copy of the report to a designated recipient
Export	Brings up the filter criteria window
Format	Brings up the window used for font choice and number display
Hide or Show Header	Enables you to either display the header or hide it to increase the room available for information on the report
Collapse or Expand	Enables you to specify the amount of transaction detail shown on a report; can be used to make a summary or standard report even more compact
Refresh	Refreshes the screen and updates transaction data consistent with the preferences you selected, as discussed earlier in the chapter

Memorizing and Recalling Reports

When you memorize a report, what you are actually memorizing are the customized settings and filter criteria — not the transactions themselves. For example, assume you want to create a report of transactions involving a certain Item from a specific date to the present, and you want to set up columns showing percentages of gross sales. The format for this report is the same each time you recall it, but the transactions are updated.

To memorize a customized report format and/or filtering criteria, follow these steps:

1. After you customize a report, click Memorize on the button bar (previously shown in Figure 30-19). The dialog box shown in Figure 30-20 appears.

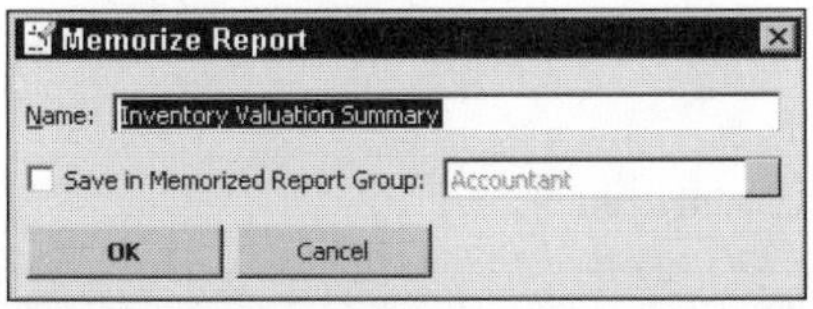

Figure 30-20: Save your memorized format and filtering criteria under a unique name using this dialog box.

2. If you have changed an existing memorized report, indicate whether you want QuickBooks to replace the earlier report (under the same name) or create a new memorized report (under a new name).
3. In the Memorize Report window, enter a title for the report.
4. (Optional) Indicate whether you want to save the report as part of a related group of reports. (Doing so allows you to access and modify all of the reports in the group more easily.)
5. Click OK.

To recall a memorized transaction, follow these steps:

1. Go to Reports ➪ Memorized Reports. The Memorized Report List submenu shown in Figure 30-21 appears.
2. Select the report that you want to recall from the submenu.

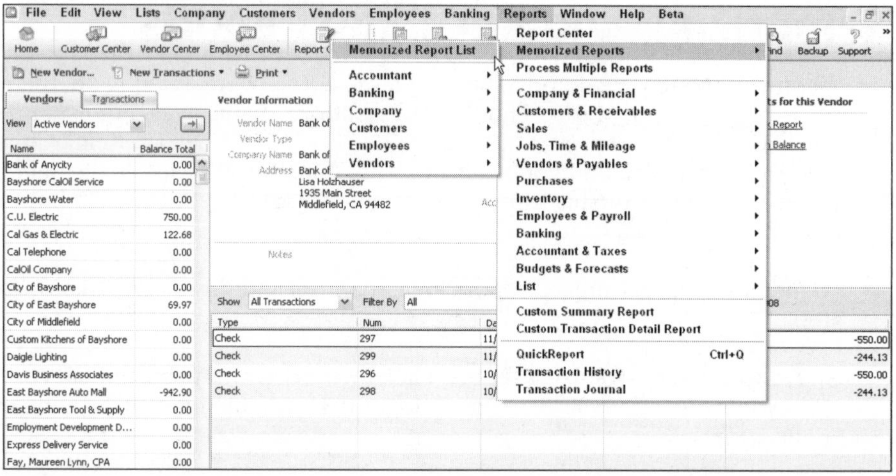

Figure 30-21: Use this submenu to access the list of previously memorized reports.

If you want to edit the report, follow these steps:

1. Go to Reports ➪ Memorized Reports. A list of memorized reports appears as shown in Figure 30-22.
2. Double-click the report you want to modify. The previously memorized report appears on-screen.
3. Edit the report, making any needed changes.
4. Click Memorize. You'll receive the message, "The report you are memorizing is a memorized report. Would you like to replace the original memorized report or create a new one?"

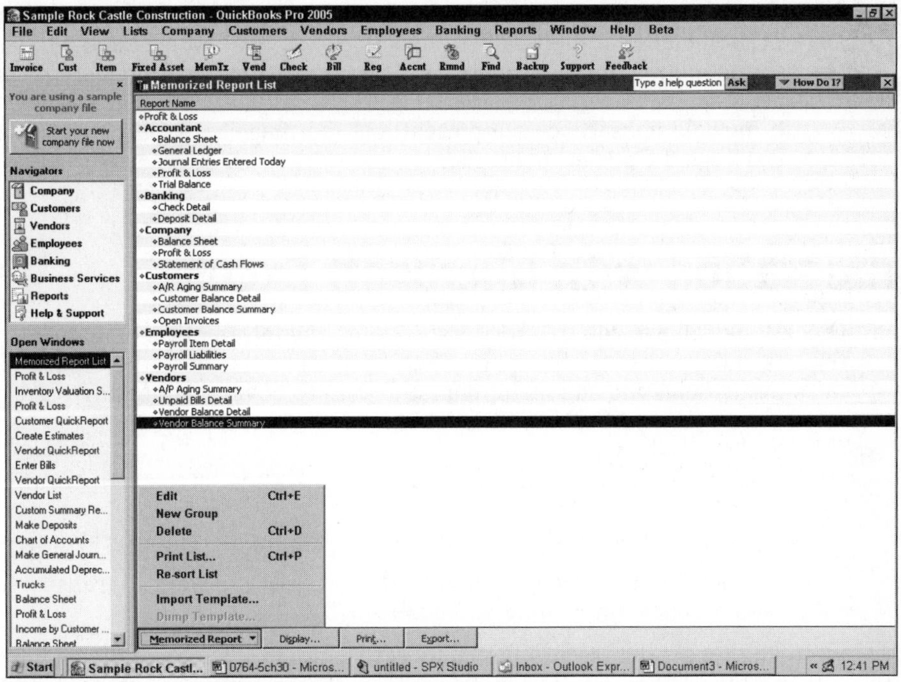

Figure 30-22: A list of previously memorized reports.

5. To replace the original memorized report and use the same name, click Replace.
6. To create a new memorized report with a new name, click New.
7. Assign a name to the report.
8. Click OK.

Caution

Be sure to change the name so that you can identify the new report in the list. You also have the option to Save in Memorized Report Group and choose a report group from the drop-down list.

Zooming In on Reports and Graphs

The Zoom function is a useful and innovative program feature that allows you to see the underlying transactions that make up any number shown on a report. Simply move the mouse pointer over the amount you want to analyze.

As you move your mouse pointer over a report, you'll see the pointer change to the symbol of a magnifying glass. This is called the QuickZoom symbol. Whenever you see this symbol, you can double-click the amount. A new report appears that lists the individual transactions from which QuickBooks calculated the summary amount. If the amount is a single transaction, you can double-click it to see that transaction in its original form, for example, an invoice or a payment receipt.

Tip If multiple transactions are present, put the magnifying glass over any one and you'll see the original transaction

Integration with Microsoft Excel

QuickBooks allows you to effortlessly "pour" the information contained in its reports and graphs into Microsoft Excel spreadsheets. Once the report data is on the spreadsheet, you can manipulate the data to cover a wide range of assumptions and formats as your business needs dictate.

To transfer report data to Microsoft Excel, follow these steps:

1. Click the Export button that appears at the top of the report window.
2. On the screen that appears, indicate whether you want to transfer the report data to a new or existing spreadsheet.

   The report data is automatically converted to a Microsoft Excel spreadsheet, and the Microsoft Excel program is opened simultaneously from within QuickBooks, as shown in Figure 30-23.

	A–F	Type	Date	Num	Name	Memo	Class
1		Type	Date	Num	Name	Memo	Class
2	Ordinary Income/Expense						
3	Income						
4	Construction						
5	Labor						
6		Invoice	10/05/2007	40	Teschner, Anton:Sun Room	Removal labor, removed shed and graded area for su	
7		Sales Receipt	10/15/2007	3	Natiello, Ernesto:Kitchen	Removal labor	
8		Invoice	10/15/2007	42	Cook, Brian:Kitchen	Removal labor	
9		Invoice	10/15/2007	42	Cook, Brian:Kitchen	Framing labor	
10		Invoice	10/15/2007	42	Cook, Brian:Kitchen	Installation labor	
11		Invoice	10/15/2007	43	Teichman, Tim:Kitchen	Removal labor	
12		Invoice	10/15/2007	43	Teichman, Tim:Kitchen	Framing labor	
13		Invoice	10/15/2007	43	Teichman, Tim:Kitchen	Installation labor	
14		Invoice	10/23/2007	44	Jacobsen, Doug:Kitchen	Installation labor	
15		Sales Receipt	10/25/2007	4		Removal labor - cleaned up backyard in preparation f	
16		Sales Receipt	10/25/2007	4		Installation labor - installed new deck	
17		Invoice	10/26/2007	46	Pretell Real Estate:155 Wilks Blvd.	Framing labor	
18		Invoice	10/26/2007	46	Pretell Real Estate:155 Wilks Blvd.	Installation labor	
19		Sales Receipt	10/30/2007	6		Removal labor	
20		Invoice	10/30/2007	50	Cook, Brian:Kitchen	Framing labor	
21		Invoice	10/30/2007	48	Pretell Real Estate:155 Wilks Blvd.	Removal labor	
22		Invoice	10/30/2007	49	Cook, Brian:2nd story addition	Removal labor	
23		Invoice	10/30/2007	50	Cook, Brian:Kitchen	Installation labor	
24		Invoice	11/15/2007	51	Pretell Real Estate:155 Wilks Blvd.	Framing labor	
25		Invoice	11/20/2007	82	Melton, Johnny:Dental office	Installation labor	
26		Invoice	11/25/2007	57	Cook, Brian:Kitchen	Removal labor	
27		Invoice	11/25/2007	57	Cook, Brian:Kitchen	Framing labor	
28		Invoice	11/25/2007	57	Cook, Brian:Kitchen	Installation labor	
29		Invoice	11/25/2007	59	Jacobsen, Doug:Kitchen	Installation labor	
30		Invoice	11/25/2007	59	Jacobsen, Doug:Kitchen	Framing labor	
31		Invoice	11/25/2007	75	Burch, Jason:Room Addition	Installation labor	

Figure 30-23: You can open Microsoft Excel and create a spreadsheet like this one directly, simply by clicking the button at the top of the report window.

Tip Click the tab QuickBooks Export Tips at the bottom of the Excel window to view useful tips about creating spreadsheets and exporting data.

The Graph QuickZoom Function

A picture may be worth a thousand words, but sometimes it's nice to know how many thousands your picture is worth. QuickBooks lets you do this. You can access a number of graphs from the Reports menu. Figure 30-24 shows an Accounts Receivable Graph.

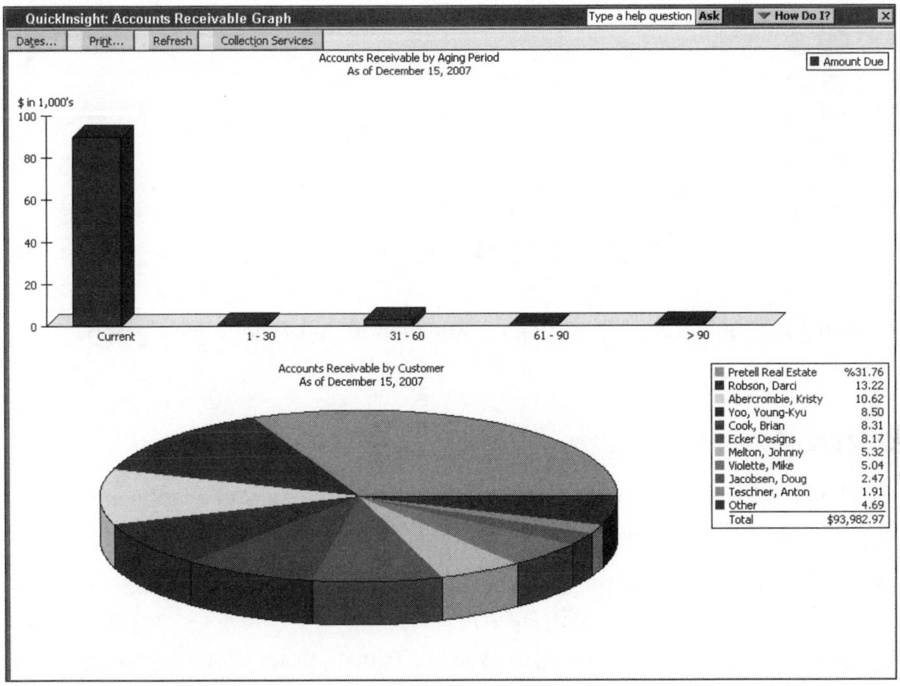

Figure 30-24: A sample Accounts Receivable Graph.

With a click of the mouse on a portion of the graph, you can see a more detailed QuickZoom graph, representing that portion of the graph, as shown in Figure 30-25.

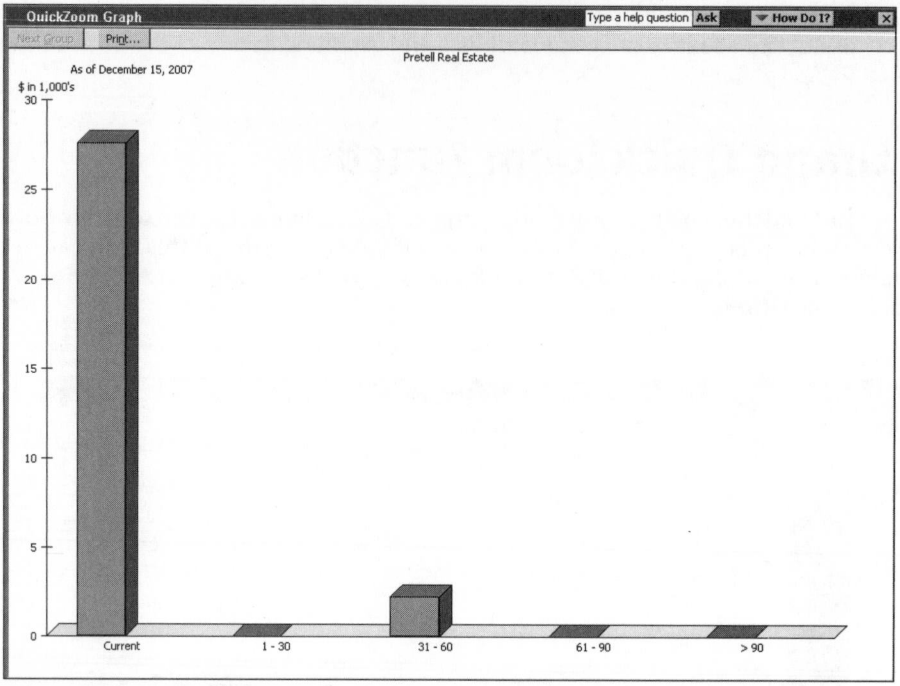

Figure 30-25: A QuickZoom graph representing a portion of the original graph.

Summary

QuickBooks allows you to create over 50 types of reports and graphs and to customize them to your liking. The possibilities are endless!

✦ Standard reports are the traditional reporting forms used to convey business performance and net worth for a selected period.

✦ QuickReports provide you with a list of transactions that affect specific customers, vendors, or Items.

✦ Summary reports summarize transaction totals and can be shown on either a cash or an accrual basis.

✦ Transaction reports list specific transactions and are always shown on an accrual basis. Transaction detail reports provide more information and detail and can be shown on a cash or an accrual basis.

- Reports can be customized and formatted to display the information you specify in the way that you want to see it. You can memorize and recall report formats that you have created.
- The Zoom function allows you to see the underlying transactions that make up a number shown on a report or a section of a graph.

✦ ✦ ✦

CHAPTER 31

Budgets

In This Chapter

Setting up budgets

Budget reports

Customizing budgets

Changing budgets

Grouping data

Using graphs to compare budgeted and actual performance

Budgets are like diets — they only work well if you adhere to them. Instead of calories and fat grams, QuickBooks monitors income and expenses. And at the end of the fiscal period, you don't step on a scale; you produce a vivid graphic representation comparing budgeted and actual performance. It's a compelling moment of truth!

Setting Up Your Budget and Defining Your Goals

The QuickBooks budgets enable you to compare your company's projected performance to the actual results. You can prepare a budget based on anticipated amounts for the following:

- Individual account balances
- Customer:Job revenue and expenses
- Revenue and expense amounts for a particular class

You can create budgets for either Profit and Loss or Balance Sheet accounts, but they must be account-based. You can create a budget from scratch, from actual data from the previous fiscal year, or from the previous fiscal year's budget. A particular budget is uniquely identified by its fiscal year and the account type (either Profit and Loss or Balance Sheet), and if desired, it can be further identified by Customer:Job or Class.

Creating a Budget

After you have decided what type of information you want to compare by using a budget, you can set up a budget for your company by following these steps:

Tip You can set up specific budgets by Customer:Job or Class.

1. From the Company menu, choose Planning and Budgeting, and then select Set Up Budgets.

   If a budget currently exists, the most recent budget will be displayed in the Set Up Budgets window; otherwise, a window containing default data from prior years appears, such as the one shown in Figure 31-1.

2. Click Create New Budget. The dialog box shown in Figure 31-2 appears.

3. In the Create New Budget dialog box, choose the fiscal year for the new budget, and then choose Profit and Loss (income and expense) or Balance Sheet accounts, and click Next.

4. If you choose Profit and Loss, you can specify additional criteria of either Customer:Job or Class, if class tracking has been turned on. If you choose Balance Sheet, no additional criteria can be specified, so click Finish to create the budget.

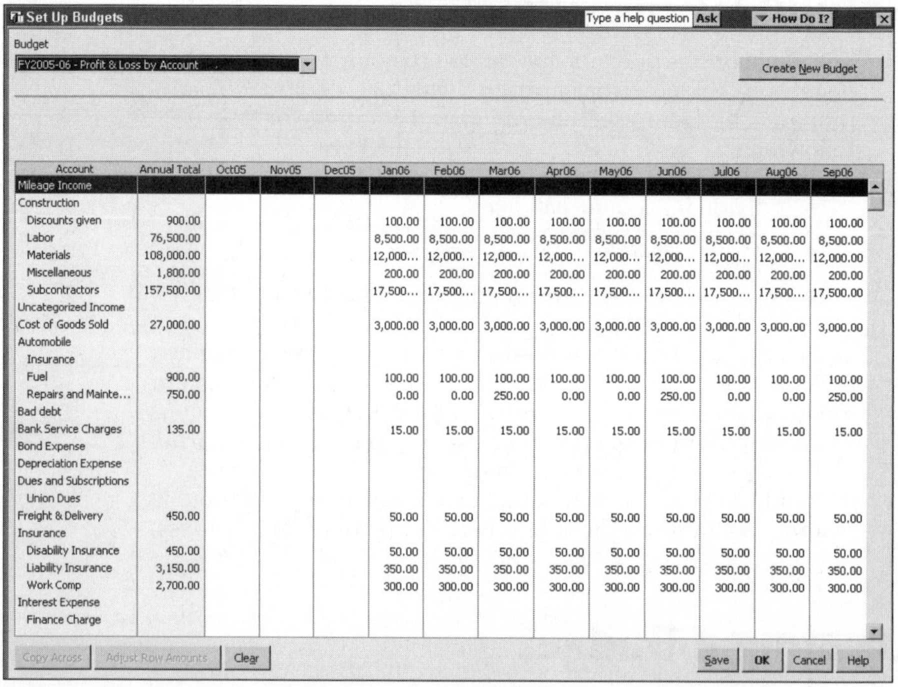

Figure 31-1: Default data used to create a budget for a particular account.

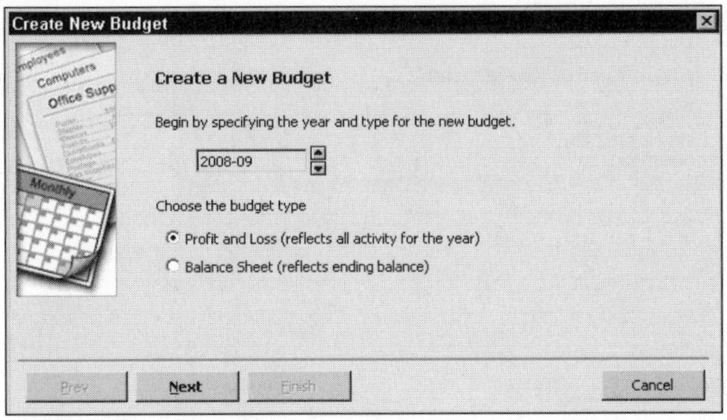

Figure 31-2: This dialog box takes you through the steps for creating a new budget.

5. Choose whether you want to create the budget from scratch or from the previous year's actual data. If you choose to create the budget from scratch (as discussed in the next section), you must manually enter amounts for each account that you want to track. If you create the budget from the previous year's actual data, QuickBooks automatically enters the monthly totals from last year for each account in the budget.
6. Click Finish to create the new budget.

Budgeting for a Customer:Job

QuickBooks enables you to set up a budget for a particular Customer:Job, which is to reflect all the accounts included within that particular Customer:Job. You can set up a budget for each Customer:Job on your company's list. To set up a budget for a specific Customer:Job, follow these steps:

1. From the Company menu, choose Planning & Budgeting, then Set Up Budgets, and then click Create New Budget.
2. In the Create New Budget dialog box, choose the fiscal year for the new budget; then choose Profit and Loss (income and expense) accounts.
3. Select Customer:Job in the dialog box that appears, as shown in Figure 31-3.
4. Choose whether you want to create the budget from scratch or from the previous year's actual data.
5. Click Finish to create the new budget.

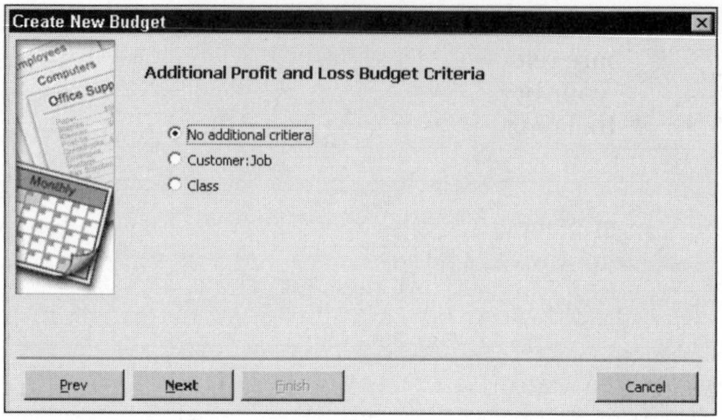

Figure 31-3: Setting up a budget with Customer:Job detail.

Budgeting by class

Budgeting by class can give you unique insight as to the performance of your company's various sectors, divisions, or activities. It is a useful tool for planning and analyzing your company's performance in critical areas. To create a Budget by Class, follow these steps:

1. From the Company menu, choose Planning & Budgeting and then Set Up Budgets. If a budget currently exists, the most recent budget is displayed in the Set Up Budgets window; otherwise a window containing default data from prior periods appears (previously shown in Figure 31-1).
2. Click Create New Budget. The Create New Budget dialog box appears.
3. Select the year and type of budget that you want to create, and click Next.
4. Select Class from the dialog box that appears (previously shown in Figure 31-3), and click Next.
5. Choose whether you want to create the new budget from scratch or from the previous year's actual data.
6. Click Finish.
7. In the Set Up Budgets window, choose the class from the Class drop-down list.
8. Enter or modify the budget amounts, and then click Save.

Budget Reports

QuickBooks offers you the option of either using preset budget reports or creating a customized budget report. You'll probably find it useful to co-opt the best of both worlds and start with a preset report, customizing it to your liking.

QuickBooks allows you to create a number of reports from budget data, the terms of which allow you to compare relevant information at a glance and instantly understand the economic trends your business is experiencing. To create and view reports that allow you to assess actual data in terms of original budget projections, follow these steps:

1. From the Reports menu, choose Budgets, and then choose the report that you want to run from the following options:
   - **Budget Overview:** Summarizes the budget for Income Statement and Balance Sheet accounts on a month-to-month basis.
   - **Budget vs. Actual:** Compares budgeted amounts.
   - **Profit & Loss Budget Performance:** This report summarizes how your actual profit and loss compare to your budgeted profit and loss. Figure 31-4 shows a sample Profit & Loss Budget Performance report.
   - **Budget vs. Actual Graph:** Compares budgeted to actual account balances as shown in Figure 31-5.
2. Use the buttons at the top of the screen to select parameters for the report.

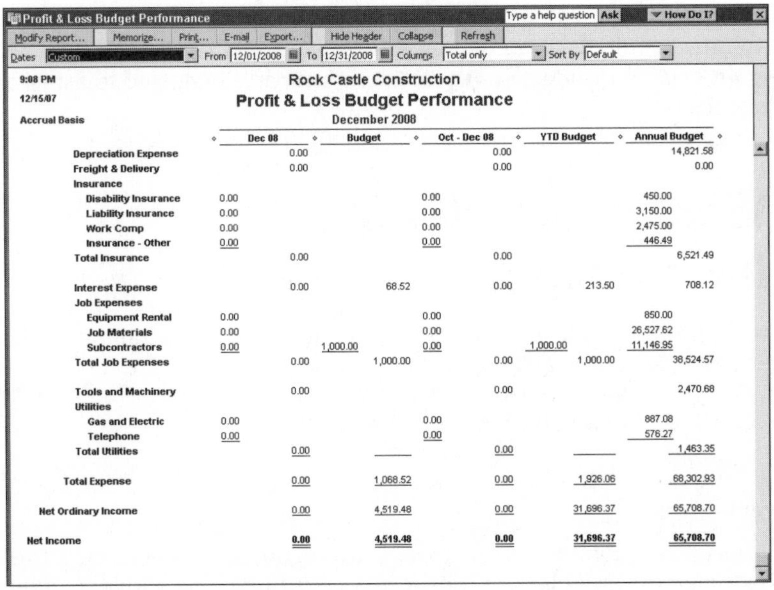

	Dec 08	Budget	Oct - Dec 08	YTD Budget	Annual Budget
Depreciation Expense	0.00		0.00		14,821.58
Freight & Delivery	0.00		0.00		0.00
Insurance					
Disability Insurance	0.00		0.00		450.00
Liability Insurance	0.00		0.00		3,150.00
Work Comp	0.00		0.00		2,475.00
Insurance - Other	0.00		0.00		446.49
Total Insurance	0.00		0.00		6,521.49
Interest Expense	0.00	68.52	0.00	213.50	708.12
Job Expenses					
Equipment Rental	0.00		0.00		850.00
Job Materials	0.00		0.00		26,527.62
Subcontractors	0.00	1,000.00	0.00	1,000.00	11,146.95
Total Job Expenses	0.00	1,000.00	0.00	1,000.00	38,524.57
Tools and Machinery	0.00		0.00		2,470.68
Utilities					
Gas and Electric	0.00		0.00		887.08
Telephone	0.00		0.00		576.27
Total Utilities	0.00		0.00		1,463.35
Total Expense	0.00	1,068.52	0.00	1,926.06	68,302.93
Net Ordinary Income	0.00	4,519.48	0.00	31,696.37	65,708.70
Net Income	0.00	4,519.48	0.00	31,696.37	65,708.70

Figure 31-4: A sample Profit & Loss Budget.

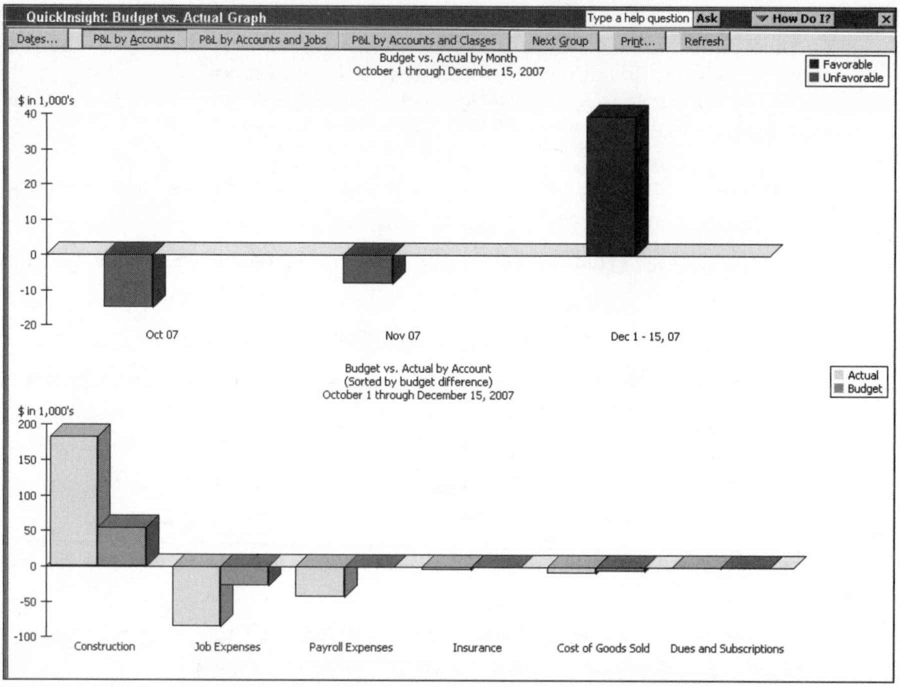

Figure 31-5: The Budget vs. Actual Graph compares budgeted to actual account balances.

If You Were Overambitious: Changing a Budget

Sometimes the goals that initially seem realistic just aren't attainable. Maybe management was naïve and overly optimistic. Or maybe there were unforeseen market factors, delays, or difficulties once the project was underway. QuickBooks enables you to change an existing budget by following these steps:

1. Go to Reports ➪ Budgets & Forecasts ➪ Budget Overview. The Set Up Budget window opens.
2. Choose the budget from the drop-down menu and, if necessary, the Customer:Job and class that describe your budget as shown in Figure 31-6.
3. When QuickBooks displays the monthly budget amounts, change the amounts as appropriate.
4. Click Save.
5. (Optional) Choose another budget (and if necessary, Customer:Job and class), and repeat steps 3 and 4.

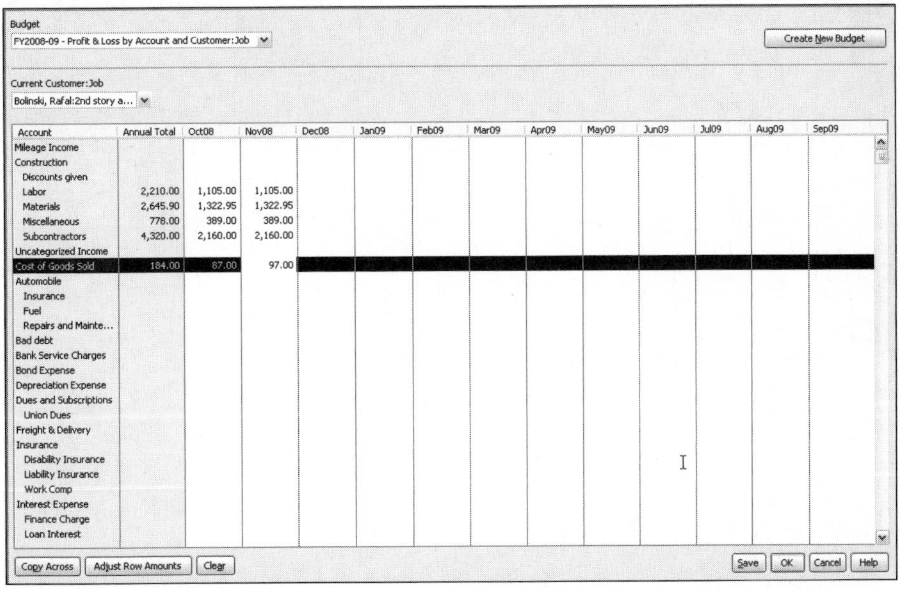

Figure 31-6: Use this drop-down menu to select the budget you want to edit.

6. When you are finished, click OK.

Caution

Remember to click the Save button when you're exiting this window. Your changes are not saved if you merely click OK. This is a frequent error.

Summary

The QuickBooks budget reports are sophisticated management tools that enable you to set goals, monitor performance, and pinpoint problems.

- ✦ You can create budgets for accounts, Customer:Jobs, or classes.
- ✦ QuickBooks offers several types of preset budget report formats that you can customize to meet the needs of your business.
- ✦ You can edit and change budgets to conform to revised company goals and projections.
- ✦ You can create a wide array of sophisticated graphs that enable you to visually compare projected and actual performance. The Budgeted vs. Actual Graph window also displays the six accounts for which the actual balances differ most greatly from the projected balances, which enables you to easily pinpoint problems or unrecognized strengths.

✦ ✦ ✦

CHAPTER 32

Dealing with the IRS

✦ ✦ ✦ ✦

In This Chapter

✦ ✦ ✦ ✦

People have been known to panic, scream, and even vomit, but there's no reason to break a sweat over a little envelope — even if the return address is from the Internal Revenue Service and you know it's not a refund check. This chapter acquaints you with the various types of screening methods for both income tax and payroll tax returns. And some good news: not all audits result in "adjustments."

How the IRS Is Set Up

It's an interesting sign of the times that the commissioner of the IRS is not a tax attorney; his background is in computer technology — and for good reason. For the most part, people do not process the returns you and your company file. Computers do. The IRS is beset with technological problems — and public relations problems. Both have prompted a series of public hearings, which were replete with testimony from taxpayers victimized by technological glitches and insensitive agents. These congressional hearings resulted in a revised "Taxpayer Bill of Rights," which governs the collection process and the promise of technological makeover.

For the 2004 fiscal year, the IRS will have a little more than 99,000 employees (full-time equivalent) and a budget of $10.185 billion. The parts of this elephantine agency with which taxpayers interact are known as *service centers*. There are several service centers located throughout the country. You file your tax returns with the center located closest to you. They all have a pretty equal distribution of work but some variation in staffing, which some experts claim makes people in certain areas of the country more or less likely to be audited. (This theory is unproved.)

The processing centers within the IRS are divided into departments — highly specialized departments full of highly specialized people. That is how the IRS ensures competent handling of complex issues — by specialization. There are people who do nothing but review 1041 forms, people who do nothing but review 941 forms, people who do nothing but look at estate tax returns all day, and so on. These people are experts on the issues in their area.

There is one more important point that you need to know about the IRS. The agency employs a lot of people to talk on the phone — people who are supposedly trained in dealing with the public. When you call the IRS, you cannot simply speak to the person who has your file. You get someone who is trained to handle calls, and not someone who is either familiar with your return or specialized in the area of tax that you are questioning. What does this tell you? It tells you two things. First, if you want to respond to a notice, do it in writing and send it to the address shown on the notice. Second, don't rely on a call to the IRS for sophisticated tax advice. In fact, in general, don't call the IRS for anything more complicated than a request for a specific form. Surveys have shown an alarming number of incorrect answers by IRS personnel in response to seemingly simple taxpayer inquiries.

The IRS Taxpayer Advocate Service

There is one exception to this rule of not attempting to solve problems with the IRS by phone. The Taxpayer Advocate Service (TAS) is an independent organization within the IRS that helps taxpayers resolve problems with the IRS and recommends changes that will prevent problems. If you have an ongoing issue with the IRS that has not been resolved through normal processes, or you have suffered or are about to suffer a significant hardship as a result of the administration of the tax laws, contact TAS.

Contacting TAS

You can contact or learn more about TAS in the following ways:

✦ Visit the TAS Web site located at `http://www.irs.gov/advocate/index.html`.

✦ Call the Taxpayer Advocate Service toll-free telephone number, 1-877-777-4778, or TTY/TTD, 1-800-829-4059.

✦ Call, write, or visit the local taxpayer advocate office for your state. You can find a list of Taxpayer Advocate Service offices in Publication 1546, The Taxpayer Advocate Service of the IRS. Appendix A of this book contains a reproduction of this publication.

Taxpayer rights

While you are visiting the TAS Web site, you may want to spend some time on its Taxpayer Rights page, located at `http://www.irs.gov/advocate/article/0,,id=98206,00.html`. You will find links to the following at this site:

- Publication 1, Your Rights as a Taxpayer (included in this book in Appendix B)
- Protecting Taxpayer Rights, Fact Sheet (which appears in Appendix C)
- The Taxpayer Bill of Rights 2, as passed by Congress
- Taxpayer Bill of Rights II, IRS Training Publication
- Low Income Taxpayer Clinics, Access to Representation

Income Tax Return Audits

According to the IRS, audits are undertaken to verify information on returns, not for the purpose of increasing your tax. The agency maintains that its employees are specially trained to explain and to protect taxpayers' rights. But this is not always the way taxpayers perceive the audit experience.

The screening process

When an individual taxpayer or entity files a return, it goes to one of the regional IRS centers. A return is put through an initial screening process to determine whether it will be selected for audit. The following is a partial list of factors that can heighten your chances of winning this unlucky lottery:

- **Incorrect Social Security number or failure to sign the return:** All returns are electronically screened for these common errors.
- **Incorrect filing status:** Returns are screened to make sure, for example, that married people don't try to pass as singles and those who claim "head of household" status are really entitled to do so.
- **Math errors:** A small mathematical error can prove costly. Statistically, returns that are incorrectly added are more likely to contain other errors, and this makes them prime audit targets.
- **Missing forms and schedules:** Even if the reported amounts are correct, if you fail to provide the required supplemental information, you have made yourself a more likely candidate for an audit.

In addition to the foregoing screening methods, which are really pretty simple, the IRS uses a more complicated process based on statistical analysis of the information contained on the returns. The Discriminate Function system (DIF) is used to compare the information on your return to various statistical norms. For example, according to these norms, it may be anticipated that a single woman living in Wisconsin having a $60,000-a-year income will make charitable contributions and have itemized deductions within a certain range. Variations from the statistical norm, and controversial deductions such as those for a home office, are assigned points under a DIF scoring system. The higher the DIF score, the more likely the return will be audited. If this Wisconsin taxpayer, in this example, has a disproportionate amount of charitable contributions and other deductions in relation to her income, the return will be given a high DIF "score" and possibly be selected for audit.

Which returns are most likely to be audited?

Factors other than the screening process itself can increase your audit potential. The probability of an income tax audit varies with the type of return, income, geographical location, and just plain luck.

In 2003, the overall audit rate for individuals was about 7.7 audits for every 1,000 taxpayers. The audit rate for businesses in 2003 was about 1.9 per 1,000.

Tip

This is less than a third of the rate in 1996, reflecting an overall decline in audits. Overall, some 618,000 individuals were audited in 2003, compared with 1.1 million in 1999. The IRS has requested funding to beef up its audit staff, which has declined 20 percent since 1995.

Someone who earns $100,000 a year has three times a greater chance of being audited than has someone with income of less than $25,000.

The type of deductions that you take may increase your audit odds. Certain deductions, such as a home office and automobile-related expenses, are assigned a higher DIF score. It's to your advantage to maintain scrupulous documentation concerning these deductions if you take them.

Being in the wrong place at the wrong time may also play a part. Someone from San Francisco is three times more likely to be audited than is someone from Milwaukee. No one knows why. Maybe it's because San Francisco has a much higher proportion of self-employed entrepreneurs.

A tax attorney also tells me that writing nasty notes in the margin of your return is a surefire way to get audited. He tells me that he actually had an old curmudgeon of a client who did this. The client was not only audited but also assessed a penalty for filing a "frivolous return."

Targeted Areas

The IRS has been recently realigning its audit resources to focus on the following notorious areas of noncompliance:

- ✦ Offshore credit card use
- ✦ High-risk, high-income taxpayers
- ✦ Abusive schemes and promoter investigations
- ✦ Nonfilers
- ✦ Unreported income

Finally, it can be just simple bad luck. The IRS selects a certain proportion of returns each year for "random" audit. Random audits are not based on criteria any more scientific than pulling a name from a hat. A return may be selected for audit for three years subsequent to its filing.

Tips for avoiding income tax audits

Obviously, you want to be sure to check your math and filing status and verify that you've submitted all the correct forms and schedules. But beyond that, it is a good idea to review your return critically for unusual or disproportionate amounts that should be explored. For example, you may have had an unusually high itemized deduction, investment, or business loss. This would normally increase your DIF score, making you a more likely candidate for audit. There's a good chance that you can head off an audit by attaching a clear explanation and documentation as to the unusual item on your return. For example, if you had a large business loss due to extraordinarily high legal fees, attach receipts for that expense along with an explanation of the action. If you have a large charitable deduction, attach a receipt from the organization clearly indicating the value of what was given.

Also, make sure that you include all your 1099 forms and W-2s with your tax return. The IRS matches information from the copies of the forms that it receives from the issuing companies to the amounts that you have reported on your return. If it is not readily apparent that you included these amounts on your return, the IRS will want to ask you about them.

Types of income tax audits

Section 7602(a) of the Internal Revenue Code gives the IRS a staggering array of powers over the nation's taxpayers. For example, the agency can do the following:

- ✦ Examine any business and personal books, papers, and records that may be relevant to the information on the return

- Summon you to appear at its offices and provide information under oath
- Summon third parties (such as your accountant, banker, or stockbroker) to provide information about you

The IRS invokes all of these powers during the infamous audit process. The agency conducts three types of audits: correspondence audits, office audits, and field audits.

Correspondence audits

A *correspondence audit* is the inquiry of choice, because it does not involve face-to-face communication. It's conducted entirely by mail. The IRS simply notifies you that documentation is missing and that an adjustment is contemplated. You have 30 days to respond. For example, if it looks like you haven't reported the amount shown on a 1099 form, the IRS might send you a letter of inquiry with a proposed adjustment. You can either accept the adjusted amount and pay it or submit an explanation as to why the amount was included on your tax return (or why it does not need to be included).

The office audit

An *office audit* is a bit more intimidating. You are invited to come to the IRS office with your records and supporting documents for a face-to-face meeting with a real agent. Usually, the notice is fairly clear as to which items the IRS is questioning—for example, your home office deduction or educational expenses.

An accountant, an attorney, or an enrolled agent who is certified to represent clients in IRS matters may accompany you. You can even give one of these persons a power-of-attorney authorization to appear without you. Or, if you are confident that your records are flawless and above reproach and that your reading of the law is beyond dispute, you can go it alone.

Audit Lore

No one knows for sure, but rumor has it that the following may serve as tip-offs to the IRS that there are auditable issues in your return:

- **Dramatic unexplained changes in income:** For example, if you earned $50,000 last year but report that you earned only $15,000 this year, this may raise your audit potential.
- **Round numbers:** For example, a round number such as "$5,000" for wages or total Schedule A deductions doesn't occur often.
- **Sloppy returns:** Math errors, missing W-2s, and other sloppiness are a tip-off to the IRS that it should be alert to other errors that can lead to collectible taxes.
- **Unrealistically low income:** If your tax return indicates that you, your spouse, and four kids live in a plush suburb on less than $10,000 a year, for example, this may be an issue.

Field audits

Field audits are conducted when the target of the audit is a business with voluminous records. In the interests of "convenience," the audit is held at the taxpayer's place of business.

Conventional wisdom has it that you want to avoid field audits. Who needs IRS agents hanging around your business premises for however long they decide to stay? And should you need to produce some records, it is probably a lot less stressful to compile them with your accountant, rather than to pull them out on the spot at the bidding of your "guests."

I know a certain taxpayer who is a regular subject of field audits. He claims that it's his practice to politely usher the agents to his conference room, graciously serve them coffee while they pore through his records — and turn off the air-conditioning so that the temperature climbs above the 100-degree mark.

Responding to a notice

The IRS initially notifies you that you are the subject of an audit by letter. The audit letter tells you which tax year is being reviewed and which items are being reviewed. The letter also tells you the type of audit and, if necessary, which records to produce.

The following sections provide a brief checklist of the things you'll want to do after the initial panic and disbelief subside.

Decide on representation

You'll need to decide whether you want to have representation at the audit or have someone help you draft your response in a correspondence audit. A CPA, a lawyer, or an enrolled agent can represent you before the IRS. They can even show up at the IRS office for you if you authorize them to do so by power of attorney. IRS Form 2848 is used for this purpose. It may be a good idea to allow a representative to appear at the audit for you, particularly if you are nervous or anxious. If the IRS agent poses any questions that your representative needs to refer to you, your representative can simply get back to the agent later.

When hiring representation for an audit, do not hesitate to ask for a written fee arrangement up front. Ask whether an hourly rate or a flat fee will be charged. If the rate is hourly, ask what the total estimated fee is likely to be in different scenarios. This will help avoid misunderstandings. You should not feel awkward asking these questions if your tax advisor does not bring them up first.

Marshal your documentation

Review the audit letter to determine the items under review and the documentation that you need to substantiate them. For example, if your educational expenses are under review, you want to make sure that you have all your receipts. If you're missing one, you'll want to contact the school.

Occasionally, deductions have been taken for expenses that obviously were incurred but for which you don't have exact substantiation as to the amount. The IRS may still allow the deduction if it is based on a reasonable approximation. For example, assume that your job requires you to travel between two cities. You have lost some records but definitely made the trips. You can work with the IRS to approximate the travel expenses as closely as possible.

QuickBooks can be extraordinarily useful in this regard. You can create a QuickReport summarizing virtually every business expense.

Exercise your rights

Under the Freedom of Information Act, you can request information directly from the IRS to help you prepare for an audit. For example, if the notice indicates that the IRS is questioning a discrepancy in the 1099 income that was reported, you can request directly from the IRS all of your 1099 forms in its records.

Tip

If the IRS has already audited your return for one of the previous two years and made no adjustment, you may be able to call a halt to the audit. Either you or your representative should write a letter notifying the IRS of the previous audit and that it resulted in no changes. Maybe the agency will consider it a waste of time to go down the same alley twice.

Tips for Handling Your Own Audit

If possible, you should have a competent CPA, lawyer, or enrolled agent represent you. In the event that you are a CPA, lawyer, or agent , or feel you are savvy enough to resolve an audit on your own, here are a few tips:

- **Give the right impression:** Convey the image that you are organized and on top of things, that you are the very type of taxpayer that is likely to know the rules and comply with them.
- **Give them only what they ask for:** If you are asked to provide documents needed to support the deduction being questioned, provide *only* documents needed to support the deduction being questioned. Never try to anticipate what may be questioned next. It may not be an issue that the examiner is going to raise, unless you alert or remind him or her to do so.
- **Never give the IRS less information than is requested:** This is a good way to irritate an agent and convey that you have something to hide.
- **Answer questions, but be brief and, of course, honest:** This is not the time to chat. Be pleasant and succinct. If it is an office audit, take a few seconds to reflect before answering the question. If you are responding to a correspondence audit, read your response and edit out extra verbiage.

✦ **Always keep track of your original documents and records:** Never send the IRS the only original of a document or leave it in their office. Have it with you, in an office audit, but take it with you when you go.

✦ **Do not allow your personality or demeanor to create complications for you:** An audit is not the time to chatter or attempt to make new friends. The goal is to make the meeting or letter brief and courteous. Never allow yourself to become argumentative or belligerent, however absurd a turn the auditor's questions may take. This is especially true for written correspondence. Do not shoot off any angry or sarcastic letter. It will not make you feel better in the long run.

✦ **Be sure to request copies of anything that you are asked to sign:** If possible, review it with an accountant or attorney before signing it. Also, ask the agent to provide you with anything relevant in their files.

Payroll Tax Notices

When your company sends its payroll tax deposits to the IRS, the funds go into an account identified by your nine-digit taxpayer identification number. The deposits are coded to correspond to each tax quarter. Your deposits are supposed to correspond to your liabilities, and they most likely will if you are using QuickBooks. (As discussed in Chapter 21, liabilities are tracked each time you record your payroll and are adjusted automatically when you make a payment.)

If your payments exceed the liabilities shown on your Form 940, and everything works as it should, you receive a refund or a credit applied to the next tax quarter. If the deposits are less than the liability shown on Form 940, the IRS will send you a notice that you owe something.

If your company fails to respond to these notices, it is deemed "delinquent." What happens if you fail to respond to the notice? Nothing—except that the IRS sends you another notice. And if you don't respond to that one, they send you another one. By the third or fourth notice, if you haven't responded, the IRS begins collection action. In fact, the third or fourth notice that you receive states that it is "for collection and demand." If you ignore this one, your company's account is transferred to the Asset Collection Service (ACS) division. The ACS has the authority to file liens and levies on the company's property and accounts.

The payroll tax deposit match game

Getting a notice from the IRS doesn't automatically mean that your company owes the money. It could be a mistake. To err is human. The IRS is not human, but it does make mistakes. Plenty of them. Agency error is attributed to "computer problems."

What constitutes a computer problem at the IRS? Usually it's a failure to make a correct electronic match of deposits with liabilities. The reason for this can be anything from crediting a wrong account to failure to note a previous correction you made to your deposits (such as adjusting for an overpayment made because you previously deposited withholding amounts for an employee when you were not obligated to do so).

Tips on avoiding payroll tax notices

For the most part, we make our own problems. The errors are attributable to something done at the taxpayer's end. Studies show that most errors are due to something like, well, a failure to read the form properly, or an incorrectly filled out deposit coupon, or a math error.

Here's the good news: QuickBooks minimizes the potential for these types of errors in several ways. The program pretty much frees you from the task of having to figure out where to enter information on the form altogether. With QuickBooks, you prepare your Forms 940 and 941 using a series of user-friendly information screens such as the one shown in Figure 32-1.

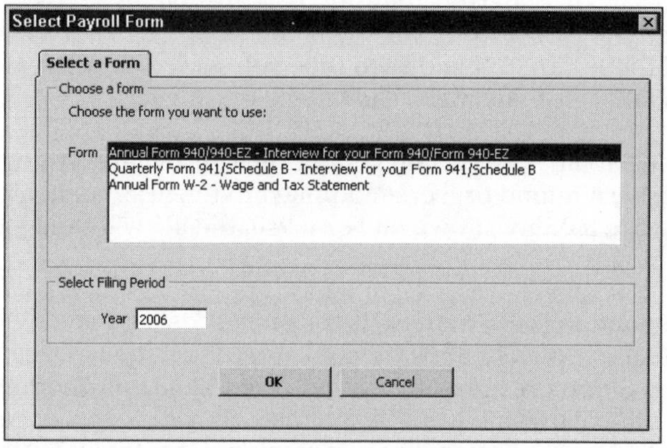

Figure 32-1: User-friendly screens guide you through the process of creating Forms 940 and 941 and decreasing your audit potential.

These screens ask you all the right questions and then enter your answers directly on the form for you. You can preview a completed form prior to printing it. As Figure 32-2 illustrates, the on-screen form looks just like the paper form and can even be edited directly using this window. (To access it, go to Employees ⇨ Process Payroll Forms and select Federal.)

QuickBooks also frees you from a lot of the calculations that are subject to error and from subsequent IRS notices. For example, you don't have to add the withholding amounts to determine your liability — QuickBooks does this for you.

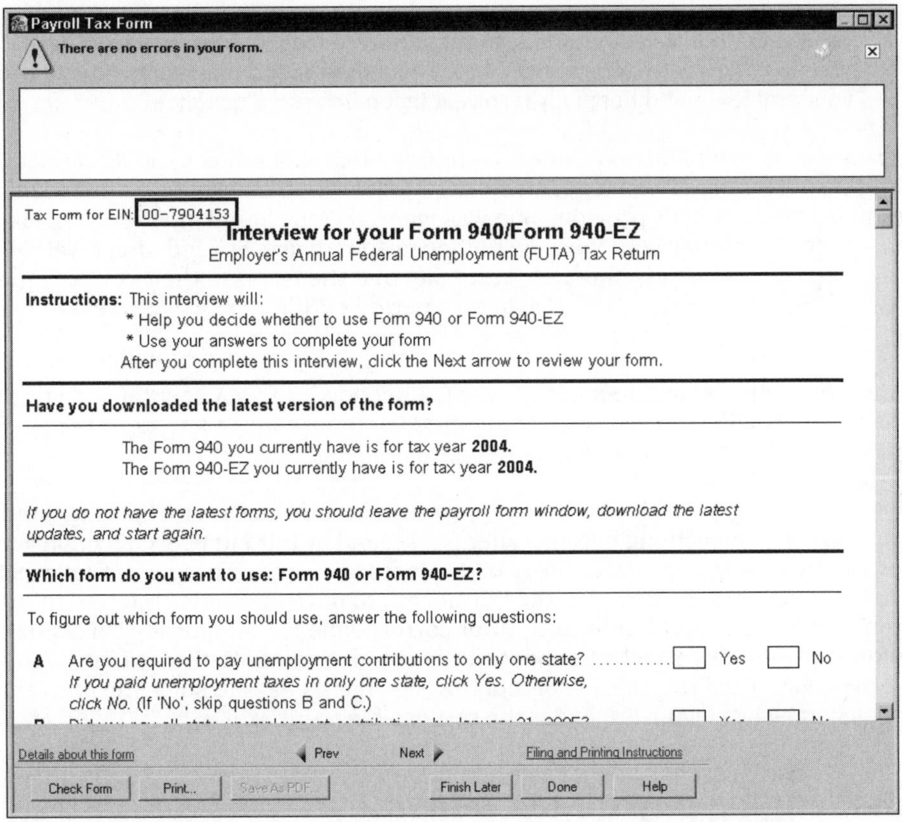

Figure 32-2: This screen looks just like the paper form and can be edited.

Responding to a payroll tax notice

If you think the IRS has made a mistake in sending your company a payroll tax liability notice, your first impulse may be to pick up the telephone and call them. After all, they do provide you with a telephone number on the notice, don't they? That they do, but I suggest that you not waste your time using it. The people on the telephone are trained to handle only inquiries. They may not have your file, and they cannot really do anything to resolve your problem.

A better approach is to write a letter. Why is this better? First, you create a paper trail of your diligent attempts to resolve the problem. This can be important if you later need to argue to have a lien lifted or penalties waived. Second, you can provide the IRS with the type of detailed information that they actually need to go ahead and resolve your problem. For example, you can send them a QuickBooks payroll tax liability report or a QuickReport on a specific employee to drive home your point. You can't do this by phone.

Tip

When you respond to an IRS notice, enclose a copy of the questioned return. Of course, the IRS already has this, but it relieves the agent from having to take the time to retrieve it, which means that the agent can spend that much more time on your problem — and hopefully resolve it that much more quickly.

Here are some commonsense rules of etiquette for responding to an IRS notice. First, do not express hostility or irritation — even if you are sending a subsequent response because your previous one was ignored. You should, however, enclose a copy of the first letter with your current correspondence. Second, don't wait for a response to your correspondence, assuming that the ball is in their court. If you have not heard from them in a reasonable period of time — say two weeks — write again.

Also, when you respond to a notice, use the encoded tear-out section and envelope provided. The IRS receives literally hundreds of thousands of letters each day. This increases the odds that yours gets to the right place.

If you get a second or third notice, and your correspondence is still being ignored, you need to do something because after the second or third notice, collection activities can begin — the agency can levy on business accounts or property. One constructive thing that you can do is call the IRS and ask to have the matter referred to the Problems Resolution Division. Your prior correspondence, supporting QuickBooks records, and overall excellent paper trail should give you a lot of credibility with these people. The Problems Resolution Division has 45 days to solve the problem and generally can light a fire under the responsible agent.

Challenging payroll tax penalties

If you get a notice from the IRS assessing a late-filing penalty, you can do one of two things. You can pay it or you can object to it. In fact, you are invited to object to it. The notice that you receive tells you to write the IRS if you feel that you have "reasonable cause." So instead of sending payment, you may want to try sending an explanatory letter. Don't do both — you can send payment later if the letter doesn't work. Payment, from the agent's perspective, resolves the problem, and this weakens your arguing position and bargaining strength considerably.

Of course, if you don't send a payment, and the issue is not ultimately resolved in your favor, the meter is ticking. The penalty and interest continue to grow until the issue is resolved. If you are not absolutely sure of your position, the recommended procedure is to pay and fight for a refund.

Reasonable cause is very subjective. What one agent finds to be reasonable cause may not fly with another agent. The agents have broad discretion. Illness is a good excuse. Management turnover or internal crisis can also be. (But don't lie — this book isn't telling anybody to lie!) You should draft a well-reasoned and very polite letter explaining that your company has always paid its liabilities in a timely manner and why it just couldn't pay in a timely manner this time around. Of course, this won't work if your company is a habitual late filer. The IRS frowns on habitual late filers.

Summary

This chapter provided you with some tips on how to coexist peacefully with the IRS. Of course, the best way is to simply avoid the IRS by not doing things that trigger an audit or notice. But if you are the target of one, this chapter provided you with a few survival tips.

- Mathematical errors, missing 1099 forms and schedules, and disproportionately high deductions can make you a more likely audit target. Other factors such as occupation, geography, and luck can also play a part.
- The IRS conducts three types of audits: correspondence, office, and field. An attorney, an accountant, or an enrolled agent can represent you.
- It is best to respond to a payroll tax liability notice in writing. If you feel that an error was made, and the agency has not responded to two written communications, ask to be assigned to the Problems Resolution Division. This division is under a time constraint to resolve your matter within 45 days.
- You can have payroll tax penalties for late filing abated for "reasonable cause." It's worth a try unless your company is a habitual late filer.

✦ ✦ ✦

CHAPTER 33

Creating Binding Contracts with QuickBooks

✦ ✦ ✦ ✦

In This Chapter

What is a contract?

Sales of goods under the Uniform Commercial Code

The Statute of Frauds

Using QuickBooks to avoid disputes over contract terms

When the very existence of a contract is challenged

Damaged goods and incorrectly filled orders

✦ ✦ ✦ ✦

Contracts are agreements that result in both parties having legal rights and obligations. Most deals go off without a hitch, but not all of them do. QuickBooks provides you with a lot of mechanisms to avoid contract disputes. QuickBooks sales forms can be used to document all the essential terms of a contract. Customer and vendor histories enable you to establish a pattern of prior dealings and performance with the other party.

What Is a Contract?

A *contract* is a legally enforceable agreement between two parties. It involves some sort of bargained-for exchange of goods, services, or rights between the parties. Not all agreements create a legally binding contract. The legal requirements for a contract are determined both by the laws passed by your state's legislature and by the common law.

The *common law* is a set of standards developed by courts on a case-by-case basis. Courts are bound to rule consistently with prior cases decided by other courts in the same jurisdiction. A decision in a case that presents facts or legal questions that have not previously been decided sets a "precedent" to be followed by other courts in the jurisdiction the next time the same issue arises. The common law is made up of precedents.

Contracts can be either express or implied. *Express contracts* meet the traditional common-law requirements for formation of a contract. *Implied contracts* are enforced by the courts in a variety of circumstances where the traditional common-law elements of a contract are not present, based on the conduct of the parties.

Elements of an express contract

All jurisdictions have well-established common-law precedents to determine whether a contract exists. Courts usually look for three elements: offer, acceptance, and consideration. If all three of these elements are readily ascertainable, the contract is considered an express contract. Express contracts may be either written or oral.

Offer and acceptance

An *offer* is an invitation to enter into an agreement. It gives the offeree the power to create a legally binding contract by accepting it. For example, if I offer to sell you my automobile for $5,000 and you accept the offer, a binding contract is created.

But what if I advertise that the auto is for sale and do not specify a price, and you offer to pay me $5,000? Our roles are reversed, but a contract may still be formed. You, the buyer, are now the offeror and I am the offeree, and I can indicate my *acceptance* of your offer to purchase.

The element of consideration

Another recognized element of a contract is *consideration*. This term basically refers to the requirement that both sides must be giving up something of value to enter into the agreement. For example, if I advertise the auto for free, that may well be an offer that you may accept. But there is no contract. Why? Because there is no consideration — only one of us has given up something of value. On the other hand, if I offer the auto to whoever agrees to tow it away, a binding contract may exist. The towing service has value and may constitute consideration.

Implied contracts

Implied contracts are contracts that, as their name suggests, are implied from the conduct of the parties and other circumstances surrounding the transaction. For example, suppose there is a milkman that always delivers milk to your house. You have never actually met him, but you take the milk in the house and drink it every week. If the court were to look for evidence of an offer and an acceptance, it might not find any. But based on the conduct of the parties, it is likely that an implied contract exists.

Implied contracts are based on the legal doctrines of *promissory estoppel* or *unjust enrichment*. Under these doctrines, a party may be disallowed (that is, estopped) from denying the existence of a contract. This happens when it is simply unfair, in the court's view, to allow a party to wiggle out of any obligations based on its overall conduct in inducing the other party to perform.

Sales of Goods under the Uniform Commercial Code

It would be pretty difficult to have a nationally based economy in this country if businesses were required to comply with different contractual laws for each of the 50 states, Puerto Rico, and the District of Columbia. Instead, we have the Uniform Commercial Code (UCC). The UCC consists of numerous articles, covering various aspects of contract law, which were drafted by a special committee. State legislatures decide whether to adopt a version of the UCC and incorporate its provisions in their state's laws. Some version of the UCC is currently in effect in all states, except Louisiana.

What contracts are covered by the UCC?

The UCC applies to sales of "goods." It does not apply to services. This can be confusing. For example, if I get my car's oil changed, is that a good or a service? It is probably a service, and the oil and grease (or whatever they put in my car) are incidental to providing the service. Accordingly, the UCC does not apply. But because the UCC is based on common law (that is, law that has evolved on a case-by-case basis), many of its provisions can be analogized to provide insight as to how contracts for services are treated.

The battle of the forms

The UCC deals with sales of goods and is especially useful in the absence of a written contract, or when a dispute arises as to specific contractual terms that cannot be resolved with reference to the written documents. The UCC provides a lot of rules for determining and implying contractual terms when no one can figure out what was originally intended by looking at the forms.

It's a sad fact of business life that most contracts are not fully negotiated and sales forms are not always clearly or correctly drafted. The process of "contracting" begins with a phone call and the dispatch of a form by one party. The buyer and seller may both dispatch their own forms "confirming" the transaction, and the terms contained in these forms may not be the same. The buyer's forms are drafted to give the buyer an advantage, and the seller's forms are drafted to give the seller an advantage. Most of the time this does not pose a problem; the deal goes off without a hitch. But sometimes, as the parties begin to perform, a dispute arises. Then everybody sits down to read their own forms and each other's, probably for the first time. The UCC attempts to deal with this common scenario that probably originated when the first contracts were carved on stone tablets.

The UCC is intended to give guidance to courts in fashioning appropriate remedies. One method that the UCC recognizes is to look to the parties past "course of performance" and "prior dealings" to figure out what they intended by the terms of the present contract. For example, assume I have purchased slaughtered chickens from you for my restaurant business for the past 10 years. Suddenly, without prior negotiation or communication, you begin sending me live, squawking chickens. This is definitely a deviation from our prior course of dealings, and the court will likely find that we have a contract for the purchase and sale of slaughtered chickens.

Tip Vendor and customer reports can be extremely useful in establishing a course of prior dealings and past performance under the UCC.

The UCC requires that contracts be sufficiently definite to be enforceable. The Code isolates five essential terms for enforcement of a contract: parties, price, quantity, time, and place of performance. Sound familiar? That because these terms are included on QuickBooks sales forms.

QuickBooks sales forms and purchase orders such as those shown in Figures 33-1 and 33-2 contain most of the essential terms necessary to create a binding contract. But what about the terms that are not specified? For example, what if the forms that you usually send out don't say anything about time of performance? The UCC anticipates this common scenario.

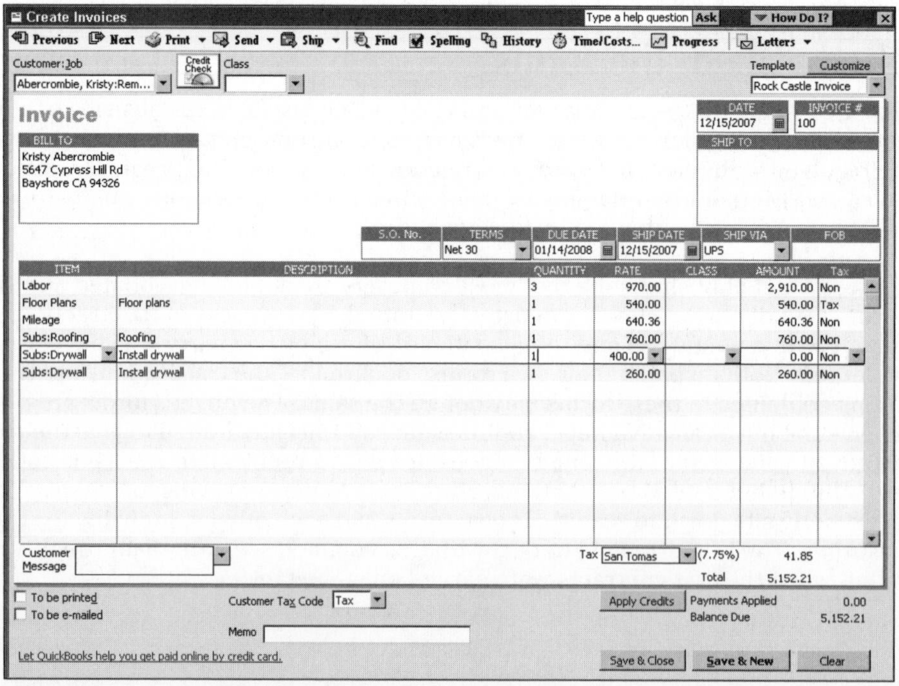

Figure 33-1: This invoice contains all the terms essential to create a binding contract under the Uniform Commercial Code.

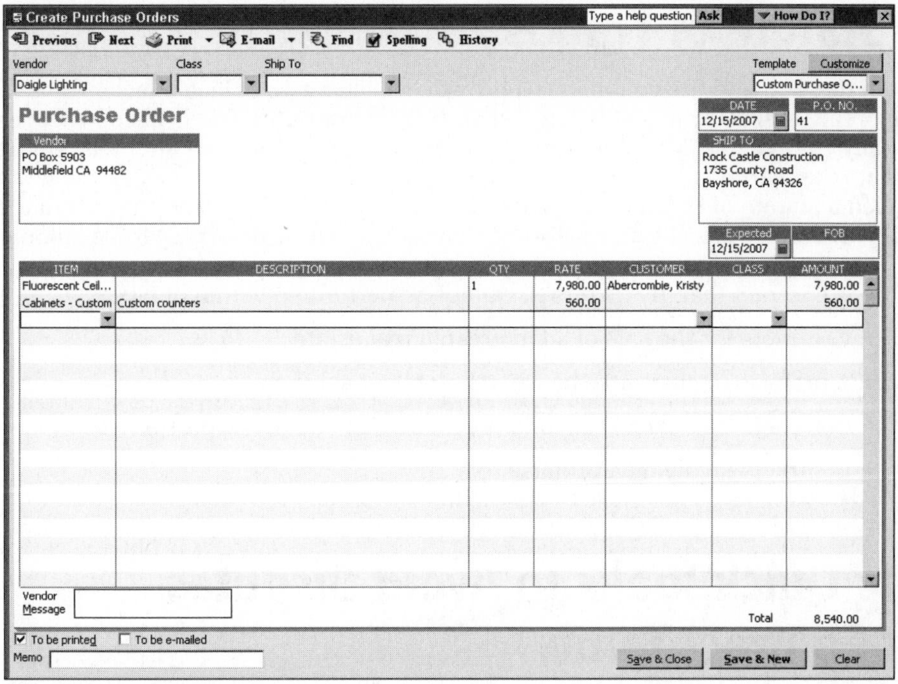

Figure 33-2: This purchase order contains all the terms essential to create a binding contract under the Uniform Commercial Code.

When one of the essential terms of a contract is not specified, the courts may look to the UCC to supply the missing term if it is reasonable to infer the existence of a contract. For example, if the invoice does not specify the time of performance, the UCC authorizes the court to assume that the parties intended a "reasonable" time frame for performance. The court looks to similar contracts within the industry to ascertain what might be a reasonable time frame.

Modifying UCC terms

It is unbelievably easy to modify the provisions of the UCC if you decide that you don't like them. Simply draft a written contract containing other terms. The provisions of the UCC apply only when the parties have specified no other terms. Any terms that the parties agree to on their own automatically supersede the UCC provisions.

The Statute of Frauds

Both the UCC and the common law provide a wide range of legal mechanisms for enforcing oral contracts and discerning their terms. But not all oral contracts are legally enforceable. Most jurisdictions in the United States have adopted requirements that certain types of contracts must be in writing. This type of state law is called a Statute of Frauds. The types of contracts covered by a Statute of Frauds vary by state. Typically, the following contracts must be in writing to be enforced:

- A contract that, by its terms, cannot be performed within one year
- Contracts for the sale of an interest in real estate
- A promise to guarantee or pay the debts of another
- Contracts that extend beyond the lifetime of one of the parties
- Contracts involving a promise to marry

Using QuickBooks to Avoid Disputes over Contract Terms

You don't want to leave any contractual terms to chance. It's infinitely better to specify them rather than risk having them imposed by a judge that is inattentive, unduly impressed by the other side's lawyer, or just plain stupid. Or to risk having to make huge concessions to the other party just to have to avoid the uncertainties of litigation. (Of course, most judges are conscientious and competent, but if they were all perfect, there wouldn't be such a thing as an appeal.)

Disputes arising over sales of goods

Some introspection is in order here. If you are selling goods, you need to give some thought to which of the five essential contractual terms — parties, price, quantity, time, and place of performance — are most subject to dispute in your line of work. You need to make sure that your sales forms are very specific as to these terms the first time around with a new customer. A simple note in the Memo portion of the form, such as the one shown in Figure 33-3, does the trick.

Cross-Reference

After you have dealt with the parties a few times, you establish a course of dealings and course of performance, which give you a certain comfort level. But prior to this point, QuickBooks gives you a lot of flexibility in customizing your sales forms and purchase orders to add information about your contractual terms. Reading Chapters 14 and 15, which deal with the subject of setting up sales forms, may save you time, grief, and legal fees.

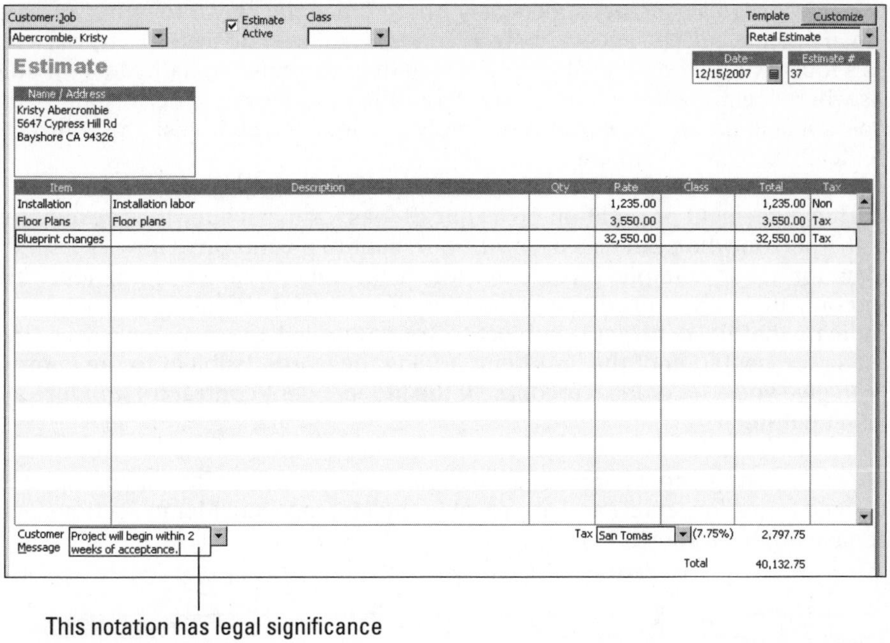

Figure 33-3: Adding a simple notation in the Memo field can save second-guessing and potential litigation later.

Disputed service contracts

If you are selling services, the UCC does not apply. But you will likely find similar protections under the common law of your state. The common law tends to favor a party who has fully performed a service. This is especially true if there are ascertainable standards for performance — such as having your oil changed or your house painted. This is the case even if you hire the owner of the company to paint your house and he sends his dim-witted son who gets his foot stuck in a paint can and leaves his footprints in your driveway. Generally, so long as the service is completed within the specified time frame, you must pay the company that provides it.

However, an exception is recognized for "personal" services. A service is personal in nature when you are clearly hiring the skills and talents of a specific person — for example, consultants, artists, astrologers, and hairdressers. Still, the law favors the performing party — so long as they perform the service (even if they have an off day or give you bad advice). But a seller generally has one important, widely recognized right, with respect to personal service contracts: the person you hire is the person you get.

Suppose you sign a contract specifically hiring Bingo the clown to entertain at your company picnic and the agency instead sends Bozo, who manages to terrify your boss's four-year-old daughter by threatening to cut a bunny in half. Most jurisdictions will recognize a breach of contract, because services by a performing artist are personal in nature. Substitutions simply are not allowed unless the contract specifically provides for them.

A written agreement or notation on a QuickBooks form can alter the presumption that the person who performs a service pursuant to a contract is always entitled to be paid for it. For example, if you enter into a contract to have a mural depicting your company's seven products painted on the side of its building, you might want to indicate that the contract is subject to your approval after you have seen the artist's representation of the first item. Adding the words "subject to the approval of" can give you a lot of legal recourse if the independent contractor you hire simply isn't cutting it.

If you are entering into a contract for the purchase of service Items, you can easily add some terms for review and approval in the Message and Memo sections of the purchase order, as shown in Figure 33-4.

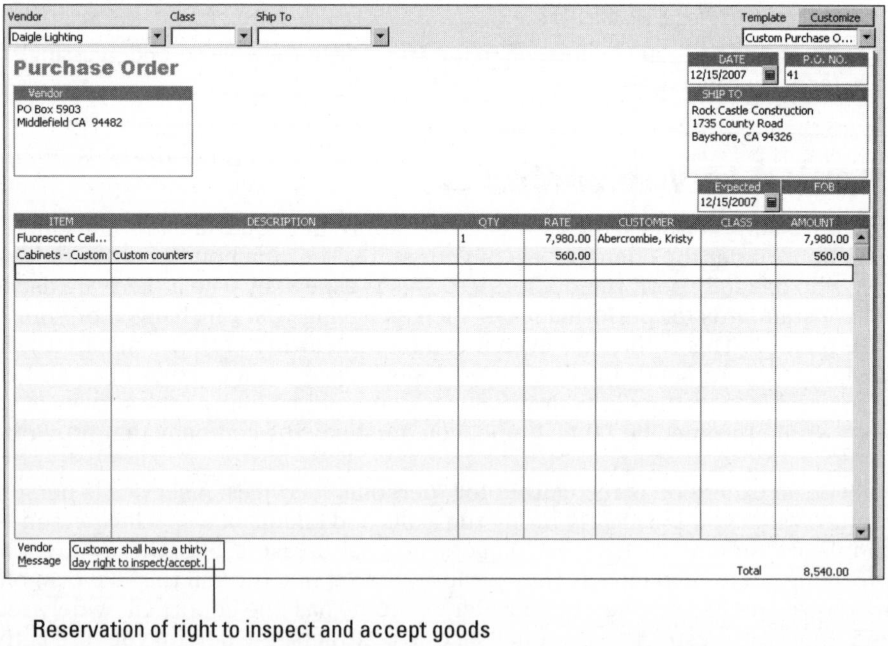

Figure 33-4: This purchase order reserves the right to inspect the counters that have been ordered prior to installation.

When a Contract's Very Existence Is Challenged

What do you do about the "customer" that claims they never got your sales form with all the crystal clear, specific terminology that you carefully drafted? Unfortunately, it happens all the time. As with the issue of a disputed term, your claim is buttressed if there have been prior dealings. For example, assume that you have delivered a shipment of lettuce every week for the past four years to the restaurant and the restaurant owner suddenly wants to claim there is no written contract. If all goes well and you have a competent judge, this ludicrous assertion should be rejected and the owner of the establishment ordered to pay for the now decomposing produce.

Similarly, if Mr. Deadbeat orders the lettuce, serves it to his customers, and then claims there is no contract, the UCC covers the situation. A contract is implied based on the fact that the goods were accepted and used. You'll be compensated at the rate normally paid for the lettuce, in the absence of evidence as to what the agreed contract price was.

The really difficult situation arises when you are dealing with a first-time customer who refuses delivery, claiming they never received your confirming sales form. For example, assume that you carefully transport a truckload full of specially created ice sculptures to a restaurant in a neighboring town. The restaurant owner claims he never ordered the ice sculptures — maybe a manager that has since been fired ordered them. In any event, the restaurant owner tells you that there is no written contract and he is not accepting any ice sculptures. There are several ways that you can protect yourself from this scenario with QuickBooks sales forms.

First, obtain signatures on all initial orders whenever possible. A facsimile signature (followed by a hard copy in the mail) should make you feel secure enough to begin performing under the contract. A signature indicates acceptance of all the terms on your sales form. But how do you know that the person who signs the form has the authority to bind the company to a contract? The answer is that you do not have to know. If the circumstances made it reasonable to assume that the person placing the order was acting on behalf of the company, the law is on your side. This legal doctrine is called "apparent authority," and it applies whenever a company places an employee in a position to convey to third parties that the employee is in a position to bind the company to contracts. So, for example, if the person tells you that she is the manager and can enter into a contract, the company will be bound by her actions.

Tip

The legal doctrine of apparent authority is a sort of double-edged sword. If you do not want your employees to obligate your company to purchase goods or services without your approval, you should have a policy identifying which employees can place orders and generate purchase orders, and advise your suppliers in writing of this policy.

What if the other party doesn't have a fax machine or it is otherwise impractical to obtain a signature before you start performing under the contract? This is also another common scenario in our fast-paced I-want-it-yesterday economy. When it arises, you can customize your sales form to enable you to enter information as to the time, date, and person with whom you spoke by phone. I suggest you obtain both the name and the job title of the person who placed or confirmed the order. The employee from your company who took the order at your end should also be identified on the sales form to further protect you in the event of a dispute as to the existence of a contract.

Damaged Goods and Incorrectly Filled Orders

I know a wholesaler of novelty items who ordered several thousand toy frogs. The frogs were supposed to make an adorable croaking sound but instead made a sickly sort of belching noise. The buyer argued that these were defective goods. The seller claimed they were just fine — they made a noise on cue. Obviously, the forms of both parties were silent as to the tenor and pitch of the simulated frog croak. What does the UCC have to say about a situation like this?

The UCC provides that a buyer has the right to inspect the goods and reject "non-conforming goods" within a "reasonable" period of time. But the buyer cannot reject the shipment of goods if he has already accepted the goods. Under Section 2-206 of the UCC, acceptance can occur in any of these ways:

✦ After a reasonable time to inspect the goods, the buyer indicates to the seller that he or she will take them. (Unfortunately, it's the buyer's problem if he or she did not inspect enough of them and doesn't catch the defect until after acceptance has already been indicated.)

✦ After a reasonable time to reject, the buyer fails to notify the seller of rejection.

✦ The buyer acts in a way that is "inconsistent" with rejection (for example, uses the goods).

Rejection of nonconforming goods is a complicated legal area. This book isn't useful insofar as providing you with a definitive answer as to anybody's legal obligations when a dispute arises. But you should be aware of the provisions of the UCC so that you don't inadvertently make representations or take actions that are going to adversely affect your interests. For example, the buyer in our croaking frog example should immediately notify the seller that he feels the goods are nonconforming. The buyer should not take acts inconsistent with rejection, such as selling some of the frogs to his customers. (If some of them are okay to sell, why not all of them?) If you are using QuickBooks, you might want to indicate on a customized purchase order template that all deliveries are subject to inspection and approval within a period of time that you specify on the form.

What if a buyer rejects goods for a trivial reason? What if the toy frogs really do sound like frogs to most people and the buyer is unrealistically insisting that they should be able to fool real frogs? This may be deemed a "wrongful" rejection under the UCC, giving the unfortunate seller a legal remedy for breach of contract.

If you are a seller, you may want to take some steps to protect yourself from rejection of goods. For example, you might customize your QuickBooks sales forms to limit the amount of time that the buyer has to reject nonconforming goods (for example, 48 hours). You might send a sample of the shipment and ask the buyer to sign off before producing, shipping, or manufacturing the remaining goods. Doing either of these things will make it harder for a buyer to argue to a judge, months later when you are sending them dunning notices on a delinquent account, that the goods were not acceptable.

Summary

This chapter discussed how you can use QuickBooks sales forms and purchase orders to create binding legal contracts. It also gave you some tips on what to do when a dispute arises.

✦ A contract is a legally enforceable agreement between two parties involving a bargained-for exchange.

✦ Contracts may be express or implied. Express contracts are formed when there is an offer, acceptance, and consideration. The existence of implied contracts is inferred from the surrounding circumstances.

✦ The Uniform Commercial Code (UCC) has been adopted in all but one of the 50 states, and in Puerto Rico and the District of Columbia. It supplants the common law in respect to transactions involving the sale of goods.

✦ The UCC provides rules for supplying an essential contract term when the agreement between the parties is silent. Service contracts are not covered by the UCC but are covered by analogous common-law provisions.

✦ Certain types of contracts must be in writing and cannot be oral. The Statute of Frauds of the particular state in which they are made governs these contracts.

✦ Goods that do not meet contract specifications can be rejected by a buyer, so long as the buyer has not previously accepted the goods. A wrongful rejection of goods by a buyer constitutes a breach of contract.

✦ ✦ ✦

APPENDIX A

Your Rights as a Taxpayer

IRS
Department of the Treasury
Internal Revenue Service
Publication 1
(Rev. August 2000)
Catalog Number 64731W
www.irs.gov

Your Rights as a Taxpayer

The first part of this publication explains some of your most important rights as a taxpayer. The second part explains the examination, appeal, collection, and refund processes. This publication is also available in Spanish.

Declaration of Taxpayer Rights

I. Protection of Your Rights

IRS employees will explain and protect your rights as a taxpayer throughout your contact with us.

II. Privacy and Confidentiality

The IRS will not disclose to anyone the information you give us, except as authorized by law. You have the right to know why we are asking you for information, how we will use it, and what happens if you do not provide requested information.

III. Professional and Courteous Service

If you believe that an IRS employee has not treated you in a professional, fair, and courteous manner, you should tell that employee' s supervisor. If the supervisor' s response is not satisfactory, you should write to the IRS director for your area or the center where you file your return.

IV. Representation

You may either represent yourself or, with proper written authorization, have someone else represent you in your place. Your representative must be a person allowed to practice before the IRS, such as an attorney, certified public accountant, or enrolled agent. If you are in an interview and ask to consult such a person, then we must stop and reschedule the interview in most cases.

You can have someone accompany you at an interview. You may make sound recordings of any meetings with our examination, appeal, or collection personnel, provided you tell us in writing 10 days before the meeting.

V. Payment of Only the Correct Amount of Tax

You are responsible for paying only the correct amount of tax due under the law— no more, no less. If you cannot pay all of your tax when it is due, you may be able to make monthly installment payments.

VI. Help With Unresolved Tax Problems

The Taxpayer Advocate Service can help you if you have tried unsuccessfully to resolve a problem with the IRS. Your local Taxpayer Advocate can offer you special help if you have a significant hardship as a result of a tax problem. For more information, call toll free 1–877–777–4778 (1–800–829–4059 for TTY/TDD) or write to the Taxpayer Advocate at the IRS office that last contacted you.

VII. Appeals and Judicial Review

If you disagree with us about the amount of your tax liability or certain collection actions, you have the right to ask the Appeals Office to review your case. You may also ask a court to review your case.

VIII. Relief From Certain Penalties and Interest

The IRS will waive penalties when allowed by law if you can show you acted reasonably and in good faith or relied on the incorrect advice of an IRS employee. We will waive interest that is the result of certain errors or delays caused by an IRS employee.

THE IRS MISSION

PROVIDE AMERICA' S TAXPAYERS TOP QUALITY SERVICE BY HELPING THEM UNDERSTAND AND MEET THEIR TAX RESPONSIBILITIES AND BY APPLYING THE TAX LAW WITH INTEGRITY AND FAIRNESS TO ALL.

Examinations, Appeals, Collections, and Refunds

Examinations (Audits)

We accept most taxpayers' returns as filed. If we inquire about your return or select it for examination, it does not suggest that you are dishonest. The inquiry or examination may or may not result in more tax. We may close your case without change; or, you may receive a refund.

The process of selecting a return for examination usually begins in one of two ways. First, we use computer programs to identify returns that may have incorrect amounts. These programs may be based on information returns, such as Forms 1099 and W-2, on studies of past examinations, or on certain issues identified by compliance projects. Second, we use information from outside sources that indicates that a return may have incorrect amounts. These sources may include newspapers, public records, and individuals. If we determine that the information is accurate and reliable, we may use it to select a return for examination.

Publication 556, Examination of Returns, Appeal Rights, and Claims for Refund, explains the rules and procedures that we follow in examinations. The following sections give an overview of how we conduct examinations.

By Mail

We handle many examinations and inquiries by mail. We will send you a letter with either a request for more information or a reason why we believe a change to your return may be needed. You can respond by mail or you can request a personal interview with an examiner. If you mail us the requested information or provide an explanation, we may or may not agree with you, and we will explain the reasons for any changes. Please do not hesitate to write to us about anything you do not understand.

By Interview

If we notify you that we will conduct your examination through a personal interview, or you request such an interview, you have the right to ask that the examination take place at a reasonable time and place that is convenient for both you and the IRS. If our examiner proposes any changes to your return, he or she will explain the reasons for the changes. If you do not agree with these changes, you can meet with the examiner's supervisor.

Repeat Examinations

If we examined your return for the same items in either of the 2 previous years and proposed no change to your tax liability, please contact us as soon as possible so we can see if we should discontinue the examination.

Appeals

If you do not agree with the examiner's proposed changes, you can appeal them to the Appeals Office of IRS. Most differences can be settled without expensive and time-consuming court trials. Your appeal rights are explained in detail in both Publication 5, Your Appeal Rights and How To Prepare a Protest If You Don't Agree, and Publication 556, Examination of Returns, Appeal Rights, and Claims for Refund.

If you do not wish to use the Appeals Office or disagree with its findings, you may be able to take your case to the U.S. Tax Court, U.S. Court of Federal Claims, or the U.S. District Court where you live. If you take your case to court, the IRS will have the burden of proving certain facts if you kept adequate records to show your tax liability, cooperated with the IRS, and meet certain other conditions. If the court agrees with you on most issues in your case and finds that our position was largely unjustified, you may be able to recover some of your administrative and litigation costs. You will not be eligible to recover these costs unless you tried to resolve your case administratively, including going through the appeals system, and you gave us the information necessary to resolve the case.

Collections

Publication 594, The IRS Collection Process, explains your rights and responsibilities regarding payment of federal taxes. It describes:

- What to do when you owe taxes. It describes what to do if you get a tax bill and what to do if you think your bill is wrong. It also covers making installment payments, delaying collection action, and submitting an offer in compromise.
- IRS collection actions. It covers liens, releasing a lien, levies, releasing a levy, seizures and sales, and release of property.

Your collection appeal rights are explained in detail in Publication 1660, Collection Appeal Rights.

Innocent Spouse Relief

Generally, both you and your spouse are responsible, jointly and individually, for paying the full amount of any tax, interest, or penalties due on your joint return. However, if you qualify for innocent spouse relief, you may not have to pay the tax, interest, and penalties related to your spouse (or former spouse). For information on innocent spouse relief and two other ways to get relief, see Publication 971, Innocent Spouse Relief, and Form 8857, Request for Innocent Spouse Relief (And Separation of Liability and Equitable Relief).

Refunds

You may file a claim for refund if you think you paid too much tax. You must generally file the claim within 3 years from the date you filed your original return or 2 years from the date you paid the tax, whichever is later. The law generally provides for interest on your refund if it is not paid within 45 days of the date you filed your return or claim for refund. Publication 556, Examination of Returns, Appeal Rights, and Claims for Refund, has more information on refunds.

If you were due a refund but you did not file a return, you must file within 3 years from the date the return was originally due to get that refund.

Tax Information

The IRS provides a great deal of free information. The following are sources for forms, publications, and additional information.

- Tax Questions: 1–800–829–1040 (1–800–829–4059 for TTY/TDD)
- Forms and Publications: 1–800–829–3676 (1–800–829–4059 for TTY/TDD)
- Internet: www.irs.gov
- TaxFax Service: From your fax machine, dial 703–368–9694.
- Small Business Ombudsman: If you are a small business entity, you can participate in the regulatory process and comment on enforcement actions of IRS by calling 1–888–REG–FAIR.
- Treasury Inspector General for Tax Administration: If you want to confidentially report misconduct, waste, fraud, or abuse by an IRS employee, you can call 1–800–366–4484 (1–800–877–8339 for TTY/TDD). You can remain anonymous.

APPENDIX B

How to Get Help with Unresolved Tax Problems

THE TAXPAYER ADVOCATE SERVICE
How to Get Help With Unresolved Tax Problems
IF YOU HAVE BEEN UNABLE TO RESOLVE AN ONGOING TAX PROBLEM THROUGH NORMAL IRS CHANNELS,
THIS GUIDE IS FOR YOU.

THE TAXPAYER ADVOCATE SERVICE

The Taxpayer Advocate Service is an independent organization within the IRS, headed by the National Taxpayer Advocate. The Taxpayer Advocate Service helps individual and business taxpayers resolve problems with the IRS by:

- Ensuring taxpayer problems which are not resolved through normal IRS channels are promptly and impartially handled;
- Assisting taxpayers who are facing hardships;
- Identifying issues that compromise taxpayer rights, increase taxpayer burden or create problems; and bringing these issues to the attention of IRS management;
- Recommending administrative and legislative changes through the National Taxpayer Advocate's Annual Report to Congress.

Each state and IRS Campus (formerly Service Center) has at least one Local Taxpayer Advocate who is independent of the local IRS office and reports directly to the National Taxpayer Advocate.

WHO MAY USE THE TAXPAYER ADVOCATE SERVICE?

You may contact the Taxpayer Advocate Service if the established IRS systems or procedures have failed to resolve the problem or dispute.

Generally, we can help if you:

- Are suffering, or are about to suffer, a significant hardship;
- Are facing an immediate threat of adverse action;
- Will incur significant costs in resolving the tax problem through normal channels (including fees for professional representation);
- Will suffer irreparable injury or long-term adverse impact;
- Have experienced a delay of more than 30 days beyond normal processing times to resolve a tax account problem; or
- Have not received a response by the date promised.

Hardship situations and other issues that are referred to the Taxpayer Advocate Service are reviewed on the individual merits of each case.

We work with the IRS to resolve your dispute or problem. However, the Taxpayer Advocate Service is not a substitute for established IRS procedures or the formal IRS Appeals process. The Taxpayer Advocate Service cannot reverse legal or technical tax law determinations.

HOW DO I REACH A TAXPAYER ADVOCATE?

- Call the telephone number listed in this brochure for the Taxpayer Advocate Service office nearest you.
- Call the Taxpayer Advocate Service toll-free phone number,

  1-877-777-4778.
- For TTY/TTD help call 1-800-829-4059.
- File Form 911, Application for Taxpayer Assistance

  Order, with the Taxpayer Advocate Service; or
- Send a written request for assistance or
- Request that an IRS employee complete a Form 911 on your behalf (in person or over the phone).

Form 911 is available by phone at 1-800-829-3676, or on the IRS internet web page: www.irs.gov. File this form by mail or fax to one of the Taxpayer Advocate Service offices listed in this brochure.

Form 911 requires Taxpayer Advocate Service to determine if significant hardship exists and what actions can be taken to relieve the hardship. In certain situations, enforcement action may be suspended while your case is reviewed.

WHAT CAN I EXPECT FROM THE TAXPAYER ADVOCATE?

Your assigned case advocate will listen to your point of view, work with you to address your concerns, and see your case through to an appropriate resolution.

You can expect your case advocate to give you:

- His or her name and phone number;
- Courteous service;
- Timely acknowledgment;
- An impartial and independent review of your problem;
- Time frames for action;
- Updates on progress; and
- Advice on how to prevent future Federal tax problems.

WHAT INFORMATION SHOULD I PROVIDE TO THE TAXPAYER ADVOCATE?

- Your name, address, and social security number or employer identification number issued by the IRS;
- Your phone number and best times to call;
- Your previous attempts to solve the problem, and the office(s) you contacted;
- The type of tax return and tax year(s) involved; and
- A description of your problem or hardship.

If you want to authorize another person to discuss or receive information about your case, send Form 2848, Power of Attorney and Declaration of Representative, or Form 8821, Tax Information Authorization. You can get these forms at most local IRS offices, at the IRS website, www.irs.gov, or by calling 1-800-829-3676.

Send correspondence to: Taxpayer Advocate Service, Internal Revenue Service, at the address in this brochure. Street addresses should be used for correspondence sent by courier; fax numbers are also listed. Addresses and phone numbers may change over time, but the most current information is always available on the TAS home page of the IRS internet web site: www.irs.gov.

TO CONTACT THE TAXPAYER ADVOCATE, CALL THE NUMBER LISTED FOR YOUR LOCAL AREA OR YOU MAY CALL THE TAXPAYER ADVOCATE TOLL-FREE (1-877-777-4778).

OFFICE OF THE NATIONAL TAXPAYER ADVOCATE

1111 Constitution Ave., NW
Room 3031, TA
Washington, DC 20224
(202) 622-4300
(202) 622-6113-FAX

Taxpayer Advocate Service 1-877-777-4778

OFFICES BY STATE AND LOCATION (IF MORE THAN ONE OFFICE PER STATE)

Alabama
801 Tom Martin Dr., Room 151-PR, Birmingham, AL 35211
(205) 912-5631
(205) 912-5156-FAX

Alaska
949 E 36th Ave., Stop A-405, Anchorage, AK 99508
(907) 271-6877
(907) 271-6157-FAX

Arizona
210 E. Earll Dr., Stop 1005 PHX, Phoenix, AZ 85012-2623
(602) 207-8240
(602) 207-8250-FAX

Arkansas
700 West Capitol St., Stop 1005 LIT, Little Rock, AR 72201
(501) 324-6269
(501) 324-5183-FAX

California (Laguna Niguel)
24000 Avila Rd., Stop 2000, Laguna Niguel, CA 92677
(949) 389-4804
(949) 389-5038-FAX

California (Los Angeles)
300 N. Los Angeles St., Stop 6710 LA
Los Angeles, CA 90012
(213) 576-3140
(213) 576-3141-FAX

California (Oakland)
1301 Clay St., Suite 1540S, Oakland, CA 94612
(510) 637-2703
(510) 637-2715-FAX

California (Sacramento)
4330 Watt Ave., Stop SA5043, Sacramento, CA 95821
(916) 974-5007
(916) 974-5902-FAX

California (San Jose)
55 S Market St., Stop 0004, San Jose, CA 95113
(408) 817-6850
(408) 817-6851-FAX

Colorado
600 17th St., Stop 1005 DEN, Denver, CO 80202-2490
(303) 446-1012
(303) 446-1011-FAX

Connecticut
135 High St., Stop 219, Hartford, CT 06103
(860) 756-4555
(860) 756-4559-FAX

Delaware
409 Silverside Rd., Wilmington, DE 19809
(302) 791-4502
(302) 791-5945-FAX

District of Columbia (Maryland)
31 Hopkins Plaza, Room 940, Baltimore, MD 21201
(410) 962-2082
(410) 962-9340-FAX

Florida (Ft. Lauderdale)
7850 SW 6th Ct., Room 265, Plantation, FL 33324
(954) 423-7677
(954) 423-7680-FAX

Florida (Jacksonville)
841 Prudential Dr., Suite 100, Jacksonville, FL 32207
(904) 665-1000
(904) 665-1817-FAX

Georgia
401 W. Peachtree St., NW, Summit Bldg., Stop 202-D, Room 510
Atlanta, GA 30308-3539
(404) 338-8099
(404) 338-8096-FAX

Hawaii
300 Ala Moana Blvd., #50089, Stop H-405, Room 1-214
Honolulu, HI 96850
(808) 539-2870
(808) 539-2859-FAX

Idaho
550 W. Fort St., Box 041, Boise, ID 83724
(208) 334-1324
(208) 334-1977-FAX

Illinois (Chicago)
230 S. Dearborn St., Room. 2855, Stop 1005-CHI, Chicago, IL 60604
(312) 566-3800
(312) 566-3803 FAX

Illinois (Springfield)
320 W. Washington St., Room 611, Stop 1005SPD, Springfield, IL 62701
(217) 527-6382
(217) 527-6373-FAX

Indiana
575 N. Pennsylvania St., Room 581, Stop TA770
Indianapolis, IN 46204
(317) 226-6332
(317) 226-6222-FAX

Iowa
210 Walnut St., Stop 1005, DSM, Room 483
Des Moines, IA 50309-2109
(515) 284-4780
(515) 284-6645-FAX

Kansas
271 W. 3rd St, North, Stop 1005-WIC, Suite 2000
Wichita, KS 67202
(316) 352-7506
(316) 352-7212-FAX

Kentucky
600 Dr. Martin Luther King Jr. Pl., Room 622
Louisville, KY 40202
(502) 582-6030
(502) 582-6463-FAX

Louisiana
600 South Maestri Pl., Stop 2, New Orleans, LA 70130
(504) 558-3001
(504) 558-3348 -FAX

Maine
68 Sewall St., Room 313, Augusta, ME 04330
(207) 622-8528
(207) 622-8458-FAX

Maryland
31 Hopkins Plaza, Room 940, Baltimore, MD 21201
(410) 962-2082
(410) 962-9340-FAX

Massachusetts
25 New Sudbury St., Room 725, Boston, MA 02203
(617) 316-2690
(617) 316-2700-FAX

Michigan
McNamara Federal Bldg., 477 Michigan Ave., Room 1745, Stop 7
Detroit, MI 48226
(313) 628-3670
(313) 628-3669-FAX

Minnesota
316 N. Robert St., Stop 1005 STP, Room 383
St. Paul, MN 55101
(651) 312-7999
(651) 312-7872-FAX

Mississippi
100 W. Capitol St., Stop JK31, Jackson, MS 39269
(601) 292-4800
(601) 292-4821-FAX

Missouri
1222 Spruce St., Stop 1005-STL, Room 10.314
St. Louis, MO 63103
(314) 612-4610
(314) 612-4628-FAX

Montana
10 West 15th Street, Suite 2319, Helena, MT 59626
(406) 441-1022
(406) 441-1045-FAX

Nebraska
1313 Farnam Street, Stop 1005OMA, Room 208
Omaha, NE 68102-1836
(402) 221-4181
(402) 221-3051-FAX

Nevada
4750 W. Oakey Blvd., Stop 1005LVG, Las Vegas, NV 89102
(702) 455-1241
(702) 455-1216-FAX

New Hampshire
Thomas J. McIntyre Federal Building, 80 Daniel St., Room 403
Portsmouth, NH 03801
(603) 433-0571
(603) 430-7809-FAX

New Jersey
955 S. Springfield Ave., 1st Floor
Springfield, NJ 07081
(973) 921-4043
(973) 921-4355-FAX

New Mexico
5338 Montgomery Blvd., NE, Stop 1005 ALB
Albuquerque, NM 87109
(505) 837-5505
(505) 837-5519-FAX

New York (Albany)
Leo O'Brien Federal Bldg., Room. 354
1 Clinton Square, Albany, NY 12207
(518) 427-5413
(518) 427-5494-FAX

New York (Brooklyn)
10 Metro Tech Center, 625 Fulton St, Brooklyn, NY 11201
(718) 488-2080
(718) 488-3100-FAX

New York (Buffalo)
201 Como Park Blvd., Buffalo, NY 14227-1416
(716) 686-4850
(716) 686-4851-FAX

New York (Manhattan)
290 Broadway, 7th Fl., Manhattan, NY 10007
(212) 436-1011
(212) 436-1900-FAX

North Carolina
320 Federal Pl., Room. 125, Greensboro, NC 27401
(336) 378-2180
(336) 378-2495-FAX

North Dakota
657 Second Ave., N. Stop 1005-FAR, Room 244
Fargo, ND 58102
(701) 239-5141
(701) 239-5323-FAX

Ohio (Cincinnati)
550 Main St., Room. 3530, Cincinnati, OH 45202
(513) 263-3260
(513) 263-3257-FAX

Ohio (Cleveland)
1240 E. 9th St., Room 423, Cleveland, OH 44199
(216) 522-7134
(216) 522-2947-FAX

Oklahoma
55 N. Robinson, Stop 1005 OKC, Room 138
Oklahoma City, OK 73102
(405) 297-4055
(405) 297-4056-FAX

Oregon
1220 SW 3rd Ave., Stop O-405, Portland, OR 97204
(503) 326-2333
(503) 326-5453-FAX

Pennsylvania (Philadelphia)
600 Arch St., Room 7426, Philadelphia, PA 19106
(215) 861-1304
(215) 861-1613-FAX

Pennsylvania (Pittsburgh)
1000 Liberty Ave, Room 1602, Pittsburgh, PA 15222
(412) 395-5987
(412) 395-4769-FAX

Rhode Island
380 Westminster St., Providence, RI 02903
(401) 525-4200
(401) 525-4247-FAX

South Carolina
1835 Assembly St., Room 466, MDP 03, Columbia, SC 29201
(803) 253-3029
(803) 253-3910-FAX

South Dakota
115 4th Ave. SE, Room 114, Stop 1005ABE
Aberdeen, SD 57401
(605) 226-7248
(605) 226-7246-FAX

Tennessee
801 Broadway, Stop 22, Nashville, TN 37202
(615) 250-5000
(615) 250-5001-FAX

Texas (Austin)
300 E. 8th St., Stop 1005-AUS, Room 136, Austin, TX 78701
(512) 499-5875
(512) 499-5687-FAX

Texas (Dallas)
1114 Commerce St., Room 1004, MC1005DAL
Dallas, TX 75242
(214) 413-6500
(214) 413-6594-FAX

Texas (Houston)
1919 Smith St., Stop 1005 HOU, Room 1650
Houston, TX 77002
(713) 209-3660
(713) 209-3708-FAX

Utah
50 South 200 East, Stop 1005 SLC
Salt Lake City, UT 84111
(801) 799-6958
(801) 779-6957-FAX

Vermont
Courthouse Plaza, 199 Main St.
Burlington, VT 05401-8309
(802) 860-2089
(802) 860-2006-FAX

Virginia
400 North 8th St., Room 916, Richmond, VA 23240
(804) 916-3501
(804) 916-3535-FAX

Washington
915 2nd Ave., Stop W-405, Seattle, WA 98174
(206) 220-6037
(206) 220-4900-FAX

West Virginia
425 Juliana St., Room 3012, Parkersburg, WV 26101
(304) 420-6616
(304) 420-6682-FAX

Wisconsin
310 W. Wisconsin Ave., Suite 1298 West Tower, Stop 1005-MIL
Milwaukee, WI 53203
(414) 297-3046
(414) 297-3362-FAX

Wyoming
5353 Yellowstone Rd., Room. 206A
Cheyenne, WY 82009
(307) 633-0800
(307) 633-0918-FAX

TAXPAYERS LIVING ABROAD OR IN U.S. TERRITORIES (A/C INTERNATIONAL)

San Patricio Office Bldg.
Room 200
7 Tabonuco St.
Guaynabo, P.R. 00966

787-622-8930 Spanish

787-622-8940 English

787-622-8933-FAX

IRS CAMPUSES (FORMERLY SERVICE CENTERS) WALK-IN SERVICE UNAVAILABLE

Andover
310 Lowell Street, Stop 120, Andover, MA 01812
(978) 474-5549
(978) 247-9034-FAX

Atlanta
4800 Buford Hwy., Stop 29-A, Chamblee, GA 30341
(770) 936-4500
(770) 234-4443-FAX

Austin
3651 S Interregional Hwy., Stop 1005 AUS, Austin, TX 78741
(512) 460-8300
(512) 460-8267-FAX

Brookhaven
1040 Waverly Ave., Stop 102, Holtsville, NY 11742
(631) 654-6686
(631) 447-4879-FAX

Cincinnati
201 River Center Blvd., Stop 11-G, Covington, KY 41011
(859) 669-5316
(859) 669-5405-FAX

Fresno
5045 East Butler Ave., Stop 13941, Fresno, CA 93888
(559) 442-6400
(559) 442-6507-FAX

Kansas City
2306 E. Bannister Rd., Stop 1005 ROE
Kansas City, MO 64131
(816) 926-2493
(913) 696-6390-FAX

Memphis
5333 Getwell Rd, Stop 13M, Memphis, TN 38118
(901) 395-1900
(901) 395-1925-FAX

Ogden
1973 N. Rulon White Blvd., Stop 1005, Ogden, UT 84404
(801) 620-7168
(801) 620-3096-FAX

Philadelphia
11601 Roosevelt Blvd., Stop SW 820, Philadelphia, PA 19154
(215) 516-2499
(215) 516-2677-FAX

OFFICE OF SYSTEMIC ADVOCACY

Executive Director, Systemic Advocacy

1111 Constitution Ave., NW
Room 3219, TA:EDSA
Washington, DC 20224
(202) 622-7175
(202) 622-3125-FAX

Director, Individual Advocacy

1111 Constitution Ave., NW
Room 3219, TA:EDSA: DIA
Washington, DC 20224
(202) 622-7175
(202) 622-1917-FAX

Director, Business Advocacy

1111 Constitution Ave, NW
Room 3219, TA:EDSA:DBA
Washington, DC 20224
(202) 622-7175
(202) 622-1917-FAX

TAXPAYER ADVOCATE

INTERNAL REVENUE SERVICE | SERVICE

The Office of the Taxpayer Advocate operates independently of any other IRS office and reports directly to Congress through the National Taxpayer Advocate.

IRS

Department of the Treasury
Internal Revenue Service

www.irs.gov

Publication 1546 (Rev. 12-2003)
Catalog Number 13266S

APPENDIX C

Protecting Taxpayers' Rights

September 1997
FS-97-20

PROTECTING TAXPAYERS' RIGHTS

The Internal Revenue Service touches the lives of almost every American. The IRS is striving to ensure that all taxpayer contacts are conducted in a courteous, respectful manner. The most important consideration for the IRS in these contacts is the protection of a taxpayer's rights. The IRS has taken many steps in written rules, in policies, in training, in guidance and in evaluations, to ensure taxpayers' rights are protected.

- All IRS employees who have contact with taxpayers are trained in IRS's commitment to the fair and impartial treatment of taxpayers. IRS employees in Collection, Examination and Customer Service all receive training on the provision of both the first and the second Taxpayer Bill of Rights as well as training in quality customer service.

- Customer Service Representatives who answer taxpayers' questions on both tax law and on individual accounts are regularly monitored, not just for the accuracy of their answers, but also for how courteously they treat taxpayers.

- Publication 1, Your Rights as a Taxpayer, is given to every taxpayer selected for an audit. This publication outlines a taxpayer's right to privacy and confidentiality, to professional and courteous service, to representation, to help from the Problem Resolution Office, and to administrative and judicial review. These rights are guaranteed by law.

- IRS's Policy Statement P-1-20, approved in 1973 and used for all enforcement officers, appeals officers and reviewers, strictly prohibits the use of enforcement results and statistics to evaluate those officers. The Taxpayer Bill of Rights, passed in 1988, made this policy law.

- Taxpayers who have encountered difficulties resolving problems through normal IRS channels may be helped by the Problem Resolution Program. Generally, if the Service has not resolved a problem within a reasonable amount of time, or after a couple of inquiries by the taxpayer, the problem qualifies for PRP handling.

(more)

- The enactment of the Taxpayer Bill of Rights authorized "Taxpayer Assistance Orders," which provide relief for taxpayers who might suffer hardships as a result of a planned enforcement action by the IRS. In 1996, the IRS received approximately 30,000 requests for relief. More than 35% of these requests were initiated by IRS employees who recognized the potential hardship and took steps to stop the enforcement action.

- Enforcement managers are required to prepare quarterly certifications for the district director to report any violations of the proper use of statistics. These certifications must give a detailed description of the violation and what corrective action was taken. The district director must then send this certification forward to the Commissioner.

- Revenue officers and revenue agents are evaluated on a variety of job standards that include customer relations. This standard requires agents to conduct themselves in a "courteous, firm and professional manner." In addition, this standard requires agents to ensure that they fully explain to taxpayers their rights under the law.

- The Collection Appeals process allows certain collection actions, such as filing of liens or seizures, to be appealed either before or after the action occurs. Normally, the IRS will stop the collection action until the appeal is settled.

The training, the policies and the procedures that the IRS has put in place contribute to ensuring that taxpayers are treated with respect and dignity, and that their rights are protected. These rights are guaranteed by law. Many of these laws are contained within the Internal Revenue Code. Some of those sections covered by the code are as follows:

Sec. 6331(d) - (added by TBOR 1) - Requires notice in writing 30 days prior to making a levy.

Sec. 6343(d) - (added by TBOR 2) - Authorizes the return of levied property in certain cases.

Sec. 6323(j) - (added by TBOR 2) - Authorizes the release of filed lien in certain cases.

Sec. 6326 - Allows for the administrative appeal of liens.

Sec. 7605 - Protects taxpayers from being subject to unnecessary audits.

(more)

Sec. 7609 - Requires notice to taxpayer when summons is made to third party.

Sec. 7811 - Authorizes Taxpayer Assistance Orders.

Sec. 7430 - Allows for awards of reasonable administrative costs and reasonable litigation costs when IRS advances unreasonable positions.

Sec. 7431 - Authorizes civil action for damages for disclosure of return and return information.

Sec. 7432 - Authorizes civil action for damages for failure to properly release lien.

Sec. 7433 - Authorizes civil action for damages for certain unauthorized collection actions.

X X X

APPENDIX D

The Sarbanes-Oxley Act of 2002: Key Points for Small Businesses

Sarbanes-Oxley (SOX) is a comprehensive statute that passed in 2002 ostensibly to make corporate management and boards accountable, and restore the public's confidence in the financial reporting process. It was a Congressional response to lapses at giant companies like Enron, WorldCom, Global Telink, and Adelphia.

Why Do Small Companies Care about SOX?

Although SOX currently applies to publicly traded companies, private and not-for-profit companies alike can protect themselves and gain a competitive edge by becoming more familiar with the standards introduced by SOX. Fairly simple control and governance measures can help non-public and not-for-profit companies do the following:

- Procure reasonable officers' and directors' liability insurance
- Pre-empt litigation by shareholders, creditors, and other entities on the basis of the company's governance practices

- ✦ Attract additional capital and favorable credit terms
- ✦ Retain large corporate clients and customers that are required to comply with SOX

Key SOX Provisions for Small Businesses

Titles III and IV of SOX can serve as a sample set of standards in many respects for smaller non-public companies. Title III deals with issues of corporate accountability and governance, and Title IV addresses issues pertaining to financial disclosures, loans, and ethics. In particular, Title VIII contains criminal fraud provisions that apply equally to public and non-public companies.

Title III: Corporate Accountability and Governance

Although non-public companies do not have to file financial statements with the Securities and Exchange Commission (SEC), and may not be required to have audited financial statements, they do have important legal duties and obligations. Private companies have legal duties to minority shareholders, creditors (including lenders and vendors), private investors, and other parties relying on the integrity of the company's financial statements. Not-for-profit companies have a critical relationship with their donors and the public.

Non-public companies should be familiar with the following procedures and requirements outlined in Title III:

- ✦ **Audit committee:** Each public company subject to SOX must form a special audit committee. Each member of the audit committee must be a member of the board of directors, but otherwise must be "independent" in the sense that he or she receives no other salary or fees from the company. Although not all non-public companies are subject to audit, many companies, such as not-for-profits, are audited. Audited companies are well-advised to voluntarily form audit committees that mirror the requirements of SOX.
- ✦ **Management accountability and certification:** Management accountability is critical to any company, and SOX provides guidance on how to achieve it. Title III also requires the chief executive officer and chief financial officer (CEO and CFO) to certify that financial statements fairly present, in all material respects, the financial conditions and results of operations of the company. The CEO and CFO must certify, among other things, that the internal controls were reviewed within 90 days prior to the report and whether any significant changes were made to the internal controls.
- ✦ **Improper influence over financial statements:** Title III spells out that it is unlawful for corporate personnel to exert improper influence upon an audit

for the purpose of rendering financial statements materially misleading. Non-public companies should adapt these standards with respect to information they provide to investors, creditors, donors, and shareholders.

✦ **Limits on bonuses:** Title III requires the CEO and CFO to forfeit certain bonuses and compensation received if the company is required to issue corrected financial statements because the company has not complied with Securities and Exchange Commission rules. Many non-public and not-for-profit companies are considering adopting analogous provisions (called *restatements*) due to the company's not complying with SEC rules.

Title IV: Financial Disclosures, Loans, and Ethics Codes

This Title contains several key SOX provisions that can be adapted to small companies, including:

✦ **Disclosure of adjustments and off-balance sheet transactions:** A portion of the law requires financial reports filed with the SEC to reflect all material corrections to the financial statements made in the course of an audit. It also requires disclosure of all material off-balance sheet transactions and relationships that may have a material effect upon the financial status of an issue.

✦ **Prohibition on personal loans extended by a corporation to its executives:** Such loans are now prohibited if they are subject to the insider-lending restrictions of the Federal Reserve Act.

✦ **Changes in inside stock ownership:** Senior management, directors, and principal stockholders also have to disclose changes in their ownership of corporate stock within two business days of completing the transaction. Non-public companies may want to consider voluntarily making similar information available to creditors and shareholders.

✦ **Internal control certification:** The now famous Section 404 of the Article provides that annual reports filed with the SEC must include an internal control report stating that the management is responsible for the internal-control structure and procedures for financial reporting and assessing the effectiveness of the internal controls for the previous fiscal year. Internal control is important for non-public companies as well, and these companies are well-advised to adapt emerging Section 404 standards, rather than reinvent the wheel for their own companies.

✦ **Code of ethics:** Article IV also requires companies subject to SOX to disclose whether they have adopted a code of ethics for its senior financial officers. Non-public companies, and not-for-profits in particular, can benefit from looking at and adapting the codes adopted by their public counterparts.

Title VIII: Criminal Fraud and Whistleblower Provisions

Title VIII of SOX imposes criminal penalties (a 10-year maximum) for knowingly destroying, altering, concealing, or falsifying records with intent to obstruct or influence a federal investigation or bankruptcy matter.

The SOX Spin-Off: Simple Software Solutions

One benefit of SOX is the "software spin-off" that can help analyze the internal control and risk of fraud within your company. Many off-the-shelf programs, such as Sarbox Pro (`www.sarbox.pro.com`) work off the information in your company's trial balance (which you can prepare in QuickBooks) to help identify the greatest risks to your company and the controls in place to mitigate the most significant risks ("key" controls).

Note At the time this book was written, Sarbox Pro cost less than $3,000.

More Information about SOX

If you are looking for more information about Sarbanes-Oxley, check out my book, *Sarbanes-Oxley For Dummies* (Wiley Publishing, Inc.). This straight-to-the-point guide presents a summary of best practices, smart business policies, and invaluable compliance checklists.

✦ ✦ ✦

Glossary

accounting period The accounting period is the period at which the company's books are closed out and started afresh. This is usually the company's fiscal year, but sometimes it is monthly or quarterly.

accounts payable Money that you owe to your vendors, customers, or others.

accounts receivable Money that customers, vendors, or others owe to you.

accumulated depreciation The total amount of depreciation recognized for an asset as of the current date. It is generally tracked in a special accumulated depreciation account established for each asset. The value of a fixed asset at any given time on a company's books is equal to the original cost of the asset less the accumulated depreciation recorded for it. This amount is sometimes referred to as the *carrying value* of the asset.

aging summary A report that tells how much each customer owes to the company, when the balances are due, and which accounts are overdue.

asset An account that tracks what your business owns.

average cost method A method of valuing inventory wherein the number of items is multiplied by the average cost per item to derive the dollar value of the inventory account.

balance sheet A snapshot of the company's financial position as of a certain date, including the balances of the asset, liability, and owner's equity accounts.

balance sheet accounts Accounts that appear on the Balance Sheet, including asset, liability, and owner equity accounts.

bills Invoices that you receive from a vendor. (Do not confuse them with QuickBooks' invoices, which are invoices that you send out.)

calendar year An actual year, from January 1 through December 31, in contrast to a *fiscal year*, which may or may not run from those dates.

capital contribution Money that the owners contribute to the business.

capital gain The profit realized on the sale of a fixed asset.

capital loss The loss taken on the sale of an asset.

carrying value See *accumulated depreciation*.

cash basis Record keeping that records actual payments and receipts, in contrast to *accrual basis*, which is record keeping on the basis of accounts receivable and accounts payable balances.

cash equivalent A payment that is not actually cash but is treated as such for accounting purposes, such as credit cards or checks.

cash sale A sale where payment is made at the time of the delivery of goods or services.

Chart of Accounts A complete list of all the accounts set up to record the activities of your business.

closing the books The process of reducing the income and expense accounts to a zero balance and determining the net income or loss. This is usually done at the end of a fiscal year.

common law A set of standards developed by courts on a case-by-case basis. Courts are bound to rule consistently with prior cases decided by other courts in the same jurisdiction. A decision in a case that presents facts or legal questions that have not previously been decided sets a *precedent* to be followed by other courts in the jurisdiction the next time the same issue arises. The common law is made up of precedents.

contract A legally enforceable agreement between two parties that involves some sort of bargained-for exchange of goods, services, or rights between the parties. Not all agreements create a legally binding contract.

cost of goods sold The cost of all goods held in inventory to produce the products that are sold.

credit limit The maximum amount of credit that you are willing to extend to a customer (or that a vendor is willing to extend to you).

current assets Cash accounts and assets that you could convert to cash within one year. Inventory goods are an example.

current liabilities Liabilities that must be paid within one year.

current ratio The company's ability to meet its short-term obligations. It is a ratio of current assets to current liabilities. The higher the ratio, the better. A ratio of 2:1 is good; 3:1 is excellent.

customer Someone who buys your products or services.

debit-to-asset ratio A measurement that shows the company's amount of debt as compared to its asset value. The goal is to have the lowest possible ratio, and to see a downward trend over years. To calculate the debt-to-asset ratio, divide debt by assets.

debt-to-equity ratio A measurement that shows the company's amount of debt as compared to its equity value. To calculate the debt-to-equity ratio, divide total liabilities by equity.

depreciation The accounting method used to offset a portion of the original cost of a fixed asset against a business's income over multiple years.

draw Money that the owner takes out of the business (for example, for their living expenses).

enrolled agent A tax professional who is certified to represent clients in IRS matters.

equity account An account that represents the value of the business to its owners. These accounts include both contributions to capital and retained earnings (in a corporation).

estimated taxes Taxes that a business or individual pays quarterly, rather than paying the entire tax liability when filing the end-of-year tax return. Most businesses are required to pay quarterly taxes or incur penalties.

expenses Money that the business is paying for operating costs, cost of goods, and other products and services needed to operate.

field audit An IRS audit in which the auditor comes to your place of business.

FIFO First in, first out — a system by which inventory that comes in first is the first to leave. Compare with *LIFO* (last in, first out).

fiscal year The 12-month period that your business uses for tax and financial reporting purposes. It may or may not correspond to the calendar year.

fixed assets Accounts that represent long-term assets but which are not expected to be converted to cash within one year such as machinery and furniture.

fixed liabilities Liabilities that can carry over from year to year. Also called *long-term liabilities.*

FOB Stands for Free on Board; the terms regarding the transportation of the merchandise from seller to buyer.

gross income All of the income before deducting expenses such as the cost of sales.

gross profit See *gross income.*

gross profit margin The company's gross profit divided by its net revenues. It tells you what proportion of each dollar of net sales revenue is actually profit. A high ratio may indicate too much administrative, salary, and overhead costs — costs unrelated to producing the actual product the company sells.

income from operations Income earned in the normal course of doing business. Compare this with other income.

inventory Materials that you keep on hand for sale to customers.

Item Short for line item, Item is the information about each product or service that appears on a bill.

job A QuickBooks project that has a beginning and an end. A job might be a wedding to be catered or a construction project to build a house. An ongoing relationship with a client is not necessarily a job.

liability An account that tracks what your business owes.

LIFO Last in, first out — a system by which the last inventory that comes in is the first to leave. Compare with *FIFO* (first in, first out).

limited liability company (LLC) A company that is taxed as a partnership but is entitled to limited liability status similar to a corporation.

limited partners Partners who share in the profits and losses of the business but whose personal assets are not at risk to creditors.

loss A negative amount after subtracting expenses from income. If this number is positive, it is called a *profit.*

net profit A measurement calculated by dividing net income by net revenues. This figure tells you the portion of your net sales or service revenue that your company actually gets to keep.

net revenues The amount of money your company made minus any returns and sales discounts.

nexus A legal term pertaining to whether a business has a sufficient presence in a particular state so as to make it obligated to pay taxes in that state. This issue can require some research, but ignoring it can be extremely unprofitable.

office audit An IRS audit in which you are invited to come to the IRS office with your records and supporting documents for a face-to-face meeting with an agent.

other income Income that is not from a normal or ongoing part of the business such as the sale of an asset.

owner's draw See *draw*.

partnership An unincorporated joint business venture between two or more individuals.

permanent accounts Accounts in which the balances carry over from one accounting period to the next. These include asset, liability, and equity accounts. In contrast, revenue and expense accounts are temporary accounts, because they are "closed out" at the end of an accounting period.

physical inventory An actual count of inventory items on hand.

posting The process of including a transaction in an account for the purpose of recalculating the account balance to reflect the transaction. For example, if you write a check and enter it into your checking account in QuickBooks, you are posting the check.

profit A positive amount after subtracting expenses from income. If this number is negative, it is called a *loss*.

purchase order An official authorization to buy. You may receive purchase orders from customers or issue them to vendors.

quick ratio The company's ability to meet an unforeseen financial crisis such as fire or flood. To calculate the quick ratio, divide the company's cash and marketable securities by its current liabilities.

register A chronological list of transactions for each asset and liability account maintained by a company to track what it owns and what it owes.

resale number The ID number that certifies that a customer is entitled to purchase items for resale rather than end-use and therefore should not be charged sales tax.

retained earnings Earnings that are retained or reinvested in the business by the owners rather than withdrawn as income.

return on investment (ROI) A measurement that evaluates the owners' return on their investment in the business. Calculate this by dividing net income by owners' equity.

revenue Money coming into the business from sales of products or services, or from other business transactions.

ROI See *return on investment.*

S corporation A special type of incorporation for small corporations (75 or fewer shareholders) that provides certain tax benefits. An S corporation pays no corporate income tax. It receives limited liability status like a C corporation, but is taxed like a partnership or sole proprietorship.

shrinkage A reduction in inventory due to spoilage, theft, or damage.

sole proprietorship A business owned wholly by one person.

SS-4 form An IRS form that you fill out to obtain a tax identification number.

start date The date that you begin tracking business activity in QuickBooks. The start date may be today's actual date, or you may want to enter several months of previous transactions, in which case it would be the date of the oldest transaction you are entering.

statement on financial condition See *balance sheet.*

stockholder equity The value of a shareholder's ownership interest in the company.

summary reports Reports that summarize groups of transactions. Compare with transaction reports.

temporary accounts Accounts that are closed out at the end of an accounting period such as revenue and expense accounts. Compare with *permanent accounts* in which the balances carry over.

terms The request you make to a customer (or that a vendor makes to you) regarding how quickly you wish your invoice to be paid. Common terms are Net 30 and Due on Receipt.

transaction reports Reports that list individual transactions. Compare with *summary reports.*

turnover ratio A measurement that shows how well the company's products are selling. To calculate the turnover ratio, divide the company's net revenues by its average of total assets for the period that the net sales cover. The ratio tells you the level of sales that the company's assets are producing.

undeposited funds A QuickBooks account that holds amounts you have received but not yet deposited into a bank account.

useful life The remaining years that a depreciated asset is expected to remain serviceable. For example, if a machine is expected to last seven years, and you have had it for three years, it has a remaining useful life of four years and is 3⁄7 depreciated.

vendor Someone who sells something that your business buys such as office supplies or inventory.

working capital The amount of money that you have to run your business. To calculate working capital, subtract the total of the company's current liabilities from its current assets.

Index

C

D

E

J

L

M

N

Q

Continued

S

T

U

Continued

Z